Canto is an imprint offering a range of titles, classic and more recent, across a broad spectrum of subject areas and interests. History, literature, biography, archaeology, politics, religion, psychology, philosophy and science are all represented in Canto's specially selected list of titles, which now offers some of the best and most accessible of Cambridge publishing to a wider readership.

Saladin

Saladin

THE POLITICS OF THE HOLY WAR

MALCOLM CAMERON LYONS
and
D. E. P. JACKSON

CAMBRIDGE
UNIVERSITY PRESS

PUBLISHED BY THE PRESS SYNDICATE OF THE UNIVERSITY OF CAMBRIDGE
The Pitt Building, Trumpington Street, Cambridge CB2 1RP, United Kingdom

CAMBRIDGE UNIVERSITY PRESS
The Edinburgh Building, Cambridge CB2 2RU, United Kingdom
40 West 20th Street, New York, NY 10011–4211, USA
10 Stamford Road, Oakleigh, Melbourne 3166, Australia

First published 1982
First paperback edition 1984
Reprinted 1995
Canto edition 1997

Printed in the United Kingdom at the University Press, Cambridge

A catalogue record for this book is available from the British Library

Library of Congress Cataloguing in Publication Data
Lyons, Malcolm Cameron.
Saladin: the politics of the holy war.
(University of Cambridge oriental publications; no. 30)
Bibliography
Includes index.
1. Saladin, Sultan of Egypt and Syria, 1137–1193 2. Islamic Empire – History – 750–1258. 3. Egypt – Kings and rulers – Biography. 4. Syria – Kings and rulers – Biography. I. Jackson, David Edward Pritchett, joint author. II. Title. III. Series: Cambridge University. Oriental publications; no. 30.
DS38.4.S2L93 956'.01'0924 79–13078

ISBN 0 521 58562 7 paperback

CONTENTS

FOREWORD

The object of this work is to re-examine and, where possible, to add to evidence for the career of Saladin in order to strengthen the frame of reference into which the judgements and conclusions of his modern biographers can be fitted. For this purpose, attention is concentrated on contemporary sources, and in particular on the extant correspondence, diplomatic and private, of the period. This adds little to our knowledge of Saladin's rise to power in Egypt or to the history of the Third Crusade, but it is of particular value for the central period of his career. The sources are, primarily, concerned with Saladin's own actions and their interpretation, but these, in turn, reflect the wider pattern of forces at work in his age.

It is hoped that this work may be of service to non-Arabists. In view of this, personal names have been arbitrarily distinguished for ease of identification. For instance, Saladin's brother al-Malik al-'Ādil Saif al-Dīn Abū Bakr Aḥmad ibn Ayyūb is referred to throughout as al-'Ādil, while another brother, al-Malik al-Mu'aẓẓam Shams al-Daula Tūrān-Shāh ibn Ayyūb is called Tūrān-Shāh. Extended forms, together with cross-references, are given in the Index. Place names are divided into three categories: (a) those which have common European forms, such as Acre and Jerusalem, which are retained; (b) less common names, transliterated from the Arabic sources; (c) names used for identification and derived not from the Arabic sources but from modern maps, etc., the forms of which have been left unaltered. In both personal and place names there are a number of variants of form and spelling. In some cases spellings have been taken from vocalised manuscripts but in general forms and transcriptions are based on a modification of the system used in the *Manuel de Généalogie et de Chronologie pour l'Histoire de l'Islam* of E. de Zambaur.

There are a number of problems of dating, including textual difficulties and variants in the identification of the first day of the lunar month. It is possible, however, in spite of mistakes made by individual authorities, to construct a calendar of events during Saladin's lifetime based on dates and days of the week that can be confirmed from eastern and western sources which shows an average discrepancy of no more than one day over a period of twenty years. As a result, the margin of error to be allowed for in the establishment of any individual date is generally small.

We owe many debts of thanks, principally to the Publications Committee of the Oriental Faculty of Cambridge University for their help in arranging for the publication of this book. We wish to acknowledge with thanks the generous grant from the Carnegie Trust for the Universities of Scotland. For both advice and encouragement we are deeply grateful to Professor Jonathan Riley-Smith. Mrs Ursula Lyons, of Lucy Cavendish College, Cambridge, has helped at all stages of the writing of the book through her valuable work on both Arabic and European sources. We must also acknowledge with gratitude the kindness and help of Mr J. Sullivan and Dr Hugh Kennedy, both of St Andrews University, as well as that of the staff of the Cambridge University Press.

May 1977

1

EARLY ADVENTURES

The history of mediaeval Islam and its civilisation provides a series of problems of definition and interpretation, but, in general, the materials necessary for their analysis are inadequate. In such a context, the career of Saladin is perhaps unique because of the volume of contemporary evidence.

Here, the narratives are, in the main, well-known.[1] Of Saladin's contemporary biographers, Ibn Shaddād's work has survived intact. Most of 'Imād al-Dīn al-Iṣfahānī's huge *Kitāb al-Barq al-Shāmī* has been lost, but its abridgement by al-Bundārī has recently been edited in part.[2] The manuscript on which this edition is based ends with the close of the year 583 A.H., where it overlaps with the start of the *Kitāb al-Faiḥ al-Quṣṣī fī' l-Fatḥ al-Qudsī* and so provides a complete cover by 'Imād al-Dīn of Saladin's career. A less partisan view is given by another contemporary, Ibn al-Athīr,[3] and facts and attitudes can be checked by reference to William of Tyre and other western writers. The *Kitāb al-Rauḍatain*, with its quotations from the lost work of Ibn Abī Ṭayy, is of particular value and local histories, such as the *Zubdat al-ḥalab min tārīkh Ḥalab* by Ibn al-'Adīm, also have their points of interest.

With the principal exception of al-Bundārī's abridgement, these sources have been covered by recent writers, whereas a valuable collection of contemporary letters has not yet received its proper share of attention. In the main, these are attributed to Saladin's administrator, the Qāḍī al-Fāḍil,[4] and they comprise both personal letters sent by al-Fāḍil himself and others drafted for Saladin. Some are quoted by the narrative historians or are found in other works; twenty-six are included, complete or in part, in a Cairo edition,[5] but a large number are still unedited. This collection is supplemented by a manuscript of letters wrongly attributed to 'Imād al-Dīn[6] and by the writings of another of Saladin's contemporaries, the North African al-Wahrānī.[7] The scope of their material is, of course, limited and they cannot compensate entirely for the dearth of official documents, but in addition to the details that they provide, many show the construction that Saladin himself wished to have placed on his actions, while others supply this with an unofficial commentary.

Gombrich, referring to "the old-fashioned biography of the 'Life and Letters' type", has pointed out in his *In Search of Cultural History*: "we know how little we know about human beings and how little of the evidence we have would satisfy a pyschologist interested in the man's character and motives".[8] It is certainly true that, in spite of the letters, Saladin's own personality can, at best, be seen in glimpses. The purpose of any new study must be to provide evidence for an analysis of his role in the context of his background. He can be seen as a hero of Islam, a dynastically-minded politician, a war-band leader or as a pawn manipulated by external forces, and it is for the insight that they give into these questions and, by extension, into the structure of mediaeval Islamic society, that the sources must be appraised.

Not surprisingly, there are no references to Saladin's birth and early boyhood in the letters and no evidence can be added to the well-known account.[9] According to this, two Kurdish brothers from Dvin near Tiflis, Ayyūb and Shīrkūh, moved to Iraq, where Ayyūb was appointed castellan of Takrīt. A report quoted by Abū Shāma says that he owed this position to the Seljuq Sultan Muḥammad ibn Malik-Shāh and that he was later confirmed in it by the powerful administrator, Bihrūz.[10] By this time, as Seljuq power weakened, the Crusaders' great opponent, Zangī, was establishing himself in virtual independence in Mosul and its adjoining territories. Ayyūb used his position at Takrīt, roughly halfway between Mosul and Baghdad (map 4), to help Zangī after his abortive expedition against Baghdad in 1132. This show of independence seems to have gone unchallenged at the time, but six years later, in 1138, Shīrkūh got his brother expelled from his post by killing a man in a private quarrel. The dead man was said to have been a Christian, which may have angered Bihrūz, "the Christians' friend".[11] At all events, Ayyūb and Shīrkūh were ordered to leave and Abū Shāma quotes the story that this coincided with the birth of Ayyūb's son Yūsuf,[12] whose title, Ṣalāḥ al-Dīn, was corrupted by western writers to Saladin.

The brothers now joined the service of Zangī, who put Ayyūb in charge of the citadel of Baalbek. On Zangī's death in 1146 Shīrkūh remained in the service of one of his sons, Nūr al-Dīn, who took over Aleppo, while another son, Saif al-Dīn, became ruler of Mosul. Meanwhile Ayyūb found himself besieged in Baalbek by troops from Damascus, then held by the Burid Mujīr al-Dīn Abaq. As no relief force came to his rescue, he surrendered the place on favourable terms and later went with his family to Damascus. When Nūr al-Dīn moved against the city in 1154, Ayyūb was chiefly responsible for arranging its surrender, after which he joined the victors.

There is nothing surprising in the geographical span of the brothers' careers or in their changes of employment. Mercenaries, scholars and pilgrims were constantly on the move in the mediaeval Islamic world, with the result that the nucleus of an administration, civil as well as military, could quickly form around an ambitious paymaster.

Saladin was reported to have had a particular fondness for Damascus,[13] as being the home of his boyhood, but his early days are, for the most part, a blank. Adolescence was a period which contemporary society tried to shorten as much as possible by emphasising the need for early maturity. For this reason al-Fāḍil told his son not to show childishness;[14] elsewhere he praised a boy for "resembling a grey-beard in his gravity",[15] and gravity is associated with youth in a eulogy of Saladin's own children.[16]

Of the process of education, Saladin wrote: "children are brought up in the way in which their elders were brought up",[17] and the influence on Islamic society of this traditional approach cannot be overemphasised. In spite of the fragmentation of its sects, Islam was a great assimilative force not least because the Quran was at the heart of its education. Admittedly, al-Wahrānī pictured the educated man as being able to answer questions on Euclid, the *Almagest*, arithmetic and law,[18] but this was an academic ideal and most obviously it was study of the Quran and "the sciences of religion" that linked the young Saladin to his contemporaries. In addition, they shared a common cultural heritage based on specifically Arab traditions. Saladin is said to have had a knowledge of the genealogies, biographies and histories of the Arabs, as well as of the blood lines of their horses.[19] More significantly, he is credited with having learnt by heart the *Ḥamāsa* of Abū Tammām.[20] This anthology offers a ready-made set of values and attitudes, emotional and at times self-contradictory, based in the main on the tribal society and Arabian background of its poets. These do not necessarily coincide with the dictates of religion, but together they provided a framework of convention that overrode racial differences for those whose education they coloured.

Study, of course, had to be backed by practical training. Al-Wahrānī added archery and the use of arms to his ideal scholar's accomplishments.[21] Ibn Jubair later reported that every evening Saladin's own sons would come out of the citadel of Damascus to shoot, ride and play polo[22] and Saladin himself must have done the same. Such training necessarily divided social groupings, but what is not so clear is the extent to which it was linked to a class structure. To the Franks, Saladin was "not of noble parents, but not a low plebeian of obscure blood",[23] and a hierarchical view of society was certainly current at the time. Usāma ibn Munqidh praised his mother's readiness to kill his sister rather than "see her captive in the hands of the peasants",[24] and references are not hard to find to the riff-raff at the bottom of the social ladder. Al-Fāḍil wrote of the "furniture and books of religion and literature" needed by the middle classes,[25] while an upper class can be provided by emirs and princelings. This vertical classification, however, was matched in importance by a horizontal division. History and geography were responsible for a number of cellular groupings in Islamic society, representing minority religions or the fragments of conquered races. But these were not confined to what had originally been the non-Arab parts of the Islamic state. The obvious Arab illustration is that of the Bedouin tribe and this clan pattern was reproduced in the sectional organisation of Islamic cities, where tribes, races and groups had quarters of their own. Even where there was no apparent reason for fragmentation, denominational differences within Islam itself provided a focus for groupings and it can be argued that for the individual his group and not his class was the determining factor of his life.[26] A qualification here is the extent to which the group represented a closed community. What could apply to a Bedouin tribe largely out of contact with the outside world has to be modified in relation to more widely developed societies. The importance of Saladin's Kurdish background can be seen throughout his career, but Ayyūb and Shīrkūh had cut themselves off from a specifically Kurdish environment and to that extent the Frankish assessment of their position on a social scale was of obvious relevance to their standing.

Not unnaturally, for Saladin's contemporaries authority was linked directly to military power which, in turn, was based primarily on cavalry. As a result, the horse was promoted to a position of importance not only as a military but also as a social factor. Amongst the settled population, as opposed to the nomadic tribes, horses could only be maintained by those who could afford to pay for their forage. Further, the characteristic Muslim battle tactic was that of the Parthian charge and retreat, where the horse was not, in the main, a weapon of shock but a vehicle for the archer, who would ride up to the enemy, shoot, in order to break his line or lure him out of position, and then retire. This required a high standard of horsemanship. How effective Saladin's troopers were can only be guessed at by approximation, but William of Tyre seems to have agreed with Napoleon in classing the professional Muslim cavalry above the Bedouin.[27] To the Bedouin, riding was a natural accomplishment, but to the professionals it was something to be practised for the specific ends of war. Military exercises, hunting and polo were all combined in cavalry training and those who were not able to spare the time for practice would be at a disadvantage when facing those who could. In such circumstances one would not expect to find citizen armies, but, rather, an employer/employee relationship in which recruits were hired, equipped and trained by a leader who could afford their services. The existence of these professional soldiers cut across class lines, but also helped channel the transmission of power within family groupings. A leader required experience and judgement in order to win acceptance from his men[28] and, in the absence of a formal command structure with opportunities for training, these could best be acquired by tuition on the battlefield. This process is illustrated by Usāma ibn Munqidh, who was initiated by his family in the Frankish wars,[29] and Saladin himself wrote that he had fought in company with his father and his uncle at the start of his career, "taking part in victories and leading troops against the unbelievers".[30]

In part, then, Saladin's education helped to identify him with his Islamic background and, in part, he was marked out for command. The scope for command, however, must have appeared limited in the context of the political situation of the day. Whatever the complexity of its underlying forces, superficially this was clear enough in so far as it affected Saladin's immediate surroundings. The Zangid dynasty was firmly in control of Mosul and Syria. It was faced with no serious challenge except on the Frankish frontier and under Nūr al-Dīn war against the Franks had come to be represented as the major activity of the state. Within Syria itself, Ayyūb and Shīrkūh were probably not the most powerful of Nūr al-Dīn's subjects[31] and although Saladin could hope for a career as a commander in the Frankish wars, reasonably enough his early ambitions, as quoted by 'Imād al-Dīn, were modest in the extreme.[32]

This was the situation when, in the summer of 1163, Shāwar, the deposed vizier of Egypt, arrived in Damascus. Egypt was in decline.[33] The foundation of Cairo in 969 had marked the start of a period of Pharaonic expansion under the Fatimids, who challenged Sunnī Islam, claiming descent from the Prophet's daughter, but by Nūr al-Dīn's time their dynasty had dwindled to the "scheming old women and conceited child" of al-Wahrānī's description.[34] With the capture of Ascalon by Baldwin III in 1153 they had lost their last foothold in the Levant and, in their isolation, they had no longer any necessary involvement in the power struggles of their neighbours. Egypt's wealth, however, and its growing reputation for weakness were dangerously enticing.[35] It was "the beautiful bride, led out by her attendants",[36] waiting for the first bold suitor.

The author of the Latin *Continuation* of William of Tyre noted that the Egyptians credited the Nile flood to the power of the Fatimid Caliph,[37] but he went on to say of al-'Āḍid, who had become Caliph in 1160 at the age of eleven, that he left all the affairs of the kingdom to his vizier – a reflection of the old Egyptian division between the divine Pharaoh and his chief servant. The vizier, however, was in an exposed position in that he could expect no help from his nominal master. William of Tyre wrote that the Caliph was unconcerned in cases of rivalry for the vizierate[38] and Ibn Shaddād added with some justification that, according to Egyptian custom, whoever could kill the vizier would be confirmed as his successor.[39] The dangers inherent in such a system finally destroyed it. Shāwar, a former governor of Qūṣ, had taken the vizierate from the powerful Banū Ruzzaik in January/February 1163. Within six months he had been driven out by Ḍirghām, a protégé of the Banū Ruzzaik, and it was at this stage that he came to ask help from Nūr al-Dīn to recover his position by force.

Not unreasonably, Nūr al-Dīn took time to reach a decision. Success in Egypt would strengthen his position against the Franks and Shāwar is said to have made him large promises of money and land.[40] On the other hand, the main road to Egypt, the Via Maris, skirting the Mediterranean, was controlled by the Franks and the land road by the Gulf of 'Aqaba across Sinai was threatened by Frankish garrisons at Kerak, Shaubak and Eilat (map 7). Too small a force would be ineffective and the failure of a large expedition would damage Syria. Shāwar's supplanter, Ḍirghām, sent an envoy to Damascus to urge, presumably with inducements, that Shāwar should be abandoned and Nūr al-Dīn appeared to agree to the proposal, "although secretly he was with Shāwar".[41]

In the event, he must have decided that the advantages to be gained outweighed the dangers and by the spring of 1164 he had abandoned secrecy and decided on an expedition. Shāwar is said to have hoped for sole command, but Nūr al-Dīn entrusted his men to Shīrkūh, whom "he had never sent on a mission in which he had not succeeded"[42] and who "paid no heed to danger"[43]. While Nūr al-Dīn watched the Frankish frontier, Shīrkūh and Shāwar moved off on 15 April 1164 to follow the line of the Rift Valley to the head of the Gulf of 'Aqaba and with them, according to Ibn Shaddād, went Saladin, who was now twenty-six years old.

Surprisingly, Saladin makes no separate mention of this expedition in an account of his career that he later sent to Baghdad.[44] Ibn al-Athīr goes so far as to quote an anecdote which, if genuine, would prove that he stayed behind[45] and, while Ibn Abī Ṭayy gives him a small part to play in the later stages of the campaign,[46] Ibn al-Athīr transfers this to anonymous "lieutenants".[47] Admittedly, Ibn al-Athīr's anecdote has the hallmark of invention, but more significantly there is no reference to Saladin in the brief account given in Bundārī's version of the *Barq*. It can reasonably be suggested, however, that Ibn Shaddād, who can be shown to have checked on points of doubt, is the best authority in this context and certainly in Shīrkūh's next campaign Saladin was thought experienced enough to have earned independent command, but there is a genuine problem here to which no firm answer can be given in the present state of the evidence.

Whatever Saladin's role may have been, for the Syrians the campaign was not entirely satisfactory.[48] They defeated an advanced force under the command of Ḍirghām's brother Mulham at Tell Basṭa, 11 miles (18 km) from Bilbais, and from then on Shāwar appears to have taken the initiative while Shīrkūh stayed in reserve. There was some skirmishing at Arḍ al-Ṭabbāla immediately to the north of Cairo (see plan of Cairo). Shāwar was forced to draw off and after marching around Cairo he camped to the south-east of Fusṭāṭ at Birkat al-Ḥabash. From there he moved to the hill of al-Raṣad overlooking Fusṭāṭ and then, apparently without any serious opposition, he took Fusṭāṭ itself. His attacking force next took up its position at al-Lūq, on the north-west corner of Cairo, and he seems to have made probing attacks on the west, south and east sides. The quarter of al-Yānisīya outside Bāb Zuwaila, the great south gate of Cairo, held firm but al-Hilālīya on the east side was evacuated and houses were burnt on the west side from Bāb al-Sa'āda to Bāb al-Qanṭara. Ḍirghām's troops were badly mauled; the Caliph refused to help him and on 24 May Ḍirghām and his brothers were killed while attempting to flee.

On 25 May Shāwar was reinstated as vizier by the Caliph. In his letter of appointment there is only a passing reference to Shīrkūh's force – "those whom you have brought with you, hoping for vengeance"[49] – but Shīrkūh himself was not to be dismissed lightly. He is now reported to have sent Shāwar a message saying that he and his men were tired of tent life and of heat and dust, clearly implying that he had not entered Fusṭāṭ.[50] At this, Shāwar sent him 30,000 dinars, but asked him to leave the country. Shīrkūh refused, saying that Nūr al-Dīn had ordered him to stay, as by the terms of their agreement Nūr al-Dīn had been promised one-third of the grain revenues of Egypt. Shāwar refused to hold to this and followed the precedent of his rival, Ḍirghām, in writing to Amalric, King of Jerusalem, to ask for help. He pointed to the dangers that would threaten the Franks were Shīrkūh to establish himself in the country and he promised them 1000 dinars for each stage of their march, together with an allowance of barley for their horses and a special grant for the Hospitallers. Amalric marched from Ascalon to Fāqūs, 26 miles (42 km) north-east of Bilbais on the Syrian caravan route. By this time Shīrkūh, having heard of his move, had retired from Cairo to Bilbais where, according to Ibn Abī Ṭayy, he had ordered Saladin to collect stores.[51]

The siege of Bilbais began in the third week of July 1164. Shāwar had now advanced from Cairo to join Amalric and according to Ibn al-Athīr Shīrkūh had only a low wall and no fosse to shelter him from their combined attack.[52] This attack, however, was not pressed. Shāwar must have been hoping to play off Franks against Syrians and he is said to have told Shīrkūh that he was deliberately holding the Franks back.[53] At the same time he made offers of land to Shīrkūh himself and to his followers in the hope of recruiting some of them into his service.[54] For his part, Amalric seems to have made no serious attempt to take the initiative and he may have been content to extort subsidies from Shāwar rather than risk his men. Meanwhile, Nūr al-Dīn took advantage of his absence to capture the castle of

Ḥārim, midway between Aleppo and Antioch (map 3), and on 10 August he crushed Bohemond of Antioch who had been reinforced by Raymond of Tripoli and by Thoros of Armenia, as well as by a Byzantine detachment sent by the Emperor Manuel. By October, after three months of stalemate, it must have been clear that none of the armies involved wanted to stay at Bilbais any longer.

Shīrkūh could not maintain himself indefinitely in the face of superior numbers. The Franks had their own weakened frontiers to guard and Shāwar must merely have hoped to rid himself of both his sometime allies. The emir Shams al-Khilāfa, whom Shīrkūh and Shāwar had captured at Tell Basṭa now acted as an intermediary between them and an agreement was reached by which Shīrkūh was to leave Egypt in return for another 30,000 dinars and a safe-conduct. The Franks made their own arrangement and the only obvious beneficiary of the campaign was Shāwar. Even he, however, had bought his return to power at the price of showing his weakness to both the Franks and the Syrians.

It is perhaps appropriate that Saladin's own part in this is obscure as it underlines the fact that for the first twenty-six years of his life we have had no picture of him at all. His uncle, small and violent, seen mace in hand watching his garrison leave Bilbais,[55] and his taciturn father, the only man allowed to remain seated in Nūr al-Dīn's presence,[56] have discernible characters, but Saladin at this stage is nothing but a name. An elder brother, Shāhanshāh, had been killed in a Frankish raid on Damascus;[57] a quotation, not necessarily authentic, notes that he was expected to rise to serve another elder brother, Tūrān-Shāh,[58] but nothing else shows him in the context of his family. There are no references to his mother, his younger brothers, al-'Ādil, Būrī and Ṭughtekīn, his sisters, or to his relations with his cousins.[59] He was brought up against a confused background of power politics, involving Seljuqs, Zangids, Fatimids and Franks, but the narratives add no fresh evidence of importance for its interpretation. It was his good fortune to coincide with a period in the decline of the Fatimid Caliphate when it could be decisively influenced by the actions of individuals, such as Shāwar and Shīrkūh, but details of their Egyptian expedition throw no clear light on the underlying causes of this process.

None of this is surprising as it merely reflects Saladin's dependence at the start of his career on what lay outside his own control. He could only prepare himself for what opportunities might arise, and it must be noted that it was presumably because of his competence that Shīrkūh chose him as an *aide-de-camp* in place of his own sons, while in 1165 Nūr al-Dīn gave him more administrative experience by appointing him to the post of *shiḥna*[60] (defined by Ibn Jubair as "police chief"[61]) of Damascus. It is here, perhaps, that he comes more nearly into focus as an individual. The poet al-'Arqala played on the Quranic story of Potiphar's wife and wrote: "go softly, thieves of Syria – this is my advice to you... The hands of women were cut because of that Joseph, but this one cuts off the hands of men".[62] On the other hand, it was presumably his Muslim enemies who supplied the Franks with the basis for the account that: "Under Noradin, sultan of Damascus, as a first omen of his power [Saladin] began by raising an infamous tribute for himself out of the venal courtezans of that city, for he would not allow them to exercise their profession until they had first purchased of him a licence".[63] He also found himself at loggerheads with the learned but difficult Kamāl al-Dīn al-Shahrazūrī, the Qāḍī of Damascus, of whom al-Wahrānī pictures overworked angels complaining to God on the Last Day that he wanted a Day of Judgement for himself alone.[64] Saladin had taken over some of his functions and 'Imād al-Dīn wrote that he used to "upset Saladin's purposes through decisions based on Islamic law".[65]

These details perhaps sketch an identifiable outline of an individual, young enough to be compared to the handsome Joseph of the Quran and to be thought an upstart by his elders, in a position to command attention, favourable and unfavourable, in his own right. The picture, however, is an isolated one and almost immediately Saladin is relegated to the background while it is Shīrkūh who continues to lay the foundations for his career.

Shīrkūh had no intention of leaving Egypt to Shāwar and made preparations on a considerable scale for two years. The Franks heard that he had collected "an infinite number"[66] of men from the east and the north and that he had written to the Abbasid Caliph of Baghdad, who had instructed "all the leaders of his false doctrine"[67] to send help. According to Ibn Shaddād, Shāwar heard of these preparations and decided to counter them by again inviting the Franks to Egypt.[68] William of Tyre, however, reported that "he was found to be supine in the matter and crassly ignorant",[69] and it was said that he got his first news of Shīrkūh's move in a letter from Amalric.[70] In fact, he had been having troubles of his own at home. Firstly, there were old scores to be settled with his enemies. Then another rival, Yaḥyā ibn al-Khayyāṭ, made an unsuccessful attempt on the vizierate and the

Berbers of the Lawāta tribe, together with a number of Bedouin from Qūṣ, staged a rising which had to be checked by his brother Najm.[71] With difficulties such as these to contend with, the threat from Shīrkūh left him little alternative but to offer the Franks the same terms as before.

Nūr al-Dīn added a number of his own emirs to Shīrkūh's force, giving a figure estimated by Ibn al-Athīr at 2000 riders.[72] Saladin wrote to Baghdad that he and his uncle had gone to Egypt "with vast armies"[73] and William of Tyre later put Shīrkūh's numbers at 12,000 Turks, 9000 of whom were fully armed, the remainder being archers.[74] Arab historians were in doubt about the sequence of events. According to Ibn Shaddād, Shīrkūh and Amalric arrived simultaneously, while Abū Shāma quotes a report that Amalric had joined forces with Shāwar at Bilbais before Shīrkūh was clear of the desert, forcing him to make a detour to the south.[75] He certainly moved south, although not necessarily to avoid a joint Frankish-Egyptian force. William of Tyre adds that his army had been endangered by a sand-storm,[76] but even without this, after a desert crossing he must have hoped to avoid battle until his horses and men were rested, and he is reported to have reached Iṭfīḥ on the Nile 42 miles (68 km) south of Cairo on 30 January 1167.[77] William of Tyre writes that before leaving for Egypt Amalric advanced some 65 miles (105 km) south of Gaza in the hopes of intercepting the Syrians on the march, but when this failed, he returned to Ascalon, mustered his men and left again by the coast road at the end of January (map 7).[78]

When the Franks arrived they camped by the Nile, apparently between the two cities of Cairo and Fusṭāṭ, "having on their left the noble and splendid metropolis commonly known as Babylon".[79] It was then decided by Shāwar and Amalric that Shīrkūh should be attacked while he was still to the south of Cairo on the east bank of the Nile, but when they reached his camp they found that he had already crossed. With the Nile between him and any pursuit, he turned north for Cairo and, rather than cross and follow him, the allies marched back the way that they had come.

Something of a stalemate now followed. As yet Shīrkūh had done no damage and had posed no threat to the Frankish-Egyptian armies, but they for their part had not been able to stop him going where he wanted and there was no certainty that he could be brought to battle. The Franks decided to take what advantage they could by threatening to return to Palestine unless they were given more money. The Qāḍī al-Fāḍil, who was in Shāwar's service at the time, is quoted as saying that he was alone in a tent with Shāwar, Shāwar's son al-Kāmil and his brother Najm when this was discussed.[80] The family were apparently agreed that they could not hold Egypt without the Franks and al-Kāmil decided to go with them if they left, while Najm planned to go to the west. Only Shāwar was determined to stay and fight, but in the event money was produced and a formal agreement was made, ratified by the Fatimid Caliph himself.

This agreement, however, brought a military solution no nearer. Shīrkūh had ensconced himself on the west bank of the Nile at Giza, almost exactly opposite Fusṭāṭ. If his force was to be destroyed, the allies had not only to cross the river but, ideally, to do it in such a way that he could not make his escape. Shīrkūh, for his part, had difficulties of his own. It could be argued that only a military Micawber would have manoeuvred himself into a position where he was faced by a superior force, cut off from his base and forced to rely for supplies on what he could collect from a presumably hostile country. It is important to realise, however, that in this he was merely following the razzia technique typical of his period, which was later practised by Saladin himself. This is an obvious development derived from the regular raiding of foraging clans. At its simplest the aim of such raids was merely to produce maximum plunder with minimum loss. Repeated, however, as part of an offensive strategy they had a dual object, in part to gain plunder with which to finance future raids, and in part to probe for weaknesses which, when found, could be exploited to destroy the enemy.

By the standards of this concept of war, Shīrkūh at Giza was well enough placed. He was sheltered by the Nile. Until Shāwar and Amalric decided what to do, he could take the initiative by moving up- or down-stream. The sight of his banners across the river was bound to weaken Shāwar's authority in his capital and to attract deserters, amongst them, according to report, being the leaders of three Bedouin tribes, the Banū Ṭalḥa, the Qurashīs and the Banū Ja'far.[81] In fact, these tribes are still found nominally in Shāwar's service after the campaign[82] and it seems unlikely that they can have done more than back both sides impartially, but of greater significance was the success of Shīrkūh's approach to Alexandria. He is said to have written to the city to ask for help, on the grounds that Shāwar had brought the Franks into the lands of Islam.[83] The account given by Abū Shāma suggests that the Alexandrians rose against Shāwar and gave charge of the city to Najm al-Dīn ibn Maṣāl, a son of the vizier of the Caliph al-Ẓāfir, who was said to have been living there incognito. There may well be some romantic elaboration in this, but the Alexandrians, either in their support of Sunnī Islam or through hopes of material advantages, were now prepared to throw in their lot with the Syrians.

Another, but unsuccessful, attempt at diplomacy is reported to have been an approach to Shāwar himself. Shīrkūh is said to have sent an envoy to suggest a joint attack on the Franks, promising that he would then leave Egypt for ever and allow no one else to attack it.[84] Shāwar could have hoped for no happier solution to his problems, but even if the account is correct and the approach was made he might well have doubted its sincerity. Instead of agreeing, he is said to have killed the envoy and then told the Franks of his message.

While Shīrkūh was trying the effects of diplomacy, the allies were slowly trying to come to grips with him. On the day after the Caliph had ratified the agreement with the Franks, they began to build a bridge of boats across the Nile from the island of Rauḍa (see plan of Cairo) to Giza. This got as far as mid-stream but then, according to William of Tyre, "fear of the enemy" prevented it from being completed.[85] The apparent folly of starting an operation which could not be carried out in the face of the enemy conceals the fact that this half-completed bridge was a threat to Shīrkūh's freedom of manoeuvre. He either had to leave enough men to guard against its completion, or else, if he moved from Giza, the bridge, when finished, would deny him its use as a base.

Frankish reinforcements now arrived with Humphrey of Toron and Philip of Nablus, and eventually Hugh of Ibelin was left to guard the bridge while the main force moved north. According to William of Tyre,[86] Shīrkūh moved down-stream to face them, but even if this is true, he had still not abandoned his camp at Giza. An eye-witness, the Sharīf al-Idrīsī, who had been sent from Alexandria with a message from Ibn Maṣāl, told of how he had been at Giza for two days when a messenger arrived with a warning that the Franks were coming.[87] Tents, cooking-pots and heavy baggage were precipitately abandoned and the Syrians made off up-river.

Shāwar now wrote an optimistic letter, noting his own services to the House of God and the House of the Prophecy;[88] from far and near men had risen up to help the family of the Prophet, whose glorious banners had been aided even by the Cross; one of his enemies had been used to fight the other and one disease was checked by another. Shīrkūh, he added, had now been driven off towards upper Egypt.

At this point the allies decided to split their forces. Hugh of Ibelin and Shāwar's son al-Kāmil were left to guard Cairo and the bridge. Another joint Egyptian–Frankish force was sent up the east bank of the Nile, while Amalric and Shāwar pursued Shīrkūh on the west bank. For the sake of speed, Amalric left his infantry behind. The pursuit continued for more than 185 miles (298 km) up the Nile until Shīrkūh reached Dilga on the west side of the Baḥr Yūsuf canal, and the allies camped some 12 miles (19 km) off to the east of it at Ashmūnain (map 6). Al-Idrīsī was still with Shīrkūh and he tells of how the Syrians had sacked Dilga and were feeding their horses in the evening when Shīrkūh ordered lamps to be lit and the march to continue. Then suddenly the order was countermanded; the men were called back and Shīrkūh camped.[89] This may reflect no more than the general confusion of a series of forced marches, a genuine change of plan on the part of the commander or even, perhaps, an attempt to mislead enemy scouts. What is clear is that, whatever the circumstances that led to the decision, Shīrkūh was now prepared to stand and fight.

The battle took place on 19 March. The ground that Shīrkūh had chosen is best described by William of Tyre, who got his information from a number of eye-witnesses.[90] It was on the border of the desert in broken country crossed by small valleys, getting its name, Bābain ("which is to be interpreted 'Gate' "), from the fact that the approach to it lay between two hills. Shīrkūh occupied the hills and William of Tyre notes that he stationed himself between them. This agrees with the account given by Sibṭ ibn al-Jauzī, which sets Saladin on the right wing, a force of Kurds on the left and Shīrkūh in the centre.[91] Ibn al-Athīr places Shīrkūh on the right wing with a picked force and he reports that Saladin was stationed by the baggage in the centre with orders to lure the Franks into a trap by a feigned retreat.[92] 'Imād al-Dīn agrees that the baggage was in the centre but does not make it clear whether the Muslims were in two divisions or three or where Saladin was posted.[93] Al-Idrīsī, although he joins Ibn al-Athīr in placing Shīrkūh on the flank, gives the Syrians two divisions, of which one, commanded by Saladin, was to attack the Franks from the rear, and he adds that "weakness entered through this".[94] According to a letter, written some years later: "Asad al-Dīn [Shīrkūh] drew up his own troops, the Ghuzz, by themselves and the Bedouin and those who were with him by themselves. He was facing the Egyptians while his Bedouin faced the Franks.".[95] This supports al-Idrīsī's battle-line, but it does not make clear to what extent, if at all, the two divisions were subdivided and what ground they held. It can reasonably be assumed, however, that Shīrkūh's plan was to persuade the allies to charge at the gap between the hills.

When the battle was joined, the Franks duly attacked Shīrkūh's centre and according to al-Idrīsī many of his men were killed or routed.[96] The evidence of the letter suggests that this must refer to Bedouin, but Shīrkūh's own position is then not clear and pride may have prompted some alterations of fact. The Franks certainly had an initial success, but the flanking hills were too steep and sandy for their horses and Hugh of Caesarea, who was attacking what William of Tyre takes as Saladin's force there, was captured. There was scattered fighting in the little valleys to the south of the main position and the Muslim centre returned to the attack. Saladin joined in from the rear and there were enough men stationed on the hills to capture the Frankish baggage train, which must have been left to the north of them. According to 'Imād al-Dīn, Shāwar himself was with Amalric[97] but there are no detailed references to the performance of his men, except for a note that the Qāḍī al-Fāḍil hurt his back by falling off his horse.[98] It was left to Amalric to extricate the attacking force. He himself had moved to the south of the hills but had apparently not taken part in the pursuit of Shīrkūh's centre. When the confused fighting had made it clear that no victory was possible, he raised his standard on a crest to serve as a rallying point for his men. He had then to retire between the enemy-held hills and, according to 'Imād al-Dīn, he could have been captured had not the Syrians seen another group of Franks retreating and broken off to engage them. This allowed Amalric's force to reach the ford of the Baḥr Yūsuf canal and from there he drew off to Minyat Ibn al-Khaṣīb, 21 miles (34 km) north of the base at Ashmūnain from where he had advanced against Dilga.

To Ibn al-Athīr, this first major field action in which Saladin is known to have taken part gave Shīrkūh one of the most remarkable victories in recorded history – "that 2000 riders should have defeated the armies of Egypt and the Franks of the Coast".[99] William of Tyre, on the other hand, puts the Frankish losses at 100 and those of Shīrkūh at 1500.[100] He then pictures Shīrkūh as gathering together his survivors and making off across the desert to Alexandria before the Franks learnt what he was doing. There is some justification for both points of view. Shīrkūh had come to Egypt with an inferior force and had then out-manoeuvred Amalric and Shāwar and induced them to attack him in circumstances in which they were lucky to escape destruction. In view of the odds against him at the start of the campaign this was a remarkable achievement, but it fell far short of total victory. In spite of their losses, Amalric and Shāwar were still in the field and they were joined by the east-bank force under al-Kāmil and Gerard de Pugi and by the Frankish infantry under Joscelin of Samosata. Shīrkūh had won himself time and prestige, but the neutral reporting of Sawīrus ibn al-Muqaffa' is perhaps the fairest comment on the battle itself: "many people of his [Shīrkūh's] army were slain and a great multitude of the Franks and the Muslims [i.e. the Egyptians] also were slain and each of them captured from the other prisoners".[101]

Shīrkūh now marched north. He made no demonstration against Cairo, where the Giza bridge was still guarded, but moved on to Alexandria. Here his earlier diplomacy proved its worth. Had Alexandria been held against him he could not have hoped to take it by storm and, with a superior force again gathering in his rear, he would have been left either to resume marching and counter-marching along the Nile or to go home. As it was, he was welcomed into the city, given money and arms and provided with a base which, if it could be held, would dramatically weaken Shāwar's position.

On hearing this news the Franks and Egyptians, who were re-grouping at Cairo, held a war council at which it was pointed out that Alexandria was dependent on river-borne supplies and could be starved out.[102] Amalric and Shāwar moved to Damanhūr, some 30 miles (48 km) south of Alexandria; patrols were sent out to enforce a land blockade and all traffic on the Nile was halted and the ships searched. It would take time before this process could be effective, but equally, if Shīrkūh did nothing to break the blockade, it would defeat him in the end. If he stayed to face a siege, he could not expect the Alexandrians to starve themselves indefinitely for his sake. He could come out to fight but this time the initiative would be with the allies and they could be expected to choose their own ground. On the other hand, if he abandoned Alexandria, his only tangible gain in Egypt, he could expect little further support. In the event, he took the bold decision to split his forces in the face of superior numbers. He himself moved out of Alexandria with the bulk of his force and marched south by a desert route to avoid the allied concentration. Such a move, in itself, would be of no more than nuisance value unless the city could be held, and this difficult and dangerous task was left to Saladin.

Amalric's first reaction was to return to Cairo, but when it appeared that the city was not threatened, he left Shīrkūh to his own devices and turned back northwards. According to William of Tyre, he was now persuaded to convert his blockade into a siege by an Egyptian who claimed to be able to arrange for Alexandria's surrender,[103] but even without this, Shīrkūh's withdrawal was a clear invitation to an assault. At this point, the Franks no longer had any cause to complain of Shāwar's laxness. When it had been a question of using one enemy to fight another, he may have been prepared to keep in the background, but now that the recovery of one of his own cities was at stake, he shouldered the burdens of war, arranged and paid for the construction of siege engines and "applied himself to all matters".[104]

This determination presented Saladin with a formidable test. He had only a small Syrian garrison. His communications with Shīrkūh were cut and his supplies blocked. The townspeople had little to gain and very much to lose by supporting him, but his only hope lay in their co-operation. William of Tyre gives no figure for Shāwar's Egyptians but he puts the Frankish numbers at about 500 horse and 4000 to 5000 foot.[105] To set against this he estimates that more than 50,000 of the besieged could bear arms and he comments on the wonder felt that so small a force could hold such numbers in check behind their walls. In fact, how many Alexandrians could or would fight for Saladin is doubtful. According to Maqrīzī, they provided him with 20,000 horse,[106] but this is not confirmed by contemporary writers. It is clear that Saladin had to husband his resources. William of Tyre reports that the Syrians rarely went into action because of their lack of numbers and the fact that they had no great faith in their Alexandrian allies. When they did fight, "they showed no great spirit and did little to hearten the others".[107]

The besiegers cut down orchards to get wood for machines and built a tower "of remarkable height",[108] from which they could look down over the whole city, but their most effective weapons were hunger and subversion. Shāwar sent messages to the citizens offering them substantial remissions of taxes and by July, three months after the blockade had started, the city was short of food. According to Abū Shāma many Alexandrians had been killed[109] and William of Tyre notes a flow of refugees.[110] It had been a remarkable achievement, diplomatic as well as military, for Saladin to have maintained his position, but clearly he could not hold out indefinitely. It was the responsibility of Shīrkūh, as commander of the expedition, to rescue him.

On leaving Alexandria Shīrkūh had marched as far as Qūṣ, 425 miles (684 km) south of Cairo. It may be that by now he had abandoned hopes of conquest, as he seems to have been looking for money and not military advantage. According to William of Tyre, he made an unsuccessful attempt to storm Qūṣ itself,[111] while 'Imād al-Dīn says, ambiguously, that he was "strengthened by it",[112] perhaps implying that the city bought him off. From there he turned north again. He brought with him a large number of Bedouin, but his army is said to have been weakened by "the difficulties that they had experienced and the terrors that they had seen",[113] and some Turkmans had been seduced from his service by Shāwar.[114] The Franks had received reinforcements by sea and were at least no weaker than they had been before the battle of Bābain. The defection of Alexandria had not led to any general movement against Shāwar in Egypt and as a result Shīrkūh's options were now limited. He could attack Cairo, where Hugh of Ibelin was still guarding the bridge; he could try to force his way through to the relief of Alexandria, or he could make peace.

According to one account,[115] he did make a move against Cairo, but it seems likely that this could have been no more than a demonstration. His best hope was for a profitable peace and this was also to Shāwar's advantage. If the Syrians were destroyed, the Franks would be left in too strong a position, while a peace treaty could free Egypt from foreign interference. Shīrkūh took the matter up with his prisoner, Hugh of Caesarea. The terms suggested included an exchange of prisoners on both sides, the raising of the siege of Alexandria and a safe-conduct home for the Syrian force. Hugh was reported to have been reluctant to serve as an intermediary lest he be thought to be acting in his own interests[116] and the approach was made by Arnulf of Turbessel. Amalric's own views are not recorded. It would obviously have been better for him to capture Alexandria and destroy Shīrkūh, but equally, he would have found it difficult to maintain his position if Shāwar wanted to make peace, and as a result, an agreement was made.

William of Tyre has left a picture of the raising of the siege of Alexandria. The townspeople came out "to enjoy conversation" with the Franks and the Franks, for their part, went to see the sights of the city.[117] Saladin himself was lodged in Amalric's camp, where he was given a guard to protect him from insults.[118] The Syrians are said to have moved out in the first week of August and on 17 August Shāwar entered with drums and trumpets as a conqueror and after extorting "a vast sum of money... he returned proudly to his camp".[119] Not unnaturally he wanted revenge. The Qāḍī of Alexandria was arrested and later ransomed by his family; others held out in the Pharos until they were pardoned and Ibn Maṣāl went into hiding until he could escape to Syria.[120] Some unrecorded provision had clearly been made in the truce terms for an anmesty, as Saladin now complained to Amalric, who sent word to Shāwar that he was breaking the agreement.[121] Saladin also asked Amalric to transport his sick and wounded to Palestine by ship. Amongst those who were taken off was al-Idrīsī who after a period of internment in a sugar refinery at Acre was allowed to go on to Damascus. Amalric himself burnt his siege machines, collected his garrison from Cairo and reached Ascalon towards the end of August, while Shīrkūh and Saladin arrived at Damascus on 5 September.

For Saladin this expedition marked a coming of age. Before it there is only his own reference to his "victories",[122] the question-mark of the first Egyptian campaign and the subordinate role of *shiḥna.* Now he had emerged from this comparative obscurity to stand alone against Amalric and Shāwar. He had led troops in a field action and carried the responsibilities of the defence of Alexandria. This is more than any of his Syrian contemporaries had achieved and his experience and success meant that, given the opportunity, his qualifications for command could not be questioned.

It was not clear, however, whether any opportunity would come. In spite of Shīrkūh's two years' worth of planning, his well-prepared army and his achievement at Bābain, he had been forced out of Egypt for a second time, having had to abandon his friends in the only city that had come over to his cause. He had no reason to hope ever to be able to defeat the combination of Shāwar and the Franks and Shāwar was well placed to meet any threat from him or from Amalric by the counter-threat of an alliance with the other. Nūr al-Dīn's position can only be guessed. Both he and his father had followed a policy of expansion. Ibn Khaldūn, however, was correct in noting the cohesive power of '*aṣabīya* (group-feeling)[123] in ensuring the survival of dynasties, and the further expansion was carried, the more diluted this force was bound to become. Nūr al-Dīn had helped Shāwar to return to power in return for promises of money and land. He had supported expansionism in backing Shīrkūh's attempted conquest, but the extent of his own commitment is less clear. '*Aṣabīya* was not directly involved as he was not seeking a kingdom for any member of his family. If Shīrkūh took Egypt, he would have a power base to rival that of the Zangids themselves and, although short-term gains could be expected, Nūr al-Dīn must certainly have been able to see possible dangers.

According to 'Imād al-Dīn, Nūr al-Dīn did not use his authority to give orders to Shīrkūh but tried to divert his attention by pointing out the difficulties – "you have exerted yourself twice but have not achieved what you sought" – and by putting him in charge of the frontier town of Homs.[124] There was obviously scope for mixed feelings. 'Imād al-Dīn had introduced himself to Saladin by writing a poem urging him to return victoriously to Egypt and to remove the Imamate from those who held it "by treachery".[125] Shīrkūh's views are not recorded but Saladin is quoted as saying: "I suffered such hardships at Alexandria as I shall never forget",[126] and he told Ibn Shaddād that he had had no wish to go back to Egypt.[127] In the winter of 1167/8 Nūr al-Dīn granted him two estates as *iqṭā's* (fiefs), one in the lands of Kafr Ṭāb, west of Aleppo, and one in the lands of Aleppo itself (map 3), and at this, according to 'Imād al-Dīn, "he thought that he had everything for which he could wish".[128]

In the event, it was neither Shīrkūh nor Nūr al-Dīn who opened the way for him. In the summer of 1168 an embassy came to Amalric from the Byzantine Emperor Manuel. According to William of Tyre, the envoys reported that it had come to the Emperor's notice that Egypt, up till then a country of moderate strength and great wealth, was now known to be ruled by weaklings.[129] It did not seem to him that this state of affairs could continue and, to prevent the country from falling into other hands, he suggested a joint attack which, he considered, would meet with an easy success. William of Tyre himself was sent to Constantinople to discuss this suggestion, but Manuel was detained by another campaign. When William returned to Palestine, he found that a decision had already been taken and that Amalric had left for Egypt.

No contemporary historian was certain of the immediate causes of this move. William of Tyre, who was in the best position to know, suggests that Amalric may have been alarmed by reports that Shāwar was in touch with Nūr al-Dīn[130] and later it appears that the Franks had heard a rumour that Saladin and Shāwar's son, al-Kāmil, were planning to marry each other's sisters in order, it was thought, to cement an anti-Frankish alliance.[131] William also suggests that Amalric may have been persuaded by the "magnanimous but unstable" Master of the Hospital, who had squandered the resources of his Order and wanted to recoup his losses by taking Bilbais and its lands, which Amalric had promised him. Ibn al-Athīr claims that Amalric, "the most courageous and wily of their kings since they first came to the Coast",[132] had been urged to attack by Franks who had been left behind in Cairo after the second expedition. In his writings Ibn al-Athīr shows a fondness for Thucydidaean speeches used not for historical accuracy but to convey arguments which he thinks appropriate and he pictures Amalric as speaking against the plan on the grounds that Shāwar was already sending them substantial sums of money, whereas, if they attacked, the whole country would oppose them; the Egyptians would then call in Nūr al-Dīn, and if Egypt was put in the charge of a man like Shīrkūh, this would prove fatal. The counter-argument was that Eygpt would have fallen before Nūr al-Dīn could muster his men and he would then be glad to treat for peace.

As far as Syria was concerned, the moment for a Frankish attack on Egypt was well chosen. In the autumn of 1168 Nūr al-Dīn was looking eastwards. Bedouin had captured the Lord of Qal'at Ja'bar, a castle strategically placed by one of the northern Euphrates crossings (map 8). He had been brought to Nūr al-Dīn, who was then concerned to force the surrender of Qal'at Ja'bar itself. Also, the death had occurred of Zain al-Dīn 'Alī-Kuchuk ibn Bektekīn, who had acted as administrator for Nūr al-Dīn's brother, Quṭb al-Dīn of Mosul, and who had held a number of important towns and castles, including Irbil, Takrīt, Sinjār, Ḥarrān and the citadel of Mosul itself. Nūr al-Dīn is said by Ibn Shaddād to have been "moved to cupidity" by Zain al-Dīn's death[133] and according to Abū Shāma the Franks were well aware that he was pre-occupied in the north and that the remaining Syrian troops had scattered to garrison the frontier.[134]

According to 'Imād al-Dīn's dating, Amalric left Ascalon in the third week of October 1168 and on 4 November he attacked Bilbais.[135] His only real chance of success lay in speed in order to forestall reaction by Nūr al-Dīn, while Shāwar must have hoped to buy time by defending Bilbais, where the garrison was commanded by his own son, Ṭayy.[136] Ṭayy is said to have been confident enough to ask Amalric: "do you think that Bilbais is a piece of cheese for the eating?", to which Amalric replied: "yes, it is cheese and Cairo is butter".[137] For the moment, it was Amalric's confidence that was justified. The town that had held out for three months under Shīrkūh fell almost immediately to a Frankish attack. Most of its houses were burnt and the people killed or taken as slaves, to be replaced, the

Arab historians had heard, by "the common people from amongst the Franks of the Coast",[138] whom Amalric had invited to settle there. Abū Shāma reports that Amalric freed those of its inhabitants who fell to his lot as prisoners[139] but this is not confirmed by William of Tyre, and the harsh treatment of Bilbais is quoted by Ibn al-Athīr as the reason for the determination of the people of Cairo and Fusṭāṭ to resist.[140]

After a five-day wait at Bilbais, the Franks moved towards Cairo, where they camped on 13 November. William of Tyre criticises the slowness of the march and claims that they took ten days to cover what was scarcely a single day's journey.[141] This is exaggerated, as his ten days include the five days that Amalric took to regroup his army, but he may be right where he adds that "those who knew the secrets of this affair" explained the delay as being due to Shāwar's intrigues. Shāwar must certainly have done his best to slow the Frankish advance, but this was not his only move. During his own campaign against Ḍirghām, although his first attack on Cairo had been beaten off, he had been able to take Fusṭāṭ without resistance. If the Franks followed his example, the fall of Fusṭāṭ, with the supplies and shelter that it could provide, might again prove fatal to Cairo and on 12 November he took the desperate step of setting fire to it. It was reported that 20,000 phials of naphtha and 10,000 torches were used.[142] Men, women and children streamed out of the city, "as though leaving their graves for the Resurrection".[143] The hire of a donkey or a camel for the brief journey to Cairo was from 10 to 30 dinars, at a time when a monthly income of 20 dinars was reckoned as wealth.[144] Goods that had to be abandoned were looted by sailors from the Fatimid fleet, in whose ships the fire had started,[145] and by the Negroes who formed a large part of the Fatimid army.

For his part, Amalric skirted Cairo and camped by Birkat al-Ḥabash, where he was met by Shams al-Khilāfa, bringing terms for a settlement. When these were found to be unacceptable, he moved up to Bāb al-Barqīya on the east side of the city and, according to Maqrīzī, he attacked so fiercely that Cairo was almost taken by storm.[146] There is, however, little evidence for this attack and the shift of camp can best be seen as an attempt by Amalric to strengthen his hand in negotiations. Shams al-Khilāfa now came out again with an offer quoted variously at 400,000, 1,000,000 or 2,000,000 dinars.[147] Eastern and western sources agree that 100,000 dinars were paid over immediately and that Shāwar asked for time to allow him to collect the rest.[148] At this, Amalric released his son Ṭayy, who had been captured at Bilbais, and drew off some 7 miles (11 km) north of Cairo to al-Maṭarīya. After eight days, during which there were "frequent but unprofitable embassies" from Shāwar,[149] he went even further north to Saryāqūs, some 20 miles (32 km) from Cairo on the road to Bilbais. His only military action was to send Humphrey of Toron to clear the Nile for the passage of a small fleet, estimated by Maqrīzī at twenty galleys,[150] which had been attacking Tanis, Ashmūn and Minyat 'Amr.

Shams al-Khilafa's son, Musā, told Ibn Abī Ṭayy that Shāwar refused to ask for help from Nūr al-Dīn[151] and that it was the Caliph al-'Āḍid who wrote, according to another account on two occasions, once after the burning of Fusṭāṭ and again after Shāwar's attempt to buy off Amalric.[152] This is almost certainly wrong, as 'Imād al-Dīn, who was employed in Nūr al-Dīn's chancellery at the time, reports the arrival of a stream of letters from Shāwar.[153] It is, of course, possible that Amalric, perhaps at Shams al-Khilāfa's prompting, discounted danger from Syria because he believed that Shawar would not invite Shīrkūh back to Egypt. William of Tyre suggests that he was badly advised by Miles de Plancy, who told him to be content with a ransom that he could keep for himself rather than to press for the capture of Cairo, whose spoils would have to be shared with his army.[154] His retreat from Cairo can certainly be explained as part of a bargain by whose terms he was to wait for money to be collected by the Egyptians, but in itself this does not account for his reluctance to strengthen his position. There is no final solution to the problem and all that can fairly be said is that his dilatoriness was matched by speed on the part of Nūr al-Dīn.

Within a month of Amalric's attack on Bilbais, Nūr al-Dīn's army was in camp south of Damascus, ready to march. He himself had been in Aleppo when Shīrkūh, hearing of the Frankish move, had ridden from Homs to meet him. Ibn al-Athīr elaborates the story by making Nūr al-Dīn send Saladin to fetch Shīrkūh from Homs and having uncle and nephew meet 1 mile from Aleppo.[155] Nūr al-Dīn then gave Shīrkūh 200,000 dinars and ordered his treasurer to supply whatever else was needed. Saladin was reluctant to return to Egypt, but at Shīrkūh's prompting Nūr al-Dīn ordered him to join the expedition. 'Imād al-Dīn reports that at this point Nūr al-Dīn went to take over Qal'at Ja'bar, while Shīrkūh was left to collect a force of Turkmans.[156] Nūr al-Dīn reached Qal'at Ja'bar on 24 October and as Amalric's march from Ascalon can be dated to the third week of October, this shows that the Syrians made their preparations on hearing of the Frankish muster without waiting for any appeal for help.

When Nūr al-Dīn returned to Damascus at the start of December, Shīrkūh was in camp to the south of it at Ra's al-Mā'. He had collected a force of over 5000 horse, to whom Nūr al-Dīn added another 2000, together with some emirs, "to share the cares with him", as William of Tyre put it.[157] Such numbers are not intended to represent the total size of the force, as they leave out of account servants and camp followers, and, in this case, Ibn al-Furāt, who only exaggerates Shīrkūh's cavalry by giving him 7000 men, not counting Nūr al-Dīn's contingent, makes the full expedition number 70,000 horse and foot.[158] This is certainly too large a figure, but the force was obviously a strong one. As a final act of generosity, Nūr al-Dīn gave each rider a bonus payment of 20 dinars and according to William of Tyre he also provided them with enough camels to carry their baggage to Egypt.

Amalric was still at Saryāqūs when word came that Shīrkūh was on the move "with an innumerable horde of Turks".[159] At this, he drew back to Bilbais, which he garrisoned to act as a base, and then in the fourth week of December, some forty days after he had first reached Cairo, he marched out to intercept the Syrians in the desert. The attempt failed and he was told by his scouts that Shīrkūh had reached the Nile. Shāwar is now said to have invited Shīrkūh to join him in an attack on the Franks, to which Shīrkūh replied that this had been his own plan on the second expedition, when the Frankish army could have been cut off west of the Nile.[160] As it was, Amalric was left with an open line of retreat and no further prospects of success. He collected his forces at Bilbais, then moved off to Fāqūs and finally left Egypt at the start of January 1169.

William of Tyre dates Amalric's retreat from Bilbais to 2 January 1169,[161] and Shīrkūh seems not to have entered Cairo until 8 January.[162] Shīrkūh may well have been reluctant to go too near Shāwar while there was still a chance that the Franks might be called back as allies and, although the picture is complicated in the Arabic sources by tales of intrigue and counter-intrigue, the logic of the position is clear. Shāwar wanted neither the Syrians nor the Franks in Egypt and he would ally himself with whichever side was less dangerous to him at any given moment. For his part, the Caliph al-'Āḍid was not concerned with changes in the vizierate and if Shīrkūh was willing to serve him, he was unlikely to object. Sunnīs had entered Fatimid service before, and they were certainly less dangerous to him than the Franks. As for Shīrkūh, it was clear both from his earlier actions and from their interpretation by 'Imād al-Dīn that he had intended to establish himself in Egypt with or without Shāwar's consent. He was acting in accordance with Nūr al-Dīn's orders, but it is wrong to overemphasise his subordinate position. In practical terms, when he left Syria, he and his force can better be seen as independent adventurers looking for fortune, than as a detachment of the Syrian army on a foreign campaign.

On 10 January Shīrkūh had an audience with the Caliph and on 18 January Shāwar was killed. Shāwar had tried to ingratiate himself by sending Shīrkūh gifts and he seems to have succeeded to the extent that the sources are generally agreed that Shīrkūh did not plan his murder.[163] According to 'Imād al-Dīn, he even sent Ḍiyā' al-Dīn 'Īsā to warn him of danger[164] and it may be that Shīrkūh himself would have been content to act as army commander, leaving Shāwar to control civil administration. This, however, did not satisfy his companions and Saladin, in particular, is said to have pointed out that, "while Shāwar holds power, we have no authority".[165]

According to the commonest story,[166] 'Izz al-Dīn Jūrdīk helped Saladin to unhorse Shāwar when he rode out on a foggy day to visit the Syrian camp. Shīrkūh was not there at the time and Saladin and Jūrdīk kept Shāwar in a tent to wait for his return. 'Imād al-Dīn wrote: "one messenger after another came from the Caliph's palace to demand Shāwar's head, and they refused to leave until they got what they wanted".[167]

A number of attempts were made by Arab writers to explain or justify the killing. According to an account given by Abū Shāma, the Caliph had discussed it with Shīrkūh when they met.[168] Another rumour was that Shāwar had planned to kill Shīrkūh at a Barmecide feast and had only been prevented by his son, al-Kāmil.[169] Ehrenkreutz stresses the importance of the role of the "palace establishment, which had become utterly disappointed with the appalling performance" of Shāwar.[170] He notes the promises made to Nūr al-Dīn, "which some reports placed at one-third the entire produce of Egypt", and suggests that with Shīrkūh's appointment "the caliph served notice [to Nūr al-Dīn] that henceforth the sultan's own commander, not the caliphate, was responsible for Egypt's wartime financial commitments".

It is reasonable to assume that there were a number of Syrian supporters in the Palace. Al-Fāḍil is the most obvious example of a man who changed masters at this period to his own advantage, but he was not alone.[171] The dangers and the drain on Egyptian resources caused by the prolonged tug-of-war between Franks and Syrians could be ended if a tamed Syrian force, loyal to al-ʻĀḍid, settled in Egypt and was kept contented by grants of land which it would be in its interests to defend against all comers. This cannot be challenged, but neither can the fact that the Syrians were the strongest single force in Egypt. If Amalric and Shāwar together had found it hard to match them, the Caliph with his Armenian archers, the questionably effective black regiments and the fragments of what had been the vizier's army, was in no position to enforce his will. As is shown by the details of Shāwar's career and confirmed by the theoreticians,[172] the revenues of the Caliph and of the vizier were separate and although the Palace resources were bound to follow the fluctuations of the Egyptian economy, whoever was chosen as vizier would be expected to carry the costs of administration. As a result, there can have been little need for a Fatimid initiative, as it is difficult to see any other end to a situation where Syrian strength and impatience was coupled with Shāwar's lack of power and what was accepted by his contemporaries as weakness on the part of al-ʻĀḍid. The extent of the intrigues cannot now be uncovered, but Shāwar does at least deserve a measure of sympathy. At no stage during his career did he have enough power to deal with his enemies. He maintained his position by daring as well as by cunning and he served, at the end of his career, to teach Saladin the lesson that wealth without military power was worse than useless.

The Caliph now followed what was quoted as Egyptian custom by confirming Shīrkūh in office.[173] He did, however, keep one weapon in his hand by briefly sheltering Shāwar's sons in the Palace. According to William of Tyre he had promised to protect them as long as they held no secret negotiations with "the Turks",[174] and when they broke this condition, they were killed.[175] What could not have been clear either to Shīrkūh or to the Caliph was how the Cairenes would react to the appointment of a Syrian vizier. Ibn al-Athīr reports that when Shīrkūh entered the city to take up office, he was met by the mob.[176] In the open, his horsemen had nothing to fear from untrained men, but in the narrow streets the mob had an advantage that it could exploit briefly and had it turned against Shīrkūh, it might have been in the Caliph's interests to produce an alternative vizier. In Ibn al-Athīr's story, however, Shīrkūh dispersed the crowds by telling them, on the Caliph's authority, to plunder Shāwar's palace. There is no other record of trouble, but Shīrkūh was anxious to clear Cairo of the refugees from Fusṭāṭ, whom he ordered to return home. They asked, pertinently, what they were supposed to use for shelter, at which Shīrkūh "made them fair promises"[177] and gradually they were removed from Cairo. When Ibn Jubair visited Fusṭāṭ in April 1183 traces of the fire were still visible, but he wrote that "most of the city is newly constructed and the buildings there are continuous".[178]

When Nūr al-Dīn heard of "the conquest of Egypt",[179] he ordered the news to be proclaimed and all his towns to be decorated. There was a strong rumour, however, that he was not pleased to learn that Shīrkūh had accepted office as Fatimid vizier. The rumour was attributed to Shams al-Dīn 'Alī, whose brother, Majd al-Dīn, was Nūr al-Dīn's foster brother and, according to Shams al-Dīn, far from being glad, Nūr al-Dīn would have preferred Egypt not to have been taken; he schemed to destroy the power of Shīrkūh and of Saladin, but was unable to do so; "one often finds in his letters to al-'Āḍid hints that Shīrkūh should be sent away and had he been able to say this openly he would have done so". By way of confirmation a sentence is quoted in which Nūr al-Dīn wrote of the need that his army felt for Shīrkūh in Syria.[180] Rumours of this kind intensified towards the end of Nūr al-Dīn's life, when there was greater justification for them. At this early period, however, he could scarcely have expected Shīrkūh to challenge the power of the Caliph. He might have preferred Shāwar to have been left as a figure-head, but he could certainly not have wanted his men to return and leave Egypt to the Franks.

Even had Shīrkūh himself thought of unseating the Caliph, he was to have little opportunity, as he died in his third month of office, on 23 March, suddenly enough to allow reports to spread that he had been poisoned.[181] There were other, simpler, explanations. He had a fondness for what Ibn Shaddād called "coarse meats"[182] and Abū Shāma records that he had a gluttonous appetite and "liked eating meat, going on doing so day and night".[183] This led to a series of illnesses and finally he succumbed to Juvenal's recipe for sudden death, a hot bath after a meal. He left behind 500 of his own *mamlūks,* the Asadīya, together with a large quantity of money, horses and baggage animals, and he also bequeathed to whoever followed him in office an opportunity to change the pattern of power in Egypt.

Saladin, in a letter of condolence sent to Shīrkūh's surviving son, Nāṣir al-Dīn, told him that Amalric, on hearing the news, had dismounted to give thanks to God and had said: "today I shall set out for Egypt".[184] In fact, the Franks were not ready to move again, but both they and the Egyptians must have been anxious to see how the Syrians would react to the death of their leader. The Syrian force was neither homogeneous nor rigidly organised with a single chain of command. The main racial groupings were those of Turks and Kurds. Of the soldiers some had been recruited by Shīrkūh, and had now lost their pay-master. Shīrkūh's own *mamlūks* were, in theory, part of his estate, but although the *mamlūk* system implied servitude it did not entail servility and they can be reckoned as watching over their own interests. In addition, there were the emirs provided by Nūr al-Dīn. They had been sent out under Shīrkūh's command, but there were no fixed rules of precedence to dictate what should happen on his death. At first sight, such a situation seems potentially disastrous, but its divisive factors were balanced by collective self-interest. The Syrians were on the brink of fortune and the profits were too large and too obvious to allow for the luxury of prolonged rivalry.

In theory, although Nūr al-Dīn's emirs might appoint an army commander of their own to replace Shīrkūh, the vizierate was a matter for the Caliph. In practice, no clear distinction was made by contemporary historians between the two positions.[185] The fall of Shāwar had made it clear that, for the moment, the Syrians were the dominant military force in Egypt and it was reasonable to assume that Shīrkūh's successor would fill both his roles, although there may have been grounds for dispute as to how and by whom he should be appointed. Ibn al-Athīr, again recording the arguments that he thought appropriate, reports that the Caliph himself picked Saladin, having been told by his advisers: "there is no one weaker or younger than Yūsuf".[186] He continues: "not one of the emirs who sought the position for themselves obeyed him or served him", but, according to this version, after some bargaining he was eventually accepted by the majority. Such an explanation might be credible if the premise is accepted that Saladin, in spite of Bābain and Alexandria, could reasonably be considered the weakest of the Syrian emirs. Not surprisingly, this is not put forward by his eulogists. Al-Wahrānī wrote: "after Shīrkūh's death the people agreed that the vizierate should be kept in his family because of the qualities of leadership and sound governance that they were known to possess and because of what had been experienced of their generosity and their military prowess".[187] 'Imād al-Dīn is less fulsome and more detailed. He wrote that after the three-day period of official mourning, during which "opinions differed", the Syrian emirs decided on Saladin and "made the Lord of the Palace invest him as vizier".[188] There had been a number of other candidates for the post, led by Saladin's maternal uncle, Shihāb al-Dīn al-Ḥārimī and the Turkish emir, 'Ain al-Daula al-Yārūqī, who was the senior with the largest train of followers. Saif al-Dīn al-Mashṭūb and Quṭb al-Dīn Khusrau, the two remaining candidates, were Kurds and according to Ibn al-Athīr, who agrees with 'Imād al-Dīn on the lists of names, the role of mediator was played by another Kurd, Ḍiyā' al-Dīn 'Īsā.

It is, of course, possible that al-'Āḍid's advisers may have pre-selected Saladin, in the hope of splitting the Syrian ranks. The evidence, however, can be no better than gossip and the identification of tenable arguments. It has to be accepted that, although the position was complicated by individual rivalries, the bulk of the Syrians must have wanted a competent leader who would further their cause. Here Saladin was an obvious compromise candidate. Thanks to his record in the second Egyptian expedition his military qualifications were impeccable. Shihāb al-Dīn and 'Ain al-Daula could be played off against one another. The Kurds, al-Mashṭūb and Khusrau, were junior to them and could be persuaded to support their fellow Kurd, Saladin, rather than 'Ain al-Daula, while Shihāb al-Dīn would naturally back his nephew if he could not have the post himself. As a result, whatever the Fatimid position, 'Imād al-Dīn cannot be far from the truth in suggesting that after the negotiations there was almost unanimous support for Saladin amongst the Syrians. The most prominent exception was 'Ain al-Daula, who left for Syria saying: "I shall never serve Yūsuf."[189]

2

VIZIER OF EGYPT

Saladin's appointment as vizier to a Fatimid Caliph in a country with which he had no connections by birth or upbringing sets off not inappropriately the combination of good fortune, intrigue and ability in his early career, to which it supplied the climax. Ayyūb and Nūr al-Dīn had been relegated to the background: Shīrkūh and Shāwar, as supporting actors, had played their introductory roles and left. This was Saladin's cue, but to the observer he is still little more than a silhouette. His qualities of leadership, his concern for his sick and for his allies, his professed reluctance to return to Egypt and the ruthlessness of his seizure of Shāwar can be juxtaposed but not composed into an integrated picture. There is no portrait of him as clear as that given by Hugh of Caesarea of the tall and swarthy al-'Āḍid, with his pleasant face and the first down of manhood on his cheeks,[1] and there is no picture at all of the men who surrounded him. To the Franks, the Egyptian emirs were "worthless and effeminate"[2] while the Syrians were mainly remembered for their violence. Even 'Imād al-Dīn later wrote of Saladin's "rough companions";[3] the Christian author, Sawīrus ibn al-Muqaffa' noted their depredations during Shīrkūh's first expedition,[4] and although they can be seen as realists, who accepted *force majeure* as a working principle and did not rebel against successful rulers, at this stage in his career Saladin must be seen as holding a wolf by the ear.

Whatever obscurities there were in the background, the immediate situation was clear enough. The complexity of the forces that affected Egypt in its position as an Islamic state, a Mediterranean power, a centre of population and a source of wealth, all operated on a level which Saladin had not yet reached. He had more power and apparent independence than ever before in his career, but his horizon was necessarily limited by his own problems. He was in the service both of the Sunnī Nūr al-Dīn and of the Shī'ite al-'Āḍid, but, immediately, he was the protagonist of the Syrians. His own quoted remark – "while Shāwar holds power, we have no authority"[5] – may not be genuine but it underlines the fact that the Syrians were observably seeking a controlling position in Egypt. At its simplest this would merely involve the substitution of one set of emirs and *iqṭā'* -holders for another. It did not even necessarily require the destruction of the Fatimid caliphate, but with religious antagonism to focus hostility, it did require urgent action.

Saladin was invested as vizier on 26 March. According to the Arabic sources he now repented of "wine-drinking and turned from frivolity"[6] to "assume the dress of religion".[7] To western audiences the point was put more disparagingly: "that patron of prostitutes whose power was among stews, his campaigns in a tavern, his studies among dice and garlic, is suddenly lifted up; he sits among princes and is even greater than princes".[8] The document of his appointment was read out to the Egyptian and Syrian emirs when he took his seat in the vizier's palace. In an obvious attempt to reconcile these rivals a reference to the Egyptians had been added which ran: "these are the Caliph's helpers in the west as your troops are in the east and both form a single band in his service against those who resist them".[9] This can have deceived no one and it is no wonder that letters to Syria expressed homesickness. 'Imād al-Dīn wrote: "our companions have conquered... but they have come amongst a people whom they do not know.... and they see faces that frown at them".[10]

Saladin later gave a rhetorical account of his difficulties and his methods in a letter to Baghdad. The Egyptian people, he said, were well disposed to him because of his championship of true religion and of the fact that he had saved them from slavery, but the land contained numerous wealthy and united armies that were more dangerous to Muslims than to unbelievers; religious law had been distorted by "interpretation" and unbelief camouflaged under another name; there was a powerful force of Christian Armenians and more than one hundred thousand Negroes who recognised no God but the (Fatimid) Caliph; secrecy and cunning were better weapons against them than open resolution and they had to be dealt with gradually, as a sword blade is worn down by a file.[11]

Saladin was concerned here to paint his difficulties in the gloomiest colours but there is no doubt that he felt the need to act carefully and as a result the first few months of his vizierate held little drama. He tried to fix his favour with the Egyptian people, spending the money that Shīrkūh had collected and treating them "with a fairness to which they were not accustomed".[12] He is also said to have made a start on moving Fatimid troops out of Cairo, beginning with the infantry.[13] But he apparently felt that he needed more reliable support than could be got from possible rivals amongst the Syrian emirs, and he wrote to Nūr al-Dīn to ask for "his brothers and his family" to be sent from Syria.[14]

At this point the rumours of Nūr al-Dīn's hostility recur. Ibn Abī Ṭayy was told by his father that Nūr al-Dīn resented Saladin's appointment as vizier and said: "how dared he do anything without my orders?"[15] Nūr al-Dīn wrote several letters on this point, according to this report, but Saladin paid no attention to what he said, without, however, abandoning his allegiance. Abū Shāma adds that what annoyed Nūr al-Dīn was the way that Saladin spent money without asking his advice.[16] According to Ibn al-Furāt, Nūr al-Dīn went so far as to order the Syrian emirs in Egypt to leave,[17] and his removal of the *iqṭā*'s of Homs and al-Raḥba (map 8) from Shīrkūh's son, Nāṣir al-Dīn, is quoted as another sign of his disapproval.

Part, at least, of the factual basis of these rumours can be established. Nāṣir al-Dīn did lose his father's *iqṭā*'s, for which he got Tell Bāshir in temporary exchange. He later recovered al-Raḥba, but it is not clear when this was. It was natural, however, that a place as important as Homs should not be entrusted to an untried man and Nūr al-Dīn, in fact, split the responsibility for it by giving the town to the emir Fakhr al-Dīn ibn al-Za'farānī, and leaving one of his own lieutenants to hold the citadel. Some Syrian emirs did leave Egypt. It has been noted that 'Ain al-Daula al-Yārūqī went home in disappointment, and according to one report Nūr al-Dīn held this against him.[18] Quṭb al-Dīn Khusrau, another of the vizierate contenders, also left, as did 'Izz al-Dīn Jūrdīk, who had helped Saladin to seize Shāwar. Nūr al-Dīn may certainly have been suspicious of Saladin, but it cannot be proved that this influenced his actions and, in fact, he did what Saladin had asked. On 7 July Saladin's elder brother, Tūrān-Shāh, was sent from Damascus.[19] He arrived in Cairo on 29 July and almost immediately after his arrival Saladin took his first decisive step.

The Fatimid Palace formed an excellent setting for conspiracies and not surprisingly during the secret-war phase of Saladin's vizierate it was a centre for intrigue.[20] The official story of the first recorded plot against Saladin is that a group of Egyptian malcontents, including soldiers and emirs, formed around the eunuch Mu'tamin al-Khilāfa, one of the powerful civilian controllers of the Palace.[21] They are said to have been feeling the effect of Saladin's measures to transfer land to the Syrians, as a result of which they decided to call back the Franks. Saladin would have to march from Cairo to face an invading force and the conspirators could then destroy his garrison and take him in the rear. They wrote a letter to the Franks, but by Bilbais a vigilant Turkman, "one of Saladin's companions", noticed a man dressed in ragged clothes carrying a new pair of sandals. The man was arrested and the letter was found concealed in the sandals. Its handwriting led the investigators to a Jewish scribe, who then conveniently apostatised, embraced Islam and revealed the plot. Saladin concealed his knowledge in order to lull al-Mu'tamin's suspicions. For some time al-Mu'tamin kept to the shelter of the Palace, but he then lowered his guard, went to visit an estate that he owned some 10 miles (16 km) north of Cairo and was killed there by Saladin's men on 20 August.

There must be doubts as to the truth of this story. Now that Saladin had been reinforced by Tūrān-Shāh, he may have thought the time ripe to clear Cairo of his enemies. The sandals and the apostatising Jew have a touch of Arabian Nights story-telling, and Saladin's own reference to the cunning with which he had to act suggests that he was not above manufacturing evidence. As he showed later, however, he himself believed the main point, that if he had to march out of Cairo to meet an attack, his enemies would rise behind him.

Amongst the most formidable of these were the Negro regiments of the Fatimids. 'Imād al-Dīn, who halved Saladin's estimate of their numbers, putting them at over 50,000 men, referred to their long and uneasy history of trouble-making in Cairo.[22] He wrote that "whenever they rose against a vizier they killed him", and added, "they thought that all white men were pieces of fat and that all black men were coals".[23] They had taken advantage of the confused situation to spread their own brand of anarchy and according to the Armenian Christian, Abū Ṣāliḥ, they had grown "insolent and violent"; "their hands were stretched out until they stopped the roads and seized the money of travellers, or shed their blood".[24]

On the day after al-Mu'tamin's death they took up position in the great square of Cairo between the West and East Palaces. There they were said to have been joined by more of Saladin's enemies, including Egyptian emirs and common people.[25] Saladin had concentrated his force in the vizier's palace, to the north-east of the East Palace. He was now faced with the prospect of fighting on ground not of his own choosing, overlooked on the flanks by buildings held by the Palace troops who might at any moment join in against him. He had no safe line of retreat and he was faced by large numbers. On the other hand, as he had precipitated the rising by killing al-Mu'tamin, he can be assumed to have made his preparations and he afterwards proved to have enough men both to maintain frontal pressure and to encircle his enemies. Perhaps in order to carry out this manoeuvre, he deliberately kept himself in reserve.

According to a later report, Tūrān-Shāh came to tell him that the Negroes were about to attack and Saladin angered him by waiting to see what the Caliph would do.[26] It must certainly be true that Saladin was watching the Palace, but presumably tactical appreciation and not dilatoriness made him leave Tūrān-Shāh, or, according to other reports, Abū'l-Haijā' the Gross, in charge of the fighting that now broke out in the square.[27] It went on for two days and towards the end of this time a number of the Caliph's Armenian archers are said to have shot at the Syrians from a vantage point in the Palace.[28] This must have been the crisis of the battle, as enfilading fire from the Palace walls could endanger the Syrian position. An order was given, either by Tūrān-Shāh or by Saladin, to burn out the Armenians with naphtha and at this one of the Caliph's officers came out to give Tūrān-Shāh a message that the Caliph wanted him to drive the Negroes away. This took the Negroes aback, as they had thought, not unreasonably, that the Caliph would be on their side, and it also freed the Syrians from the danger of a flank attack.[29] The Negroes could not now maintain themselves in the open and they were driven down the main thoroughfare of Cairo, the Qaṣabat al-Qāhira, which ran from the square down to Bāb Zuwaila (see plan of Cairo). Saladin's reserves held the heads of the side streets against them, to prevent them from out-flanking the pursuit. They made a stand at the Market of the Sword Sellers, some 600 yards (550 metres) short of Bāb Zuwaila, but this refuge was burnt down and they were driven to Bāb Zuwaila itself, which was shut against them. At some time during this fighting Saladin sent men to burn down the Manṣūrīya quarter where they lived. This completed their demoralisation and they now asked for quarter. The Arab historians agree that this was granted and it is difficult to see how they could otherwise have got clear of Cairo, but either some link is missing from the story, or else the Syrians acted unscrupulously. For when the Negroes retired from Cairo to Giza, Tūrān-Shāh followed them across the Nile and destroyed them with such thoroughness that few escaped. This act, whatever its justification, was so successful that Saladin never again had to face a military challenge in Cairo.

The Negro revolt ended on 23 August,[30] but almost immediately Saladin had another threat to meet. As has been noted, the Emperor Manuel, moved, according to Nicetas, by an untimely thirst for glory,[31] had already suggested a joint Frankish–Byzantine invasion of Egypt. According to John Cinnamus, he sent an embassy to Egypt to demand tribute, and threatened war when this was refused.[32] By the end of summer of 1169 his fleet was at sea under the command of Andronicus Contostephanus. Sixty galleys were sent to Palestine, with money for "the knights of Jerusalem".[33] Andronicus with the rest of the fleet sailed to Cyprus, off which he met a patrolling squadron of six Egyptian ships. Two of these were captured, but the others escaped to bring back their news to Egypt. Amalric had refused an invitation to come to Cyprus, and after some delay the whole Byzantine fleet re-formed, moving first to Tyre, which it reached at the end of September, and then to Acre. Nicetas put its numbers at over 200 ships,[34] while William of Tyre counted it at 150 galleys, 60 ships "with doors in their sterns" for loading horses,[35] and some 12 dromons loaded with supplies and siege engines. Saladin exaggerated the numbers and wrote that 1000 ships arrived off Egypt.[36]

Amalric had decided to take the land route. Troops were left to watch Nūr al-Dīn, who was peacefully restoring a mosque outside Damascus,[37] and the rest of the army mustered at Ascalon, while the Byzantines sailed on ahead. The time was now midway through October and it was conventionally reckoned that the Mediterranean sailing season ended in the first week of December.[38] The expedition's first goal was Damietta, chosen, Ibn Shaddād supposed, because it could be attacked by land and sea.[39] To Amalric, at least, this was only a beginning, as already in September he had been promising the Pisans concessions in Cairo and Fusṭāṭ.[40] He arrived at al-Faramā on 25 October and two days later he reached Damietta, camping to the north, between the city and the sea (map 7). The Byzantines had outstripped him and the sourness of the alliance is reflected in Cinnamus' suggestion that he delayed deliberately in order to ensure that they had to bear the brunt of the fighting.[41]

Saladin must have been expecting an attack, but he could not have been sure where it would come. William of Tyre reported that

Damietta was almost empty of troops and would have fallen to an early assault, but for three days no attack was made and the opportunity was lost.[42]

Saladin himself had apparently decided that in spite of his August victory he could not afford to leave Cairo, but he sent a stream of reinforcements, headed by his nephew Taqī al-Dīn, and including his uncle, Shihāb al-Dīn al-Ḥārimī. The expenses of the troops sent from Cairo are said to have been over 550,000 dinars[43] and Saladin is quoted as praising the generosity of the Caliph for sending him 1,000,000 dinars, as well as other gifts, during the crisis.[44] The money produced effective results and William of Tyre noted that so many well-armed troops arrived that the Muslims were able to hold their own not only behind the city walls but in the open.[45] Nūr al-Dīn sent help from Syria, including Saladin's former rival, Quṭb al-Dīn Khusrau, and 'Imād al-Dīn wrote: "reinforcements, small and great, cause talk that scatters united forces".[46] The point of this is seen in Nicetas' reference to the rumours of "eastern Arabs and vast numbers of hired Assyrian horse near at hand",[47] that dismayed the besiegers at the end of the siege.

The Byzantines and the Franks blamed each other. To the Franks, their allies were "naturally weaker" than themselves,[48] while the Byzantines resented "the haughty and over-bearing Palestinian knights".[49] Nicetas says that Andronicus had wanted to attack quickly with scaling ladders, but Amalric had insisted on waiting for a siege tower to be built.[50] Part of the wall was destroyed by mangonels, but William of Tyre claims that their bombardment was wrongly directed.[51] According to Nicetas the allowances for the Byzantine fleet had been calculated for a three-month period starting from August and they were now running out.[52] When Byzantine commanders asked for loans with which to pay their men and buy food, the Franks refused them. Byzantine soldiers had to eat roots and "the empty and senseless"[53] siege dragged on for some fifty days. Finally, according to William of Tyre, through the efforts of the Franks and the "Turkish satraps", particularly Shihāb al-Dīn, peace terms were arranged.[54] Even this was held against Amalric by Nicetas, as he claimed that a desperate attack by Andronicus was on the point of success when Amalric stopped the fighting.[55] After a brief delay, during which besiegers and besieged met and traded with one another, the machines were burnt and on 13 December the allies left for home. As a final blow, storms scattered the Byzantine fleet, sinking many ships.

William of Tyre reported that there were secret conditions attached to the armistice[56] and according to Nicetas the Muslims now sent a peace-making embassy with gifts to the Emperor Manuel.[57] But no crumbs of consolation could make up for the total failure of the expedition, which had presented Saladin with exactly the success that he needed to confirm his position. He later wrote that he had met two enemies, one hidden and one open, the hypocrites and the unbelievers; he had defeated 200,000 horse and foot and "dashed the hopes of the Egyptians, the Franks, the Byzantine Emperor, the Genoese and the races of the Rūm" – presumably the Pisans and Venetians.[58] The Egyptians were the hidden enemy, the hypocrites, and this reference bears out Maqrīzī's report that Saladin took advantage of the siege to execute a number of Egyptian leaders on suspicion of treachery.[59] He was further strengthened by the reinforcements sent by Nūr al-Dīn. Al-'Āḍid is said earlier to have asked Nūr al-Dīn to recall his men, leaving only Saladin and his personal followers. Nūr al-Dīn now replied: "the arrows of the Turks are the only answer to the lances of the Franks",[60] and the Syrians had again taken on the role of saviours of Egypt.

Some months after the ending of the siege of Damietta, Saladin's father, Ayyūb, came to Egypt. According to Ibn al-Athīr, Saladin himself had asked for him.[61] Ibn Abī Ṭayy, on the other hand, reported that the Abbasid Caliph al-Mustanjid had criticised Nūr al-Dīn for his delay in ordering the deposition of his Fatimid rival and Nūr al-Dīn had sent Ayyūb to press this on Saladin as a matter of urgency.[62] Both stories may be true, but 'Imād al-Dīn, the most reliable source in this context, merely notes that in the spring of 1170 Ayyūb asked for permission to leave Syria, which Nūr al-Dīn granted, and as a mark of friendship Nūr al-Dīn himself left Damascus to accompany him as far as Ra's al-Mā'.[63] Ibn al-Athīr suggests that Nūr al-Dīn then went on to attack Kerak, to distract the attention of the Franks,[64] but in fact Ayyūb arrived in Cairo on 16 April, while Nūr al-Dīn's attack did not take place until after April 20. Meanwhile, as a mark of unusual respect, Ayyūb had been met outside the north gate of Cairo, the Gate of Victories, by the Caliph himself and had been lodged in the Pearl Palace.[65] Saladin, by way of welcome, had offered to resign the vizierate in his favour, but the offer was refused.

Saladin's family was now strongly concentrated in Egypt. His uncle, Shihāb al-Dīn, his brother, Tūrān-Shāh, and his nephew, Taqī al-Dīn, were already there. Another brother, Ṭughtekīn, is said to have arrived with Tūrān-Shāh[66] and a third brother, al-'Ādil, together with a second nephew, Farrukh-Shāh, are found in Egypt soon afterwards, though the dates for their arrival are doubtful.[67] His brother-in-law, Zain al-Dīn 'Umar, apparently came to join him later in the year,[68] and to add to the family numbers, his eldest son was born on 17 June.

The first storms of his vizierate had successfully been weathered, but the safer he became, the more likely he was to attract Nūr al-Dīn's attention. Self-interest, if nothing more, would prompt Nūr al-Dīn to support his own men in Egypt in times of danger, but this did not mean that he had to allow Saladin free rein. As an extreme measure, Saladin could be ordered home, but short of this, Nūr al-Dīn might insist on measures, such as the overthrow of the Fatimid Caliphate, that went against Saladin's judgement or his wishes. For Saladin was still inclined to feel his way carefully, and it was part of the sequence of his good fortune that Nūr al-Dīn's attention was now diverted.

After his withdrawal from Kerak, Nūr al-Dīn had camped by Tell 'Ashtarā, 20 miles (32 km) north of Deraa (map 8) on the Damascus road. 'Imād al-Dīn, who was with him at the time, has described how, when he was sitting in his tent on the morning of 29 June, he suddenly felt the earth heaving beneath him like the sea in a storm wind.[69] The epicentre of the earthquake seems to have been in northern Syria. Damascus was not badly affected, but the citadel of Baalbek was in danger of collapse; Homs and Hama were severely damaged and half of Aleppo was said to be in ruins. The Aleppans moved to tents outside their city and corpses were still being recovered from the rubble a year later. In this Michael the Syrian saw divine punishment for the sufferings inflicted on Christian prisoners, who were not allowed to enter the churches of Aleppo except on Sundays,[70] while 'Imād al-Dīn in a letter to Baghdad wrote that the only consolation was that the Christians had suffered the most, as they were in their churches at the time to celebrate a feast day.[71] It was, in fact, the feast of St Peter and St Paul and William of Tyre wrote that no man could remember so severe an earthquake. "The greatest cities of Syria and Phoenicia, famous throughout the centuries, were razed to the ground."[72] Both Franks and Muslims had suffered and, as William put it, while each feared the anger of the Judge, they were afraid to hurt others and a brief truce was observed.

Nūr al-Dīn marched north from 'Ashtarā on the day after the earthquake and for some time he was busy with reconstruction work.

Then, on 6 September, his brother, Quṭb al-Dīn, who was some forty years old, died in Mosul. Saladin himself had no hand in the sequel to this, but it helped shape his future career. Of Quṭb al-Dīn's sons, 'Imād al-Dīn Zangī, the eldest, had married Nūr al-Dīn's daughter and had been nominated as his father's successor, but then replaced by his brother Saif al-Dīn Ghāzī. This was said to have been the result of a plot on the part of Saif al-Dīn's mother, the daughter of Timur-Tāsh, an Ortoqid prince of Mārdīn, and Quṭb al-Dīn's administrator, the eunuch 'Abd al-Masīḥ.[73] 'Abd al-Masīḥ's power was certain to attract envy, but the position was embittered by the fact that he was a Christian. Nūr al-Dīn claimed to have received "thousands" of complaints about him[74] and decided to move to Mosul to settle affairs to his own satisfaction. He crossed the Euphrates at Qal'at Ja'bar and reached al-Raqqa on 14 September. This was briefly defended against him, and after taking it he moved up the line of the Khābūr river northwards to Niṣībīn, where he arrived some time before 14 October. 'Imād al-Dīn was now sent to Baghdad to explain his master's actions to the Caliph – he was merely going to his own home and the home of his father to set it in order[75] – after which he returned to find Nūr al-Dīn, reinforced by troops from Ḥiṣn Kaifā, besieging Sinjār, which fell at the start of December.

Nūr al-Dīn now moved to the north of Mosul, where his men forded the Tigris, strung out "like a single thread" behind a Turkman guide.[76] Saif al-Dīn and 'Abd al-Masīḥ had asked for help from Ildeghiz of Hamadan, but by crossing the river Nūr al-Dīn had cut the city off from the east. There was no fighting and terms were quickly made. 'Abd al-Masīḥ was removed, and later sent north to Sīwās. This must have seemed to some Muslim writers an inappropriate penalty for a persecutor of the godly and an unreliable account says that he was converted to Islam and his name changed from 'Abd al-Masīḥ to 'Abd Allāh.[77] But the decision crucial to Saladin's career was that Mosul should be left to Saif al-Dīn, while Nūr al-Dīn's son-in-law, Zangī, had to be content with the far less important town of Sinjār. The Qāḍī Kamāl al-Dīn al-Shahrazūrī is quoted as telling Nūr al-Dīn that this would destroy his house as Zangī, the elder, would not obey Saif al-Dīn and Saif al-Dīn, the king, would not obey Zangī.[78] Nūr al-Dīn, however, was not deflected from his decision and after a brief pause he marched back west, reaching Ḥarrān on 23 February and Aleppo on 14 March. In May he was in Damascus and not until June is there any reference to orders being sent to him from Egypt.

Saladin in the meanwhile had been strengthening his hold on Egypt and widening the basis of support of his regime. He gave his father the *iqṭā's* of Alexandria and Damietta and, in upper Egypt, Tūrān-Shāh was put in charge of the Red Sea port of 'Aidhāb, as well as of Aswān and Qūṣ (map 6), where he appointed as his deputy the emir Shams al-Khilāfa, a surprising survivor of Shāwar's intrigues.[79] In Cairo Saladin ordered the demolition of a site on which to build a college for the Mālikites, the oldest of the orthodox denominations in Egypt, and at the same time a prison in Fusṭāṭ was converted for use by the Shāfi'ites, his own denomination. These foundations must have had the immediate aim of weakening the Fatimid position, but it was an act of general prudence for Muslim rulers to win the favour of *faqīhs* and scholars. The organised power of the Christian church was not duplicated in Islam but careers based on education in religion and religious law attracted able and ambitious men. Their main function was to serve as judges and administrators, but they could, less tangibly, provide a link between their military masters and the ideal Islamic state.

In theory, Islam was a theocracy guided by the Prophet's successor, the Caliph, God's representative on earth, in whom Muslim historians saw a parallel to the Pope, but who was originally more closely akin to a Caesaro-Papist Byzantine emperor. All Muslims formed a single religious community, the *umma*, in whom the power of Islam was vested and the consensus of whose opinion was an infallible guide to action. As a concept, as a general stimulus and on a personal level this notion maintained some validity, but in political terms the *umma* was either utopian or irrelevant. The Caesaro-Papist view of the Caliphate scarcely outlasted the earliest days of Islam and as the Caliphate declined in importance and was fragmented, the powers necessary to maintain social organisation had to be channelled through smaller and more practical administrative units. Characteristically, these were provided by family or clan dynasties, but there were obvious grounds for challenging the theoretical *raison d'être* of such intermediaries in a theocracy, in which any or all of them could be regarded as parasites. To counter this challenge rulers needed the help of scholarship and religious propaganda. If, for instance, the basis of their rule could be linked to one of the fundamentals of Islam, then their position within the Islamic framework would need no further justification. This is a lesson that Nūr al-Dīn taught by example in that his own rule was joined in practice and propaganda to the Islamic concept of the Holy War.

Saladin now showed that he had taken this lesson to heart. He gathered his troops outside Cairo in November 1170, collecting, as the Franks heard, forces "from all Egypt and from the regions of Damascus and swelling their ranks with a number of plebeians and men of the lower classes".[80] According to a letter written by al-Fāḍil the army moved from its camp by Birkat al-Jubb, some 11 miles (18 km) from Cairo, on 26 November and on Tuesday 8 December it was in southern Palestine.[81] On the next day it attacked Dārūm, 9 miles (14 km) south of Gaza. A small fortress had been built here by Amalric and a number of settlers had been attracted to it, according to William of Tyre, because it was easier for men of limited means to make a living there than in the cities.[82] Their settlement fell on the first day of the Muslim attack and the Muslims then brought up a mangonel against the fortress itself, as well as using Aleppan sappers to bring down one of its towers. The attack had started on Wednesday 9 December and on Friday 11 December news came that Amalric was marching south from Gaza.

Saladin now moved north with a force estimated by William of Tyre at 40,000 horse, drawn up in 42 "cohorts".[83] The Muslims considered it necessary when fighting the Franks to adopt a flexible formation based on numbers of small self-contained units, so that when the Franks charged one of them, the others could move without confusion to attack their flanks and rear.[84] The tactical unit was the *ṭulb* (squadron) which was defined as a body of not more than 200 horse, commanded by an emir.[85] If William of Tyre's cohorts can be taken as 200-man *ṭulbs*, this would give a figure of 8400 horse, not including servants and retainers. William's figures are a flimsy basis for theorising, but at least it is clear that the Muslims dangerously outnumbered Amalric, who was credited by William with 250 horse and 2000 foot.

According to al-Fāḍil, the Muslims surrounded the advancing Franks and waited for the expected charge, which did not come.[86] William of Tyre explains that the Franks were alarmed by the enemy numbers and closed their formation. The Muslims attacked to try to split them, but they pressed even more tightly together and continued to move towards Dārūm. The Muslims harassed their march until Friday evening, but when Amalric did not offer battle, Saladin left him and moved on Saturday to attack Gaza. Here Miles de Plancy, whom William of Tyre had already blamed for giving bad advice in Egypt, was said to have refused to allow the citizens to take shelter in the citadel[87] and the Muslims captured or killed a number of them, as well as seizing horses, cattle and stores and freeing a number of their own prisoners. Saladin returned to Dārūm on the same day, but as Amalric still made no move, he left for Egypt on Sunday. The army arrived in Cairo on 22 December and was welcomed home by the Caliph.

The Dārūm expedition was not Saladin's only effort during the winter campaigning season of 1170/1, and although the dating and details are not clear, it is known that he also attacked and captured the castle of Eilat. This was built on an island some 7½ miles (12 km) from the head of the Gulf of 'Aqaba, close to its western shore (map 7). The southern route from Syria to Egypt passed down through the eastern hills at the head of the gulf, crossed the flat land at its tip and then climbed through a low pass to the hinterland of Sinai. The castle, which relied for its water on cisterns and on a mainland spring, could not accommodate a large garrison and neither during Shīrkūh's expeditions nor at the time of Ayyūb's move to Egypt is it mentioned as being a threat to the Muslims' passage. Obviously, however, it could menace smaller parties and Saladin decided to clear it from his path.

Al-Fāḍil is quoted as saying that Saladin had ships made in sections, which were loaded on camels.[88] A large force escorted them from Cairo and the castle was attacked by land and sea. It is said to have fallen on 31 December, the garrison being killed or captured, and Saladin then occupied it with a garrison of his own. In part, this story is contradicted by a letter preserved by Qalqashandī, which notes that the castle was extremely strong and could only have been taken by a long siege, but when the Muslims camped by the sea-shore, its garrison asked for quarter and surrendered.[89] It must be doubtful if Saladin himself was there at the time. He could have left Cairo immediately after returning from Dārūm and arrived before 31 December, or he could have crossed Sinai from the coast road to Egypt without returning to Cairo at all. In both cases, however, some note would be expected in the Arabic sources. 'Imād al-Dīn does, in fact, credit him with two expeditions, but he confuses the issue by dating the end of the first to November[90] and connecting the second with the arrival of a caravan bringing more, unspecified, members of Saladin's family to Cairo, which is best dated to February 1171.[91] It has been suggested that Eilat was, in fact, Saladin's main objective,[92] but if his attack on the Coast was diversionary it is difficult to see why he then gave Amalric clear passage from Dārūm to Eilat before the castle had fallen. It may be agreed, however, that while he himself marched on Dārūm he must have sent a blockading force to Eilat. If Qalqashandī's letter is authentic, he may have been thinking in terms of a long siege to which he could later come himself. But had the castle then surrendered quickly, he might have decided to visit it at his leisure to supervise the posting of a garrison and this he could reasonably have combined with the task of escorting his family to Cairo.

A successful campaign and the arrival of more family reinforcements encouraged him to make further changes in Egypt, but although the pace was accelerated, he did not move rashly. First he checked his defences. Towards the end of February Tūrān-Shāh left for upper Egypt on an expedition against marauding Bedouin that lasted until half-way through May. In May Saladin himself paid the first visit of his vizierate to Alexandria, where he ordered the fortifications to be strengthened. He improved the position of Sunnī Islam by the dismissal of all Shī'ite judges in Egypt and their replacement by Shāfi'ites. In particular, the post of Qāḍī 'l-Quḍāt of Cairo and Fusṭāṭ was given to the Ash'arī Shāfi'ite Ṣadr al-Dīn ibn Durbās, a Kurd who, in the view of al-Wahrānī, added to intelligence and sound judgement the merit of "keeping himself from bribery and banquets".[93] Saladin's nephew, Taqī al-Dīn, founded another Shāfi'ite college in April and according to Maqrīzī, "the people professed the doctrines of Mālik and al-Shāfi'ī from that year on and the doctrine of the Shī'ites was hidden away until it was forgotten in Egypt".[94]

In the Palace, however, the centre of Fatimid Shī'ism still remained intact. According to a report quoted earlier, the Abbasid Caliph al-Mustanjid had already pressed for the overthrow of his rival. Al-Mustanjid himself was murdered on 20 December 1170 while Nūr al-Dīn was moving on Mosul, but the point was taken up by his successor, al-Mustaḍī'. Ibn Abī Ṭayy, who relished stories of dissension between Nūr al-Dīn and Saladin, said that Saladin's delay led Nūr al-Dīn "to suspect and revile him".[95] In theory Saladin could have played off al-'Āḍid against Nūr al-Dīn, had he been recalled from Egypt, a point that must have occurred to both of them, but, in fact, the history of his moves agrees exactly with his claim to Baghdad that he had had to act slowly and with cunning to chip away at the base of the column of Fatimid power. There was an uncomfortable historical parallel to his own position in the reign of the eighth Fatimid Caliph, al-Mustanṣir, when Fatimid rule had been threatened by the proclamation of allegiance to the Abbasids by Nāṣir al-Daula ibn Ḥamdān in northern Egypt. In the event, it was the Caliph who survived and Nāṣir al-Daula who was killed. It was reasonable for Saladin to move with prudence to avoid making the same mistake.

According to 'Imād al-Dīn, Nūr al-Dīn wrote to Saladin in June 1171 telling him to establish the Abbasid *khuṭba* in Egypt, and Saladin waited for two months to co-ordinate his plans.[96] There are the usual stories of hesitancy and intrigue.[97] Saladin is said to have asked advice from his emirs, who were split on the question of changing the *khuṭba*, "but it was not possible to do anything except obey Nūr al-Dīn's orders".[98] He is also said to have asked for a decision about the legality of the position, and the Shāfi'ite *faqīh*, Najm al-Dīn al-Khābushānī, is credited with pressing the case against the Fatimids.[99] It is reported that a concerted attack was made on Egyptian emirs, whose houses were surrounded by Syrian troops. Al-'Āḍid was told: "the emirs whom we are killing are men who have rebelled against you".[100] Al-'Āḍid then fell ill. One account makes him take poison, while according to another he was injured in a fall.[101] In his illness he asked Saladin to visit him and one of his sons is quoted as saying that, when Saladin came, he asked him to look after his children, "who were all young".[102] The commonest story, however, is that Saladin, fearing treachery, refused to go and regretted it afterwards.[103]

It is difficult to disentangle what truth there is in these accounts. Saladin can be expected to have sounded the feelings both of his emirs and of the religious leaders. His relations with al-'Āḍid are variously reported. On the one hand, he is said to have acted in al-'Āḍid's lifetime to break his power by taking away all his possessions, including his horses, thus preventing him from showing himself to the people in the state processions,[104] while another report says that the two were on such friendly terms that Saladin would disappear into the Palace for days at a time, alone and without an escort.[105] Whatever Saladin's personal feelings, however, al-'Āḍid was a potential source of danger to himself, his family and his Syrian troops. The timing of his move may have been affected by al-'Āḍid's illness, but the logic of power politics had made it clear that the Fatimid Caliphate could no longer survive.

On the first Friday of the new year 567 A.H., 10 September 1171 A.D., the Abbasid *khuṭba* was introduced in Fusṭāṭ.[106] Ibn al-Athīr says that a Persian emir, whom he remembered seeing at Mosul, went to the pulpit before the preacher and pronounced the prayer for al-Mustaḍī'[107]. Ibn Abī Ṭayy said that Saladin entrusted the task to his father for fear of what might happen and his father threatened to kill the preacher if he pronounced the *khuṭba* in al-'Āḍid's name. The preacher then left out all names from the prayer, excusing himself on the grounds that he did not know al-Mustaḍī's titles. Al-'Āḍid asked for whom the *khuṭba* had been pronounced and was told that no one had been named. "Next Friday", he said, "it will be for a named man."[108]

Here again, whatever the accuracy of these details, it appears that Saladin intended to move in two stages, taking his first step on 10 September and testing reaction to it, before introducing the Abbasid *khuṭba* into Cairo itself.[109] On 11 September he paraded 147 out of a total of 167 squadrons of his army through the Cairo streets in front of crowds that included Frankish and Byzantine envoys. Al-Fāḍil wrote: "those who saw this review thought that no king of Islam had ever possessed an army to match this".[110] Two days later, on Monday 13 September, al-'Āḍid died. Although he had held the Caliphate for some eleven-and-a-half years, he was said to have been ten days short of his twenty-first birthday at his death.

3

LORD OF EGYPT

On the second Friday of Muḥarram 567 A.H., 17 September 1171 A.D., the Abbasid *khuṭba* was pronounced in Fusṭāṭ and Cairo. Saladin described his reaction to al-'Āḍid's death in a letter to Majd al-Dīn Mubārak ibn Munqidh, the military governor of upper Egypt. He stressed, disingenuously, his own fidelity; he had acted with the greatest respect towards the dead Caliph, accompanying his corpse to the graveside, comforting his children and establishing them in his palace; affairs were proceeding smoothly and there was no unrest; the governor was to give orders for the *khuṭba* in his district to be pronounced in the name of "the ruler who commands the united obedience of Islam", the Abbasid Caliph al-Mustaḍī', "whose name and titles are to be clearly stated"; anyone who by word or deed tried to stir up the people or to meddle in the affair of "the one who has gone and the one who stands in his place" was to be punished; "as far as we can see, the world is safe".[1]

In spite of Saladin's euphemistic reference to the establishment of al-'Āḍid's children in the palace, it must have been obvious that the Fatimid dynasty had now ended. All the remaining Fatimids were "kept from women lest they breed",[2] but provided with allowances for food and clothing and 'Imād al-Dīn, writing at the end of Saladin's reign, noted that they were still there "to this day... but their numbers have diminished."[3] The death of al-'Āḍid, however, was a landmark but not a turning-point; although the palace may have been a focus for anti-Syrian feeling, he himself had been a cypher. Saladin still had enemies in Egypt and he was still under the shadow of Nūr al-Dīn. At that, however, the early history of his career in Egypt is at least superficially one of reaction to external dangers. The struggle for Syrian dominance in Egypt gives it coherence, but Saladin was the executive rather than the originator of a policy which in itself was a simple reflection of the view that Shīrkūh had "conquered" Egypt. Now that at least some of the pressure had been removed his scope had widened and it can be argued that for the first time he now had the opportunity to impose his own pattern on events rather than merely react to external promptings.

His first action was to show himself in the role of champion of Islam. According to 'Imād al-Dīn, he had agreed with Nūr al-Dīn to launch a joint attack on Kerak and Shaubak to clear the eastern route between Syria and Egypt.[4] This agreement must, at best, have been tentative on Saladin's part as far as timing was concerned since he could not have been sure whether or not the Abbasid *khuṭba* would lead to trouble in Cairo. His success, however, allowed him to leave the city on 25 September and he marched by way of Bilbais on an expedition that lasted until halfway through November and that appears to have produced no results, except, according to Ibn al-Athīr, for a worsening of his relations with Nūr al-Dīn.[5] Ibn al-Athīr reported that when Saladin wrote to tell Nūr al-Dīn that he was leaving Cairo, Nūr al-Dīn himself moved south from Damascus. Saladin had been so successful in his attack on Shaubak that the garrison had asked for quarter, with a ten-day delay before the castle had to be surrendered. It was now pointed out to Saladin that if he attacked the Coast from one side while Nūr al-Dīn attacked from the other, the Frankish kingdom would fall and his own position in Egypt would be in danger. More immediately, if he were to meet Nūr al-Dīn at Shaubak, he could be refused permission to return to Egypt. As a result, Saladin marched back to Egypt, claiming to have heard news of Fatimid plots, "but Nūr al-Dīn did not accept the excuse".[5]

This story is certainly exaggerated. To assume that Saladin had to have the danger from Nūr al-Dīn pointed out to him is naive. William of Tyre, who has no hesitation in giving details of Frankish difficulties and losses, makes no reference to the proposed surrender of Shaubak but writes that Saladin wasted his time there for some days and then left after seeing that he was making no headway.[6] But the rumours cannot be dismissed entirely. Even the faithful 'Imād al-Dīn, who is always concerned to show Saladin in the best light, merely notes vaguely that "something happened" to prevent his meeting with Nūr al-Dīn and he adds that Saladin had lost horses and baggage animals on his journey.[7] These losses and the strength of Shaubak, which was never taken from the Franks by assault, may well have been reason enough for Saladin's withdrawal, but the fact that he never met Nūr al-Dīn after December 1168 must have some significance and had Nūr al-Dīn wanted to replace him or curb his power, the fall of the Fatimids would have given him a convenient opportunity. It is to be assumed, however, that Saladin's move from Cairo, within a fortnight of al-'Āḍid's death, was primarily intended as a *beau geste* and, in view of the need to consolidate his position in Egypt, he cannot have been looking for a long siege. His decree cancelling taxes in Fusṭāṭ and Cairo had been published in his absence and he must have been anxious to investigate what rumour claimed to be the vast treasures of the Fatimid Palace.

The opulence of the Fatimid court, the splendour of their public processions and their magnificent gifts naturally led to a belief that they were endlessly wealthy. It seems that when Saladin took over the Palace, the reality proved something of a disappointment. There were treasures of various kinds, including a stone jar containing 700 jewels, a huge emerald, 100 chests of splendid clothes and 2 ribs of a "huge fish" which, when set upright, could conceal a mounted man. But these were interesting rarities rather than major contributions to Saladin's treasury. Ibn Abī Ṭayy notes that not much money was found because of the sums that Shāwar had given to the Franks[8] – and, he might have added, because of the million dinars given to Saladin during the siege of Damietta. That Saladin was disappointed seems to be confirmed by the persistent rumours of undiscovered secrets. According to a Shī'ite story, he tortured a man who was thought to know where the secret treasure was hidden by having beetles fixed to his skull – "no-one could endure this for an hour without the beetles working through to his brain".[9] In this case, the story goes, the torture failed because the victim had carried the head of the martyred Imām of the Shī'a, al-Ḥusain ibn 'Alī, when it had been brought from Ascalon to Egypt for re-burial and the beetles did not attack him. This is hostile fantasy, but the early existence of the rumours themselves is confirmed by 'Imād al-Dīn, who says of Ibn 'Abd al-Qawī, whom Saladin crucified in 1174, that he knew the secrets of the Palace and its hidden treasures, but died without revealing them.[10]

Treasure or no treasure, however, Saladin had already taken steps to buy popularity by cancelling the *mukūs* taxes in Fusṭāṭ and Cairo.[11] Taxation in early Islam was concentrated on persons and property but their expansion had brought the Arabs into contact with many long established service taxes (the *mukūs*) and, as these had no Islamic precedent, they had, strictly, to be considered illegal.

On the other hand, as they were usually intended to defray, if not cover, the cost of the services to which they were attached, after each periodic cancellation they were regularly reintroduced.

Saladin's decree of abolition[12] was read out on Friday 6 October. It covered "Cairo, Fusṭāṭ and all traders visiting there"; these men were to be allowed to come and go, leave money, bring it or lend it, and trade by land and water, by ship and on horseback, in secret and openly, without having to reveal what they had concealed, without being asked about what they were exporting or importing and without being stopped on the road. "All governors who read this or to whom it is read, men of the sword or the pen, overseers or inspectors, must obey it." The value of the cancelled taxes was put at 100,000 dinars a year. Although the timing can be questioned, it is clear that Saladin intended that similar taxes should be repealed throughout Egypt. In an undated letter to Ikhmīm in upper Egypt he is found writing:

> It has come to our notice that the various branches of *mukūs* taxes have not yet been abandoned in Ikhmīm... and that those who come and go, those who live there and those who travel, all have to share in their payment... and have not yet tasted the sweetness of our benefaction... The people of its lands have not shared in the concessions that we made at the start of our reign... The rich are hurt and the poor are crushed... Such taxes are a punishment for those who delay paying the *zakāt* [alms tax] and who follow their lusts.

The decree of repeal was to be read in the old mosque at Ikhmīm; all the people, inhabitants and travellers, were to be informed of it, lest any doubt should remain; no one was to open a register to cover such taxes in future "or to set up a balance" (to weigh payment). Saladin had agreed to compensate the *iqṭā'* holders, who had benefitted from the taxes, and they were to obey "both now and in the future".[13]

Qalqashandī wrote that Saladin replaced the *mukūs* taxes by spoils of war,[14] but at no period of his career was this true. Perhaps he had some hopes of balancing an initial loss against the treasures of the Palace and the fact that on his return to Cairo he is reported to have removed silver ornaments from mosques in Cairo and Fusṭāṭ may show that he was trying to make up for their inadequacy.[15] A reliance on windfalls, however, would obviously have been unsound policy and he had already taken steps to raise revenue from a tax with an impeccable Islamic pedigree. This was the *zakāt* or alms tax, an *ad valorem* levy on certain types of goods and property which according to Islamic law was obligatory on all Muslims, as opposed to the voluntary alms (*ṣadaqa*), which they could give as they wished.

In theory the individual could distribute his *zakāt* himself, but there were obvious practical difficulties and Saladin was able to treat it as a state tax without legal criticism. When the money had been collected it was not entirely at the disposal of the ruler, as the headings under which payments could be made from it were laid down by law. A certain percentage was to be paid out as social security benefits to the poor and in other good causes, but the rest could be spent by the state under headings which could be stretched to accommodate war, diplomacy and administration.

According to al-Fāḍil, in the first distribution of the *zakāt*, which is dated to November 1171, the Treasury took half of the total.[16] Ibn Jubair, visiting Alexandria in 1183, noted that the Treasury's share then was three-eighths.[17] Ibn Ḥamdān, who was employed in the *zakāt* office, signed a balance sheet for the Muslim year 588 showing a total of 52,000 dinars.[18] Unfortunately, it is not clear whether this figure represents the total collected or the Treasury's share, in which latter case it could be argued that the *zakāt* more than replaced the estimated loss on the cancelled taxes.

It could, of course, be objected that Saladin had merely substituted one burden for another at the cost of what can be seen from the Ikhmīm letter as considerable administrative inconvenience. The optimistic references in his decree to the free passage of merchants have to be set against Ibn Jubair's complaints of persistent ill-treatment of merchants and pilgrims at "places such as Ikhmīm, Qūṣ and Minyat Ibn al-Khaṣīb".[19] Ibn Jubair wrote of the *zakāt* collectors:

> They feel the waists of the merchants to see that they are not carrying anything under their armpits and they have long needles mounted on handles that they stick into sacks etc., to see that nothing is being smuggled... It would be more fitting to give *zakāt* to pilgrims rather than to take it from them... It reminds them of the days of the *mukūs* taxes and they are humiliated.

This coupling of the *zakāt* with the *mukūs* might be taken as proof of the failure of Saladin's move had Ibn Jubair not added: "Saladin would put a stop to this if he heard of it."[20] Islam was concerned with social welfare, and to collect and distribute money for this purpose by methods clearly derived from religious law underlined the relationship of the regime to fundamental Islamic principles. Imperfections and inadequacies could be blamed on subordinates; the ruler's position was strengthened.

Saladin's concern to associate himself with his Islamic background had a wider application to his administration of Egypt. It was popularly claimed that if a wall were to be built round Egypt, cutting it off from all other lands, its people would be self-sufficient[21], and in Saladin's time, apart from its need for certain strategic imports, notably timber for ship-building, Egypt could certainly exist with the minimum of dependence on the outside world. This meant that a strong ruler whose primary concern was with Egypt itself could establish a Pharaonic state whose external relationships would be subordinated to its own interests. On the other hand, if Egypt were merely regarded as a transit land or as a base for some wider enterprise, then its needs could be expected to take second place.

Although it has been claimed that an Egypt-first policy was, in fact, advocated,[22] Saladin, together with the Kurds and Turks who made up the bulk of his army, must naturally have thought of an Islamic centre of gravity as lying farther east. From the standpoint of religious propaganda Egypt was part of the patrimony of Islam, a base for the Holy War but not as convenient a one as Syria. Further, the immediate lesson of the fall of the Fatimids was that Egypt had proved too weak to stand alone. This might be explained as the accidental result of political disturbance, while to Ibn Khaldūn it could illlustrate inevitable degeneration following the dilution of '*aṣabīya*. In economic terms, however, it may suggest that, without growth, administration and defence were inevitably top-heavy at this period, or more widely, that in view of the sociological factors involved growth was needed to absorb energies which would otherwise be self-destructive or decline to apathy. To what extent any of these points can be justified in this context must be seen from Saladin's later career. It is immediately clear that, while Nūr al-Dīn held Syria, Saladin was forced to think in Egyptian terms, but he invariably based the justification for his actions on Islam and as soon as he found it practicable, he turned to expansion, linking this to the imperatives of an Islamic policy.

No coherent policy, however, was possible without power. Saladin had earlier been shown by Shāwar the disadvantages of wealth without military backing, but the converse also held good in that military power could not be maintained without wealth. This might be won by conquest, in which case the army could be considered as a producer and not merely as a consumer, but Saladin's history shows how comparatively unproductive conquest was, and for the most part state revenues relied on primary production.[23] The importance of production was, of course, obvious enough in Egypt, whose revenue depended directly on the annual Nile flood, but Saladin had also to take account of the power structure that controlled it. Here economic factors and population statistics gave even the humblest primary producers a measure of importance. Préaux, writing of the flight of peasants from their villages in Lagid Egypt, noted that this succeeded as a method of exerting pressure in circumstances where "those who abandoned their tasks could not immediately be replaced".[24] In an account of the Fayyūm written some fifty years after Saladin's death al-Nābulsī mentioned the lack of cultivation caused by the withdrawal of labour and he referred to what could not be brought back into cultivation "without the fear of driving the inhabitants to have recourse to flight".[25] If there was quantifiable power at the lowest end of the scale of producers, it can be taken for granted that the full interrelationship of power and wealth was too complicated to be manipulated easily or arbitrarily by a leader exclusively for his own purposes.

An obvious expedient in such cases, where the ruler's main interests lay elsewhere, was for him to barter land, together with the responsibility for its administration, in return for support. Niẓām al-Mulk is credited by Muslim historians with introducing the idea of making grants of the usufruct of lands and villages in place of money, as he is said to have thought that this would ensure the better management of estates in a large empire. Saladin followed the same pattern in Egypt where, according to Maqrīzī, his reign marked the start of a period in which all lands were held as *iqṭā's* by the Sultan, his emirs and troops.[26] Maqrīzī also noted another change which he dated, by implication, to this period, where he wrote that neither in Fatimid times nor earlier did the army have the type of *iqṭā's* that were seen in his own day. Formerly the lands had been leased to any of the emirs, prominent men or soldiers who wanted them, in return for sureties and a guaranteed sum to be paid to the Treasury. In his own time, by contrast, the cultivators had become "slaves born in the house of the *iqṭā'* holders, except that they can never hope to be sold or freed"[27] – presumably because of the replacement of the leasing system by one of long-term or permanent grants. This passage, however, should not be taken as proof that Saladin himself made dramatic and uniform changes to Fatimid *iqṭā's*. Contemporary sources are, in the main, silent on this point and clearly there was no uniformity. Ibn Mammātī mentions land leased on surety and without survey on the west bank of the Nile, which he contrasts with east-bank lands leased on an acreage tax with a cadastral survey.[28] In addition to leases, long-term grants of land were made which must certainly have encouraged *iqṭāʿ* holders to try to keep their farmers and peasants tied to the soil, but in spite of this the remark already quoted from the survey of the Fayyūm shows that the peasants' weapon of flight was still effective.[29]

Intricacies peculiar to Egyptian administration added their own difficulties. Egypt depended on the Nile and to control the Nile flood there had to be a system of interdependent dykes and channels, the maintenance of which required large-scale organisation of labour. As a result Egypt was by tradition a centralised bureaucracy. If the bureaucratic machine were allowed to become inefficient, the country would suffer and the ruler would lose revenue. Contemporary accounts give a bewildering mass of detail about the complexity of the every-day processes involved which were, in the main, inherited from Dynastic times. The Nile flood obliterated landmarks and changed the condition of the soil, which meant that agricultural land had to be re-surveyed every year. The procession that used to set out for this purpose comprised an overseer (*mushārif*), an administrator (*ʿāmil*), the surveyor (*masīḥ*), the witness (*shāhid*), the guides, the most important farmers and the men with the measuring poles.[30] They had to establish not only the acreage but also the precise condition of the land and here Ibn Mammātī notes thirteen possible variants which determined the tax assessment.[31] The unloading of a ship needed the same kind of multiplication of functionaries. These included the man who carried the key to the dockyard, the man who weighed the goods, men to unpack them from their containers, a storekeeper to put them in a warehouse, another man who was responsible for opening and closing the warehouse, guards for the ship, searchers at the dockyard gates, guards to protect the goods, boat crews to ferry them from the ship and porters to carry them.[32]

These are, of course, no more than symptoms. What they indicate is the existence of bureaucratic processes that could provide Egypt with a managed economy, where agriculture, largely dependent on a state-controlled water-supply, could be further controlled by variable tax rates to produce the crops required, and state monopolies could regulate the major trading products as well as the supply of money. The tax system did, in fact, extend state influence throughout Egypt, not only to the living but even to the dead. In Saladin's time undertakers were not to proceed with a funeral until the appropriate government department had been notified. If the dead man had heirs, his estate would be released to them, but if it fell to the state itself, then the department would pay the funeral expenses.[33] Non-Muslim Egyptians were liable for a special tax and government clerks were told to enter in the register not merely their names but "what would not change with the days, such as tall, short, white or black".[34] It was noted in the Fayyūm in the Muslim year 641 that out of 1142 such non-Muslims, 849 were in residence, 139 were in the south and 154 in the north. Soldiers had their descriptions as well as their names entered in the army lists, as clerks had to keep track of them throughout their service to check on their pay and equipment. If they died or were discharged, the equipment provided by the state had to be returned, except where a man had fallen on active service. No claim was then made and a cross was entered against his name on the list.[35]

The proliferation of controls, however, does not obscure the fact that Saladin had taken over a mixed economy, and the type of poor relief financed by the *zakāt* shows that he was prepared not merely to endure but, at a low level, to encourage it by providing funds for private trade. State officials, such as al-Fāḍil, traded on their own account with North Africa and India. Land reclamation was undertaken by private enterprise and Ibn Mammātī noted that the state lost money by giving long-term leases of building land, on which developers could make a 300 per cent profit.[36]

The functions of the various *dīwāns* which administered these controls have been recorded and studied,[37] but the measure of their effectiveness is difficult to determine. The evidence of letters points to confusion caused by the duplication of private and public *dīwāns*. Bureaucrats tried to extend their own powers, acting independently of their masters, and had to be checked by an apparently erratic appeals procedure whereby complaints were forwarded to Saladin himself by members of his court. Thus a letter had to be sent to an official telling him not to act roughly or to use threats when measuring the land of a dead emir as the emir's son had not been "abandoned or ignored" by Saladin.[38] A deed of grant to another beneficiary warned "the hand of the *dīwān* not to oppose him", while "the tongues of its employees" were not to challenge his description of his land, presumably by insisting on a survey.[39] In the case of Ibn al-Ṣāliḥ b. Ruzzaik, officials in upper Egypt had seized a press that he owned there and had confiscated his written proofs of ownership, while the governor and overseers at Aswān had taken his dates, cotton, wheat, barley and ships, all of which they were ordered to return.[40]

The difficulty that Saladin seems to have had in keeping his bureaucrats under effective control must have been increased by their relative scarcity. There were few Muslims to be employed. Al-Makhzūmī wrote that clerks in the *Dīwān al-Ḥarb* were usually Jews, while taxation clerks were Christian Copts. He added: "as Christians and Jews were unable to share rule with the Muslims, they shared with them in the general running of affairs, providing tax clerks, army clerks and doctors. I can only think that this is an affliction sent by Almighty God to test the Muslims." He noted that these non-Muslims passed on their professions from father to son, adding that young Muslims, having been brought up on the Quran and Arabic literature, naturally wanted to get some profit from what they had learnt and were unwilling then to study under non-Muslims. As a result, though they were constantly criticised, non-Muslim clerks could not adequately be replaced.[41]

The extent to which Saladin himself took an interest in civil administration can, perhaps, never fairly be assessed. He cannot be shown to have made any genuine efforts to tighten state control by strengthening the bureaucratic basis of a managed economy in Egypt. He was concerned with the shuffling of his dynastic cards, as he moved members of his family from one post to another, and also in the disposal of important *iqṭā's*. He was urgently interested in finance, as without money he could not maintain his forces, and he was also the final court of appeal. But at a lower level the efficient running of his administration must have depended largely on the calibre of the men whom he picked to control it.

The name that occurs most obviously in this context is that of the Qāḍī al-Fāḍil, who has some claim to be thought the most famous of all Saladin's Muslim contemporaries. He was a poet, a littérateur, an administrator and a statesman, and his letters form one of the most fruitful sources of information not only about Saladin's career but about the age in which he lived. 'Abd al-Laṭīf al-Baghdādī has left a description of him: "we came into the presence of al-Fāḍil and saw a frail old man, all head and heart. He was writing and dictating to two people, with all kinds of movements of the face and lips caused by his eagerness to get his words out. It is as though he was writing with his whole body."[42] He was some three years older than Saladin and had been sent to Egypt from Ascalon, where his father had been the Shāfi'ite Qāḍī, to enter the service of the Fatimids. He was first employed in the *Dīwān al-Inshā'* in Cairo and then moved for a time to Alexandria. When he returned to Cairo, he served first in the *Dīwān al-Ḥarb* and then again in the *Dīwān al-Inshā'*. When Shīrkūh became vizier al-Fāḍil was seconded to his service, according to malicious report in the hope that he would be involved in his master's expected fall, and after Shīrkūh's death he passed into Saladin's service. The author of the *Sūq al-Fāḍil* wrote: "no scribe is known to have reached a position with regard to his master comparable to that achieved by al-Fāḍil with Saladin. It was said that the lands were not conquered by the armies of Saladin but by al-Fāḍil's pen."[43] According to Ibn Mammātī, the ideal scribe should take care not to give the impression that his employer is in need of him,[44] but al-Fāḍil is quoted as violating this canon and writing of the letters that he composed for Saladin: "other men send their messages to the Sultan, but the Sultan is my messenger in the letters that I send".[45]

Neither al-Fāḍil nor Saladin had roots in the country that they governed and the history of Saladin's vizierate has not made clear how important this is to an interpretation of their society. On the one hand there is the picture of Islam as a monolithic structure. At its simplest, this is reflected in the view of Saladin as the restorer of true religion and it can be refined by suggesting that thanks to the basic unity of its institutions the mediaeval Islamic world had roughly interchangeable parts. On this argument, Saladin's following of soldiers, administrators and religious leaders channelled the powers needed to control society and were as integral a part of the country as those whom they replaced. In contrast, however, Egypt can be seen as a cellular society in which racial groupings, such as those of the Turks, Kurds, Armenians, Negroes and Bedouin were uneasily juxtaposed. Religious differences provided their own divisions and sub-divisions of Christian, Muslim and Jewish sects, while the compromise between managed and mixed economy added its own administrative fragmentation. Saladin's Syrians could fit into this pattern as a war-band which, finding a country capable of supporting it, exercised only the measure of control needed to ensure its own advantage. Such a band might itself be a cell, united by *'aṣabīya*, or it could be seen as unit of a mobile professional class either serving or exploiting the country of its choice. Such questions can be multiplied at will; no simple answers are to be found nor would they necessarily be mutually exclusive. Saladin, however, now established as a major figure in his own right is at least well placed to provide some acceptable evidence through the details of his career as ruler of Egypt.

4

THE SHADOW OF SYRIA

After his return to Cairo in November 1171, Saladin had some time to concentrate on administrative problems without external distractions. He himself kept to his old quarters in the vizier's palace. His father still lived in the Pearl Palace and the North Palace was given over to a number of Syrian emirs. Now that the Fatimids had fallen, coins were minted in Egypt with the name of the Abbasid Caliph al-Mustaḍī' on one side and that of Nūr al-Dīn on the other. Nūr al-Dīn had sent Sharaf al-Dīn Ibn Abī 'Aṣrūn, described as a man who never made a mistake or took a bribe,[1] to bring the official news of the death of al-'Āḍid to Baghdad and he came back with robes of honour for both Nūr al-Dīn and Saladin. The envoys bringing them arrived at Cairo on 7 March and on 8 March a number of Cairene dignitaries visited their pavilion. The city streets were decorated and on 9 March Saladin put on the robes and rode across Cairo to Bāb Zuwaila.

There can have been little to celebrate for the rest of the year, which seems to have been marked by a continued persecution of Fatimid supporters. Ibn Abī Ṭayy wrote: "when a Turk saw an Egyptian, he took his clothes",[2] and "things went so far that any Turk who liked a house would drive out its owner and settle there".[3] Maqrīzī refers to a Nubian army on the southern frontier, a plague of mice in the sugar cane plantations and, in the spring of 1172, huge hail-stones that destroyed crops.[4] He adds that there was rioting in Cairo in the summer of 1172, while Abū Ṣāliḥ wrote of "the ruin brought upon the Armenians",[5] which led their Patriarch to leave Egypt for Jerusalem in November 1172. According to Maqrīzī, there was a flow of gold and silver from the country[6] and, in a letter to Baghdad, Saladin commented on unfavourable trading terms with European merchants.[7] In the spring of 1172 he discussed a plan to expand westwards to Barqa because he had "too little money and too many men".

Riches and military power, as he had seen, were interdependent and any imbalance between them could be destructive. If he already had too many men, Egypt must have been acting as a magnet. Hopes of profit could at first be satisfied by local pillage, as described by Ibn Abī Ṭayy and confirmed by the Armenian Abū Ṣāliḥ together with the Christian Sawīrus ibn al-Muqaffaʿ, but when they were translated into administrative policy, in a context of limited resources, there had to be external growth. This has also to be seen in relation to the Islamic system of polygamy and concubinage which, together with the ease of divorce, allowed for a measure of family planning in the sense that a man could readily increase the number of his children. Saladin himself had no children, recorded or acknowledged, until he was in his thirties. Then, after he had settled in Egypt, he fathered some four sons before the summer of 1173. Al-Fāḍil later wrote of them: "they have children [of their own] and the Sultan has spread out hopes for them... He has said to them: 'beget, and I shall dower the females and enrich the males'."[8] More generally he noted of Saladin's followers: "everyone who produces children and adds to the size of his family is trusting to the grace and generosity of our master".[9] This is a classic statement of the expansionist position and its application to Saladin in Egypt cannot have been obscure to his contemporaries. The more urgent his need for growth became, the more difficult it must have been to reconcile it to his nominal subservience to Nūr al-Dīn and not surprisingly for the next two years relations between Syria and Egypt were uneasy.

As has been noted, a Nubian army was reported on the Egyptian border in the summer of 1172 and al-Fāḍil wrote to tell Baghdad that the Nubians had been joined by Armenian refugees, as well as by other "disgraced soldiers" and by a number of common people.[10] According to Ibn Abī Ṭayy, this force decided to lay siege to Aswān.[11] The surrounding country, which was Bedouin territory, suffered from Nubian plundering expeditions, and the emir Kanz al-Daula, of the Bedouin tribe of Rabīʿa, sent to Saladin for help. Saladin replied with reinforcements under al-Shujāʿ al-Baʿalbakkī, and the Nubians then withdrew. The fighting that followed was indecisive and Tūrān-Shāh, who had already campaigned in the south in 1171, was sent out again in December 1172/January 1173. He advanced beyond Aswān and al-Fāḍil wrote of the enemy that "they were the ants whom Solomon has crushed".[12] Tūrān-Shāh gave quarter to "the common people and the cultivators", a reference that can be taken to show the scarcity value of farmers to the Egyptian state, after which he attacked and captured the Nubian town of Ibrīm, 34 miles (55 km) north of Abu Simbel (map 6) and 728 miles (1172 km) from Cairo.

The Arabic sources go to some pains to paint a picture of primitive conditions in Nubia.[13] The Ibrīm garrison was reported to have had no defence against arrows. The Nubian capital, Dongola, where Tūrān-Shāh sent an envoy, was a mere collection of huts, where the only sizeable building was the palace.[14] The land was narrow; there were no crops except maize and the king's present to Tūrān-Shāh's envoy consisted of flour. Ibn al-Athīr was quick to assume that Saladin was looking for a possible refuge from Nūr al-Dīn and he explained Tūrān-Shāh's return on the grounds that the country was not rich enough to attract him.[15] In fact, geographical difficulties and, in particular, the barrier of the cataracts ensured that, except through prodigious efforts, there was little to be achieved in Nubia beyond punitive expeditions. The Muslims did try to keep a footing in Ibrīm, but they only succeeded in holding it for two years, after which it was evacuated and then reoccupied by the Nubians.

There is no entirely reliable record of Saladin's own movements. He later claimed to have campaigned against the Franks every year during this period and there are obscurities in the accounts of both William of Tyre and 'Imād al-Dīn which may conceal some manoeuvring during the campaigning season of 1172. It is not until 1173, however, that he can definitely be shown to have been on the move again. Nineteen months had now passed since the death of al-'Āḍid, during which Nūr al-Dīn had taken no action with regard to Egypt. But clearly he expected some return from his investment. On 'Imād al-Dīn's figures he had provided Shīrkūh with 200,000 dinars, to which can be added further expenditure on his men.[16] By way of return, Saladin made a selection of Fatimid treasures, including "wonderful manufactured goods",[17] some jewels, 60,000 dinars, an ass of the finest breed and an elephant. He left Cairo either in April or towards the end of May 1173. At the beginning of July Nūr al-Dīn was at Mar'ash (map 3), some 110 miles (177 km) north of Aleppo, by which time he had received the treasures but not the elephant. This supports the April date for Saladin's march and implies that the treasure was sent on ahead to Damascus, presumably after it had been escorted past Kerak, to be followed by the elephant, perhaps with other heavy baggage.

According to 'Imād al-Dīn, Nūr al-Dīn thanked Saladin, but said: "we did not need this money... He knows that we did not spend money on the conquest of Egypt out of a need for [more] money."[18] This remark, however, cannot be taken at face value. Elsewhere 'Imād al-Dīn wrote: "since the time when Egypt was taken Nūr al-Dīn had wanted an agreed sum of money to be contributed which would help him meet the expenses of the Holy War... He was waiting for Saladin to suggest this on his own account and did not ask him for it."[19] On the arrival of Saladin's gifts and before leaving himself for his northern frontier, he decided to call for an audit of the finances of Egypt. It is clear that he was not looking for presents, however exotic, but for regular payments which, from the point of view of the Egyptian economy, would amount to an annual Egyptian subsidy for Syria.

Saladin in the meanwhile, after seeing his caravans on their way, took the opportunity to attack Frankish territory. Amalric, who was wary of being outmanoeuvred so as to leave the Coast unguarded, camped to the south of Hebron at Carmel of Judaea overlooking the Dead Sea,[20] round whose southern end he could march to the relief of Kerak or Shaubak if they were in danger (map 7). But Saladin did not press an attack against the castles and contented himself with ravaging the countryside. One of his main aims, he told Nūr al-Dīn, was to drive away the Bedouin who lived in Frankish territory. He wrote: "the servant knows that the master wants to attack the unbelievers. One of the most helpful things in his opinion is that no Bedouin should remain in their lands... so that when they come up... they may not find before them any guide."[21]

The Bedouin scouted for the Franks and provided them with supplies, but their refusal to change their way of life to fit in with the wishes of settled government made them unpopular with both sides. Al-Fāḍil wrote: "the Bedouin are like colocynths; the more you give them sweet water, the bitterer are their fruits",[22] and William of Tyre commented on their treachery: "as long as the issue of a battle is in doubt, they watch from afar. Then they join the victors and pursue the vanquished as though they were enemies, to enrich themselves from their spoils".[23] In fact, the Bedouin were the supreme example of the independent cell, to whom external political patterns were largely irrelevant. Saladin's attempt to remove them from Kerak was one of a number that he made and it certainly had a valid military purpose. By this time, however, he must have heard of Nūr al-Dīn's reception of his gifts, together with the proposal to hold an Egyptian audit, and he may be credited with some harmless malice as he passed the administrative problems, as well as the expense involved, back to his master and wrote: "had these Bedouin wanted to go to Egypt, the servant would have taken them there... but their desire is for Syria... Were the master to give them a region and a great *iqṭāʿ*, it would cut them off from the land of the unbelievers."[24]

Ibn al-Athīr misinterpreted Saladin's expedition and took it to be part of another plan for a concerted attack on the Franks from Egypt and Syria. He represented Saladin's gifts – "too splendid to be described" – as being brought to Damascus by Ḍiyā' al-Dīn ʿĪsā to accompany excuses for his withdrawal.[25] It is clear, however, that at this time Nūr al-Dīn could have had no intention of involving himself in a long siege of Kerak as he was preoccupied with the north.

In the north there was a long-standing confusion of frontiers and politics. The Byzantines shared an unstable border with Seljuq Rūm. The Christian state of Lesser Armenia had a foothold both in the mountains and in the Cilician plain and the minor Muslim dynasties of the Danishmendids and the Ortoqids maintained their hold on a number of strategic cities. Of these, the Ortoqids, from their position in Mārdīn and Ḥiṣn Kaifā, had a particular importance in feuds involving Mosul and, as has been seen, it was from Ḥiṣn Kaifā that Nūr al-Dīn received reinforcements when he moved on Mosul in 1170. Now, according to Ibn al-Athīr, it was the Danishmendid Lord of Sīwās (map 1) who gave him an excuse for marching north by claiming that Qilij-Arslān had attacked his lands.[26]

Qilij-Arslān, the Sultan of Rūm, had no direct involvement in Nūr al-Dīn's affairs, but both in terms of power politics, and in the context of the Holy War, he could be seen as a potential rival. Geographically he had a strong defensive position. The Turkman tribes, who used his land for pasturage, were a favourite source of recruits for the armies of the time.[27] Unlike Nūr al-Dīn, who had only one son, Qilij-Arslān had eleven, an obvious inducement to expansion, and he shared Nūr al-Dīn's own claim on the gratitude of Islam in that he was in the forefront of the battle against the infidel.

Nūr al-Dīn decided to make use of the complaint that he had received and from his base at Aleppo he moved against Marʿash, near the river Jaiḥān, and he attacked it on 2 July. After the place had surrendered, he turned east and took Behesni, which lies between the Jaiḥān and the Euphrates. Other small fortresses and towns were taken or came to terms and by the start of the Muslim year 569 (12

August) he was apparently ready to close his campaign. Qilij-Arslān, a man whom Nicetas described as "seeming always to act cautiously and advisedly",[28] had not moved to his frontier and Nūr al-Dīn would have been running a considerable risk had he extended his lines of communication by advancing any further.

'Imād al-Dīn, oddly, gives no account of any peace settlement but writes: "Nūr al-Dīn conquered these lands and gave them as *iqṭā's* to his army."[29] He makes no mention of Sīwās, which was temporarily recovered, and appears to suggest that when its momentum ran out, the campaign simply stopped. This was denied by Ibn al-Athīr, who wrote that Nūr al-Dīn sent a detachment which captured Sīwās, leading Qilij-Arslān to sue for peace.[30] Nūr al-Dīn, who had heard disquieting news of the Franks, was ready to agree to this and a letter is quoted giving his conditions.[31] Qilij-Arslān was to marry his daughter to Saif al-Dīn Ghāzī of Mosul; he was to renew his formal profession of the Islamic faith – and a note adds: "he was suspected of following the doctrines of the philosophers"; he was accused of having abandoned the Holy War against the Byzantines and was told to send troops, whenever asked, to fight either the Byzantines or the Franks. The fact that these conditions, which would certainly have appealed to 'Imād al-Dīn, are not given by Bundārī, must cast doubt on them. At that, however, they are still important as showing the extent to which Nūr al-Dīn's apologists felt that they had to destroy the prestige that Qilij-Arslān might have hoped to enjoy as a result of his defence of the north against the Byzantines.

Nūr al-Dīn now threatened the Armenian town of Qal'at al-Rūm (map 8) but allowed himself to be bought off with 5000 dinars and returned in poor health from Aleppo to Damascus.[32] Meanwhile in Egypt on 31 July Saladin's father Ayyūb had met with a riding accident and by 9 August he was dead. Ibn al-Athīr gives a twist to the story by saying that Saladin had advanced his father's ill-health to Nūr al-Dīn as a pretext for not meeting him at Kerak and had then returned to Egypt to learn of his death. "Many a word", he added, "says to its sayer: 'let me be'."[33] Ibn al-Athīr's dating is muddled as Nūr al-Dīn was not then advancing on Kerak, but it may be that Ayyūb's death did interfere with some plan for an autumn campaign. The Arabic sources give no exact date for Saladin's return to Egypt and William of Tyre makes him delay in Frankish territory until "about the end of September".[34] He was faced by no urgent problems on Ayyūb's death, but he can be expected to have gone back to deal with his estate and his *iqṭā's* as soon as military circumstances allowed.

Nūr al-Dīn was now prepared to carry through his plan for a full audit of Egyptian revenues and resources, including what had been taken from the Palace, and for this purpose he chose one of his leading officials, al-Muwaffaq ibn al-Qaisarānī. No certain date is given for al-Muwaffaq's arrival in Egypt, but as he had left again for Syria by the middle of May 1174, he must presumably have come at latest during the winter of 1173/74. According to Ibn Abī Ṭayy, the prospect of an audit had led Saladin to think of throwing off his allegiance, but he then changed his mind and showed al-Muwaffaq what he wanted to see, including the registers of his troops with lists of their various *iqṭā's* and allowances.[35] 'Imād al-Dīn quotes him as pointing out the costs of Egyptian administration; "a country like this cannot be run except with a large amount of money"; "the great men of state" were accustomed to ease and luxury; the places that they controlled could not be removed from them and the flow of their revenues could not be halted.[36] For all these pleas, however, it must have been obvious that Nūr al-Dīn would require an annual tribute from Egypt and that there would be a serious crisis if it were not forthcoming.

Amongst "the great men of state" was Saladin's brother, Tūrān-Shāh, a man of extravagant generosity who, at his death, was said to have accumulated debts of some 200,000 dinars. Al-Fāḍil was once forced to defend him to Saladin by writing: "the master should not hold him to account for what he gives away, for when the master gives him gifts, he makes him an intermediary between himself and those who ask".[37] This type of special pleading, however, was out of place at a time when money was short. Tūrān-Shāh must have been seen as a liability in Egypt, where his *iqṭā's* were said not to satisfy him.[38] He had not wanted to settle in the south and clearly it was in Saladin's interests to find some convenient foreign part to which he could be sent. The choice fell on Yemen.

Saladin himself explained the attack on Yemen as having been prompted by the evil way of life of 'Abd al-Nabī, the ruler of Zabīd (map 5). He accused 'Abd al-Nabī of being a heretic who was leading the Muslims astray; he had blasphemously called his father's tomb the Ka'ba and he had unjustly seized the wealth of his subjects. Saladin noted for good measure that 'Abd al-Nabī enslaved pious women and sold them at low prices.[39] Ibn Abī Ṭayy, who also stressed the personal motives of the expedition, said that Tūrān-Shāh was encouraged by the Yemeni poet 'Umāra and that support had been promised him by an enemy of 'Abd al-Nabī's, Hāshim ibn Ghānim of the Banū Sulaimān, who had held power in Zafar, Ṣa'da and Ta'izz.[40] Abū Shāma quoted poems written by 'Umāra, including the lines: "in front of you is the conquest of Yemen and of Syria", and: "create for yourself a kingdom in which you will not be joined to another".[41] To Ibn al-Athīr, Yemen was merely another Ayyubid bolt-hole for use in case of an attack by Nūr al-Dīn.[42]

These motives, worthy and unworthy, may all have had some relevance but they must be set in the context of Saladin's need for growth. Yemen was an ideal target for the strategy of the razzia. Qalqashandī wrote: "the Lord of Yemen has no enemies as he is cut off by sea and land",[43] but in fact an Egyptian expedition could safely muster at Mecca and then march south. If it ran into difficulties, it could return to the same sanctuary and all the while its base in Egypt would be in no danger.

Yemen itself contained a mixture of sophistication and backwardness. Ibn Jubair described the Yemeni tribesmen whom he saw bringing food to barter for clothes at Mecca as being simple Bedouin, untouched by civilisation. He wrote: "there is nothing in the comic stories of the Arabs that is funnier than Yemeni prayers", in which the worshippers showed none of the regular forms of ritual, "but only sincerity of intent".[44] But Yemen was the centre for one of the principal trade routes of the east. Aden, as Ibn al-Athīr noted, was the port for India, the African coast, as well as Abyssinia, Oman, Kirmān, Kīsh and Fars – a list that covers both Indian Ocean traffic, north and south African trade and routes through the Gulf to Persia (map 4).[45]

Individual Egyptians may well have wanted to strengthen their trading position on these routes, but although Tūrān-Shāh's debts may suggest reliance on money-lending merchants, there is no evidence that private enterprise had any responsibility for his expedition. Saladin himself can have needed little prompting. For him Yemen was "a treasure house".[46] By attacking it, he could thin out his forces, keep his brother occupied, look forward to great profits in return for no real risk, and still claim to be serving Islam. Not surprisingly, he helped fit out the expeditionary force. Tūrān-Shāh was allowed to keep a year's worth of the revenue of Qūṣ for his own purposes and Saladin provided him with extra men and provisions. Tūrān-Shāh left at the start of the month of Rajab 569 (5 February 1174) and on 9 March he was writing to Saladin from Yanbu', the port of Medina, on the eastern shore of the Red Sea.[47] From there he marched to Mecca.

His move was followed by the discovery of what was claimed as another Fatimid plot, to pave the way for which, according to one lurid suggestion, he had been enticed out of Egypt by 'Umāra.[48] The plot was said to have involved various classes of Fatimid supporters, including officials, soldiers, Negroes, Armenians and Isma'īli zealots, all of whom complained that their allowances had been cut off and their property seized. They were alleged to have been in touch with the Franks, who had been in the habit of sending a messenger to Cairo, ostensibly with friendly messages for Saladin. This man would ride out at night, or pretend to be going to church in order to conceal his meetings with "the retainers and servants of the Palace", the Egyptian emirs and the Christians and Jews, who were "their dogs and scribes". During the spring harvest season, which covers March, April and May in upper and lower Egypt, many of Saladin's men would be supervising the work on their *iqṭā's* and if a Frankish fleet were sent, a joint attack could be co-ordinated. The plotters are also said to have asked for help from Sinān, the Assassin leader in Syria, who himself had made an approach to the Franks in 1172. But there were difficulties – premature, as it turned out – about the choice of a Caliph and of a vizier for the restored Fatimid kingdom. According to 'Imād al-Dīn the plot was brought to light by "a member of the army". Ibn al-Athīr said that a Christian, used by Saladin as an undercover agent, disclosed it. According to another account Najm al-Dīn ibn Maṣāl, who had helped Saladin during the siege of Alexandria, was party to it and then betrayed it, while yet another version names the traitor as Zain al-Dīn 'Alī, who asked for the property of one of his fellow-conspirators by way of reward.[49] The leaders, including 'Umāra and Ibn 'Abd al-Qawī, the man who was said to know the secrets of the Palace, were arrested and then crucified on 6 April.

This was the second major conspiracy claimed by Saladin to have been directed against him by his Egyptian enemies and, as was the case with the earlier plot, there is bound to be a question-mark to set against it. Adherents of the old regime could have been expected to rise had they seen a chance of success. 'Umāra, who had continued to praise the Banū Ruzzaik after their eclipse by Shāwar, maintained his support for lost causes by writing poems regretting the passing of the Fatimids. A Sicilian fleet did arrive at Alexandria in July and Ibn al-Athīr accounts for the fact that Amalric did not move by saying that he had heard of the collapse of the plot, while the Sicilians had not. On the other hand, the July date cannot be made to fit into the spring harvest plan. Egypt had had advance warning of the Sicilian preparations and a rising could have been planned to coincide with their attack without the need for an interchange of messages. Saladin was at least as strong now as he had been during the Damietta expedition, the failure of which should have discouraged conspirators, unless they were desperate. The appearance of the names of Ibn Maṣāl and Zain al-Dīn ʻAlī is interesting. Saladin is quoted as saying of Ibn Maṣāl on his death: "I shall never have another friend like him."[50] Zain al-Dīn ʻAlī was an equally unlikely recruit for a conspiracy. He was a Damascene by birth, on friendly terms with al-Fāḍil, and later to be chosen by Saladin for the signal honour of preaching in Jerusalem after its capture.[51] Ibn Maṣāl had married off one of his slave girls to Zain al-Dīn's son, ʻAbd al-Karīm,[52] an arrangement that implies a patron-client relationship, and if either or both were acting as Saladin's *agents provocateurs*, this link between them could help explain the variant accounts.

The main reason for the suspicion that Saladin must at least have brought the plot to a head is its timing. As on the previous occasion, this coincided exactly with his needs. In 1169 he had been threatened by a Byzantine fleet and had cleared Cairo of possible trouble-makers, and he was now seen to be doing the same thing under the threat of a Sicilian attack. More immediately, in April al-Muwaffaq's mission to Egypt was coming to an end and he was about to take his report back to Nūr al-Dīn. Saladin could not be confident about Nūr al-Dīn's reaction and a first-hand account of a dangerous conspiracy would help to underline the delicacy of the situation in Egypt as well as to emphasise the difficulties and responsibilities of his own position.

In the early summer of 1174 Nūr al-Dīn was seen to be mustering his men. He had sent his summons to Mosul, Diyār Bakr and al-Jazīra, and the Mosul vanguard, with the eunuch Gumushtekīn, had left by the middle of May. Ibn al-Athīr was sure that the target was to be Egypt.[53] According to him, Saladin had slackened his attacks on the Franks and Nūr al-Dīn, whose only concern was the Holy War, had realised that this was because he wanted a Frankish state to act as a buffer between him and Syria. Ibn al-Athīr had earlier given a circumstantial account of an Ayyubid family council called to discuss the threat from Nūr al-Dīn.[54] Ayyūb had publicly criticised Taqī al-Dīn for making a bellicose speech, but had privately told Saladin that, although Nūr al-Dīn was to be treated tactfully with a show of obedience, if he came to Egypt he would not be allowed a single sugar-cane. Saladin confirmed to Ibn Shaddād that he had heard that Nūr al-Dīn might attack him; his emirs, he said, had advised resistance and he alone had opposed them.[55] Clearly, the "knife cuts and needle pricks"[56] from Nūr al-Dīn of which he had complained, together with "unendurable things" contained in letters from Syria, might well have been preparing the way for war, and while Nūr al-Dīn was calling up his reinforcements, Saladin collected his own troops outside Cairo at Birkat al-Jubb. The explanation which he later sent to Syria was that in the previous year he had seen the chance of success at Kerak and he was now planning to join Nūr al-Dīn in a concerted attack on it.[57] This need not be accepted at face value and, if Ibn al-Athīr was right, Saladin's muster can be seen as preparation for the defence of Egypt. On the other hand, al-Muwaffaq had not yet reached Damascus. He was accompanied by Saladin's envoy Ḍiyā' al-Dīn 'Īsā, together with gifts, money and a statement of Egypt's finances and even if relations were near breaking-point, some time could clearly be allowed for diplomacy. It can be suggested that Saladin was showing his teeth by way of warning, but it is significant that in a letter sent to Tūrān-Shāh in the middle of May he could offer to send reinforcements to Yemen.[58] This must suggest that Ibn al-Athīr was arguing ahead of events. Had Nūr al-Dīn claimed a subsidy from Egypt, Saladin would have been trapped between his need for growth and the certainty that Nūr al-Dīn would not be able to tolerate refusal. War would have been as likely an answer here as any but, for the time being, his letter suggests that Saladin had no particular fears.

In the event, Nūr al-Dīn never received al-Muwaffaq's report. There were celebrations in Damascus on Sunday 5 May to mark the circumcision of al-Ṣāliḥ, his only son. On 6 May he flew into an uncharacteristic fit of rage while playing polo. He went back to the citadel of Damascus, where he fell ill. The doctors wanted to bleed him, but he said: "a man of sixty is not bled", and "as he was a man who inspired awe, they did not press him again".[59] He died on Wednesday 15 May. William of Tyre wrote of him that he was "the greatest persecutor of the Christian name and faith, but a just ruler, astute and far-sighted and, according to the traditions of his race, a religious man".[60]

5

INDEPENDENCE

It is difficult to over-stress the influence of Nūr al-Dīn on Saladin's political education and on his career. Nūr al-Dīn was an exponent of the politics of growth allied to the ideal of the Holy War, a manipulator of religious propaganda and a ruler who showed the value of setting men before money. With his death and that of Ayyūb the dominant figures of Saladin's youth had been removed. Ayyūb himself had died without upsetting any balance of power or, apparently, altering in any way the pattern of Saladin's life. Nūr al-Dīn, however, left him as a legacy something approximating to real political independence. The facts of their relationship may, perhaps, never be discovered. All that is left is rumour based arguably on hostility to Saladin, to Nūr al-Dīn or to both. What is irrefutable is that Saladin had lived under Nūr al-Dīn's shadow. Egypt as seen from Syria was a conquest paid for by Syrian money. Saladin's policy of expansion was either irrelevant or a drain on resources that might otherwise have been used by Syria. Egypt was certainly a base for the Holy War but observably in this period no successful pincer attack on Palestine had ever been mounted. Economically the two countries had remained isolated without any recorded attempt being made to pool resources. Nūr al-Dīn's death ended any prospect of an immediate Egyptian subsidy for Syria and left Cairo and Damascus in a position where neither had any necessary links with the other.

This meant that Saladin could determine his own policy. If the evidence can be trusted,[1] during the first years of his reign Egypt had been a net importer of men. Saladin had merely processed them as Ayyubid supporters and attempted to re-export numbers of them to North Africa and Yemen. There is no indication that he had thought it possible to increase Egypt's own capacity to absorb them, but it may be argued, with Ibn al-Athīr, that his policy of external growth had been determined, at least in part, by a need to expand beyond any possible control. With the death of Nūr al-Dīn his choice was now unforced. The Fatimid empire, based on Cairo, could be reproduced by an Ayyubid state. The Mediterranean, the Red Sea, the Nile, or all three, could be allowed to shape his plans, or they could be subordinated, as before, to a Syrian-centred policy whose end – or means – was the Holy War, with Saladin taking over the role of Nūr al-Dīn.

The only qualification here is that Syria could not yet be used as a factor in Saladin's calculations until the dust of disturbance had settled, and here the dead Nūr al-Dīn had a final lesson to teach.

A state, as he had shown, could be run successfully by one man who commanded the obedience of semi-independent members of his own family and who controlled a group of subordinates whose position relative to one another need not be defined. For a dynasty, however, the power structure needed clarification so that authority could be transmitted easily from one generation to another. At Nūr al-Dīn's death, his son, al-Ṣāliḥ, was eleven years old. His eldest nephew, and son-in-law, 'Imād al-Dīn Zangī, was relatively powerless in Sinjār, while Saif al-Dīn Ghāzī, in Mosul, was unable to count on Zangī's loyalty. But neither Sinjār, nor Mosul nor the young al-Ṣāliḥ in Syria had resources or experience to match those of Egypt and of Saladin, the tried commander and tested administrator.

Saif al-Dīn now celebrated his uncle's death by allowing wine to be drunk openly in Mosul and by pushing back his own boundaries to the Euphrates.[2] From Sīwās his former administrator, 'Abd al-Masīḥ, came to join him and advised him to swallow up Syria as well, but he was not to be persuaded and returned home. In Syria, al-Ṣāliḥ was too young to hold real power and the strongest single family grouping was that of the brothers known as the Banū 'l-Dāya. The eldest, Nūr al-Dīn's foster brother Majd al-Dīn, had died in 1170, but at the time of Nūr al-Dīn's death the rest of them seemed to be impregnably based in and around Aleppo. 'Alī, described as "the greatest of the Nūrid emirs", held Shaizar: 'Uthmān held Qal'at Ja'bar and Tell Bāshir, while Ḥasan held Ḥārim (map 8).[3]

'Alī now moved to the citadel of Aleppo, but he was a sick man and there was trouble in the town of Aleppo itself, where the Sunnīs supported the Banū 'l-Dāya, but a strong Shī'ite faction followed the lead of Ibn al-Khashshāb. Meanwhile in Damascus a number of Nūr al-Dīn's officials, including Raiḥān, "the chief of the servants",[4] the vizier al-'Adl ibn al-'Ajamī, and the treasurer Ismā'īl, assumed a measure of independence, took an oath to act together and appointed Ibn al-Muqaddam as army commander. Ibn al-Muqaddam could call on the Damascus garrison, but the group's main advantage lay in the fact that al-Ṣāliḥ, who had stayed in Damascus, was under their control.

The Franks reacted predictably to their good fortune. Amalric collected a Frankish force and attacked Bāniās, by the head-waters of the Jordan, which Nūr al-Dīn had taken from him in 1164. According to William of Tyre, Nūr al-Dīn's widow, "showing more than feminine strength", acted in her husband's stead and tried to buy a truce.[5] Amalric continued the siege for a fortnight in the hopes of getting better terms, but then broke it off on finding that the garrison's morale was improving while his own health had suffered. He agreed to the terms offered by the Muslims and drew back to Tiberias. The Arabic sources do not mention the part played by Nūr al-Dīn's widow, but say that Ibn al-Muqaddam moved out towards Bāniās and sent envoys to arrange a truce, using as an argument the threat of a move by Saladin from Egypt.[6]

Saladin was the unknown factor in the equation. Ibn Abī Ṭayy wrote that, after Nūr al-Dīn's death, the Syrian emirs swore to break with him and to arrest any of his supporters whom they found in Syria.[7] According to Ibn al-Athīr, Kamāl al-Dīn al-Shahrazūrī urged them to consult Saladin on Syrian affairs – "Let us not remove him from amongst us, or else he may remove himself from our allegiance... he is stronger than we are." In fact, immediately after the death of Nūr al-Dīn, 'Imād al-Dīn wrote a letter to Saladin on behalf of al-Ṣāliḥ. In it he referred to the fact that all the Syrian emirs had agreed to take the oath of allegiance to al-Ṣāliḥ and "there is nothing here to concern the heart except for the Franks". A veiled appeal was made to Saladin's loyalty; Nūr al-Dīn had trusted him to do what was necessary in such circumstances.[8]

Saladin himself had written to an unnamed Syrian emir from his camp at Birkat al-Jubb. He said, cryptically, that "news" of Nūr al-Dīn had reached him "from the side of the enemy"; he hoped that it was false, but were it to prove true, then "kings nurture the growth of their kingdoms for their children"; he had already received instructions from Nūr al-Dīn that al-Ṣāliḥ was to succeed him, with Gumushtekīn acting as his administrator; if this was not accepted by Syrians, then Saladin would act "for this boy... as a sword against his enemies". He warned the Syrians that they were surrounded by enemies "on all sides", and promised that if the Franks attacked, he would march against them; if the news proved to be false, "the armies of Nūr al-Dīn" would attack Kerak as had been arranged.[9]

On 6 June, three weeks after Nūr al-Dīn's death, Saladin sent an official letter of condolence to al-Ṣāliḥ. He referred to "the earthquake shock" of this calamity; Islam had been deprived of her Alexander, but "the servant's" two hands were in the service of his son, one closed on the sword-hilt and one open to distribute bounty; if the enemy were to attack, he would pursue them "as the night follows the day". The letter was dated to the first Friday on which the *khuṭba* was pronounced in Egypt in the name of al-Ṣāliḥ and it ended with a prayer that God might preserve his kingdom for ever.[10]

On 5 July, some four weeks after Saladin's letter of condolence and after the conclusion of the truce with Amalric, 'Imād al-Dīn wrote again from Damascus, apparently in reply to a letter of reproach which has not been preserved. He offered excuses for the fact that Saladin had not been kept informed about the situation; there had not been time to write again "and I thought that the first letter would be enough". He may be excusing the vagueness of his earlier letter where he added: "news of the unbelievers is not hidden", and he explained the need for the truce by saying that the Franks had brought up a large force of infantry and cavalry at a time when the garrison of Bāniās was off its guard and short of stores.[11]

Just over a week later Saladin wrote to the Qāḍī Ibn Abī 'Aṣrūn from Fāqūs on the coast road to Palestine (map 7); on hearing of the Frankish advance from the governor of Bāniās he had advanced four stages with his army, only to be met by news of the truce, which was an act of disobedience to God, His Apostle and all pious Muslims; Damascus alone was covered by its terms;

> if we complete our march, other than what we wish will be thought of us, while if we sit still, the enemy is not far from the other frontiers that are not covered by the truce... If we disperse our forces, it will not be easy to collect them again later... We have decided to send a message to Shams al-Dīn 'Alī and his brothers [the Banū 'l-Dāya] to let them know of the dangers... We have kept our men from dispersing for fear lest the enemy move towards Ḥārim, using the money with which they have been strengthened... While they know that we are assembled... they will be deterred from moving.[12]

Saladin was faced with a difficult decision. He could combine an Egypt-first policy with concern for the Holy War and either move independently against the Franks or else wait in Egypt until he was invited by al-Ṣāliḥ to come to his help. His position, however, with the resources of Egypt at his back, was stronger than that of any of the Syrian groupings and according to the logic of dynastic expansion he should take over the country before it could fall into the hands of a possible rival. He could – and did – claim that Syria was a better base for the Holy War than Egypt but he could not yet expect to be accepted as the protagonist of Islam to whom such a base should be granted as a right. Appeals to Islamic principle would appear hypocritical if he were seen to be attacking the lands of his former master, this being the point of his remark to Ibn Abī 'Aṣrūn about the suspicions that would be aroused if he advanced. Ideally, he needed either an invitation to Syria or the excuse of either anarchy or danger from the Franks. A move by Amalric against Ḥārim, to which he had referred, might have served his purpose, but by the time that the letter had been written, this threat had vanished.

Amalric had complained of feeling unwell during the attack on Bāniās. When he returned to Tiberias, he fell ill with dysentery and he died on 14 July. Saladin wrote to his nephew Farrukh-Shāh that reliable news of the king's death had come from Dārūm – "may God curse him and abandon him and lead him to punishment as bitter [*murr*] as his name... We give abundant thanks to God as this is the fulfilment of the most for which we could have hoped."[13] Amalric was succeeded by Baldwin the Leper and Saladin wrote him an official letter of condolence: "the master of a house cannot but be saddened by the loss of his neighbours... The king must know that we have a sincere affection for him, as we had for his father... Let him rely on us."[14]

This can be taken as diplomatic usage rather than as hypocrisy but there was some room for ambivalent feelings. Amalric's death had cleared a powerful piece from the chessboard of the Holy War, but in Saladin's diplomatic manoeuvring it could block a line of advance. If the Franks were inactive, the Syrian emirs would have time to set their house in order and an Egyptian march on Damascus would seem indefensible in Islamic terms. On the other hand, with the deaths of Amalric and Nūr al-Dīn Saladin had seen the two greatest military commanders of Syria and Palestine removed from his path. He told Farrukh-Shāh that he had heard that the Franks had not yet agreed on Amalric's successor, that news had come of the death of Shams al-Dīn 'Alī – who was, in fact, ill but alive – and that a stroke had left Qilij-Arslān incapable of movement.[15] This apparent clearing of the field must have tempted him even more strongly to move without invitation. For the moment, however, a decision could be postponed as Egypt itself had to face the threat of another invasion.

According to Saladin's account, after the failure of the Franks and the Byzantines at Damietta in 1169, the King of Sicily had determined to show his strength and had spent five years in building and equipping a fleet; Saladin had been warned of it by the Emperor Manuel himself, whose territories were thought to be threatened, and it had alarmed the Almohades in the west.[16] In spite of warnings, however, the garrison of Alexandria was taken by surprise when the Sicilians arrived on Sunday 28 July and there was only a small force to resist them. "This", wrote Saladin, "was at a time when those appointed to watch were off their guard, not when the news was hidden."[17] More and more Sicilian ships came into sight throughout Sunday afternoon, but they made no attempt to land.

On Monday the fleet was lying off Alexandria in strength; it was thought that a landing could not be prevented and that, if any immediate resistance was attempted, the townspeople might be trapped on the beaches. "A number of intelligent Turks",[18] presumably Saladin's professionals, advised that they should be drawn back and stationed near the city walls. According to Maqrīzī, the Sicilians disembarked on "the mainland by the Pharos",[19] which appears to mean that they anchored their ships in the Pirates' Haven, the north-facing bay on what had been the island of Pharos. They then attacked down the peninsula by which this had become attached to the mainland and the Muslims had to take to the shelter of their walls. The Sicilian fleet rowed round to the harbour, but the Muslims claimed to have denied them prizes by scuttling or burning those of their own ships that were at anchor there. Monday's fighting went on until evening, when the Sicilians pitched 300 tents, and on Tuesday they brought up three large mangonels, supplied with black stones from Sicily.

News of the attack seems to have been slow in reaching Saladin, who was still in camp at Fāqūs some 120 miles (193 km) away. According to his own account, a message, brought by pigeon, arrived on Tuesday.[20] The governor of Alexandria had presumably been waiting to see whether the Sicilians were in earnest or whether they were merely feinting to force Saladin to concentrate on Alexandria before pressing home an attack elsewhere. Saladin, in fact, took no chances, and reinforced Damietta, as well as sending help to Alexandria.

At Alexandria itself the Muslims made a sally on Wednesday 31 July, during which they burnt the Sicilians' mangonels. The Sicilians were seen to be weakening and in the afternoon a messenger reached the city with the false but heartening news that Saladin himself was only 20 miles (32 km) away to the east. The Muslims then made a successful evening attack, killing or capturing a number of the enemy, including a force of 300 horsemen whom they had managed to cut off and surround. After this reverse the fleet put to sea again on Thursday 1 August. No one knew what its destination was, but Saladin in his letter claimed that it no longer had any fighting capacity.[21]

On the heels of the Sicilian attack there was more trouble in upper Egypt. Another army of Negroes, Bedouin and "the people of the lands" had gathered there and a leader named 'Abbās ibn Shādhī had attacked the districts of Qūṣ from a base at Ṭūd, some 12 miles (19 km) south of Luxor (map 6).[22] This in itself was no more than one of a number of sporadic movements by Fatimid supporters who took advantage of the remoteness of Cairo and the difficulties of the country to launch their raids. What does call for comment is the fact that this time the malcontents were joined by Kanz al-Daula, the governor of Aswān, who in 1172 had asked for Saladin's help against the Nubians. No explanation is given for this *volte-face*, which may, of course, be more apparent than real. Al-Kanz, a Muslim Bedouin, could well have been hostile to Nubian Christians, but not to the Fatimid supporters who had joined them, and although it is worth looking for some particular action that might have antagonised him, no evidence for this has been found.

In the event, the trouble was not serious. The rebels killed the brother of Abū' l-Haijā' the Gross and Abū' l-Haijā' himself moved south. He was supported by Saladin's cousin, 'Izz al-Dīn Mūsik, who was almost certainly governor of Qūṣ at this time, and by Saladin's brother al-'Ādil. Ibn Shaddād wrote of al-'Ādil's force that it comprised men who had already tasted the delights of possession in Egypt and were afraid of losing them.[23] In the face of their determined self-interest the rebellion failed and both 'Abbās and Kanz al-Daula were killed. The defeat of Kanz al-Daula is dated to 7 September and by the 28th al-'Ādil had returned to Cairo.[24]

By this time Saladin himself was on the point of leaving. External and internal dangers had allowed him to postpone for a time the crucial decision on whether or not he should march on Syria without invitation or clear excuse. In spite of the possible risk to his reputation, it had been obvious, to al-Faḍil at least, that sooner or later the move would have to be made. In a letter to Tūrān-Shāh, he had referred to Tūrān-Shāh's journey from Syria to Egypt to meet his brother in 1169, and had added that "one day" it would be matched by another, this time from Yemen to Syria.[25]

The Syrians themselves were providing at least a partial opening. 'Imād al-Dīn, who was in Damascus at the time, has left an account of the intrigues that he saw. According to him, the leaders distrusted one another; administration suffered and decisions made one day were reversed on the next. One of the Banū 'l-Dāya, 'Uthmān, was sent by his elder brother 'Alī to bring the young al-Ṣāliḥ from Damascus to Aleppo, where he would be under 'Alī's protection, as well as that of Gumushtekīn, an arrangement which tallied with what Saladin had claimed to be Nūr al-Dīn's wish. 'Uthmān, however, who was "far from subtle and not experienced in the management of affairs", was out-manoeuvred by al-'Adl ibn al-'Ajamī, one of the group of Damascene leaders. Al-'Adl, a man whom 'Imād al-Dīn obviously disliked and feared, arranged to go to Aleppo with the returning delegation in order to discuss al-Ṣāliḥ's position. When 'Imād al-Dīn took his leave of 'Uthmān outside Damascus he tried to indicate to him that he should be on his guard, but "he was a foreigner who could not be alerted by an expression". 'Imād al-Dīn then spoke to him in private, but 'Uthmān passed on what he had said to al-'Adl. At Aleppo al-'Adl presented his services to 'Alī, who "because of the purity of his faith believed in that of al-'Adl", and it was then formally agreed that al-Ṣāliḥ should be brought to Aleppo, at which 'Alī would give up his own lands and act as his adviser.

Al-'Adl, who was angry with 'Imād al-Dīn because of his meddling, now went back to Damascus with 'Uthmān and Gumushtekīn. 'Imād al-Dīn approached Gumushtekīn

> thinking of him as an old friend... Gumushtekīn said: "leave me until I can straighten out your affair"... I knew then that they had put 'Uthmān's head in the bag (*sic*)... I had to fall in with this and remain on friendly terms with them as I had fine possessions, wealth, horses and equipment. If I abandoned these and escaped myself, then my sun would set... I let them believe that I was with them and came to Aleppo with them.[26]

Al-Ṣāliḥ left Damascus on 25 July. Ibn al-Muqaddam, the army commander, Raiḥān, the castellan of the citadel, and the Qāḍī Kamāl al-Dīn al-Shahrazūrī stayed behind. Gumushtekīn, al-'Adl and

Ismā'īl the treasurer, went with al-Ṣāliḥ, who was escorted by 'Uthmān. When they reached Tell al-Sulṭān, one post-stage from Aleppo on the Hama road, they were met by messengers from 'Alī. They then travelled through the night and arrived at Aleppo at dawn. 'Alī was too ill to leave the citadel and his brother, Ḥasan, came out to greet al-Ṣāliḥ. Immediately, he and 'Uthmān were seized and before the news could reach 'Alī the Damascenes had entered the citadel where the castellan, Shādhbakht, "was with them in secret".[27] The three brothers, 'Alī, 'Uthmān and Ḥasan were now held as prisoners and Ibn al-Khashshāb, the Shī'ite leader, was killed.

In spite of 'Imād al-Dīn's account, there are obscurities both in the details and the motives of this plot. According to one report Ibn al-Khashshāb was killed by the Banū 'l-Dāya before their fall.[28] Another story says that a group, including al-'Adl, paid to have him killed and the man whom they hired was 'Izz al-Dīn Jūrdīk, Saladin's associate in the seizure of Shāwar.[29] Certainly Jūrdīk seems to have had some part to play, as he managed to antagonise both Gumushtekīn and the Banū 'l-Dāya. Ibn al-Athīr makes Gumushtekīn go twice to Damascus and says that on the first occasion he was driven off by troops sent out by Ibn al-Muqaddam.[30] In part, the motives of the plot were straightforward. The Banū 'l-Dāya, weakened by the death of Majd al-Dīn and the illness of 'Alī, were obvious targets for envy. But the relationship between Damascus and Aleppo is not clear. To move al-Ṣāliḥ to Aleppo had the tactical purpose of deceiving the Banū 'l-Dāya and opening the way to the citadel. It might have been that, as 'Alī is said to have claimed, al-Ṣāliḥ's presence at Aleppo would make his cousin, Saif al-Dīn of Mosul, less inclined to interfere in Syria,[31] and he was certainly further away from Saladin. His removal, however, made it less invidious for Saladin to move against Damascus and it has to be asked whether Ibn al-Muqaddam was party to the plot and, if so, whether his fellow-conspirators were relying on him to hold the border.

Some light is thrown here by letters quoted by 'Imād al-Dīn. Saladin wrote to Ibn al-Muqaddam to express his anger at the seizure of the Banū 'l-Dāya: "how have they dared to do this to the supporters of the dynasty and its props?" Ibn al-Muqaddam had no difficulty in interpreting the motives behind this indignation and he replied: "let it not be said that you have designs on the house of the one who established you... This does not befit your good character." Unless 'Imād al-Dīn is wrong in quoting this as the reply to Saladin's complaint about the Banū 'l-Dāya, at this stage Ibn al-Muqaddam must certainly have been on the side of the conspirators. Saladin then wrote again:

> we choose for Islam and its people only what will unite them, and for the Atabeg house only what will preserve its root and its branches... Loyalty comes only after death...[32] I am in one valley and those who think evil of me are in another... If we had inclined to any other path, we would not have chosen the way of consultation and writing.[33]

It can hardly be that this claim to good faith was in itself enough to make Ibn al-Muqaddam change his mind, but in fact he did break with Aleppo decisively enough to gain the credit of being the first to invite Saladin to Syria. One of the reasons suggested for this is that the Damascene emirs, including, presumably, Ibn al-Muqaddam himself, afraid lest they should be treated like the Banū 'l-Dāya, had offered the city to Saif al-Dīn of Mosul, who refused it.[34] The approach to Saladin was linked to an agreement then made between Gumushtekīn and Saif al-Dīn, which implies that after Saif al-Dīn's refusal the Damascenes may have hoped to enjoy independence by playing off Aleppo against Mosul, and were then confounded by the prospect of an Aleppo–Mosul pact. The young al-Ṣāliḥ, surrounded by a self-interested court, was in no position to exercise authority. Because of their mutual suspicions, his controllers tended to cancel each other out. Saif al-Dīn lacked strength, foresight or ambition enough to advance his frontiers west of the Euphrates. The Franks, thanks to the death of Amalric, were not immediately menacing, but the threat that they posed was too close to Damascus to be ignored and it is difficult to see how the city could have prospered for long in a divided and anarchic Syria. Saladin was almost certain to march, whether he was invited or not, and Ibn al-Muqaddam, who appears as a stubborn man, neither particularly ambitious nor subtle, may simply have been at a loss to know what to do in a difficult situation. Whatever his immediate motives, his *volte-face* was unquestionably adapted to the political and military realities of the situation.

6

FROM EGYPT TO SYRIA

Saladin had presumably gone back to Cairo from Fāqūs after the dispersal of the Sicilian fleet and, according to 'Imād al-Dīn, he moved out to his camp site at Birkat al-Jubb at the beginning of September.[1] For the rest of this month al-'Ādil, whom he was intending to leave as his deputy in Egypt, was dealing with Kanz al-Daula's rebels in the south and it was not until October that Saladin began his march. Invitations to Syria had reached him not only from Ibn al-Muqaddam but also from Shams al-Dīn Ṣadīq of Buṣrā. Shams al-Dīn was a man of no great power, with a local reputation in the Ḥaurān as an extortionate ruler, but Buṣrā, some 70 miles (113 km) from Damascus, was a convenient base where an invader could muster reinforcements and test the reactions of the Syrians before committing himself to an attack.

According to a date quoted by Abū Shāma, Saladin moved from Birkat al-Jubb to Bilbais on 12 October[2] and by the 23rd he had reached Buṣrā. A nine-day march from Ṣudr, two days' journey from Cairo, to Kerak was considered fast[3] and if Abū Shāma's date is correct, Saladin's force must have moved with remarkable speed. In itself this tends to confirm the report that he took with him no more than 700 riders.[4] He clearly expected reinforcements from Syria itself, and on the day of his arrival at Buṣrā he wrote to tell his nephew Farrukh-Shāh that he had already been joined by "emirs, soldiers, Turks, Kurds and Bedouin" – "The emotions of their hearts are to be seen on their faces." Letter after letter, he claimed, had come from Damascus saying that the lands could now be brought under control; he himself was planning to leave Buṣrā on Thursday (24 October) and he had prepared a stock of guarantees of immunity to help open his way to Damascus; there was no fresh news from Aleppo, where al-Ṣāliḥ's emirs were still busy with their internal feuds. As for the

Franks, he reported that "on this blessed journey we camped in their lands like those who have authority."[5]

According to another letter Saladin, in fact, left Buṣrā on Wednesday 23 October, accompanied by Shams al-Dīn Ṣadīq.[6] This time the pace of his march was slower and he camped at Jisr al-Khashab, some 60 miles (97 km) from Buṣrā and 10 miles (16 km) south of Damascus, on Sunday 27 October. On the previous day he had been joined by Sa'd al-Dīn ibn Anar and by Shīrkūh's son Nāṣir al-Dīn Muḥammad. Sa'd al-Dīn's father had held Damascus in the service of the Burids, from whom Nūr al-Dīn had taken it, and Nūr al-Dīn had then married his sister. Saladin's cousin, Nāṣir al-Dīn Muḥammad, must have been hoping to mend his fortunes, Tell Bāshir, which had been given him as a substitute for his father's Syrian *iqṭā's*, had later been transferred to 'Uthmān of the Banū 'l-Dāya and was now under the control of Aleppo. Gossip suggested that he himself was on uneasy terms with Saladin and that he claimed, as his father's son, to have a greater right to the Sultanate of Egypt.[7] The one recorded letter of his addressed to Saladin in Egypt, although polite, shows no particular sign of respect,[8] and it may be that he had expected to win more profit from his father's success. For the moment, however, his immediate hopes were pinned on Saladin's success.

Ibn al-Athīr dramatised the dangers of the situation in a conversation said to have been held between Shams al-Dīn of Buṣrā and al-Fāḍil. Shams al-Dīn, commenting on Saladin's small force, said: "if the garrison of Damascus keep you out for one hour, the people of the countryside will destroy you. But if you have money with you, then things will be easy." Al-Fāḍil said: "we have a large sum of money - 50,000 dinars". Shams al-Dīn struck his head and said: "you are lost and you have destroyed us". In fact, Ibn al-Athīr added, "all that they really had was 10,000 dinars".[9]

Saladin wrote that when he halted at Jisr al-Khashab troops flocked out from Damascus to join him, the only ones to hold back being those who were restrained by what they thought was prudence.[10] He then appears to contradict himself by reporting that on Monday (28 October), when he marched on the city, "a not inconsiderable part" of the Damascus army was drawn up to bar his way. It seems that Ibn al-Muqaddam had either contented himself with staying in the background, or else did not have enough influence over his troops to prevent a show of opposition.[11] At that, however, there was no serious resistance and al-Fāḍil wrote of the Damascenes that "they knew that chaff is winnowed by the wind".[12] They drew back to shelter behind their walls and asked for quarter. This was granted and Saladin entered the city.

At first sight, it appears that he had broken the rules of razzia strategy by committing himself too far and with too small a force in a position where his line of retreat would be threatened if anything went wrong. This seems inconsistent with the policy of caution that he had followed since coming to power in Egypt and the key, as William of Tyre noted, must surely have been money. William wrote that Saladin had been invited by the leaders of Damascus while "their rightful Lord" was at Aleppo and that, after hurrying across the desert, he had taken over the city. He then went on: "he was a man prudent in council, energetic in war and of more than common liberality, a point which caused particular anxiety to the more far-sighted of us. For by no other bond to-day can the hearts of subjects and even of other men be better won over to leaders... than by liberality."[13] Ibn Shaddād referred to the great sums of money that Saladin gave away in Damascus[14] and al-Fāḍil wrote later that he had spent the wealth of Egypt on the conquest of Syria.[15] If he was certain of being able to buy help, then the choice of a small force was the obvious answer to the problem of how to avoid the Franks and strike at Syria, before counter-measures could be taken. This does not necessarily contradict Ibn al-Athīr's remark about his 10,000 dinars. He must have expected to take over public funds in Damascus, and, as can be seen elsewhere in his career, he made use on his campaigns of a form of credit transfer (*ḥawāla*) by which notes of hand were given authorising the recipients to obtain payment elsewhere.[16]

Meanwhile in Damascus Raiḥān, one of Ibn al-Muqaddam's former colleagues, had shut himself up in a citadel and on Tuesday Saladin sent his brother Tughtekīn to surround it "with a sea of steel".[17] He then opened negotiations by pointing out that he had come "only to serve the Nūrid house",[18] and at this Raiḥān agreed to terms. Saladin laid stress on the warmth of his welcome: "we dawned on the people like light in darkness";[19] "the people rushed to us both before and after we had entered the city in joy at [the coming of] our rule... Had we not made haste to come to them, they would have hastened to us."[20] His first action was to pray in the Umayyad Mosque. The markets which had been shut were re-opened and proclamations were made prohibiting looting, cancelling *mukūs* taxes and reassuring those who "repented of their opposition".[21] No blood was shed. Tughtekīn did not bring the women out of the citadel or "do what is normally done when places surrender".[22] The virtues of Saladin's rule are contrasted in his propaganda with the evils that he found; there were unlawful practices, including the farming of a tax on wine; the people had been badly treated and the wages and allowances of the troops had been cut.[23] "The bright lamps of the Nūrid house were extinguished",[24] and Saladin was quick to point the moral and link what his enemies would see as crude expansionism to Islamic principle. He had not taken Damascus, he wrote, out of personal greed but because of his concern for it;[25] it was a step on the road to the conquest of Jerusalem and "to hold back from the Holy War" – as he accused his opponents of doing – "is a crime for which there can be no excuse".[26]

In his letters Saladin was obviously doing his best to paint a picture of a triumphal progress in a just cause, but he had certainly met with no serious opposition and there had been no brutality to alienate support. He paid a visit to the old opponent of his *shiḥna* days, the Qāḍī Kamāl al-Dīn, to calm any possible fears and this peaceful takeover contrasted with the violent intrigues of al-Ṣāliḥ's emirs in Aleppo. But he could not rest on his laurels. Ibn al-Athīr's point about the dangers that faced his expedition may have been exaggerated, but it underlined the ephemeral position of would-be rulers who had no more than a superficial relationship with their subjects. Further, if a check might dangerously have limited his scope, success imposed its own restrictions of choice. A reliance on local recruits pointed the way to the cycle of expansion. Victories attracted men, to pay for whom further successes were needed, attracting in their turn more recruits. From a strategic point of view Damascus was the key to southern Syria and an ideal base for operations against the Latin Kingdom. At that, however, if it were not protected from the north, its position would be compromised by the fact that it would have to be defended against its Muslim neighbours as well as against the Franks. Finally, in the war of words, Saladin was claiming to have come to Syria to restore al-Ṣāliḥ to his proper position. He could not reconcile this with the straightforward seizure of Nūr al-Dīn's former capital. Rather, he was forced to pursue a collision course with Aleppo in order to be seen as rescuing al-Ṣāliḥ from his evil counsellors.

While Saladin was still at Damascus he received an embassy from Aleppo. This was headed by Quṭb al-Dīn Ināl, one of the emirs whom

Nūr al-Dīn had sent to Egypt with Shīrkūh's third expedition. His message, according to Ibn Abī Ṭayy, was one of "thunder and lightning".[27] He is pictured as pointing to his sword and saying to Saladin: "these swords that gave you the kingdom of Egypt will drive you back". In reply, Saladin claimed to have come to Syria only to unify the cause of Islam, to see to the upbringing of al-Ṣāliḥ and to rescue the Banū 'l-Dāya. This was not accepted. The envoys said: "you want the kingdom for yourself; go back where you came from".[28] This interchange was presumably intended to do no more than define positions. Aleppo was concerned to represent Saladin as an aggressor who was betraying his master, while Saladin claimed to be acting in the interests of Islam. Both sides were looking for a propaganda advantage, but Saladin was the first to move to strengthen his position in the field.

On Sunday 8 December 1174, forty days after the surrender of the citadel of Damascus, he camped outside Homs, which marks approximately the halfway point in the 200-mile (322 km) journey from Damascus to Aleppo – although exact distances vary with the routes taken (map 8). Saladin himself usually took the road by Baalbek through the valley of the Biqā', between the ranges of Lebanon and anti-Lebanon. On this occasion, however, he makes no reference to Baalbek, which was held by a hostile garrison, and it may be guessed that he moved to the east of anti-Lebanon.

He was not looking for sieges but for a quick campaign to win popular support. His numbers were growing. He wrote to his brother al-'Ādil: "up to this point we have collected about 7000 riders and the armies have swollen to such an extent that they cannot be numbered",[29] and on the day after he had camped by Homs he was joined by one of Nūr al-Dīn's leading emirs and former army commander, Fakhr al-Dīn ibn al-Za'farānī, who had held the *iqṭā'* of Homs at Nūr al-Dīn's death.[30]

In spite of this support, however, there was still resistance at Homs and after an unsuccessful attempt to come to terms, Saladin had to attack on Tuesday 10 December. The town was captured without difficulty and he wrote to Zain al-Dīn 'Alī in Egypt, repeating his earlier claims: "our move was not made in order to snatch a kingdom for ourselves, but to set up the standard of the Holy War... These men had become enemies, preventing the accomplishment of our purpose with regard to this War". He added that he had not intended to damage the city, "knowing how close it was to the unbelievers", and he ended by saying that he had given his customary orders for the checking of unlawful practices.[31]

In a similar letter to Quṭb al-Dīn al-Nīsābūrī in Damascus he talked of conciliatory messages that he had sent without effect into the city until "the fire of anger was kindled"; then, when the people of Homs saw "the jaws of death gaping", they agreed to the terms that they had earlier rejected and all were given quarter.[32] The note of self-justification is less in evidence in a letter that he wrote to his nephew, Farrukh-Shāh. He did remark that fair dealing was his "key to the lands", and he criticised "the feeble minds" of the people of Homs, but he allowed himself mundane comments on the winter climate which "in those parts is more than the body can bear". He was also explicit about his real objective; news of his complete victory would, God willing, soon be on the way. Punning on the Arabic name of Aleppo (*Ḥalab* = milk), he added: "we have only to do the milking and Aleppo will be ours".[33]

His optimism proved ill-founded. What is not mentioned in the letters is the fact that only the town of Homs had surrendered. The citadel still held out, but Saladin had pinned his hopes on the quick collapse of resistance at Aleppo and merely left a force to mask it. He then took another eighteen days to deal with the problem of Hama, which lies some 30 miles (48 km) further north on the direct route to Aleppo. This delay, which is not explained by 'Imād al-Dīn or noted in any of Saladin's extant letters, is said to have been caused by attempted diplomacy. The citadel of Hama was held by Saladin's former associate, 'Izz al-Dīn Jūrdīk. According to Ibn Abī Ṭayy, when Saladin reached al-Rastan on the Orontes, some 13 miles (21 km) north of Homs, Jūrdīk came out to meet him and after a day and a night of talks it was apparently agreed that the town of Hama should be handed over but not its citadel.[34] Jūrdīk left this in the charge of his brother, while he himself went to Aleppo to try to arrange a general peace. When he got there, however, he was arrested and imprisoned with the Banū 'l-Dāya, one of whom, according to Ibn Abī Ṭayy, threatened to kill him as he was being lowered into the bottle dungeon of the citadel.[35] Why Jūrdīk was treated like this is as obscure as are most of the intrigues of al-Ṣāliḥ's court, but his arrest lost Aleppo a useful base. Saladin had moved north of Hama, and on hearing the news, he turned back and Jūrdīk's brother handed over the citadel to him on 28 December.

Two days later Saladin reached Aleppo, the key to northern Syria, without which he could neither follow a policy of dynastic expansion in the east nor whole-heartedly pursue the Holy War. The old town of Aleppo lies to the east of a small river; there are low hills nearby, but the town itself is dominated by its formidable citadel, built on what Ibn Jubair described as "a round table", some 160 feet (49 metres) high.[36] Saladin sent a letter from his camp to tell Farrukh-Shāh that he had arrived: "we are hoping that God, Exalted be He, will cause things to proceed peacefully without the need of war".[37] Not long afterwards he wrote to Farrukh-Shāh again: for eight days he had been using the flat of his blade and not the edge and he had been trying to damp down the fires of war; he had been welcomed by soldiers and others in Aleppo, who had hurried to take refuge with him, but the town and the citadel were strong and it would take time before "their hardness could be softened".[38]

In fact, in spite of its deserters, Aleppo had no intention of surrendering. The young al-Ṣāliḥ himself had been brought out to address the people and he appealed to them for protection, breaking into tears in the middle of his speech. According to Ibn Abī Ṭayy, "the people fell under his spell",[39] and the spell was then confirmed by a bargain which restored to the Shī'ites a number of privileges that had been abolished by Nūr al-Dīn. This was a serious blow for Saladin, who had never yet had to face a city where both garrison and people were resolutely hostile. Further, as Ibn al-Athīr pointed out, the Aleppans, living as they did near the Frankish border, were experienced fighters.[40] They made a habit of coming out to attack the besiegers and Saladin's only real chance of success lay in breaking their attachment to al-Ṣāliḥ or in winning over al-Ṣāliḥ's counsellors.

Al-Ṣāliḥ's situation was reasonably secure, but his emirs were not content merely to keep Saladin at bay. They tried for a coup to remove him once and for all and approached Rashīd al-Dīn Sinān whose followers, the Isma'īlī Assassins, were entrenched in the Nusairi Mts to the west of Hama. While Saladin was in camp outside Aleppo, a group of these men approached his tent but were recognised by Khumartekīn, Lord of Bū Qubais, which bordered their lands. Khumartekīn was killed and in the exchange of blows that followed one Assassin attacked Saladin, but had his head struck off by an emir coming to the rescue. 'Imād al-Dīn added that "the others were not killed until they had killed a number of people".[41] Saladin wrote to tell Farrukh-Shāh what had happened: the Aleppans had realised that they could not fight him openly and so they had taken the almost unbelievable step of approaching the Assassins; at the time of the communal meal, thirteen of them armed with knives had launched an attack; he himself had been protected by his *mamlūks*, friends and emirs, but Khumartekīn had been killed.

Farrukh-Shāh was then himself told to be on his guard sleeping and waking, by day and night, at rest or journeying; he should only employ men whose religious faith he knew or who were guaranteed by those who had reason to fear the consequences of treachery, for "the knives have been distributed" and large sums of money shared out amongst Assassins. Saladin added that he was writing from outside Aleppo where the tents could not keep out the winter rain and fires could not ward off the cold, but "men's minds are hardened by the expectation of victory". Farrukh-Shāh was invited to come to Syria – "there is a horizon here in which you can rise".[42]

In an earlier letter Farrukh-Shāh had referred to expenses connected with Damietta, which was in his charge at the time and to which extra troops had been drafted.[43] In a reference to this Saladin wrote: "we have no doubt that you will carry the expense yourself", an indication, perhaps, that his own funds were running low. To keep a large force camped outside Aleppo was an expensive business and in spite of his remark about the expectation of victory, he can have had little reason for hope. Raymond of Tripoli had gathered a force which was camping by the Nahr al-Kabīr, a river which follows the line of the Homs/Tripoli gap, where he was well placed for a move against Muslim territory. Arab historians claimed that the Aleppans had approached him to ask for help,[44] and William of Tyre said that overtures had been made by the garrison of the citadel of Homs. Frankish hostages were still being held in Homs for the final settlement of the ransoms of both Raymond himself and of Reynald of Châtillon, who had been captured by Nūr al-Dīn and released shortly before his death. The Franks hoped to recover these hostages and also to be given money "if they gave help against this pestilent man". As a result, they moved on Homs, but found, according to William of Tyre, that there was no substance in the promises and that the garrison of the citadel was now hoping to be rescued by a relief force sent by Saif al-Dīn of Mosul.[45] William of Tyre confused the issue by assuming that the Lord of Mosul, "the most powerful of the Parthians",[46] was still Nūr al-Dīn's brother, Quṭb al-Dīn, who had died in 1170, but he made no mistakes about the Mosuli interpretation of Saladin's position. Saladin had "spurned the laws of humanity; he had forgotten his own condition and, showing no gratitude for the benefits conferred on him by the father of the boy [al-Ṣāliḥ], he had risen in rebellion against his Lord". To counter this kind of propaganda Saladin made a virtue of what seems to have been a necessity and drew off from Aleppo, claiming again to be defending Islam from the Franks. He returned to Hama and from outside the town al-Fāḍil wrote a personal letter to Farrukh-Shāh: Saladin had moved by a forced march from Aleppo leaving the weak and the stragglers to look after themselves and the hardships of the journey had had their effect on al-Fāḍil's own strength; the Franks, however, in spite of their large numbers, had been forced to retire with their money wasted and their expectations confounded.[47] Saladin himself wrote to al-'Ādil that when he reached Hama and began to draw up his men in battle order, the Franks drew back to Ḥiṣn al-Akrād (map 3). "This is a victory opening the gates of men's hearts."[48]

It did not open the way to the citadel of Homs. Saladin had left Aleppo on 26 January 1175. On 2 February he was reported to be at Hama and the citadel of Homs did not fall until 17 March. According to 'Imād al-Dīn, he spent a month besieging it[49] and during the fortnight which is left unaccounted for, he was presumably either waiting for another Frankish move or trying the effect of diplomacy. When nothing happened, he had to bring up mangonels and begin a siege. The citadel, which he described in one letter as being "like a howdah on a hill",[50] and in another as "wearing the clouds as a turban",[51] stands on a mound some 200 feet (61 metres) high and he watched the fighting from the vantage point of a room at the top of Homs' only college. Although he later denied his own losses, both sides suffered casualties and eventually a number of the besiegers made an abortive attack on the citadel gate and were captured. This success, however, seems to have prompted the garrison to take the opportunity of coming to terms. According to Saladin, his sappers had undermined the walls, his mangonels had destroyed the defences until "the towers were like doors",[52] but he gave the defenders quarter "for the sake of those who had been captured".[53] He wrote to the Qāḍī 'l-Quḍāt in Egypt to tell him of this victory which had been granted to him in particular and to the people of Islam in general,[54] and in a letter to Baghdad he congratulated himself on the fact that the citadel was taken peacefully, with lives and women being spared; "the faces of our friends are open, laughing and cheerful, for none of them were lost".[55]

By this time the Mosuli relief force was not far away, but it was weaker than it should have been and the prophecy made to Nūr al-Dīn about the ruin of his house was being fulfilled. Saif al-Dīn Ghāzī of Mosul had summoned his elder brother 'Imād al-Dīn Zangī to join him, but Zangī had refused. Saladin is credited with a share in widening the family split by encouraging Zangī and even by reinforcing him with troops.[56] As a result, while the crucial campaign was taking place in Syria in March and April 1175, Saif al-Dīn himself was busy attacking Zangī in Sinjār, and it was his younger brother 'Izz al-Dīn Mas'ūd who was sent west with troops that could be spared. He was accompanied by Zulfindār, an emir to whom Ibn al-Athīr attributes a whole series of mistakes that ruined the Mosuli cause during this period, and after marching by Aleppo, where he was joined by a number of al-Ṣāliḥ's troops, he led his combined force southwards against Hama.

Saladin himself had moved south from Homs to the valley of the Biqā', where he took Baalbek without a fight on 29 March (map 8). When the Mosulis advanced on Hama, according to his own account, a constant stream of his men were sent to reinforce it and the Mosulis were forced to draw off.[57] They then sent a message to his commander there, 'Alī ibn Abī'l-Fawāris, saying that they were hoping for peace and unity and this message was passed on to Saladin at Baalbek. He moved quickly with a small force and was outside Homs on 2 April. There was now an interval for bargaining. Gumushtekīn and al-'Adl were doing the negotiating for Aleppo and Mosul and according to 'Imād al-Dīn, who had now joined him, Saladin agreed to return "the fortresses" – presumably Homs, Hama and Baalbek – to Aleppo and only to keep Damascus, where the *khuṭba* was to be in al-Ṣāliḥ's name. 'Imād al-Dīn went on to suggest that Saladin's amenableness, and the fact that he had not come with many men, led the allies to underestimate him – "what we have heard about him is not true".[58] They demanded al-Raḥba, on the Euphrates, which was refused on the grounds that it belonged to Nāṣir al-Dīn Muḥammad ibn Shīrkūh. They then left and although Saladin sent messengers after them, they refused to return.

This account raises some questions. If Saladin was willing to give up Homs, Hama and Baalbek less than three months after having written about his hopes for final victory, it suggests that he was taking his failure at Aleppo very seriously. He could reasonably have argued that if he could not take Aleppo quickly, he could probably not take it at all in the near future, as a besieging force would always be exposed to attack by the Mosulis, the Franks or both. A peace settlement would at least allow him to use Damascus as a base or, if it were broken, it would give him a propaganda advantage in a renewed war. 'Imād al-Dīn's insistence on the smallness of his force is surprising. During the course of the campaign, Saladin himself talked of his own huge numbers,[59] and these are mentioned again in Ibn Abī Ṭayy's note on the capture of Baalbek.[60] He might reasonably have left the bulk of his troops behind while he himself rode north in the hope of reaching a peaceful settlement, but Baalbek is no more than 90 miles (145 km) from Hama as the crow flies and matters did not come to a head until a fortnight after its fall. The question of al-Raḥba is also obscure. There seems no reason to doubt the statement found in Abū Shāma that Nūr al-Dīn removed it from Nāṣir al-Dīn Muḥammad after Shīrkūh's death.[61] He may certainly have got it back by this time, although there is no reference to this, but it might also be that Saladin was deliberately confusing the negotiations.

It is clear from his letters that he saw the Franks as the key to the problem. He wrote to Baghdad to complain to the Caliph about the agreement that the Aleppans and Mosulis had made with them, of which he claimed to have written evidence with which to confute them if they tried to deny it; a number of leading Frankish prisoners were to be released and the allies were to hand over to the Franks captured Ayyubid supporters so that the Franks could use them to exchange for those of their own men whom Saladin was holding; Ḥārim and its territories were to be given back, together with the cave fortress of Shaqīf Tīrūn in the hills flanking the plain of Sidon, which the Muslims had captured in 1165; the Franks had been supplied with hostages, including the brother of Gumushtekīn and the son of the Lord of Manbij (who was almost certainly Saladin's enemy Quṭb al-Dīn Ināl), together with the nephew of Saladin's "old friend" (as he was later described[62]), 'Alam al-Dīn Sulaimān, and a son of the emir Fakhr al-Dīn ibn al-Za'farānī, who had joined Saladin before the fall of Homs.[63]

On the day after the breakdown of the negotiations, 'Izz al-Dīn Mas'ūd advanced up to the east bank of the Orontes near Shaizar, some 16 miles (26 km) north of Hama, and Saladin himself then moved his own tents north to the foot of the hills known as the Horns of Hama. He had written to Farrukh-Shāh in January inviting him to Syria and this invitation had been reinforced in al-Fāḍil's message sent on the march to Homs, to which he had added a sentence to say: "Saladin's wishes are to be followed."[64] Letters must also have been sent to Taqī al-Dīn and Shihāb al-Dīn al-Ḥārimī, as all three had arrived in Syria and were converging on Hama at the start of April. It emerges, however, that Saladin's real answer to the prospect of a joint attack by his enemies was to try to come to terms with the

Franks himself. This is nowhere recorded by his contemporary biographers and in his indignant letters to Baghdad he took care not to mention it. But he wrote to Farrukh-Shāh: "God knows that we are reluctant to make a truce with the Franks and that we are eager only for the welfare and advantages[65] of the people of Islam, but we are afflicted by a people like butterflies or even lighter brained."[66]

This same letter gives the most vivid account of the position immediately before the armies met. Saladin told Farrukh-Shāh that, as he was writing, the Aleppan squadrons were coming back towards his army and he was having to move out to meet them: he was between two enemies – presumably the Franks and 'Izz al-Dīn Mas'ūd's troops – with neither of whom had he yet settled; he had sent word to Shihāb al-Dīn and Taqī al-Dīn[67] to say if the journey was too hard for them and they wanted to take their time, they were to send their troops ahead to reinforce him; as for Farrukh-Shāh himself: "God, God, let him not finish reading this letter without having put his foot in his stirrup." At this point the letter breaks off to give news that had just come in by carrier pigeon that the Franks had agreed to terms; the details would not be known until Saladin's envoy returned, and he was sure that the Franks would have asked for more than the agreed offer taken back to them but it is clearly implied that any settlement would be ratified. The letter ends by deploring the need for such a truce and writing of the Aleppan/Mosuli allies that they had committed more acts of treachery than they had drawn breaths.

This picture of hectic activity, diplomatic and military, with the last-minute rush of reinforcements and flurry of messages, poses an obvious problem. Saladin admittedly was covering Hama but he had earlier been prepared to let its garrison look after itself while he took Baalbek. If he was in desperate need of reinforcements he could have moved south to meet them, rather than stay in an unnecessarily exposed position. On the other hand, were 'Izz al-Dīn Mas'ūd's force to be destroyed away from the shelter of the walls of Aleppo, Saladin would recover prestige and could perhaps hope for al-Ṣāliḥ's surrender. 'Izz al-Dīn Mas'ūd might be encouraged to fight by the joint inducements of the weakness of Saladin's army and the prospect of Frankish aid, but a premature settlement by Saladin with the Franks or the arrival of Egyptian reinforcements could frighten him off. The explanation that Saladin was deliberately baiting a trap would alone cover the timing given in the letter and it is tempting to apply it to the negotiations themselves. In what he wrote Saladin had shown that his aim was the conquest of Syria. It was better for him to win a battle than to agree to a peace that would block his hopes of expansion and there must be a strong suspicion that he wanted the negotiations to fail. At the least, it can be said that he out-manoeuvred his enemies strategically as well as tactically so as to induce them to throw away their advantages by attacking him.

The battle was fought on Sunday 13 April. Saladin put the total numbers involved on both sides at some 20,000.[68] He himself was in the centre of his line, with his Egyptian reinforcements on the wings, and 'Imād al-Dīn, standing behind the ranks, was watching the dust and listening to the noise.[69] After a time he saw that the dust was getting further away and he added, without giving more details, that Saladin drove the allies away from "their baggage, their beasts and their infantry". In fact, they were completely routed. Ibn al-Athīr blamed Zulfindār for cowardice and ignorance of war. He said that 'Izz al-Dīn Mas'ūd stood for a time in an impossible situation, causing Saladin to exclaim: "he is either the bravest of men or else he knows nothing of war", but then he, too, was driven off the field.[70] Saladin himself wrote that he broke the enemy like glass and that no single man, "known or unknown", was lost.[71] This may be an exaggeration, but it shows that there was no real resistance. There was talk of bribery[72] and possibly because of this or through fear of treachery the Aleppans and Mosulis seem to have been unwilling to fight their way out of a difficult situation, as long as Saladin left them room for retreat.

Saladin could have had no interest in a bloody victory.[73] His best chance of success at Aleppo was still to enter by invitation and the more of its men he killed, the larger would have to be his own contribution to garrisoning northern Syria against the Franks of Antioch. Furthermore, the professional soldiers of the day fought for their pay-masters, but were content to transfer their allegiance when circumstances changed. It scarcely causes surprise to find a Muslim garrison soldier being transferred to Frankish service when his castle changed hands,[74] and it was common to see Muslim troops fighting for Muslim rulers whom they had earlier opposed. Saladin could hope that, given time and success, his present enemies might serve under his own command and, not surprisingly, he gave orders that no fugitives or wounded men were to be killed. Prisoners were taken but then released and Saladin's men contented themselves with plundering the enemy camp. Saladin wrote to Baghdad to say that he had decided not to pursue the routed, to take prisoners or to refuse quarter to those who asked for it.[75] He told Zain al-Dīn 'Alī in Egypt that he had freed his prisoners out of respect for the principles of Islam; his men had seized equipment and horses; "there is no rider of ours who does not have led horses by his side and no foot-soldier who cannot outstrip the riders thanks to the many horses that he has taken"; it was a day which had given promise of future happiness; it had confirmed and added, given security and spread fear. He ended his letter with an apparent contradiction of what he had written to Baghdad, telling Zain al-Dīn that he was moving in pursuit of the routed enemy in the hope of cutting them off from their base.[76]

Although he may have hoped to avoid bloodshed by leaving clear an immediate line of flight from the battlefield, he must certainly have wanted to reach Aleppo as soon as possible to exploit his success. According to 'Imād al-Dīn, he was planning another siege,[77] but in fact he merely camped to the west of the city telling Baghdad that he was trying to cut if off from contact with the Franks.[78] At this he went on, the Aleppan emirs broke off their alliance with the Franks and asked for peace. The effect of the battle can be seen in the terms offered. It was now suggested that Saladin should keep all his conquests, with al-Ṣāliḥ holding only north Syria as far as Hama. In return, al-Ṣāliḥ's name was to be retained on the coinage and in the *khuṭba* throughout Saladin's dominions.[79] Saladin improved the bargain by insisting on being given Ma'arrat al-Nu'mān, 35 miles (56 km) north of Hama and within 50 miles (80 km) of Aleppo. Ibn Abī Ṭayy, who claimed to have seen Saladin's signature on the document of agreement, added that one of its conditions was that Saladin was to come in person to help if al-Ṣāliḥ were attacked.[80] Saladin left this out of his account to Baghdad and gave its converse, which was that the Aleppo troops were to serve with him in the Holy War.[81] "The Nūrid emirs and *mamlūks*" were to be released. 'Izz al-Dīn Jūrdīk, together with 'Uthmān and Ḥasan of the Banū 'l-Dāya, had survived, but the sick 'Alī can fairly be assumed to have died in prison. The Aleppo negotiators made it a condition that Saladin should make peace with Saif al-Dīn of Mosul, and he himself interfered again in Atabeg family quarrels by stipulating that Saif al-Dīn should make peace with his brother Zangī and raise the siege of Sinjār. 'Imād al-Dīn claimed later that the Aleppans were not to undertake anything without consulting Saladin,[82] but although Saladin may have wanted this, he did not himself claim it to Baghdad as part of the agreement. On 25 April he celebrated the 'Īd al-Fiṭr outside Aleppo and by 6

May the agreement had been signed; he had returned to Hama and the Frankish force had dispersed.

7

WAR AND DIPLOMACY

The peace treaty with Aleppo marked the end of the first phase of Saladin's Syrian campaign. In spite of his successes he had failed in his explicitly stated aim of taking Aleppo and as a corollary to this the nature of his expedition had arguably changed. He had been drawn to Syria by a power vacuum rather than by any external threat to Islam. The size of the force that he took with him appears to confirm that this was not the migration of a war-band; he was relying on recruiting the soldiers and administrators who formed part of the mobile professional class, and the figures quoted suggest that in its first month his army had increased by a factor of ten. It is during the winter siege of Aleppo that there is the first recorded summons sent to Farrukh-Shāh and by April 1175 Saladin's Syrian supporters were stiffened by family reinforcements, bound to him by *'aṣabīya.* It is not yet clear how far this point can be taken but it may suggest uncertainty in the prospects for growth that had attracted the early influx of recruits or, less tangibly, a refusal to accept Saladin's self-selected Islamic role. Saladin had set his claim to be serving Islam against the obvious accusations of disloyalty to his dead master and of self-seeking. He claimed to have received a popular welcome and he accused the Aleppans and Mosulis of mistreating peasants and "drawing the sword of sedition",[1] but he had not been accepted as the only leader in the Holy War or acknowledged as having a right to rule in the name of al-Ṣāliḥ, and where the interests of the people and of the ruling group coincided, as had happened at Aleppo, he had been repulsed. With the peace treaty the military position had been settled as an official stalemate but the basic conflict between Saladin's policy of growth and the Zangids' attempt to hold their own had not been reconciled and there was no break in the propaganda war.

Saladin had outlined his position in a long letter sent to the Caliph at the start of his Syrian invasion, in which he rehearsed his services to Islam and justified his move: Egypt was too far away to be used as a base for the recovery of Jerusalem, whereas from Syria it could be attacked by large armies with horses that had not been tired out by a desert crossing,[2] he had a greater right to look after the upbringing of al-Ṣāliḥ than those who were claiming to serve him loyally but were, in fact, eating up the world in his name. Accordingly, he asked the Caliph for a diploma of investiture to cover not only Egypt, Yemen and the Maghrib, but also Syria "and all the lands contained in the Nurid state, together with everything that may be conquered for the Abbasid cause by our swords and our armies".[3]

The reaction to this came after his truce with Aleppo when he had returned to camp outside Hama. Here he was met by the Caliph's envoy, Shihāb al-Dīn Bashīr, who brought him robes of honour and a diploma of investiture, covering the lands that he already held.[4] The Caliph was taking a neutral position. He had also sent robes of honour to al-Ṣāliḥ and Saladin later complained of the propaganda advantage that this had given to the Aleppans. Saladin was told to maintain friendly relations with al-Ṣāliḥ and Aleppo and its districts were specifically excluded from the diploma of investiture, which covered Egypt, Yemen and the rest of Syria. Saladin, the message went on, now had no excuse for abandoning the Holy War. He was reminded of the need to guard the coast of Egypt, "for the enemy, distant as he is, is near to it", and he was told: "the Caliph wishes you to attack the lands held by the enemy as a deliverer and not as a raider... especially Jerusalem". In reply he wrote: "the dawn has risen on the night of waiting". He made no overt criticism of the omission of Aleppo, but he obviously felt the need to counter Mosuli propaganda: "the Lord of Mosul has wronged the Caliph's servant and used his tongue and his pen against him, as his hand has proved powerless... In one of his letters he called him a *khārijī* [heretic, rebel] although it was by the servant's sword that God killed the *khārijīs*". He then went on to give details of his victory and of the treachery of the Aleppans and Mosulis, claiming again that his own sole aim was "to exalt the pulpits of religion".[5]

Although he did not try to reopen the question of Aleppo, he was concerned to stress the full range of his difficulties and he ended by saying that he was now being forced to move against the fortress of Ba'rīn (map 8). This lies some 15 miles (24 km) south-west of Hama and it was being held for Fakhr al-Dīn ibn al-Za'farānī by one of his lieutenants. Fakhr al-Dīn had joined Saladin with what was described as a strong force before the attack on Homs, hoping, it was said, to be reappointed as army commander and perhaps also expecting the return of his former *iqṭāʿ* of Homs. Saladin, however, had no intention of surrendering command of his army and his family now had the first claim on major *iqṭāʿs*. Homs was given to his cousin, Nāṣir al-Dīn Muḥammad, and Hama to his uncle, Shihāb al-Dīn. Fakhr al-Dīn then left and Saladin, who was said to have paid no attention to him when he was there, was annoyed by his defection. He told the Caliph that Fakhr al-Dīn was relying on the Assassins and the Franks: Baʿrīn was one of the frontier posts of Islam; "there is no advantage to Islam and the Muslims in this fortress remaining in his hands... Very frequently he talks of removing it from Islam and handing it over to the unbelievers." The place was surrendered to Saladin on terms of quarter and Fahkr al-Dīn himself joined the service of Mosul and is next found east of the Euphrates, where he was given al-Ruhā (Edessa).

Saladin now moved south to Damascus by Homs and Baalbek and there followed some months of comparative quiet.[6] Outside Damascus on 22 July he met Frankish ambassadors, including an envoy from Humphrey of Toron. According to ʿImād al-Dīn, the Franks had come to negotiate a truce and they agreed to all Saladin's demands[7] – an interpretation which would still allow Saladin to criticise Aleppo and Mosul for buying support from the infidels. ʿImād al-Dīn, however, had not mentioned Saladin's negotiations with the Franks before the battle of Hama and it seems that the embassy was not, in fact, negotiating an agreement with Damascus, where the earlier truce that Saladin had criticised was still in force, but finalising or perhaps extending the Hama agreement. According to William of Tyre this allowed Saladin to attack al-Ṣāliḥ and his allies without interference from the Franks in exchange for the return of Frankish hostages held in the citadel of Homs. Humphrey of Toron, a man said to have been connected to Saladin "by bonds of too great familiarity",[8] is named as the mediator in this and William pointed out, fairly, that it was against the interests of the Franks, who should have done everything that they could to prevent Saladin from becoming more powerful.

After the cold and rain of winter, Syria was now suffering from a drought and Saladin did what he could to relieve the burden on the country by sending back some of his Egyptian reinforcements. Shihāb al-Dīn stayed in Hama and Taqī al-Dīn was appointed governor of Damascus in place of Ṭughtekīn. Farrukh-Shāh, however, returned to Egypt accompanied by al-Fāḍil, whose first reported absence this was from Saladin's service since his rise to power. He left a vacancy to be filled and 'Imād al-Dīn wrote: "Saladin, in spite of his intense desire with regard to me, was hesitant."[9] 'Imād al-Dīn's detractors had pointed out that "his business is letter-writting and this is the post of al-Fāḍil". He had an advocate, however, in Najm al-Dīn ibn Maṣāl, who had gone to Syria with Saladin, and al-Fāḍil underlined the fact that Saladin's dominions were now scattered and that he himself could not be present on every occasion. As a result, to his own great satisfaction, 'Imād al-Dīn was now officially appointed to act as al-Fāḍil's deputy.

It may have been 'Imād al-Dīn who drafted an optimistic letter to Farrukh-Shāh sent by Saladin from Damascus on 24 October, in which he wrote: "things are going in the best of ways. Men's hearts are united in our favour and our orders are obeyed." The only doubt was about the Franks; "we do not know whether they will keep to the Damascus truce or break it, cut short its time or extend it". Farrukh-Shāh was ordered to leave Damietta, which did not have to be guarded after the close of the sailing season, and to move to the eastern province of Egypt to guard against possible raids from Sinai. The most important part of the letter comes in a section in which Farrukh-Shāh was told to collect the tax from the non-Muslims of the western province and to send money to Saladin who was "submerged in seas and floods of expenses". Saladin went on to say that if Farrukh-Shāh did not help or if he delayed the repayment of loans – presumably made to him from state funds – then "ears will feign deafness, although tongues have answered the summons, and hosts will disperse".[10]

Farrukh-Shāh could have had no doubt why Saladin needed money. By the time that the letter had been written, Saif al-Dīn Ghāzī had moved west to Niṣībīn, some 120 miles (193 km) from Mosul. Under the terms of the Aleppo agreement he and Saladin were to have made peace and Saladin had sent an envoy to Mosul while an envoy from Saif al-Dīn had come first to Aleppo and then to Damascus. According to 'Imād al-Dīn, the Mosuli envoy had been summoned for an interview with Saladin. He had put his hand into the sleeve of his gown to bring out his copy of the draft peace agreement between Saladin and Saif al-Dīn but by mistake, instead of this, he took out the text of a pact between Aleppo and Mosul. Saladin looked at it and merely remarked that perhaps this was the wrong copy. When the envoy realised his mistake, Saladin asked:

"how can the Aleppans have made an alliance with the Mosulis when it is a condition of their agreement [with us] that they should not undertake anything without consulting us?" 'Imād al-Dīn added that from that day onwards Saladin realised that the pact with Aleppo was broken.[11] The story is repeated in a letter from Saladin to Baghdad:

> the messenger from the Lord of Mosul returned to hear us take the oath [to ratify the peace treaty]. When he came with the documents, he made a gesture with his hand to bring it out, but what he brought out was the document of an oath between the Mosulis and the Aleppans, the gist of which was an agreement directed against us... Gumushtekīn and others had sworn to this, breaking their [earlier] oath.[12]

It is difficult to know what to make of this tale. On the face of it, it seems no more than a circumstantial and elaborate excuse on Saladin's part for breaking off negotiations and his later career shows how determined he was to discredit the Mosulis and destroy their influence. On the other hand, Saif al-Dīn had not yet put out his full strength and may have had an interest in engineering a breakdown. Finally, the suspicions on both sides must have been such that any mistake could have been interpreted, rightly or wrongly, as part of a plot.

Whatever the truth of the story, Saif al-Dīn appears now to have moved to Niṣībīn. Ibn al-Athīr criticises his timing and points out that his men, who could normally have expected to spend the winter on their lands, were kept at Niṣībīn from autumn until spring, by which time they were not only disgruntled but running short of money.[13] Saif al-Dīn was not an experienced field commander, but it is hard to believe that this was simply a mistake on his part. It turns out that he was looking for help from Mārdīn and Ḥiṣn Kaifā, both of which are nearer to Niṣībīn than to Mosul and it may be that he had been hoping for a quick muster which would allow him to strike at Saladin in the absence of his Egyptian reinforcements. Saladin, however, was careful not to be taken at a disadvantage. There is no mention of Saif al-Dīn's move in the October letter to Farrukh-Shāh, but news of it must have come soon afterwards and 'Imād al-Dīn was told to send word to al-'Ādil.[14] In his turn, he was to pass on instructions to the emirs, telling them to make their preparations for a return to Syria. Meanwhile, Saladin himself sent a letter of complaint to Baghdad. The Caliph was asked either to warn Saif al-Dīn not to break "the covenant of God" or else to allow Saladin "to draw the noose tight". He also asked, presumably with Ḥiṣn Kaifā and Mārdīn in mind, that all "the lords of the outlying districts" should be ordered to help him against the Franks with the object of capturing Jerusalem; if they were not willing to do this, "at least they should not act as helpers against the Caliph's servant, turning him aside from his purpose".[15] In another letter, accusing the Aleppan emirs of treachery, he told the Caliph that he was returning a second robe of honour that had been sent to him apparently in order that he should forward it to al-Ṣāliḥ; he had informed the Aleppan emirs of its arrival, but had then learnt that they were preparing to abandon their pact with him "and making the same claims about this robe of honour as they had done about the first, which they had followed up with injustice... They were claiming independence for this child and not obeying the edict which made the servant [Saladin] his guardian"; as a result, Saladin had thought it right to return the robe to Baghdad "as it was he [and not al-Ṣāliḥ] who had been intended [by the Caliph] to benefit from it".[16]

There is no record of a reply from Baghdad, but clearly nothing could have reconciled the two sides, who were again intent on war. Saif al-Dīn crossed the Euphrates at al-Bīra, some 75 miles (120 km) north-east of Aleppo, in the early spring of 1176. Before continuing his march, he was concerned to come to terms with Gumushtekīn and al-Ṣāliḥ, presumably with a view to dividing the spoils should Saladin be driven out of Syria. This bargaining, premature as it was, led to difficulties and according to Ibn Shaddād, on several occasions Saif al-Dīn made up his mind to return home, but finally things were settled to his satisfaction.[17] He moved south and camped outside Aleppo, and when al-Ṣāliḥ came out to meet him, he shed tears and the two embraced. Saladin had been at Damascus when he heard that the Mosulis had reached Aleppo and he marched out on his way north in the month of Ramaḍān (March/April 1176). On 7 April he reached Marj Bū Qubais, the pasture-land at the south end of the Ghāb depression, north of Hama.

From an earlier halting-place, al-Ghasūla, south of Homs, he had written to Tūrān-Shāh who had now left Yemen and arrived in Syria.[18] The reason for this move is not certain. A letter dated to August 1175 referred to a serious illness which had attacked Tūrān-Shāh; his son had died and for fifty days after this he had taken no food.[19] There had been "one blow after another" from which he had suffered, all of which may have given him the distaste for Yemen which Ibn Abī Ṭayy attributed to him,[20] but it may also have been felt that he would now be more use in Syria. Saladin began his letter with a Quranic quotation from the story of Joseph in Egypt: "I am Joseph and this is my brother", and went on: "praise be to God who has removed sorrow from us, given us a fair gift and watered Syria with a cloud coming up from Yemen". In a letter of his own al-Fāḍil echoed this by comparing Tūrān-Shāh's arrival to rain for the thirsty and sunrise for the lost night-traveller. He went on to say that he himself had come back from Egypt, when the enemy, having broken their oath, had begun to move; there was no doubt that it was right to fight them and "we hope that Almighty God will continue to give the Ayyubid house its customary victory".[21]

Tūrān-Shāh reached Damascus on 19 April. Saladin had not waited for him, but had already crossed the Orontes. Ibn Shaddād reported that Saladin had had to send for Egyptian troops, "who were delaying on their own affairs, not realising that delay spelt disaster",[22] but this seems to be either an exaggeration or else a confusion with the 1175 campaign. Al-Fāḍil's letter proves that at least some of the Egyptians were with Saladin during his march from Damascus and there is no reference by 'Imād al-Dīn to any late arrivals. On the contrary, he notes that, although Saladin had only 6000 men, he decided to advance as he himself expected no more reinforcements. 'Imād al-Dīn numbered Saif al-Dīn's force at 20,000 riders, over and above their camp followers, and he claimed that they had a pledge of help from the Franks.[23] His numbers were challenged by Ibn al-Athīr, who said that he had seen the Mosuli muster roll and order of battle, which had been drawn up by his brother Majd al-Dīn. He himself put the total at between 6000 and 6500 riders and added: "would that I knew how large Mosul and its territories up to the Euphrates could be that it should have 20,000 horsemen".[24] In this context, both authors appear disingenuous. Ibn al-Athīr leaves the Aleppo troops out of his reckoning, although al-Ṣāliḥ himself was with the army, and 'Imād al-Dīn glosses over the fact that Saladin moved without waiting for Tūrān-Shāh, who can certainly be presumed to have brought troops with him from Yemen. There is nothing in the account of the fighting that followed to suggest that either side was badly outnumbered and it seems fair to conclude that 'Imād al-Dīn was exaggerating and perhaps adding in servants to Saif al-Dīn's numbers.

On 13 April, almost a week after his arrival at Marj Bū Qubais, Saladin was still in camp, celebrating the 'Īd al-Fiṭr. He then heard that the allies had moved some 23 miles (37 km) south of Aleppo to

Tell al-Sulṭān, and at this news he crossed the Orontes by Shaizar and sent his heavy baggage back to Hama. He had almost 50 miles (80 km) to cover to reach Tell al-Sulṭān, and he took two days for the march, Tuesday and Wednesday 20 and 21 April. Saif al-Dīn's scouts saw his cavalry scattering to water their horses on the Wednesday evening and Ibn al-Athīr blames Zulfindār for advising against an immediate attack.[25] There is too little evidence to show whether Saladin was in danger of being surprised but he may have relied on orthodox generalship on the part of the enemy which would require enough daylight for a set-piece battle. On Thursday 22 April, both armies were drawn up in conventional formation, each with a centre and two wings. The mid-point of Saladin's line was marked by a tell which masked his reserves. His left was commanded by Shams al-Dīn Ṣadīq of Buṣrā. The commander of the right wing is not named, but may have been Farrukh-Shāh, who was noted as taking a prominent part in the battle.[26] Saif al-Dīn was in the allied centre with Zulfindār. His right wing was commanded by Muẓaffar al-Dīn Keukburī, a son of the former Mosuli administrator Zain al-Dīn 'Alī-Kuchuk, and the commander of his left wing is not named.

When the battle was joined the left wings on both sides were defeated. Two of Saladin's emirs were killed, apparently trying to rally Shams al-Dīn's men, but Saif al-Dīn got into more serious difficulties while trying to help his own left. This must presumably be taken in connection with an ill-ordered charge by his centre whose riders, according to 'Imād al-Dīn, started their gallop too soon: "they arrived racing against one another and scattered... Before the thousands were hundreds, before the hundreds tens and before the tens scattered ones."[27] Saladin then launched his own cavalry against this disjointed formation and drove them back. According to Ibn Abī Ṭayy, when Saif al-Dīn moved to support his left, he was thought by his men to have been routed[28] and Ibn al-Athīr also notes that there was confusion amongst the allies, which he blames on the fact that Zulfindār had set up the standards where they could only be seen from near at hand.[29] Ibn al-Athīr claimed that only one man was killed and certainly it seems that once Saif al-Dīn had lost control of the situation, there was no more serious fighting. The allies were driven from their camp and made no attempt to rally. Al-Faḍil wrote: "I have written this letter at Tell al-Sulṭān, where I am in Saladin's company... The trees of Saladin's spears bear fruit, while those of the enemy cast no shadow."[30]

As he had done at the Horns of Hama, Saladin contented himself with his victory and made no attempt to destroy the enemy force. He again gave quarter and spent what was left of the day plundering the allied camp. Saif al-Dīn's own tent was given to Farrukh-Shāh as a reward for his services in the battle and 'Imād al-Dīn described how, in addition to treasure-chests, wine, musical instruments and singing girls, Saif al-Dīn had brought with him a collection of birds, including doves, nightingales and parrots, which Saladin returned with the message: "tell him to go back to playing with these birds, for they are safe and will not bring him into dangerous situations".[31] The captured emirs, including 'Abd al-Masīḥ, were taken to Hama, but then allowed to go free. According to Ibn Abī Ṭayy, the Aleppo troops returned "naked, bare-foot and impoverished, blaming one another for oath-breaking"[32] – presumably a reference to suspicions of treachery. Ibn al-Athīr noted that they were joined in Aleppo by 'Izz al-Dīn Mas'ūd, Saif al-Dīn's brother, but Saif al-Dīn himself had apparently bypassed the city and gone straight to Buzā'a, some 23 miles (37 km) to the east of it, from where he moved off across the Euphrates on his way back to Mosul.[33]

Saladin made no serious demonstration against Aleppo, although Ibn Abī Ṭayy reports that he camped outside it for several days.[34] The city had no intention of surrendering and Saladin turned his attention to cutting its communications and capturing the neighbouring castles. He first attacked Buzā'a, which surrendered on 4 May. He left one of his Kurds in charge of it and advanced north-east to Manbij, then held by his enemy Quṭb al-Dīn Ināl, who was claimed by 'Imād al-Dīn to have been one of those chiefly responsible for Saif al-Dīn's move to Syria.[35] Ināl surrendered on 11 May and Saladin surprisingly tried to buy his allegiance by offering to allow him to keep the contents of the citadel, valued by 'Imād al-Dīn at 300,000 dinars.[36] Ināl, however, was not to be won over and preferred instead to join the service of Saif al-Dīn.

Saladin now turned west, keeping at approximately the same distance from Aleppo, and at the end of the second week of May he laid siege to A'zāz. William of Tyre had noted A'zāz as marking the halfway point on the journey from Antioch to Edessa[37] and, under the name of Hazart, it had been a fief of the Frankish principality of Edessa. Saladin claimed to be afraid lest it should be handed back to the Franks but 'Imād al-Dīn added simply, "his siege of A'zāz was, in fact, a siege of Aleppo".[38] The castle, which stood on an artificial hill, was strong, well garrisoned and well supplied. Saladin set up mangonels and both sides suffered losses. Then on 22 May he was again attacked by the Assassins, one of whom cut his cheek with a knife. The man was killed by Shīrkūh's former *mamlūk*, Saif al-Dīn Yāzkūj; two others were cut down on the spot, and a fourth was then hacked to pieces by the bystanders. One of Saladin's rescuers later died of his wounds and Saladin himself went back to his own tent with his cuirass pierced through and blood streaming from his cheek. Ibn al-Athīr said that he was like a man in a panic[39] and Ibn Abī Ṭayy reported that "the army was disturbed and people were afraid of one another".[40] 'Imād al-Dīn, an eye-witness, wrote that Saladin's tent was now protected by a stockade; he would not talk to anybody whom he did not recognise; "when he rode out, if he saw anyone in his entourage whom he did not know, he had them removed. Afterwards he would ask about them and if they wanted intercession or help, he would help them."[41] A reassuring message was sent to al-'Ādil in Egypt – "there was only a scratch with some few drops of blood... there is nothing to cause distress"[42] – and the siege went on.

After five-and-a-half weeks, the walls of A'zāz had been undermined and it surrendered on 21 June. Saladin had now marched in a half-circle round Aleppo. He had met with uninterrupted success, but it is during the siege of A'zāz that 'Imād al-Dīn for the first time talks of restlessness amongst his troops.[43] 'Imād al-Dīn himself complained about the difficulties of communication.[44] As far as he was concerned the roads were cut and he could not get money from Damascus to meet his expenses. The spirit of the Aleppan troops was not broken and they were trying to catch Saladin off guard. 'Imād al-Dīn tells a revealing anecdote of a captured Aleppan raider whom Saladin, after consulting "his rough companions", decided to treat as a thief. 'Imād al-Dīn claimed that it was only because of his own intervention that the man's hand was not cut off in accordance with the penalty laid down by Islamic law,[45] and this underlines an obvious problem. It could not seriously be claimed that the Aleppans were violating any legal code in defending al-Ṣāliḥ. If they were treated harshly Saladin's reputation would suffer, and yet if he simply left the city and moved south, he could not hope to hold his recent conquests, which would be isolated between Aleppo and the lands of Saif al-Dīn.

As a result, he decided to march from A'zāz to Aleppo itself, a move which had the effect of taking Gumushtekīn by surprise. Gumushtekīn had assumed that the attack would continue around the fortified perimeter of Aleppo and that the next threat would be to his own *iqṭā'* of Ḥārim on the road to Antioch. He went there to defend the place himself, a move which 'Imād al-Dīn doubtless deliberately misrepresented in a poem in which he wrote: "Aleppo banishes its Gumushtekīn as [Quṭb al-Dīn] Qaimāz was banished from Baghdad."[46] When Saladin, marching by Marj Dābiq, arrived at Aleppo, Gumushtekīn tried to recover from his mistake by asking permission to return to the city to arrange for a peace. Saladin agreed, apparently on the understanding that an agreement was to be made immediately. Abū Shāma's account suggests that hostages were exchanged on both sides,[47] but 'Imād al-Dīn, who was sent into Aleppo with Saladin's envoy to Baghdad, Shams al-Dīn ibn Abī'l-Maḍā', claimed that he was acting as an envoy and that it was only the Aleppans who had to supply hostages.[48] 'Imād al-Dīn was clearly out of his depth, and has left an indignant and confused account of what happened: "they removed our servants and left us in a narrow place with no lights, no privy and no bread or water. We passed the night hungry and thirsty, without any bedding, guarded by people who rejoiced at our misfortune." In the morning they were taken into the presence of al-Ṣāliḥ and 'Izz al-Dīn Mas'ūd, Saif al-Dīn's brother; "the document of the oath [to a peace treaty] was presented to us and we were dismissed without anyone taking any [further] notice of us"[49] The document that 'Imād al-Dīn had been given presumably contained terms unacceptable to Saladin and it was realised that this was a trick to get Gumushtekīn into Aleppo. 'Imād al-Dīn wrote: "Gumushtekīn did not cease acting with hypocrisy and dissembling and Saladin blamed me and attributed their wrong-doing to me."

These abortive negotiations lasted for some time. Saladin wrote from Aleppo on 2 July:

> we are wrapped in safety, with abundant good fortune... For a month, both before and after the capture of [A'zāz?] and before and after the [Assassins'][50] attack... we have been accepting advice and listening to peace proposals... we were conciliatory and not distant, soft and not rough, and we agreed to give up part of what we held and what we had given as *iqṭā's* to our army... but every time we made a good proposal, they refused, in accordance with their past custom.[51]

After the move to Aleppo, "they wrote to us many times, secretly and openly, claiming to want peace... On each occasion, we agreed to what they wanted... or to most of it... drawing the line only at what we knew they intended to use as a cause for injury." The recipient of this letter, an unnamed religious leader, was asked to pass this information around his own circle, as it was a true account of the situation and not merely "words patched together".[52]

While these negotiations were going on, Saladin did not press an attack but instead sent agents to collect revenues from Aleppan estates. Inside the city, however, both Shīʿa and Sunnī were united in support of al-Ṣāliḥ and according to Ibn al-ʿAdīm, they were eager to take the offensive.[53] These were "the common people" whom Ibn al-Athīr represented as attacking Saladin's troops, inflicting losses and stopping him from coming close to the city.[54] Ibn al-Athīr may well be exaggerating, but Saladin was certainly in a difficult position. His pacific policy towards the vanquished at the Horns of Hama and Tell al-Sulṭān had produced no obvious results and the more united the opposition became the less weight his own claim to be acting in al-Ṣāliḥ's interests could carry. The loss of Buzāʿa, Manbij and Aʿzāz might weaken Aleppo in time, but in the short term they were no more than useful bargaining counters. If his troops had been restive during the siege of Aʿzāz, it would have been foolhardy to force them to start on a far more difficult and costly siege. The Aleppans for their part could hold their city and could hope in time for another expedition from Mosul, but for the moment they could do nothing to remove Saladin from their lands.

Not surprisingly this stalemate again led to peace. Saladin gave up his claim to be in charge of al-Ṣāliḥ, who was confirmed in his possession of Aleppo and its territories. Saladin appears to have kept Buzāʿa and Manbij, but Aʿzāz was given back. A romantic account tells of an evening meeting between Saladin and Nūr al-Dīn's daughter after peace had been made; Saladin "kissed the ground and wept for Nūr al-Dīn," at which the girl asked him for Aʿzāz.[55] ʿImād al-Dīn, however, who copied out the peace agreement, appears to suggest that the return of Aʿzāz was included in its terms.[56] The peace was to cover Aleppo, Mosul and Diyār Bakr.

The agreement was dated by Ibn al-Athīr to 29 July[57] and Saladin moved from Aleppo on 31 July. He still had some scores to pay off and he chose to march on the stronghold of Sinān, the Assassin leader, at Maṣyāf, some 90 miles (145 km) as the crow flies from Aleppo in the shelter of the Nusairi Mts. Here he gave the impression of being about to start on a siege and had his mangonels set up, while his men spread out to plunder what they could of the Assassins' lands. But by 10 August, the attack had been broken off and Saladin was a day's march away at Hama. If three days are allowed for the march from Aleppo, one day for the erection of the mangonels and one for the move to Hama, this gives a maximum of six days for the attack, which was clearly not pressed home. ʿImād al-Dīn's explanation is that the Assassins had sent unspecified threats and inducements to Saladin's uncle, Shihāb al-Dīn, who held the *iqṭā'* of Hama, as a result of which he had persuaded Saladin to leave.[58] Ibn al-Athīr reported that they had threatened to kill Shihāb al-Dīn himself, as well as the rest of Saladin's family and his emirs, and he also says that Saladin's army was tired after its campaign,[59] while Ibn Abī Ṭayy links the withdrawal to a threat of Frankish raids.[60]

While Saladin was at Maṣyāf he had been sent a number of Frankish prisoners who had been captured in the Biqā', but the news from the south was not reassuring. In July the Franks had seen that Damascus was "without troops and without a ruler". Amalric's successor, Baldwin the Leper, had crossed the headwaters of the Jordan, and, passing the forest of Bāniās, he had raided up to Dārayyā, a village within 6 miles (10 km) of Damascus.[61] On 1 August, seeing that Saladin was still preoccupied, he attacked again. He himself marched on the Biqā' valley from Sidon in the south, while Raymond of Tripoli attacked from the territory of Jubail in the north. Baldwin followed the usual Sidon – Damascus road, skirting Jabal Nīḥa and coming out at Mashgharā on its eastern slopes. He then moved up the Biqā', finding a land "flowing with milk and honey, as the saying is",[62] while Raymond marched along the line of the Adonis river to cross the main ridge of the Lebanon range by al-Munaiṭira, north of Baalbek. Ibn al-Muqaddam, who held Baalbek, is credited with the destruction of a Frankish raiding party,[63] but he failed to link up with Tūrān-Shāh, who had led his troops over the pass from Damascus. The Arab historians placed the battle that followed at 'Ain al-Jarr, on the Damascus side of the floor of the Biqā' by the main Damascus–Beirut road.[64] William of Tyre reported that after Baldwin had reached 'Ain al-Jarr, his men had ravaged the countryside, forcing the people to take refuge in the hills or else to drive their cattle for shelter into the marshes.[65] Baldwin then moved north to meet Raymond and presumably the combined force turned back to confront Tūrān-Shāh. Tūrān-Shāh's regular troops were reinforced by local levies, but he was decisively defeated and forced to take to the hills, losing "many dead, more wounded and innumerable prisoners".[66] Baldwin and Raymond returned with their spoils and the only loss that William of Tyre notes was that of a number of stragglers who had been plundering in the marshes and were then cut off.[67]

According to Ibn al-Athīr, the battle of 'Ain al-Jarr encouraged the Franks to further daring,[68] but with the imminent return of the army from the north, this threat does not seem to have been taken seriously either by Tūrān-Shāh or by Saladin. Tūrān-Shāh did not stay to guard Damascus, but almost immediately after his defeat he must have left for Hama, where he met Saladin for the first time since the start of his Yemen expedition. Another visitor to Hama at this time was the poet Abū Ḥassān al-Ḍarīr who came to complain of the governor of Tadmur and who wrote a poem in which he shows that it was now widely held that Saladin was on his way back to Egypt and that he had only a small force left.[69]

Saladin moved back slowly to Damascus which he reached on 25 August. Nūr al-Dīn's Qādī of Damascus, Kamāl al-Dīn al-Shahrazūrī, had died in July. The post of Qāḍī had been held temporarily by one of his deputies, al-Auḥad Da'ūd, but after some negotiations it was given to Ibn Abī 'Aṣrūn, who was rewarded for having left Aleppo to join Saladin's service. Saladin had also lost his envoy to Baghdad, Shams al-Dīn Ibn Abī 'l-Maḍā', who died in the third week of August. 'Imād al-Dīn noted his useful friendship with Ẓahīr al-Dīn ibn al-'Aṭṭār, a man of influence at al-Mustaḍī's court, as well as his services to Saladin in the field of public relations.[70] When he was sent on a mission to Baghdad, "he would make liberal gifts to poets... and often come back in debt". He was replaced by Ḍiyā' al-Dīn al-Shahrazūrī and as a final gesture towards both past and present Saladin "adorned his unadorned rule"[71] by marrying 'Iṣmat al-Dīn Khātūn, the widow of Nūr al-Dīn and the sister of Sa'd al-Dīn ibn Anar, who had joined him before his capture of Damascus in 1174. He then appointed Tūrān-Shāh as his deputy in Syria and on 10 September he left for Egypt, feeling secure, according to Ibn al-Athīr, because of his victories and because of the treaties that he had made.[72]

8

EGYPTIAN INTERLUDE

Ibn al-Athīr's remark about Saladin's feeling of security is not convincing. There was now no treaty between the Franks and Damascus and Saladin could hardly have been encouraged by Tūrān-Shāh's performance at 'Ain al-Jarr. The Holy War, in fact, had come a poor second to dynastic expansion during the whole of Saladin's stay in Syria. He took credit for having driven Raymond of Tripoli away from Homs but he himself had fought no battle and taken the offensive on no occasion against the Franks. He had criticised his opponents for buying Frankish support and had then made his own bargain with them, ignoring the Caliph's instructions that he should concentrate on the recovery of Jerusalem. None of this necessarily indicates hypocrisy but it does show that the Franks were only of incidental relevance in the immediate context of Saladin's power struggle.

Circumstances had not accommodated themselves to idealistic over-simplification or, in fact, to simplification of any kind, in that the claims of Egypt, the Holy War and dynastic growth had not been resolved. Saladin had taken Egyptian money with him to Syria and, as was shown in his letter to Farrukh-Shāh, had sent back for more. Syria, however, at the start of what was to be a prolonged drought, can have been in no position to make good Egyptian losses. The pattern of growth, by which one conquest could pay for the next, had been interrupted. A symptom of the difficulties that this entailed is perhaps to be seen in references to unrest in Saladin's army and its lack of numbers.

Saladin himself, wherever possible, preferred men to money, as is shown by his attempt to buy Quṭb al-Dīn Ināl. This reflects the optimist's view that a cycle of expansion can continue until equilibrium is somehow reached and, in more general terms, there is certainly an optimistic tone in the letters covering this period. Superficially, both these and 'Imād al-Dīn's account show Saladin as the simple-minded enthusiast, convinced of the benefits that he was bringing, believing that Aleppo should and would open its gates, dismayed by the baseness of Aleppan dealings with the Franks and the Assassins, and turning to irritation when balked. This may be dismissed as window-dressing but Saladin's own hopes and the amount of effort that he put into explaining and defending his actions remain clear.

To whom the defence was primarily addressed is less obvious. At this period Baghdad was not a serious military rival to Damascus and Cairo and unlike the Pope, to whom he was compared, the Caliph did not enjoy the backing of a hierarchical religious organisation. In theory, however, only the Caliph could grant the lands of Islam to their rulers and in the story cycle of al-Ẓāhir Baibars, it is the Caliph who is shown as giving Egypt to the Ayyubids because of their service to him. This, of course, was intended for vulgar consumption and in part Saladin may have aimed his propaganda at the common people who wielded the powerful "weapons of prayer".[1] Other possible targets were recruits, in particular administrators, one of whose qualifications was an attachment to their Islamic background. Further evidence is needed but at least it is clear that, whatever his motives, Saladin persevered in his attempt to cope with a basic contradiction, that the hereditary principle was recognised in Islamic practice – "kings nurture the growth of their kingdoms for their children"[2] – and that he wanted Islamic sanction in order to disregard it in the case of al-Ṣāliḥ. He had left Syria with the problem unresolved and without any clear line of future policy. There was no advantage to be got in attacking Aleppo again unless there was a chance of success. On the other hand, if he accepted the situation in Syria, he was left without room for expansion in the east and sooner or later he could expect another Zangid counter-attack.

At this point he sent a letter to 'Aḍud al-Dīn, the Caliph's vizier, explaining what he had done and hinting at future plans. He started by referring to an earlier letter that he had sent on his return to Damascus and he repeated his version of the settlement with Aleppo; he had agreed to peace in the north and to the return of lands that had been taken from al-Ṣāliḥ by the sword, hoping by this to win the Caliph's favour; "the emirs of the outlying regions" – a reference, perhaps, to Mārdīn and Ḥiṣn Kaifā – had earlier sent messages asking him to reach an accommodation with Saif al-Dīn, but he had turned away their envoys, pointing to what Saif al-Dīn had done in the past: then, eventually, he had agreed to a settlement on condition that the troops of Mosul were to help him in his wars. At this point, Saladin started to prepare Baghdad for another northern campaign in 1177 and he told the vizier that "the lesser tyrant of Rūm", (the Lord of Armenia), had moved near to the lands of Islam and was proposing to attack in the spring; the Lord of Sicily had also prepared a strong fleet and had promised to help the Franks of the Coast. As for his own move, "it is well known that Syria has been suffering from drought this year... and it is this that has driven the Caliph's servant and his men from the country". He noted that on his journey to Egypt he had escorted a large number of Muslim merchants, saving them from the heavy taxes that they would have had to pay on their goods had they gone through Frankish territory. He ended by praising al-'Ādil's administration of Egypt; the people were tranquil, the roads safe, the frontiers protected and justice enforced; he himself was reviewing his troops and preparing stocks of weapons and provisions in readiness for the spring; he was then proposing to send out not only an army but also the Egyptian fleet, so as to "grind the unbelievers as with a file from both sides", land and sea.[3]

He began by concerning himself with his fortifications. 'Imād al-Dīn explained that the walls of Cairo and Fusṭāṭ were thought to be weak and two separate garrisons were needed for defence.[4] Instead of strengthening each individually, Saladin now ordered a single wall to be built around both cities and a citadel to be constructed. On 11 February 1177 he wrote to Tūrān-Shāh in Syria to tell him of work that had been done to improve the fortifications of Damietta and to build up a citadel at Tanis; an unnamed person, presumably Farrukh-Shāh, had spent large sums of money on this, thus laying up treasure in heaven, and Saladin himself was intending to visit both places and also Alexandria, where in just over a year 40,000 dinars had been spent on repairs to the city wall; the Franks of the Coast were hoping to get help from overseas, but he himself intended to force a battle and had fixed a time for the muster of his troops. He included a reference to the dangers of the route from Syria and the difficulties of correspondence. Tūrān-Shāh was warned only to send news that could do no harm if it fell into the wrong hands – "we have already expressed the desire that his letters be free of anything which could be damaging if it were made known". Code was to be used for important messages.[5]

On 23 February Saladin left Cairo for his promised visit to the

Mediterranean, taking with him his two eldest sons, al-Afḍal, who was nearly seven years old, and 'Uthmān, who was five. After inspecting Damietta, he went on to Alexandria where he visited the sheikh Abū'l-Ṭāhir al-Iṣfahānī and listened to traditions of the Prophet for three days in the first week of March. In his earlier letter to 'Aḍud al-Dīn he had talked of his plan to attack the Franks by land and sea and he made use of his visit to inspect his fleet. According to Ibn Abī Ṭayy, he found that the ships were worn out and their equipment damaged, and he ordered timber and craftsmen to be collected and construction work to begin.[6] With the decay of Fatimid power the Egyptian fleet had served as little more than an instrument for the slave trade and on this occasion 'Imād al-Dīn noted that a large number of captives had been brought into Damietta, from amongst whom Saladin gave him a girl of his own choice.[7] For more serious purposes, however, the fleet suffered from two weaknesses, one of which was a shortage of materials, more particularly, suitable timber, which had to be imported from Europe. Periodic attempts were made to halt this trade and Saladin wrote that "the Muslims sought these things and the Rūm blocked their export",[8] while in another letter he instructed an envoy sent to Genoa to do his best to buy up and send off anything that was lacking or in short supply for the fleet.[9] An equally serious problem was that of man-power. Naval service was neither popular nor highly regarded. Saladin later complained of "the unknown hordes",[10] recruited to man his ships, and Maqrīzī noted that it was an insult in Egypt to call a man a sailor.[11] A strong Egyptian fleet, however, could have great strategic importance. William of Tyre wrote of the alarm felt by the Franks at the prospect of large numbers of ships coming from Egypt to attack the Coast in support of any army.[12] What was even more to be feared, he added, was that an Egyptian fleet might interfere with, or entirely block, the passage of Frankish reinforcements in the shape of pilgrims from Europe.[13]

Saladin left the Mediterranean coast on 16 March and wrote on 19 March to tell Tūrān-Shāh that he had seen to the preparation and the manning of the fleet and had watched how quickly the ships were being built. "Men have been collected whom bad administration dispersed in the past, including a number of Maghribīs, whom the enemy fear"; as for the rest of Egypt, there was prosperity and a good harvest; "praise be to God, there is no injustice uncovered in the lands", and "the hearts and tongues of the inhabitants were united in praise of the regime".[14] He added that he was expecting to be attacked by the Franks; Tūrān-Shāh had promised him the gift of an exceptional horse, but this should not be sent while danger still threatened. Meanwhile, Tūrān-Shāh himself had been trying to negotiate a truce with the Franks. Saladin was not enthusiastic but wrote that "those who are present can see what the absent cannot"; there would be no objection if the truce covered only one part (Damascus and not Egypt), and did not involve disadvantages for the Muslims; Syrian troops, however, must be allowed to move to Egypt in case of need without being accused of breach of faith.

Saladin went on to raise the problem of Muslim trade passing through Frankish territory. In his account to Baghdad of his return to Egypt in 1176, he had referred to transit taxes levied by the Franks. He now wrote:

> no reply has come to our letter about the need to stop the passage of the Muslim caravans... and it may be that this was lost because of enemy action and never arrived. The disease of the caravans is proving intractable and its cure is difficult. These merchants are risking their lives, reputations and goods and they also take the risk of strengthening the enemy. Every time that we decide to mete out harsh punishment to those of them who arrive here... the wounds that the Franks have given them are still bloody... and everyone pleads for them and says: "do not add distress to distress".

He underlined the importance of public opinion for his decisions by insisting that "the foolish people" must be stopped by Tūrān-Shāh at Damascus,

> otherwise, how can we stop them here? If we prevent them from leaving Eygpt, it will be said: "these are men who want to go back to their homes and their children", or if we stop them from coming in, then we will be told: "these are people who have suffered at the hands of the enemies of Islam".[15]

The political union of Cairo and Damascus may have encouraged trade but the Syrian exports to Egypt listed by Maqrīzī are for the most part minor agricultural products which had no significance for the Egyptian economy.[16] It may be that the merchants of whom Saladin complained were transporting more valuable goods from farther east, which he would have preferred to have sent through his own port of Aden, but his remarks can reasonably be taken at face value, on the assumption that he wanted no advantage to accrue to the Franks from the internal trade of his dominions.

The same letter contains a reference to the document of an oath which , he said, had not arrived in Cairo. He wrote that, were it not for his reluctance to refuse any request by Tūrān-Shāh, he would not have wished to sign this himself as Tūrān-Shāh's own signature would have been sufficient. This appears to be a reference to the Aleppo settlement. According to 'Imād al-Dīn, before Saladin left for Egypt, he sent his envoy, Sa'd al-Dīn Abū Ḥāmid, to Mosul and Diyār Bakr in order to administer the oath confirming the treaty.[17] Sa'd al-Dīn had returned with representatives from Mosul, Mārdīn and Ḥiṣn Kaifā, and an oath had been taken from Tūrān-Shāh in Damascus. After this, the leader of the Mosul delegation, a son of the Qāḍī Kamāl al-Dīn al-Shahrazūrī, had gone home, but the others had been persuaded to go on to Egypt. Sa'd al-Dīn had decided not to take them on the long detour to the east of Kerak, but to cross Frankish territory, on the assumption that if the crossing could be completed in two days, the Franks would be taken by surprise. The plan failed. The envoys of Ḥiṣn Kaifā and Mārdīn were captured and the others escaped only with difficulty.

At the start of June Saladin was at Birkat al-Jubb outside Cairo and by the end of the month he had moved further down the caravan road to Palestine and was in camp at Fāqūs (map 7). He was plagued by the difficulties of communication that had been underlined by the misadventure of the eastern envoys. He wrote from his camp to comment on the fact that in a letter just received from Tūrān-Shāh there was no reference to the arrival of any of his own letters from Egypt; he himself had had news, but not all of it was credible, and there were rumours which only added to his confidence "that God will not allow Islam to be abused"; the one clear indication that the enemy was planning an attack by sea was the fact that no Rūmī merchant ship had arrived in Egypt that year – presumably after the opening of the sailing season in March; nevertheless, "our only object here and our only purpose in this life which has been lent us is to fight against the infidels, whether we are believed in this or disbelieved". Tūrān-Shāh had obviously been painting a picture of hardship and poverty in Syria and Saladin commented that he did not want to be forced to go there himself "lest this movement import a second famine for the inhabitants". As an illustration of the difficulties, Tūrān-Shāh had talked of the straitened circumstances of a Syrian *iqṭā'* holder. Saladin wrote: "if his [Tūrān-Shāh's] purpose is to let us know of this, then we have taken note of it... but if he wants us to give the man another *iqṭā'* in exchange, while Syria is hard pressed this year by the general drought, this is a door which, if opened, will be entered by many". In fact, at this point he himself, and, by extension, Egypt, was either unwilling or unable to subsidise Syria, and he added by way of explanation: "there is no merchant we know of in Egypt who will take money from us on a bill of exchange to be paid by his deputies or associates in Damascus".[18]

The main source of Saladin's concern was the Count of Flanders, who had come on a pilgrimage, while envoys from Constantinople had also arrived at Jerusalem to suggest another joint attack on Egypt. This was followed by prolonged discussions and Saladin wrote another letter while he was still waiting for news: "up to the time of writing we are still in our camp with our forces gathered and our intention set on raiding the enemy by land and sea, seeking him out if he does not attack". He went on to say that his troops were rested and well supplied with money; the ports were strongly fortified and the fleet well off for funds; its raids had been successful, except in one case where a commander had landed to take on water, "because of intense thirst", and had then been caught unawares; there was no reliable news of the Sicilian fleet; some said that it had been delayed and others that it was on the point of attacking Egypt; similarly, there were various stories about another (Byzantine) fleet – "eyes and ears are alert for news of it".[19] Some time after this the rumours were replaced by definite information. Saladin wrote to tell Tūrān-Shāh that news had come from one of his informants on the Coast that a muster had been proclaimed and that the King and his nobles had gone (to Acre) to inspect the Byzantine ships; they could not have chosen a better time from his own point of view, he claimed, as his armies were strong and well equipped; Tūrān-Shāh was to make preparations for a muster of Syrian troops so that they might be ready to move towards Egypt in accordance with the plan that had already been drawn up; "we are content to pass on the news and we do not choose to dwell at length on the measures that the situation requires".[20]

In the end the Franks did not come out. According to William of Tyre, the Count of Flanders was unwilling to move against Egypt.[21] He had heard of the difficulties caused by the Nile flood and men familiar with the country had warned him that this was not a suitable time for an attack. He had also been told that "an infinite number of Turks" had gathered there and, in spite of an offer of 600 camels, he was afraid of a shortage of supplies on the journey. After some time he was induced to change his mind, but by then the Byzantines had left for home. Some suspected Bohemond of Antioch and Raymond of Tripoli of having arranged this breakdown deliberately in order to secure the Count of Flanders' help for themselves.

While Saladin was watching his frontiers, his court was relaxing and, in particular, 'Imād al-Dīn was enjoying his first visit to Egypt. His only duty was to write letters to Syria, "and that not constantly",[22] for every department had its own scribes. He described his life as one of listening to songs and poems, visiting colleges, exchanging traditions of the Prophet, and investigating literary and legal topics. He claimed to have been in attendance on Saladin every evening for consultation on affairs of state and went on:

> Saladin was very fond of sitting with his particular friends from amongst men of intelligence... When he wanted to break up the gathering, he would rise to perform the evening prayer...and the candles would be removed. If he needed a letter written...he would dictate what he wanted to me and I would remain awake that night and bring it to him in the morning.

In his free time, 'Imād al-Dīn paid his first visit to the Pyramids, where he camped with his friends and sat discussing the Pyramids and their builders in the moonlight. On the way past Gīza he had seen a circle of men dressed in mantles like those of Iraqi or Syrian *faqīhs*. He thought that they must be students, but they ran away and "I was told that they were beer drinkers".[23] The Fatimid library was still being sold off at twice-weekly sales. The books had been on shelves properly catalogued, but Qara-Qūsh who was in charge of the Palace – "a Turk who knew nothing about books"[24] – had been advised by the auctioneers to take them out and pile them on the floors. The auctioneers would then go through the piles and where they found a work in more than one volume, they would split up the individual parts, have them bought up cheaply by their own agents, and then reassemble them. 'Imād al-Dīn wrote: "when I saw what was happening, I went to the Palace and bought in the same way as they did".[25]

This account of 'Imād al-Dīn's dignified leisure with its strong Islamic overtones, has to be contrasted with the lurid pictures painted by the North African satirist al-Wahrānī, a man who represented Saladin as refusing to believe that he was a true Muslim – "even if I saw you walking on water".[26] Al-Wahrānī wrote of 'Imād al-Dīn's homosexual darling, the singer al-Murtaḍā,[27] of orgies where the host ran naked on all fours, barking like a dog, and of wine drunk from the navels of singing girls.[28] He described mosques with their doors covered by spiders' webs, with doves nesting in their prayer niches, and others used as stores or bake-houses.[29] He accused Saladin's new Qādī of Damascus, Ibn Abī 'Aṣrūn, of not believing in the Resurrection,[30] adding, in a reference to his subordinates, "whoever uses wolves as sheep dogs is a wrong-doer".[31] Similarly, he wrote that the Qāḍī of Cairo, Ṣadr al-Dīn ibn Durbās, had appointed as judges Kurdish donkey-thieves and cattle-rustlers.[32]

Details of this kind are not to be taken literally. A reference to a man who wrote to his mother that he was making a living by stealing shoes from mosques to pawn with the Jews in order to buy wine in brothels[33] is meant as a joke, but one which was acceptable to the conventions of the time, and it must be noted that details of orgies were sent in a letter to Saladin's nephew Taqī al-Dīn, whose words were "sweeter than a beating with a prostitute's slipper". This serves as a corrective to the one-sided picture presented by 'Imād al-Dīn, which is that of the formalised Arabic eulogy, whereas al-Wahrānī follows the equally formalised pattern of satire. Literary convention decreed that both forms were permissible, whatever their relationship to fact, but for satire there were political limits that could only be set by the ruling group.

One of the best known poets of Saladin's day, Ibn 'Unain, was banished from Damascus because he was thought to have gone too far. The notorious line attributed to him, describing Saladin's rule in Damascus, runs: "our Sultan is lame, his scribe is blear-eyed and his vizier hump backed".[34] He described al-Fāḍil's head coming through the neck of his gown as looking like that of a rat peering out of its hole[35] and he laughed at Ibn Abī 'Aṣrūn for having gone on campaign with Saladin, remarking that a bow for carding cotton was no good for shooting arrows.[36] The danger of his approach, as opposed to al-Wahrānī's exaggeration, is that it seems to have been based on a sense of superiority. Ibn 'Unain was proud of his Arab ancestry and he insulted Saladin's Egyptian followers in Damascus by equating them with their former enemies, the Negroes, and writing: "if I were black with a head like an elephant, bulky fore-arms and a huge penis, then you would see to my needs, but as it is, I am white".[37] He was not impressed by Saladin's successes and wrote of his lack of real opposition: "do not rejoice at your conquests, for time is sleeping".[38] This criticism was too barbed for an administration that was looking for popular support and Ibn 'Unain was exiled, at which he wrote: "why have you sent away a trustworthy man who has committed no crime and no theft? Banish the muezzins from your lands if you are sending away all those who speak the truth."[39]

The double standard of eulogy and satire is important to the understanding of Saladin's own position at this time. His Arab biographers credited him with the heroic Arab virtues of courage, fidelity and generosity. From a hostile point of view, however, he could be represented as a hypocrite set on a policy of selfish expansion, the implications of which seem to have been so commonly accepted at the time that in a letter to Najm al-Dīn ibn Maṣāl, al-Wahrānī could add Dārā to a list of places affected by Saladin's campaigns,[40] although Saladin did not reach it until four years after Ibn Maṣāl's death. To the eulogists, Saladin's internal administration was in the best traditions of Islam, but to the satirists it was run by pompous weaklings or petty criminals. Neither view should be accepted, but it must be clear that at this stage of his career, though Saladin's power and resources had been increased, he was far from having established his position in the eyes of his contemporaries. His able manipulation of force in Syria had not won him acceptance even from such old associates as 'Izz al-Dīn Jūrdīk, let alone the more deeply committed supporters of the Zangid house. If he was to maintain or strengthen a connection between his own expansionist position and Islamic principle, he badly needed another success against the Franks.

9

DEFEAT AND DIFFICULTIES

In October 'Imād al-Dīn's pleasant interlude came to an end. As the Franks had not attacked Egypt, Saladin kept his promise by taking the offensive himself. William of Tyre connected this with the Frankish threat to the north, where the Count of Flanders was preparing for an attack on northern Syria.[1] This seems to be supported by undated letters, in one of which Saladin said that he was moving because the enemy were looking covetously at a frontier town, presumably Ḥārim, which, although not in his territory, could at least be defended by him. "If the enemy comes through this door... he will enter the house."[2] The second letter is one of a series addressed to Tūrān-Shāh. In it Saladin referred to the enemy's intention to attack unspecified lands, adding that he hoped to send his next letter from the edge of Frankish territory; if the Franks moved (against the north), he could attack from the rear, and if they stayed where they were, "the lance points would be in their breasts"; Tūrān-Shāh had suggested that Saladin should himself return to Syria, and this might be possible later; after the present expedition had ended, he would march (again) through the middle of Palestine and enjoy a second spring there.[3]

Saladin left Cairo on 28 October and on 30 October he camped outside Bilbais. 'Imād al-Dīn has left an account of his own share in the subsequent preparations. He had, or so he said, a presentiment about the expedition and he claimed to be ill-equipped – "The way was all on sand and my camels and mules were not able to carry [what I needed]." From Bilbais he wrote to his "dearest friend", the Qāḍī Shams al-Dīn Muḥammad ibn al-Farrāsh to ask what he should do. Shams al-Dīn replied: "go with Saladin and do not abandon him and he will recognise your resolution and your sincerity". 'Imād al-Dīn wrote an indignant poem to express his disapproval of this advice and his narrative continues: "Saladin said: 'are you with me or do you intend to leave us?' I said: 'the decision belongs to my master and whatever he chooses for me is better'. He said: 'go back and pray for us'."

'Imād al-Dīn's caution was quickly justified in commercial terms. He wrote: "I had gone to the army market to buy my provisions and found that prices had begun to rise. So I told my servant... 'sell my loads and my baggage and take advantage of these high prices'."[4]

No date is given for the start of the expedition, but 'Imād al-Dīn wrote some lines of poetry from the camp on 14 November when preparations must almost have been completed. Saladin moved by way of al-'Arīsh, where he left part of his heavy baggage under guard, and from there, bypassing Dārūm and Gaza, he reached Ascalon on Wednesday 23 November (map 7). Baldwin had been warned of his move and had collected what force he could. His position was weakened by the absence of a hundred knights who were helping with the Count of Flanders' northern campaign, where they had been joined by the Hospitallers and most of the Templars, the rest of whom had shut themselves up in Gaza. William of Tyre numbered Saladin's force at 26,000 horse, "not counting those mounted on mules and camels", of whom 8000 were *ṭawāshīs*, the cream of the professional cavalry, and 18,000 *qaraghulāmīs*.[5] The Egyptian army list of 577 A.H. showed a total of only 6976 *ṭawāshīs* and 1553 *qaraghulāmīs*.[6] Saladin himself, as has been seen, had been writing throughout the year of the strength of his forces and he can be argued to have recruited extra troops for this campaign, but even so William of Tyre's figures, in relation to professional soldiers as opposed to servants, must be exaggerated. Baldwin, however, was obviously out-numbered. He drew up his troops outside Ascalon but was advised not to risk a battle, and, after some skirmishing, he retreated within the shelter of the city walls at evening.

Baldwin's reluctance to fight in the open now led Saladin to make a serious error of judgement. He followed orthodox razzia strategy by allowing his troops to go off on plundering raids which extended northwards up the coastal plain as far as Qalqilya by Arsūf (map 2). Ramla and Lydda were attacked and William of Tyre quoted from the Book of Lamentations: "how hath the Lord covered the daughter of Zion with a cloud in his anger".[7] But the application of this strategy depended on the assumption that the main Muslim force could not seriously be challenged and Baldwin, who was not prepared to see his lands ruined, now marched out of Ascalon on

Friday 25th November. He was joined by the Templars from Gaza and instead of striking inland, where he could expect to meet Saladin's foragers, he followed the line of the coast to preserve as much as he could of the element of surprise.

The meeting-place of the armies is difficult to determine. Arabic sources talk of the battle of Ramla and William of Tyre mentions "Mons Gisardi".[8] The site must be marked by a hill and have a river nearby. Further, if Baldwin, who was hoping for a surprise attack, can be assumed to have marched on the day of the battle itself, it has to be within half a day's march of Ascalon. Tell Gezer, which was earlier identified as Mont Gisart, is at least 25 miles (40 km) from Ascalon and so is presumably too far away to qualify, as are the surroundings of Ramla. Further, 'Imād al-Dīn notes the river as being one "on which Tell al-Ṣāfiya stands".[9] Tell al-Ṣāfiya itself lies to the west of the Wādī al-Sanṭ and the plain from which it rises is traversed by a number of water-courses. The Tell itself is the site of the castle of Blanchegarde, which is not mentioned in any account of the battle; anywhere to the east of it seems too near a line where Saladin's march would have been interrupted by foothills, and although the point cannot be proved, a western site, such as that of the present settlement of Kefar Menahem, some 16 miles (26 km) from Ascalon,[10] can be suggested as a possibility.

Saladin had enough warning of the Franks' approach to try to collect those of his troops who were within earshot by sounding his trumpets and beating his drums. His men were scattered, however, and he was having difficulty with his baggage. Ibn al-Athīr and 'Imād al-Dīn both note that the baggage train had caused bunching at an unspecified river crossing,[11] and Saladin wrote that not only was the baggage mixed with the cavalry, but a number of his own men were so ill prepared that they had to go off to collect weapons and armour. Saladin also commented on the close formation of the Franks and William of Tyre wrote that the whole Frankish force, "all eager to avenge their wrongs and divinely inspired to manly courage by the fires which they could see on all sides and by reports of the slaughter of their own people, hurried on like one man".[12] Before the battle was joined, Saladin altered his formation. He later explained that, on the advice of his emirs, he had given orders for the right wing to close to the left and the left wing to move toward the centre, so that a tell by which they were marching would be at their backs when the attack came.[13] The implication of this command is that a formation comprising two advanced wings and a retired centre, with a tell to the right rear, was ordered to face half left, and this fits reasonably with an assumption that Saladin was moving westwards to meet Baldwin advancing from Ascalon. The normal Muslim tactic to counter a Frankish charge was to give way at the point of impact and then attack round the flanks and rear, but Saladin's manoeuvre could easily have caused his centre temporarily to be masked by one of its wings, thus making it impossible for his men to draw away in order to absorb the charge.

William of Tyre noted that the Muslims had given their horses no rest since their move from Egypt[14] and this too was confirmed by Saladin, who said that some of his men had overtired their mounts. Even with his disadvantages, however, he still had the weight of numbers on his side and according to William of Tyre, the issue of the battle was at first uncertain. Saladin's nephew, Taqī al-Dīn, distinguished himself. Ibn al-Athīr noted that he had advanced to the front of the Muslim line,[15] presumably because he was in command of one of the advanced wings, and 'Imād al-Dīn said that he stood firm in the face of attack.[16] His son, Aḥmad, charged the enemy and was then sent back by his father on a second charge and killed.[17] As the fighting continued, the Franks got the upper hand. The Muslims scattered behind their baggage and, with his army now defeated, Saladin himself had to be rescued by his guards from an attack by three Frankish horsemen.

Razzia strategy required that the raiding force should always be able to make good its retreat either by having a safe line open to it or by its ability to outrun pursuit. The Franks had won a surprising victory thanks not only to the fighting spirit of their men but to Saladin's over-confidence and it remained to be seen whether his mistakes had compromised his retreat. The battle had started in the early afternoon and William of Tyre noted that the pursuit reached Cannetum Esturnellorum, where it was interrupted by nightfall.[18] If Cannetum Esturnellorum is correctly identified as 'Uyūn al-Qaṣṣāba and if the battle itself was near Kefar Menahem, this would give a chase of about 17 miles (27 km). Over such a distance a victorious force with sufficient resources to conduct an organised operation of pursuit and destruction could be expected to wipe out a defeated enemy. Baldwin, however, seems to have been under no illusions about his capacities. He himself went back to Ascalon, leaving the pursuers to cut down stragglers, but without making any serious attempt to challenge Saladin himself, who was reported to have retreated by short stages in the hopes of re-forming his men. At this point, Saladin's gravest difficulties appear to have been caused by shortage of provisions and the fact that his scattered forces were no longer in a condition to march as an organised unit. William of Tyre reported that for ten days, starting on 26 November, the day after the battle, there was such rain and cold that "it could truly be believed that even the elements had conspired against the enemy".[19] Then, when the Muslims reached the desert, they had to contend with a lack of water; many of their overworked horses died and 'Imād al-Dīn wrote of the lack of water, fodder and guides.[20] Al-Fāḍil, who had presumably stayed at al-'Arīsh, hired Bedouin and went into the desert, from which he helped to extricate Saladin himself. Saladin's friend, Ḍiyā' al-Dīn 'Īsā, together with his brother and their companions, were betrayed to the Franks by their guide and taken prisoner, while others were reported to have given themselves up of their own accord rather than starve to death. William of Tyre noted that the Bedouin, "this treacherous race", had caused the rearguard at al-'Arīsh to panic by spreading news of the defeat. They had then pursued the stragglers and William commented: "that which the locust hath left hath the cankerworm eaten".[21]

Saladin got back to Cairo in the second week of December. Messengers had already arrived and optimistic rumours had spread. 'Imād al-Dīn wrote: "I rode out to listen to what they had to say and to hear how God had given victory to the Muslims. But I heard them saying: 'good news! The Sultan and his family are safe and are arriving with spoils.'" 'Imād al-Dīn knew the niceties of official phraseology and he went on: "they would not be giving good news of his safety unless there had been a defeat".[22]

Saladin was obviously concerned about the injury to his reputation. Anything that damaged the morale of his troops and his supporters could lead to unrest, and on 9 December he wrote to tell an unnamed emir that "the Franks had lost many times more than the Muslims";[23] although the battle had started well for them, it had ended in the Muslims' favour and in spite of the distance and the lack of water and guides only a very few had been lost on the way home and none of any importance; "we carried the weak and the helpless and went slowly so that the stragglers could rejoin the main body". The emir was asked to read out the letter to the leading men of his town so that they could join in thanking God and be assured that the army was safe and that attacks on the enemy had not been broken off. On the whole, apart from the concealment of 'Īsā's capture, the details given in this letter do not violate Qalqashandī's rule that detectable lies should be avoided in reports of defeats,[24] but Saladin strayed further in a letter to the Caliph's vizier in which he wrote: "if one hundred Muslims were martyred, yet thousands of unbelievers were killed... The people said that it was a defeat but through the blessing of the Caliphate it was a victory."[25] A third letter, to a *faqīh* who was asked to pass on its contents to his circle, talked of God's grace, which had led the Muslims through waterless deserts; no-one with a name had been lost, but only beasts that had died of thirst or fatigue; Saladin had given orders that the returning troops were to be met with provisions at the boundary of his own territory, and as the letter was being written, the army was re-forming.[26]

In spite of these attempts to minimise his losses, one fact that Saladin could not conceal was that Baldwin had stopped him for a time from taking any effective part in the defence of north Syria. The situation in Syria itself was not encouraging. The country was weakened by drought and Tūrān-Shāh had not proved an effective leader in Damascus. According to 'Imād al-Dīn, he was "plunged in the sea of his own pleasure" and had paid blackmail to the Franks to protect his own lands and crops from attack;[27] in spite of famine conditions in Syria he had exported 1000 *ardabbs* of grain to the Franks, although here Saladin expressed approval, but wished that he had made a better bargain.[28] 'Imād al-Dīn went on to say that every emir had gone his way in his own lands and the Franks had seen the weakness of the country. Further north, in Aleppo internal feuds had again weakened al-Ṣāliḥ's position. Al-'Adl had been acting as his vizier and had appeared to be winning the power struggle against his main rival, Gumushtekīn, when he was murdered by the Assassins on 31 August. Gumushtekīn had a brief interval of "sleeping soundly in his bed", but his rivals accused him of responsibility for the murder and told al-Ṣāliḥ: "you are the Sultan... and this Gumushtekīn despises you". Gumushtekīn was arrested on 5 September and forced to write to his garrison, ordering them to surrender Ḥārim to al-Ṣāliḥ. They refused, and although Gumushtekīn was tortured to death, they proceeded to maintain themselves in the castle as rebels against al-Ṣāliḥ's authority.[29]

The Franks, then, had reason to feel optimistic about the chances of an attack, and the Count of Flanders, with Raymond of Tripoli, arrived at Hama on 14 November. Hama was a good choice as a target in that al-Ṣāliḥ could not be expected to help Saladin's garrison by sending any relief force from the north, and, as it happened, Saladin's uncle, Shihāb al-Dīn, who held the town, was ill. In the event, however, Saif al-Dīn 'Alī al-Mashṭūb, who was in the neighbourhood, came to reinforce it and after four days the Franks withdrew. According to William of Tyre, they had merely made a demonstration, "not without loss to the enemy", and were now marching north to join Bohemond of Antioch,[30] but obviously the town had been in some danger. Saladin heard of the attack from al-Mashṭūb and wrote to Baghdad of "the good news that has come to us from our dominions in Syria". To add indignation to the tale he accused the Franks of having broken the truce, referring to the pact that he had made with Raymond of Tripoli in 1175. This was a propaganda point, as was shown by 'Imād al-Dīn, who noted with reference to the Count of Flanders, that if any leader arrived whom the Franks were bound to obey they might do so and then, when he left, the truce would be resumed.[31] Saladin went on to say that the Franks had reached Hama on a Monday and attacked on Tuesday, their cavalry fighting on foot; al-Mashṭūb had told him that they had suffered more than a thousand casualties, and had then withdrawn, partly because the troops of Damascus, Homs and Baalbek had linked up and were planning to attack their camp. The Frankish raid, Saladin added, was a clear violation of the agreement that had been made and an attempt to take advantage of Syria when it was "wounded by famine".[32]

Following on the Frankish withdrawal, Shihāb al-Dīn died on 5 December, four days after the death of his son. 'Imād al-Dīn wrote: "that time coincided with the battle of Ramla and this was a calamitous month".[33] Meanwhile, the Frankish force had moved to Ḥārim. The castle of Ḥārim stands on an isolated hill in a plain under the Amanus mountains some 40 miles (64 km) to the west of Aleppo and 20 miles (32 km) east of Antioch (map 3). It had been captured by Nūr al-Dīn and its recovery would be of particular value to Antioch. Ibn al-'Adīm listed a number of points in the attackers' favour, amongst them being the facts that the garrison were rebels, al-Ṣāliḥ was still a boy and Saladin was in Egypt.[34] Before the Franks arrived, al-Ṣāliḥ had sent out a force under the emir Ṭumān who, after failing to persuade the garrison to surrender, remained to watch the Franks, but was unable to challenge them openly. The Franks for their part invested the castle but the expected success did not come. William of Tyre was particularly critical of the Count of Flanders, who dismayed the besiegers and gave heart to the besieged by frequently talking of going home. The fact that Antioch was so close at hand was a mixed blessing. Supplies could easily be brought up, but William wrote of the besiegers that "they were given to dissoluteness and paid more attention to dice and other harmful pleasures than military discipline and the laws of siege warfare demanded". They were constantly hurrying off to Antioch, where they indulged themselves with "baths, feasts, drunkenness and other lubricious pleasures".[35] As a result, the siege dragged on throughout the winter and was still in progress in February 1178.

Meanwhile in Egypt Saladin was re-equipping his army. 'Imād al-Dīn wrote that "he concerned himself with generosity", making gifts and allowances, ransoming such prisoners as he could and replacing lost beasts. The drain from his funds must have been considerable. At a later period he was found paying from 100 to 150 dinars compensation for a lost horse,[36] at which rate to replace 400 horses would cost more than the previous year's expenditure on the walls of Alexandria. On the other hand, he could not afford to be seen to have suffered a major setback which might prevent him from intervening in Syria, either as a champion of the Holy War or even as the defender of his own borders. By 17 February, he had moved out of Cairo to Birkat al-Jubb, where he waited for more than a month until 23 March. By this time the situation in Ḥārim had simplified itself into a stalemate between Aleppo and the Franks. The Ḥārim garrison had fallen out of the reckoning as a separate force by coming to terms with al-Ṣāliḥ's commander, Ṭumān, who had sent picked men through the Frankish lines to reinforce it.[37] It was obvious, however, that if Saladin was allowed an opportunity to break the stalemate and relieve the castle this would be to the disadvantage of both sides, as he could be expected then to keep it for himself. As a result, terms were arranged by which the Franks were bought off. The Count of Flanders went to Jerusalem for Easter and then sailed from Latakia, leaving William of Tyre to record his ineffectiveness. 'Imād al-Dīn tried to give Saladin some direct credit by writing that the Franks did not abandon the siege until Saladin had left Egypt,[38] but Ibn Shaddād dates the Frankish move to 11 March[39] and apparently Saladin first got news of it from his agent Yūsuf al-Ṭarābulusī in Dārūm, which implies that he was still in or near Egypt. He wrote to tell Farrukh-Shāh that Yūsuf had warned him of the possibility of another attack by the Assassins and had also given the news that the Franks had withdrawn, "although it was not clear how".[40]

On 29 March Saladin was at Ṣudr at the western edge of Sinai. He had crossed to Eilat by 1 April and he reached Damascus on 15 April. He was met by Tūrān-Shāh, to whom he had sent some verses written by 'Imād al-Dīn, and 'Imād al-Dīn took care to note: "whether I was travelling or at rest, there were always people who wanted sparks from the flint of my inspiration".[41] He was also met at Damascus by messengers from Baghdad where the Caliph had agreed to accept his intercession for his protégé, 'Izz al-Dīn Aq-Burī, who had fled to Syria in the wake of an earlier disturbance in Baghdad. As it happened, however, the Caliph's vizier, 'Aḍud al- Dīn, "a man from a stock that was always killing or being killed", was murdered by Assassins on 21 April. Aq-Burī had apparently been relying on his good offices, and after having set off for Baghdad, he turned back when he heard the news. This must have been a further blow in a disappointing season for Saladin, not simply because, according to al-Fāḍil, he only "endured Aq-Burī's superficial roughness because he knew that he was sound at heart",[42] but also because he must have wanted to see him restored to a position of influence at the Caliph's court. By way of compensation, however, 'Aḍud al-Dīn was succeeded as vizier by a man on friendly terms with Saladin, Ẓahīr al-Dīn ibn al-'Aṭṭār.

According to 'Imād al-Dīn, the Caliph's letter had also included an offer of men and money.[43] From Saladin's replies it seems that this must have been tied to a proposal for a campaign against the Franks, and he was quick to defend himself against any possible suggestion of slackness. Before news of 'Aḍud al-Dīn's death had reached Damascus, Saladin had written to him to say that the famine in Syria was such that he could not muster a large army or even collect the troops already stationed there.[44] He expanded this point in another letter in which he wrote that the years of drought had caused things to get out of hand in Syria; no army could be mustered there, as this would be a crushing blow to the inhabitants; in Egypt, however, he had strengthened his defences and was now free from anxiety about the country; he had ordered the Egyptian fleet to attack Frankish bases and if the drought ended, the next spring, God willing, would see the capture of Jerusalem.[45]

Al-Fāḍil, who was intending to make the pilgrimage to Mecca, had been left behind in Egypt with al-'Ādil and there was a constant interchange of news, rumours and opinions between him and his correspondents in Syria. In the first of a series of letters quoted by 'Imād al-Dīn there is a reference to a Frankish raid on Ṣudr that must have followed Saladin's march to Damascus; according to deserters, the Franks had even thought of attacking Saladin's former base at Fāqūs, but had given up the idea because of their lack of numbers; they had apparently scented weakness in Egypt and were said to be planning to attack again; a letter had come from Manbij, reporting distcontent, presumably directed against Saladin, in Aleppo and Mosul,[46] and al-Fāḍil wrote: "what the Lord of Manbij reports about Aleppo and Mosul is mere supposition or hearsay... They have devoted their days to pleasure and have been defended by Saladin from their foes."[47] Both Saladin and al-Fāḍil were clearly convinced that Aleppo and Mosul were no longer aggressive and that the treaty of 1176 had effectively stabilised the situation. Saladin himself had referred in another letter to a report that the Aleppans had acted against an unnamed supporter of his. He had dismissed this, saying that he did not believe that they would have broken their agreement; "our hand, praise be to God, is strong".[48] It can be assumed, then, that at this point his remark about the capture of Jerusalem was to be taken seriously in so far as it implied that, in his view, al-Ṣāliḥ and Saif al-Dīn Ghāzī would not act as obstacles to any attack on the Coast in 1179. Before he could concentrate on this, however, there were other problems to be settled.

'Imād al-Dīn had painted a picture of the disintegration of government in Syria which reinforces remarks made in a letter from Saladin in which he had written apparently of Tūrān-Shāh's administration: "one can overlook small faults and keep silent about minor matters, but where the whole land is eaten up... this shakes the pillars of Islam".[49] 'Imād al-Dīn now put the position more tactfully and wrote of the power that Tūrān-Shāh had exercised and of his faithful and compassionate treatment of al-Ṣāliḥ, adding that when Saladin returned, "he was restricted to the continuance of his pleasures and his authority was ended".[50] Not unreasonably, he wanted a city of his own and as nothing new had been added to the Ayyubid state since Saladin's initial success in Syria, his choice was bound to upset existing arrangements. In the event, he asked for Baalbek, where he had been brought up as a boy. This was held by Ibn al-Muqaddam, who was not only a senior Nurid emir, but the man who had first invited Saladin to Syria after Nūr al-Dīn's death. Tūrān-Shāh's intention was obviously known before Saladin arrived, and 'Imād al-Dīn noted that Ibn al-Muqaddam did not come to Damascus to pay his respects as usual since "he knew that if he came he would find it difficult to get back".[51] Messengers were sent openly and in secret and Ibn al-Muqaddam was offered a larger *iqṭā'*, but he refused to leave Baalbek. Saladin apparently felt that he had to give Tūrān-Shāh what he wanted but he was unwilling to risk his reputation by harsh treatment of his followers. After some time, according to 'Imād al-Dīn, Tūrān-Shāh was given permission to march on Baalbek but there is no further account of this and if Tūrān-Shāh did move, it was without success.

This was the most important but by no means the only problem for Saladin. It is at this point that al-Fāḍil mentioned Tūrān-Shāh's debts and heavy expenses, telling Saladin that he should not hold him to account for his generosity.[52] He noted other causes for dissatisfaction; Syria was suffering from high prices; in Egypt, Saladin had given orders that the open performance of actions objectionable to Islam must be stopped;[53] al-'Ādil had passed on the message with a reprimand to one of his officers, but the man had pointed to "certain quarters" that protected houses of ill-fame and said: "if the wood were straight, the shadow would not be crooked"; al-'Ādil himself was accused of being a partner in the business, the implication being that the state was again short enough of funds to have to take revenue from brothels. External affairs, however, were seen in a more optimistic light. Al-Fāḍil commented on the fact that Saladin's envoy had been well received by the Mosulis, who were offering their services against the enemies of Islam; the Assassins had been putting out peace feelers and the King of Nubia was not worth a stone to stop him barking. On a domestic note, al-Fāḍil regretted the illness of Saladin's son 'Uthmān, who had gone with his father to Syria, and warned him against eating fruit or imported meat in Damascus. Other waters, he added are drunk, but that of Damascus is eaten.[54]

Saladin now sent Farrukh-Shāh to the Ḥaurān to guard against Frankish raids, while he himself moved to Homs, camping nearby on the Orontes. The Syrian famine and the unsolved problem of Baalbek meant that he was in no position to do more than watch his borders and al-Fāḍil had to console him for his inability to carry on the Holy War by writing: "God does not ask the doer about the completion of his deed but about his intention."[55] There was no serious military activity on the Frankish side, but a band of Franks "and the unbelieving wolves who had joined with them"[56] – a reference to eastern Christians – had been raiding round Hama, where according to 'Imād al-Dīn the regular garrison numbered less than 100 men. The raiders were eventually defeated and the prisoners brought to Saladin, who ordered them to be killed by "men of piety". 'Imād al-Dīn was summoned and thought that he was being called to "some important task that could not be carried out by anyone else". The prisoner whom he was chosen to kill turned out to be a boy, whom he asked to be allowed to keep as a slave. Saladin then decided to exchange him for a Muslim prisoner held by the Franks, and told 'Imād al-Dīn that he could have one of the captives taken by the Egyptian fleet. 'Imād al-Dīn was not prepared to credit himself with any compassion for the victim, but wrote: "I turned from that deed lest the company might laugh at me as they did at the others."[57] Saladin did not invent this form of execution by non-combatants where prisoners were killed as an amusing spectacle[58] ("homo hominem non iratus, non timens, tantum spectaturus occidit"), but it did not win universal approval and al-Fāḍil wrote: "to kill a prisoner with his hands tied... is a foul action. Men's souls must always be naturally inclined to find it disgusting."[59]

In August al-Fāḍil wrote that there was neither a peaceful nor a military solution to the problem of Baalbek[60] and Saladin still took no decisive step but stayed in his camp by the Orontes. Then, according to 'Imād al-Dīn, in the autumn when the winds were blowing down the leaves, the emirs wanted to disperse and said to him: "this is the time to go". Saladin, however, pointed out: "if we ignore the matter of Ibn al-Muqaddam, the covetousness of the Franks may be aroused against us and the secret evil brought into the open... His religion is strong... and maybe he will not force us into a long affair."[61] In effect, Saladin had accomplished nothing since he had moved to Syria in the spring, and if he allowed a successful challenge to his authority, he could expect to find it increasingly difficult to attract support. Before he moved from Homs, he wrote to the Caliph's vizier to say that Ibn al-Muqaddam had collected a force of "ignorant scum" at Baalbek, and he himself was having to send his troops there to guard the crops and protect the eṣtates from the Franks.[62] He then marched his men down the Biqā' and according to 'Imād al-Dīn, he "flattered Ibn al-Muqaddam for all his age like a baby", but as this produced no result, he had to camp outside Baalbek at Ra's al-'Ain. There was no serious fighting and he rode out to hunt each morning. Snow fell and the besiegers had to huddle round their stoves, "as though in the cells of anchorites".[63] During the course of the blockade, Saladin wrote again to Baghdad to say that Ibn al-Muqaddam was suspected of being in correspondence with the Franks; he himself, if he wanted, could take Baalbek by force and make an example of him, but he was acting with clemency while Ibn al-Muqaddam was acting with folly.[64]

At the start of January 1179 Saladin moved back to Damascus, but he posted a blockading force at Baalbek under Ṭughril al-Jāndār. As late as March, al-Fāḍil, who was now at 'Aidhāb on his way across to the Ḥijāz (map 5), was still writing to 'Imād al-Dīn of "the intractable affair" of Baalbek, which he hoped would not distract Saladin from the Holy War or give the Franks an opportunity and he emphasised that Saladin would have to overlook Ibn al-Muqaddam's disobedience.[65] In fact, Ibn al-Muqaddam was in a desperate position. Saladin had left himself no room for a change of heart, and even if he did not use force, sooner or later he could starve out the Baalbek garrison. As a result, some time in the spring, Ibn al-Muqaddam at last agreed to an exchange and gave up Baalbek in return for the fortress and lands of Ba'rīn, the town of Kafr Ṭāb and villages and estates in lands of Ma'arrat al-Nu'mān (map 8).

The generosity of this settlement led to a reconciliation and Ibn al-Muqaddam remained loyal to Saladin for the rest of his life. Damage, however, had been done elsewhere. The series of Saladin's reverses and his apparent show of weakness had encouraged his enemies, and the confidence that he and al-Fāḍil had expressed as regards their relations with Aleppo and Mosul now vanished. In his letter from Baalbek to Baghdad Saladin had again accused their leaders of abandoning the path of religion and of having made approaches to the Assassins and the Franks.[66] The Franks for their part had taken advantage of his preoccupation and in October Baldwin, "with the whole strength of the realm",[67] had moved to the Jordan where work was started on building the castle of Bait al-Aḥzān. This controlled the crossing at Jisr Banāt Ya'qūb of one of the main routes to Damascus and was sited at the start of the Jordan's course through the low hills that block the south end of the Huleh basin (map 2). The site itself is not particularly strong, but it had considerable strategic importance and Saladin unsuccessfully offered the Franks up to 100,000 dinars to stop their work on it. According to 'Imād al-Dīn, he was warned that "when they strengthen this fortress the Islamic frontier will be weakened... for between it and Damascus is [only] a day's journey. He said: 'when they have finished it, we shall go there and destroy it'. He was patient because of the strength of his religion."[68] This may have been a choice forced on him by his difficulties with Ibn al-Muqaddam, but he may also have felt that, in view of his problems, it would be better to trust to a siege, where he would be risking no more than a check if he were unsuccessful, than to attack Baldwin again at a place where a second defeat might prove disastrous.

10

CONSOLIDATION AND EXPANSION

The transfer of Baalbek marked the end of a slow and unhappy period in the development of Saladin's rule. He was no longer the invincible general or the administrator riding the wave of popular support. From al-Fāḍil's absence on pilgrimage may be inferred a stand-still in internal administration and foreign policy. As long as Aleppo and Mosul held to the terms of the peace settlement of 1176 Saladin could not excusably expand to the north or east and as a result his range of choice was narrowing.

On a personal level he was tenacious in continuing to prepare for dynastic growth, should the opportunity arise. According to information that he gave 'Imād al-Dīn, he had fathered five sons before he left Egypt in 1174.[1] A letter preserved by Qalqashandī quotes Da'ūd, born in May 1178, as his twelfth son,[2] while on 'Imād al-Dīn's list he appears as the seventh. Of these, Mas'ūd was born in September/October 1175, nine months after Saladin had been campaigning at Aleppo and the mother of Ya'qūb, who was born in Egypt in October 1176, must have accompanied Saladin back from Syria. Apart from references to Nūr al-Dīn's widow, 'Iṣmat al-Dīn Khātūn, whom he married in September 1176, there are almost no details to be found about his wives or the slave girls who bore him children, but some, at least, stayed with him over a period of years. The mother of his eldest son, al-Afḍal, who was born in 1170, gave him another son in the Muslim year 573 (1177/8 A.D.); Shamsa,[3] the mother of 'Uthmān, who was born in 1172, gave birth to Ya'qūb in October 1176; Ghāzī and Da'ūd were born to the same mother in 1173 and 1178 respectively and the mother of Isḥāq, born in 1174, gave birth to another son in July 1182.

Both al-'Ādil and Taqī al-Dīn were also producing large families and even if their contemporaries were unwilling to concede the

Ayyubids any privileged position as Islamic champions, at least the '*aṣabīya* basis of their support was being strengthened.

The Holy War, however, was still the best justification for Saladin's position in Syria and with the start of the new campaigning season in the spring of 1179, his intelligence service told him that the Franks were planning a raid.[4] He ordered Farrukh-Shāh, who had less than a thousand men with whom to guard the Damascus frontier, to watch for the attack and then to retire, avoiding battle and lighting warning beacons on the hills, at which he himself would march out. The Franks for their part were not expecting resistance. They had been told that unguarded flocks and herds were on the pasture grounds to the east of the Golan heights, and as they did not want their quarry to escape they climbed the heights by night to launch a surprise attack in the morning. Farrukh-Shāh was waiting for them but he had apparently not thought that they would move in the dark and his advance guard was caught up in a fight before it had time to retreat. The Franks, however, had no idea of the seriousness of their position and some scattered for plunder while Baldwin, who was leading the raid, advanced too rashly, presumably in pursuit of Farrukh-Shāh's advance guard. Farrukh-Shāh had concentrated his force at Tell al-Ḥāra, some 12 miles (19 km) south-east of Qunaitra (see map 2) and its size was concealed by the boulder-strewn country and perhaps by the Tell itself. His Turkish *mamlūks* engaged the King's squadron, shooting down at them, killing horses and causing extensive damage. The Franks were forced off in disarray and Saladin, who had been summoned by pigeon, was met with news of the victory. The Franks had carried back their wounded and, according to 'Imād al-Dīn, the Muslims did not realise the extent of their success until "someone arrived who had seen them in their lands", and who reported that all their knights were wounded.[5] Amongst the casualties was Humphrey of Toron, the Constable, who had been wounded while defending Baldwin and who died after having been carried to his castle of Ḥūnīn.

With this gratuitous victory presented to him, Saladin decided to call in more troops. Although some rain had fallen, Syria still could not support a large force and he contented himself with asking al-'Ādil to send 1500 horse from Egypt, to be exchanged for Tūrān-Shāh. In a letter to al-'Ādil he explained that he was sending back Tūrān-Shāh first "to relieve the burden on Syria in a year like this"; secondly to deter the Sicilian fleet from attacking, and also in the hopes that this would give al-'Ādil himself more liberty of movement.[6] According to 'Imād al-Dīn, Tūrān-Shāh was induced to go by "additional grants promised him in Egypt", a phrase which, together with a reference to his presence in Cairo, may imply that the *iqṭā'* of Alexandria, which was eventually given him, was still being negotiated. His tenure of Baalbek had been as short as the difficulties it caused had been protracted. He left his agents there, but lost the town to Farrukh-Shāh at the end of the year, possibly as part of the Alexandrian bargain. He moved out of Damascus on 3 May, taking with him the usual train of merchants and non-combatants and on 7 May he left Buṣrā, it being thought that he would meet the troops coming from Egypt at or near Eilat. Al-Wahrānī wrote that he celebrated his arrival in Egypt by distributing some 170,000 dinars to "buffoons and panders" – "it was as though it had fallen into a well".[7]

Saladin himself was still concerned with the Syrian border. Taqī al-Dīn was sent to Hama where he was reinforced by Ibn al-Muqaddam and al-Mashṭūb, while Nāṣir al-Dīn Muḥammad held Homs. They were to stay "lurking in their lairs",[8] ready to repel attacks and, in particular, they were to recruit more men. There had been a grazing dispute between Turkmans and Bedouin, in which a number of Turkmans had been driven away,[9] and because of their value as potential recruits messengers were sent to try to conciliate them and to persuade them to return. Saladin was also concerned to establish his position further north. There was trouble between Qilij-Arslān and the Ortoqid Nūr al-Dīn Muḥammad of Ḥiṣn Kaifā and in a letter written at this period Saladin claimed that the Lords of Diyār Bakr were afraid of Qilij-Arslān and had sent messengers to Damascus to ask for protection. In the same letter he mentioned the arrival of an envoy from Qilij-Arslān himself with a message of loyalty and affection, and he ended by repeating: "all our efforts are exerted to incline everyone to the Holy War".[10]

Qilij-Arslān's immediate aim was to recover places that had been taken from him by Nūr al-Dīn in the northern campaign of 1173, and he claimed that al-Ṣāliḥ was willing to return him Ra'bān. This was an uncomfortable argument for Saladin. His right to Ra'bān, which was held by agents of Ibn al-Muqaddam, was based on possession rather than law and there is no recorded attempt to refute Qilij-Arslān's claim. The matter was resolved by force. Qilij-Arslān sent out troops and Saladin replied with a relief force commanded by Taqī al-Dīn. He tried to cover his action by claiming that Qilij-Arslān's men were plundering the lands, that Qilij-Arslān himself had made a truce with the Byzantines and had given presents to the

Franks, that his own concern was for the people of the lands and that he had sent Taqī al-Dīn "out of necessity".[11] Whatever its justification, the move was successful. Taqī al-Dīn with a force put at either 800 or 1000 riders surprised and routed Qilij-Arslān's army whose numbers were variously quoted at 3000, 20,000 or, in a letter from Saladin to Mosul, 30,000.[12] This was a decisive battle in that Qilij-Arslān was now discouraged from trying to expand southwards at Saladin's expense and from now on it was Saladin's turn to take the offensive.

For the moment, however, Saladin was occupied with the Franks. He made two reconnaissances of the castle of Bait al-Aḥzān, on the first of which he showed it to an envoy from the Caliph, who left for Baghdad in April, and he returned to it on 16 May, staying for five days. This time he made some probing attacks and, according to William of Tyre, his army left in dismay because an important emir had been killed by an arrow.[13] 'Imād al-Dīn explained that he had found the castle "easy to take", but did not want to commit himself to a siege until his reinforcements had arrived from Egypt.[14] He then moved to the pasture-land east of Hermon, and when the grass there was used up, he circled the mountain and came down to the head-waters of the Jordan by Bāniās.

Winter-sown wheat and barley are harvested in Syria in May and this was the season when the Bedouin from the eastern deserts were in the habit of coming to get their grain. Their arrival in this year provided a problem for Saladin, who did not want either to antagonise them or to see Syrian supplies depleted. He tried to resolve the difficulty by sending them to raid the lands of Sidon and Beirut, but, according to 'Imād al-Dīn, this was not wholly successful, the implication being that unsupported Bedouin raiders could not penetrate far enough into Frankish territory. Saladin was then reported to have held a council at which he said:

> you know the high price of grain, the shortage of supplies, the appearance of the Bedouin of the desert and the disappearance of the grass. We have taken the crops of the enemy that are near at hand and nothing remains now but to send out our troops in rotation to provide food until the time comes to return.[15]

This agrees with the account given by William of Tyre, apart from the fact that William apparently credited Saladin himself with having attacked the lands of Sidon before settling in camp between the town of Bāniās and the river Dan.[16] Saladin's attack on Sidon may be confirmed by an undated letter from al-Fāḍil, criticising him for not having taken the opportunity to capture the town, and adding that it was "meaningless to concern himself with a war against his fellow Muslims" – presumably Qilij-Arslān.[17]

For the moment, Saladin had no time to concern himself with Muslim wars, as his raids now stirred the Franks to action. Baldwin moved north from Tiberias with a considerable force and then instead of following the low road past Jisr Banāt Ya'qūb to the head of the Huleh basin, he swung west through the hills, passing by Ṣafad and Tibnīn and coming out at a point on the western boundary ridge overlooking the plain of Marj 'Uyūn. From there, William of Tyre noted, there was a view to "the roots of Lebanon" over the whole region below, and the Franks could see the enemy's camp fires and their movements.[18] They had, in fact, caught Saladin unawares and it may be that their detour by the mountains had taken them out of range of scouts watching the southern approaches. As it happened, the Muslims were on the point of moving. Supplies in the neighbourhood were running short and it had been decided that the whole army should move north to the Biqā'. On the night of 9/10 June, on which the Franks camped on the hills above, Farrukh-Shāh was sent out on a final raid. Had Baldwin been better informed or more alert to realise what was happening he could have concentrated his attack either on Farrukh-Shāh's raiding force or on Saladin's base. As it was, on the morning of Sunday 10 June, he moved his men down the hill at a pace that was uncomfortably fast for his infantry and they stopped "for some hours", according to William of Tyre, to consider what to do.

In the meanwhile, warning of danger had reached both Farrukh-Shāh and Saladin.[19] Marj 'Uyūn, where the Franks had halted, was hidden from Saladin's camp at Tell al-Qāḍī by the higher ground of the Metullah hills. Saladin himself, riding out with the governor of Bāniās, had been met by herdsmen who told him that they had seen a Frankish force. At first he would not believe that his spies could have failed him so badly, but when the news was confirmed, he rode back to Tell al-Qāḍī, sent his heavy baggage to the shelter of Bāniās and brought out his men in battle formation. Farrukh-Shāh was on the Frankish side of the Litani river which near this point runs southwards near the castle of Beaufort before making a sharp west turn towards the sea. He decided to try to rejoin Saladin and according to William of Tyre part of his force re-crossed the river, which is fordable there in summer, and was destroyed by the Franks.

'Imād al-Dīn wrote that the Muslims "did not stand in the face of the Franks but left their baggage", which was then plundered by the Frankish infantry. Farrukh-Shāh himself, according to one of his companions, came back to the river with fewer than 30 men and saw 600 mounted Franks on a hill on the far side. He argued that if he halted the Franks would cross and wipe out his force and so he forded the river with his handful of riders. This encouraged the rest of his men who were apparently hanging back and by the time that he had reached the Franks he was at full strength. There is no reference in this account to his baggage, which presumably would not have been sent back into obvious danger and the explanation of 'Imād al-Dīn's reference may either be that his baggage train had returned earlier, before it was realised how near the Franks were, or that what the Franks met was baggage moving up from Saladin's camp in preparation for the journey to the Biqā'.

Their initial success had the effect of splitting the Frankish force. The infantry, after plundering the intercepted baggage, camped by the river. A group including the Master of the Templars and Raymond of Tripoli – perhaps the horsemen seen by Farrukh-Shāh – climbed a hill by the river, presumably in order to get a view of the enemy, but they appear to have had no real notion of the seriousness of their position, now that they had lost the advantage of surprise. William of Tyre implies that they thought that they had already won the battle, which would mean that they had entirely miscalculated Saladin's numbers. As it was, far from being able to time their attacks so as to destroy a divided force, they now found themselves caught in the simplest of traps. As Farrukh-Shāh crossed to challenge them from the west, Saladin arrived from the south-east. Resistance was ill co-ordinated and ineffective. After two charges the cavalry was cut off on a hill and many killed or captured. The infantry scattered. Some got away across the Litani and either took refuge in Beaufort or else went down the river towards Sidon. Raymond of Tripoli escaped, but the Master of the Templars, Hugh of Tiberias and Baldwin of Ramla were amongst those captured. The Muslims heard that the King himself had been carried from the battle by one of his servants, who hid him that night and escaped with him the next day. 'Imād al-Dīn sat beside Saladin to copy down the names of the prisoners in a register. He wrote: "I and Saladin's personal attendants numbered no more than twenty and there were more than seventy prisoners there ", and he went on to add that, in addition to these, there were at least another 270 important prisoners not counting those of lower rank.

This was the second consecutive success presented to Saladin by the Franks' enthusiasm for offensive strategy coupled with tactical mistakes. It left them in an obvious state of weakness but Saladin seemed disinclined to press home his advantage and he waited for almost seventy days to strengthen his position before moving against Bait al-Aḥzān. Taqī al-Dīn had now rejoined the army after his relief of Ra'bān together with Nāṣir al-Dīn Muḥammad who no longer had to guard Homs against any immediate threat from Tripoli. Saladin wrote to Baghdad that "the tail of his army had lengthened", and that he had recruited Turkmans, together with Bedouin, and provided them with food, fodder and money in spite of "the extent of the expenditure, which is more than can be afforded".[20]

He struck camp on 18 August and halted by Bait al-Aḥzān on 24 August. He may have been slowed down by his baggage and perhaps by the need to hold back for reinforcements, but it is also possible that he had been waiting for word of the Franks. Baldwin's losses at Marj 'Uyūn had to some extent been made good by the arrival of reinforcements from Europe including Henry of Champagne, and Saladin told Baghdad that, on hearing of his muster, the Franks had mustered again themselves. In fact, Baldwin had moved to Tiberias and on 25 August, the day after his arrival at Bait al-Aḥzān, Saladin drew up his army in battle order and marched southwards towards Tiberias, passing beneath the high hills that form the western boundary of the Huleh basin, at the southern end of which stands the castle of Ṣafad. This demonstration drew no reply from Baldwin and the Muslims raided the lands of Ṣafad, destroying fruit trees and cutting vines, the stalks of which could be used for mantlets or for burning in saps. By midday on 25 August Saladin had returned to Bait al-Aḥzān.

The castle stood close to the west bank of the Jordan, which is about 80 feet (24 metres) wide at this point. William of Tyre described its site as being a hill "of moderate height",[21] but in fact it is little more than a sizeable mound, overlooked by the higher ground that flanks the Jordan as it cuts its way down through the ridges to the Sea of Galilee. Saladin had the choice either of trying to capture it quickly and without interruption, or of deliberately drawing out a siege in order to force Baldwin into another field action, where the prize could be the destruction of the Frankish army. In the event, in spite of his success at Marj 'Uyūn and the arrival of reinforcements, he preferred to try for speed. Although the high ground behind the castle provided an obvious platform for mangonels, at the suggestion of 'Izz al-Dīn Chāulī it was decided to begin with a trial assault. The castle mound has been estimated at about half a mile (800 metres) in circumference. Part of its summit was occupied by the castle itself and part by a settlement sheltering under it walls. It was against this latter that 'Imād al-Dīn saw "a young man of the common people", in a tattered shirt, leading the Muslim stormers up slopes described by Saladin as so steep that footholds had to be cut with axes. This attack succeeded and the Templar garrison drew back to the castle itself. Saladin was afraid that if his men stayed where they were, the garrison might surprise them by a night attack, but the Franks were concentrating on defence and had lit fires behind their gates in case the Muslims burst through. As a result Saladin's sappers were able to work without interruption in an attempt to undermine the castle walls. At first this was unsuccessful and the work had to be restarted. Enlarged saps were fired on the night of Wednesday/Thursday 28/29 August, and on the Thursday, while 'Imād al-Dīn was watching – "and we had been waiting for a long time in expectation" – part of the wall collapsed. The garrison lit firewood piled behind the breach, but the flames were blown back at them and Saladin later wrote that the castle was like a ship in a flood of fire. The Franks then asked for quarter, but this was refused and the Muslims entered by force. Saladin put the total numbers of the garrison at over 1500, of whom more than 700 were taken prisoner. He is said to have interrogated them himself and Muslim apostates were killed on his orders, together with crossbowmen, whose efficiency the Muslims had cause to dislike. 'Imād al-Dīn added that most of the others were killed, without orders, by "the volunteers and the assembled ruffians" of the Muslim army, while 100 Muslim prisoners, who had been used for stone-cutting and building work, were freed.

To William of Tyre the loss of Bait al-Aḥzān was "greater confusion piled on previous loss", and he quoted: "the judgements of the Lord are a great deep".[22] The military lesson was clear. Castles were only effective in conjunction with a field army, for which they could provide an offensive base or a refuge, or for which they could buy time, and which, in turn, had to relieve them if they were attacked. In themselves, their fortifications were of limited value, particularly in view of the Muslims' skill at sapping. Saladin could not destroy the Latin Kingdom except by a field action, but for their part the Franks could not defend themselves indefinitely by declining challenges and in the last resort they were dependent on men and not on walls.

Saladin now demolished the castle and wrote to Baghdad to say that he had pulled out the foundation stones with his own hands. The Muslims were impressed by the depth of the castle well, which took the corpses of the garrison and their beasts and still left room to be filled with earth and lime, and by the thickness of the walls, which 'Imād al-Dīn compared to the rampart of Gog and Magog.[23] In spite of this, however, Saladin claimed only to have spent three days on the work of demolition, after which he moved off to raid the lands of Tiberias, Tyre and Beirut. He returned to Damascus on 13 September and then suffered an unexpected reverse. More than ten of his emirs – and presumably a proportionate number of common soldiers – died of a disease that 'Imād al-Dīn thought had been caused by the hot weather and the corruption of the corpses at Bait al-Aḥzān. Taqī al-Dīn and Nāṣir al-Dīn Muḥammad fell ill, and although they both recovered, the loss was more serious than any recorded in Saladin's battles up to this date.

The approach of winter now brought an end to any serious land fighting. According to a letter quoted by Abū Shāma, the Egyptian fleet had increased its numbers to sixty galleys and twenty *ṭarīdas*, and it closed its raiding season with an October attack on the harbour of Acre where in two days of fighting a number of Frankish ships were claimed to have been destroyed.[24] This was the fleet's second raid of the year, as it had already put out in May and returned on 17 June with a reported total of 1000 prisoners. A Frankish force of 40 galleys was then said by al-Wahrānī to have approached Alexandria, "but when they saw the numbers of those who came out against them, they retired".[25] Apart from these successes, however, it had been a difficult summer in Egypt. The level of the Nile had dropped so low that Pharaoh's throne – or, according to Maqrīzī, Joseph's grave[26] – had been uncovered, and its flood had been delayed until it was feared that "the Kings of the Abyssinians had diverted it to the lands of the Negroes". Prices had been high because of the belated flood, and in August/September an attempt had been made to cut allowances paid in the form of poor relief by the state. Saladin had disapproved of this and three-quarters of the original payments had been restored, but the official in charge insisted that the recipients had no legal right to the money and it was expected that further cuts would be made. By contrast, the emir 'Izz al-Dīn Mūsik had held a feast to celebrate the circumcision of his sons at which he slaughtered 700 sheep and spread silk under the hoofs of al-'Ādil's horse. His wife had then given another banquet of equal splendour, while in November the circumcision of a number of Saladin's sons and sons of al-'Ādil had been celebrated "with great magnificence". Al-'Ādil himself, having presumably been freed by Tūrān-Shāh's arrival in Cairo, had spent most of the summer in the eastern province, from which a series of Bedouin raids had been launched against Frankish territory. His brother Ṭughtekīn had fallen ill, and had then, in a fit of repentance, "listened to traditions of the Prophet and held discussions with *faqīhs* in his house every evening until God Almighty granted him health and restored to him his full intellect". In November Tūrān-Shāh went to Alexandria, and on his way there 300 of his men deserted and left for Barqa.[27]

The references to financial problems in Egypt are to be added to Saladin's own complaints about the expenses of his army and his earlier difficulties with the Syrian harvest. As has been quoted, he had told the Caliph of his hopes for an attack on Jerusalem but, in spite of his victories, it could be argued that he was not yet strong enough economically for a major campaign, in which case he could perhaps have been expected to return to Egypt. Surprisingly, however, his letters show that he was concentrating neither on the Holy War nor on the administrative problems of his dominions, but on his feud with Qilij-Arslān. He had ended his letter to Baghdad about Bait al-Aḥzān with an attack on Qilij-Arslan, who had "broken the staff of Islam"; his evil-doing had to be stopped as he was stirring up other trouble-makers. Saladin asked the Caliph to send him orders; if he disobeyed them, he would be guilty of a crime which would make it lawful to fight against him. Saladin went on to explain, disingenuously in view of his earlier criticisms of Mosul and Aleppo, that he could not cope with both Qilij-Arslān and the Franks and in order to leave his arm free, he would have to make a truce with the Franks.[28]

The next reference to this truce comes in a letter from al-Fāḍil, who had come to Damascus from Mecca after completing his pilgrimage in 1179. In March 1180 he started on a second pilgrimage, with the intention this time of going back to Cairo, and before he left, he sent an undated letter to Farrukh-Shāh. In part, it is a catalogue of personal difficulties. Saladin and Farrukh-Shāh were in camp, apparently by the Frankish frontier, and Saladin had been forwarding to al-Fāḍil a number of letters from Egypt, all containing requests, but none from any of his agents or from any close friend. Al-Fāḍil was afraid either that his correspondents were concealing disasters or that their letters had been kept back by people wanting to spare him bad news, or that they had fallen into careless hands and been lost. Farrukh-Shāh had asked al-Fāḍil to come to see him, but he was reluctant to move because of the dangers of the roads – "this is something that affects all roads and is reported by all tongues"; further, most of his companions were ill and his house had become a hospital and a chemist's shop; his baggage animals were being used to carry barley as prices showed that there were going to be enormous difficulties in the coming year; he had spent 200 dinars in 15 days and was afraid of burdening himself with debts that would force him to sell one of his houses in Egypt. The Frankish truce comes into this catalogue of woe in a reference to the fact that he knew that terms had been agreed and he was afraid that, if he did move from Damascus, he would arrive at the camp when everybody else was leaving and he might also miss the chance of a military escort on his journey south. Turning from his own difficulties, he then discussed the political situation: there were constant rumours in Damascus about movements in Aleppo and Mosul, but he himself still considered that possible enemies there were too weak and lacking in numbers to concern Saladin. He also discounted rumours of a gathering of Negroes who were said to have been ravaging upper Egypt, but it was necessary for Saladin to go back to Egypt to deal with financial problems, and because of this the conclusion of peace with the Franks was a definite advantage. Apparently he could not understand why Saladin was staying in Syria. He made no reference to Qilij-Arslān, but wrote that if preoccupation with Aleppo was delaying the move, it should be noted that Aleppo was now at its weakest and "the enemy whose power was to be feared", the Franks, were covered by a truce; if Saladin felt that he could not leave under these conditions, what would happen if Aleppo was reinforced?[29]

Although discussion about the need for a Frankish truce had been going on since September 1179, it was not until the early summer of 1180 that it was concluded. Al-Fāḍil's letter must be dated at the latest to March 1180 and on 15 April Farrukh-Shāh, with men from Bāniās and the surrounding regions, made a raid on Ṣafad.[30] William of Tyre reported that Saladin himself was in camp by Bāniās, which would fit with al-Fāḍil's remarks, and that he had made an abortive attack on Tiberias.[31] He seems to have had no intention of going back to Egypt. During this period, according to 'Imād al-Dīn, he was negotiating with a stream of envoys sent on behalf of Nūr al-Dīn Muḥammad of Ḥiṣn Kaifā, who was at odds with Qilij-Arslān.[32] His envoy, Ḍiyā' al-Dīn al-Shahrazūrī, was in Baghdad in March, and on the evidence of the Bait al-Aḥzān letter it can be supposed that the Caliph was being asked to sanction a northern expedition.

As far as the Franks were concerned, Saladin had no need to hurry; the Kingdom of Jerusalem was faced by internal troubles and any delay might win better terms. According to William of Tyre, every day the signs of Baldwin's leprosy were becoming more apparent.[33] A visit by Bohemond of Antioch and Raymond of Tripoli, who had come with an armed escort, was said to have alarmed him and he hurried on the marriage of his sister Sibylla, the widow of William de Montferrat, to Guy de Lusignan. Frankish messengers were then sent to Saladin who was still at Bāniās, and a truce was made by land and sea on terms that William of Tyre described as "humble enough on our part". William, who did not know of Saladin's preoccupation with the north, went on to add that he had agreed to a truce not because he had any fear of the Franks, but simply because the drought, which had affected Syria for almost five years, had caused so serious a shortage of food and fodder of all kinds in the region of Damascus that a settlement of some kind was inevitable.

While these negotiations were still going on and while Diyā' al-Dīn al-Shahrazūrī was still in Baghdad, the position there changed abruptly with the death on 29 March of the Caliph al-Mustaḍī'. The vizier Ẓahīr al-Dīn ibn al-'Aṭṭār administered the oath of allegiance to his successor, al-Nāṣir, but died soon afterwards. 'Imād al-Dīn merely reported that he had fallen ill,[34] but according to Ibn al-Athīr he was arrested five days after al-Mustaḍī's death, and nothing more was heard of him until his dead body was carried out for burial. The mob, following the tradition of mediaeval Baghdad, pounced upon it and dragged it through the streets before cutting it in pieces, and this, as Ibn al-Athīr adds, was in spite of the kindness with which he had treated them.[35] Ẓahīr al-Dīn was replaced as vizier by Majd al-Dīn ibn al-Ṣāḥib and the new Caliph promptly sent out an envoy, Ṣadr al-Dīn, the Shaikh al-Shuyūkh, to underline his claims to religious leadership and presumably also to investigate the realities of the political situation.

Ṣadr al-Dīn went first to al-Pahlawān, the ruler of Hamadan, Isfahan and the lands of Khurasan (map 4). It was reported that al-Pahlawān at first showed reluctance to have the *khuṭba* pronounced in al-Nāṣir's name, but Ṣadr al-Dīn then told his soldiers that they were not to obey him until he did, an indication at least of the Caliph's supposed authority.[36] Saladin may have regretted the loss of the well-disposed Ẓahīr al-Dīn, but he had nothing to gain by any show of opposition and he quickly changed the *khuṭba* throughout his dominions. Al-Fāḍil heard of Ṣadr al-Dīn's mission when he was at Mecca on his second pilgrimage and sent him a letter from Fusṭāṭ after his return there in July 1180. In this he underlined Saladin's virtues, referring again to his repeal of the *mukūs* taxes and stressing the extent of his empire, from the amber and pearl coast of Yemen to Barqa in North Africa; as for Syria, Saladin had freed Islam there from the tribute that previous rulers in their fear of the Franks had paid "in the vicious situation known as a truce"; the tables had now been turned on the Franks and they had been forced by the sword rather than bribed to make peace. Al-Fāḍil added that Sicilian envoys had come to ask for terms and he hoped that Saladin himself would now be able to go to the Ḥijāz and fulfil his Islamic obligations to make the pilgrimage.[37]

In this al-Fāḍil was putting the Frankish truce in the best possible light, leaving out any reference to the reason why it was necessary. He could have advanced William of Tyre's point about the distressed state of Syria but Saladin had already compromised this argument by talking of his need to clear the way for a march to the north.

At the start of June 1180, the Egyptian fleet appeared off Beirut, where it learnt that the truce with Baldwin had been signed. It kept to the truce terms, which had specifically covered the seas, and sailed north to attack the lands of Tripoli, following Saladin's own example. The Arabic sources give no exact picture of the details of Saladin's movements, but William of Tyre shows that he was concerned to make a demonstration in force against Raymond of Tripoli.[38] Raymond had camped at 'Arqa, to the north of Tripoli, and the Hospitallers shut themselves in Ḥiṣn al-Akrād while Saladin's army moved between them, cutting their communications. This suggests that Saladin had come north up the Biqā', and then turned west through the Homs/Tripoli gap, the eastern end of which is overlooked by Ḥiṣn al-Akrād. Raymond was said to be prepared to give battle, but Saladin was not looking for more victories and after his men had plundered the country another truce was made. William of Tyre reported that Saladin then returned to Damascus, but in fact it seems certain that he must have continued his march north. At the end of June he was in camp by the Geuk Su, which flows into the

Euphrates some 30 miles (49 km) north of al-Bīra and about 300 miles (483 km) as the crow flies from Damascus (map 1).

The ostensible reason for this march was a matrimonial quarrel. Nūr al-Dīn Muḥammad, the Ortoqid ruler of Ḥiṣn Kaifā, had married the daughter of Qilij-Arslān, but according to 'Imād al-Dīn, he was a man "addicted to singing girls", one of whom became his favourite wife. Qilij-Arslān's daughter, "of Seljuq stock, with the pride of the Sultanate", was not disposed to meek acceptance and her father threatened Nūr al-Dīn Muḥammad who asked for help from Saladin, who in turn apparently offered to mediate. Qilij-Arslān refused the offer, catalogued his son-in-law's shortcomings, and insisted on the return of territory that had been handed over as part of his daughter's dowry. This was a difficult point to challenge and 'Imād al-Dīn wrote simply: "we replied saying that he could not attack Nūr al-Dīn Muḥammad as we had made an agreement with him".[39] Saladin's position, in fact, was so weak in terms of any possible Islamic justification that Ibn Shaddād preferred to ignore the whole episode. But the rumours that al-Fāḍil had quoted about unrest in Mosul and Aleppo, however much he might discount them, underlined the fact that the Ortoqids as potential allies were too important to be abandoned, and when Saladin was joined at the Geuk Su by Nūr al-Dīn Muḥammad and his brother, Abū Bakr, he held a reception for them and presented them with gifts, valued by 'Imād al-Dīn at more than 100,000 dinars. This lavishness must have been calculated not only to cement an Ortoqid alliance but to impress the other northern princelings, enemies and potential friends alike.

As has been noted Saladin arrived in the region of the Geuk Su at the end of June and he was still there at the start of October. 'Imād al-Dīn telescoped the intervening period and only reported that Qilij-Arslān's leading emir, Ikhtiyār al-Dīn al-Ḥasan, came to present his master's submission, after which an agreement was drawn up.[40] According to Ibn al-Athīr, Saladin was at Ra'bān, not far to the west of the Geuk Su, when he was met by a messenger with another complaint from Qilij-Arslān about the treatment of his daughter. At this, he flew into a rage and threatened to attack Malaṭīya, some 75 miles (121 km) to the north, saying: "it is two days' march from me and I shall not dismount until I am in the city". Qilij-Arslān was alarmed by the threat and decided to negotiate. Ibn al-Athīr again quoted arguments which were appropriate if not necessarily authentic. Qilij-Arslān was made to reproach Saladin – "one of the greatest of the Sultans" – for having made peace with the Franks, collected an army from far and near and spent huge sums of money, all for a singing girl: "what will be your excuse with God Almighty and with the Caliph and the kings of Islam?" Saladin acknowledged that Qilij-Arslān was in the right, but said that he could not abandon Nūr al-Dīn Muḥammad, who had taken refuge with him. It was finally agreed that the girl should be sent away for a year and that if Nūr al-Dīn Muḥammad failed to do this, Saladin would abandon his support.[41] There is no evidence to confirm Ibn Al-Athīr's details, except to the extent that Malaṭīya certainly played some part in the affair. An undated and unaddressed letter from al-Fāḍil mentions "the affair of Malaṭīya" in a context which shows that he was talking of this campaign. He referred to the Nile as having reached its flood level, which it did on 20 August in this year,[42] and he then went on to say with reference to Malaṭīya that he approved of the fact that an envoy had (now) been sent (presumably to Qilij-Arslān) with a mildly-worded letter. He added his comment on the campaign as a whole: "we hope that God, Exalted be He, may free us from the necessity of waging a war where final victory would almost be a matter for regret, and that He may reconcile the hearts of the Muslims".[43]

One unforeseeable factor which affected Saladin's plans was the death from illness at the end of June of Saif al-Dīn, the Lord of Mosul. Saif al-Dīn's ten-years rule had been successful at least in the negative sense that after the Tell al-Sulṭān campaign in 1176 there had been no further open breach between him and his brother Zangī, and he had lost no territory to Saladin. He was said to have wished to leave Mosul to his twelve-year-old son, Sanjar-Shāh,[44] but his advisers were, not unreasonably, afraid of what Saladin might do. As a result, it was Saif al-Dīn's brother, 'Izz al-Dīn Mas'ūd, who succeeded him as Lord of Mosul, while Sanjar-Shāh was given the town of Jazīrat ibn 'Umar, 90 miles (145 km) north of Mosul on the Tigris; his younger brother Nāṣir al-Dīn was given Qal'at 'Aqr al-Humaidīya and Zangī was again forced to content himself with Sinjār. Saladin was threateningly close at hand. The polymath, Fakhr al-Dīn Ibn al-Dahhān, was sent to him as an envoy from 'Izz al-Dīn Mas'ūd and produced a copy of the oath of agreement that had confirmed Saladin's peace treaty with Saif al-Dīn. According to 'Imād al-Dīn, he asked Saladin: "by what interpretation do you seize what 'Izz al-Dīn holds?" Saladin answered that the oath only applied during the lifetime of the contracting parties and that he was going to consult Baghdad.[45] The present tense, "you seize", is perhaps a touch of rhetoric, as there is no evidence that Saladin had done anything of the kind but he may certainly have started to advance to add weight to his claims.

The claims themselves were extensive.[46] Saladin was demanding a triangle of towns, Sarūj, al-Ruhā and Harrān, within a radius of 60 miles (97 km) to the east of the Euphrates at al-Bīra and within some 120 miles (193 km) of Aleppo. Of these, al-Ruhā had been handed over to Nūr al-Dīn by Quṭb al-Dīn Ināl in exchange for an *iqṭā'* that included Sarūj, and both had been taken by Saif al-Dīn in 1174 after Nūr al-Dīn's death. At the same time Saif al-Dīn had also recovered Ḥarrān, which had been removed from the *iqṭā's* of Mosul by Nūr al-Dīn in his winter campaign of 1170/1. Saladin also claimed three other places that shared the same history, in that they had been taken by Nūr al-Dīn in his winter campaign and then taken back by Saif al-Dīn in 1174. They were al-Raqqa, by a Euphrates crossing some 105 miles (169 km) east of Aleppo, al-Khābūr, at this period a town on the Khābūr river, which joins the Euphrates about 100 miles (161 km) downstream from al-Raqqa, and Niṣībīn, roughly midway between Ḥarrān and Mosul (map 8). If Saladin held these towns he would in effect cut Mosul off from Aleppo. He told the Mosuli envoy that he had earlier been granted them by the Caliph and that he had left them in the hands of Saif al-Dīn on condition that Mosuli troops would be sent to reinforce him in times of need. This was a standard formula used by Saladin in most of his peace agreements and it need not be questioned that some form of co-operation was written into the 1176 treaty. Saladin's claim to the towns, however, is more than doubtful. There is no mention of them in the diploma of investiture sent him in Baghdad in 1175 which granted him Egypt, Yemen and Syria, apart from Aleppo and its districts.[47] It might have been possible to argue that the term "Syria" loosely covered all the lands held by Nūr al-Dīn, including those to the east of the Euphrates, but this cannot be supported by any contemporary letters and that the Caliph should have intended to give Saladin a town as far east as Niṣībīn in 1175 seems incredible. Saladin, however, did his best with a weak case and a letter to the Shaikh al-Shuyūkh shows the arguments used. Saladin's services to the Caliphate were rehearsed again. It was pointed out that Egypt was still not free from danger, both within, from Fatimid supporters, and without, from foreign enemies; it required a large army for its own protection, but Egyptian troops had had to protect Syria as well, where high prices had caused them five years' worth of hardship and expense; they were needed there because the towns that should have supplied a garrison for Syria had been "cut off from it" and their troops removed – an obvious attempt to replace political boundaries by Saladin's own version of strategic geography.[48] The reply from Baghdad has not been recorded, but it can be seen that his arguments were not accepted. The towns were left with 'Izz al-Dīn Mas'ūd and for the time being Saladin let the matter drop.

According to Ibn Shaddād, the end of Saladin's stay by the Euphrates was marked by a general treaty covering the lands of Qilij-Arslān together with Diyār Bakr and Mosul.[49] This is not mentioned in specific terms by Saladin's other contemporary biographers, but there is no doubt that his double set of negotiations did lead to some form of agreement. As far as Mosul was concerned, he cannot be shown to have won any immediate advantage from Saif al-Dīn's death, but he had at least blocked the way for Qilij-Arslān and put the Ortoqids under an obligation. As an Islamic epilogue to his campaign, he now turned briefly against the Armenians. Since the fall of Nūr al-Dīn's client Mleh, which had followed closely on his patron's death, the Armenians under Roupen III had been hostile to the Muslims. Roupen was now accused of having treacherously attacked Turkmans whom he had invited to pasture on his lands, and, in general, "there were many complaints from the Muslims about the harm that he had done them".[50] Ibn Shaddād's peace treaty was dated to 2 October and Saladin then moved from the Euphrates to the Nahr Aswad, a river that flows beneath the eastern slopes of the Amanus Mts. A hill fortress which Roupen's troops were preparing to evacuate was captured before its stores had been destroyed and Roupen then offered to release Muslim prisoners and "exerted himself to win Saladin's favour". The captured stores had not lasted for long and the Muslims were finding provisions difficult to get. Peace was made and 'Imād al-Dīn wrote: "it was God's mercy that he submitted so that we could march away quickly".[51] By early November Saladin had returned to Hama.

From Hama the army moved south to Homs, where it camped by the Orontes. It was here that Saladin heard the news of the death of his brother, Tūrān-Shāh. It was said that the climate of Alexandria had not suited Tūrān-Shāh and that he had had recurrent attacks of colic, from one of which he died.[52] He left behind a reputation for generosity fondly recorded by poets, as well as debts said to amount to more than 200,000 dinars,[53] which were paid off by Saladin, and, as emerged from al-Fāḍil's letters, a reputation for unreliability with both money and power. He had proved to be an incompetent administrator in Syria and, on the evidence of his quarrel with Ibn al-Muqaddam, an uncomfortable associate. Irresponsibility may have been exacerbated by jealousy and he was said to have been in the habit of speaking against Saladin when drunk.[54] Within the limitations of his own character, however, he can be said to have done good service to the Ayyubid dynasty, as much in the battle with the Negroes in 1169 as in the conquest of Yemen. When Saladin heard the news of his death, he spent the day alone and, according to 'Imād al-Dīn, "he called for books of elegies in his grief to study them".[55]

Various dates for Tūrān-Shāh's death are given, one of the latest being 1 July,[56] and as 'Imād al-Dīn was with Saladin on the campaign, his report that Saladin did not hear of it until November can scarcely be challenged. The delay, of course, may have been accidental or designed to prevent distraction, but the simplest explanation is that Saladin on the Euphrates was virtually out of touch with Egypt. This, of course, is by no means an unusual position for a field commander on a distant expedition but it does reopen the question of whether Saladin was, or had become, primarily a war-band leader or whether he should be thought of as a territorial ruler, in which case communications and the machinery of administration were of the first importance. The details of his invasion of Syria appear to discount the war-band theory, at least in its simplest forms, and this is reinforced by the fact that while he was in Syria he did still concern himself to some extent with Egyptian affairs. The letter which mentions his interference with the cuts in poor relief in Egypt also notes rumours that he was proposing to dismiss the Qāḍī Ṣadr al-Dīn Ibn Durbās.[57] Further evidence, and another aspect of the problem, is to be seen in a letter from al-Fāḍil in which he wrote that on his way back from Mecca he passed by the town of Ikhmīm, some 320 miles (515 km) south of Cairo. Here the inhabitants complained to him about their governor while praising his predecessor, whom they wanted to have returned to them.[58] This in itself is commonplace, but the interesting point is that al-Fāḍil thought it worthwhile to ask for a letter of support from Farrukh-Shāh in Syria. It is not clear whether it was Saladin or al-'Ādil who was expected to make the final decision, but the implication is that the machinery of Egyptian bureaucracy was unable to correct its own defects. Help had to be asked from men whose authority depended on their place in the group surrounding Saladin, however far away they happened to be at the time, and although this peripatetic administrative nucleus was not a single war-band, its territorial links were obviously far more tenuous than those of non-expansionist regimes.

On his return to Damascus from the north, Saladin received the Caliph's envoys, Shihāb al-Dīn Bashīr and the Shaikh al-Shuyūkh. The Shaikh al-Shuyūkh was persuaded to accompany him to Egypt, although for some reason he made it a condition that he would not enter Cairo but would spend two days at al-Shāfi'ī's shrine and then leave for Mecca.[59] Shihāb al-Dīn Bashīr returned to Baghdad with Ḍiyā' al-Dīn al-Shahrazūrī, and an envoy was sent from Saladin to Mosul. Farrukh-Shāh was left in charge of Syria and Saladin started from Damascus on 8 December and arrived in Cairo on 2 January 1181.

11

OPPORTUNITIES

When he had left for Syria in February 1178 Saladin was under the shadow of his defeat by Baldwin. Syria was suffering from both drought and inefficient administration. In spite of their failure at Ḥārim, the Franks were a threat to the frontiers. Al-Ṣāliḥ in Aleppo and Saif al-Dīn in Mosul were keeping to the terms of their settlement and offering Saladin no excuse for expansion. Qilij-Arslān, with the prestige of a victory over the Byzantines at Myriocephalum behind him was in a position to claim precedence in the Holy War. By the end of Saladin's stay some at least of these clouds had cleared. He had weathered the difficulties caused by Ibn al-Muqaddam's defection and established his military superiority over both Franks and Muslims. The deaths of Saif al-Dīn and of al-Mustaḍī' at least offered a chance that patterns and policies might change. For the moment, however, after the settlement in the north, there were no more prospects for advancement than there had been in 1178 and Saladin's position, although stronger, had not radically changed.

What emerges from his letters during this period is the tenacity with which he maintained the justification for his actions. In spite of financial pressures, difficulties of communication and administrative problems, he concentrated on his claim to be the champion of the Holy War, to whom territories should be ceded in the interests of Islam. He had done his best to weaken any claim that Qilij-Arslān might have to share in this role and had reserved for himself the right to decide how and when the war should be waged. How far he was justified in this is, of course, arguable. He can be accused of self-seeking or defended on the grounds that, in spite of his optimism about an attack on Jerusalem in 1179, he was not yet strong enough for a major campaign. In fact, what is conveyed by the letters is a clarity of outline and obscurity of detail. The Holy War is the dominant concept, but how it is to be pursued is left blurred and Saladin constantly shifts to distractions and irrelevancies. These may be camouflage, concealing expansionist ambition, or the difficulties of an over-burdened administrator. They may also be the reflection of a genuine difficulty. The black and white of the Holy War, however fairly it might convey Saladin's own ideals, was an over-simplification in respect of the need for an immediate, practical and coherent policy. An obvious stumbling block for such a policy was the position of al-Ṣāliḥ. As long as he could be treated as a child, rivalry amongst his emirs and fears of his uncle in Mosul might leave Aleppo isolated and weak, but if he grew up and produced sons of his own, Saladin could expect constant pressure for the return of southern Syria. In that case, he might never be able to launch a full-scale attack on the Franks from Damascus and this problem may well have appeared insoluble.

According to Abū Shāma, Saladin intended to spend the fast of Ramaḍān (19 January - 17 February) in Egypt and then make the pilgrimage to Mecca. Abū Shāma quotes letters to Ayyubid governors in Yemen in which they are ordered to prepare the way for his coming by sending money, supplies and robes of honour to Mecca in greater quantities than usual.[1] For some reason, however, he then changed his mind and is next seen riding out from his new fortifications by al-Maqs to inspect the Nile banks in June.[2] He was again becoming embroiled with the Bedouin. He was said to have removed two-thirds of their Eygptian *iqṭā's* to use as compensation for the *iqṭā'* holders of the Fayyūm which he intended to take over.[3] Not surprisingly, there are accounts of trouble. At the start of the Muslim year 577 (May/June 1181) the Bedouin in the eastern province were accused of trading with the Franks; their grain was confiscated and they were forced to move westward.[4] Later in the year warships were sent out against Bedouin river pirates, who had been plundering the shores of the Lake of Tanis and who had impenetrable refuges in its reed-beds and thickets.[5] The clearest picture of anti-Bedouin feeling comes in a letter from al-Fāḍil to Farrukh-Shāh who was having to cope with the Bedouin of Syria. Al-Fāḍil wrote of their innumerable wrong-doings, which made them "an enemy within the ribs"; if the Franks were strong, then the Bedouin were a hand for striking, and in their periods of weakness the Bedouin were an eye for spying; Saladin had done them services, the least of which would have been sufficient to bring them into the right path, if this could have been achieved by kindness, but bitter colocynth cannot be sweetened by water; on Frankish expeditions they acted as guides and helped with water and transport and they befriended escaping Frankish prisoners; they drew allowances for men who were on the *dīwān* list as names but who had never served the state,[6] and they neglected their duties of gathering information and protecting the roads, for which they had been given *iqṭā's*; Saladin had taken *iqṭā's* from "the Turks" to give to the Syrian Bedouin in exchange for a promise that they would move from Dārūm; a few of their leaders did go, but most of their people were left in Frankish lands and they took refuge in incredible statements; they were supposed to provide Saladin with 5500 riders, and had they done so, Dārūm would have been abandoned, peasants in Frankish territory would have been unable to work their lands and the Muslims living there would have had to move. Al-Fāḍil outlined Farrukh-Shāh's alternatives; he could either give them a large grant in exchange for the districts whose crops they were in the habit of taking, or else he could detain their leaders; to detain them would not violate their written safe-conduct, as this covered life and property, both of which would be preserved, but it should only be done if most of the leaders could be gathered together and seized at one and the same time.[7]

The bitterness of these feelings may have been increased by the threat of an expedition against the Holy Cities of Arabia by Reynald de Châtillon from Kerak. Maqrīzī implies that Saladin received advance warning of this in June[8] and al-Fāḍil referred to a letter from the castle of Eilat which reported that the garrison were in a state of alarm.[9] The land route from Kerak to Mecca and Medina passes Tabūk, which is 120 miles (193 km) as the crow flies from the head of the Gulf of 'Aqaba, then Taimā', which is another 130 miles (209 km) on, and from Taimā' the distance to Medina is well over 200 miles (322 km). (See map 5.) If the Franks had any real intention of attacking the peninsula by land, they would undoubtedly have needed Bedouin support. On a later expedition Reynald's men are known to have had Bedouin guides and al-Fāḍil's remarks about the ways in which they helped the Franks with water, transport and local knowledge are almost certainly relevant in the present case. For the moment, however, no great harm was done on either side. There are no reliable dates for the start of Reynald's move, but this cannot have been before the rainy season, as 'Imād al-Dīn notes that he was helped by the fact that there was grass in the desert this year.[10] He left a force at 'Aqaba to mask the Muslim garrison at Eilat and advanced towards Tabūk. Farrukh-Shāh collected his troops and, according to Ibn al-Athīr, ravaged the lands of Kerak. 'Imād al-Dīn merely says that he remained opposite the Frankish force in the desert,[11] a confrontation which is known to have been going on in December and Reynald, who must obviously have been unwilling to leave a Muslim army in his rear, was eventually forced to retire. As he must presumably have expected Farrukh-Shāh's move, it is open to question whether he was intending anything more than a reconnaissance in force.

Meanwhile in Egypt 'Imād al-Dīn had again been enjoying a life of ease. In the summer of 1181 he was invited to visit the emir Majd al-Dīn Mubārak, who had formerly been Tūrān-Shāh's deputy in the Yemeni town of Zabīd, a post in which he had been succeeded by his brother Hiṭṭān. Majd al-Dīn had an estate outside Cairo where 'Imād al-Dīn went "with a company of excellent men". They spent the first day being royally entertained and on the next day the emir took them down the Nile in boats "laden with good things". When they returned he had sheep slaughtered for them, after which they retired for a siesta. They were woken by a disturbance. The emir's gardens were surrounded by a force led by Saladin's former controller of the Palace, Qara-Qūsh, who had come to arrest him. 'Imād al-Dīn and his companions, for all their dignity and importance, ran in confusion, each concerned with his own safety and not one of them "taking another by the hand", until they got back to Cairo. There their friends made jokes at their expense, asking them "if they had been associated with the emir in some evil deed". The explanation turned out to be that Saladin's intimates had accused Majd al-Dīn of misappropriating the revenues of Zabīd. Saladin, according to 'Imād al-Dīn, had replied that there was no proof of this, but they pointed to the preparations for his party which they construed as signs of imminent flight. After Majd al-Dīn's arrest, Saladin realised the mistake and had him released, but this cost him 80,000 dinars which he had to pay to Saladin, and other sums, which were claimed by al-'Ādil and by another of Saladin's brothers, Tāj al-Mulūk Būrī.[12]

'Imād al-Dīn's "excellent men" had included Muwaffaq al-Dīn Ḥamza, who had recently returned from an embassy to Mosul, and Shams al-Dīn ibn al-Farrāsh, who had been Nūr al-Dīn's *Qāḍī al-'askar*, and to whom Saladin entrusted affairs of the first importance, but in spite of the links that bound them to Saladin, they were not part of the inner group of his counsellors. The implications of one incident cannot be pressed too far. It does not show whether this group was primarily the war-band or the family, although the mention of al-'Ādil and Būrī may suggest the latter, nor can the range of its influence be judged in a single context. What is clear, however, is that it was possible for the group on occasion if not to control Saladin at least to urge him along lines of its choice disregarding legal justification and using power for its own profit.

In more immediate terms, the fiasco of Majd al-Dīn's arrest was part of the discontent associated with the aftermath of Tūrān-Shāh's conquest of Yemen. When Tūrān-Shāh left, his agents continued to send him money, but centralised authority was lacking and there were quarrels, in particular between Ḥiṭṭān in Zabīd and 'Izz al-Dīn 'Uthmān in Aden. Saladin wrote in a letter to al-'Ādil: "this Yemen is a treasure house... We conquered it, but up to this day we have had no return and no advantage from it. There have only been innumerable expenses, the sending out of troops...and expectations which did not produce what was hoped for in the end."[13] It is not surprising, in view of this attitude, that Saladin should suspect that he was being robbed by the local governors. In an undated letter al-Fāḍil is found writing to 'Uthmān in Aden to remind him that he owed his position to Saladin's habit of giving the lands that he had conquered "to strangers rather than to relatives", that Saladin took nothing for himself and "did not even look at what others would have stretched out their hands to grasp"; he had spent money on Yemen and got no return and 'Uthmān, who had apparently requested subsidies for some new expedition, was asked to provide accounts of his revenue so that "the excuse may be truthfully established".[14] Saladin sent out a mission "to investigate the sources of wealth" and "to examine what was hidden". In particular, he proposed to leave clerks on whose trustworthiness he could rely in Zabīd and Aden, where they would be responsible to him and not to the governors.[15] Later, as a more drastic move, a former governor of Cairo, Ṣārim al-Dīn Khuṭlubā, was sent out to Zabīd and finally in the summer of 1182, Saladin's brother Tughtekīn went to re-establish direct Ayyubid control.

Problems, however, both in Egypt and Yemen were overshadowed for Saladin by the situation in Syria. On 18 November 1181 al-Ṣāliḥ fell ill in Aleppo. On 2 December the citadel gates were closed and on Friday 4 December al-Ṣāliḥ died after a seventeen-day illness. He was some nineteen years old at the time, "the most handsome of men", according to Ibn Abī Ṭayy,[16] with all the advantages of his father's reputation to help him. He had cultivated his father's piety, to the extent that, in spite of his doctor's recommendation, he refused to drink wine in his last illness. He had won remarkable loyalty from the people of Aleppo. Had he lived to control his own affairs, Saladin's future, together with the whole pattern of Syrian–Egyptian relations, would almost certainly have been significantly changed. In some ways his was the most fortunate of the series of timely deaths that marked the course of Saladin's career, in that it opened what was perhaps the only path by which expansionism and the Holy War could be combined in a credible grand design. Not unnaturally, there was talk of poison and 'Alam al-Dīn Sulaimān and Yāqūt al-Asadī were named as suspects.[17] Yāqūt seems to have been a nonentity, but 'Alam al-Dīn Sulaimān later had a profitable career in Saladin's service. At that, however, apart from any other consideration, Saladin's botched arrangements go far to show that, whatever the cause of al-Ṣāliḥ's death, he himself bore no responsibility for it.

His immediate plans are shown in a letter that he wrote to Farrukh-Shāh after he had heard the news of al-Ṣāliḥ's illness "and the fact that no-one is allowed in to see him."[18] He had ordered a double line of communication; Taqī al-Dīn and Nāṣir al-Dīn Muḥammad had been told to send carrier pigeons to Aleppo from Hama and Homs, and in both these towns Damascus pigeons were to be waiting; from Damascus the two lines were to join and Farrukh-Shāh was told to send the Buṣrā pigeons to Damascus, while Saladin himself sent couriers to wait at Buṣrā; meanwhile, Farrukh-Shāh was to send troops to reinforce Taqī al-Dīn, ostensibly because of another quarrel involving Diyār Bakr, and Taqī al-Dīn himself was to move north-east from Hama to Manbij to watch the Euphrates and cut off Aleppo from the east. Saladin wrote: "we hold Bālis, Qal'at Ja'bar, Manbij and Tell Bāshir and these are all the roads". Of these, Bālis and Qal'at Ja'bar are on the Euphrates itself; Manbij watches the crossing at Qal'at Najm and Tell Bāshir that of al-Bīra (map 8). While Taqī al-Dīn held the Euphrates, Saladin himself planned to strike at Aleppo and he told Farrukh-Shāh: "if the news of his death is confirmed, we shall reach you faster than any answer... The troops are rested...and the advantage in moving is clear."

This plan was unfortunate in its timing. Farrukh-Shāh was in no position to help as he had been forced into the desert to confront Reynald, and during this critical period when Taqī al-Dīn could expect no reinforcements, 'Izz al-Dīn Mas'ūd of Mosul crossed the

Euphrates. A number of Aleppan emirs were said to have been in favour of his brother Zangī, and it was pointed out to al-Ṣāliḥ in his last illness that Nūr al-Dīn had loved Zangī and had taken charge of his upbringing, but al-Ṣāliḥ realised that Zangī did not have the resources to hold Aleppo and that only 'Izz al-Dīn could withstand Saladin.[19] As it stands, this argument, which is another of Ibn al-Athīr's reconstructions, is unconvincing in that al-Ṣāliḥ himself had been in a weaker position than Zangī, but his emirs may well have felt that they would be safer with the power of Mosul to protect them. On 12 December, eight days after al-Ṣāliḥ's death, 'Izz al-Dīn's envoys arrived in Aleppo to administer the oath of allegiance. 'Izz al-Dīn himself, with Mujāhid al-Dīn Qaimāz, his principal administrator, moved to al-Bīra, where the Aleppan emirs were summoned to meet him. According to Ibn al-'Adīm, Taqī al-Dīn thought of trying to interfere, but was met by reluctance on the part of some of his men.[20] Tell Bāshir, from which the crossing at al-Bīra might have been blocked, was held by Saladin's ally Badr al-Dīn Dildirim, but he could not be expected to act alone, and as a result, 'Izz al-Dīn arrived unopposed to take over Aleppo on 29 December.

Because of the distances involved it took Saladin some time to realise that his plans had failed. On 7 January, before he could have heard what had happened, he wrote to the Lord of al-Rāwandān, a town some 50 miles (80 km) from Aleppo to the west of Tell Bāshir:

> the emir knows of the recent death of the Lord of Aleppo, which is our territory. In quest of it we shall not turn aside our reins as it is covered by the diploma of investiture given us by the Commander of the Faithful and we only left it with al-Ṣāliḥ, after administering its territories and taking its castles and fortresses, in order to respect the rights of his father... We have kept faith with the dead, but now the face of truth is clear for us... Taqī al-Dīn is near it with his troops... The emir is asked to help... Let him come himself with his men... Let him act as a man acts in his own interest.[21]

After the opportunity for a quick attack had passed one report suggested that Saladin gave up hope of taking Aleppo but this is not confirmed by his letters, which show that he was opening a new campaign of propaganda. In the middle of Ramaḍān he wrote to the Caliph's vizier, Majd al-Dīn Ibn al-Ṣāḥib: "the Lord of Mosul has coveted Aleppo and stretched out the hand of injustice to grasp it. He has broken his oath." He repeated his claim that Aleppo had been granted to him by the Caliph al-Mustaḍī' and went on to say that the only reason why 'Izz al-Dīn had been able to reach it was the fact that Farrukh-Shāh was "at the farthest edge of Frankish territory at the start of the desert of the Ḥijāz", where "a Frankish tyrant" was threatening Taimā', "the gateway to Medina". "It is a matter of wonder that we should be defending the Prophet's grave...while the Lord of Mosul is trying to take something from our lands with the hand of injustice... The Mosulis take the unbelievers as friends in place of the Muslims and carry treasures to them." In this context Saladin mentioned that 'Izz al-Dīn had sent envoys to the Franks and that they had moved against Ḥārim, while troops from Aleppo had attacked al-Rāwandān; if 'Izz al-Dīn did not acknowledge that he was in the wrong, this would lead to war as he would be disobeying the Caliph's commands, although Saladin himself would prefer to spend his brief life attacking the unbelievers, "who have made Jerusalem into a place of filth".[22] In another letter, Saladin accused the Mosulis of being in touch with the Assassins, to whom they had promised castles and estates, using them as go-betweens with the Franks; "this is not a slander" – their envoy was with Sinān, his was with the Count and the Count's was with the King; Saladin himself had a prior claim on Aleppo and one based on justice; "entering a house does not confer possession on the one who seizes it"; the basis of the agreement between Saladin, Aleppo and Mosul had been that they were not to attack each other's lands and that they should unite to repel an oath-breaker. Saladin again repeated that if the Mosulis did not give up Aleppo, their refusal to obey the Caliph's orders would justify him in attacking them "or rather, mowing them down". He suggested that, as a test of sincerity, the Caliph should order them to give up one village and order him to give up a province, and he claimed to have letters giving evidence of their dealings with the Assassins and the Franks, the most recent of which he was sending to Baghdad.[23]

It is difficult to judge the effectiveness of these arguments. Saladin's claim that Aleppo was covered by his diploma of investiture is contradicted by the document preserved by Qalqashandī, which granted him all Syria except for Aleppo and the territories held by al-Ṣāliḥ. Sophistry might suggest that, when al-Ṣāliḥ died, the exception no longer applied and Syria in its entirety belonged to Saladin. Whether or not, however, he was relying on some such argument as this or on another, unknown, diploma, it is obvious that his legal claim was too weak to be taken seriously in Aleppo as otherwise some reference to it would have been expected in the detailed accounts of the transfer of power. If Saladin's remark about the tripartite treaty was not a deliberate irrelevance, he must presumably have been implying that al-Ṣāliḥ had in some way acknowledged his right to Aleppo as part of the conditions of the treaty, which is not only unrecorded but an inconceivable admission for Nūr al-Dīn's son to have made. The reports of the Frankish move on Ḥārim were false, and as Saladin had urged the Lord of al-Rāwandān to attack Aleppo, he could scarcely complain if the Aleppans retaliated.

Clearly, accusations of this type were so hackneyed a theme of propaganda that, true or false, they can have made little impression on Baghdad. The crucial point was whether or not the Caliph would accept Saladin's last and simplest argument: "if the sharing of Syria continues, it will lead to a weakening of unity".[24] This was self-evident and the weakness could compromise the chances for the recovery of Jerusalem. On the other hand, the Caliph was being asked to take sides in a case where Saladin, the stronger party, had demonstrably the weaker claim, if only because he was demanding land that neither he nor any of his family had ever held. Saladin could urge, by implication, that he deserved Aleppo as the champion of Islam, but this had neither been admitted nor convincingly demonstrated. The missing half of the evidence, that of Mosuli letters sent to Baghdad, might perhaps explain the crudity of his approach. Saladin is found referring scornfully to "borrowed gifts"[25] made by the Mosulis and his reaction could arguably be seen as defensive rather than offensive. It may be, in fact, that what both sides were hoping for, at best, was a measure of neutrality from Baghdad and that each was primarily concerned to cancel out the other's claims.

While the sighting shots of the propaganda campaign were being fired Saladin was settling his affairs in Egypt. He had been freed from the fear of another Sicilian attack, as the Sicilian fleet had gone on a disastrous cruise to the Balearics, but nevertheless, at the end of February, before the start of the sailing season, he made a visit of inspection to the coast. In Alexandria he found time not only to inspect the walls but to study the *Muwaṭṭa'* of Mālik, and he then returned to Cairo by way of Damietta.[26] It was important to him to leave behind a contented Muslim population and one inexpensive move in this direction was the enforcement of an order stopping non-Muslims, even doctors and clerks, from riding on horses or mules.[27] As a more positive measure, on 16 March he gave orders for a hospital to be opened in Cairo. It was to be provided with a monthly income of 200 dinars from state funds, together with grain from the Fayyūm, and was to be staffed with servants, overseers, physicians and surgeons. Arrangements were made to reopen the old hospital of Fusṭāṭ, which was given a monthly income of 20 dinars.[28] On 18 March Saladin moved out of Cairo to camp at Birkat al-Jubb where al-'Ādil joined him and at the end of the month dynastic links were strengthened by the arrangement of marriage contracts between four of Saladin's sons and al-'Ādil's daughters.

Meanwhile in Aleppo things had not been going smoothly. The Aleppan emirs were not inclined to pay deference to the Mosulis and in particular to 'Izz al-Dīn's administrator, Mujāhid al-Dīn Qaimāz. Ibn Shaddād reported that they considered, not unreasonably, that they had chosen 'Izz al-Dīn and, on this reckoning, it was he who was in their debt.[29] Further there was a split within their own ranks;[30] Ḥusām al-Dīn Ṭumān, who had supported Zangī, was involved in a quarrel with the Mosul troops over the matter of a village whose safety he had guaranteed. The Mosulis had wanted to sack it, at which he threatened to go to the Franks, and this had led to his arrest. 'Izz al-Dīn later released him and he remained loyal to the Atabek house, but Zangī's other main supporter, 'Alam al-Dīn Sulaimān, fled to Saladin. Meanwhile Zangī himself had suggested the exchange of Aleppo for his own town of Sinjār. When 'Izz al-Dīn rejected this, Zangī is said to have threatened to hand over Sinjār to Saladin[31] but even without this 'Izz al-Dīn may well have been having second thoughts. He was reported to have refused to press an attack on Damascus,[32] but Aleppo itself was proving unprofitable. Further, if he left either Aleppo or Mosul to a subordinate, he would, in effect, be setting up another possible rival and not surprisingly he changed his mind and accepted Zangī's proposal. To give himself what profit and prestige he could he married al-Ṣāliḥ's mother and emptied the citadel of Aleppo of the weapons and stores held in its armouries. Then on 22 February he left to meet Zangī on the Euphrates at al-Raqqa. An agreement was reached on 27 February and agents were sent to make the arrangements for the transfer of Aleppo and Sinjār. During the interregnum the disloyalty that the situation encouraged came briefly into the open when Muẓaffar al-Dīn Keukburī, who had been left in charge of the town of Aleppo, made an abortive attack on the citadel, but was foiled by Shādhbakht.[33] Zangī then sent on his son, Quṭb al-Dīn, to Aleppo and followed with his wife, who was Nūr al-Dīn's daughter. He confirmed the Shī'ites in their privileges and was reported to have treated the people well, but by the time that he reached the city, on 18 May, Saladin had already left Egypt.

After moving to Birkat al-Jubb in March, Saladin had waited 54 days before leaving for Syria. Sometime before this a Frankish pilgrim ship had been wrecked off Damietta. William of Tyre numbered the pilgrims at 1500,[34] while according to 'Imād al-Dīn the ship carried 2500 people, of whom some 1676 were captured and the rest drowned.[35] The terms of the 1180 truce "by land and sea"[36] had been intended to cover situations like these, but William of Tyre reported that Saladin had no intention of allowing so large a prize to escape. He sent an embassy to Baldwin, making impossible demands and when these were refused, he broke off the truce. In fact, William had already noted that the truce was for a two-year period, starting in May 1180, and the Arabic sources, including Saladin's letters, merely refer to it as coming to an end. Saladin was undoubtedly in the wrong over the pilgrim ship, and he produced what can be seen as an excuse when he wrote that the Franks themselves had earlier acted with treachery by seizing a number of merchants and others at sea.[37] In general, however, he was sensitive to accusations of oath-breaking and one of the reasons for his delay at Birkat al-Jubb may have been that he wanted to attack the Franks on his march with a clear conscience. The date given for his departure is 11 May. Half the Egyptian army is said to have gone with him while half remained to guard the country.[38] Al-'Ādil was to stay behind as Saladin's deputy and Qarā-Qūsh was ordered to complete the Cairo–Fusṭāṭ wall. On the evening before he left, Saladin sat with his companions, remarking on the breeze and the scent of the flowers. The tutor of one of his sons quoted a line of poetry: "enjoy the scent of the ox-eye plant of Najd, for after this evening it will come no more."[39] This was taken as an evil omen and, in fact, Saladin never saw Egypt again.

In addition to his Egyptian troops Saladin took with him an unusually large group of non-combatants, comprising not only merchants but also refugees who had left Syria because of the famine and who now wanted to go home. Large stores of provisions and baggage animals had been collected and in a letter to Baghdad he invited admiration for having escorted such numbers for so long a journey, quoting the average time for the passage from Egypt to Syria, for those travelling at a gentle pace, as thirty days.[40] The expedition reached Eilat after five nights and word then came that the Franks had mustered at Kerak. Each side, in fact, was well-informed about the other. The Franks knew of the situation in Aleppo and they had heard of Saladin's muster and of his long tail of civilians. According to William of Tyre, "the whole might of the kingdom" had assembled at Kerak, but he added that Raymond of Tripoli, who was on bad terms with Baldwin, was there against his will and it was felt that the king had been over-persuaded to help Reynald de Châtillon defend Kerak, while leaving the rest of his lands open to attack.[41] In fact, the Frankish concentration was strategically correct, provided that they intended to force a battle and not merely to defend Kerak. The lands that had been left unguarded might well suffer, but the best long-term protection for the kingdom was for Saladin himself to be caught at a disadvantage.

From Eilat Saladin moved away from the Rift valley through the eastern hills, following the line of the modern road from Ma'ān to 'Aqaba (map 7) and he halted by the edge of Frankish territory at al-Qaryatain. According to 'Imād al-Dīn, he stayed there for ten days, raiding Frankish lands, and then said: "our provisions will not allow us to stay [longer] as we have this large number with us, both noble and humble". He then split up his men and sent the civilians under the escort of his brother Būrī by a safe detour to the east, where the Syrian pilgrimage route crosses the Transjordan plateau, while he himself advanced on Kerak.[42] According to William of Tyre he stopped at Gerba, a name derived from the Wāḍī Jarba, some 10 miles (16 km) south of the castle of Shaubak, which he reached after twenty days.[43] William also claimed that had the Franks denied him access to the water that he found there he would have had to retire, as his "huge multitude of civilians" was running short of water.[44] There is a discrepancy here as on 'Imād al-Dīn's account his force must already have been split, but the total of twenty days is reasonable. Al-Qaryatain has been correctly identified as al-Qurain,[45] some 6 miles (10 km) north of the Ashtar pass on the Ma'ān–'Aqaba road, over 30 miles (48 km) south of Shaubak and 50 miles (80 km) from 'Aqaba. It would be plausible to give Saladin 5 days for his move to Eilat, 4 to al-Qaryatain/al-Qurain, 10 for raiding and 1 for the move to Gerba.

The Franks, to William's disgust, were not prepared to challenge him either at Gerba or at the crossing of the Wādī Ḥasā some 15 miles (24 km) south of Kerak. Saladin wrote to tell 'Izz al-Dīn 'Uthmān in Aden that they had come out to bar his way, but had then retired and were only prepared to fight behind fortifications.[46] It is possible that they had been hoping to take advantage of his non-combatants and had gone on to the defensive when they found that his force had been split. William was wrong in suggesting that the whole Muslim army could have been turned back at Gerba, but it would fit with Saladin's letter if the Franks had reconnoitred this part and then retired on seeing him in battle order. This, however, is only conjecture. What is clear is that the strategic value of their concentration was wasted. Saladin did not attack Kerak itself, but rejoined Būrī safely at Qaṣr al-Azraq some 50 miles (80 km) east of Amman, and in the meanwhile an attack had been made on the undefended west bank of the Jordan.

Farrukh-Shāh in Damascus had taken advantage of the ending of the truce to launch a raid. According to William of Tyre, he was reinforced by troops from Buṣrā, Baalbek and Homs and he made his preparations quickly so as not to lose the advantage of surprise. While the Franks were at Kerak, he crossed the Jordan and attacked Dabūrīya (map 2) at the foot of the western slopes of Mt Tabor. It was harvest time and men had come in from the surrounding countryside to help with the work. The inhabitants woke one morning to find the town surrounded and although they had time to take refuge in a tower, this was quickly mined and 500 of them were captured.[47] Saladin described the place as having a strong citadel and a settlement as big as a town. Farrukh-Shāh, he said, had sent his raiders as far as the lands of Acre, and had killed or captured 1000 men and women and had driven off 20,000 head of beef cattle and working oxen.[48]

Farrukh-Shāh's other major success was his capture of the cave fortress of Ḥabīs Jaldak some 14 miles (23 km) east of the Sea of Galilee. This consisted of a number of chambers hollowed into the face of a precipice that overlooks a wadi running southwards to the Yarmuk river. The surrounding country, known to the Franks as the land of Suhite, was fertile and the possession of Ḥabīs Jaldak, in addition to its military value, ensured them a share of its grain revenues. The disappointed Franks at first suspected that Farrukh-Shāh had bought the surrender of the fortress by bribery and then the blame was shifted to "Syrians",[49] who were in command of the garrison and who had surrendered when Farrukh-Shāh's men seized the lowest chamber and started tunnelling through to the others. This account is confirmed in part by Saladin, who wrote that the place had been taken by mining, and he went on to say that Farrukh-Shāh had left "an ample garrison" of his own to hold it.[50]

After his raids, Farrukh-Shāh went to meet Saladin at Buṣrā, and from Buṣrā Saladin himself moved on to Damascus which he reached on 22 June, forty-three days after leaving Egypt. Less than three weeks later he was on the move again, finding no rest, according to 'Imād al-Dīn, except in labour.[51] He had a joint force of Egyptians and Syrians, which he split into three divisions, the right under Taqī al-Dīn, the left under Farrukh-Shāh and the centre under his own command.[52] He left Damascus on 11 July and on the evening of 12 July he camped on the east bank of the Jordan at the foot of the Sea of Galilee, in a position to threaten the nearby town of Tiberias. Raymond of Tripoli, who had married the Lady of Tiberias, was ill, but reinforcements were called in from the castles of Safad in the north and Kaukab in the south, and these entered the town on the night of 12/13 July. Saladin heard of this on 13 July and as he was hoping to provoke a battle, he sent his left wing under Farrukh-Shāh to cross to the west of the Jordan. The challenge was not accepted and he told Baghdad that he found himself calling out the deaf. Rather than press an attack against Tiberias itself, he then decided to force the Franks out by marching in the opposite direction, down the Jordan, to attack Baisān, some 15 miles (24 km) further south. He left on the evening of 13 July and next day Farrukh-Shāh was ordered to begin the assault on Baisān, while Saladin watched for a relief force from Tiberias. After ravaging the town, Farrukh-Shāh started to mine the citadel only to be discouraged, according to William of Tyre, by the fierce resistance of the garrison. In fact, his attack was not pressed home as news now came that the Franks were on the move.

The relief force advanced down the Jordan valley with the river to their left and the hills on which Kaukab stands to their right. There was no serious fighting during the first day's march and in the evening the Franks camped on the hillside rather than risk being surprised on the valley floor. On 15 July, as "the dawn broke on them in anger and the east drew its sword against them", the Muslims saw them coming down from the hills. William of Tyre wrote that they reached the plain between Baisān and Forbelet, the modern Taiyiba, and Saladin said that they were intending to march to Mt Tabor. From Baisān the Harod valley runs westward, between the mountains of Gilboa on the south and, on the north, a wide tongue of high ground that continues on the line from Mt Moreh towards the Jordan. Kaukab is on the eastern tip of this ridge, overlooking the Jordan valley, some 7 miles (11 km) north of Baisān. On their march from Tiberias, the Franks must have passed beyond it and camped nearer Baisān on the south-east corner of the hills, where the Harod valley joins that of the Jordan. If Saladin was right about their plan of march they presumably intended to draw off the Muslims by moving westwards along the Harod valley and then to turn north beneath Mt Moreh, where an easy crossing of the high ground would bring them out in the direction of Tabor.

Saladin gave no estimate of his own numbers, but William of Tyre wrote that he had 20,000 fighting men, the largest Muslim force seen since the Franks had first come to Syria. To set against it, the Franks themselves had barely 700 lances and an unspecified number of foot-soldiers. When they came down from their hillside, they saw Taqī al-Dīn's wing at a distance and the Muslim centre halted and waiting for Saladin, who was busy co-ordinating his tactical plan. When he realised that the Franks were intending to move to the west, he ordered Farrukh-Shāh with his left wing to block their way. Taqī al-Dīn's right wing had presumably been guarding the Jordan valley in case the Franks turned back along it to Tiberias. He was now ordered up and the Franks were hemmed in from three sides, with Farrukh-Shāh to the west, Taqī al-Dīn to the east and Saladin's centre to the south. The Frankish cavalry charged and Saladin used his extra numbers to contain them and to attack the infantry who were waiting behind them. William of Tyre was certainly right in thinking that the Muslims were trying to surround the Frankish force, but although Saladin claimed that the infantry scattered up the hillside, the attempt at encirclement failed. After some hard fighting, the whole Frankish force was able to draw off up the slope to the castle of Forbelet 4½ miles (7 km) west of Kaukab, leaving Saladin to complain that the Muslims had dispersed to water their horses and that the intense noonday heat had robbed him of complete victory. William of Tyre echoed his remark about the heat, writing that as many died of heat stroke on both sides as fell in the battle, and he went on to say that few knights but a number of common people had fallen on the Frankish side. The Muslims had buried their dead by night to conceal their losses, but these were put at 1000. Saladin did not refer to casualties, but 'Imād al-Dīn wrote that "in this fierce encounter...destructive to the enemy...a number of Muslims were martyred". The Muslims spent the night of the battle, 15/16 July, camped by Forbelet, but Saladin appears to have been unwilling to force the matter any further and by 18 July he had re-crossed the Jordan and was in camp at al-Fawwār in the Ḥaurān.

The army did not remain for long at al-Fawwār which was found to be infested by snakes and frogs and where "the water was heavy, the air pestilential",[53] and "the market of the doctors did a roaring trade".[54] Saladin moved to healthier quarters at Ra's al-Mā', 35 miles (56 km) south of Damascus, and from there he went north to the Biqā'. The Franks, who had now gathered at Sepphoris to the north of the Nazareth hills, were uncertain of his intentions.[55] Some thought that he was preparing to attack Beirut; others argued that he was pre-occupied with Aleppo and a number of well-informed counsellors thought that there would be a war with Mosul, as 'Izz al-Dīn Mas'ūd was reported to be besieging Ayyubid towns in the region of the Euphrates. In fact, every one of these theories was correct. From the valley of the Biqā', Saladin sent patrols up onto the Lebanon range from where they could watch for the fleet that he had summoned from Egypt. When this came, he crossed the mountains himself and attacked Beirut, while on the southern frontier al-'Ādil had brought up Egyptian troops to raid round Dārūm and Gaza. This appeared to be a serious and well co-ordinated attack. The Egyptians had thirty galleys, according to William of Tyre,[56] or forty, according to Saladin,[57] and the Frankish ships were still fitting out at Acre and Tyre. Baldwin did not have enough men to allow him to oppose both al-'Ādil and Saladin, and in order to halt the movement of a relief force to Beirut, Saladin had ordered a detachment to hold the coast road, where the Franks reported that they were blocking the narrows with stones. Saladin himself, however, had brought no siege train, which led the Franks to wonder whether he was over-optimistic or whether he thought that he would not have time to use it, but it is clear from William of Tyre's description that his attack on Beirut was not a mere demonstration. He used his numbers to keep up constant pressure, allowing the garrison no rest. His arrows "filled the city and the walls like hail"[58] and his sappers did their best to undermine the walls. The garrison, however, dug successful counter-mines and an attempted assault with scaling ladders was abandoned when the emir who had suggested it was wounded. Meanwhile Baldwin, who had decided to ignore al-'Ādil, had reached Tyre on his way north and after three days of attacks Saladin called off his men. He spent the fourth day doing what damage he could to the surrounding country and then disappeared over the mountains.[59] Ibn Shaddād wrote that he had failed in his purpose.[60] 'Imād al-Dīn explained that he had realised that a siege of Beirut would be a long business,[61] and he himself told Baghdad that he had drawn off with the intention of returning when he was free from his other cares.

The capture of Beirut would have been a spectacular triumph, but

Saladin could scarcely have hoped to hold it had it fallen. It may be that he had deliberately left his options open, either to press an attack if the chances seemed good, or to ravage the countryside and withdraw, but another possibility is that he changed his plans during the siege itself as it was now, according to Ibn al-Athīr, that he received an invitation to cross the Euphrates from Muẓaffar al-Dīn Keukburī.[62]

It had been clear before Saladin moved from Egypt that the Franks were not his main, or immediate, concern. He had followed up his earlier propaganda campaign by writing to the Caliph, before the ending of the Frankish truce, that "the unbelievers in the distant parts" had united and were intending to send out huge armies to the Coast; help would be needed from Aleppo and Mosul, as he had to have troops to protect Egypt from a sea-borne invasion, Damascus from the Franks of the Coast, Hama and Homs from Tripoli and Tell Bāshir, Ra'bān and al-Rāwandān from the Armenians; as a result, his own forces were scattered while "the emirs and sultans of Islam are sleeping in their kingdoms"; Aleppo had made a truce with the Armenians and with Bohemond, while Qilij-Arslān had made a truce with the Byzantines.[63]

When he wrote to the Caliph in July about his attack on Baisān, he claimed that the Muslims had now taken the measure of the Franks; after the fast they had arrived at the feast; he himself, however, had been distracted and provoked beyond measure by Muslim enemies; in particular, the Lord of al-Bīra, [the Ortoqid Shihāb al-Dīn Maḥmūd] a member of an old and loyal house, had sought his protection and had wanted to serve in the Holy War, but had then been besieged and reduced to desperate straits by his own cousin Il-Ghāzī of Mārdīn, who had been authorised to attack him by 'Izz al-Dīn of Mosul. Saladin added that one of the merits of the Lord of al-Bīra was that "he never claimed that his town was an inheritance", a reference to his argument that the Zangid princelings had no right to inherit towns such as Mosul and Aleppo, which were in the gift of the Caliph. He also pointed out that it was bad policy to use Egyptian troops to defend Syria, as this showed weakness to the enemy and Egypt had foes of its own, open and secret; the only answer lay in a united Syria. [64] In another letter, written after the Beirut raid, he complained of gifts of money to the Assassins "to take the life of one whose friend and master is the Commander of the Faithful" (presumably himself), of the offer of fortresses to the Franks for the defeat of armies that were in the Caliph's service and, again, of the attack on al-Bīra.[65] He added, perhaps naively, that he was presenting an excuse before he had been accused of being in the wrong, but there is no doubt that the Caliph knew what the charge would be. The policy of Ayyubid expansionism that had been blocked by the peace treaty of 1176 was about to be renewed. Saladin was laying claim not only to Aleppo, but to any other town whose troops could be shown to be needed for the Holy War. This could not be accepted either by 'Izz al-Dīn in Mosul or by Zangī in Aleppo and Saladin's sincerity in turning his back on the Franks to fight his fellow-Muslims was bound to be called in question.

12

THE CAPTURE OF ALEPPO

On his return from Beirut, Saladin sent Farrukh-Shāh to Damascus to watch the Frankish frontier. Taqī al-Dīn was told to arrange for the safety of the Hama–Tripoli border and then to join Saladin, and Saladin himself marched to Baalbek. He was not in a hurry. He later explained to Baghdad that he had deliberately taken forty days to move from his own lands to the Euphrates, although a shorter time should have served "to awaken the foolish and alarm the forgetful",[1] and on this reckoning he must have moved from the vicinity of Baalbek at the end of the second week of August. According to 'Imād al-Dīn, he went to Homs by Zarā'a at the northern end of the Biqā' valley,[2] but there was a loop in his route, as on 6 September he was at Ṣadad, some 20 miles (32 km) south-east of Zarā'a on the far side of Anti-Lebanon (map 8). A letter that he sent from Ṣadad to an unnamed recipient explains both the slowness of his march and its purpose. He wrote that constant reinforcements were reaching him, including troops from the frontiers, so that, by the grace of God, he had more men than ever before; "the emirs of the lands" were sending him envoys and coming to join him, all with "wide hopes", and all having to be favourably received; his expedition had two motives, the first of which was to take lands which could be given as *iqṭā's* to those emirs who would otherwise disperse – a frank statement of the expansionist position; the second was the stubbornness and procrastination of the Aleppans and the Mosulis, who were looking for help "from those behind them who were weaker and fewer in numbers than themselves," a disparaging reference to al-Pahlawān; Saladin had offered them a settlement, but they had replied with anger and so he was having to move in spite of the cold and the rain, with snow lying on the hill-tops.[3]

There is no reason to doubt that many emirs did send messages to

Saladin at this time, but only the comparatively obscure Bektash of Kafr Lāthā is known to have joined him.[4] Near Aleppo, however, he was met by an envoy from Muẓaffar al-Dīn Keukburī who later arrived himself. This was of crucial importance to Saladin's future. Keukburī was a son of the former administrator of Mosul, Zain al-Dīn and had commanded a wing against Saladin at the battle of Tell al-Sulṭān. Ambition had led him to overreach himself in his abortive attempt on the citadel of Aleppo, but he had been left by 'Izz al-Dīn of Mosul to hold the town and citadel of Ḥarrān. He was now preparing to change sides and was said to have sent a message to Saladin during the attack on Beirut inviting him to cross the Euphrates.[5] He came to press his point in a personal interview. His argument was that Aleppo would be left isolated if Saladin established himself east of the Euphrates and, according to 'Imād al-Dīn, he said: "these lands are yours... You have general affection and complete awe... Will anyone come forward to disobey you when I am I?"[6] This advice must have fitted with Saladin's own wishes. He had no reason to be optimistic about his chances of taking Aleppo. A bleak exercise in siege warfare as winter set in could be expected to disperse his new recruits and the longer that he took to overcome Muslim resistance, the less acceptable would be his claim on the gratitude of Islam. By contrast, a lucrative campaign east of the Euphrates, where Keukburī could arrange at least some show of popular welcome, would be attractive both to his followers and from the point of view of propaganda. In military terms it held out more opportunities than risks. The Aleppans were formidable in the shelter of their own walls and they could interfere with his communications, but they were not strong enough to trap him if he left them in his rear. If he attacked Aleppo, a relief force could be expected from Mosul, but if he crossed the Euphrates, 'Izz al-Dīn would arguably be forced on to the defensive.

Saladin reached Aleppo on 19 September 1182. His troops spread out to the east of the city, but there are no reports of fighting. Instead Saladin tried to negotiate with Zangī, the suggestion being that he should reverse his previous exchange and take back Sinjār, now held by 'Izz al-Dīn.[7] After a few days Saladin moved away, marching by Tell Khālid to al-Bīra, with the question of this exchange apparently having been left open. The siege of al-Bīra by the Lord of Mārdīn had been raised some time earlier and Saladin was welcomed by Shihāb al-Dīn Maḥmūd, who handed him the keys of his citadel, which Saladin then returned to him.

Saladin now wrote to tell Baghdad that the Mosulis were reported by eye-witnesses to have an eleven-year agreement with the Franks, promising an annual payment of 10,000 dinars, "the surrender of the frontier posts of the Muslims", Bāniās, Shaqīf Tīrūn and Ḥabīs Jaldak, and the release of all Frankish prisoners held by them or found in places recovered from Saladin. The Mosulis, he wrote, had thought that he could not attack them unless he made a truce with the Franks and they themselves had moved up to Niṣībīn, while the Franks were planning an attack on Syria; to prevent this, Farrukh-Shāh was stationed at Ra's al-Mā', while al-'Ādil had been ordered to the Frankish border; Saladin himself had moved slowly with his Egyptian troops in the hope that the Mosulis would give up what they had seized, but they had refused, claiming kingship to be hereditary and ignoring the rights of the Caliph. Near the Euphrates, he went on, he had been met by Keukburī of Ḥarrān, "the leader of their armies" and by the Lords of Sarūj and al-Bīra; letters had come from Mosuli *iqṭā'* -holders and people whose wealth had been seized by illegal taxes; they were complaining that in spite of their nearness to the seat of the Caliphate, the Caliph's writ did not run amongst them. Saladin added that the Mosulis had approached "a certain quarter from which the Caliph's favour had been turned", another reference to al-Pahlawān, and he stressed his own commitment to the Holy War and to the needs of Islam by telling the Caliph of attacks by the Egyptian fleet on Syrian ports and by reporting that the common people in the lands of Islam were raising their cry for help to the heavens.[8]

From al-Bīra he marched east towards al-Ruhā. He had written both to Farrukh-Shāh and to al-'Ādil asking them to send him money, as he wanted popularity and not plunder from the places that he was hoping to take. He told al-'Ādil that no resistance was expected – "we have only to get to those cities and halt there" – and he wrote to Farrukh-Shāh: "hurry to produce the money, for every time that the cities open their gates, desires open their mouths".[9] Farrukh-Shāh never replied. He had gone on an expedition against the Franks, become over-tired and, falling ill, had returned to Damascus, where he died. He left a reputation for generosity, bravery and a fondness for literature. He was a friend of the learned Tāj al-Dīn al-Kindī, whose exposition of a line of Mutanabbī had begun their acquaintanceship. He had quoted Mutanabbī at the battle of Marj 'Uyūn[10] and he was himself reckoned to be a competent poet, for a prince. According to 'Imād al-Dīn, he was a man on whom Saladin relied[11] – more than on all the rest of his family and his emirs, Ibn al-Athīr added.[12] His death was clearly a blow to Saladin's plans for containing the Franks, but the Mosul campaign was too far advanced to allow for any turning back. Instead, Saladin sent his "chief emir",[13] Ibn al-Muqaddam, to take charge of Damascus, while Farrukh-Shāh's son, Bahrām-Shāh, was confirmed in possession of Baalbek.

The town of al-Ruhā was held by Nūr al-Dīn's former army commander, Fakhr al-Dīn Mas'ūd ibn al-Za'farānī. As has been shown, he had briefly been in Saladin's service in 1174, and he now resisted long enough to come to terms and re-enter it, after which, according to Ibn al-Athīr, the commander of the citadel was bribed to surrender.[14] 'Izz al-Dīn of Mosul, who had moved westwards from Niṣībīn to Dārā, had turned back when Saladin crossed the Euphrates, but sent troops to reinforce al-Ruhā. They failed to arrive in time and presumably returned to Mosul, but Saladin did not pursue them. Instead, he turned off at a right-angle and moved past Ḥarrān down the line of the river Balikh to al-Raqqa some 90 miles (145 km) away on the Euphrates. Al-Raqqa was an important crossing point and Saladin may have wanted to strengthen his lines of communication south of Aleppo. It should be noted, however, that he was following the path of Nūr al-Dīn's winter campaign of 1170, where there had been no question of danger from the rear, and it may be that the motive in both cases was psychological, to turn a military expedition into a triumphal progress. Al-Raqqa itself was held by Saladin's old enemy, Quṭb al-Dīn Ināl, from whom he had captured Manbij in 1176. This time, Quṭb al-Dīn, seeing the size of Saladin's force, made little attempt to resist and surrendered on condition that he could keep his own property. Saladin promptly impressed the inhabitants with the benefits of his rule and had a decree published proclaiming "good news for his subjects"; all his governors had been instructed to cancel *mukūs* taxes and to erase all mention of them from treasury records because "the most miserable rulers are those whose purses are fat and their people thin"; the decree was to be read out in the house of God, so that the angels might bear witness to it.[15]

From al-Raqqa Saladin moved across to the fertile but unhealthy valley of the Khābūr, whose inhabitants were described by a contemporary traveller as living dead,[16] and here he took over al-Fudain, al-Ḥusain, Māksīn, Durain, 'Arabān and the town of al-Khābūr itself within a stretch of some 80 miles (129 km). There are no reports of fighting and the only details that 'Imād al-Dīn adds are that Saladin was met by "the qāḍīs, leaders, men and women of 'Arabān", and that the town of al-Khābūr then offered its allegiance.[17] During his march up-river Saladin had a choice of routes open to him. He could move eastwards under Jabal Sinjār, on the south side of which was the town of Sinjār itself. A westward route along the upper Khābūr valley would lead to Ra's al-'Ain, some 50 miles (80 km) east of Ḥarrān, which is, in fact, listed amongst the conquests of this campaign. It does not appear, however, that Saladin went there himself and 'Imād al-Dīn reported that he crossed the bridge at al-Tunainīr, and then marched some 40 miles (64 km) north-eastwards to Niṣībīn.[18] Niṣībīn itself was of no great importance. Ibn Jubair, who visited it two years later, described it as being of medium size, and resembling a Spanish town from the outside, whereas inside there was only the confusion of the desert and nothing worth looking at.[19] In spite of that, however, it had an important strategic position between Mārdīn and Mosul, within easy reach of the northern towns of Diyār Bakr (map 1), and it was the base where Nūr al-Dīn had collected troops for his own move on Mosul. The town offered no resistance and its citadel soon surrendered. Saladin then held a council to decide on his next move. According to Ibn al-Athīr, the choices open to him were to attack Sinjār, Mosul itself, or Jazīrat Ibn 'Umar, which was within 60 miles (97 km) of Niṣībīn on the Tigris and which had been given to Saif al-Dīn Ghāzī's elder son. Ibn al-Athīr added that, in view of the news from the west, a number of emirs suggested that the expedition should now be abandoned altogether.[20]

In Aleppo Zangī had been playing mouse to Saladin's cat.[21] When Saladin disappeared across the Euphrates, Zangī came out to raid to the north and east, destroying the fort at Bālis and burning the Euphrates bridge at Qal'at Ja'bar (map 8). He attacked Manbij and Qal'at Najm and crossing the Euphrates himself, he raided Sarūj. In a second expedition, he demolished his own citadel at A'zāz and destroyed fortifications at al-Karzain and Buzā'a. He attacked Tell Bāshir, whose Lord, Dildirim al-Yārūqī, had joined with Saladin, and he moved south of Aleppo to take Kafr Lāthā from another of Saladin's recruits, the emir Bektash.

Meanwhile the Franks had been listening to news of Saladin's progress.[22] They heard that it had only taken a few days to capture al-Ruhā, Ḥarrān "and almost the whole region that had been under the power of the Lord of Mosul," as much by bribery as by force of arms.

The Lord of Mosul was said to have been virtually abandoned by his supporters and there was a story that an attempt had been made to poison him. Other reports, however, claimed that the eastern leaders had banded together and that Saladin's army had been roughly handled. William of Tyre does not mention the death of Farrukh-Shāh, but this must have been known to Frankish spies and not surprisingly the Franks decided to use their opportunity, being the more indignant, as William noted, because Saladin had dared to leave without making any truce with the King. In October 1182, they raided up to the edge of the lava plateau of the Lajāt, within 10 miles (16 km) of Saladin's camp site at Ra's al-Mā', and on their way back they recaptured Ḥabīs Jaldak, where Farrukh-Shāh's "ample garrison" proved to be seventy "strong and warlike men",[23] who surrendered the place in exchange for a safe conduct to Buṣrā.

The loss of Ḥabīs Jaldak is not mentioned by 'Imād al-Dīn and must have been a source of chagrin to Saladin, who had held it for less than six months, but sporadic raids were not enough to make him turn back. 'Imād al-Dīn referred to a flow of embassies and troops to Niṣībīn.[24] The services of Nūr al-Dīn Muḥammad of Ḥiṣn Kaifā were bought with the promise of Āmid and numbers of Turks and Kurds in the pay of Mosul deserted to join the invaders. According to Ibn al-Athīr, Keukburī and Nāṣir al-Dīn Muḥammad of Homs were pressing for a decisive attack.[25] Keukburī had gambled heavily on Saladin's success and if the gamble failed he could hardly hope to maintain himself east of the Euphrates. Nāṣir al-Dīn Muḥammad was looking for a position of greater independence and authority and was said to have offered to pay Saladin for the *iqṭā'* of Mosul. Saladin himself stood to gain not only territory but security for his position in Syria, as the fall of Mosul would bring down Aleppo. He must have been encouraged by the support that he had received and as yet he had not been faced with any serious resistance. Early in November, then, he marched from Niṣībīn across the district known as Bain al-Nahrain and down the Wādī al-Murr to the Tigris at Balad, some 25 miles (40 km) north of Mosul itself. 'Imād al-Dīn could then boast that, in one and the same year, "we had watered our horses from the Nile, the Euphrates and the Tigris".[26]

At this point, however, Saladin had to cope with the double difficulty of attacking a large city and of justifying what he was doing. In the case of Aleppo he could claim, even if unconvincingly, that al-Mustaḍī' had intended it to pass to him, but this could not possibly apply to Mosul and the Mosulis must have done their best to drive the point home to the Caliph whose vizier, Majd al-Dīn Ibn al-Ṣāḥib, was said to favour them, and a few days before Saladin arrived Ibn Shaddād, who was then in Mosuli service, was sent to ask for help.[27] He covered the distance to Baghdad, over 200 miles (322 km) away as the crow flies, in 50 hours by sailing down the Tigris, but his mission did not prosper. The role that the Caliph had chosen in a difficult situation was that of peacemaker, and he sent out the Shaikh al-Shuyūkh to mediate between the two sides. According to Ibn Shaddād, Saladin had arrived at Mosul on 10 November.[28] Three days earlier, in a letter to Baghdad, he had referred to the fact that messages from the Caliph had already urged him to come to terms with 'Izz al-Dīn and he added that it was unthinkable for him not to obey the Caliph's commands; the only conditions on which he insisted were that the Mosulis should show obedience to God and the Caliph, help the Caliph's friends, shun his enemies, and send aid when it was needed; the Caliph's messenger (presumably the Shaikh al-Shuyūkh himself or one of his companions) was at that moment waiting in Mosul for a reply to this, which he would then pass on to Saladin himself.[29]

Saladin was, of course, being disingenuous. He had left out any reference to his recent conquests and any agreement on the apparently innocuous terms offered would presumably have been on the basis of *uti possidetis*. 'Izz al-Dīn could not be expected to accept this and Saladin now began the siege. In Nūr al-Dīn's winter campaign, Mosul had surrendered without any real resistance. After the battle of Tell al-Sulṭān Saif al-Dīn Ghāzī was said to have thought of abandoning it, if pressed, and, according to Ibn al-Athīr, Keukburī had spread the same rumour on this occasion about 'Izz al-Dīn.[30] But unlike Saif al-Dīn in 1170, 'Izz al-Dīn and Qaimāz had taken steps to prepare their defences. Men and equipment had been collected from the remaining Mosuli cities, Jazīrat ibn 'Umar, Sinjār and Irbil, and Qaimāz had spent large sums of his own money. Ibn al-Athīr paints a picture of Saladin's discomfiture in another of his analytical exercises. He makes Saladin tell Keukburī and Nāṣir al-Dīn Muḥammad that they had misled him and that he should have attacked another city, so as to maintain his reputation for invincibility; if he attacked Mosul and was forced to withdraw, the psychological advantage would be lost. Taqī al-Dīn was made to suggest the use of mangonels and Saladin was quoted as replying: '"one does not set up mangonels against a city like this... Even if we destroyed a tower...who could enter the city when there are so many people there?"[31]

It is certainly true that after his experiences at Aleppo, Saladin cannot have been optimistic when he saw that the Mosulis were determined to fight it out, but he did set his troops in position.[32] His brother Būrī had the north-west section, while he himself and Nūr al-Dīn Muḥammad of Ḥiṣn Kaifā watched the rest of the western and southern approaches, and Taqī al-Dīn, perhaps in imitation of Nūr al-Dīn's tactics, was sent across the Tigris to block the city from the east. There was some fighting, but apparently no serious assault. Ibn al-Athīr reported that Chāulī al-Asadī was struck by a nailed boot thrown from the wall and refused to attack and that Qaimāz sent out a stage army with torches by night from the postern gate of the citadel, each man then extinguishing his torch, and coming out again with another.[33] According to the story, these tactics frightened Saladin off but, in fact, when he did move, he took care to provide himself with a face-saving excuse.

'Imād al-Dīn wrote that he was at Saladin's side when the Shaikh al-Shuyūkh, together with Shihāb al-Dīn Bashīr and a number of the Caliph's officials came to his camp.[34] He also noted the arrival of a messenger from al-Pahlawān's brother, Qyzyl-Arslān, and Ibn al-Athīr added that an envoy had also been sent from Shāh-Arman of Khilāṭ.[35] Word spread that there was going to be a peace settlement. The Turks and Kurds who had come over to Saladin became alarmed and changed sides again, excusing themselves to 'Izz al-Dīn, and 'Imād al-Dīn added: "a number of our companions who were eager for robes of honour also deserted". In the meanwhile, Taqī al-Dīn and Būrī kept up their attacks on the city, to the annoyance of the Shaikh al-Shuyūkh, who asked them to stop until he had sent messengers to the Mosulis. It was at this point, according to 'Imād al-Dīn, that Saladin retired, ostensibly out of deference to the Shaikh al-Shuyūkh, "to a place that was not too far away for messengers to reach".

In response to the Shaikh al-Shuyūkh's invitation, negotiators now came out from Mosul to his tent and Saladin sent al-Fāḍil, Ḍiyā' al-Dīn 'Īsā and 'Imād al-Dīn to listen to what they had to say. 'Imād al-Dīn reported that the Mosulis spent the whole of the first day in making complaints but promised to come back with proposals. These proved to be demands for the return of all their lost lands and for Saladin to withdraw to the Euphrates, after which there could be a peace conference. Negotiations dragged on for nearly a month without any conclusion being reached. Al-Fāḍil had withdrawn after some days, followed by 'Īsā, which left 'Imād al-Dīn on his own. He wrote: "the Shaikh al-Shuyūkh was accusing us of not wanting to settle things... We then agreed to everything that he wishes and it was decided that the Mosulis should give us back [*sic*] Aleppo and that we should return to 'Izz al-Dīn everything for which he asked." It was decided that the Shaikh al-Shuyūkh should enter Mosul to get confirmation of the agreement, but at this point, the Mosulis changed their position and are reported to have said: "if Saladin wants to reach agreement with us, he must give back our lands and retire from us. We shall leave him a clear passage to Aleppo, but he is not to ask for aid from us against it, as we have an oath that binds us to our brother, 'Imād al-Dīn Zangī."

The withdrawal of his senior negotiators seems to confirm that Saladin was not taking these discussions seriously and the situation, in fact, was another siege-induced stalemate. The Mosulis could not drive Saladin away, but he was losing men by desertion. He could not hope to take Mosul by assault and if he waited for a lengthy blockade, his position in Syria could be endangered and the eastern rulers might unite against him. 'Izz al-Dīn was clearly not going to agree to unnecessarily humiliating terms and Saladin had to find a way of withdrawing, without damage to his reputation, while still keeping up some military pressure. His solution was to attack Sinjār, some 75 miles east of Mosul, held by 'Izz al-Dīn's brother, Sharaf al-Dīn, whose troops had been attacking his lines of communication.[36] Taqī al-Dīn was sent out ahead of the main force and intercepted a column of Mosuli reinforcements. He followed Saladin's usual policy towards Muslims, taking their horses and equipment and keeping their leaders as prisoners, but sending the rest back to Mosul on foot. Saladin then moved himself, accompanied by the Caliph's envoys. He deployed his men around Sinjār and here the Kurdish tribesmen brought in by Nūr al-Dīn Muḥammad of Ḥiṣn Kaifā disgraced themselves by wantonly cutting down trees in the orchards, behaviour that 'Imād al-Dīn contrasted with the disciplined conduct of Saladin's own troops. Saladin wanted to take Sinjār with the minimum of damage and he now tried to induce the garrison to surrender, "sending people near the wall to speak to them...teaching them right guidance – but they did not understand". After this, he was forced to attack with mangonels and sappers and he succeeded in breaching the outer fortifications. There is some discrepancy in accounts of what happened next. Ibn al-Athīr refers to treachery on the part of a Kurdish emir in the garrison[37] and Ibn Shaddād, who dates the fall of Sinjār to 2 Ramaḍān (30 December) says that it was taken by storm.[38] 'Imād al-Dīn, however, says that the attack slackened off in the month of Ramaḍān. There was continuous rain and the army were "in the guise of monks" and "were taking care not to shed blood".[39] The garrison was made careless by this delay, and one night a man came to tell Saladin that the guard were asleep in the breach, a point which may explain Ibn al-Athīr's reference to treachery. In a sudden assault a number of leaders were captured, and in dismay at their loss Sharaf al-Dīn sued for peace. A letter confirms that Sinjār was taken peacefully[40] and Ibn Shaddād's account, together with his early Ramaḍān date, must be assumed to be wrong.

Sharaf al-Dīn was allowed to leave Sinjār with his drums, banners, fighting men and retainers. The leading citizens came out and were well received by Saladin and he repaired the damage that had been done during the siege. The town was given as an *iqṭā'* to Taqī al-Dīn and Saladin's brother-in-law, Sa'd al-Dīn Ibn Anar, was left in charge of the citadel.[41] Ibn al-Athīr added that its capture confirmed Saladin's gains east of the Euphrates. Before, his only fortress there had been that of al-Ruhā, but now Sinjār "was like a wall for all his conquests".[42] Saladin promptly sent letters to Baghdad suggesting that the Caliph should persuade the Mosulis to accept their losses in return for being allowed to keep what was left of their lands. He told the Caliph that the reason for his attack on Mosul was that the Mosulis had induced the Franks to attack Syria; he had been welcomed in the places that he had taken "as though he was coming to his own house", but he had left Mosul out of respect for the intercession of the Shaikh al-Shuyūkh; the troops of Sinjār had tried to cut his supplies and he had decided to add their town to the places covered by his diploma, as he was determined not to leave the lands until he had silenced the tongues that refused to acknowledge the grace of the Caliph.[43] In another letter, he repeated that he had left Mosul after receiving the Caliph's command to make peace; he had obeyed, as was his custom, but this had led the Mosulis into self-deception; his own companions had slackened their efforts and when the soldiers and people of the lands of Mosul, who had joined him, had realised that he was not going to take the city, they had gone back to 'Izz al-Dīn; meanwhile, the Aleppans and the Mosulis had been tempting the Franks into making abortive attacks on Syria, and Saladin insisted that if the Caliph was concerned about the Mosulis, he should tell them to be satisfied with what was left in their hands; this would ensure their survival, whereas otherwise "today will be followed by tomorrow".[44] This same point was explained in a letter to Majd al-Dīn Ibn al-Ṣāḥib in which Saladin claimed that the Mosulis were not steadfast in battle, nor faithful to their agreements when they made peace; they must be told to be content with what they had, as there was enough left them to satisfy their ambitions; they could keep this if they stayed quiet, but they should not seek what lay beyond their grasp.[45]

Saladin now held a council to decide on his next move. In Syria the Franks had raided round Damascus, and in the north the Mosulis were trying to recruit help from the Lords of Diyār Bakr. Shāh-Arman of Khilāṭ had sent his leading emir, Bektimur, to Saladin's camp during the siege of Sinjār, and when Saladin had refused to accept his intercession for Mosul, Bektimur had left in anger. It was now January; there had been heavy rainfall with snow on the hills, and Saladin agreed to a suggestion that he should go into winter quarters and continue his campaign in the spring. He marched northwards to Niṣībīn, where he found the citizens complaining about his governor, Abū'l-Haijā' the Gross, and according to Ibn al-Athīr, "regretting the just rule of 'Izz al-Dīn".[46] This kind of dissatisfaction was dangerous, and Abū'l-Haijā' was quickly replaced.

The Shaikh al-Shuyūkh and Shihāb al-Dīn Bashīr left for Baghdad, towards the end of Ramaḍān (27 January), and Saladin gave them a letter for the Caliph in which he had written: "the servant has sent continuous messages to the Caliph's court explaining his affairs and revealing the secrets of his excuse". He pointed out that when the Caliph had ordered peace to be made, he had consented and then, when things were almost settled on terms agreed in the presence of the Shaikh al-Shuyūkh, the Mosulis "had loosed it before it was tied"; they were hoping to get help from Aleppo in the spring and for immediate reinforcements from Diyār Bakr. Saladin revealed that the Shaikh al-Shuyūkh had asked him to give up his conquests, which he still claimed to be covered by his diploma. He would have agreed to this, he said, as he had no wish for more territories, had he not been forced to add to the numbers of his men for the Holy War. His justification was that he used what he had in the service of Islam and he wrote: "if any of those who claim kingship to be hereditary and who consider the lands to be their inheritance were forced to repel the infidel enemy, the days would teach them what they do not know".[47]

On a personal level, relations were still maintained between the invaders and the Mosulis. A private letter had been sent from Mosul by Fakhr al-Dīn Ibn al-Dahhān to al-Fāḍil, who was asked to pass on greetings to 'Imād al-Dīn.[48] A reply was sent from Niṣībīn, referring to "the messages and messengers exchanged between the two sides", and the intervention of the Shaikh al-Shuyūkh, and ending uncontentiously: "God Almighty knows the desire of the one addressed in this letter for a settlement."

For all his messages of self-justification, Saladin's diplomacy was not purely defensive. An important letter has been preserved which he sent to Mujāhid al-Dīn Yurun-Qush, one of Zangī's principal officers in Aleppo. He referred to conversations that Yurun-Qush had had with Zangī, in which they had presumably discussed the question of exchanging Aleppo. The town and citadel of Sinjār had now surrendered on terms of quarter and so "the substitute that had been asked for" was ready to hand, a reference to the negotiations that Saladin had conducted with Zangī when he passed Aleppo in the autumn. He could not expect to get Aleppo, he said, without giving something in return, as that would damage good relations between himself and Zangī. He then went on to suggest that if Zangī wanted to take all the lands of Mosul, he himself, for a suitable consideration – presumably the surrender of Aleppo – would help him to become head of his house and independent in his rule. He mentioned the regular interchange of envoys and letters that had been maintained "up to the last minute", and then apparently broken off because of a recent estrangement. He claimed on many occasions to have been offered a pact against Zangī, but always to have refused, and he pointed out that he had turned away from Aleppo to attack Mosul instead. He ended by saying that he was prepared to overlook the damage that Zangī had been doing in his lands – "up to this present moment we have love for him in our hearts".[49]

How seriously Saladin expected this to be taken is not clear. That Zangī, Nūr al-Dīn's eldest nephew, son-in-law and favourite, must have hoped in the course of time to be acknowledged as rightful Lord of Mosul and head of his house can scarcely be doubted, but his career shows that he was not prepared to become Saladin's pensioner. The reference to Saladin's refusal of offers of a pact aimed against him seems a particularly cynical distortion. It may have been true of the time of Zangī's dispute with Saif al-Dīn Ghāzī, but 'Imād al-Dīn's account makes it clear that Saladin had recently been pressing 'Izz al-Dīn to help him take Aleppo and 'Izz al-Dīn's refusal had contributed to the breakdown of negotiations. Saladin, however, must have realised that Yurun-Qush would have heard the details of this bargaining and the sentence is better taken not as an ineffective diplomatic lie but as a threat. Translated from the past to the future it could imply that, if Zangī did not agree to Saladin's terms, Saladin, with Sinjār added to his conquests, would have a stronger leverage to apply to Mosul and 'Izz al-Dīn might then feel more tempted to recover his lands – the bait that Saladin had already offered – at the expense of his brother. To keep up the psychological pressure, Saladin moved west from Niṣībīn to Dārā and then across to Ḥarrān, some 115 miles (185 km) from Aleppo.

Saladin reached Ḥarrān at the end of February 1183 and it was shortly after this on 2 March that al-'Ādil wrote from Egypt to tell him the alarming news that the Franks had struck at the heart-lands of Islam.[50] Reynald de Châtillon had already reconnoitred the land route to Arabia in the winter of 1181/2, and, according to a letter, he had spent two years in having ships constructed in sections so that they could be carried on camel-back.[51] Camels were hired from the Bedouin and early in the new year 1183 the ships were brought down to the Gulf of 'Aqaba. In part, Reynald's motive was self-defence, in that his lands had been damaged by the Muslim garrison at Eilat. Saladin claimed that he had found the castle too strong to storm and as a result he had decided on a blockade to cut the garrison off from their source of drinking-water, a mainland spring; only two ships were thought necessary for this and the rest of the flotilla had been sent out of the Gulf to the Red Sea itself.

It is important not to read too much significance into this move. As was shown later, Reynald had scarcely enough men and resources to defend Kerak itself against a full-scale attack. Unless he managed to capture Eilat, he had no naval base at all and even if he took it, its earlier surrender to Saladin was a poor guarantee that he could hold it. This must be construed, then, not as a serious attempt to extend Frankish influence into the Red Sea or to capture its trade routes, but merely as a piratical raid. It might, of course, have been intended as the first of a series, but unless Reynald seriously thought that he could control the land routes along the Rift valley from Kerak to 'Aqaba – and so cut off Egypt from Syria – he could have had no far-reaching plans for naval dominance.

The raid itself, however, was sufficiently alarming. 'Imād al-Dīn wrote that the Muslims "were unaccustomed to attacks by the infidel in that sea",[52] and Ibn al-Athīr added that they had no experience of the Franks either as fighters or as traders there.[53] Ibn Jubair, who arrived from Spain at Alexandria at the end of March, was told that the Franks had burnt sixteen ships and had then crossed to the west coast at ʻAidhāb (map 5), where they captured a pilgrim ship and a caravan coming overland from the Nile. He also heard that they had planned to attack Medina and remove the Prophet's body[54] and Maqrīzī later supplied the other half to this rumour by saying that the body was then to be taken to Frankish territory where Muslims would have to come on pilgrimage to visit it.[55] From ʻAidhāb the flotilla re-crossed the Red Sea and attacked the east coast, from Rābigh, 90 miles (145 km) north of Jedda, to al-Ḥaurā', an anchorage on the route from Egypt to Medina.

Fortunately for the Muslims, al-ʻĀdil did not allow the affair to get out of hand. Saladin later told the Shaikh al-Shuyūkh that his brothers had built ships in order to meet the Frankish threat and that "he had considered its consequences when first he had heard the news".[56] In fact, he had to transfer ships from Fusṭāṭ and Alexandria to the Red Sea and although he may have had some advance warning of Reynald's plans, the Franks were given a start estimated by Ibn Jubair at one-and-a-half months.[57] The Muslim fleet, under the command of the Armenian admiral Lu'lu', began by breaking the blockade of Eilat. The Frankish ships there were destroyed and those Franks who made their escape into the hinterland were reported to have been tracked down by Bedouin. Lu'lu' then sailed south to ʻAidhāb, where he arrived too late to intercept the rest of the flotilla, but he followed it across the Red Sea and caught it at anchor. The Franks beached their ships and took to the desert, where Lu'lu' pursued them. Saladin remarked that the Franks had been joined by Bedouin as impious as themselves who had guided them to the weak spots of the Muslims and Maqrīzī elaborated this by saying that during the pursuit Lu'lu's men had purses full of silver fixed to their lances to buy back the Bedouins' loyalty.[58] According to Saladin, the chase lasted for five days and nights and the Franks were eventually trapped.[59] They asked for quarter and the whole force, numbered by Saladin at 170 men, was captured.[60]

Ibn Jubair saw prisoners from this raid being led into Alexandria, mounted backwards on camels and escorted with drums and trumpets. He heard that others had been sent to different places to be killed, some being taken to Mecca and Medina.[61] ʻImād al-Dīn wrote that two were brought to Mecca and the rest to Cairo, where Saladin sent a letter ordering their execution, "so that not one of them may remain who knows that road".[62] In itself this is unsurprising, and the Franks would certainly have had no scruples about killing Muslim raiders caught on their own coasts. Saladin's letters, however, show that there was a complication. He sent a reply to al-'Ādil's message of 2 March, congratulating him on a victory that had preserved the sanctity of the sacred territory and on the recovery of Muslim prisoners whom the Franks had abandoned as they fled. He had read Lu'lu's own despatch, he wrote, which he had then forwarded to the Caliph and he quoted from the Quran: "he has taken every ship by force". He then went on to say that the captured Franks had uncovered the hidden parts of Islam; if any disaster were to happen, "the enemy would flood into the sacred territory" and "tongues in the east and west would blame us"; "the earth must be purged of their filth and the air of their breath".[63] This letter is presumably the one referred to by 'Imād al-Dīn in which the order was first given for the prisoners' execution. Saladin then had to send another letter to al-'Ādil. He began: "if we wrote our brother...as many letters as need and motive prompted, we would spend our whole time in writing and he in reading". He then repeated his congratulations and went on:

> there is no need to refer back to the question of killing the prisoners... There is no good to be got out of preserving any one of them, nor any excuse that God will find acceptable for closing our eyes to them. The judgement of God on men like these is not a problem for scholars nor is it obscure. Let the decision to kill them be carried out... Their attack was an unparalleled enormity in the history of Islam.[64]

Abū Shāma quotes a phrase from a third letter in which Saladin referred to "the repeated talk" that there had been about the prisoners.[65]

Al-'Ādil's reluctance and the fact that he apparently suggested taking legal advice, as is indicated by the reference to scholars, shows that this was not a straightforward execution of men captured by force. The clue is given in 'Imād al-Dīn's account of the pursuit in which he noted that the Franks had asked for quarter and in a phrase in Saladin's first letter to al-'Ādil in which he wrote: "if in these circumstances faith is kept with the unbelievers it will cause a rent [amongst the believers] that can never be mended".[66] The only reasonable explanation of this is that the Franks must have been promised quarter and, in spite of al-'Ādil's representations, Saladin refused to allow the promise to be honoured.

Saladin may arguably have felt the need to make an example of the Frankish raiders not only because of their sacrilegious plans, but because of the possible criticism of his own position. It was his absence on an anti-Muslim war that had given Reynald his opportunity and his determination to continue his campaign, in spite of difficulties caused by the death of Farrukh-Shāh, could be taken as showing that he was putting his own dynastic interests before those of Islam. From his own point of view, although in terms of territory the war had been going well for him, he had not yet managed to achieve his main objective, the destruction of the independent power of Mosul and Aleppo, and his army was now shrinking in size.[67] Nāṣir al-Dīn Muḥammad had apparently left and Taqī al-Dīn had taken his men back to Hama. This encouraged 'Izz al-Dīn and his allies to think of taking the offensive. Shāh-Arman, whose proposals Saladin had rejected during the siege of Sinjār, came down from Lake Van (map 1), bringing with him Daulat-Shāh, Lord of Bitlīs. They were joined by Il-Ghāzī of Mārdīn, and late in February 'Izz al-Dīn went out from Mosul with a light force and no heavy baggage. The allied army gathered at Ḥarzam, beneath the hills of Mārdīn, some 90 miles (145 km) from Saladin at Ḥarrān, and they were reinforced from across the Euphrates by troops from Aleppo. Saladin appears to suggest that they hoped to defeat him before he could gather his men,[68] but in fact there is no report of any movement on their part throughout March and they seem to have been content to see whether their muster would frighten him away. In itself this would not prevent him from gathering his men again and returning but it would detract from his prestige and allow an opportunity for the recapture of lost lands.

For his part, however, Saladin was not to be bluffed. His lines of retreat were open and he could not easily be taken by surprise from a base 90 miles away. He could afford to wait in comparative safety and call back Taqī al-Dīn, who covered the distance from Hama to Ḥarrān, 175 miles (282 km) as the crow flies, in five days. This was not the urgency of alarm. 'Imād al-Dīn wrote that both Taqī al-Dīn and Saladin wanted to advance, "and we said: 'they are in great numbers and we should be careful of failure. Also, these are the blessed ten days of Dhū'l-Ḥijja'."[69] Saladin, in fact, stayed at Ḥarrān to perform the prayer on the 'Īd al-Naḥr (6 April) but then, without waiting for the arrival of Nāṣir al-Dīn Muḥammad or of his other troops, he moved out against the allies, marching eastwards to Ra's al-'Ain. This uncompromising pugnacity was successful. The allies debated whether or not to risk battle but could not agree amongst themselves. As Saladin put it, they dispersed by mutual consent, without the intervention of the hand of fate or the tongue of dearth.[70] He told the Shaikh al-Shuyūkh that they had been sure that he would wait for the 'Īd al-Naḥr and so they themselves retreated from Ḥarzam on the day before it, 5 April.[71]

At first sight it is difficult to judge how serious a risk Saladin was running when he decided to move. He obviously relied on the discipline of his own men, trained in the Frankish wars, whereas 'Imād al-Dīn wrote of the men of Diyār Bakr in this campaign that they had no experience in war at all.[72] It is also clear that he could have waited longer at Ḥarrān in complete safety. If the allies had not challenged him before Taqī al-Dīn arrived, they were unlikely to do so while he was waiting for Nāṣir al-Dīn Muḥammad. The fact that they had made no move may have led him to believe that they could never act decisively and they were, of course, faced with the difficulties of joint command. 'Izz al-Dīn by not bringing a baggage train had presumably showed that he did not want a long campaign. If the Mosulis were unwilling to fight, Il-Ghāzī of Mārdīn would have every reason for retreating to his own walls, while, according to Saladin's propaganda, Shāh-Arman was foolish or senile – "a grown man who has entrusted his affairs to women;... He has lost the two most pleasant things [enjoyment of food and drink and of women]."[73] If Saladin was correct in saying that the allies had dispersed before he moved, this implies that they had some definite grounds for believing that he was about to march. Each side, in fact, can be presumed to have had information about the other and both may have been bluffing. If the point of the concentration at Ḥarzam had been to drive Saladin off without fighting, it had already failed. If Saladin had let it be known that he was intending to force an action, the fact that he did not move until the allies had dispersed may suggest that this was what he had been waiting for, and on this interpretation his tactics can be seen as effective and totally safe.

Saladin now moved to the allies' former camp site at Ḥarzam, where he halted to plan his next move. Shāh-Arman had returned to Khilāṭ and 'Izz al-Dīn had gone to Mosul taking with him the Aleppan troops, who only reached home by making the long detour to cross the Euphrates at 'Āna (map 8). Il-Ghāzī of Mārdīn had gone back to his citadel under the shelter of its mountain a mere 10 miles (16 km) away from Ḥarzam, but this was reckoned to be too strong to attack. He then wrote to Saladin excusing himself for having urged the allies to fight and asking for peace. Saladin noted that he had sent a reply "which did not close for him a door which he wanted to open".[74]

It was apparently at this stage that a message came from the Caliph authorising Saladin to take Āmid, some 50 miles (80 km) north of Mārdīn, a not over-generous reply to a request for diplomas covering Mosul and the whole of the Jazīra.[75] Āmid stands on a rock ridge by the Tigris and was reported by William of Tyre to be almost impregnable because of the numbers of its inhabitants, its strong fortifications and its site.[76] Its basalt walls gave it the name of "the black town",[77] and 'Imād al-Dīn reported a conversation that he had had with the Lord of al-Suwaidā', who said to him: "this Sultan of yours has sworn to do the impossible", referring to Saladin's promise to give the town to Nūr al-Dīn Muḥammad, to which 'Imād al-Dīn replied: "his good fortune comes from God".[78] For all this, Āmid was not proof against assault. It was the scene of the famous siege described by Ammianus Marcellinus, who was present when it was unsuccessfully defended by eight Roman legions against Sapor's Persians when the Gauls in the garrison hacked at the gates with their swords in their eagerness to be allowed out to fight. Saladin had smaller numbers and less formidable opponents to fear. The town was administered for an elderly emir by a certain Ibn Nīsān, who was both unpopular and, at this period, apparently incompetent. 'Imād al-Dīn wrote that the townspeople were prepared to welcome Saladin, "and our aim was to free the place from Nīsānid slavery".[79]

Saladin was clearly optimistic about the expedition as he felt able to send back to Syria not only a number of emirs but Taqī al-Dīn himself and he wrote to tell Baghdad that, were it not for custom's sake, he would not take any troops with him, but would rely on the Caliph's diploma.[80] He reached Āmid on 13 April and waited for three days before attacking. It was presumably at this point that he wrote to Khuṭlubā, whom he had sent to restore stability in Yemen: "this letter comes from Āmid...we are hoping for its conquest...and the indications of victory are apparent". He went on to stress his need for money. "You know how the least of these moves drains our treasuries... Yemen is a treasury and we have no trustier guardian of it than you."[81]

In contrast to Saladin's liberality, it was Ibn Nīsān's meanness, according to Ibn al-Athīr, that lost him his town. 'Imād al-Dīn wrote that he had collected a considerable force, thinking that Saladin would tire of the siege "but every day found our strength increasing". One of his companions had pointed out to him that "the enemy are not infidels that the people should fight for their lives", but in spite of this he distributed neither money nor food to buy support.[82] After his three-day wait, Saladin used his mangonels, including one called al-Mufattish (The Examiner), to destroy the battlements, so as to clear the archers from the walls. Next, infantry with scaling ladders captured part of the outer fortifications and the mangonel bombardment was turned against the main walls themselves, which were also attacked by sappers. At this, 'Imād al-Dīn wrote that "the help given Ibn Nīsān by the townspeople slackened off".[83] Ibn Nīsān became afraid of treachery and an arrangement was made by which he was allowed three days to move his own possessions, but not the stores and arms held in the town, which was then to be handed over to Saladin. The exact date of the transfer is not clear,[84] but it must have been on or just before 29 April. According to Saladin, there were three days of actual fighting to add to the three days' delay on his arrival, and three more days were taken up with moving Ibn Nīsān's goods, leaving almost a week for negotiations. After the agreement had been made, Ibn Nīsān sent a message to Saladin to say that his servants had deserted him and he was unable to move his valuables. Saladin sent his own men to help but, according to Ibn Abī Ṭayy, nobody brought out anything without stealing half of it or more, and when the three days were up, only one-tenth of the goods had been moved.[85] "The tongue of Saladin's standard then spoke in the mouth of the citadel" and the city was handed over to Nūr al-Dīn Muḥammad, together with its stores. These may have been magnified by rumour but they were clearly impressive. 'Imād al-Dīn remarked on an inventory which noted a total of 80,000 candles,[86] and Ibn Abī Ṭayy, who reported this as 100,000 candles, added a tower full of arrow-heads and a library of 1,040,000 books. In return for a diploma granting him the city, Nūr al-Dīn took Saladin's hand in token of allegiance. He was to follow Saladin in every expedition of the Holy War, repair the damage done to the city and cancel the *mukūs* taxes.

The fall of Āmid won over another piece of the diplomatic chess board, as Il-Ghāzī of Mārdīn now agreed to enter Saladin's service. Those of his lands that Saladin had taken were returned to him on condition that he was to send his troops whenever Saladin needed them and as a result of these moves, in Aleppo, against which Saladin was now preparing to move, Zangī no longer had any room for manoeuvre. In a private letter to Sa'd al-Dīn at Sinjār al-Fāḍil had discussed whether Sinjār and Niṣībīn would be used as an exchange for it or whether they would be left with Taqī al-Dīn and some alternative bargaining counter found.[87] There was no hint that the exchange might not be accepted and Saladin was already looking further ahead.

He was obviously determined to pursue his quarrel with Mosul and he kept up his barrage of letters to Baghdad in which he ignored Aleppo and concentrated on the problems of Mosul and of the Jazīra. He claimed that had he been given a diploma covering Mosul it would have fallen to him; it was Egyptian troops who had taken Āmid after a year's active service and two campaigns against the Franks, while the rest of his army was in Syria guarding the frontiers; if the Jazīra were added to his lands, then all the armies of Islam would be ranged against the infidel.[88] In another letter he wrote that Āmid had been opened by the key of the Caliph's diploma, while the fact that he had not yet been sent the key to Mosul had kept it from him; every other ruler of Islam busied himself with eating, making money and playing polo and the only blows they saw were on the exercise field; if he were given Mosul, there would be a united front against the enemies of truth, and were a diploma to arrive covering the Jazīra as well, this would be light added to light. The Caliph was asked whether Saladin or 'Izz al-Dīn was the more faithful and diligent in his service and whether any other Islamic ruler, apart from Saladin, was a source of damage to the unbelievers.[89]

An immediate reaction to these protestations was brought by Ḍiyā' al-Dīn al-Shahrazūrī, who must have told Saladin that the Caliph was not prepared to do what he asked. As a result, on 7 May he sent a long letter from Sarūj in which he developed his arguments, re-stating his criticisms of 'Izz al-Dīn, defending his own position and playing on the Caliph's desire for temporal power in addition to spiritual authority. He was clearly annoyed by what he must have seen as 'Izz al-Dīn's influence in Baghdad and he wrote: "as the servant is grateful for the good treatment that he has received, so he complains of [the Caliph's] turning away from him". He referred to "those who only look to Baghdad in time of trouble", instancing the Mosulis who had not "knocked at the door of the Caliphate" until they were frightened; as for his own position, the commands of Baghdad were carried out throughout his dominions; his envoys were at the Caliph's doors and his letters in the Caliph's chancery; he had waged the Holy War beneath the black banners of the Abbasids and he was not like those who wore arms for adornment only and who were like figures painted on the walls.

He tried to alarm al-Nāṣir with the thought that the Mosulis were working to restore the influence of the Seljuq sultanate; when the power of the Seljuqs had weakened, the Caliphate, thanks to its manipulation of sword and pen, had regained its independence, but the desire of Saladin's enemies was to restore Seljuq rule; if this were disbelieved on six days of the week, Saladin would call the seventh to witness, as Seljuq names were mentioned in the Friday *khuṭba* at Mosul. He briefly noted the unsuccessful attempt by the Mosulis to force him away and added that after the break-up of their forces at Ḥarzam they had taken refuge in a mirage that could not give drink to the thirsty, and the bird of hypocrisy had returned to its nest.

He himself, however, was not without hypocrisy when he reminded al-Nāṣir of the struggle for independence of an earlier Caliph, al-Mustarshid, claiming that the Mosulis had persecuted al-Mustarshid's followers, just as they persecuted Ayyubid supporters in their lands, but failing to refer to the help given by his own father to Zangī after his attack on al-Mustarshid in 1132.

Amongst those whom Saladin claimed to have been persecuted by the Mosulis was Keukburī, whom 'Izz al-Dīn would have had every reason to consider as a deserter, and for good measure he accused them of seizing money from orphans and stealing religious endowments; it was no secret that they were an obstacle to the Holy War; "they are not content not to fight, but they prevent those who can"; they had asked for help from the Franks and the Assassins; had the treasure in the citadel of Aleppo a tongue, it would have cried out its wrongs; it had been carried to the infidels and used to buy lances to strike at the breasts of the believers and what had been left of it in Aleppo had been shaped into goblets for the drinking of wine forbidden by Islam.

In the same letter, Saladin again defended his own conduct. Referring to his return to Damascus after Nūr al-Dīn's death, he said that he had come to Syria to fight the unbelievers, to end the heresy of the Assassins and to remove wrong-doing from the Muslims; the Mosulis had distracted him from this for three years and these had been followed by the years of drought; he had retired to Egypt to rest his army and to collect money and when he came back to Syria he had continued to wage the Holy War, paying no attention to them; they had then seized Aleppo and its lands without justification and distracted him when he was in the middle of the lands of the unbelievers; he had taken their towns and territories but had continued to invite them to a peaceful settlement; if he were given Mosul, this would lead to the capture of Jerusalem, Constantinople, Georgia and the lands of the Almohades in the west, "until the word of God is supreme and the Abbasid caliphate has wiped the world clean, turning the churches into mosques". He stressed that all this would happen by the will of God and that, far from asking for money for help, he would give the Caliph Takrīt, Daqūqā, al-Bawāzīj Khuzistan, Kīsh and Oman. Of these, the first three are in a triangle bordered by the Tigris and the Little Zab, with Takrīt, at 100 miles (161 km), being the nearest to Baghdad. Khuzistan is south of Baghdad at the head of the Persian Gulf and Kīsh is a Gulf island. Were Saladin to take them all, he would virtually have encircled Baghdad and whether he was well advised to catalogue such wide-ranging ambitions is difficult to judge. His own view was obviously that it might sound unconvincing, not dangerous, and he added: "if this hope is thought to be too great...what has already happened [i.e. the conquest of Egypt and Yemen] is greater than the conquests that are expected". He went on: "the servant is more righteous in asking for this diploma than are those who advise it to be delayed".[90] As an appendix to the letter he wrote to Majd al-Dīn in Baghdad to stress that he did not want money or men or the removal of a governor whose dismissal would be a blow to Islam, but only legal justification and the Caliph's approval for his actions; a diploma would be like a grain of corn producing seven ears, each with a hundred grains.[91]

Of the extant letters of the period, this gives perhaps the fullest statement of Saladin's propaganda position in which all his actions are justified and the arguments of his opponents refuted in terms of Islamic principle. It also indicates how far the Holy War could be used as a basis for expansion. Saladin could not attack the Christian kingdom of Georgia without first moving through the lands of its Muslim neighbours. An invasion of Byzantine territory would involve the swallowing up of Qilij-Arslān and the Moroccan and Spanish bases of the Almohades could only be attacked if Saladin expanded along the whole of the North African coast. Coupled with his references to Khuzistan, Kīsh and Oman, this gives the picture of a projected Ayyubid state stretching from Spain to the Caucasus, monopolising almost all the temporal power of Islam. In such a grandiose context, raids and counter-raids in Palestine and even the recovery of Jerusalem would sink into comparative insignificance and it has to be questioned whether Saladin seriously thought that he could now afford to treat the Franks of the Coast as an incidental problem and concentrate on establishing a vast monolithic Islamic state, or whether it was merely annoyance with his lack of diplomatic success that led him to a series of rhetorical exaggerations.

For the moment he was prepared to leave Mosul behind and from Sarūj he moved across the Euphrates to Tell Khālid, some fifty miles (80 km) north-east of Aleppo.[92] His brother Būrī had been sent on ahead to invest it and mangonels were set up, but both the town and the citadel surrendered as soon as Saladin himself arrived on 17 May. He gave the place to Badr al-Dīn Dildirim, Lord of the neighbouring Tell Bāshir, and sent off letters to call in reinforcements for the siege of Aleppo. It seems that he was anxious both to swell his numbers and also to force emirs who showed signs of independence or hostility to make a public gesture of loyalty. He wrote to an unnamed recipient: "this letter has been written after we crossed the Euphrates, came to Tell Khālid and received the peaceful surrender of its garrison... Letters have been sent to all the emirs, summoning them to what will be of advantage to them... You must abate your pride, abandon obstinacy and show compliance."[93]

According to 'Imād al-Dīn, after leaving Tell Khālid Saladin made a detour northwards to 'Ain Tāb, which was held by Muḥammad, son of Khumartekīn of Bū Qubais, who had been killed while defending Saladin against the Assassins in 1175.[94] Muḥammad's brother, Mankūrus, still held Bū Qubais and had commanded the troops of Hama in Saladin's service. 'Ain Tāb, however, had been part of the *iqṭā's* of the Banū 'l-Dāya and on their fall it had remained within the territories of Aleppo. There is no record of any part played by Muḥammad in the wars between Saladin and Aleppo and he may have been enjoying some modest independence. Now, however, when Saladin's army turned towards him, he offered his services and was confirmed in possession of 'Ain Tāb quickly enough to allow Saladin to move back another 60 miles (97 km) to Aleppo within four days of having left Tell Khālid.

On 21 May Saladin camped outside Aleppo.[95] He himself took up his station to the east of the citadel by the Maidān al-Akhḍar, with his troops encircling the suburb of Bānaqūsā to the north-east and spreading round to Bāb Janān on the west side. At this stage he seems to have been deploying his men dangerously close to the city in the hopes of an early success. He had been negotiating with Zangī, at least intermittently since September 1182 and, according to 'Imād al-Dīn, Zangī was regretting having left Sinjār and did not want to fight.[96] His monthly expenditure on his army and his emirs was 30,000 dinars and Saladin was cutting off his sources of revenue. It was apparently at this stage of the siege that Saladin wrote to Keukburī to tell him that Zangī had sent out Ṭumān as an envoy; Ṭumān had met Taqī al-Dīn to discuss an exchange of territory and a message had been sent by the Caliph, apparently urging acceptance of what had been proposed. Saladin, however, had not agreed to it for a number of reasons, amongst them being the fact that he already held the estates, castles and wealth of Aleppo and he did not see why he should give up more than he would receive; another reason was that, although all the proposals from Aleppo were placatory on the surface, there was an evil object behind them; the Aleppans wanted to loosen the noose and to win time, as they were expecting help from the unbelievers. He added that news had just come in that the Franks had mustered with the intention of attacking Syria; the Mosulis, too, were on the move and must have been summoned by the Aleppans, for otherwise they were too feeble and too short of numbers to challenge him; he himself was waiting for his troops to flock in, for it was clear that the siege of Aleppo required a large force.[97]

That the muster of the Franks and the reported movement of the Mosulis should be quoted as a reason for Saladin's refusal to agree to an exchange underlines the fact that he was relying on being able to force the issue quickly. He may well have been right in his assessment of Zangī's weakness, but the people of Aleppo were still determined to resist. According to Ibn al-'Adīm, 10,000 of them came out each day to fight and there was skirmishing morning and evening. 'Imād al-Dīn wrote that Saladin did not want to inflict losses on the Aleppans – "they are, after all, the soldiers of the Holy War" – but his "young men" were pugnacious and he had difficulty in holding them back.[98] Then, in a skirmish, his brother Būrī was wounded in the knee and after this Saladin decided to shift camp. If the psychological effect of his position by the Maidān al-Akhḍar had failed to force a surrender and if he was not going to use it as a base for an assault, then it was unnecessarily exposed. He moved round to the west, across the river Kuwaik, and camped on the slopes of Jabal Jaushan, where he ordered his builders to lay the foundations of what he wanted the Aleppans to believe would be a permanent settlement. This may have been a bluff, but at least it appears to show that he was no longer afraid of an immediate Frankish attack.

The Franks themselves, as is clear from William of Tyre's account, were not thinking of taking the offensive.[99] They realised that the fall of Aleppo would virtually complete the encirclement of their lands by Saladin, but they thought defensively in terms of strengthening their own fortifications. Bohemond of Antioch, "troubled by the nearness of so great an enemy", went to meet Baldwin at Acre, taking with him Raymond of Tripoli, and he was given a force of some 300 knights from the Kingdom of Jerusalem to help him defend his lands. Saladin knew of this, although he referred in a letter to Raymond rather than Bohemond, and he detached 'Izz al-Dīn Chāūlī from the army to help Ibn al-Muqaddam watch the frontier. Instructions were sent from the camp at Aleppo on 6 June: Chāūlī was to obey Ibn al-Muqaddam, the senior emir in Saladin's service, and enforce obedience to him; anyone who acted without or against his orders, who had fallen short in his service or who had been summoned and was slow to come, was to be reprimanded severely; "tell the emirs that it is those to whom Ibn al-Muqaddam is grateful who will earn our gratitude". Chāūlī was told that the Franks might ask about a truce, as they had been trying to negotiate on a number of occasions during the year; they had offered terms to which they would not keep, as when they saw what they coveted, they did not distinguish between right and wrong; Ibn al-Muqaddam would tell him of the interchange of messages and of the terms asked for and offered; the most recent development was the return of Taqī al-Dīn's envoys from Raymond of Tripoli, accompanied by Raymond's own messenger, who had said that his master was prepared to join in a truce and to help negotiate it (with Baldwin); Raymond said that he had gone to Jerusalem (presumably a reference to his visit to Baldwin) only for this purpose. But, for all these claims, Chāūlī was warned, only one thing was clear, which was that Raymond was mustering his men and joining forces with the other Franks. "His insincere nature is known; he says what he does not do and promises what he does not perform." Saladin added that he himself was in a situation where he had to overlook this, as he was seeking what would bring advantages in the longer term to Islam; as a result, if Chāūlī was approached about a truce, he was first to try to secure the release of Taqī al-Dīn's son (who had been surprisingly trapped by an offer of Frankish lands). He was then, apparently, free to make an agreement if the Franks accepted the conditions offered by Ibn al-Muqaddam, but if they demanded a stiffer price, then he was to consult Saladin.[100] The fact that Chāūlī was to obey Ibn al-Muqaddam, but then left to negotiate on his own, presumably shows that he had been sent to watch the frontier by Hama in Taqī al-Dīn's absence, where he would be expected to negotiate with Raymond of Tripoli, while Ibn al-Muqaddam at Damascus dealt with Baldwin.

Meanwhile, according to 'Imād al-Dīn, Saladin was acting with forbearance, clemency and an assumption of ignorance[101] – a reference to the line: "An ignorant man is not the leader of his people, but the leader is one who pretends to be ignorant." In spite of the absence of any real threat from the Franks, he had now changed his mind about the question of an exchange. The arguments against this were still the same. If he gave Sinjār and Nisībīn, then, as al-Fāḍil had pointed out, Taqī al-Dīn would certainly ask for replacements and he could probably stay at Aleppo without risk long enough to bankrupt Zangī. The most likely reason for his second thoughts was the fierceness of the Aleppan resistance. A long siege would damage his reputation and leave a legacy of resentment. At this stage he must have realised that his best chance was to come to terms with Zangī, who was negotiating through Ṭumān behind the backs of his own supporters.[102] Ṭumān's instructions are said to have been to press at least for al-Khābūr and Sinjār in exchange for Aleppo and to try to get al-Raqqa for himself. He succeeded in this and Saladin's need for a settlement can perhaps be seen in the fact that he added in Sarūj and Niṣībīn as well.[103] The arrangement, confirmed in writing by Saladin, was made on the evening of 11 June and on 12 June the citadel gates of Aleppo were opened.

Zangī's move took the emirs and people of Aleppo by surprise and Ibn al-'Adīm wrote that nobody knew what was happening until Saladin's standard was hoisted over the citadel.[104] Saladin himself had nothing to gain by taking advantage of this confusion and he sent in a conciliatory message. The Aleppans then picked two emirs to negotiate with him, one being Zain al-Dīn Bilik and the other 'Izz al-Dīn Jūrdīk, a man who, Saladin wrote, had been like a brother or a son to him in the days of Nūr al-Dīn, but who had remained faithful to the service of Aleppo from the time of the Syrian campaign of 1174.[105] Jūrdīk now entered Saladin's service and it must be assumed that arrangements were made for a general transfer of power. The only point of detail noted in the sources is that, according to Ibn al-'Adim, Saladin agreed to leave the offices of *khaṭīb* and *qāḍī* with the Hanafites, but then broke his promise on the prompting of Ḍiyā' al-Dīn 'Īsā and replaced the Hanafite holders – Ibn al-'Adīm's uncle and father – by Shāfi'ites.[106]

Zangī himself came out to a tent that had been pitched for him by Saladin, and, with his vizier Shams al-Dīn ibn al-Kāfī acting as intermediary, he began to settle the details of his move. There are some discrepancies of dating, but Saladin held a reception for Zangī probably on 13 June when, according to 'Imād al-Dīn, "it seemed as though two moons had met".[107] During the course of this, word was brought to Saladin that his brother Būrī had died of his wound but he hid his feelings and did not interrupt the reception. Zangī then ordered Ṭumān to hold the citadel until news came that the exchange had been completed and he himself left on 17 June. On 20 June word arrived that Sinjār, Niṣībīn and al-Khābūr had been handed over by Saladin's agents and on the next day Saladin entered the citadel, where Ṭumān entertained him.

Saladin had allowed Zangī to take with him all of the citadel's stores that he could remove and Ṭumān was left to sell off the remainder, a quantity of which was bought by Saladin himself.[108] Saladin was making good his claim that he wanted only "the stones of Aleppo"[109] and he was, in fact, acting with considerable generosity as he himself was short of money. He had written to tell al-'Ādil that "the word of Islam" was now united but he had again underlined the problems of expansion; the more money he had for disposal and the more lands that were added to his empire, the more recruits flocked to him, as a result of which there was no limit to his expenses.[110] In this context, he had noted elsewhere[111] that Yemen was of little use, as it was still in a state of confusion. Ṭughtekīn had been ill.[112] Khuṭlubā's men were apparently restive and al-'Ādil had been told to send out replacements so that the *iqṭā'* holders could return to their *iqṭā's*.[113] Khuṭlubā had arrested and then released Hiṭṭān, his predecessor in Zabīd, and had to be told not to drive 'Izz al-Dīn 'Uthmān in Aden to open disobedience. Saladin wrote to al-'Ādil: "up to now the lands are dependent on Egypt. We send letters there which are hopes and they come back as money."[114]

In spite of his earlier hesitation about the need for an exchange Saladin had no doubts about his success. To him Aleppo was "the key to the lands",[115] and he wrote to Ṭughtekīn: "this city is the eye of Syria and the citadel is its pupil".[116] In another letter he claimed: "we have given Zangī places that have not left our possession", a condition of the agreement being that Zangī was to come himself with his troops whenever he was needed, and Saladin added: "we have taken the dinar and given him the dirhams".[117] The people of Aleppo agreed with his estimate. Ibn al-Athīr wrote: "one of the common folk brought a wash-tub and water and shouted to Zangī: 'you are not fit to be a king but only to wash clothes'."[118] According to Ibn al-'Adīm, this same man complained that the Aleppans had fought without pay – "so what had led you to do what you did?"[119] In fact, Zangī, whose whole career had been one of disappointment, was paying for his imprudence in trying to establish himself west of the Euphrates. Any pretensions that he had as a contender for power had been decisively weakened and he had lost both money and reputation. A popular song was sung with the words: "this Zangī is mad", and the people shouted a catch-phrase about the donkey who had sold Aleppo for Sinjār (fresh for sour milk).[120]

13

EMPIRE-BUILDING AND THE HOLY WAR

For Saladin, the capture of Aleppo marked the end of some eight-and-a-half years of waiting since he had told Farrukh-Shāh, "we have only to do the milking and Aleppo will be ours",[1] and it closed the first major campaign that he had undertaken since al-Ṣāliḥ's death had opened his way to the north and east. From the standpoint of the Holy War a finite goal had been achieved and Saladin could now threaten the whole length of the Frankish coast. As his letters show, however, he was finding that the logical end to the cycle of expansion, where power depended on conquests, attracting recruits to be paid for by further conquests, was a power monopoly co-terminous with the frontiers of Islam. The obligation of the Holy War was still being stressed and a contemporary poem took the fall of Aleppo in the month of Ṣafar as an omen of the fall of Jerusalem in Rajab,[2] but it remained to be seen how far Saladin's inclination or circumstances would allow him to pursue it.

After spending one night in the citadel of Aleppo, he moved out to Ḥārim (map 3), the gambit pawn advanced towards Antioch. Since the fall of Gumushtekīn and the attack by the Count of Flanders in 1177/78, it had been held by Surkhak, described by 'Imād al-Dīn as "a minor Nurid *mamlūk*".[3] According to Ibn Abī Ṭayy, Saladin had offered him Buṣrā, property in Damascus, 30,000 dinars in cash and 10,000 dinars for his brother in exchange for the castle, but in an attempt to get better terms he had written to the Franks.[4] Not everyone believed this convenient accusation and another version, also quoted by Ibn Abī Ṭayy, makes Ḥasan of the Banū 'l-Dāya point out that the same thing had been said of him when he had held Ḥārim.[5] It is clear, however, that, whether or not any approach had been made to the Franks, there had been a quarrel amongst the troops of the garrison themselves. Surkhak was shut out of the castle and seized by Taqī al-Dīn, who had come with an advance guard, and when Saladin himself arrived, the castle gates were opened. Surkhak was later released, but not given any employment with Saladin.

Saladin explained the position by saying that Surkhak had been in touch with him, but had been making conditions – presumably asking for more than he had been offered; the garrison had then forced him out of the castle and proclaimed their allegiance to Saladin.[6] In another letter he described Surkhak as a man without religion or intelligence and said that he had arranged to hand Ḥārim over to Bohemond of Antioch, as was proved by his letters and witnessed by his envoys; he had conspired with men known as al-Shamsīya (sun worshippers), who acknowledged no Creator and "worshipped what they saw swimming in the river of day and setting in the ocean of the dark"; the garrison had expelled him and scattered his followers, after which he himself had been arrested outside Ḥārim by Taqī al-Dīn; Saladin had then received the castle's surrender and arranged for its defence. He added to this letter his own account of the capture of Aleppo, in which he claimed that Zangī had been betrayed by the Aleppan troops and people; "he then entered by the gate of supplication, which is never shut in the face of an entrant", and after that the Aleppans themselves had produced "their greatest plea, which was that they were brother Muslims"; Saladin had obeyed the Caliph's command to sheathe his sword and his wish was now that the armies of Islam should march together to attack their enemies and not be split by envy. He would not object to sharing command if this were possible in war, but, in fact, there could only be a single commander.[7]

In other letters he stressed that the conquest of Aleppo was merely a mile-stone in the road to victory in the Holy War. In one he wrote that, in gratitude to God, he was now going to attack the Armenians.[8] More generally, he told the governor of Baalbek, who was looking after Farrukh-Shāh's young son, Bahrām-Shāh, that he was planning to take steps that would anger the unbelievers.[9] He wrote to Hiṭṭān in Yemen that as all Muslim lands were now held either by himself or by his friends, he would show his gratitude by attacking the Franks[10] and in a letter to Ṭughtekīn he wrote: "Islam is now awake to drive away the night phantom of unbelief."[11]

Before he could move, however, there were a number of administrative details to be settled. He agreed to a truce with Bohemond of Antioch, who released a number of Muslim prisoners as a gesture of conciliation, and he gave A'zāz to 'Alam al-Dīn Sulaimān, who had earlier left Aleppo to join him. Aleppo itself was administered in the name of al-Ẓāhir, his fourth son, who was now ten years old, and the citadel was held by Saif al-Dīn Yāzkūj, a former *mamlūk* of Shīrkūh's, who had helped to rescue him during the assassination attempt at A'zāz.

A decree was read out abolishing the *mukūs* taxes – "none of our governors, emirs or officials is to stretch out his hand for these things" – "we give away lands and do not seek them as gifts".[12] It is likely to have been at this time that another decree forced non-Muslims in Aleppo to wear distinctive clothes, perhaps in an attempt to reconcile Shī'ites as well as Sunnīs to Ayyubid rule, but this proved too popular with the "fools and trouble makers"[13] of the city, who had to be restrained from insulting and abusing them.

'Imād al-Dīn wrote a number of diplomas for officials and professional men, three of which he recorded in the *Barq*.[14] One was for the Shaikh 'Alā' al-Dīn Mas'ūd, who was put in charge of the Hanafite colleges in Aleppo and al-Raqqa – although this latter town had been given to Ṭumān – with control over their endowments and the power to appoint or dismiss teachers. A diploma for the *muḥtasib* of Aleppo instructed him to ensure that the Shī'ites did not slander those of the Prophet's companions of whom they disapproved; competent craftsmen, certified by "knowledgeable men", were to be allowed to continue the practice of their craft, but shoddy work and fraudulence were to be checked; quacks were to be kept from treating patients and from prescribing or selling unknown drugs; jugglers and soothsayers were to be banned and the *muḥtasib* was to see that mosques and "houses of worship" were not used as shops or stores. Another diploma was for a doctor, "skilled in dissecting limbs...with a knowledge of the four elements", who was given a fixed salary and ordered to continue his service in the citadel. In his case it is not stated whether he could appoint his own deputies, but this permission is found in another diploma, written for one of Saladin's own doctors, Ibn al-Miṭrān.[15]

The details in these diplomas are duplicated in many other Islamic documents and they are quoted here only to show how the ruling group could influence society by controlling crafts and professions both directly and by the extension of its authority through its own nominees. In more general terms, the problems of the relationship of a dynasty to the large number of groups that comprised its subjects could be simplified and the dynasty strengthened if a stratified concept of society was superimposed on its cellular structure, that is, specifically, if a professional class could be encouraged to develop, divorced as far as possible from its origins, in direct dependence on and relaying the orders of, a ruling class.

Saladin's arrangements took time and it was not until 14 August that he was able to move. He took with him troops from Aleppo and from across the Euphrates, as well as a number of Turkmans, and marching on average some 20 miles (32 km) a day, he followed his usual route by Hama, Homs and the Biqā' valley to Damascus, which he reached by 24 August. The Franks were taking care not to be caught off guard and had mustered at Sepphoris. Unfortunately for them, Baldwin, who was becoming more gravely affected by his leprosy, had fallen ill at Nazareth and his condition was so serious that his brother-in-law, Guy de Lusignan, was appointed as his lieutenant, a position which, in the opinion of many, he was unfitted to hold. There were various suggestions as to what Saladin might do.[16] Some thought that he would return to Beirut and others that he would try to take the castles of Ḥunīn and Tibnīn to the east of Tyre. There was an obvious possibility that he might make for Kerak or Shaubak again, while optimists hoped that after his long campaign he would return to Egypt to rest his army and collect supplies. Saladin himself stayed at Damascus for just over three weeks and then moved out on 17 September to camp at Jisr al-Khashab 10 miles (16 km) to the south.

Sometime before his expedition he had received a message from the Caliph. In reply to his letter of complaint from Sarūj, the Caliph had sent him a diploma phrased with some finesse to avoid any definite reference to lands or cities. It did not mention Mosul or the Jazīra, but covered all territories that Saladin could take from those who disobeyed the Caliph's orders. Saladin replied: "to the foot of the Caliph the Muslim says: 'would that I were a clod of earth' "; steps were being taken to spread news of the arrival of the diploma, "removing its contents from being absent on paper to being present in men's minds". He interpreted it as giving him what was held by all those "whose actions in their lands are not sound and the balance of whose loyalty does not incline to Baghdad"; his gratitude would be shown by deeds rather than by words and he was beginning to fulfil his obligations by attacking the infidels, "before waging a Holy War on those who have abandoned their allegiance" (a clear threat that he intended to march again on Mosul); his letter was sent as he was setting out with the defenders of the faith and the friends and servants of the Caliph. Before he left, however, he had been approached by envoys from Ḥadītha and Takrīt, whose masters, he said, wanted to join his service but were afraid of the Mosulis. These towns, on the Euphrates and the Tigris respectively, were within some 130 miles (209 km) of Baghdad and any troops sent there would be within a week's march of the Caliph (map 8). This clearly called for tact and Saladin wrote that, although he considered that the towns were covered by the terms of his diploma, because of their position he wanted special permission to include them in any possible peace settlement or to defend them if the Mosulis chose to remain hostile; he would obey the Caliph's orders and not act on his own – "Were it not for the fact that to disregard the future benefit of these people would harm others who are obedient to the Caliph, the servant would not have brought the matter to the Caliph's knowledge nor written of it."[17]

On 21 September he sent a second letter to Baghdad from Jisr al-Khashab, which again showed that he was not exclusively concerned with the Franks. He started by saying that he was about to attack the unbelievers in the heart of their lands, where they had mustered their men and brought out the Cross. They had raised large sums of money to prepare their defences, but "the servant offers himself before his money, his money before his family and his family before his men"; other Muslim rulers had either had the power to attack the Franks but not the will, or else the will without the power; he did not say this in order to criticise his predecessors, but merely to remind himself of it, lest he should feel over-confident and believe that this could not happen to him; other rulers were concerned to conquer lands to gain wealth, while he himself not only did not exact illegal dues from his subjects, but gave away his lawfully gathered wealth to the poor: he was not, he complimented himself, in the habit of mentioning these things, but he wanted the Caliph to know that he had a servant who only took what was legally allowed him and who "entered houses through their doors".[18]

A week after he had written this letter, Saladin moved from Jisr al-Khashab on his way to the Jordan. According to 'Imād al-Dīn, he crossed on 29 September by the ford of al-Ḥusainīya and attacked Baisān, which was found to be empty.[19] If this ford is to be identified as that of Shaikh Ḥusain, which lies almost due east of Baisān, it would mean that he had not repeated his march of July 1182, when he had passed directly beneath the castle of Kaukab, but had stayed on the east side of the Jordan. This is partially confirmed by William of Tyre, who wrote that the people of Baisān fled to Tiberias,[20] which would have been impossible without a long detour had Saladin been advancing down the west bank (map 2).

On 30 September, after sacking and burning the empty town, he moved westwards up the Harod valley, the scene of his earlier battle with the Franks. He sent out an advance guard commanded by Chāūlī, who had presumably rejoined him on his march past Hama, and 'Izz al-Dīn Jūrdīk, whose first campaign this was in his service. They intercepted Frankish reinforcements from Kerak and Shaubak, who were marching on the Nablus road, and took a number of prisoners. Meanwhile, the main Frankish force had been waiting for news and when they heard that Saladin was at Baisān, they moved from Sepphoris over the Nazareth hills to al-Fūla, in the Jezreel valley west of Mt Moreh. This is a direct distance of less than 10 miles (16 km), but must have represented a day's march for a large force across a range of hills. According to William of Tyre, they numbered 1300 cavalry and 15,000 infantry,[21] a figure that agrees well enough with 'Imād al-Dīn's estimate of 1500 lances, 1500 Turkopoles and 15,000 foot.[22] Their march from Sepphoris can be dated to 30 September and on 1 October Saladin heard that they were at al-Fūla. He himself had moved 9 miles (14 km) up the Harod valley from Baisān to 'Ain Jālūt, by the modern settlement of Gidona. He now sent out 500 skirmishers against the Franks and drew up the rest of his army in battle order. William of Tyre wrote that he had taken up his position, "with a huge force of excellent and carefully picked men", "near the waters".[23] In this context William mentioned "the spring of Tubania", which can be identified as 'Ain Tuba'ūn, 1 mile from 'Ain Jālūt on the north side of the stream known as Nahr Jālūt. 'Ain Tuba'ūn is in open country, but 'Ain Jālūt itself is directly beneath the slopes of Gilboa.

When the Franks advanced, to their surprise Saladin did not give battle but unexpectedly moved off down the Nahr Jālūt. The Frankish force was reckoned to be the largest that the Kingdom had ever produced from its own resources. At that, however, it was clearly outmatched by the Muslims, who were reported by the Arab historians to be "in vast numbers",[24] and Saladin's move can best be explained in terms of geography. His 500 skirmishers were presumably intended to test the discipline of the Frankish march and to see whether they could be tempted to break formation. If this had happened in open ground, then Saladin's numbers could have been used to engage their cavalry and infantry separately in the hopes of destroying them piecemeal. In fact, however, the Franks kept their cavalry screened by their infantry, thus protecting their horses to some extent from Muslim arrows. Saladin could not halt their advance altogether without committing his squadrons to a massed formation vulnerable to an armoured charge. He could still, of course, harass them as they marched, but any troops posted to block off 'Ain Jālūt itself could be crushed against the steep hillside behind it. By drawing back, he was losing an immediate chance of fighting a decisive battle, but apparently he was content to wait for his opponents to make mistakes.

The Franks now established themselves at 'Ain Jālūt with their backs to the hill. Saladin himself camped temptingly close, while his raiders spread out to ravage as much unguarded territory as they could reach. They attacked Zar'īn within 2 miles of 'Ain Jālūt itself on the slopes to the west of it, and Forbelet (Taiyiba) on the northern boundary ridge of the Harod valley. According to William of Tyre, some even climbed Mt Tabor, where the monks, helped by refugees from the surrounding countryside, defended the fortified monastery.[25] Raiders were seen on the hills above Nazareth and many of the townspeople were said to have been crushed to death as they fled for shelter into the principal church.

Meanwhile, the Frankish army was running short of food. Saladin's attack had coincided with the end of the pilgrimage season, which closed with the approach of winter and rough weather at sea. Pilgrims and the Italian sailors who were about to take them back had left their ships to join the muster, but had taken no provisions with them. It seems from this that if Saladin had concentrated on cutting off their supply lines, he must have succeeded in forcing an action. It may be that he did not realise his opportunity or that his men were too concerned with plunder. William of Tyre reported some Frankish losses but said that escorted convoys got through and the Arabic sources make no reference to any plans for starving out the Franks.

In spite of this, there was discontent in the Frankish army. "Simple people without experience of the malice of the leaders"[26] could not understand why no attack was made on Saladin's camp. There was an encouraging historical precedent. Gideon had "pitched beside the well of Harod", at or near the Frankish position, while "the Midianites and the Amalekites and all the children of the east lay along in the valley like grasshoppers for multitude",[27] and the night attack of his 300 men had routed this vastly superior force. Guy de Lusignan, however, "a man totally useless in affairs of this magnitude",[28] had neither the imagination nor the authority of Gideon. It was suggested that jealousy of his position caused the other leaders, including Raymond of Tripoli, to remain inactive, but it was also argued that Saladin's camp was too strong to attack and that his forces were waiting to surround the Franks if they came out. 'Imād al-Dīn wrote that Saladin had been hoping for a Frankish attack – "every day we expected them to charge, rushing into battle as was their custom"[29] – but he was not prepared to break the stalemate himself and by 5 October his emirs were themselves complaining of a shortage of provisions. He decided to draw off and marched out of the valley towards Mt Tabor, claiming that he was still hoping for a battle: "they may pursue us and we shall then turn back against them".[30] The Franks did, in fact, now move back to their base at Sepphoris, across the Nazareth hills. Saladin implied that they had retired into their mountains in order to avoid battle, but by this time it was clear that he had no plans for staying west of the Jordan. He re-crossed to the east bank and William of Tyre was left to console his readers with a minor miracle of the fish that had providentially appeared in the waters of 'Ain Jālūt during the period of the army's stay, although normally there were few if any to be found there.[31]

On his return Saladin wrote to tell the Caliph that the Franks appeared unwilling to risk an action, however large their numbers might be and however much damage might be done to their lands; he himself was planning to go to Kerak, from where he would send back his Egyptian troops and meet their replacements. He ended his letter with an oblique reference to the Mosulis, remarking that the Caliph should know that his servants were only kept from carrying out the obligations of Islam (the Holy War) when "someone" prevented them.[32]

Although this had not been mentioned in Saladin's letter, the *rendezvous* for the Egyptian forces at Kerak was more important than usual on this occasion. Al-'Ādil himself was leaving Egypt and Taqī al-Dīn was being sent to take his place. This was the first major administrative reshuffle since Tūrān-Shāh had been sent back from Syria and it is not clear how much significance should be read into it. Al-'Ādil, as 'Imād al-Dīn noted,[33] had been the virtual ruler of Egypt in Saladin's absence, but in spite of this it is he who is credited with the initiative, as he wanted to be given Aleppo. According to an account quoted by Ibn Abī Ṭayy, Saladin had been forced to borrow at least 150,000 dinars from him, after which he had asked for

Aleppo. Ibn Abī Ṭayy's version goes on to say that al-'Ādil asked for a bill of sale, but Saladin insisted that Aleppo could only be given as an *iqṭā'*: "do you think that [these] places can be sold and do you not know that they belong to the people who are stationed in them?... We are the treasurers of the Muslims."[34]

At first sight, Aleppo seems a poor substitute for Egypt, even though the lands that went with it extended to Ra'bān in the north, the Euphrates in the east and Hama in the south. Al-'Ādil, however, must have known that another clash with Mosul was almost inevitable and he may have hoped to extend his power by moving east of the Euphrates. Taqī al-Dīn, as al-Fāḍil had suggested, must presumably have been asking for replacements for the *iqṭā's* of Sinjār and Niṣībīn, and this exchange allowed Saladin to satisfy both him and, apparently, al-'Ādil without the need for further conquests. The loser in the exchange was Saladin's son al-Ẓāhir, who later talked of his distress at being forced to leave Aleppo after only six months, but he was as yet too young to have to be considered seriously.

Saladin left Damascus on 22 October and, after moving through the Sharāh district to the east of the Dead Sea, he camped at al-Rabba, 6½ miles (10 km) north of Kerak. The local Muslims asked him for protection and 'Imād al-Dīn wrote: "Muslims had lived in these parts from ancient times, but their children had been brought up under Frankish rule. They had been afraid to show their affection for us and so had concealed it."[35] The castle of Kerak itself stands on a north/south tongue of land surrounded by wadis. It is cut off on the south from the higher ground of the hill Umm al-Thalj by a deep fosse and another fosse separated it on the north from the township with which it shared its plateau. Reynald de Châtillon was said to have had warning of the attack and to have brought in what were thought to be enough troops to defend it.[36] When Saladin moved up from al-Rabba, Reynald refused to allow the townspeople to move their goods into the shelter of the castle and tried, mistakenly, to defend the plateau itself. Its sides are steep but by no means unscalable and the out-numbered garrison failed to hold them. The Muslims were almost able to force an entrance into the castle itself as they followed the retreating Franks and the town with all its contents was plundered. Saladin now used it as a base and set up seven mangonels, which kept up a day-and-night bombardment of the castle.[37]

Al-'Ādil arrived on 22 November, bringing with him a caravan of Egyptian merchants as well as his own household and replacements for Saladin's troops. Al-Fāḍil sent a letter to Taqī al-Dīn to give him the news, adding that the towers of Kerak were prostrate in worship; the veils of their mantlets had been removed and their noses cut off; when Taqī al-Dīn arrived, the promised hour of victory would not be slow in coming.[38] Al-Fāḍil's optimism complements the pessimistic picture painted by William of Tyre. Saladin's attack had coincided with the marriage of Humphrey IV of Toron, the step-son of Reynald and son of Etiennette de Milly, to Isabella, the younger sister of King Baldwin.[39] The castle was full of actors, minstrels and the like, who had come for the wedding and the numbers of these useless mouths were increased by the local "Syrians" with their wives and children. There were so many of them that the garrison could not move freely about their duties; the one mangonel they managed to set up attracted such a barrage of stones that it was never used and the Muslims became daring enough to let themselves down by ropes into the fosse to plunder whatever they found there.

Surprisingly, Saladin did not press home his advantage. According to 'Imād al-Dīn, he had not brought with him a large enough siege train,[40] which appears to be contradicted by the evidence. Ibn al-'Adīm said that, although the walls were breached, the Muslims were unable to fill in the fosse and so were prevented from attacking.[41] The Franks had prepared a relief force which moved to the southern end of the Dead Sea. According to 'Imād al-Dīn, Saladin heard of this at the end of the month of Rajab (18 November),[42] that is, before the arrival of al-Ādil and Taqī al-Dīn, but in spite of his claim to the Caliph that he was looking for battle, he made no move to challenge the rescuers. Taqī al-Dīn was sent off to Egypt on 3 December and Saladin himself raised the siege and marched north with al-'Ādil on the next day.

It is clear from this that the attack on Kerak, fierce as it was, was not intended to be pressed home at all costs, nor was Saladin prepared to go out of his way to force a field action. One problem that he faced was how to get the best out of his men and here there was no rigid code of discipline on which he could rely. Sanctions could be taken against *iqṭā'* holders and others dependent on him for money, and in extreme cases it was thought reasonable for a commander to kill those who disobeyed his orders. But there was a constant problem of desertion and Saladin, who preferred to encourage rather than to punish, seems to have taken considerable care not to press his troops too far. Sieges were unpopular; the fast of Ramaḍān was approaching and 'Imād al-Dīn wrote that the army was tired.[43] Saladin himself had his diplomatic campaign to wage and in view of all these points it is not surprising that he slackened his pressure. His attack had served to interchange his Egyptian troops; for the first time he had forced his way into the township of Kerak and explored the possibilities of using it as a base for an attack on the castle and he had added credit to his account in the Holy War. He returned to Damascus on 12 December and the Syrian troops were allowed to rest, "in preparation", 'Imād al-Dīn wrote, "for the coming year".[44]

Al-'Ādil was now given a diploma covering Manbij, one of Taqī al-Dīn's former *iqṭā's*, as well as Aleppo, and he left Damascus for the north on 19 December. His secretary, al-Ṣanī'a b. al-Naḥḥāl, was sent on ahead to make arrangements for the transfer of the city and the citadel, and al-'Ādil himself arrived at Aleppo on 8 January. The Aleppans were quick to find a grievance. Al-Ṣanī'a, who was now put in charge of al-'Ādil's chancellery, was a Christian who had turned to Islam in order to marry a Muslim girl[45] and the number of Christians whom he employed prompted a poem: "the religion of the Messiah has the upper hand over all others in the reign of al-'Ādil. There is a Christian emir, a Christian vizier, a Christian governor and a Christian overseer of the *dīwān*."[46]

Al-Fāḍil had gone to Egypt with Taqī al-Dīn, with instructions to come back to Saladin as quickly as possible. He kept up his usual flow of letters and the volume of this correspondence can be judged from the fact that, when he wrote to 'Imād al-Dīn from Eilat, three-and-a-half days after having left Saladin at Kerak, he had already received one letter from him and one from Saladin.[47] To start with, he was concerned about the difficulties of the journey. He wrote from Ṣudr, which he reached in eleven days from Kerak, including those of departure and arrival, to say that it had not been a question of tiring the riding beasts but of killing them through forced marches, first to avoid the Franks and then, on the second stage from Eilat to Ṣudr, in order to reach water.[48] After his arrival in Egypt he had more serious problems to record. In a letter to Saladin in Ramaḍān (18 December 1183/16 January 1184) he explained that he was not going to use code, as this would destroy the pleasure of those who looked at his letter or listened to it being read out; there was nothing in it that would be harmful if it fell into enemy hands, except for what he had to say about Egyptian finances; the affairs of Egypt, however, were in an extraordinary state and if he started to explain them, he would be opening doors that should be kept closed; the difficulties were caused by those who had come back from the Syrian campaign; soldiers had official notes granting them increases in pay or authorising money to be transferred to them, without the place from which it was to be taken being specified; merchants had credits from the treasury that had to be paid off and rich emirs would send in their servants or companions, who had to be shown favours; "some of even higher rank, our sultans", were doing the same thing and al-Fāḍil made it clear to whom he was referring, when he added that al-'Ādil had given orders that had to be obeyed. He went on to say that in the case of other rulers, shortness of money was caused either by meanness of spirit or lack of lands, but Saladin's difficulties were caused by the numbers of his men; army pay for one district of Egypt came to a figure of 5 million dinars: money paid to *faqīhs*, Quran reciters, teachers and doctors, as well as under such headings as poor-relief, robes of honour and gifts for kings, expenditure on fortifications and on the fleet, etc, came to a million dinars (a year); men had recorded with admiration the generosity of kings who had perhaps once in their lives given someone 10,000 or 5000 dirhams: "how would it be were they to see one who gives away every day in one district of his empire 17,000 dinars?"[49]

In his letter, al-Fādil referred to the arrival of messengers from "the kings" at Damascus and 'Imād al-Dīn wrote that envoys from Ḥadītha and Takrīt had reached an agreement with Saladin and that other envoys had come from Sanjar-Shāh of Jazīrat ibn 'Umar and from Zain al-Dīn Yūsuf of Irbil.[50] Sanjar-Shāh, who was now about twenty years old, had been promised Mosul by his father, Saif al-Dīn Ghāzī, and was said to bear a grudge against his uncle, 'Izz al-Dīn. Zain al-Dīn Yūsuf, the brother of Keukburī of Ḥarrān, had been allowed by the Mosulis to succeed his father, Zain al-Dīn 'Alī-Kuchuk in the possession of Irbil. Jazīrat ibn 'Umar is on the Tigris some 85 miles (137 km) north of Mosul and Irbil is some 50 miles (80 km) to the east of it (map 8). Geographically, both form part of the upper Tigris region and in terms of recent history both were within the sphere of influence of Mosul. The fall of Aleppo, however, had obviously weakened Mosul and for all Saladin's insistence that he was now turning to the Holy War, no formal treaty had been made to resolve the quarrel between him and 'Izz al-Dīn. 'Izz al-Dīn had mistakenly arrested his administrator, Qaimāz, another false move attributed by Ibn al-Athīr to the evil genius of Zulfindār,[51] and Sanjar-Shāh together with Zain al-Dīn Yūsuf, freed from Qaimāz's control, saw an opportunity for self-advancement. By 25 February 1184, when an embassy arrived from Mosul accompanied by the Shaikh al-Shuyūkh, Saladin had agreed to support the dissidents, thus throwing down a deliberate and unavoidable challenge to 'Izz al-Dīn.

There are some missing pieces to account for here. 'Imād al-Dīn quotes a letter from Saladin to Taqī al-Dīn in which he said that there was now abundant pasturage and they had no excuse for abandoning the Holy War in this year; he was preparing to move to Aleppo at the end of February and was calling for a muster of his troops there.[52] Aleppo was the base for an attack on Antioch but any muster there could also threaten Mosul. A letter from al-Fāḍil shows that before the arrival of the Shaikh al-Shuyūkh, an envoy from Saladin had returned from Mosul bringing a conciliatory message from 'Izz al-Dīn. Al-Fāḍil went on to say that the door of Saladin's clemency was always open, that it was a characteristic of his that he would not dispatch a wounded man and that nothing now remained except the Holy War.[53] Obviously, 'Izz al-Dīn was the "wounded man", whom al Fāḍil thought should now be left alone, and the implication may be that Saladin, by broadcasting his intention of gathering troops, had frightened 'Izz al-Dīn into granting some concessions, after which he gave up the idea of an early spring muster. At that, however, whether or not 'Izz al-Dīn had been ready to come to terms before the attempted defection of Sanjar-Shāh and Zain al-Dīn Yūsuf, the loss of their lands was more than he could allow to pass unchallenged.

His supporters, including al-Pahlawān's brother Qyzyl-Arslān, Shāh-Arman, 'Imād al-Dīn Zangī and Qilij-Arslān, had sent messengers to Damascus, but it was the Mosul embassy under the Qādī Muḥī al-Dīn al-Shahrazūrī that had to conduct the vital negotiations, with the Shaikh al-Shuyūkh to hold the ring. Muḥī al-Dīn had earlier criticised the Shaikh for his behaviour in 1182, asking: "were you sent as an envoy or to provoke slaughter?",[54] but according to Ibn Shaddād, who was himself with the Mosulis, 'Izz al-Dīn had asked the Caliph to send him "as a messenger and an intercessor", on the grounds that he was respected both in Baghdad and by Saladin.[55] His visit started unhappily with the death of his son, who had fallen ill on the journey and had been carried to Damascus on a litter. Three days were spent in mourning and 'Imād al-Dīn wrote: "the heat of the embassy was chilled".[56] Gloom spread as far as Egypt. Al-Fāḍil wrote to 'Imād al-Dīn that rumours had been heard from Turks and Bedouin about the loss; he had thought of sending a letter of condolence to the Shaikh, but had hoped that the news might prove false and for two days he had had no pleasure in food, drink or conversation; he had then decided not to write, as it was said that condolence after three days was a renewal of misfortune.[57]

The negotiations themselves were equally unfortunate. Muḥī al-Dīn had been a fellow-student of 'Imād al-Dīn's at the Niẓāmīya College in Baghdad and 'Imād al-Dīn wrote: "this time they [unspecified] turned him aside from taking counsel with me and prevented him from talking to me. Had he asked my advice, I would have told him the proper approach."[58] Instead of this, he behaved "as though he were Gabriel, bringing down the revelation from heaven",[59] thinking that he was doing his master a service; Saladin "matched his roughness with smoothness", but his intransigence was a bar to agreement.

In fact, the real bar was the fact that Saladin had already committed himself to support those whom 'Izz al-Dīn had every right to consider as rebels against his authority. 'Imād al-Dīn went on to say that he was summoned by Saladin one morning and told to prepare a draft agreement, presumably to preserve the *status quo*, and he pointed out that Saladin would have to make an exception "for those who trusted in your word [Sanjar-Shāh and Zain al-Dīn Yūsuf]...but these Mosulis will not agree to any exception". Saladin said: "write me something that may keep me from breaking my word", and 'Imād al-Dīn then suggested that the lords in question should be allowed to choose which side they wanted to join. Saladin told him to go to the Shaikh al-Shuyūkh to get his consent and also to approach the Qāḍī Muḥī al-Dīn, as on this basis he himself would be prepared to swear to a treaty. The Shaikh agreed, but Muḥī al-Dīn, not unreasonably, refused – "These men are in our lands and are our deputies and under our authority. If they come out against us, then obviously this is a breach of unity... Excuse yourselves to them by saying: 'we only received you at a time of anger, but now there is perfect peace'."[60]

At this point negotiations broke down. Saladin had called in al-'Ādil from Aleppo to help, but neither he nor anyone else could find a way out of the impasse. Al-'Ādil arrived on 19 March and on 22 March the Mosul delegation left Damascus. The Shaikh al-Shuyūkh refused to accept the customary presents marking the end of a mission, normally a sign of anger but in this case a gesture attributed by 'Imād al-Dīn to the lofty spirit that made him give away even the food provided for him to his escort.[61] According to this account Saladin now had second thoughts and said: "I feel shame before the Shaikh al-Shuyūkh." He sent 'Imād al-Dīn to tell the Shaikh that he would allow him to dictate the terms of an agreement and word was also sent to the Mosulis. Muḥī al-Dīn, however, "on seeing Saladin's humility exalted himself and said: 'After what has happened I have no desire to exchange messages until I have returned to my master who singled me out for this embassy... We have one who is joined to us, protects us and inclines to us' – by which he meant al-Pahlawān." This annoyed Saladin and 'Imād al-Dīn went on: "the Qāḍī had been sent to quench the fire, but had kindled it." Saladin had been lukewarm about marching again on Mosul, but was now prompted to do so – "All these things can be attributed to that speech."

The full implications of this are obscure. 'Imād al-Dīn's reference to the hardening of Saladin's resolve to attack Mosul may be true in its context. The propaganda campaign had shown that ever since he had left Mosul he had been thinking of going back, but there was no point in this if he could get what he wanted without fighting. Muḥī al-Dīn's remark: "now there is perfect peace", reinforces the suggestion that 'Izz al-Dīn was ready to be conciliatory and al-Fāḍil, at least, seems to have thought that no expedition would be needed. It had been shown, however, that the Mosulis still had a sticking point, beyond which they would turn for help to al-Pahlawān, and this must have convinced Saladin that if he wanted his own way, he would have to fight for it. It is difficult to see exactly what he meant by his final offer to accept the Shaikh al-Shuyūkh's terms. If he broke his word and abandọned Sanjar-Shāh and Zain al-Dīn Yūsuf, his position east of the Euphrates would be endangered. Similarly, if Muḥī al-Dīn was about to be granted favourable terms, petulance alone on his part seems too naive an explanation for a lost opportunity. The Shaikh al-Shuyūkh may have had some compromise of his own, but there is no word of what it could have been. All that is clear is that Saladin convinced at least his own apologists that he was not responsible for breaking off the talks. The Shaikh al-Shuyūkh went back to Baghdad to report and Saladin was apparently prepared to wait without moving against Mosul until he returned.

At the start of the Muslim year 580 (14 April 1184) Saladin instructed 'Imād al-Dīn to write a diploma for Zain al-Dīn Yūsuf, covering, amongst other territories, Irbil and its citadel, Shahrazūr and the basin of the Great Zāb.[62] He presumably claimed the right to dispose of these lands, which he had never himself held, by his interpretation of the Caliph's last diploma and in itself this was no more than a gesture on his part, to which the Mosulis replied with an ineffective one of their own. 'Izz al-Dīn released his former administrator, Qaimāz, who was sent to get help from al-Pahlawān and from his brother Qyzyl-Arslān, Lord of Azerbaijan. Qyzyl-Arslān provided him with a force of 3000 horse for an attack on Irbil, but they proved to be undisciplined and incompetent. Zain al-Dīn Yūsuf surprised them when they were busy looting his villages and they were routed with the loss of their plunder and their equipment. Ibn al-Athīr quoted Qaimāz as saying on his return to Mosul: "I saw those '*ajamīs* doing things which I thought no Muslim would do to fellow Muslims. I used to forbid them, but they would not listen."[63]

In the meanwhile Saladin was slowly mustering men for another campaign against the Franks. There had been heavy rain together with snow in the winter which had made movement difficult and had led al-Fāḍil to hope that this was the soap which would wash clean the filth of unbelief.[64] In April, when "the grip of the cold had slackened", Saladin moved to the Biqā' and Maqrīzī noted that on 21 April letters from him arrived in Egypt calling for men, money and arms.[65] On 31 May Nūr al-Dīn Muḥammad arrived in Aleppo to pay of his debt of gratitude for the gift of Āmid. His vizier, 'Imād al-Dīn's friend Qawwām al-Dīn 'Abd Allāh, went on ahead to present his master's services to Saladin and Nūr al-Dīn Muḥammad himself left Aleppo in the company of al-'Ādil on 8 June. They were obviously in no great hurry and were met by Saladin in the Biqā' on 20 June. In the month of Rabī'a I (12 June – 11 July) Saladin wrote to tell the Shaikh al-Shuyūkh that reinforcements had been summoned from Egypt, while troops had been collected from Syria and east of the Euphrates; Nūr al-Dīn Muḥammad had arrived, as had the forces of the Lord of Mārdīn, together with the Lord of Dārā and Sharaf al-Dīn,[66] a brother of 'Izz al-Dīn of Mosul and a surprising addition to the list. 'Imād al-Dīn, who quoted Saladin's letter, makes no further reference here to Sharaf al-Dīn and as he was credited with leading the troops of Sinjār, who were, in fact, commanded by Ṭumān, Saladin was perhaps deliberately exaggerating the contrast between 'Izz al-Dīn, obstinately unreconciled, and his brother who was content to serve the Islamic cause.

After camping outside Damascus for some time, Saladin finally moved towards Ra's al-Mā' on 13 July and according to 'Imād al-Dīn he reached Frankish territory on 16 July.[67] He apparently slanted eastwards, following the line of the modern route from 'Ammān to Ziza and then crossing towards the head of the valley of the Arnon to come down the line of the Wādī Sanīna to al-Rabba (map 2). Taqī al-Dīn, bringing with him al-Fāḍil and the remainder of al-'Ādil's household, had left Egypt on 12 July and Saladin occupied the time until his arrival at the end of the month by ravaging Frankish territory. According to Maqrīzī, the Aleppan troops reached 'Ammān on 18 August and Kerak on 22 August,[68] which agrees with Ibn Shaddād's remark that Kerak was surrounded on 23 August.[69]

Saladin presumably had more than one reason for not bringing up his whole force simultaneously. He needed men to contain the garrison, to serve his mangonels and to make the necessary preparations for an assault across the castle fosse. This, however, had a frontage of no more than 150 metres and too large a force would merely drain his supplies for no gain in efficiency. Further, an offensive/defensive detachment left by the Damascus frontier might deter the Franks from moving round to the south of the Dead Sea as they had done during the 1183 siege, and if they crossed to the north of it, Saladin could trap them by a pincer attack. Finally, according to Ibn Wāṣil, he was anxious to prevent Nūr al-Dīn Muḥammad from running blindly into difficulties and may well have been glad of an excuse to leave him in reserve under the supervision of al-'Ādil.[70]

Meanwhile he himself, together with Taqī al-Dīn, prepared the way for an assault. The township of Kerak was again taken as a base. Nine mangonels were set up against the north front of the castle and the outer defences were destroyed so that 'Imād al-Dīn could write that the only remaining obstacle was the wide, deep fosse.[71] Abū Shāma quoted from optimistic letters in which al-Fāḍil wrote: "no Frank can put his head out without receiving an arrow in the eye... The towers and fortifications opposite the mangonels have been destroyed...nothing remains but to fill in the fosse... Not one of us is to be heard grumbling or is discontented. This assault, God willing, will lead to victory."[72] Saladin protected his sappers by having covered ways constructed and in a letter to Nūr al-Dīn Muḥammad he reported that work on filling the fosse had progressed so far that a fettered prisoner had been able to jump down from the wall and make his escape unharmed.[73] It was presumably at this stage that the reserves were called in for a final effort. Al-'Ādil and Nūr al-Dīn Muḥammad arrived on 26 August; on 30 August, newly-erected mangonels joined in the bombardment, but at this point a Frankish relief force moved to the rescue.

When Saladin heard that the Franks had crossed the Jordan, he promptly raised the siege, burnt his machines and moved over 40 miles (64 km) north to Ḥisbān. Here he had a commanding position at the edge of the plateau of Moab and was well placed both to observe and to block any Frankish advance. Ibn Jubair, who was in Damascus at the time, heard that the Franks had tried to cut his supply lines and that the two armies had raced each other to "the water", the race being won by Saladin.[74] If he had been in a hurry, his cavalry could have made the 40-mile journey in a day, but, similarly, the journey from Jerusalem to Ḥisbān is no more than a day's ride and unless Saladin had raised the siege prematurely, Ibn Jubair's version must be wrong. Ibn Jubair did not himself know the country and his "water" may be Ma'īn, in this case the wadi that bounds Ḥisbān on the east, while the reported Frankish camp site at al-Wāla has been identified as El-Al (Elealeh), an isolated hill 2 miles (3 km) north of Ḥisbān across the plateau. 'Imād al-Dīn, however, wrote that the Franks could only be reached by rough and difficult ways[75] and the *Chronicle* of Ernoul, which has telescoped the 1183 and 1184 sieges, made Saladin camp within two leagues of them.[76] This distance, together with 'Imād al-Dīn's description, would better suit 'Ain Awaleh, some 6 miles (10 km) from Ḥisbān near the head of the Wādī Nuṣarīyat, but the point cannot be proved as no further details are given, 'Imād al-Dīn wrote: "we said: 'we shall blockade them...and wait patiently until they come out' ",[77] but after some time when they had made no move, Saladin drew off. According to Ernoul, the Franks were convinced that he was going home, but the Arabic sources insist that he was trying to tempt them from their camp in order to force a battle. Chāulī was ordered to watch them, but the Franks caught him off guard by a night march through "the narrows", a side road over rough ground, according to Ibn Jubair,[78] and 'Imād al-Dīn was left to write: "we regretted the lost opportunity and the escape of the bird from the net".[79]

Saladin had not apparently distinguished himself. No irreparable damage had been done to Kerak, which still stood as "an obstruction in the throat" of Islam.[80] If he had really wanted a field action, then he had thrown away the advantage of a far stronger tactical position. The Franks had waited until he had called in his forces from the Damascus border and had then drawn him from Kerak merely by halting on his lines of communication. Kerak was the centre of a cultivated region and had he temporarily risked his supplies to press an assault on the castle, the relief force would presumably have had to fight him on his own terms. As it was, they outmanoeuvred him and broke the siege without a blow being struck. It may be that he had been afraid of being caught between the garrison and the relief force, but another possibility is that, in spite of the scale of his operations, he was still thinking in razzia terms. In that case, it could be argued that it was he who had outmanoeuvred the Franks. He had brought them to the east of the Jordan and while they marched south to Kerak, he could pick his point for a raid on the now vulnerable west bank.

In the event, he chose to attack Nablus, which suggests that his army went up to Wādī al-Fāri'a from the Jordan. There is some doubt about his own actions. Ibn Shaddād states definitely that he sent raiders out and they later returned to him,[81] while 'Imād al-Dīn merely confuses the issue with ambiguities.[82] Baldwin had no doubt that Saladin himself was on the west bank[83] and it seems likely that he crossed the Jordan and then sent out raiding parties from the main body of cavalry that accompanied him. At Nablus the Muslims plundered and burnt the town, but were not able to take the citadel. They then went northwards with their prisoners, both Franks and Samaritan Jews, to the isolated hill of Sebaste, where the Muslim shrine of Zakarīyā (John the Baptist) had been made into a church. Its bishop arranged terms with the attackers and his town was spared in exchange for the release of eighty Muslim prisoners, after which the Muslims moved further north to Jenin. Here they undermined the tower in which the inhabitants had taken refuge and more booty and prisoners were taken, although Maqrīzī added that the Muslims lost a number of sappers who were trapped by the tower's fall.[84] They then moved by night, passing Zar'īn, 'Ain Jālūt and then Kaukab, on their way to the Jordan. According to Maqrīzī's dating, Nablus was attacked on 8 September and the Muslims re-crossed the Jordan on 10 September, which would mean that Sebaste and Jenin, which are within 20 miles (32 km) of Nablus, were both attacked on 9 September. The speed of this move through relatively undefended country shows that, whatever Saladin's hopes may have been when he attacked Kerak, he was now intent on plunder and a demonstration of force, rather than on a serious military operation.

It may be argued that he was not yet strong enough to press home an attack on the Coast, or that he was merely campaigning for propaganda effect with an eye to his feud with Mosul, but whatever his motives, the pattern that he was following was not that of total war. This was reflected at all levels, as is shown by Ibn Jubair who left

Damascus for Acre on 13 September, two days before Saladin returned from his campaign. He noted that while Saladin was at Kerak caravans were still coming from Egypt by way of the Coast; Muslims were going from Damascus to Acre and Christian merchants were arriving in Damascus. Muslims and Christians paid their dues in each other's lands and Frankish territory was considered to be "extremely safe". He added that the same thing happened in the civil wars between Muslim rulers, in that these did not affect the ordinary people and the merchants.[85] The armies did not, of course, campaign against one another in a vacuum but, while "the men of war were occupied with their wars", the groups that made up contemporary society maintained as far as possbile their own characteristics and patterns of life.

Saladin himself now returned to the problem of Mosul. While he was still at Kerak, his second son, 'Uthmān, had written to tell him that the Shaikh al-Shuyūkh and Shihāb al-Dīn Bashīr had now come back to Damascus.[86] They had brought with them robes of honour from the Caliph for Saladin, al-'Ādil and Nāṣir al-Dīn Ibn Shīrkūh. Saladin gave his to Nūr al-Dīn Muḥammad of Ḥiṣn Kaifā as a token of gratitude and Nūr al-Dīn left for the Euphrates on 27 September. Unfortunately, there are no details of the Shaikh al-Shuyūkh's message or of Saladin's reply. Ibn al-Athīr reported that nothing came of the discussions that were now held[87] and this seems to be confirmed by the vagueness of 'Imād al-Dīn's account. The mission, in fact, was ill-omened as well as unproductive. 'Imād al-Dīn noted that "the weather was very hot and diseases spread".[88] Both the Shaikh al-Shuyūkh and Bashīr fell ill, and although Saladin tried to persuade them to stay, they insisted on leaving. Bashīr was carried from Damascus in a litter and died at al-Sukhna. The Shaikh al-Shuyūkh, accompanied by Ṭumān with the troops of Sinjār reached al-Raḥba, a place with an unhealthy reputation as the dwelling of the angel of death.[89] He had refused to consult a doctor, preferring "to rely on God",[90] and he died there in the month of Sha'bān (7 November – 5 December). It must have been suspected that his insistence on leaving Damascus reflected Saladin's refusal to agree to his proposals, but 'Imād al-Dīn was ready to counter this by adding: "Saladin did not cease in heart and tongue mentioning him and thanking him."[91]

14

THE END OF EMPIRE

The death of the Shaikh al-Shuyūkh marks the end of any real hope that the dispute between 'Izz al-Dīn and Saladin could be settled by diplomacy. In spite of the extent of Saladin's territory, the existence of an unsubdued and unreconciled opponent could act as a focus of discontent for all those whom his ambitions had alarmed. By his attack on Kerak and his raid west of the Jordan he had paid at least perfunctory tribute to the obligations of the Holy War and he could now turn his attention to clearing the way for a spring campaign across the Euphrates.

In November Taqī al-Dīn left for Egypt. According to a report given by Maqrīzī, a formal arrangement had been made that he was to administer the country in the name of Saladin's second son, 'Uthmān, while al-'Ādil held Aleppo in the name of al-Afḍal, his eldest son. If either of the two boys were to die, one of his brothers would take his place and when they were considered to have come of age, the arrangement would end.[1] Saladin spent Ramaḍān (6 December – 4 January) in Damascus, after which he moved northwards to the Biqā'. At the start of the Muslim year 581 (4 April) he was in camp outside Hama, having now finally made up his mind to march on Mosul.

A letter was sent to Taqī al-Dīn from Hama on 6 April to say that messengers had come from Antioch and that Saladin's own envoy, al-'Adl[5] had returned "from Frankish territory"; Raymond of Tripoli had freed a number of Muslim prisoners and had sent a letter "with a request about the Antioch truce". Antioch had sheltered behind this since the fall of Aleppo in 1183 and the Franks must have been the more anxious to extend it because of the death in March of King Baldwin. After the 'Ain Jālūt campaign Guy de Lusignan had been removed from his office and Baldwin's six-year-old nephew crowned as co-king with his uncle. Ibn Jubair on his visit to the Coast had been told that Baldwin did not show himself to the people because of his leprosy and that power was held by "the damned Count, Lord of Tripoli and Tiberias".[2] Raymond, in fact, took over as regent on Baldwin's death and must be assumed to have been negotiating at this point not merely for Antioch and Tripoli but for the Kingdom of Jerusalem as well. In 1182 Saladin had crossed the Euphrates without having made a truce with the Franks, but this had left the Damascus frontier exposed. He himself had accused his enemies too often of coming to terms with the infidels to find it anything but embarrassing to do the same thing himself, but he had to balance a propaganda point against military danger. This time he chose caution and a general truce was arranged. It is significant that no reference is made to this by any of his contemporary biographers, who also ignore the treaty that he made with the Emperor Andronicus before the latter was deposed and killed by Isaac Angelus.

The letter to Taqī al-Dīn noted that another frontier where defence was needed was that of Armenia where the Armenians "were still asking for" a truce. This allowed Saladin to confer a small favour on Qilij-Arslān. He agreed to a truce on condition that the Armenians released those of Qilij-Arslān's men whom they were holding prisoner and if they refused, he threatened to lead his army over the passes against them.

No explanation is given in the letter of the move against Mosul. Taqī al-Dīn was promised a full account of what was happening from Saladin's envoy there, but the only detail added is that the arrival of messengers from Antioch coincided with that of envoys from Mosul who had thought that Saladin would be preoccupied with the ending of the Frankish truce – a reference to another unsuccessful Mosuli mission which met Saladin at Hama. There is the usual comment on expenses; news of Saladin's move had brought in envoys from friend and foe; they had to be given hospitality and in return for the little presents that they brought from their masters, Saladin had to send back more splendid gifts; as a result, "the expenses are large and the outgoings greater than normal", but none of this had weakened Saladin's resolution. The letter ends with a reference to an ambitious plan that Taqī al-Dīn had been considering for an attack on the Almohades in the Maghrib. Although Saladin had listed the Almohades as a suitable enemy in his blueprint for Islamic domination, he must have been anxious not to over-extend himself. As a result, Taqī al-Dīn had to be discouraged. There had been a break in his letters and the writer added that he hoped that this was not

> in fulfilment of the threat that he [Taqī al-Dīn] had made in reply to the disapproval we expressed about trifles, which were replaced by good deeds... There is no need to mention his march to the Maghrib... Although this would be desirable, he has been ordered to consult [Saladin] about it and although it is a dangerous frontier for Islam, the wall of Taqī al-Dīn's name defends it.[3]

Al-Fāḍil wrote from Damascus to tell al-Afḍal that envoys from "the kings" had flocked to Saladin's camp at Hama; they were bringing "gifts" which were, in fact, the tribute of their lands and their troops were ready to serve Saladin, wherever he might lead.[4] Less cheerfully, he hinted to 'Imād al-Dīn that there had been an estrangement between himself and Saladin. The reason, he suggested, might be that he had broken his custom of being present during important affairs, such as the forthcoming expedition; he had left himself in the position of the Muslim who was neither saved nor damned at the Last Judgement, as he was going neither to the Euphrates nor to the Nile; he had crossed the threshold of his sixtieth year and his powers were weakening. He quoted the line: "why, when I have not been present at the battle, do I pass the night as though badly wounded?" and he told 'Imād al-Dīn: "if there is a gap, then block it with the excuse of weakness, but otherwise there is no need to reveal the face of the eclipse". He congratulated 'Imād al-Dīn on his having been promised an estate and a house in the lands of Mosul but advised him to be tactful in his requests and he ended by saying that he expected a successful outcome from Saladin's march.[5]

This letter, together with some later evidence, suggests a possible difference of opinion about the way to deal with Mosul. Before Zain al-Dīn of Irbil and Sanjar-Shāh had complicated the issue, al-Fāḍil had thought that it was time for a settlement so that Saladin could turn his whole attention to the Franks. Since then, letters had come from Keukburī complaining of the attack by Qaimāz on Irbil,[6] but 'Imād al-Dīn has already been quoted as saying that it was the Mosuli threat to look for help from al-Pahlawān which had tilted the balance.[7] Saladin clearly felt that he had to make a pre-emptive attack and al-Fāḍil may well have disapproved. One risk was that Saladin could find himself caught in a spider's web of eastern wars, which would leave him no time for the Holy War itself. Another was that too much territory might weaken central control, and if the Ayyubid bubble grew too big, it could burst.

Risk or no risk, however, Saladin was not now to be turned aside and he moved from Hama to Aleppo by Tell al-Sulṭān, where he was met by al-'Ādil with the Aleppan troops. He camped outside Aleppo and then moved north along the line of the Kuwaik before striking across the plains towards al-Bīra (map 8). According to 'Imād al-Dīn, he halted at a place two parasangs down-stream from al-Bīra and took three days to ferry his army across the Euphrates, after which he moved some 60 miles (97 km) further on to Ḥarrān.[8] There is a discrepancy in the dating of his march. Ibn Shaddād wrote that he was met at al-Bīra by Keukburī on 15 April and that he reached Ḥarrān on 25 May.[9] No explanation is given for this delay and the account is not supported by 'Imād al-Dīn who accompanied the expedition. Although he adds no exact dates, 'Imād al-Dīn makes Saladin both leave Aleppo and reach Ḥarrān in the month of Ṣafar (4 May – 1 June) and he does not mention any meeting with Keukburī at al-Bīra. On the other hand, Keukburī can be expected to have helped Saladin's working parties sent on to collect boats for the river crossing and it may be assumed that Ibn Shaddād confused his facts. Saladin camped outside Ḥarrān for some days in late May and then, after playing polo with Keukburī one day, he dismayed his supporters by having him arrested.

'Imād al-Dīn sent an immediate note to al-Fāḍil who replied that he had been expecting this blow for some time, but "God knows my sorrow and concern for what has happened". Keukburī's offence, he commented elliptically, was only one of over-boldness and weak-mindedness and it was not that he had been looking for a change of allegiance and preparing to play the turncoat; he himself had done all that an absent man could, by writing letters; had he been present he would have spared no efforts to aid Keukburī, but he could rely on the tactful help of 'Imād al-Dīn; he had no doubts that by the time his letter reached Ḥarrān Keukburī would have been released, but nevertheless his heart was constricted.[10] He wrote in the same terms to the Qāḍī Najīb al-Dīn al-'Adl, who had also sent word of the arrest:

> I have no doubt that Saladin's kindly feelings will soon appear... The cause of offence was only over-boldness... My absence at a time like this, by God, is hard for me to bear and the choice was not mine... I can remember the heat and dust of Ḥarrān and can still feel the effect of it although I am sheltered by a roof... But if – and may God forbid it – you see something that requires my presence, I will come even if I have to travel by mule and endure the heat even without a tent. In this I would be serving myself and giving ease to my heart... Minds are disturbed and thought confused as a result of what has happened."[11]

He wrote to the powerful Sonqor al-Khilāṭī, "one of the leaders and intermediaries in whatever is good", and repeated that the cause of offence was the fact that Keukburī had presumed too far on Saladin's generosity, but "the mercy of the Sultan is near at hand".[12]

'Imād al-Dīn gave his own version of the background to the arrest. Keukburī had supported Saladin in his attacks on Mosul, Sinjār and Āmid and had continually urged his brother, Zain al-Dīn Yūsuf of Irbil, to change sides and abandon the Mosulis. "He was an example to all who wished to serve us." In Ramaḍān 580 (December – January 1184/5) he had sent letters to Damascus urging Saladin to march east. His envoy had made lavish promises, offering to supply provisions and to pay the expenses of the troops and, in particular, he had guaranteed Saladin 50,000 dinars to be handed over on the day that he reached Ḥarrān. Saladin did not ask for the money, "as modesty was part of his nature", but when Keukburī made no move to pay it, "the slanderers" suggested that he must have come to an arrangement with the Mosulis. 'Imād al-Dīn was sent with the Qāḍī Shams al-Dīn Ibn al-Farrāsh, to investigate the matter and to remind Keukburī of his envoy's promise. Keukburī guessed their errand and before they could broach the matter, he produced a copy of the Quran, laying his hand on it to take an oath. It fell open at the verse: "O you who believe, keep your covenants." 'Imād al-Dīn drew the moral from this, but Keukburī persisted in disclaiming responsibility for what his envoy had said. His arrest followed on the next day.[13]

'Imād al-Dīn's story, which is confirmed by Ibn al-Athīr, can be accepted as giving one of the reasons for the quarrel but another point emerges from a Fāḍilī letter to Saladin himself. Al-Fāḍil, commenting on the arrest, wrote to say that there was no doubt that Saladin with his generous and easy nature, "the source of pure, sweet, water", would not have gone to this extreme without having previously endured and overlooked Keukburī's faults and clearly he was to be excused and Keukburī blamed; nevertheless, Keukburī's earlier record of service made it important that he should be treated well; when he had collected his wits and looked at the position honestly, he would realise that the reason why Saladin had not given him what was held by his brother, Zain al-Dīn Yūsuf, was the agreement, confirmed by oath, between Zain al-Dīn and Saladin; Keukburī himself had asked for this agreement and had acted as an intermediary in it; other allies who were bound to Saladin by similar compacts should be glad when they saw the care that he had taken to keep his word and this was a point to stress in all letters sent to those who might be upset by the news; there was no doubt that Keukburī would be the better for his lesson and that he had gone too far, but al-Fāḍil hoped that by the time his letter arrived the knot would have been undone. He went on to say that the lands and the people were quiet and safe; administration was proceeding with justice; tongues were calling down blessings on Saladin and hands were raised in prayer. For all that, however, "the servant sees that the gap is widening for the master in expenditure and that there is an urgent need for money". He was afraid, he said, lest the fact that Saladin had to have money quickly might lead him to "underestimate certain affairs whose consequences should be thought of and to enter into certain dangers against whose harmful results he could not be secure".[14] There is, unfortunately, no explanation of this cryptic remark but the early financial strain and the possibly unwise measures that it could prompt may be taken as confirming al-Fāḍil's dislike of the whole expedition. What is unquestionably clear is that Keukburī had been demanding territory held by his brother and that Saladin had refused. It may be guessed that at this point Keukburī withheld his promised subsidy, but at any rate the quarrel had now come to a head. 'Imād al-Dīn must have known the facts, but he edited them to conceal Keukburī's apparently discreditable attempt to get the better of his brother. Finally, al-Fāḍil's reference to those who might be upset by the news underlines the diplomatic damage that could be expected and bears out a remark by Ibn al-Athīr that Saladin "was afraid lest the people in the lands of the Jazīra turn away from him... They all knew what Keukburī had done for him."[15]

As al-Fāḍil had hoped, the affair was quickly settled. 'Imād al-Dīn suggested that it was Saladin's emirs who had been urging stern measures.[16] Some advised him to transfer Keukburī to the citadel at Aleppo lest he should escape, others thought that he should be killed and the camp was in an uproar. 'Imād al-Dīn himself, the Qāḍī Ibn al-Farrāsh and Ḍiyā' al-Dīn 'Īsā then pointed out that the offence was not unduly serious, "and this was Saladin's own view". They were told to visit Keukburī and calm his fears. 'Imād al-Dīn wrote: "he said: 'I shall give Saladin all my lands and hand over all my possessions, new and old, and I shall go with him and serve him.' We said: 'show your submission by handing over the citadels of al-Ruhā and Ḥarrān.' He said: 'I shall accept all that you advise.' " According to Ibn Shaddād, Keukburī was released on 2 June and the citadels that had been taken from him were returned.[17] There is no reference to his promised subsidy, but in view of Saladin's need for money, it seems more than likely that it was now paid.

Al-Mashṭūb had been sent with the advance guard to Ra's al-'Ain and Saladin followed from Ḥarrān on 3 June. 'Imād al-Dīn had written to al-Fāḍil just before the army left and al-Fāḍil replied on 14 June, thanking God for 'Imād al-Dīn's good health, which He was asked to leave as a deposit not to be recalled, and adding that he expected an early victory.[18] At the same time, according to Ibn Shaddād, a messenger came from Qilij-Arslān to warn Saladin that "all the kings of the east" had agreed to fight him if he did not draw back from Mārdīn and Mosul.[19] Saladin, however, was not to be frightened off and from Ra's al-'Ain he went to Dunaisir in the plain below Mārdīn, where he was joined by troops under the command of Nūr al-Dīn Muḥammad's brother, Abū Bakr. Nūr al-Dīn himself had been prevented from coming by an illness, from which he died on 15 June. He left two youngs sons and Abū Bakr, who wanted to take over his brother's towns of Ḥiṣn Kaifā, Āmid and Khartpirt, promptly asked for leave to go.[20] Saladin made no move against Mārdīn, where Quṭb al-Dīn Il-Ghāzī, who had come to terms with him during the 1183 campaign, had died in the autumn of 1184. The town was now governed in the name of his elder son, a ten-year-old boy, by Niẓām al-Dīn Alpqush, a *mamlūk* appointed by Quṭb al-Dīn's maternal uncle, Shāh-Arman. Niẓām al-Dīn had shut himself up behind his walls and Saladin moved away eastwards by Dārā and Niṣībīn. On leaving Niṣībīn he was joined by Sanjar-Shāh of Jazīrat ibn 'Umar and according to 'Imad al-Dīn he took the most direct route, reaching Balad at the end of the month of Rabī'a 1 (1 July) and then moving nearer to Mosul and halting at al-Ismā'īliyāt.[21]

When Saladin reached Balad, he sent his envoy Ḍiyā' al-Dīn al-Shahrazūrī to explain to the Caliph the reason for this return to Mosul. The main points were the same as before, but Sanjar-Shāh and Zain al-Dīn Yūsuf were used to reinforce the argument, the basis of which was that 'Izz al-Dīn had been acting against the Caliph's orders; the name of the Seljuq Sultan was pronounced in the *khuṭba* in Mosul and appeared on Mosuli coins; 'Izz al-Dīn had levied illegal taxes; he was getting support from al-Pahlawān and had been corresponding with the Franks; Saladin himself had not come to Mosul "out of a desire to add to his kingdom or to destroy an ancient house... His whole purpose was to bring the Mosulis back to obedience to the Caliph and to make them aid Islam...as well as to force them to do their duty by guarding their clients and giving their rightful due to their relatives"; the Lord of Irbil, whose father had defended the Mosulis and who was their client, had complained of their injustice; 'Izz al-Dīn had cheated Saif al-Dīn Ghāzī's heir, Sanjar-Shāh, out of his inheritance and "had he been able to do so, he would have shed his blood". Saladin went on to say that Sanjar-Shāh would not have asked a stranger to help him against his own uncle had he not been in a state of fear.[22]

According to Ibn al-Athīr, while Saladin was at Balad, 'Izz al-Dīn sent him a deputation including his own mother and the daughter of Nūr al-Dīn of Syria, who had come from Aleppo with her husband 'Imād al-Dīn Zangī. Other ladies and state dignitaries accompanied them and they asked Saladin to agree to a peace settlement by whose terms the Mosuli troops would be sent to his service whenever they were needed. Ibn al-Athīr added that 'Izz al-Dīn and his court were confident that this would be accepted, but Saladin held a council at which Ḍiyā' al-Dīn 'Īsā and al-Mashṭūb, both Mosuli Kurds, argued that Mosul should not be abandoned for a woman and that 'Izz al-Dīn had only sent out the embassy because he knew that he could not hold his city. "This coincided with Saladin's wishes", and he sent back the embassy "making unacceptable excuses",[23] of which, Ibn al-'Adīm added, he later repented.[24] Ibn al-Athīr was in Mosul at the time and he wrote that Saladin's rejection of the embassy angered the common people so that they kept up constant skirmishing against his troops. The violence of this opposition led Saladin to regret that he had lost "both his good reputation and his chance to take the city". He was angry with his advisers and letters arrived from al-Fāḍil and others "who had no desire for Mosul", criticising what he had done.[24]

It is difficult to challenge Ibn al-Athīr's first-hand account and it is certainly true that Saladin was again faced by determined resistance from Mosulis, but one problem is that 'Imād al-Dīn implies that the Atabek ladies came out later in the year, not long before Saladin finally left Mosul. He noted that Saladin had received them with courtesy and had said: "We have come to unite the word of Islam and to restore things to order by removing differences... I accept your intercession...but there must be an agreement."[25] 'Imād al-Dīn, however, is not concerned to define the date and, together with his tendency to gloss over less creditable points in Saladin's career, this suggests that, unless two approaches were made, Ibn al-Athīr's version should be accepted.[26]

Saladin was in no hurry to launch an assault on Mosul. Keukburī crossed the Tigris and camped to the east[27] of the city, where he was reinforced by his brother Zain al-Dīn Yūsuf. Saladin himself sent troops forward every day to test the morale of the defenders but his main concern seems to have been to break their spirit by distributing Mosuli *iqṭā's*. 'Imād al-Dīn was given property that had belonged to a former vizier of Mosul, to the annoyance of treasury officials, who told Saladin that an offer of 15,000 dinars had been made for it.[28] Al-Mashṭūb, with other Hakkārī emirs and tribesmen, was sent to take over the Hakkārī region, while Humaidīya Kurds were sent to their native district around al-'Aqr, some 50 miles (80 km) away to the north. The weather had become very hot and Saladin allowed his men not to wear mail. According to 'Imād al-Dīn, he said: "we shall act slowly and not hurry...it is enough for the people of Mosul that they are imprisoned there".[29] Al-Fāḍil passed this information on to al-Afḍal and wrote optimistically of "the nearness of the great victory". Saladin, he said, was in camp at al-Ismā'īlīyāt and the lords of the region, the army leaders and the governors had come to him; the most recent arrival had been that of Zain al-Dīn Yūsuf with a force of nearly 1000 *ṭawāshīs*; Shāh-Arman, al-Pahlawān and his brother had sent envoys, gifts and messengers, "each preparing his own way and negotiating with Saladin for himself"; the delay in giving Mosul the *coup-de-grâce* was caused by the heat which made it impossible to bear arms, but snow was being imported, prices were low and there was an abundance of fodder; the huge estates of Mosul had been shared out amongst Saladin's men; 'Izz al-Dīn was imprisoned behind his walls; he knew that there was no one to help him and his subjects were fighting against him with the weapons of prayer.[30]

In spite of al-Fāḍil's optimism, in military terms the siege was making no progress and at this point an idea was put forward that the Tigris should be diverted so as to cut off Mosul's water-supply. According to 'Imād al-Dīn, although at first this seemed ridiculous, the plan was approved by one of the leading engineers of the day, Fakhr al-Dīn Ibn al-Dahhān, who had now left Mosul to join Saladin's service.[31] Ibn al-Athīr had heard of it, but wrote that Saladin gave up the idea because it would take too long and involve too much labour.[32] Saladin himself referred to it,[33] but gave a different explanation for having abandoned it. On 21 July news had reached him of the death of Shāh-Arman of Khilāṭ. Some of his advisers suggested that the army should march immediately to Lake Van, others thought that the siege should continue and a third group considered that there were enough men for both. 'Imād al-Dīn wrote: "we spent the night torn between these three views", but in the morning letters arrived from "our friends in those parts", urging

Saladin to come to them.[34] As a result, Zain al-Dīn Yūsuf was sent back to Irbil and reinforced by al-Mashṭūb. Nāṣir al-Dīn Muhammad was ordered to take the vanguard of the army to Khilāṭ and was reinforced by Keukburī while Saladin himself wrote to ask for a diploma of investiture from the Caliph; Shāh-Arman had left no heir; "his lands are masterless, with the greedy mouths of the *'ajamīs* gaping at them"; his widow was the daughter of al-Pahlawān, "who had only married her to him out of desire for his kingdom"; all Diyār Bakr was empty; at Mārdīn Quṭb al-Dīn's elder son was ten years old and the younger, two; the son of Nūr al-Dīn Muḥammad was ten; Daulat-Shāh, Lord of Arzan and Bitlīs, had had a stroke and was like "meat on a butcher's block"; as for Mosul itself, "since the servant came down against it, he had not busied himself with the siege...because of the heat"; he had planned to divert the Tigris and had collected engineers; the work was found to be easy and they had started digging diversion channels, but then news had come of Shāh-Arman's death; Saladin had been in doubt whether to go or stay, but then letters had come from the leading men there inviting him and expressing their dislike of al-Pahlawān. Saladin ended by again asking the Caliph for a diploma covering all Diyār Bakr and Mosul, as well as the lands of Shāh-Arman.[35]

The army now moved off from Mosul on its way north. While his vanguard marched on Khilāṭ, Saladin himself turned to Mayyāfāriqīn, which lies to the west of Lake Van, one day's march from Āmid (map 1). The town had been left by Quṭb al-Dīn of Mārdīn to his younger son and it was held by his widow, a sister of Saladin's former ally, Nūr al-Dīn Muḥammad of Ḥiṣn Kaifā. Mayyāfāriqīn had been in the hands of the Ortoqids since 515 A.H., when it had been taken from the Bektimurids of Khilāṭ, but according to Ibn al-Athīr at this time it was counted as part of the lands of Shāh-Arman and was garrisoned by Khilāṭī troops under the command of a Mārdīn emir, Asad al-Dīn Yurun-Qush.[36] Saladin was not expecting resistance, but Asad al-Dīn had prepared for a siege and 'Imād al-Dīn wrote: "we saw what we had not looked for and found difficult what we had thought easy".[37] The place itself was considered stronger than Āmid and Yāqūt, writing at the turn of the century, noted that it had never been taken by assault.[38] There was fierce fighting and a number of sallies, as a result of which Saladin quickly turned to diplomacy. According to 'Imād al-Dīn, he sent messengers to Asad al-Dīn saying that he would respect the rights and obey the commands of Quṭb al-Dīn's widow and he wrote to her:

"we have a better right to protect your house... We shall not enter the city except in accordance with your wishes... We shall ally ourselves to you by the marriage of one of your daughters." He then played off one against the other. Asad al-Dīn was told: "the Lady is inclined to make terms", while she was warned that Asad al-Dīn was weakening. This psychological pressure succeeded and an agreement was made by which Asad al- Dīn was to join Saladin's service in return for an *iqṭā'* and Quṭb al-Dīn's widow was allowed to keep her property and given the fortress of al-Hattākh.[39] Saladin's fifth son, al-Mu'izz Isḥāq, who was not far short of his eleventh birthday, was betrothed to one of her daughters and 'Imād al-Dīn added: "Saladin was quick to agree to everything for which they asked for fear of some hindrance."[40] On 29 August the Qādī Ibn Abī 'Aṣrun entered the town for the betrothal ceremony, at which 'Imād al-Dīn acted as deputy for the bridegroom. Saladin held a reception for the leading men and then prepared to turn his attention to Khilāṭ.

In reply to a letter giving him news of the fall of Mayyāfāriqīn, al-Fāḍil, who had already heard of it in letters from al-'Ādil and 'Imād al-Dīn, wrote to congratulate Saladin on the fact that "the dynasty is established in that region and the door has been opened to the conquest of the lands"; the people there were accustomed to "kings who devour them", whereas Saladin would remove illegal taxes and check injustice and immorality. He told Saladin that "his sons, the kings", were in good health; the roads were safe, his subjects and his troops obedient, and the Franks were abiding by the terms of the truce.[41] In private letters, however, he was less cheerful. In his reply to a letter from 'Imād al-Dīn, dated to 28 July, that reached him in Damascus on 12 August he still seems to have been concerned about his own relations with Saladin. He wrote to say that he was constantly engaged in making précis of news coming in from the army to forward on to Egypt and other letters had to be sent out to the various Ayyubid dominions; if 'Imād al-Dīn were asked, he was to tell Saladin that al-Fāḍil was fully occupied in doing what would harm his foes and delight his friends. He added, cryptically: "there remains what I have not indicated and what I cannot mention of the fact that the means fall short of the desired end".[42] This seems to refer to money. In the reply to a letter sent from Mayyāfāriqīn he wrote to tell 'Imād al-Dīn not to forward requests, presumably for money or favours, at this time, as it exposed those who asked to rejection and those who interceded for them to snubs.[43] In another letter sent to

Mayyāfāriqīn he described 'Imād al-Dīn's attempt to get a money transfer to Egypt as "a hope to be hoped, not money to enrich"; there was no chance of success in the present year, as there were already more of these transfers than the lands could bear and letters from Egyptian officials were full of discontent. Appparently al-Fāḍil had been sent the draft of a letter that Saladin was planning to forward to Baghdad. His advice was that the Caliph should not continually be pressed for diplomas – "the water in the spring must be allowed to fill up". He himself had asked for permission to make another pilgrimage in the coming year, when al-'Ādil was hoping to go too, but he had received a reply "which was like a rejection". At this stage in his career he apparently did not hesitate to threaten disobedience if he did not get his way; "if the refusal continues", he wrote, "and the time comes for me to make up my mind, necessity will call me to go".[44]

Saladin soon had causes of his own for discontent. In the official letter sent to tell al-Afḍal of the fall of Mayyāfāriqīn al-Fāḍil had written of the arrival of messengers from Khilāṭ; they had brought news that Shāh-Arman's widow, the daughter of al-Pahlawān, had been expelled from the town and that both troops and people were eager to join Saladin's service because of his "justice and generosity in which all the people of this age have a share". Saladin, al-Fāḍil added, was about to march there with his army and after that he would move irresistibly to the fulfilment of world conquest (*sic*).[45] Mayyāfāriqīn, however, had given Khilāṭ too long a breathing space. Shāh-Arman's vizier Majd al-Dīn Ibn Rashīq, "pretending friendship",[46] had written to the commanders of Saladin's vanguard, Nāṣir al-Dīn Muḥammad and Keukburī, asking them to halt short of the town, so as not to alarm the inhabitants. In the town itself, power was now held by one of Shāh-Arman's *mamlūks*, Bektimur, who had come as an envoy to Saladin in the winter of 1183/84. He did, in fact, send back al-Pahlawān's daughter, but he also took care to return the money that her father had left with Shāh-Arman, presumably as her dowry. Then, when al-Pahlawān himself arrived, Bektimur and Majd al-Dīn began to play him off against Saladin. Saladin sent Ḍiyā' al-Dīn 'Īsā to Khilāṭ and Majd al-Dīn, who was credited with having invited both of them, pointed, disingenuously, to al-Pahlawān's arrival and Saladin's slowness and added: "had you hurried, what is now hard would have been easy".[47] According to 'Imād al-Dīn's account, al-Pahlawān now had a meeting with 'Īsā and had to be reassured that Saladin was not planning to attack him.

'Īsā returned to Saladin, apparently with friendly messages, but 'Imād al-Dīn added briefly: "we realised that the honey of Khilāṭ had been protected by its bees".[48] Bektimur was left to enjoy his diplomatic success; Saladin abandoned his attempt and al-Pahlawān's army withdrew. 'Imād al-Dīn gave the result as a stalemate, but according to Ibn Shaddād it ended marginally to al-Pahlawān's advantage, in that he married off another of his daughters to Bektimur and was able to assume at least some responsibility for the town by confirming Bektimur in possession of it.[49]

Saladin himself had evidently advanced some way towards Lake Van. 'Imād al-Dīn wrote to al-Fāḍil from between Bitlīs, at the western end of the lake, and Mayyāfāriqīn, showing "violent discontent" in his letters.[50] Another letter, dated 17 September, was brought by Ibn al-Muqaddam's courier to Damascus and this gave the news that Saladin was now intending to go back to Mosul. Al-Fāḍil prayed that "good might be associated with this return", but he added that he had not been pleased by "the sending of the letter to Baghdad".[51] This presumably refers to the draft that he had seen earlier, when he had advised that the Caliph should not be pestered with more requests for diplomas. Saladin marched by Dārā and Niṣībīn and at this stage he was warned in a message from Āmid that Bektimur was planning to attack Mayyāfāriqīn. 'Imād al-Dīn wrote: "we did not raise our heads at this...knowing that while we were at rest, he would not move".[52] The weather seems to have been uncertain. Ibn Shaddād noted that it was very hot,[53] but the start of the month of Rajab (28 September) was marked by thunder and lightning, giving warning, 'Imād al-Dīn explained, of the start of the cold season.[54] During the march back to Mosul Saladin lost one of his most daring commanders, 'Izz al-Dīn Chāūlī, who broke a leg putting his horse at a water-jump, never recovered from his injury and died in Damascus. Saladin himself left Niṣībīn and halted at Kafr Zammār, to the west of Mosul, in the month of Sha'bān (28 October / 25 November). The gates of Mosul were now shut, but no attempt was made to lay siege to it.

Al-Fāḍil explained Saladin's move to Kafr Zammār in a letter to al-Afḍal by saying that he had gone "to settle the affair of Irbil and to send an army there". In fact, Saladin was making an attempt to remove from the control of Mosul the basins of both the Great and the Little Zāb, separated by the plain of Irbil (map 8). This would, in effect, isolate Mosul and give him a secure base east of the Tigris from which he might later hope to control all Iraq.[55] Al-Fāḍil went on to report that the Mosulis were approaching Saladin with requests for peace, but that his acceptance would depend on their sincerity; he was intending to pass the winter at Ḥarrān or Niṣībīn – a point which is apparently contradicted by 'Imād al-Dīn, who said that he planned to stay by Mosul[56] – and al-Fāḍil implied that in the spring he would renew his campaign; "the lands have no defender and it is as though they have been gathered together for their true Sultan". A second letter to al-Afḍal repeated this point and said that all lands were either rejoicing in past conquests or looking forward to future ones, while the Mosulis were continually asking for peace, offering to remove the name of al-Pahlawān from the *khuṭba*, to send their troops to Saladin when he needed them and to abandon "such and such" lands.[57] In a third letter al-Afḍal was told that Saladin's orders were being carried out and that his affairs were in good order; envoys and messengers had been sent to Mosul and received from the Mosulis; they had agreed to remove the injustices of which Saladin disapproved and to change the *khuṭba* and the coinage.[58]

Saladin, of course, was in a strong position, in that 'Izz al-Dīn could not challenge him in the field, but the campaign was dragging on too long after the fiasco of Khilāṭ and not everything was going smoothly. The second letter to al-Afḍal, quoted above, gave the first mention of a feud between Turkmans and Kurds which broke out at this time and which spread through the whole of Diyār Bakr, while the third letter questioned the morale of Saladin's own troops. Al-Fāḍil wrote: "it may be that an agreement will be made, if God wills, for winter is established and the troops are disgruntled".

In spite of this, no immediate steps were taken to reach a settlement. Saladin had taken Mayyāfāriqīn at the end of August and at the start of December he was still at Kafr Zammār, assiduously reading the Quran and fasting because it was the month of Ramaḍān. Then, on 3 December, the vizier al-Qawwām was murdered at Āmid as a result of a conspiracy amongst the Ortoqid *mamlūks* and on the same day Saladin was attacked by a fever. This was concealed for as long as possible, but Saladin apparently felt that the time had at last come to make peace and he called on the services of Zangī of Sinjār. Zangī sent his vizier, Shams al-Dīn Ibn al-Kāfī, who had helped to negotiate the exchange of Aleppo in 1183, and he was accompanied to Mosul by Saladin's own envoy, the Qāḍī Ibn al-Farrāsh. Saladin did not wait for their return, but left Kafr Zammār on Christmas Day for Niṣībīn and, after a brief pause there, he went on to Ḥarrān. In spite of his illness he had refused to ride in a litter.

On 21 December ʿImād al-Dīn had written to al-Fāḍil and the letter reached Damascus on 6 January 1186. In his reply al-Fāḍil cautiously avoided any direct reference to Saladin's illness and wrote that he hoped that news from the army would not be delayed, "so that hearing may serve in place of sight. Otherwise, there is no rest on a bed of coals... My master [ʿImād al-Dīn] knows to what I am referring." He also added that efforts should be made to rescue the family of al-Qawwām – "the true man answers the summons of the grave". He mentioned the Turkman troubles and said that he himself was prevented from joining Saladin by the dangers of the journey and by his own poor health.[59] Another letter of excuse shows that he was not taking Saladin's illness very seriously and was more concerned about his own difficulties. He wrote: "I have tried by every means...to bring myself to set out on the road and to relieve my eyes of the burden of having to rely on my ears for information about my master...but I have not been able to find the strength to do this." He complained of the cold and the snow. People could not bear to turn their faces to the wind and strong men could not walk in Damascus, let alone the weak. His advice was that an agreement must be made with Mosul to allow the burden of war to be dropped and he ended by saying that ʿImād al-Dīn's presence made up for his own absence "and removes me from the position of one who should be blamed to that of one who is excused".[60] In reply to another letter sent on 16 January he was still complaining about his health and he apologised for his shaking hand and uncouth script. He thanked God for the news that ʿImād al-Dīn had sent him of Saladin's complete recovery and he went on to add a banal request for an *iqṭāʿ* for one of his protégés.[61] He was obviously convinced that Saladin was in no danger and he wrote to explain to al-Afḍal that the disease had been a quartan fever which had passed off at the ninth attack; Saladin was now able to ride long distances and, generally, to enjoy food and sleep.[62] In another note to al-Afḍal he said that he had received letters written in Saladin's own hand; he had no pain left in his body, no digestive troubles and no fever spots on his face; a shoulder litter had been prepared for him – a reference to his journey to Ḥarrān – but "he then found strength from his noble soul and ordered a mule litter, then he found strength from his noble limbs and ordered horses to be brought up".[63]

The news, however, turned out to be misleading. Saladin had not thrown off his illness and at Ḥarrān, where he camped outside the town, doctors were summoned from Syria and he dictated his will. 'Imād al-Dīn was in constant attendance and wrote: "as his pain increased, so did his hope in God's grace".[64] Al-Fāḍil sent a letter from Damascus some time after 26 January to say that hearts were palpitating and tongues full of rumours, "especially when doctor after doctor is seen going off and one messenger arrives after another, but the news that they bring is concealed"; people close to Saladin were sending reports from the camp that caused anguish and confusion; the land was without a protector and the prudent man had to look to the future. Al-Fāḍil went on to say that he had already suggested in an earlier note that Saladin should be brought as fast as possible to Aleppo; Ḥarrān was not part of his kingdom and there he was "beneath a tent whose pole will not hold in the winter"; his army was weak, as the bulk of his troops had dispersed; if Aleppo, which was traditionally restive, could be kept under control, the lands beyond it would be safe, but any disturbance there would cause the mischief to spread. It might be argued that Damascus was even more vulnerable because of the Franks, and here al-Fāḍil told 'Imād al-Dīn that Bohemond had gone to Tyre, but that this was said to have been in support of Raymond of Tripoli. He insisted that there was no time to wait for a reply from Mosul and that the only thing to do was to move to the nearest part of Saladin's own lands, provided that he was still able to ride and did not have to be carried on a litter. He then told 'Imād al-Dīn that Saladin's wife, 'Iṣmat al-Dīn, had died in Damascus on the night of 26/27 January; to shield Saladin from the shock of this news, 'Imād al-Dīn was to censor his letters and to warn all those who had access to him.[65] 'Imād al-Dīn himself reported that every day during this period Saladin would call for paper and write a long letter to 'Iṣmat al-Dīn, the news of whose death was not broken to him until March.[66]

One of the crises of Saladin's illness came on 1 February. Al-Fāḍil wrote for details and asked 'Imād al-Dīn if possible to send a daily report. He repeated his advice that Saladin should not stay at Ḥarrān; there was danger from the Turkmans and the fact that Saladin's troops had dispersed was known to friend and foe; "I do not think that gentle movement would produce incapacity...and there is an obvious advantage in reaching the frontiers of the Sultan's lands." He referred to differences of opinion about the proper treatment of the disease; Ibn al-Miṭrān, one of Saladin's personal doctors, had left for Ḥarrān and had been followed by al-

Riḍā' al-Raḥbī; neither had taken much in the way of supplies, as they were relying on being given tents, food and fodder when they arrived. 'Imād al-Dīn was asked to attend to this and the *ṭawāshī* Qaimāz was to look after them so that they could devote themselves to caring for Saladin.[67]

Not long after this, there was a change for the better. A letter written by 'Imād al-Dīn, apparently on 11 February, gave "the pleasantest of good tidings in this world and the next",[68] and al-Fāḍil was sure that there could no longer be any unpleasant consequences. He later sent word to Qarā-Qūsh in Egypt that a *mamlūk* had arrived in Damascus on 12 February with a letter containing a few lines written in Saladin's own hand; Saladin had said that, when all the devices of men had been exhausted, grace had descended on him from heaven. The letter itself had been sent by al-Fāḍil to Taqī al-Dīn and "no doubt our friends will read it and share in the joy". He added that the lands were being properly administered and that there had been no attempt at revolt.[69]

This recovery too was short-lived. Al-Fāḍil received news in a letter dated to 18 February that Saladin was again unable to sit up – "which prevented me from lying down and robbed me of my rest" –, that he had suffered from a recurrence of pain, and that his faculties were weakened and his limbs emaciated. Al-Fāḍil had heard that Saladin "often thinks that I am on my way to him... By God, I have had this intention since the start of my illness"; rumours, however, were spreading in Damascus and in the lands of the Franks and all responsible people left in Damascus had asked him to stay – presumably to help keep the situation under control; also, the evil doings of the Turkmans had spread and they now had "a stranglehold on the road"; if he left for Ḥarrān he would have to take a large caravan with him, but he did not have enough force to resist an attack. He added some recommendations for 'Imād al-Dīn; when letters were sent to Damascus there must be one for Ibn al-Muqaddam, for he was "the leader and the man to whom people point in the town"; Saladin should come back to Aleppo and give up turning towards other regions for additional gains, and in this context al-Fāḍil added that a Frankish raid seemed not far off; finally, 'Imād al-Dīn was to keep the peace amongst the doctors and to see that there was no harmful rivalry amongst them, so that they could concentrate on their service and not on their expected gains.[70]

At Ḥarrān 'Imād al-Dīn wrote: "we were afraid of the strength of the rumours and the spread of bad news which could not be concealed, especially when the doctors went out and said that there was no hope... Then you could see people sending off their treasures". At this stage, however, al-'Ādil arrived from Aleppo and his presence, according to 'Imād al-Dīn, "removed all fear".[71] Saladin's second son, 'Uthmān, was also at Ḥarrān, and two of his youngest sons, Tūrān-Shāh and Malik-Shāh, were brought with their mother from Damascus. His cousin, Nāṣir al-Dīn Muḥammad, had been in the camp but had returned to his *iqṭā'* of Homs where on 3 March he died of a disease "faster than the blink of an eye".[72] The speed and unexpectedness of this led to rumours. Nāṣir al-Dīn could plausibly have been thought to feel that more was owed him than he had received during Saladin's reign. He was said to have distributed money and collected men in Aleppo as he passed on his way from Ḥarrān to Homs[73] and he was credited with having made what could be thought of as treasonable approaches to Damascus. He died after drinking wine and one story suggested that he had been poisoned by Saladin's agent, al-Nāṣiḥ Ibn al-'Amīd, a man whom Saladin had put in charge of the *dīwān* of Aleppo in 1183.[74] Not surprisingly, there is no hint of this in the letters and in these Nāṣir al-Dīn's death is subordinated to the good news of Saladin's final recovery and to the conclusion of peace with Mosul.

Ibn Shaddād had arrived at Ḥarrān with another envoy from Mosul at the start of the month of Dhū'l-Ḥijja (23 February).[75] Saladin's life was still thought to be in danger but he then recovered sufficiently to receive the envoys and a treaty was finally concluded on 4 March. On this day al-Fāḍil received a letter from al-Afḍal to which he replied by referring to the widely-spread good news of Saladin's health. He added that Nāṣir al-Dīn had died of a disease too rapid to be treated; it was hoped that this would be the last of the disasters, but it was hard for al-Fāḍil to write of it as tears were flowing from his eyes and if he expressed his real sorrow, blood would be flowing with the tears; nothing could minimise the loss, except to balance it against the greater gain, and if al-Afḍal compared the one taken to the one left, he would realise that the balance was tilted to congratulations rather than to condolence.[76]

In another letter al-Fāḍil told al-Afḍal that Saladin's disease had now completely gone; the doctors had been alarmed by the state of his urine, but this was now healthy and he had recovered his natural desires. Al-Fāḍil added: "the grace is perfected by his acceptance of a pact with Mosul"; 'Izz al-Dīn had agreed to swear obedience, to come in person and with his troops at need, to add Saladin's name to the *khuṭba* and to drop that of al-Pahlawān; he was to remove injustices from his lands, to break with the '*ajamīs* and to give up the places that had entered Saladin's service, that is, Jazīrat ibn 'Umar and Irbil; he was also to abandon his claims to what lay beyond the Zāb, including Shahrazūr, Ḥadītha, Takrīt and 'Āna. Al-Fāḍil ended by saying that the Franks had kept to their agreement and there had been no raids; nevertheless there had been difficulties (unspecified) in Damascus and great anxiety for Saladin; now, however, everyone was rejoicing in the unification of Islam and their aim must now be the Holy War.[77] A letter was sent to Yemen to tell Ṭughtekīn of the agreement; Mosul had been left with 'Izz al-Dīn on condition that he accepted Saladin's authority and this now extended throughout the Jazīra and Diyār Bakr.[78] According to Ibn Shaddād, Saladin took the district of Bain al-Nahrain, east of Niṣībīn, from Sanjar-Shāh and gave it to 'Izz al-Dīn, presumably as a gesture of reconciliation.[79]

In some ways this agreement with the Mosulis and the circumstances that surrounded it marked the nadir of Saladin's career. Since the autumn of 1174 he had spent some thirteen months fighting the Franks and thirty-three in campaigns against his fellow-Muslims. The sequence of letters written after the death of al-Ṣāliḥ show his unswerving determination to improve his own position at the expense of any possible Muslim rival. Qilij-Arslān, 'Izz al-Dīn Mas'ūd, 'Imād al-Dīn Zangī, Shāh-Arman and al-Pahlawān were all indicted as enemies of Islam, disparaged as incompetents or attacked on both grounds for no better reason than that they tried to deny Saladin lands to which he had no acceptable claim. During his stay in Syria, it was only to the east of the Jordan that he seems seriously to have intended to seize and hold Frankish fortresses and this can be seen as no more than an attempt to improve his communications with Egypt. He effected no lodgement elsewhere in Frankish territory and neither at Kerak nor at 'Ain Jālūt, in spite of his numbers, did he press for a decisive battle. He might have been absolved from responsibility for claims made in his name had it not been shown that al-Fāḍil dissociated himself from the attack on Qilij-Arslān, the second Mosul expedition and the pressure brought to bear on the Caliph. 'Imād al-Dīn's account makes clear the limitations of his own influence and although counsellors such as Ḍiyā' al-Dīn 'Īsā may take their share of blame, Saladin and not his scribes must be seen as the prime mover in the campaign of propaganda.

The successes that he achieved have to be set against the objectives that this propaganda revealed. The grand design of a united Syrian front was arguably realised by the Mosuli settlement, but the pan-Islamic empire was a chimera. It had observably distracted his attention from Palestine and its titular head, the Abbasid Caliph, had kept himself as far as possible from taking Saladin's part. Saladin constantly referred to the exactions and unpopularity of his rivals but the measure of his own control over his lands has to be questioned. Order was maintained in the cities, but roads were dangerous and communications interrupted. Specifically, in spite of his campaigns east of the Euphrates and his claims to lands beyond the Tigris, al-Fāḍil could point to the risks that he ran by staying even at Ḥarrān and the Turkman/Kurdish feud "threatened the lands with eclipse". The picture is one of superficial authority, fluctuating with the size of the army that imposed it.

The supreme importance of Saladin's army to his calculations can be seen in the figure of Egyptian expenditure already quoted from al-Fāḍil. The details may be exaggerated, but the pattern shown is clear, with five times as much money being spent on the army as under all other heads of expenditure, which in themselves included fortifications and the navy. Such a distortion goes beyond the bounds of a managed economy, however flexible. This is confirmed by the fact that Saladin is shown living, at times, hand to mouth on private loans and extortions and it must be concluded that, far from exercising real control over the economy, Saladin concentrated his attention as an administrator on the men/money equation, which he tried to resolve by expansionism.

His death at Ḥarrān could only have left him with the reputation of a moderately successful soldier, an administrator with a cavalry commander's view of economics and a dynast who used Islam for his own purposes. The gentle side of his character, so attractive to his eulogists, is blurred by his estrangement from al-Fāḍil, his arrest of Keukburī and his rejection of the Atabek embassy. Repeatedly expressed hopes for quick victories cast doubts on his intelligence. He held to one idea, the importance of military strength, and allowed himself to become its prisoner, trapped in the cycle of expansionism. The defence of this policy, that it paved the way for the conquest of the Coast, could not have been accepted unless he had left behind a united kingdom. As it was, in addition to the suspicions aroused by Nāṣir al-Dīn Muḥammad, there were rumours that Taqī al-Dīn was preparing to oust al-Afḍal from Egypt and even al-'Ādil was said to have tried to engineer an oath of loyalty to himself.[80] The Franks could confidently have looked forward to a period of discord after his death and the capture of Jerusalem would have been as far removed as ever.

In the event, Saladin was given a second chance, not only by his recovery, which allowed him the opportunity to repair his reputation, but by the death of al-Pahlawān in March 1186. The normal pattern of expansion dictated that one conquest had to be defended by another until some form of equilibrium was reached. Thus Saladin's successes west of Mosul had led to the approach from Irbil which, in turn, had led to the second Mosul expedition. This had now given Saladin lands beyond Irbil and to defend these he could have expected sooner or later to have to fight against al-Pahlawān and his brother. Al-Pahlawān's death, however, broke the pattern. It was followed by violent disturbances which affected the transmission of power. Saladin was not in a position to try to take advantage of these troubles, but what was of the greatest importance was the fact that he did not immediately have to defend his eastern dependencies. It can be argued that had it not been for the accidents of war he would have returned to Iraq, but in fact he never campaigned east of the Euphrates again and it may be that he was genuinely determined to spend the life that had been left him in the service of the Holy War. He was said to have vowed during his illness that if he survived he would devote himself to the capture of Jerusalem at whatever cost in lives and money. 'Imād al-Dīn, who never allowed himself any serious criticism of his master wrote: "that sickness was sent by God to turn away sins...and to wake him from the sleep of forgetfulness".[81]

15

PREPARATIONS

At the start of the Muslim year 582 (24 March 1186) Saladin left Ḥarrān and moved to Aleppo. He was met at the Euphrates by Shīrkūh, the thirteen-year-old son of Nāṣir al-Dīn Muḥammad, who was now formally confirmed in possession of his father's lands. 'Imād al-Dīn quoted from the diploma granting him "all the lands, estates, castles, *iqṭā's* and administrative regions" that had been held by his father, including those of Homs, Tadmur and al-Raḥba.[1] On 6 April Saladin reached Aleppo, where al-'Ādil had prepared a reception for him, and al-'Ādil then accompanied him southwards four days later. At Hama they were welcomed by Mankūrus, the son of Khumartekīn of Bū Qubais, who was acting as Taqī al-Dīn's deputy, and from there they went to Homs, where Saladin inspected the treasures and stores left by Naṣīr al-Dīn, valued by 'Imād al-Dīn at over one million dinars. Saladin's sister, Naṣīr al-Dīn's widow, was given her share and the rest was divided amongst his children in accordance with the Islamic laws of inheritance. 'Imād al-Dīn insisted that Saladin took nothing for himself, but Ibn al-Athīr claimed that he had removed most of the money, horses and weapons.[2] He added that Saladin asked the young Shīrkūh how far he had got in memorising the Quran, and Shīrkūh replied: "as far as the verse: 'Those who eat the property of the orphan unjustly are feeding their bellies with fire.' "[3] From Homs Saladin moved towards Damascus and 'Imād al-Dīn was told to send on word of his approach. He reached the city on 23 May after an absence of more than a year and 'Imād al-Dīn wrote of the delighted reception given to him by the Damascenes who could now see for themselves that he was safe.[4]

In the meanwhile, al-Fāḍil had continued his correspondence with al-Afḍal, who reached his sixteenth birthday in June 1186. He had attracted a personal following in Egypt but according to 'Imād al-

Dīn's account there had been friction between him and Taqī al-Dīn.[5] Taqī al-Dīn had written to complain of the situation, saying that he could neither run counter to al-Afḍal's wishes nor could he govern the country properly, and during his stay at Ḥarrān Saladin had invited al-Afḍal to move to Syria. According to 'Imād al-Dīn, al-Afḍal had been eager to accept, seeing in this "the achievement of his aims".[6] Al-Fāḍil wrote to him at this stage to say: "my master should know that the Sultan does not move him from one frontier post except to another, from one affair except to another important affair or from one sultanate except to another... For he is...the eldest of the sons."[7] Al-Afḍal replied that he had already moved out of Cairo but was waiting to collect enough troops to ensure a safe journey,[8] a precaution of which al-Fāḍil approved. At this point, however, Saladin sent him orders to wait. The reason turned out to be "news from the damned enemy", of a reported Frankish raid on Bedouin by the Egyptian border, which al-Fāḍil considered to be a good thing; "if it is true that the Franks have broken the truce after having asked for it, then the wheel of ruin will turn against them".[9] Al-Afḍal was to wait until Saladin reached Damascus, when new instructions would be sent to him. Al-Fāḍil himself had joined Saladin outside Aleppo in April and had told him, or so he reported, of al-Afḍal's excellent deeds and laudable character. From Damascus he wrote another letter to tell al-Afḍal that every doubt was now settled; Syria was awaiting his arrival as she awaited the rain-clouds.[10]

Al-Afḍal arrived outside Damascus on 11 August[11] and the leading men of the city were sent to escort him to the citadel in "a procession like that of the Sultan". 'Imād al-Dīn added that at this point Saladin wrote to tell Taqī al-Dīn that "his thirst could now be quenched by his absolute power in Egypt", at which Taqī al-Dīn made the mistake of appearing overjoyed. 'Imād al-Dīn wrote: "had he shielded himself behind Saladin's son and said: 'there is no governance in your lands except through the rule of your son and I shall be responsible for his upbringing and be his agent in the government', then it would have been difficult to move him".

'Imād al-Dīn then gave details of what he obviously thought was the correct way of approaching Saladin. Al-'Ādil, who may now have been regretting his move from Egypt, came to Damascus in June, where he went to al-Ẓāhir and said: "I have left Aleppo for you and I shall be satisfied with *iqṭā's* from my brother, wherever they may be, and shall remain with him and not leave him. If you want Aleppo, you should ask for it from your father." He then told Saladin: "in spite of my desire for Aleppo, I think that one of your sons has a greater right to it", and he suggested that it should be given to al-Ẓāhir. Saladin shelved the affair for the moment, saying that the pressing problem was to send 'Uthmān – his second son – to Egypt, "for I must have a son there on whom I can rely".

A dramatised view of the difficulty is quoted by Ibn al-Athīr, who represents 'Alam al-Dīn Sulaimān as having earlier told Saladin that he was taking less thought for his children than a bird for her fledgelings: "you have given the fortresses to your relatives and left your children on the ground." He went on to point out that Aleppo was held by al-'Ādil and Homs by Nāṣir al-Dīn, while Taqī al-Dīn not only held the *iqṭā'* of Hama but could drive al-Afḍal from Egypt whenever he wanted.[12] Egypt, in fact, was perhaps the only real danger here and Taqī al-Dīn had already shown signs of discontent and independence. If he was to be removed, al-'Ādil was the obvious replacement. Al-'Ādil himself later quoted to Ibn Shaddād a conversation that he had had with 'Uthmān and al-Ẓāhir, in which he warned them that mischief-makers would do their best to cause trouble. Significantly he added that they would try to make 'Uthmān afraid of him; he relied on al-Ẓāhir to put things right, "for your brother may listen to what they say".[13]

Al-Ẓāhir entered Aleppo on 27 August, while 'Uthmān and al-'Ādil prepared to leave for Egypt. Up to this point the reshuffle had gone smoothly, but according to 'Imād al-Dīn, when Taqī al-Dīn heard the news he "rebounded" across the Nile to Giza.[14] He had already talked of leaving Egypt in order to attack the Almohades and he now revived this plan, writing to Saladin to say that his heart was set on a new kingdom "and climes with long shadows". His generosity had made him popular with the Egyptian army and Saladin was obviously afraid that he would attract recruits. 'Imād al-Dīn quoted him saying: "the capture of the Maghrib is important but that of Jerusalem is more important... If Taqī al-Dīn takes my veterans away with him, then my life will be spent in collecting men, whereas if we capture Jerusalem and the Coast [first], then we can attack these provinces."[15]

'Imād al-Dīn went on to say that Saladin "knew Taqī al-Dīn's obstinacy",[16] and so decided to invite him to Syria for a visit in order to give him advice. Al-Fāḍil added his own remonstrances – which would have applied equally to Saladin himself – and wrote: "how shall we turn aside to fight with Muslims, which is forbidden, when we are called to war against the people of war?",[17] and he quoted from the Quran: "Is there not amongst you a man rightly guided?"[18] Ibn al-Athīr dramatised the story by writing that Ḍiyā' al-Dīn 'Īsā was sent to Egypt to remove Taqī al-Dīn. He arrived unexpectedly in Cairo and when Taqī al-Dīn asked for a delay, 'Īsā refused. Taqī al-Dīn then threatened to march west, only to be told by 'Īsā: "go where you want".[19] On Saladin's invitation Taqī al-Dīn then left his men behind and came to Damascus at the start of November 1186, having presumably passed al-'Ādil and 'Uthmān on their way to Egypt. According to 'Imād al-Dīn, Saladin treated him with extreme kindness and generosity and promised him all the *iqṭā's* that he had earlier held in Syria. A more important grant was that of Mayyāfāriqīn, together with all the castles "in that clime".[20] This opened up prospects of expansion in the north and east and Taqī al-Dīn now agreed to call off his attack on the Maghrib and to abandon Egypt.

Saladin completed his dynastic precautions by arranging, or approving, the marriage of al-Ẓāhir to Ghāziya Khātūn, one of al-'Ādil's daughters, and of al-Afḍal to Safrā Khātūn, the daughter of Nāṣir al-Dīn Muḥammad. For the rest, the seriousness of his illness required a long convalescence, which appears to have been enlivened only by hawking, hunting and pious discussions. 'Imād al-Dīn arranged for an edifying concourse of preachers and *faqīhs* during Ramaḍān,[21] but Saladin objected to the *faqīhs* because their debates always led to quarrels and rancour.[22] Another diversion was provided by the astrologers who said that the world would end with a great storm of wind in the autumn of 1186, a prediction which Michael the Syrian claimed to have heard over a period of thirty years.[23] This allowed Saladin's court to "laugh at the feeble minds"[24] of those who had dug shelters or prepared caves stocked with food and water. On the night in question, according to 'Imād al-Dīn, Saladin was seated with his attendants in an open place, discussing the traditions of the Prophet by candlelight. No breath of wind came and "we never saw a night as calm as that".[25] Al-Fāḍil tried his own form of therapy. He was quoted as saying that when Saladin returned to Damascus he was still in considerable pain and thought that his life was drawing to a close. One Friday, to divert his mind, al-Fāḍil told him to vow to God that if he recovered he would never fight Muslims again but would devote himself to the Holy War. He was also to promise that if he captured Reynald de Châtillon or Raymond of Tripoli he would kill them, "for victory can never be complete until after their deaths".[26]

Raymond of Tripoli was soon to be seen in a different light. The Muslims had an informed interest in their neighbour's politics and both 'Imād al-Dīn and Ibn al-Athīr give virtually the same account of the background to the coronation of Guy de Lusignan in the summer of 1186. Raymond – the greatest of the Franks, the bravest and wisest in council, as Ibn al-Athīr describes him – had married "the Countess, Lady of Tiberias", and on the death of Baldwin the Leper, he had acted as agent for Baldwin's nephew. This boy had died and to Raymond's disappointment the kingdom passed to his mother (Sibylla). 'Imād al-Dīn wrote that, after marrying one of the western Franks, "she summoned the Barons and Hospitallers and the Templars and said: 'this is my husband and I have transferred my kingdom to him'. They then placed the crown on his head." Raymond was asked to account for his stewardship and Ibn al-Athīr added that he was accused of misappropriating money for his own ends.[27]

These versions, although inaccurate, reflect the story recorded in the Latin *Continuation* of William of Tyre which reports that on the death of the boy king at Ascalon it had been decided that Sibylla, who had already married Guy de Lusignan, should take the kingdom on condition that she divorced him. At an assembly of the nobles, however, she turned to Guy and said: "my Lord Guy, I take you as my husband; I give myself and the kingdom to you and I publicly proclaim you as the future king." Raymond alone objected, "although more would have agreed with him had they not feared the queen's anger".[28] He withdrew without leave from the assembly and a later addition to the *Continuation* says that on his way back to Tripoli he met Saladin's nephew and agreed to come to terms with the Muslims.[29] He paid Saladin formal homage for Tripoli and moved with his permission to Tiberias, where his wife was staying.

The nephew referred to here must have been Taqī al-Dīn, who could be expected to have returned to Hama in November and might well have been in touch with his Frankish neighbour. This detail is not given in the Arabic sources, but 'Imād al-Dīn notes that Raymond "sought for refuge with Saladin and sent messengers offering obedience".[30] Some suspected a trick, but Saladin thought that this represented a genuine split amongst the Franks and he released a number of Raymond's knights whom he was holding prisoner and for whom large ransoms had been demanded. 'Imād al-Dīn added that the frontier – presumably by Tiberias – was secure and that a number of Muslim raiding parties entered and left

Frankish territory that way without hindrance; "had it not been for fear of his co-religionaries, Raymond would have become a Muslim".

If Raymond had temporarily been struck off the list of Saladin's enemies, Reynald de Châtillon kept his position by attacking a Muslim caravan. 'Imād al-Dīn wrote of him that he was the most treacherous of the Franks and that "we used to raid his lands each year", until he asked for a truce.[31] How much reliance the Muslims ever put on this is open to doubt in the light of the remarks about al-Afḍal's need for an escort from Egypt to Syria. It may have been felt, however, that as Reynald was allowed to levy tolls from passing Muslims, it would not be in his interests to break the truce except for some particularly tempting prize or the Muslims may simply have become careless with the passing of time, since, "when the opportunity for treachery arose", as 'Imād al-Dīn put it,[32] Reynald was able to capture a large Egyptian caravan with its military escort. Saladin demanded that all prisoners should be released and all property returned, but Reynald refused. Both 'Imād al-Dīn and Ibn al-Athīr agree that Saladin now swore to kill him[33] – for the second time, if al-Fāḍil's account is correct. The Latin *Continuation* added that Raymond of Tripoli took the matter up, but Reynald, who was on bad terms with him, prepared to resist any attempt at coercion and Raymond was left to report his refusal to Saladin.[34]

The seizure of the caravan may have envenomed Saladin's relations with Reynald, but it was obvious even without this that the Holy War was about to be resumed. Saladin had at his disposal troops from Egypt, Syria, the Euphrates and the Tigris, and for the sake of his reputation he needed a victory against the Franks. Accordingly, now that he was fully recovered, he summoned his armies and moved out of Damascus at the start of the Muslim year 583 (13 March 1187) to camp at Ra's al-Mā'. Taqī al-Dīn was sent north to watch the Armenians and the Antioch frontier; al-Afḍal was left to muster the new arrivals at Ra's al-Mā' and Saladin himself marched south towards Buṣrā (map 8). He was concerned to protect the pilgrims returning to Syria from Mecca, amongst whom was his sister, the widow of Nāṣir al-Dīn Muḥammad, and her son by an earlier marriage, Ḥusām al-Dīn Muḥammad. He also intended to meet the troops whom he had called up from Egypt and to repay Reynald by ravaging his lands and making yet another attack on Kerak.

On the evening of 26/27 April al-Fāḍil wrote from Saladin's camp to tell al-Afḍal that a messenger had just arrived from Egypt; he had left the Egyptian troops at Ṣudr on Monday (22 April) and they were expected to reach Eilat in four days; "men's minds were gladdened and strengthened at this news and the rumours [unspecified] that had spread were cut off"; Saladin had renewed his attack on the township of Kerak on 26 April, burning and destroying houses as well as killing a knight; the Turkmans had ravaged the countryside; vines had been cut down, villages destroyed, and the peasants had gone off with their wives and children to the lands of Islam. Al-Fāḍil ended by writing: "good counsel has been sent by letter to the master [al-Afḍal] telling him to move [his men] if an opportunity arises, but to stay behind in camp himself... The servant knows that the master is sometimes hasty, but to follow the injunction of the Sultan is more useful."[35]

Almost immediately after this al-Fāḍil sent al-Afḍal another letter on the day on which it was reckoned that the Egyptian troops would have passed Eilat; Saladin was still camped at Kerak and there was no news of Reynald or of his wife "the wood-carrier";[36] the Franks were reported to be still "sitting in their lands", and meanwhile Saladin was destroying the cornfields of Kerak; al-Afḍal had been told to seize any opportunity that arose to attack the Franks "in that quarter" (the Damascus frontier) and to send out his men, if he was sure that this could be done safely, but Saladin had now changed his mind; he thought it better for al-Afḍal's troops to stay where they were in readiness for the Holy War and he himself, God willing, would not be long in returning.[37]

Saladin's change of mind seems to have been followed by an alteration of the plan for his own return. According to 'Imād al-Dīn he went down to meet the Egyptian troops at al-Qaryatain and he stayed there to ravage the lands of Kerak and Shaubak until late May.[38] Al-Afḍal, meanwhile, who later claimed that his orders from Saladin to stay in camp had been delayed,[39] had moved from Ra's al-Mā' to al-Qaḥwānī at the foot of the Sea of Galilee and his troops crossed the Jordan to raid Frankish territory. In a letter giving news of this to Ṭughtekīn, Saladin wrote that: "the leader of our force was Keukburī and with him was our *mamlūk* Ṣārim al-Dīn Qaimāz".[40] 'Imād al-Dīn added that Keukburī led the contingents from east of the Euphrates and Qaimāz those of Damascus and he also noted the presence of a third leader, Badr al-Dīn Dildirim, who was in command of the Aleppans.[41] The Arabic sources reported that they made a night march to Sepphoris, where they were attacked by "Templars, Hospitallers, Barons and Turcopoles".[42] According to the anonymous author of the *Libellus de Expugnatione Terrae Sanctae*, the raiders were seen from the hills of Nazareth and a force went out to meet them, including the Master of the Templars and the Master of the Hospitallers, who happened to have been passing on a mission to Raymond.[43] Frankish numbers were put at 130 horse and 300–400 foot,[44] while another account credited "Manafaradin admiral of Edessa" (i.e. Muẓaffar al-Dīn Keukburī) with 7000 men.[45] The Master of the Hospitallers, Roger des Moulins, is said to have told his companions not to be afraid of "these raging dogs, who flourish today but tomorrow will be cast into a lake of fire and brimstone",[46] but the Franks were surrounded and destroyed, although Gérard de Ridefort, Master of the Templars, managed to escape. The Arabic historians note the death of the Master of the Hospitallers and add that prisoners were taken and that the raiders returned safely with their booty.[47]

There is some question about the part played by al-Afḍal himself. He wrote a letter to his father in Rabī'a 1 (11 May/9 June) about his victory on "the first battlefield that he had witnessed":

> the first fruits of merit are like virgin girls, splendid in their beauty but difficult to attain, who are led in marriage only to those who can look after them and pay the high cost of their dowry... The servant has obtained one of great value after a short courtship... This letter contains the first good news given to the master of the prey seized by his cub, who stood in his father's place and struck with his sword.[48]

It is clear both from the narrative accounts and from Saladin's letter to Ṭughtekīn that al-Afḍal was not, in fact, present at the battle, but it is difficult to see how he could have written so glowingly in his own praise if he had seen no action at all. This, together with a remark in the Latin *Continuation* that the Muslims moved on Tiberias "with all kinds of engines",[49] suggests that al-Afḍal himself moved from al-Qaḥwānī to threaten Tiberias, while his flying column rode westwards by night towards Sepphoris (map 2) and then rejoined him after their battle.

It appears from a Fāḍilī letter that al-Afḍal had thought of moving from al-Qaḥwāni to meet his father. Al-Fāḍil approved of this because of the help that he would be able to give "with his tongue when he counselled and with his resolution when he took an affair in hand",[50] but this would have repeated the pattern of the 1184 campaign, where the Franks had taken advantage of al-'Ādil's move from Ra's al-Mā' to entrench themselves at al-Wāla. Saladin himself was determined to force a battle and the latest news of the Franks was that their army had moved from Jaffa northwards up the coast to Arsūf. This must have suggested that they had no immediate intention of marching to Kerak and if he wanted to fight, he would have to cross the Jordan. A move south, then, on the part of al-Afḍal would be pointless and, as a result, he must presumably have been ordered to stay by the frontier.

Taqī al-Dīn, meanwhile, who had entered Aleppo on 29 March, had been watching the northern frontier. On 20 April he moved out to Ḥārim, "so that the enemy might learn that this side was not neglected";[51] and, to reinforce the lesson, in May he sent out troops under the command of his son Sa'd al-Dīn to raid the lands of Antioch and Darbsāk (map 3). Saladin himself was still in the south. Nothing remained in the territories of Kerak he wrote, except for "one little citadel", which could not hold out for ever; there were no crops left in the lands of Shaubak except in the rough ground of the Sharāh region; the districts were empty, the villages ravaged and the inhabitants had gone. Al-Fāḍil, who passed this information to al-'Ādil, told him that there had been a reconciliation between Raymond of Tripoli and his fellow Franks, but "Islam is not disquieted by one who leaves its ranks nor pleased by one who enters its contract"; when the muster at Ra's al-Mā' was completed, Saladin would be able to strike and perhaps his banners and those of al-'Ādil would meet to answer the summons of God.[52]

Raymond of Tripoli's defection is mentioned in a letter sent to the Byzantine Emperor Isaac. Isaac had written to ask for Saladin's help in bargaining for the release of his brother who was being held by Raymond. Saladin replied first to congratulate him on his successes against "his Frankish enemies", and then to tell him that, after negotiations, Raymond had agreed to release his prisoner for a ransom; Saladin had earlier been on close terms with Raymond, who had implored his support – "He used us in order to set to rights his own affairs and to terrify his fellow Franks"; Saladin had thought that he would remain faithful to his compact, but instead he came to terms with the Franks and broke the agreement that had been made at his own request – "we had not wished to use him, but to be of use to him". Saladin then suggested that the Emperor might prefer not to enter into a huckster's bargain; he himself had collected the armies of the east and the west and had already used some of them to attack part of the enemy's territory; if the Emperor wished to move against the Franks, he would find support from the Muslims; "a rescue by the sword is nobler than one where money has to be weighed out".[53]

Saladin's appeal to kingly pride was presumably not intended as more than rhetorical seasoning for his letter and he cannot have been hopeful of his chances of luring Isaac into a full-scale war with the Franks. His diplomatic technique, however, was based on a form of optimistic simplification of situations where he was hoping to win friends rather than to achieve a specific result and according to Ibn al-Athīr he had tried this same method on Raymond by promising him a kingdom.[54] The Franks, however, seeing the danger of this muster of "Parthians, Bedouin, Arabs, Medes, Kurds and Egyptians",[55] had approached Raymond and a reconciliation had taken place. At this stage al-Afḍal, for all his inexperience, had apparently taken it on himself to send orders to Taqī al-Dīn telling him not to enter Raymond's lands and not to send al-'Adl to hand over "the prisoners", a reference, presumably, to more of Raymond's men whom Saladin had been on the point of releasing. Al-Afḍal is praised in this context by al-Fāḍil for his "alertness at seeking news and his subtlety in uncovering secrets hidden by the enemy",[56] which may imply that he had been the first to hear of Raymond's move. Al-Fāḍil went on to tell al-Afḍal that Saladin was now definitely coming to meet him; he was to investigate the question of pasturage and if his present camp site was short of grass, they would *rendezvous* at al-Fawwār. In fact, the meeting took place at Nūr al-Dīn's old camp at 'Ashtarā on 27 May.

Taqī al-Dīn now made a truce with Bohemond of Antioch "in the last ten days of the month Rabī'a I"[57] (31 May – 9 June), after which he moved south to join the muster. He brought with him troops from Mārdīn and a force from Mosul under the command of Fakhr al-Dīn Ībn al-Za'farānī. Sinjār, Niṣībīn, Āmid, Irbil and Diyār Bakr are also listed as having supplied men and together with the forces of Syria and Egypt this made up what 'Imād al-Dīn described as the most blessed and the largest army that he had ever seen.[58] Saladin boasted to the Caliph that the widest plain was too narrow for it and that on the march its dust darkened the eye of the sun.[59] Both 'Imād al-Dīn and Ibn al-Athīr put the number of the professional cavalry at 12,000 and Ibn al-Athīr adds an unspecified number of volunteers.[60] It is, of course, impossible to reach an exact figure. As has been shown, a muster role of some 6000 regulars at the battle of Tell al-Sulṭān gave a total estimated at 20,000. A letter to Pope Urban put Saladin's numbers at 80,000,[61] which is certainly a gross exaggeration as far as trained soldiers were concerned, but the 12,000 regulars, with their own retainers and servants, could not unreasonably provide an army of at least 30,000. There is no basis for any guess as to the number of volunteers and irregulars, but it was shown later in the campaign that they represented a sizeable force. To set against this, the best estimates of the muster now held by Guy de Lusignan give him 12,000 knights and from 15,000 to 18,000 infantry and Turcopoles.[62] Saladin, then, could fairly have hoped to outnumber the Franks by at least three to two and still have a large, though less disciplined, reserve.

In spite of this advantage, another letter reinforces the point made earlier by al-Fāḍil[63] that a number of Saladin's advisers were reluctant to attack. It implies that the Franks had made some tentative diplomatic advances and notes suggestions made to Saladin that he should take the pledges offered and recover Muslim prisoners, whom presumably the Franks had promised to release.[64] Ibn al-Athīr, giving his dramatised account of a war council, took care to point out that Saladin's reputation required a battle. Most of the emirs, he said, suggested that they should launch raids on Frankish territory. One unnamed leader, however, advised a march through Frankish lands, "and if any Frankish army stands before us, we shall meet them... For the people of the east curse us and say: 'Saladin abandoned the fight against the infidels and came to attack the Muslims.' My advice is that we should do something to establish our own excuse and check the tongues."[65] Saladin himself wanted to fight "with all the Muslims against all the infidels... 'For affairs do not run according to human desire nor do we know how much is left of our lives.' "[66]

16

ḤAṬṬĪN

Saladin's decision to fight proved to be correct, but political rather than purely military considerations tilted the balance in its favour. At 'Ain Jālūt in 1183 and during Baldwin's march from Tiberias in 1182, he had been unable to destroy a Frankish force fighting a defensive action on favourable ground. He could only hope to succeed now either if his swollen numbers could be put to effective use or if the ground or Frankish tactics played into his hands. On the other hand, although constant raiding might eventually bring down the Latin Kingdom, he was vulnerable to the criticisms suggested by Ibn al-Athīr and he could not hope to muster his easterners over a period of years unless he took some dramatic action. Fortunately for him, Guy de Lusignan's position was even weaker. He did not have the respect of the Franks; his coronation had caused resentment and, specifically, he had been criticised for his tactics at 'Ain Jālūt where, after his dangerous march in the face of the enemy, he had entrenched himself in a strong position and simply waited for Saladin to leave.

Saladin stayed at 'Ashtarā for a month, presumably to complete his preparations. He then held a review of his troops at Tell Tasīl, some 6 miles (10 km) north of 'Ashtarā on one of the main routes to the Jordan. The Parthian tactics of charge and retreat used by the Muslims were well adapted to small formations highly trained in the individual skills of fighting on horseback. Troops of this type could be expected to follow their leaders and to react on their own initiative to changing situations, but in the case of larger units, a source of tactical weakness was the fact that commanders did not have professional staff officers to transmit their orders. Saladin was no exception. On the battlefield his men could learn something from watching his banners or listening to his drums and he must have used servants to carry messages, but reactions are shown to have been slow or uncertain. Because of this it was particularly important that everyone should know where his station was, so that parts of the army could if need be act alone. As has been shown, the smallest tactical unit was the squadron (*ṭulb*), and these were assigned to larger formations named after their notional place on the battlefield. 'Imād al-Dīn wrote that at Tell Tasīl Saladin organised his army with a right, a left, a centre, two wings, a vanguard and a rearguard, together with skirmishers supplied by each squadron.[1] Unfortunately 'Imād al-Dīn is not reliable in such contexts and this may be no more than a rhetorical exaggeration of the normal organisation, with a centre and two wings. If it is accurate, however, it would imply that, with the extra size of his army, Saladin now felt it necessary to multiply its self-contained units. No further details are given, apart from the fact that Taqī al-Dīn commanded the right wing and Keukburī the left, while Saladin himself was in the centre.

The army moved from camp on Friday 26 June and halted after a short march of some 8 miles (13 km) at Khisfīn on a tongue of plateau bounded on the west by the Sea of Galilee and on the south-east by the Raqqad tributary of the river Yarmuk (map 2). On Saturday 27 June a 20-mile (32-km) march brought it down from the plateau to the south end of the Sea. Saladin was repeating almost exactly the opening move of his 1182 and 1183 campaigns, in both of which he had then turned south down the Jordan to attack Baisān. The Franks for their part were repeating their own counter-move and mustering at Sepphoris. Nothing happened on Sunday or Monday, as each side waited for the other, but on Tuesday Saladin showed his hand by leaving his heavy baggage and climbing westwards from the Jordan to Kafr Sabt. His position there was described by Ibn Shaddād as "on the flat top of the mountain",[2] this being the shoulder of a ridge to the north of Kafr Sabt that borders the plateau of the Horns of Ḥaṭṭīn. Kafr Sabt itself was 8 miles (13 km) north-west of Saladin's camp at the end of the Sea and almost halfway to Sepphoris. From it Saladin could threaten both Tiberias, which was now to his rear, and Sepphoris, which was in front of him, as well as the lines of communication between them, while he himself had an open retreat down easy slopes to the south-east.

At Sepphoris Guy de Lusignan was still not prepared to move. He may have been hoping for a stalemate – that Saladin would not challenge him on his own ground or dare to split his forces and so repeat his mistake of 1177, while if the whole Muslim army went to attack a Frankish town or castle, a relief force could move to its rescue without hindrance. The hill of Sepphoris itself is a strong defensive position in broken country within 5 miles (8 km) of Nazareth, dominated on the south-east by the Nazareth range and on the north-east by Mt Turan. Saladin wrote to his brother Ṭughtekīn that this was where he had wanted to fight and on Wednesday 1 July, the day after his move to Kafr Sabt, he rode up to the Frankish camp but then retired, telling Ṭughtekīn that the Franks were still not willing to come out.[3] If this is true and Guy refused to fight when the Muslims were 20 miles (32 km) from safety, it seems that Saladin must have followed his 'Ain Jālūt tactics and halted where he could dare the Franks to come against him over unfavourable ground. How far Saladin's letter can be trusted is, of course, arguable. He obviously had no intention of attacking Guy's camp and he may merely have been exaggerating what had only been a reconnaissance in force. His move to Kafr Sabt, however, shows that he was unquestionably looking for a battle, albeit on his own terms. When his challenge failed, he returned to Kafr Sabt and he added in his letter that he then reconnoitred the plain of Lūbiyā and found it suitable for a battle.

If he was to get his battle, however, he had to force the Franks out into the open and he now took the decision to split his army. At dawn on Thursday 2 July he himself attacked Tiberias with his own guards, "the burning coals of the Muslims",[4] together with a force of sappers and masons, while the bulk of the army were left at Kafr Sabt. An attempt was made by the Tiberias garrison to buy him off, but this was refused by "one who hoped to win God's reward by fighting against his enemies". He wrote: "when the people realised that they had an opponent who could not be tricked and would not be contented with tribute, they were afraid lest war might eat them up and they asked for quarter... But the servant gave the sword dominion over them."[5] The attack was concentrated on one tower which was mined and brought down during the course of the day. The Muslims stormed the breach and used scaling ladders on the walls. The townspeople were either killed or taken prisoner; the town was plundered and its combustible stores, of cotton and oil, were burnt.[6] Saladin boasted of the heaped piles of gold and silver that he had taken, together with horses and vast numbers of cattle.[7] The Frankish garrison, with Raymond's wife, the Countess Eschiva, had taken refuge in the citadel, which Saladin described as being strongly protected by a deep moat. The Muslim sappers were preparing for another attack, but at this point word came that at last the Franks were on the move.

News of Saladin's success had reached Sepphoris without delay. It was not in Saladin's interests to cut off calls for help and Guy's scouts may have been watching from the hills. On Thursday evening Guy held a war council. This was presented by some western sources as a tragedy with a peripeteia in the form of a disastrous midnight change of plan by the weak-willed King, misled by his evil genius, in this case the Master of the Templars.[8] The Arab historians ignored the drama but quoted arguments and attitudes. Ibn al-Athīr gave Raymond of Tripoli the role of the Thucydidean reasoner, producing the points that could best have been made in the circumstances,[9] and this is supported by a number of Frankish accounts.[10] In spite of the fact that his wife was in danger, Raymond was said to have advised Guy to abandon Tiberias; this was the largest and strongest Muslim army that he had ever seen, but if Saladin took Tiberias, his men would certainly want to disperse and go home. Ibn al-Athīr then made Reynald de Châtillon argue against Raymond and accused him of siding with Saladin, at which he promised to go with the rest of the Franks if they wanted to advance. 'Imād al-Dīn, on the other hand, wrote that on hearing of the capture of the town, Raymond said: "if Tiberias falls, all our lands are taken",[11] and this agrees with a statement in a letter to Pope Urban that Guy was urged to move by Raymond and by his step-sons who pressed him, "with tears", to go to their mother's rescue.[12]

The Arabic accounts are based, at best, on hearsay and guesswork and because of the personal feuds involved none of the Frankish reports can be accepted as unbiased.[13] Another important point is that the tactical plan behind Guy's march is unlikely to have been as suicidal as it has been represented, but the events that followed overshadowed and oversimplified the problems both for his contemporaries and for later historians. All that can safely be said is that Guy himself must have been under great pressure to move, especially because of the criticism of his actions at 'Ain Jālūt. It must also be true, as Ibn al-Athīr hinted, that had he taken his Fabian tactics to their logical end and left the citadel of Tiberias to fall – or had it been evacuated before the Muslim attack – Saladin might have found it difficult to avoid giving battle on Guy's terms rather than on his own, but the point was never put to the test.

Early on Friday 3 July the Frankish army moved out of Sepphoris on its way east. From Sepphoris the nearest part of the Sea of Galilee, to the north of Tiberias, is 15 miles (24 km) away as the crow flies. Although Guy could choose a reasonably direct route, every man on such a march would have to cover far more than this minimum distance. It must be remembered that in 1183 Guy's army had advanced 6 miles (10 km) from al-Fūla to 'Ain Jālūt in the face of the enemy. On 15 July 1182 the Frankish army, without serious opposition, had covered a straight-line distance of some 17 miles (27 km) from Tiberias to its bivouac south of Kaukab. On the next day, when it had had to fight its way through the Muslims, it had managed to complete no more than 8 miles (13 km).

As far as the terrain is concerned, the dominating feature of the first stage of the march from Sepphoris is the narrow east/west line of Mt Turan on the north side of the flat basin of Buṭṭauf (Bet Netofa). Had Guy traversed this basin he would have had the mountain between himself and Saladin's troops at Kafr Sabt, but he could have been intercepted without difficulty at the eastern end. Instead, he marched past the northern end of the Nazareth range onto the floor of a straight valley which runs for about 5 miles (8 km) between a lower prolongation of the Nazareth hills in the south and Turan in the north. His army was split into three divisions – the vanguard, led by Raymond of Tripoli, the centre, which he led himself, and the rearguard commanded by Balian of Ibelin. They must be presumed to have started in column of route.[14]

As soon as Guy moved, the Muslim scouts sent word to Saladin at Tiberias. The news was said to have reached him at the time of the dawn prayer[15] and he immediately left to join the bulk of his army some 6 miles (10 km) away at Kafr Sabt. The Frankish advance was watched by the Muslims, but no serious attempt was made to interfere with it until Saladin arrived. By this time, according to a letter to Baghdad, Guy had reached "one of the waters".[16] This can best refer to the spring by the site of the village of Turan, indented in the south face of Mt Turan, a position in tactical terms not unlike that of 'Ain Jālūt. According to Saladin, "the hawks of the Frankish infantry and the eagles of their cavalry hovered around the water", but then "Satan incited Guy to do what ran counter to his purpose", and he left the spring and marched on.

The Muslims did not know why Guy had advanced and as the western sources are silent, evidence has to be looked for on the ground itself. The eastern end of the valley by Turan is shut off by the high ground of a ridge system. This has a number of geographical complexities but in tactical terms it is a simple right-angled barrier to a force advancing eastwards along the valley. Its highest ground is at the south above Kafr Sabt and at the north by the peak of Nimrīn, and there is a considerable dip as it comes opposite the eastern end of Mt Turan. Behind it lies the plateau to the Horns of Ḥaṭṭīn. One road to Tiberias skirted this plateau to the south and another struck across the lower ground of the ridge and went down into the valley that flanks the plateau to the north.[17] On the floor of this valley is the village of Ḥaṭṭīn, which has a plentiful supply of water.

From his position by the spring of Turan Guy may not have seen the full extent of Saladin's army, but he can have been in no doubt as to where it was. Of the choices that were open to him, the first was to camp where he was, repeating the tactics of 'Ain Jālūt in the hope that Saladin might attack. Saladin, however, had never challenged the Franks in a strong defensive position and there was no reason to expect that he would do so now. Another choice was to press on to Tiberias itself. Here, however, the Franks still had a straight-line distance of some 9 miles (14 km) to cover. According to Saladin it was now almost noon,[18] which meant that Guy had only half a day for a longer march than had previously been achieved in a full day against the resistance of Saladin's troops. If he took the southern route, he would have to fight his way through Saladin's main concentration at Kafr Sabt. The northern route, across the ridge and down to the village of Ḥaṭṭīn, followed the line of a road and led to water, but this was of less importance for an army in action than the fact that the slopes, although far from precipitous, would make it more difficult to keep formation.

Rashness, stupidity or pressure could perhaps have led a commander to risk his troops on a march of this length and difficulty and these factors may have had their part to play in Guy's decision. This, however, can be condemned without reservation only if it is accepted that he must have been aiming for Tiberias. It should be noted here that both Mt Turan and the hills to the south stop short of the transverse north/south ridge, allowing the valley to open out so as to provide an obvious battlefield. Guy knew that the Muslims were holding the line of the high ground. If they came down to fight, a charge could pin them against the ridge itself. If they stayed where they were and their position appeared to be too strong to break or turn, he could return to the water at Turan and counter the threat to Tiberias by repeating his challenge as often as it was needed, while if he won any early advantage against Saladin's opposition, he could still decide to continue with his march. With these possibilities open to him, he cannot fairly be criticised for rashness and the suggestion must be that, far from behaving irresponsibly, he was challenging Saladin on a battlefield that looked not unfavourable and that his advance might have been accepted as a sound tactical move, apart from his one miscalculation, which was that of the effect of Saladin's extra numbers.

Saladin countered with his usual tactics. He always tried to outflank and then surround the Franks where the ground allowed, a manoeuvre that was merely an adaptation on a larger scale of the standard procedure of dealing with a Frankish charge. If this was to be successful, however, the Muslims had to be strong enough to prevent the surrounded Franks from cutting their way out again. On this occasion, when Guy moved towards the ridge at noon, Saladin sent both his wings, under Taqī al-Dīn and Keukburī, round the Frankish force to seize its water and block its retreat.[19] He himself had enough men to hold the ridge and this single manoeuvre won him the battle. The Franks later credited Taqī al-Dīn with 20,000 men,[20] and however exaggerated this may be, both wings together must have been strong enough to prevent Guy from thinking of drawing back, while the ridge itself helped hold up his advance. The Franks had presumably watered their horses at Turan, but the weather was very hot and they could not take up a defensive position for long without fresh supplies. The evidence suggests that Raymond now tried to save the situation by taking the army down the northern road towards the village of Ḥaṭṭīn. The move failed as the pressure was too heavy to allow the Franks to maintain their formation and they were shepherded up amongst the rocks towards the plateau. There they were forced to camp, hemmed in by Saladin's army, without water and without hope of any supplies or reinforcements.

Saladin himself spent the night of Friday/Saturday 3/4 July bringing up his supplies and reorganising his men. In spite of his success and the apparently hopeless position of the Franks, he still took care to see that skirmishers were detailed by name from each squadron. The Muslims were relying heavily on their archers to counter the armoured Frankish knights. Horse armour was uncommon at this period[21] and 'Imād al-Dīn noted that although the Frankish knights themselves were virtually indestructible, the loss of their horses could make them useless.[22] In view of this, 400 loads of arrows were distributed and arrangements were made for further supplies to be brought up in readiness.[23]

On the morning of Saturday 4 July both sides prepared to move.[24] The Muslim skirmishers started the battle, but Saladin did not commit the bulk of his troops until he saw which way Guy was intending to go. This implies that he thought that the Franks might still try to retire to Turan, but in the event they took "the road to the lake". The direction of the fighting supports the view that they were trying to keep to the south of the plateau. Saladin must have stationed his centre on the flank of this line, and it now marched out ahead of the Franks and then turned across their front. Western sources state that the Frankish infantry "formed into a single body and quickly climbed to the summit of a high hill",[25] refusing to come down at Guy's summons. This may have happened later in the battle but the Arabic accounts make it clear that to start with the Franks were still keeping formation, with the infantry shielding the cavalry, and Saladin suffered an initial loss when one of his own *mamlūks* charged without support and was killed. At this, however, the Muslim skirmishers renewed their attacks and although the Franks made a number of charges, "their lions", 'Imād al-Dīn wrote, "had become hedgehogs".[26]

The Franks were already suffering severely from heat and thirst and the Muslims now added to their miseries by starting a scrub fire,[27] the flames of which were blown down on them by a west wind which got up at noon. A number of Franks deserted and to the horror of their contemporaries[28] renounced their faith. In this desperate situation, Raymond of Tripoli, supported by Reginald of Sidon and Balian of Ibelin, charged Taqī al-Dīn's wing. According to the author of the *Libellus*, they had been cut off from the King who was with the Hospitallers and Templars and, seeing the destruction of their infantry, they decided to fight their way clear, as they could not get back to defend the Cross.[29] This may be wrong and the charge can perhaps be seen as part of a defensive move, since Taqī al-Dīn was pressing at the time, but in that case it failed. Taqī al-Dīn had enough space to open his ranks and allow the charge to sweep through while his archers shot at the riders as they passed. 'Imād al-Dīn added that Raymond went off at an angle "into the wādī", and so escaped with a handful of men.[30] Taqī al-Dīn's wing can be assumed still to have been to the west of the Franks, the position which it had taken up after it had outflanked them, and this would place it now at the north-west of the plateau under Mt Nimrīn. In that case Raymond would have been charging towards Mt Nimrīn and must then have gone over the side of the plateau into the valley after which he made for the castle of Ṣafad in the hills to the north. According to the author of the Latin *Continuation*, his escape was held against him by those who thought that he had played the traitor.[31] Saladin himself wrote that "although he has escaped in the short term, we shall catch up with him in the long term",[32] and taunted him with having taken to his heels "when he saw that the wheel was turning quickly against him".[33] In fact, however, it is difficult to see what he could have done when once he had passed through Taqī al-Dīn's ranks. With tired horses, and after the losses that his men had suffered, he could not have hoped to fight his way back or to alter the result of the battle, which was now irretrievably lost.

Saladin went on to tell the Caliph that the other Frankish leaders "remained firm with the firmness of those rushing on death...there was a hill which they climbed for protection... They charged again and began the fight anew."[34] The hill was that of the Horns of Ḥaṭṭīn. The Horns themselves can be seen from the south as two low heights joined by a short ridge overlooking the plateau that slopes down from the higher ground by Mt Nimrīn and tilts up gradually from the south. On the north the steep side of the valley over which they stand lends them height and dignity but acts as an effective barrier for horsemen. The Franks tried to camp in the shelter of the high ground. One of the western sources speaks of three tents being pitched, but Saladin and the Arab historians were only interested in the red tent of the King. The scene was described by al-Afḍal who was watching the battle by his father's side. He was quoted by Ibn al-Athīr as saying:

> when the King reached the hill with that company, they launched a savage charge against the Muslims opposite them, forcing them to retreat to my father. I looked at him and saw that he had turned ashen pale in his distress and had grasped his beard... Then the Muslims returned to the attack against the Franks and they went back up the hill. When I saw them retreating with the Muslims in pursuit, I cried out in joy: "we have beaten them". But the Franks charged again as they had done before and drove the Muslims up to my father. He did what he had done before and the Muslims turned back against them and forced them up to the hill. I cried out again: "we have beaten them". My father turned to me and said: "be silent. We shall not defeat them until that tent falls." As he spoke, the tent fell.[35]

The best line of charge from the slopes of the Horns is to the south-west, which fits with a picture of a Frankish advance towards the south-east blocked by Saladin's centre, which then shepherded them northwards across the plateau, with Taqī al-Dīn to their left front. When they were driven up to the Horns, they turned and charged back at the centre which had swung round behind them. With the failure of their charges there was no possibility of further resistance. The Frankish survivors were captured and the Cross itself taken.

Saladin, according to 'Imād al-Dīn, gave thanks to God for his victory.[36] He then had Guy de Lusignan brought to him together with Reynald de Châtillon, and he reproached Reynald for his treacherous conduct, at which Reynald replied through an interpreter that he had only followed the normal practice of kings. Guy was given iced water to relieve his thirst. He passed this to Reynald, at which Saladin told his interpreter: "say to the King: 'it is you who have given him to drink' ". Ibn Shaddād added that it was one of the laudable customs of the Arabs that when a captive had been given food or water by his captor, his life was safe. After an interval, Guy and Reynald were again summoned to Saladin's pavilion. Guy was left in the antechamber and Reynald was taken into Saladin's presence and offered conversion to Islam. When he refused, Saladin struck him with his own sword; his head was then cut off and his body dragged out past Guy. Guy himself was now brought in and Saladin told him: "it is not the custom of kings to kill each other, but he had overstepped the limit".[37]

The author of the Latin *Continuation* suggested that Saladin was either "following his own rage" or was envious of a man of such distinction as Reynald.[38] Ibn al-Athīr heard that Saladin had twice sworn to kill Reynald, the first time being when he had tried to attack the Holy Cities and the second when he took the Egyptian caravan by treachery.[39] 'Imād al-Dīn, who obviously found the action surprising, wrote that "he did not cease to investigate the reason for it", until he heard of the oath that al-Fāḍil had made Saladin swear.[40] Saladin himself wrote to Baghdad: "the servant had sworn to shed the blood of the tyrant of Kerak, a man who had afflicted the lands of Islam with death and captivity and who had fought previous battles [with the Muslims]... His loss was the greatest blow suffered by the unbelievers."[41]

On the night of Saturday/Sunday 4/5 July the Muslim army camped by the battlefield and on Sunday Saladin went to Tiberias, where the Countess Eschiva had no choice but to surrender the citadel. She was generously allowed to remove her possessions, money, family and followers, after which she left for her husband's town of Tripoli and Saladin added a reference in his letter to this fresh victory "before the sword had been sheathed or the horse unsaddled".[42] He could only hope now that all his past actions would be vindicated, his constant requests to be granted Muslim lands justified and his position as the hero of the Holy War finally and unconditionally acknowledged. He told the Caliph that he was planning to march on the enemy's lands; "all that has been mentioned and will be mentioned of achievements leading to glory in this world and nearness to God in the next comes about through the merits of the guiding dynasty [the Abbasids]".

Before he could leave, however, he had to clear his camp. The captured Frankish leaders were sent off to Damascus on Monday 6 July and their escort was ordered to get a receipt for their delivery from Saladin's treasurer, al-Ṣafī Ibn al-Qābiḍ.[43] The Cross was fixed upside down on a lance and carried into Damascus by the Qāḍī Sharaf al-Dīn Ibn Abī 'Aṣrūn. For the rest, a number of Saladin's men "dispersed for ever", taking their captives with them. Ibn Shaddād said that he had been told by a reliable witness that one Muslim with a tent rope had been seen leading some thirty Franks in the Ḥaurān[44] and 'Imād al-Dīn talked of "thirty and forty" bound by the same rope.[45] The price of a prisoner in Damascus fell to 3 dinars and Abū Shāma heard that one had been sold for a shoe. When his captor was asked about this, he said: "I wanted it to be talked about."[46]

Saladin now had second thoughts about the Templars and the Hospitallers. According to 'Imād al-Dīn, there was no advantage to be got from keeping them alive as it was not their habit to offer ransom and they could not be put to use in captivity. They were also, in the general opinion of the Muslims, the most formidable of the Franks and Saladin had already shown at Bait al-Aḥzān that he was prepared to kill dangerous prisoners. He did not expect their captors to give them up voluntarily, but offered 50 dinars for each man. Word was sent to al-Ṣafī at Damascus that every Templar or Hospitaller who had been taken there was to be killed and those who were still with the army were put to death on Monday. No one was killed without having been offered conversion to Islam, but according to 'Imād al-Dīn only a few accepted, although those who did became good Muslims. The rest were given over to amateur executioners chosen from amongst the *ṣūfīs* and "men of piety", some of whom appointed substitutes lest they be laughed at, while Saladin watched "with a glad face".[47] The author of the Latin *Continuation* added that the bodies of these "holy martyrs" were left unburied for three nights and were seen to be bathed in rays of heavenly light.[48]

Saladin entrusted Tiberias to Ṣārim al-Dīn Qaimāz, who had led the Damascus troops at Keukburī's battle, and on Tuesday 7 July he moved out with drums and trumpets to camp not far from Kafr Sabt. According to his own estimate, his army had killed over 40,000 Franks.[49] Other accounts put the dead at 30,000 with 3000 prisoners, and the number of those who escaped was variously set at 3000, 1000 or 200.[50] No amount of exaggeration can obscure the fact that the Frankish field army, and with it the offensive capacity of the Kingdom of Jerusalem, had been destroyed. To the north, Tripoli and Antioch were left with some strength but for the moment no Frankish force could meet the Muslims in the field. Saladin was challenged, however, by time and distance. Sooner or later a relief force was certain to come from Europe. It could either arrive by sea or else follow the path of the First Crusade through Asia Minor, where Qilij-Arslān could not be expected to put Saladin's interests before his own. As for the sea route, from Gaza to al-Suwaidīya, the Franks held some 350 miles (563 km) of coastline, with fortified harbours at Ascalon, Jaffa, Acre, Tyre, Sidon, Beirut, Jubail, Ṭarṭūs, Jabala and Latakia. Inland was the network of castles from Shaubak in the south to Darbsāk and Baghrās, north of Antioch. Without a field army, these had no chance of ultimate survival, as even if they could not be taken by storm, they had no answer to the besiegers' ultimate weapon of starvation. Were Saladin allowed time, he could deal with them one by one without difficulty, but if they were still in Frankish hands when a relief force came, then their old importance would return. Finally, as a complication, there was the position of Jerusalem. Jerusalem itself, isolated in its hills, had no real strategic importance, but it represented tangible proof not only of Saladin's success but of his sincerity. It had been the focal point in his efforts to win support and it had to be recovered before he could fairly test whether or not he had finally won his point.

17

THE CAPTURE OF JERUSALEM

The first essential now was speed, and Saladin sent an urgent summons to al-ʻĀdil[1] and moved off himself on Wednesday 8 July on a march of some 25 miles (40 km) to Acre. He rode with his guest, the emir of Medina, and ʻImād al-Dīn, who took naive pleasure in distinguished company, got as near as he could, "so that they could hear me and I could hear them".[2] The Muslims were not expecting opposition and were taken aback when they saw men and banners on the walls of Acre, but then apparently realised that this was an empty gesture of defiance and "spent the night moved by delight as though the wine cup was going round".[3] On Thursday 9 July they were drawn up in battle order, but envoys came out of the town to ask for quarter and terms were arranged.

Acre proved a particularly rich prize in that, according to Ibn al-Athīr, traders had been finding the markets sluggish and had stored goods there which now fell to the Muslims.[4] The town and its estates were given to al-Afḍal, while the property and lands of the Templars went to Ḍiyā' al-Dīn ʻĪsā. Taqī al-Dīn took over the sugar refinery and ʻImād al-Dīn had a house assigned to him the contents of which were sold for 700 dinars. ʻImād al-Dīn allowed himself one amicable criticism of Saladin's generosity and pointed out that had the wealth of Acre been kept in his treasury, it could have ensured the success of all his plans.[5] The passage was read out to Saladin some years later and he transferred the blame to ʻĪsā, Taqī al-Dīn and al-Afḍal. ʻImād al-Dīn wrote: "by my life, what he said was true", but added loyally that al-Afḍal had not wanted the money for himself but for his companions. Ibn al-Athīr pointed out that Saladin himself as well as al-Afḍal had given away what had been found at Acre and, although al-Afḍal had distributed more, this was because he had stayed longer in the town.[6]

To have hoarded the spoils as a precaution against future

difficulties would have been quite unlike Saladin's normal policy and the context of his success could not have encouraged prudence. For the Muslims were now spreading out. In normal circumstances Saladin disliked giving his subordinates independent command and was quoted as saying: "I never send out any of my companions or my family on an expedition without being fearful for them."[7] Now, however, there were no serious risks to be run and according to a Frankish letter the Muslims scattered "like ants, covering the whole face of the country from Tyre to Jerusalem."[8] Keukbūrī cleared the route from Tiberias to Acre by taking Nazareth. Sepphoris was found abandoned but full of stores. South of Nazareth the Templar castle at al-Fūla had only a few servants left by way of a garrison. They surrendered on terms of quarter and the Muslims then took Dabūrīya at the foot of Tabor, Tabor itself and Zar'īn on the hills above 'Ain Jālūt (map 2). Saladin's nephew, Ḥusām al-Dīn Muḥammad, moved into the hills of Samaria to Sebaste, which Saladin's raiders had passed in September 1184. According to 'Imād al-Dīn, the monks had only allowed Muslims to visit the shrine of John the Baptist there if they brought costly gifts[9] and these treasures were now collected on Ḥusām al-Dīn's orders. He "acquired all that for himself", and left only the furnishings and utensils necessary for a mosque, into which the church was then transformed. 'Imād al-Dīn went on to note that most of the villagers round Nablus, some 5 miles (8 km) south-east of Sebaste, were Muslims. When they were sure that the Franks were irremediably beaten, they staged the only local rising reported at this period and blockaded the citadel of Nablus, whose garrison then surrendered to Ḥusām al-Dīn.

Meanwhile, Badr al-Dīn Dildirim and a number of emirs had moved south down the coast from Acre. Haifa and Arsūf surrendered and Caesarea was taken by force. From the opposite direction al-'Ādil had come up on the coast road from Egypt by al-'Ārish. He appears to have bypassed Dārūm, Gaza and Ascalon, but Majdal Yābā, some 13 miles (21 km) inland from Jaffa, had surrendered to him, which put him just over 20 miles (32 km) from Ḥusām al-Dīn at Nablus and within 15 miles (24 km) of the Muslim force at Arsūf. His most important conquest was that of Jaffa itself, which he took by storm, and according to Ibn al-Athīr "its people suffered what no others in that country suffered". Ibn al-Athīr went on:

> when I was at Aleppo I had a slave girl from Jaffa. She had a baby about a year old. It fell from her grasp and grazed its face. She shed many tears over it and I calmed her and told her that there was no

> harm done to the child that needed tears. She said: "it is not for it that I am weeping but for what happened to us. I had six brothers, all of whom were killed, as well as a husband and two sisters, and I do not know what happened to them."[10]

With the Muslims advancing through Samaria and in virtual control of the southern coastal plain, Jerusalem was almost cut off. Saladin himself, however, rightly ignored it and turned his attention to the north, sending out Taqī al-Dīn to attack Tibnīn and Tyre. In part, this may have been a mistake since in the present campaign Tibnīn's position as the eastern bastion of Tyre had already been turned. Saladin's communications were not in danger, while Tyre itself was a vital strategic harbour which he had to deny to the Franks. He may simply have miscalculated the chances of resistance. Ibn Shaddād noted that the garrison of Tibnīn were "heroes, fierce in their religion",[11] and Taqī al-Dīn was forced to send back a stream of letters asking for reinforcements.[12] Saladin left Acre on Friday 17 July and was still to the south of Tibnīn, which is some 28 miles (45 km) in a straight-line distance from Acre, on Saturday night. He attacked it on Sunday 19 July, bringing up mangonels, and the garrison sent out Muslim prisoners to arrange terms for surrender. Saladin, however, showed no sense of urgency. He allowed the Franks a delay of five days to remove their possessions, during which time some of their leaders came out to act as hostages. Under the surrender terms, arms, horses and provisions had to be left behind, but the garrison removed anything else that they could take and were then sent under escort to Tyre.

Tyre itself had been held briefly by Raymond of Tripoli, who had halted there after his escape from Ḥaṭṭīn, but Ibn al-Athīr heard that he left it for Tripoli, thinking that its garrison was too small to resist and being sure that Saladin would attack.[13] Saladin himself, however, appeared for the moment to ignore it. Tibnīn had finally been handed over to him on Sunday 26 July and according to 'Imād al-Dīn, who was with the army, the Muslims then came down from the hills to the plain – which could refer to a march by Tyre or to one crossing the Litani river to the east of it – and reached Sidon within two days (map 8).[14] Sidon is some 23 miles (37 km) north of Tyre and Saladin in fact arrived there on Wednesday 29 July. 'Imād al-Dīn's two days cover Tuesday and Wednesday and Saladin must either have spent Monday at Tibnīn or else 'Imād al-Dīn has left out a march on that day to Tyre. According to the author of the Latin *Continuation*, Saladin did come to Tyre with the intention of attacking it, but he then saw that a siege would need "no small number of days".[15] These details are important only because he appears to have been making a serious mistake and this could best be excused had he reconnoitred the place and decided that it would have to be isolated before it could be taken. The timing, however, makes it clear that even if he went there at all, he could not have made any serious attempt to probe its defences and on these grounds it is difficult to clear him of a charge of carelessness.

While Tyre was enjoying its immunity, Saladin now led his army past the orange groves and flowers of Ṣarafand and received the immediate surrender of Sidon. He wasted no time there, but marched up the coast towards Beirut, 25 miles (40 km) away. He camped to the south of the town on Wednesday night and attacked on Thursday 30 July. There was some fierce resistance and 'Imād al-Dīn described how the Franks came out to fight in front of the outworks,[16] a tactic used to prevent mining. It was this, however, that led directly to the fall of the town. When the defenders were eventually forced back within the walls, the townspeople thought that the Muslims had broken in and rushed to the harbour to try to escape by sea. In the confusion that followed, it was thought that the only safety lay in immediate surrender and Saladin agreed to terms of quarter. 'Imād al-Dīn himself was ill and Saladin summoned all his clerks, "thinking that everyone who carries a pen is a scribe".[17] None of them could produce a document setting out the surrender terms to his satisfaction and 'Imād al-Dīn – according to his own account – had to dictate it from his sick-bed. He was then invalided home to Damascus, and for the events of the next two months he had to rely on hearsay.

During the course of the siege of Beirut, Hugh Embriaco, who had been captured at Ḥaṭṭīn, was brought from Damascus and ransomed himself by arranging for the surrender of his town of Jubail, some 20 miles (32 km) further up the coast. This marked the furthest point of Saladin's northern thrust and he now turned back. Beirut surrendered on 6 August and on 23 August Saladin was 170 miles (274 km) away at Ascalon. On his march he again passed Tyre, but according to the Arabic sources he did not think seriously of attacking it. Ibn Shaddād pointed out that his troops were dispersed throughout Frankish territory; "every man was off taking what he could for himself and they were tired of fighting", while "every remaining Frank on the Coast" was in Tyre.[18] 'Imād al-Dīn noted that Tyre was "the strongest city on the Coast", and added that Saladin merely reconnoitred and left it.[19]

According to report, Tyre had received reinforcement in the person of Conrad de Montferrat. The date of his well-known adventure at Acre, where he put into harbour not knowing what had happened, and then escaped thanks to al-Afḍal's inexperience, has been given as 14 July.[20] This is almost certainly wrong, as Saladin was still there at the time. According to the Latin *Continuation* Conrad arrived at Tyre from Acre, just in time to block a move to surrender,[21] presumably when Saladin was on his way back from Beirut. The only clue given in the Arabic sources is that at Tyre he found refugees from Beirut,[22] which would narrow the chances of his having forestalled Saladin's return, but, whether because of his presence or not, Tyre was left undisturbed.

'Imād al-Dīn wrote that Saladin was now anxious to join forces with al-'Ādil who had sent him a letter urging an attack on Jerusalem.[23] In spite of what happened later, al-'Ādil obviously thought that his advice had been sound. He was quoted as saying years afterwards in Hama:

> one of the arguments that I advanced when I was speaking to Saladin and urging him to take the opportunity of capturing Jerusalem was this: I pointed out that he was liable to attacks of colic and I said: "If you die of an attack tonight, Jerusalem will stay in the hands of the Franks"... He said: "I shall do what you order and advise."[24]

The harbour of Tyre was strategically far more important than Jerusalem and in terms of comparative Muslim/Frankish strength al-'Ādil's point appears absurd. He was arguing, however, in terms not of strength but of cohesion. Had Saladin died, individual princes and emirs, judging from later history, would almost certainly have split to look after their own interests. It might be argued that, even so, Jerusalem would not have survived without reinforcements, but at the least it could have hoped for a prolonged breathing space and it was this that Saladin was proposing to deny it.

As a preliminary to his attack, he decided to clear the road to Egypt by removing the Franks from Ascalon, Gaza and Dārūm. He reached Ascalon on Sunday 23 August, but waited until Tuesday 25 August before setting up his siege engines. He had brought with him Guy de Lusignan and the Master of the Templars, having promised them their freedom in exchange for what one account gives as the surrender of Ascalon itself and another as that of all the remaining Frankish strongholds. Guy sent a message to Ascalon, presumably on Monday, but, according to 'Imād al-Dīn, "it was realised that he was acting under duress".[25] Ibn al-Athīr added that Guy promised to "set the lands alight against the Muslims and to ask for help from the Franks beyond the sea".[26] but the garrison still refused to give up and Saladin began his attack. He told his nephew, Ḥusām al-Dīn, that Ascalon had two sets of outworks, of which the smaller was just beyond its walls and the larger at some distance from them.[27] The garrison did not think itself strong enough to fight in front of its fortifications and the outer defences were mined on Wednesday 26 August. Mangonels were brought up towards the city walls; the second line of outworks fell, and the bombardment was then directed against the walls themselves. Resistance had been fierce and the Muslim dead included a leading Kurdish emir.[28] Saladin, however, unquestionably had the upper hand and Guy was now allowed to summon "intelligent men" from the city. He told them that as their walls were about to fall, they had a clear excuse for surrendering and that, unless they did, Saladin would destroy them. They agreed to ask for quarter and Saladin told his nephew: "we granted them this in the conviction that they were only being preserved from one fate for another...and out of pity, to spare the wives and children of the Muslims in the town from the violence of the army, as well as to protect the town itself from being ravaged by pillagers". The garrison were allowed their property as well as their lives and they and their families left Ascalon on 5 September.

While Saladin delayed for some days at Ascalon, Gaza and Dārūm surrendered. Further north, Ramla, on the coastal plain 13 miles (21 km) south-east of Jaffa, and Yubnā, another 7 miles (11 km) further to the south-west, had already fallen (map 2). In part exchange for the release of their Master, the Templars agreed to surrender Latrun, on one of the main routes from Jaffa through the Judaean hills to Jerusalem. 'Uthmān had now arrived from Egypt and as the Egyptian fleet under Lu'lu' had also come and could guard against any Frankish landing, Saladin was able to move on Jerusalem with complete confidence. Amongst the places mentioned as having fallen at this time are Bait Jibrīn, Hebron and Bethlehem,[29] which were captured by troops moving northwards along the spine of the Judaean hills, but an emir in command of an advance party was intercepted and killed at al-Qubaibāt, 7 miles (11 km) north-west of Jerusalem on the road from Bait Nūbā, and it is reasonable to assume that the Muslims converged on the city from more than one side.

Saladin himself arrived outside Jerusalem on Sunday 20 September. He camped to the west, where he told the Caliph that there were deep wadis, towers and a wall curving like a bracelet, but this flank was guarded by the Tower of David, "the structure built of mighty hewn stone", as William of Tyre had described it,[30] and Saladin decided that it was too strong to attack. According to Ibn al-Athīr, the Muslims were disconcerted by the apparent strength of the garrison, and Ibn Shaddād and 'Imād al-Dīn both spoke of the city as being packed with more than 60,000 fighting men.[31] 'Imād al-Dīn suggested that the defenders were so confident that they wanted to fight a field action, saying: "we shall take vengeance from the Muslims for the day of Ḥaṭṭīn", but "their experienced knight", (presumably a reference to Balian of Ibelin), had advised them to hold the city, "the place of your Lord's tomb".[32] As a result, they had strengthened the fortifications, deepened the fosse and set up mangonels, while a guard had been posted outside the walls. The author of the Latin *Continuation* agreed that there had been a great influx of refugees who were relying, he said, on the city's sanctity rather than its strength,[33] but he added that in all these numbers there were scarcely fourteen knights. Priests and men of religion joined in the fighting, but the common people begged the Patriarch and Queen Sibylla to make terms with Saladin.

On 25 September, after five days spent in reconnoitring, Saladin moved his camp. "The men of Jerusalem lifted up their eyes and saw, as the clouds of dust rolled back, that the Saracens had struck their tents, as though about to go, and they were very joyful and said: 'the king of Syria has fled because he is not able to destroy the city as he planned!' "[34] Saladin, however, was merely shifting his camp, following exactly the pattern of the First Crusade in which siege engines had been transferred to "that part of the city which lies between the Gate of St Stephen [the Damascus Gate] and the tower at the corner on the north".[35] The Franks tried to challenge his move and according to Ibn al-Athīr both sides suffered casualties, one of Saladin's emirs being amongst the dead.[36] Finally, however, the challenge was beaten off and the Muslims managed to cross the fosse and to undermine part of the wall. According to the author of the *Libellus* Saladin divided his force, using 10,000 or more archers, "well armed down to their heels", to shoot at the walls, while another mounted force of 10,000, armed with lances and bows, waited to repulse any Frankish sallies and the rest of his army was drawn up round the siege engines. When the Muslims had broken through to the walls, the defenders tried to drive them away with stones and molten lead, as well as with arrows and spears, but this failed, as did an attempted sortie. After this, "there was not found in the whole city a man bold enough to dare stand guard for a single night for a hundred besants' reward". "I myself", the author of the *Libellus* went on,

> heard with my own ears a herald...proclaiming on the part of the Patriarch and the other magnates of the city that if fifty strong and daring servants were found who would guard the corner that had been destroyed for that one night, they would be given what arms they wanted and receive five thousand besants. But they were not to be found.[37]

After the wall had been breached, Balian of Ibelin asked for a meeting with Saladin. Saladin was unwilling to grant terms, preferring to take the city by force as the Crusaders themselves had done, and, according to the *Libellus*, he claimed to have heard that it could only be cleansed by Christian blood.[38] Balian, however, first offered what was described to the Caliph as "more than the most hopeful and avaricious man could expect".[39] He then threatened that if the Franks were not given quarter, they would kill all the Muslim prisoners in Jerusalem, estimated at from 3000 to 5000, and destroy the shrines, including the Dome of the Rock and the Aqṣā Mosque.[40] This bold approach was successful. Saladin told the Caliph that the emirs had advised him to accept Balian's offer and grant quarter, as otherwise lives would be lost in achieving a victory that had already been won. He held a council meeting followed, according to 'Imād al-Dīn, by some further negotiation,[41] and terms for surrender were finally settled on 2 October.

These terms, "to be lamented rather than recorded", according to the author of the Latin *Continuation*,[42] – "the heir has paid a price in order to be deprived of his heritage" –[43] fixed a scale of ransom at 10 dinars for a man, 5 for a woman and 1 for a child. Forty days were allowed for payment and all those who could not pay were to be taken as slaves. The Franks were allowed to keep their possessions, except for horses and military equipment. Balian himself contributed 30,000 dinars on behalf of the poor. Others tried to raise money by selling their goods to eastern Christians who hoped to be allowed to stay in the city and 'Imād al-Dīn noted that what was worth more than 10 dinars was fetching less than 1.[44] What could not be carried away, chests, bedsteads, marble etc, had to be abandoned and there was an influx of merchants who traded with the Muslim soldiers. 'Imād al-Dīn himself, who had been recuperating at Damascus, arrived at Jerusalem on 3 October and quoted Saladin as saying that it was part of the grace of this victory that it should coincide with his return.[45] He watched with disapproval the organisation of the ransom collection. The city gates had been shut and in theory no one could leave without getting a receipt for payment from a clerk and showing it to the gate guards. In fact, these clerks were "the partners and not the agents of the treasury". There was no system of counter-checking receipts, and 'Imād al-Dīn was told that clerks often wrote them "for men whose money was in their own purses".[46] As far as he could see, everyone who paid a bribe went free. Some were lowered from the city walls; others were smuggled out in panniers and a number left disguised as Muslim soldiers. Keukburī asked for the ransom money of 1000 Armenians whom he claimed to come from his town of al-Ruhā; the same request was made in the case of another 500 Armenians by Shihāb al-Dīn of al-Bīra and according to Ibn al-Athīr, other emirs asked to be assigned numbers of Franks whose ransoms they could keep.[47] 'Imād al-Dīn criticised Saladin's own generosity. He had allowed the widows of Amalric and of Reynald de Châtillon to leave without payment, and the Patriarch had removed the treasures from the Church of the Holy Sepulchre. 'Imād al-Dīn objected that these were worth 200,000 dinars and although the surrender terms allowed the Franks to keep their own possessions, they did not cover church property. He then quoted Saladin as saying: "we shall deal with them according to the superficial meaning of the words", and in the *Fatḥ* Saladin was made to add: "we shall not leave them to accuse the people of the Faith of breaking faith".[48] 'Imād al-Dīn went on to write that al-'Ādil and a number of others thought, correctly, that the ransom money should be stored away, and he quoted al-'Ādil as saying that, while he was in charge of its collection, he had sent Saladin 70,000 dinars one evening and in the morning Saladin's treasurer came to ask for more as it had all been given away.[49]

This point was repeated by al-Fāḍil, who was absent at the time, and who wrote to say that if the money was collected and kept, "it will enable the master to conquer the rest of the lands". This, however, was the only qualification to his congratulations; Saladin was "the light that shines in every dawn that brings darkness to the unbelievers"; by "releasing the brother shrine of Mecca from captivity" he "has become my master and the master of every Muslim".[50] Saladin himself clearly hoped that "every Muslim" would share this view. He had recovered for the Caliph the Dome of the Rock which was "the jewel of the signet ring of Islam".[51] He wrote to point out that all his exertions had been directed to this great end; he had fought against those Muslims who had sought to delay him only in order to unite Islam so that the word of God should be supreme; to seek such a goal was to run risks, but sitting still could not fulfil the duty imposed by God, nor could it have allowed him to carry out the orders of the previous Caliphs; undoubtedly they had bequeathed the joy that they would have felt as well as their throne to their purest successor [the present Caliph]; as for Saladin himself, tongues had injured him and the cauldrons of men's thoughts had boiled against him, but he had quenched the fire with patient endurance.[52] On the day of his return to service, 'Imād al-Dīn had written seventy letters of this type,[53] and Saladin was obviously determined to press home the point that he had been wrongly criticised.

He celebrated the recovery of the shrines with a solemn performance of the Friday prayer on 9 October. According to 'Imād al-Dīn, all the men of virtue and learning who had flocked to Jerusalem wanted to have the honour of being the first to preach and Saladin's choice fell on Muḥī al-Dīn Muḥammad, who had been appointed Qāḍī of Aleppo after its conquest in 1183.[54] The shrines themselves were now restored. Saladin wrote that the unbelievers had turned Jerusalem into a garden of paradise, filling the churches and the houses of the Templars and Hospitallers with marble,[55] but 'Imād al-Dīn allowed them no credit and talked of a latrine in the Ḥaram al-Sharīf and pictures of pigs in a church on the Rock.[56] The doors of the Church of the Holy Sepulchre were closed and a council meeting was held to consider its position. Some emirs wanted to destroy it so that the Christians would no longer come on pilgrimage, but the majority pointed out that the Caliph 'Umar had not interfered with it and that what the Christians worship is "the place of the Cross and the grave, not the buildings which can be seen. They would not stop coming even if the earth [on which it stands] was scattered in the sky."[57] Saladin agreed with this and did no damage to the church, where a number of priests were allowed to stay without payment of the ransom. The eastern Christians negotiated through Ḍiyā' al-Dīn 'Īsā and were saved from explusion by agreeing to pay the poll tax as well as their ransom.

The forty days' grace for the ransom payment ended on 10/11

November. ʻImād al-Dīn gave a figure of 7000 men and 8000 women who had been unable to pay and who were then taken as slaves.[58] He estimated that there had been more than 100,000 men, women and children in the city[59] and he also said that the ransom money collected came to about 100,000 dinars.[60] This seems too small a figure. As has been seen, al-ʻĀdil was quoted as saying that he had given Saladin 70,000 dinars on one evening and he added that another 30,000 dinars had been sent on the next day. Ibn Shaddād heard that 220,000 dinars had been collected, but said that when Saladin moved from Jerusalem, none of this money was left.[61]

Whether or not Ibn Shaddād's report was correct, it is clear that practical difficulties were crowding on the heels of Saladin's triumph. In the same letter in which he had told the Caliph of the huge sums offered him by the Franks, he had gone on to talk of his strained resources; the long campaign was draining army funds; the territories of the Franks had been plundered and their grain used up, as a result of which, instead of their being a source of revenue, money would have to be spent on them; ships had to be made ready; garrisons were needed and fortifications had to be repaired. It was certain, he wrote, that the Franks would not draw back their hands from their former lands until these hands were cut off.

Saladin himself did not wait for the ransom period to end. Letters had come from al-Mashṭūb, who had been given Sidon and Beirut, urging him to attack Tyre, "the only arrow left in the quiver of the infidels"; "every day there is an opportunity which cannot be grasped when once it has gone".[62] Al-Afḍal was the first to leave Jerusalem, followed by Taqī al-Dīn, and then Saladin himself moved out with al-ʻĀdil on Friday 30 October. ʻUthmān, who had left his stores of weapons behind to supply Jerusalem with an arsenal, accompanied his father on the first stage of his journey and then turned south for Egypt. On Wednesday 4 November Saladin camped outside Acre on his way north.

18

SUCCESS AND FAILURE

Conrad de Montferrat had used the breathing space that Saladin had given him to strengthen the fortifications of Tyre, digging out the fosse across the neck of Alexander's causeway and building up the outworks. Saladin clearly did not feel confident about his chances of a quick success. He left Acre on Sunday 8 November, but took four days for the 26-mile (42 km) march and halted to the south of Tyre on Thursday 12 November. His force was short of siege engines and, by the standards of his recent campaign, lacking in men.[1] Al-ʻĀdil had returned to Jerusalem; al-Afḍal apparently stayed at Acre; Keukburī was intending to make the pilgrimage; ʻUthmān had left for Egypt and a number of emirs were watching Frankish castles. Western sources say that fighting started in the second week of November,[2] but Saladin himself stayed for almost a fortnight at what ʻImād al-Dīn called "the river",[3] presumably Nahr al-Manṣūra, 6 miles (10 km) south of Tyre. When he had collected his mangonels, he moved up on 25 November to camp at what appears to have been Tell Maʻshūq, to the east of the causeway and within a mile-and-a-half (2 ½ km) of the city walls. At this time, al-Ẓāhir arrived with troops from Aleppo[4] and Saladin tried to press an assault. The causeway was some 600 yards wide at its western end and at first the Muslims found themselves exposed to enfilading fire from Frankish ships moored alongside it. Saladin then called up ten of his own ships from Acre and others arrived from Beirut and Jubail forcing the Franks to keep to the harbour and allowing ʻImād al-Dīn to write: "our men were heartened by the fact that the sea was empty".[5] ʻImād al-Dīn himself was at the siege and had written a cheerful letter to al-Fāḍil at Damascus, to which al-Fāḍil replied some time after 5 December. ʻImād al-Dīn had told him of the repulse of a Frankish sally and of the killing by al-Ẓāhir of "the one who is known there" – a captured Frankish leader, mistaken for Conrad and promptly killed by al-

Ẓāhir to mark his own first battle. Al-Fāḍil replied that he was sure that Tyre would soon fall, as the signs of success were clear and undoubted.[6]

Al-Afḍal now came up from Acre and al-'Ādil arrived on 8 December. In a second letter al-Fāḍil commented on the flow of reinforcements and added that, God willing, the army would soon regain its former strength. He went on to ask how 'Imād al-Dīn was coping with the continuous rains and whether his beasts and tents were affected.[7] In fact, the army was not in good spirits. The weather was cold as well as wet and 'Imād al-Dīn wrote that the Muslims had become used to easy victories. At Tyre they were forced to abandon "the soft life to which they had grown accustomed", and instead of being able to live on plunder, they were having to spend their own money on food and fodder.[8]

It was at this particularly unpropitious moment that Saladin received the Caliph's reaction to his capture of Jerusalem. 'Imād al-Dīn claimed to have warned him that care should be taken in the choice of a suitable messenger to carry the news to Baghdad[9] but Saladin had thought that speed was all-important. He picked a young Iraqi whom 'Imād al-Dīn evidently disliked but who, he said, was supported by a number of influential men. This choice in itself was reported to have made a bad impression, but politically the collapse of the Latin Kingdom was not necessarily to be welcomed in Baghdad. The implications of Saladin's plan for a pan-Islamic empire could be disregarded as long as his army was tied to the Syrian frontier, but if the Coast were conquered, he would be free to swallow the whole of Iraq, including Baghdad itself. His Iraqi envoy was said, while drunk, to have passed remarks that led the Caliph's advisers to say: "this man [Saladin] thinks that he will overturn the Abbasid dynasty"[10] and it was decided to send 'Imād al-Dīn's brother Tāj al-Dīn, who was in the Caliph's service, to find out what his real intentions were. Tāj al-Dīn arrived in Damascus while Saladin was at Tyre and left for the camp in early December. He brought a letter from the master of the Caliph's household with a list of criticisms. Not surprisingly, there was no open expression of Baghdad's fears and the letter concentrated ungratefully on minor grievances; the Caliph disapproved of what he had heard of sectarian disputes in Syria; men exiled from Iraq, "for whatever reason", had been welcomed by Saladin. Ṭughtekīn was accused of causing trouble in the Ḥijāz, disturbing pilgrims and promulgating heresies, while Saladin himself had usurped the Caliph's *laqab* (title), al-Nāṣir; there had been many rebels durings the history of the Abbasid dynasty who had caused mischief in the lands, but not one of them had dared to do this. The most serious point came at the end. Saladin was accused of corresponding with Turkmans and Kurds on the borders of the Caliph's own territories, "causing their feet to slip and blunting their resolution... They should know [only] that they are Iraqi subjects."[11] It was abundantly clear that even the recapture of Jerusalem could not compensate in the Caliph's view for the spread of Saladin's influence down the Tigris and the Euphrates.

This rebuff was clearly meagre reward for victory in the Holy War and al-ʿĀdil, Taqī al-Dīn and a number of emirs suggested that Saladin should show his resentment. According to ʿImād al-Dīn, however, Saladin ordered Tāj al-Dīn to be treated with respect,[12] a remark which may conceal part of the story. Al-Fāḍil wrote to express his grief at what he had heard about "the circumstances of Tāj al-Dīn", both because of his affection for him and because his own repeated advice had been thrown away.[13] Al-Fāḍil has been shown to have urged restraint in dealings with Baghdad – this, presumably, being the advice that was thrown away – and the implication is that Tāj al-Dīn must have met with an immediately hostile reaction. Saladin, however, did not allow things to get out of hand. He had a private meeting with Tāj al-Dīn and ʿImād al-Dīn at which he said: "the Caliph is too great to allow such harsh words to be written".[14] A letter was drafted to allay suspicion but it is noticeable that in his account, ʿImād al-Dīn makes no reference at all to the problems caused by Saladin's influence in Iraq, and only points out that his *laqab* dated from the time of al-Mustaḍīʾ and that his sole purpose was "to complete the conquests for the Commander of the Faithful".

This diplomatic disappointment was not offset by any progress in the siege. Al-Fāḍil was reduced to pointing out that difficulties would double the reward to be expected in heaven and he refused to approach Saladin with requests on behalf of individual Egyptians and Syrians, as: "alms and gifts come at a time of joy".[15] It was at this point that Conrad produced his master-stroke. The Muslims were using five galleys for a night blockade of the harbour. Conrad prepared a force, put in a letter to King Henry II of England at seventeen galleys and ten small craft,[16] and at dawn on 30 December these put out to attack the blockaders. According to ʿImād al-Dīn, the Muslims had kept watch throughout the night, but had fallen asleep at dawn and woke only when they were boarded.[17] Some jumped overboard, but the rest were captured, including two of the principal officers of the fleet. The remaining Muslim ships, now thought to be too few to face the Franks, were ordered back to Beirut. They were intercepted, however, and when the Egyptian sailors saw the enemy bearing down on them, they ran their ships on to the beach, "having been terrified by what had happened to their companions".[18] By contrast, a ship from Jubail, "like a small mountain", manned by experienced sailors, managed to make its escape, and 'Imād al-Dīn concluded that the officers responsible for fitting out and manning the fleet in Egypt had been careless in their duties and had picked poor crews. The beached galleys were now broken up to prevent the Franks from towing them off.

Small as the Muslims' loss had been in terms of equipment, this was Saladin's first significant military reverse since the battle of Ḥaṭṭīn. His war council had been advising retreat and 'Imād al-Dīn quoted the emirs saying to one another: "we have been here for a long time and our target is out of reach. Our men have been killed and wounded and our funds are running low." To counter this Saladin was made to say:

> The other fortresses and castles that they [the Franks] hold border our territories on the mainland and it will be easy to take them when once their garrisons have despaired of getting help from the sea... If we go and scatter, when shall we muster and return?[19]

The point was over-dramatised, since with Tripoli and the northern ports still in Frankish hands, even the fall of Tyre would not have cut off sea-borne reinforcements, but it would have proved conclusively that the Franks could no longer hold even the strongest position. The Muslim army, however, could not be forced to fight. Saladin had tried to buy enthusiasm by distributing money and as late as the end of December he had sent 1000 dinars to Acre to attract recruits.[20] His generosity, however, was limited by a lack of funds and Ibn al-Athīr remarked that one of the reasons why the wealthy emirs wanted to leave was their fear lest Saladin should refill his treasuries by borrowing money from them.[21] The Aleppan stalwarts Ṭumān and 'Izz al-Dīn Jūrdīk, together with Ḍiyā' al-Dīn 'Īsā, were said to have voted to stay,[22] but the best that Saladin could do was to compromise by launching one final general assault.

According to western writers, this followed immediately on the loss of the ships[23] and the Arabic sources confirm that it must have taken place on either 30 or 31 December. The army was drawn up across the causeway and attacked in waves, with the cavalry at times wading into the sea in pursuit of Franks. For all their effort, however, "the day ended with weapons blunted and the soldiers spent the night grumbling".[24] 'Imād al-Dīn was sure that a series of such attacks would have won the city, but with the emirs eager to leave, a single repulse was enough to end the siege. On 1 January 1188 Saladin withdrew to his earlier camp site by the river and the army began to disperse. Ibn al-Athīr wrote: "this was Saladin's custom. When a town held out against him, he would weary of it and of the siege and leave." Ibn al-Athīr admitted that the army had not wanted to stay, but went on: "no one can be blamed in this matter except Saladin, for it was he who sent armies of the Franks to Tyre[25] and helped it with men and money from Acre, Ascalon and Jerusalem".[26] In part, this was an unfair criticism, as the surrender terms granted to the Franks had saved the Muslims both men and time. Saladin's mistake seems to have been that he did not attack Tyre earlier and his real weakness lay in the control he had or was prepared to exert over his army. It is unprofitable to guess at what might have happened had he insisted on remaining, but of an earlier siege Napoleon was quoted as saying: "he can have no idea of war who blames this prince [Alexander the Great] for having spent seven months in the siege of Tyre. Had it been myself, I would have remained there seven years if necessary."[27]

From the camp outside Tyre Taqī al-Dīn now left with the troops of Mosul, Sinjār, Jazīrat ibn 'Umar, Diyār Bakr and Mārdīn. He marched east to Damascus, passing the castle of Ḥūnīn on the hills above the Huleh basin, which had surrendered in the last week of December, and Saladin himself moved south to Acre (map 2). The weather was bitterly cold and he had difficulty with his baggage.[28] He had destroyed all the siege engines that could not easily be moved, but the camels of his baggage train still took a week to pass over the Ladder of Tyre, and a number of emirs had to be left to guard against Frankish sorties. He then camped at Tell al-Fukhkhār outside Acre. From here al-'Ādil left for Egypt and al-Ẓāhir for Aleppo, while Dildirim of Tell Bāshir asked for permission to return to his lands. Al-Afḍal had taken up his quarters in the Templars' Tower in Acre and Saladin remained in camp with his bodyguard until a combination of wind and snow drove him to take shelter in the citadel, where he stayed until the end of the Muslim year (1 March).[29]

One final misfortune had occurred before then. A letter, apparently from al-Afḍal's secretary, described the peculiar appropriateness of the pilgrimage at this time – "I shall never find another year like it" –[30] and this feeling was shared by large numbers of Saladin's followers, who wanted to celebrate the recapture of Jerusalem and to visit other shrines recovered from the Franks, such as that of Hebron.[31] Amongst those who asked leave to go was Ibn al-Muqaddam. Saladin tried to persuade him to delay for a year, but he was quoted as replying that his life was nearly over: "his hope had been achieved and his grey hairs were giving warning".[32] He won his point and was put in charge of the Syrian pilgrims. Word then came back that he had been fatally wounded in a brawl with the Iraqis on the day of the ceremonies at 'Arafat (9 February). There were various accounts of the circumstances.[33] The Caliph's representative, the Iraqi emir Tāsh-Tekīn was said to have ordered Ibn al-Muqaddam not to beat his drums and another account says that Ibn al-Muqaddam raised Saladin's standard at 'Arafat, which the Iraqis then threw down. Ibn al-Athīr wrote that Ibn al-Muqaddam refused to obey Tāsh-Tekīn's orders, on the grounds that Tāsh-Tekīn was only in charge of the Iraqi pilgrims, and the Iraqi riff-raff then plundered the Syrian camp. Ibn al-Muqaddam himself was wounded in the eye and Tāsh-Tekīn, who had presumably never meant things to go so far, had him carried to his own tent, where he died.[34] According to 'Imād al-Dīn, Tāsh-Tekīn then forced "the leaders of the pilgrimage to follow his wishes and they wrote unwillingly" to support his version of what had happened. The Caliph later dismissed him from his position, but not as the immediate result of this riot, which had shown in the clearest manner that it was not court rivalry alone that prevented Saladin from being recognised as the protagonist of Islam. Distrust and dislike were more widely, and perhaps deeply, spread and the heroes of Islam, men whose hair had been turned white by the battles of the Holy War,[35] were not to be allowed to lord it over their co-religionaries.

For Saladin this marked an unhappy end to what had promised to be an *annus mirabilis*. He had achieved what he had so often claimed to be his life's ambition. The Frankish army had been destroyed; almost all the territories of the Latin Kingdom of Jerusalem had been taken and Jerusalem itself recaptured. To set against this, he had won neither recognition nor gratitude. The expansionist phase of the Ayyubid dynasty was at least temporarily coming to an end. His emirs could look forward to the conquest of the remaining Frankish castles and of the lands of Tripoli and Antioch, but the failure to take Tyre outlined the fact that a Frankish counter-attack was bound to come. At the end of October Pope Gregory had sent a letter to summon the Princes of Christendom and in January Philip of France and Henry II of England had been reconciled by the Papal legate at Gisors. Saladin was under no illusions about the future and held a council meeting to discuss the defences of Acre. 'Imād al-Dīn may have exaggerated the apparent pessimism but he cannot have invented the suggestion that Acre itself should be destroyed so as to deny it as a base to the Franks, with Tell Qaimūn being fortified in its place.[36] Tell Qaimūn, some 13 miles (21 km) inland from Haifa, is in a defensive position covering both the east/west entrance to the plain of Acre along the line of the Kishon and also one of the north/south routes through the Carmel spur. Saladin is said to have been on the point of agreeing to raze Acre when he was won over by the argument that it was the key to control of the sea and "a lock for the lands of the Coast".[37] As a result, he called up Qarā-Qūsh from Egypt, where he had been in charge of work on the Cairo wall, to supervise the strengthening of its defences.

He told his brother Ṭughtekīn that he was allowing his troops a two-months' rest and intended to muster them again at the beginning of March[38]. It is not clear how many of them had, in fact, returned by then but in mid-March he himself moved from Acre to the Hospitaller castle of Kaukab. Both this and the Templar castle of Ṣafad, 26 miles (42 km) to the north of it, had been watched by Muslim troops since the end of August 1187 and Saladin waited there until the end of April, but then decided that the castle still could not be stormed and moved off to Damascus. After a brief five-day stay in the city, which he had not seen for fourteen months, he left on 10 May, in response to news that 'Imād al-Dīn Zangī himself had arrived with troops from the east. He marched north up the Biqā' valley while Zangī moved to Qadas, just south of the Lake of Homs. This was the first time that the two had met since Zangī had been forced out of Aleppo in 1183. They dismounted to greet one another, to emphasise equality of rank, and each held a reception for the other. It was the season of the favourite Damascus delicacy, the apricot, quantities of which had been brought to the camp and 'Imād al-Dīn, who enjoyed contrasting luxury with the austerities of war, described the fruit as stars rising in the zodiac signs of their plates.[39]

The army remained in camp by Qadaṣ for some time. By his own standards, Saladin's force was not large. Taqī al-Dīn and al-Ẓāhir had been ordered to camp by the Antioch border to watch for any movement. Al-'Ādil was still in Egypt and al-Afḍal at Acre, while emirs were watching Kaukab, Ṣafad, Kerak and Shaubak. Saladin told Ṭughtekīn that he had left a force to watch Tyre, but there are no further details of this. Reinforcements of Bedouin and Turkmans were expected and when a number had arrived, the army moved to the plain of Buqai'a at the eastern end of the Homs/Tripoli gap. This plain was watched over by the great castle of Ḥiṣn al-Akrād (map 3) but Saladin was not looking for difficulties. It would have been unfortunate for his prestige had he involved Zangī in a fruitless siege, and although he is said to have reconnoitred the castle for one day, he then decided to ignore it.

According to 'Imād al-Dīn, a plan was now made to attack 'Arqa, some 15 miles (24 km) from Tripoli at the south-west end of the gap, as, "if this was taken, Tripoli would fall".[40] The baggage was left on the Buqai'a plain and Saladin moved off with Zangī and Keukburī. 'Imād al-Dīn claimed that he took the castle of Yaḥmūr (Chastel Rouge), 11 miles (18 km) south-east of Ṭarṭūs, but this is not confirmed by Ibn al-Athīr who was also with the army, and who merely noted that Saladin raided Yaḥmūr and two other castles to the north of the gap, Ṣāfītha (Chastel Blanc) and al-'Uraima. No attack was made on 'Arqa. Saladin contented himself with reconnoitring lines of approach to Tripoli and capturing large numbers of pasturing animals. By the end of June he had returned to his baggage without having launched any major assault.

At this point six months had passed since the Muslims' last success of any note, the surrender of Ḥūnīn. Saladin was faced with two alternatives. He could try to complete the conquest of the whole Coast, in which case he had to attack strategically important Frankish strong-points, such as Tripoli and Tyre, before they became even stronger, or he could decide that complete victory was out of reach for the present and concentrate on removing unguarded pawns from the board. A factor that had to be taken into account was the loose structure of his army. His allies had no reason to give him whole-hearted support. For his own emirs and professional soldiers he and his family were merely successful members of their own class; his dynasty was bolstered by no divine right of kings and the religious sanction it had claimed had been denied it by Baghdad. During the period of its expansion it had been profitable to join his side, but profit and numbers were inextricably linked. If his military accounts began to show a loss, his numbers could be expected to diminish and his dynasty in its turn could be threatened by other Muslim expansionists. It is not surprising, then, that he chose the second alternative. During the period of his reconnaissance he had been visited by the Muslim Qāḍī of the Frankish town of Jabala, some 75 (121 km) north of Tripoli, who had warned him of the strength of Tripoli and advised him to move north.[41] Messengers had also come from Muslims in the hill country overlooking the northern coast, and on Friday 1 July he began his march.

The army moved in three divisions, the right wing under Zangī acting as vanguard, with Saladin commanding the centre, and Keukburī with the left wing bringing up the rear. There was a strong literary contingent, as Saladin's biographer Ibn Shaddād had joined his service and was accompanied by 'Imād al-Dīn and Ibn al-Athīr. They marched westwards through the Homs/Tripoli gap, reaching al-'Uraima on 2 July, and then turning north to cover the 15 miles (24 km) to Ṭarṭūs on Sunday 3 July. Saladin had intended to by-pass Ṭarṭūs, but was tempted by its vulnerability and sent orders to recall Zangī, whose wing was already to the north of it. The city walls were stormed while the servants were still putting up the tents and they left to join in the looting. Resistance was concentrated in the two strongholds, one of which surrendered to Keukburī but the second proved to be impregnable and its Templar garrison shot down a number of the attackers, who then drew off. Saladin stayed until 11 July, during which time the town was reduced to ruins. Al-Fāḍil wrote from Damascus to say: "news has come that our master has passed Ṭartūs and taken it by force, turning it upside down so that nothing remains except the ruins... An affair which has begun like this...will lead to the accomplishment of our aims."[42]

On 11 July Saladin continued his march. After committing himself to a northern campaign he had called up al-Ẓāhir with the troops of Aleppo, who now joined him some way to the south of Jabala. Below the Hospitaller castle of Marqab the army had to run the gauntlet of a Sicilian fleet which had been sent to the relief of the Coast by William II and which, after calling at Tripoli and Tyre, had sailed north. It was in position to enfilade a narrow passage on the coast road but the Muslims, covered by their own archers, passed safely and reached Jabala on 15 July, leaving Marqab in their rear. As the Qāḍī had promised, the townspeople of Jabala came out to welcome Saladin, and the Franks in the citadel were persuaded to surrender on terms of quarter, abandoning their arms, stores and horses. The fortress of Bikisrā'īl in the hills to the east of Jabala also surrendered, clearing a line of communication inland to Hama. The next target was Latakia, some 15 miles (24 km) further north. Saladin left Jabala on 20 July and camped to the south of Latakia that night. The town itself fell on the next day and terms were agreed with the Frankish garrison of the citadel on 23 July. Saladin sent an enthusiastic description to Ṭughtekīn – "there is no harbour like it or anchorage for ships"[43] – and 'Imād al-Dīn, who regretted the damage done by pillagers, was impressed by its marble, its fine buildings and the gardens attached to each house.[44] The Sicilian fleet arrived belatedly and its admiral had a personal interview with Saladin in which he asked him to spare "this frightened people". This was elaborated by Ibn al-Athīr as a request for the return of Frankish territories, in exchange for which the Franks would acknowledge Saladin's overlordship and provide him with troops.[45] Both Ibn al-Athīr and 'Imād al-Dīn agree that the admiral threatened that if Saladin refused, the kings from "the seven seas" would attack him, but he belittled this threat and the admiral crossed himself and withdrew.

The army left Latakia on 24 July and moved across difficult country 18 miles (29 km) north-east to Ṣahyūn. This castle has a spectacular site on a steep-sided spur projecting from a mountain-side but the area to be defended made it merely a matter of time before it fell. Saladin reached it on 26 July; it was invested on 27 July and the garrison surrendered on 29 July, having agreed to ransom themselves on the scale fixed for Jerusalem. While Saladin was at Ṣahyūn, his troops took Balāṭunus, which the Franks had evacuated, as well as the minor forts of 'Aidho and Jamāharīya. Balāṭunus, which is some 17 miles (27 km) east-south-east of Latakia, controls a pass under Jabal Arba'īn, but Ibn al-Athīr noted that, of the two roads to the northern coast, the one by Bikisrā'īl was difficult, while the easy road – presumably the route across the main Nusairi ridge by Maṣyāf – was partly in the hands of the Assassins.[46] This point was important because the coastal roads to Jabala and Latakia were still controlled by Franks, to the south at Marqab and to the north at al-Suwaidīya.

From Ṣahyūn Saladin moved north-east to the Orontes, where he attacked the double castle al-Shughr-Bakās on 2 August. Bakās had been evacuated, but according to 'Imād al-Dīn Saladin could see no way to attack al-Shughr except by mangonels[47] and a long siege was in prospect. Then unexpectedly the garrison asked for terms with a three-day delay to allow them to consult Antioch, after which Saladin's flag was hoisted on 12 August. On the next day al-Ẓāhir was sent some 7 miles (11 km) south to attack the fort of Sarmānīya, which surrendered on 19 August. Saladin himself then went past it to the castle of Burzey on the hills opposite Afāmīya, "proverbial for its strength throughout the lands of the Franks and of the Muslims".[48] The castle stands on an eastern spur with high ground to the west of it, where Saladin moved his camp on 21 August. He had mangonels set up, but these were put out of action by stones from the castle, whose mangonels Ibn al-Athīr saw being directed by a woman.[49] As a result, it was decided to try an assault, and the army attacked in waves on 23 August. The Franks were too far outnumbered to maintain their resistance and were forced to ask for quarter. At this, 'Imād al-Dīn wrote, the main body of the Muslim troops halted to wait for Saladin's orders, but "some cunning persons amongst his own guard" cheated both the garrison and the rest of the army, apparently by pretending that quarter had been granted.[50] They then collected the garrison, whom they took as their own prisoners, "and dispersed for ever",[51] forcing Saladin to buy back the Lady of Burzey and her family from their captors in order to pay a debt of gratitude to her sister, Bohemond's wife Sibylla, who, according to Ibn al-Athīr, had been in the habit of sending him information.[52] 'Imād al-Dīn now wrote in a letter: "we have conquered from the borders of Tripoli to those of Antioch... Antioch remains, but cannot survive... None of its castles are left except for al-Quṣair, Darbsāk and Baghrās."[53] Al-Fāḍil had evidently been expecting quicker progress against Antioch itself, but wrote to congratulate Saladin, adding, "the servant no longer considers the news of Antioch to be too slow".[54]

Saladin now moved north up the line of the Orontes and halted for some time at Jisr al-Ḥadīd within 17 miles (27 km) of Antioch. He waited for some days, according to 'Imād al-Dīn to rest his troops,[55] but also presumably to test the resolution of the defenders, and to calculate the morale of his own men. Antioch itself was a prize of the first importance. Apart from its own value, its capture would help block the land route for Frankish reinforcements and so transform the campaign from a triumphal progress into a strategically effective operation, but in spite of his successes Saladin still postponed any direct attack. Instead, he moved north and reach Darbsāk, guarding the end of the Beylan pass, on 2 September. The Templar garrison resisted fiercely. A breach was made by Saladin's mangonels and then a tower was undermined, but Ibn Shaddād saw the Templars acting as a human wall,[56] "each stepping in his comrade's place". Eventually, they too were forced to ask for quarter and the castle was handed over on 16 September. Al-Fāḍil passed on the news of its fall to Saladin's cousin, 'Izz al-Dīn Mūsik. The Templars, he wrote, had given up their stores, grain and weapons and had agreed reluctantly to pay a heavy ransom; money for this had to be taken from their treasury and this was something unheard-of as far as they were concerned. He added that Saladin had now moved to Baghrās, from which he could see the walls and towers of Antioch; this was being raided by Muslim cavalry morning and evening and men's ears there were filled with cries and their breasts with whispers. For the rest, he added that Turkmans had ravaged the lands of the Armenians, humiliating their leader and seizing plunder.[57]

Saladin reached Baghrās on 17 September and forced its surrender on 26 September. The stage now appeared to be set for the climax of the campaign and the final destruction of Antioch. Surprisingly no attack came and, instead, a truce was made, to run for eight months from 1 October. One clause was reported to have laid down that if no help reached the city during this period it was to be surrendered, and another provided for the release of all Muslim prisoners. 'Imād al-Dīn pointed out that the city could not regain its strength in this short time, thanks to the loss of its castles, and that the truce would end in May before the harvest was ripe.[58] Al-Fāḍil put a good face on it and stressed the admiration of the Muslims for the fact that Saladin had rescued the prisoners by the sword and not the dinar,[59] but nothing could conceal the disappointment of anticlimax. The promise of future surrender would, if anything, be an invitation to the Franks to use the land road left open for them and it is not even clear how seriously the promise itself was taken. There is no reference to it later in the Arabic accounts and 'Imād al-Dīn's point that Antioch could not recover seems more relevant to an anticipated siege than to a surrender.[60] Both Ibn Shaddād and 'Imād al-Dīn laid the blame on discontent in the army. 'Imād al-Dīn said that Saladin himself had wanted to fight, but "the foreign troops" were tired of the campaign, and Ibn Shaddād glossed this by saying that Zangī was asking for leave to go home. From Zangī's point of view the fall of Antioch would leave Saladin more powerful than before; its survival was no threat to his own lands and there was no reason for him to show an excess of zeal in what was not at the moment a life-or-death matter. The behaviour of Saladin's own troops at Burzey showed that, in spite of an uninterrupted run of success, discipline was becoming lax and Saladin must again have felt that this was not the time to press a full-scale siege.

His concern for the basis of his power can be seen in his disposal of the captured towns and castles. Bikisrā'īl and Jabala were given to Sābiq al-Dīn 'Uthmān of the Banū'l-Dāya. Latakia went to Taqī al-Dīn, Ṣahyūn to Mankūrus ibn Khumartekīn of Bū Qubais, al-Shughr-Bakās to Gharas al-Dīn Qilij, one of Shīrkūh's Egyptian veterans, Burzey to 'Izz al-Dīn Ibrāhīm, son of Ibn al-Muqaddam, and Darbsāk and Baghrās to 'Alam al-Dīn Sulaimān. The only direct Ayyubid gain was Latakia. Of the emirs, Mankūrus and the son of Ibn al-Muqaddam were second-generation Ayyubid supporters and all were men of moderate power and substance. With the possible exception of Gharas al-Dīn, they held property near the places that they had been given and with the consolidation of their power, Saladin could hope to be strengthening the middle class of his supporters. This comprised the independent lords who could either produce money and men or else cause trouble, not by open disobedience but merely by slackening in their service. The limitations of their loyalty were underlined in a note added by 'Imād al-Dīn to the effect that 1000 *ghirāras* of grain found at Baghrās were handed over to 'Alam al-Dīn. There was a shortage of grain at Antioch, where a *ghirāra* was fetching 12 dinars. 'Imād al-Dīn suspected that 'Alam al-Dīn would sell his grain and then advise that the castle should be dismantled and this, he added, was exactly what happened some years later.[61]

After the conclusion of the truce, Saladin moved camp on 27 September and returned to Damascus "some few days before the start of Ramaḍān"[62] (24 October). It was suggested to him that during this "month in which men join their families",[63] he should allow his troops to rest, but he was said to have repeated his remark: "life is not guaranteed".[64] Rain and mud made travel unpleasant, but he crossed the Jordan at Bait al-Ahzān and climbed up the barrier of its western hills to Ṣafad (map 2). Here the garrison's supplies were running low and when they saw that an attack was going to be pressed home, they sent out Muslim prisoners on 30 November to ask for quarter. Terms were arranged; the garrison left for Tyre and the castle was handed over to Saladin in early December.

A further triumph had been the surrender of Kerak in November. Here al-'Ādil had been left to organise a blockade after the garrison had refused pleas from Reynald's widow to exchange the castle for the release of her son Humphrey. According to Ibn al-Athīr, they had now eaten all their animals;[65] it was certain that no help could reach them and, as 'Imād al-Dīn put it, "they had established their excuse with their own people".[66] On a smaller scale, another success was the interception of a party of 200 Franks who had made their way from Tyre with the aim of slipping through the Muslim blockade in order to reinforce Kaukab. The only jarring note was struck by news from Egypt that twelve men had gone through the streets of Cairo one night shouting Fatimid slogans in the hopes of starting a popular rising.[67] No one had joined them and they had then been arrested, leaving al-Fāḍil to point out that Saladin should be glad of proof that there was no support for revolution. Saladin himself, however, was said to have been disturbed and this incident, occurring as it did at the peak of his success against the Franks, again underlined the point that victory in the Holy War was not in itself enough to settle old scores.

After the fall of Ṣafad, Saladin moved south against Kaukab. Here the defenders were still determined to resist and 'Imād al-Dīn quoted them as saying: "were only one of us left, the House of the Hospitallers would still be guarded".[68] The weather was bad. Saladin wrote of snow on the hills[69] and Ibn Shaddād complained of rain and wind and of mud that hindered all movements of men and horses.[70] 'Imād al-Dīn described how the tents sank in the mud or collapsed with broken guy-ropes because of the weight of rain, while in spite of this there was a shortage of drinking-water.[71] A wall had to be built to protect Saladin's tent, which was within range of the castle, and a number of the besiegers were killed by stones and crossbow bolts. The baggage and the heavy tents were apparently sent down to the shelter of the Jordan valley and after persistent attacks the Muslims succeeded in reaching the Frankish outworks. With the Muslim archers giving cover to their sappers, these defences fell and the main wall of the castle could then be mined. At this the garrison asked for terms and the castle was surrendered in early January 1189. It was offered to a number of emirs who refused it and was then given against his will to Ṣārim al-Dīn Qaimāz.

The fall of Kaukab marked the end of Saladin's winter campaign. The emirs and troops were now allowed to go and al-Fāḍil left for Egypt, where the abortive revolt may have suggested that more supervision was needed. Saladin himself remained by Baisān until the end of the month of Dhū 'l-Qa'da (20 January), after which he visited Jerusalem with al-'Ādil. In spite of his run of successes, the tone of a letter that he now sent to Ṭughtekīn was not optimistic. He told Ṭughtekīn that Kaukab, the nest of the Hospitallers and a base at the junction of roads, had fallen and that nothing remained "in this region" except Tyre; in the coming year he himself would attack Antioch and Taqī al-Dīn Tripoli; al-'Ādil, however, would have to stay in Egypt which was threatened with an attack and the countless nations of the Franks were not to be consoled for their losses; letters had come from agents in Alexandria, from the frontiers of the Maghrib and from the Emperor of Constantinople, warning him that they had united and were planning to attack both Syria and Egypt. As for Ṭughtekīn himself, his conduct had been one of the points of which the Caliph had disapproved and the letter indicates that he had been called back from Yemen at the time of Saladin's illness. Saladin now tried to summon him again, conveying, as from an elder brother and the head of his house, an appeal of mixed criticism and flattery. Referring to the dangers of a Frankish attack he wrote that none but great kings could stand in the face of great kings and so

> we now seek aid from our brother...and hope that he will come quickly to help us himself with his men and his treasuries... Even if he sat back and did not visit us during the sickness of the body, he should not abandon us during the sickness of Islam... He must draw a sword that will act as a lock for what we have conquered and as a key for what has yet to be conquered... By God, we are more eager to give the family of Ayyūb the splendid gifts of the next world than the transient gifts of this world. It does not please us that our brother should spend his life in fighting other than unbelievers... There is no doubt that were his sword joined to a tongue that could speak and a mouth, it would say: "while I am here, I am not there"... Let him understand our wishes... Let him come so that he may see his nephews who are sorrowful at being cut off from him.[72]

Shortages of money, as well as fears of a Frankish counter-stroke, were again souring the aftermath of success. 'Imād al-Dīn had fallen ill at Baisān and returned to Damascus, from where he wrote in early April to complain to al-Fāḍil about his expenses and the cutting-off of his sources of revenue. Al-Fāḍil replied: "were he to see the state of affairs in Egypt and the straitened circumstances of its people, who are now at their last gasp, he would realise that things in Damascus, may God guard it, are a mere drop in this ocean".[73] The roads were dangerous, which may explain 'Imād al-Dīn's complaint about his revenues, and in another letter written on 6 April al-Fāḍil referred to the murder of a messenger who had been sent with money from Egypt to Syria. As for 'Imād al-Dīn's debts and expenses, the answer, al-Fāḍil suggested, lay in Saladin's generosity, but he advised 'Imād al-Dīn to accept an *iqṭā'*, if it was offered, even for a lesser amount, rather than an allowance, as an allowance "was always striking the ears and cutting off new hopes and desires".[74]

'Imād al-Dīn did manage to get some of his requests answered, but he ran into difficulties in an attempt to have money assigned to him from Acre. Al-Fāḍil had approached the Qādī al-Murtaḍa on this point,[75] but later he spoke of "the lack of progress in the matter of this allowance" and of "the shortcomings of those who fell short" – "not everyone can go to the Sultan" – and he suggested that Ibn Shaddād, who was then at Saladin's camp, might be able to help.[76]

In themselves, these complaints, together with the search for favours, are unremarkable but what is surprising is how far 'Imād al-Dīn was prepared to press his point. He had apparently stayed at Damascus when Saladin moved out in the spring and al-Fāḍil suggested that the time had come for him to rejoin his master – for "the absent one to return to his family and for the one seeking his homeland to settle in his own place".[77] Far from doing so, however, 'Imād al-Dīn threatened to leave Saladin's service altogether and al-Fāḍil had to write:

> granted that he may have thought of cutting himself off from the Sultan's service, how can he have thought of abandoning his friends? I know that he will not, in fact, leave his service... I would prefer friendly association with him in error to being alone in the right. My tongue will obey me in gratitude and disobey me in censure.[78]

There may, of course, have been personal reasons, over and above the points mentioned by al-Fāḍil, to account for 'Imād al-Dīn's behaviour. What is clear, however, is that continuous warfare was straining the economies of both Egypt and Syria and the fact that Saladin's eulogist-in-chief could have thought, even if only half seriously, of abandoning him shows something of the extent of the problems that were to be faced.

19

CRUSADERS AT ACRE

For Saladin the military situation, as always, took precedence over everything else and from Jerusalem he now went on a tour of inspection. He was accompanied to Ascalon by al-'Ādil, who was on his way back to Egypt, and from there, he moved north again to Acre, returning to Damascus in the third week of March. On 21 April he marched out again and after waiting for his troops to assemble he moved by Bāniās to Marj 'Uyūn, which he reached on 5 May. At about this time, news came of the surrender of Shaubak and he wrote to tell the Caliph that, except for Tyre, he now held all the kingdom of Jerusalem from al-'Arīsh to the borders of the Ḥijāz and up to the northern limits of the lands of Beirut; south of the Armenian border all the territories of Antioch had been captured except for al-Quṣair and Antioch itself; the County of Tripoli, however, had only lost Jubail and the Franks still held all its fortresses. He himself, he wrote, was now setting out to attack it, having left Al-Afḍal in charge of the Coast to the south of it from Jubail to Ascalon.[1]

The attack never took place. At Marj 'Uyūn Saladin found the vicinity of Reginald of Sidon's castle of Beaufort an immediate temptation and according to Ibn Shaddād he rode from his camp every day to reconnoitre it. Then some time in the second week of May, when Frederick Barbarossa and the German Crusaders were marching from Ratisbon, Reginald himself suddenly appeared and asked for an interview, at which he promised to hand over the castle on condition that he should be given a house in Damascus and *iqṭā's* for himself and his family. His family, however, had to be removed from Tyre without Conrad de Montferrat being led to suspect treachery, and he asked for a three-month delay both for this and to collect his grain revenue after the harvest. Saladin agreed and from then on Reginald, who could speak Arabic and knew something of

Islamic history and *ḥadīth*, used to come "at all times"[2] to discuss religion with him. He was allowed to buy provisions from the army market and the only restriction placed on him seems to have been a condition that no building work should be done at Beaufort, lest the fortifications should be strengthened. Saladin was now apparently content to wait. Not only did he not advance against Tripoli, but he had apparently given up his earlier plan of moving to Antioch when its truce expired and instead of attacking it, according to Ibn al-Athīr, he went on to the defensive and sent Taqī al-Dīn north to guard against a possible attack.[3]

These changes of plan cannot be credited to Reginald alone. Ibn al-Athīr gives the clue by noting that Saladin was disturbed by news from Tyre, where the Franks had been receiving constant reinforcements and where there had been a reconciliation between Conrad de Montferrat and Guy de Lusignan.[4] For Ibn al-Athīr, this explained Saladin's concern with Beaufort whose garrison could threaten his rear if he was forced to move on Tyre, but the reconciliation was mentioned by al-Fāḍil, with greater optimism, where he wrote to tell 'Uthmān that the kings of the earth were coming to the doors of Saladin's pavilion at Marj 'Uyūn and his armies were choking the breath from the unbelievers; Conrad and Guy had made an alliance and Guy was outside Tyre with a band of Franks, but they were taking refuge in the hills in fear of death, and although Saladin's armies were challenging them to battle, they shrank from it.[5]

Guy, who had been released by Saladin in the previous summer, had taken an oath not to fight against him again, but had been absolved from this by his priests on the grounds that "an oath should not be kept where religion is in danger".[6] The breaking of his word was noted by Ibn Shaddād,[7] but, unlike the often-quoted treachery of Reynald de Châtillon, it seems to have aroused no hard feelings. From Saladin's point of view Guy was likely to be a source of division among the Franks and it may be that his oath, like the Antioch agreement, was never taken seriously. Guy himself had gone first to Tripoli and then to Tyre, where the Muslims heard that Conrad had at first refused him entry.

The pendulum, then, was swinging against Saladin. His failure to crush all Frankish resistance after Ḥaṭṭīn had lost him the initiative to the extent that he had had to concentrate his whole attention on the Coast to guard against a counter-strike. Now, it appeared that he could not even take the offensive where and when he wanted, but instead was forced to wait to see where the Frankish attack would come.

At this point al-Fāḍil wrote to tell him of the birth of a son to the seventeen-year-old 'Uthmān on 17 June and he added: "God Almighty does not let any time go past without granting our master the addition of sons or the conquest of more lands."[8] The second half of this was now wishful thinking and on 3 July word came that the Franks had crossed the Litani bridge, some 5 miles (8 km) north of Tyre, and were intending to move on Sidon. A Muslim force had been watching them from the north bank and Saladin immediately rode out to reinforce it, arriving only to find that the Franks had been driven back and that one of his own *mamlūks* had been killed. He waited, according to Ibn al-Athīr, in the hope of "taking vengeance for the Muslim dead",[9] and, as the Franks did not move, he rode out on 5 July to reconnoitre their position from the hills to the east of the plain. This misled a number of Bedouin and volunteers who had attached themselves to the army and who thought that he was going out to fight. They themselves, 'Imād al-Dīn noted, "had no experience in fighting the Franks";[10] and they now swarmed across the river. Saladin saw their danger and sent a detachment to bring them back, but this ran into difficulties as the Franks, who had at first suspected an ambush, grasped their opportunity and attacked. The Muslim survivors were pursued acrosss the Litani: 'Imād al-Dīn tried to console his readers by reporting that eighty Franks were drowned on their way back,[11] but Ibn Shaddād wrote: "the Franks never had a success like this in all the battles that I witnessed".[12] Saladin held a war council and decided to advance against the Frankish camp, a plan that was said to have brought in a flood of volunteers from Damascus and the Ḥaurān, but when he moved out on 13 July he was met by news that the camp had been abandoned.

As the coast road to the north was blocked against him, the two obvious targets for Guy de Lusignan were the castle of Tibnīn and Acre itself. Saladin went to visit both on a quick tour of inspection and then returned to Marj 'Uyūn on 22 July. His losses in the Litani battle could not have been significant as far as his actual strength was concerned, but he had to look to his prestige. Frankish foragers with a cavalry escort had been reported in the country around Tibnīn and he produced a plan for the garrison of Tibnīn to draw them into an ambush where he himself would be waiting, while the troops of Acre attacked their camp from the rear. The combined force was organised in eight squadrons, twenty men from each being selected to act as bait, but the plan was over-ambitious in view of difficulties of communication. In the event, there is no record that the Acre garrison moved at all. The party that was supposed to lead the Franks into the trap stayed to fight and Saladin, who did not know what was happening, had to commit his reinforcements piecemeal. The Franks withdrew, having killed four Bedouin emirs, and Saladin returned to Marj 'Uyūn on 26 July. According to Ibn Shaddād he was victorious and glad,[13] but this seems an unconvincing embellishment of a tactical failure.

The three month's grace allowed Reginald for the surrender of Beaufort was due to end on 13 August. On the evening after his return from Tibnīn Saladin ordered his tents and baggage to be shifted from the plain of Marj 'Uyūn to the hill-side near the castle. He told Reginald that this was because the plain was becoming unhealthy and Reginald now asked for a nine-month extension of the agreement on the grounds that his family were still trapped at Tyre. This was too much for Saladin's credulity; Reginald was not allowed to leave the Muslim camp and a blockading force was posted by the castle. On 13 August Reginald was taken there under escort and a priest came out to meet him. The Muslims had not brought an interpreter and could not follow what was being said, but 'Imād al-Dīn added: "it was as though Reginald was ordering him to resist".[14] The garrison refused to surrender, and it became clear that Saladin had been tricked into wasting three vital months of the campaigning season. He had scored no single success and every delay added to his expenses and to the dangers of the mustering Crusade. Reginald was taken to Bāniās and brought back a week later to be threatened, but to no avail. He was then sent to join the other Frankish prisoners at Damascus and on 22 August Saladin moved up to the high ground behind the castle, but on this day word came that the Franks were again on the move.

A small Muslim force had been left at al-Iskandarūna on the coast road 10 miles (16 km) south of Tyre and this was now reported to have been attacked and forced to retire by "the Franks from Tyre and those with the King".[15] At Tyre, according to the Latin *Continuation*, Guy had proclaimed that those who were on the Lord's side should join him in order to take vengeance on the Muslims and he collected a force put at 400 horse and 7000 foot, in addition to camp followers.[16] At 'Ain Jālūt he had acted cautiously and been criticised; at Ḥaṭṭīn he had been slightly less cautious with disastrous results, and he now took the desperate risk of moving through difficult enemy-held country to attack a strongly fortified city in the knowledge that Saladin was bound to bring up the whole weight of his army against him, thus leaving himself with a task described by the *Continuation* as "hard and humanly speaking almost impossible".[17]

According to report, the Franks quickly seized control of the dangerous sections of the road and arrived at Acre unexpectedly. This is certainly wrong, as when al-Iskandarūna was attacked the garrison can be expected to have sent warning not only to Saladin but to Acre as well. Saladin got his first news on Tuesday 22 August[18] and on Saturday 26 August word came that the Franks were at 'Ain Baṣṣa and that their vanguard had reached al-Zīb. Al-Zīb is within 9 miles (14 km) of Acre (map 2), some 3 miles (5 km) south of the village of al-Baṣṣa, and both are on the south side of the headland of Ra's al-Naqūra. At Beaufort Saladin was 32 miles (52 km) away from al-Zīb as the crow flies and by 26 August he could no longer have had any chance of catching the Franks, who reached Acre next day. If the dates given in the Arabic sources are correct, they had taken three days to cover less than 10 miles (16 km) round Ra's al-Naqūra, but it must be remembered that Saladin's own baggage train had spent a week on this same difficult passage in winter conditions in January 1188. 'Imād al-Dīn claimed that Saladin had wanted to attack the Franks in "the narrows" and that he had been dissuaded by the emirs.[19] In July he had moved from Marj 'Uyūn to the mouth of the Litani in less than a day and had he left on 22 August he could presumably have caught Guy by 24 August, but this claim cannot be accommodated to an equally positive remark by Ibn Shaddād that he waited deliberately in case the Frankish move was a ruse to draw him from Beaufort.[20]

Whatever plans he may have considered, in the event he acted with his usual caution and before moving he sent off written orders for reinforcements to be called in. A detachment was to move south-westwards, parallel to the Franks' line of march, but he himself chose to follow the outer sides of the rectangle Beaufort, Tyre, Acre, Tiberias.[21] He left Marj 'Uyūn on 27 August and halted in the Huleh basin at midday, reaching al-Minya on the Sea of Galilee that night, after a march of some 30 miles (48 km). Next day he must have passed by Ḥaṭṭīn as he climbed from the lakeside to march down the valley beneath Mt Turan, and in the afternoon he halted at Kafr Kanna. Sepphoris, immediately to the west of Kafr Kanna, had been fixed as the *rendezvous* for the flanking detachment, which arrived on 29 August, claiming some successes against the Franks. Saladin himself left his baggage and rode westwards across the low barrier of hill country that shuts off Sepphoris from the coastal plain until he came out on the hill-side of al-Kharrūba, by the town of Shafar'am, from where he could see the plain and to the north-west the town of Acre itself.

According to the Latin *Continuation*, the Franks had not waited for the usual mangonel bombardment but had launched an assault on the day after their arrival, that is 29 August, and the author claimed that they had been on the point of success when news came of Saladin's approach. "He had only a small force, but fear suggested that it was innumerable",[22] and the Franks withdrew to their camp at Toron (Tell al-Fukhkhār). Saladin sent reinforcements to Acre that night and then for a fortnight both sides waited for more men. Saladin was joined by Taqī al-Dīn, recalled from his task of watching Antioch, and by Keukburī, as well as by troops from Mosul, Sinjār and Diyār Bakr, but looking out to sea 'Imād al-Dīn saw Frankish ships arriving one after the other and lying moored by the shore "like tangled thickets,"[23] and Ibn Shaddād now put what was considered to be the Franks' minimum number at 2000 horse and 30,000 foot.[24]

When the Muslim army was mustered, Saladin moved down from the hills to deliver his challenge. His centre was at Tell Kaisān, an isolated mound 5 miles (8 km) south-east of Acre; his right wing was at Tell al-'Ayyāḍīya at the Acre end of an east/west ridge that marks the northern boundary of the plain, and his left rested on the Nahr Na'mān. The exact position of the left wing on the river cannot be established, but the front may be estimated as covering some 10,000 yards in a triangle whose apex was at Tell Kaisān, while at its nearest point, Tell al-'Ayyāḍīya, it was within 2½ miles (4 km) of the Frankish base at Toron. 'Imād al-Dīn had kept al-Fāḍil in touch with events and al-Fāḍil wrote from Egypt on 17 September to say: "news of the enemy's muster that you are confronting has distracted every nursing mother from her child... Hands have no other occupation [now] except to be raised to God at the time of prayer".[25]

Saladin apparently hoped that the Franks would attack him. Al-Fāḍil, who had been suffering from colic and was worried by private affairs, wrote of the pressure on Acre by land and sea and went on to say: "in spite of the numbers and power of the enemy I do not think that they will come out... It is to be hoped that God will arbitrate between us and He is the best of arbitrators."[26] At the end of the month of Rajab (13 September), the Franks felt strong enough to tighten their blockade and they surrounded Acre "like a circle round its centre".[27] Saladin's war council decided to cut a way through by a general assault timed to coincide with the Friday prayer on 14 September. The Franks, however, stood "like a compact building with no cracks in it",[28] and the day's fighting was inconclusive. Next morning the Muslims were more successful. The Franks had only a light force to hold the line north of Acre, which was farthest removed from the bulk of Saladin's army. Taqī al-Dīn was sent round to attack them and he succeeded in driving them in towards Toron and clearing the approach from the St Anthony's Gate by the citadel to the northern shore. 'Imād al-Dīn implicitly criticised the fact that the Muslims did not press home their advantage, quoting the emirs as saying, "the affair is easy", after which they dispersed to water their horses. This allowed the Franks time to re-form by Toron and they "stood like a wall behind their mantlets, shields and lances, with levelled crossbows".[29]

The Muslims had not seen such hard fighting since the siege of Tyre and the army was reported by Ibn Shaddād to be tired and discontented.[30] There were differences of opinion about what to do next. Some advised that the attack should be resumed for a third consecutive day and that, as the Franks were not using their cavalry, the Muslims should advance on foot. Another suggestion was that the Muslim infantry should be sent into Acre and a co-ordinated attack launched from inside and out, while others advised Saladin to draw back in the hopes of luring the Franks onto the open plain. Some hopes were pinned on the Egyptian fleet and an argument for doing nothing at all was that winter was coming on; the Frankish ships were bound to scatter and the Franks themselves would then run short of provisions and either have to retire or else fall an easy prey to the waiting Muslims. Saladin himself was clearly worried and Ibn Shaddād was told by his doctor that he only took a small quantity of food from Friday to Sunday.[31] The way to Acre was open but on 21 September the Franks launched an attack of their own which made no headway but showed growing confidence. On 24 September Saladin moved up closer, with his centre resting on Tell al-'Ayyāḍīya, his left on the river and his right on the sea. The emir Ḥusām al-Dīn Sunqur had died of dysentery on 10 September and on 26 September Ṭumān of al-Raqqa died at Tell al-'Ayyāḍīya, having asked to be lifted on to his horse, so that he could claim martyrdom in the Holy War.

Al-Fāḍil wrote of a Baghdad letter that came at this point: "we are engaged in something more important than the exchange of words and messages",[32] but nevertheless an optimistic official account of the fighting was sent to the Caliph: Saladin was confronting an enemy who had been thrown up by the sea and had come in floods, like those of the Caliph's liberality; after a year's fighting they had tried to surprise him by concealing their plans and moving by stealth on Acre; he had followed and the besiegers had become the besieged; a path had been cut to the city through their throats and they had been forced to one side, so that after being like the brow around the eye, they had now become like the eye surrounded by the eyebrow; nothing remained except to act speedily and give them the *coup de grâce*.[33] 'Imād al-Dīn must have written in similarly hopeful terms to al-Fāḍil, as al-Fāḍil noted that he had delayed his reply so as to be able to offer congratulations on the departure of the Franks. He went on to qualify this by adding that there were too many mouths and too little food in Acre itself and this could prove more dangerous than a shortage of equipment; if Frankish reinforcements continued to arrive by sea, they might trample down all Syria, but "if we can deal with them to-day, it lies in God's power to help us deal with what they may do tomorrow".[34]

There was no real cause for Muslim optimism. Saladin scored a small success by arranging for his Bedouin to ambush Frankish foragers by the river, but the Franks had been receiving reinforcements and entrenching their camp. They were now credited with over 100,000 men,[35] and on 3 October they were seen to be making ready for some unusual effort. The Muslims for their part prepared to meet an attack. Saladin's order of battle from centre to right was himself; his sons al-Afḍal and al-Ẓāfir; Mosulis under Ẓahīr al-Dīn Khiḍr; troops from Diyār Bakr with the fifteen-year-old Lord of Ḥiṣn Kaifā, Quṭb al-Dīn Suqmān; Saladin's nephew, Ḥusām al-Dīn, now Lord of Nablus; Ṣārim al-Dīn Qaimāz, presumably with the troops of Damascus, and, on the extreme right, Taqī al-Dīn. From the centre to the left the line comprised the Kurd al-Mashṭūb, the emir Mujalla ibn Marwān with Mihrānī and Hakkārī Kurds, then the troops of Sinjār under Mujāhid al-Dīn Yurun-Qush, then Keukburī and then the Asdī *mamlūks* with Saif al-Dīn Yāzkūj.

The Franks began their attack to the north of Acre. They were reported to have strengthened their left wing until it outnumbered the Muslim right, and Taqī al-Dīn threw out his skirmishers to cover a tactical retreat. He himself, together with Qaimāz and Ḥusām al-

Dīn, fell back in the hope of drawing the opposing Frankish wing out of line but the Franks did not rise to the bait and halted. Saladin, meanwhile, had misunderstood the point of Taqī al-Dīn's move and weakened his centre by sending off a number of its squadrons to his support. The Franks saw their opportunity and turned against the nearest part of the Muslim line, the troops of Diyār Bakr who had been left exposed by Ḥusām al-Dīn's withdrawal. The Diyār Bakris had a poor reputation, and both Ibn Shaddād and 'Imād al-Dīn stressed their inexperience in war.[36] A Frankish charge broke them; other contingents were involved in their rout and the Count de Bar reached Saladin's own tent on Tell al-'Ayyāḍīya. 'Imād al-Dīn, who had been watching the battle from the Tell with "a number of men of virtue...not thinking that it would reach us",[37] turned tail and was so convinced of disaster that he got as far as the Sea of Galilee in his flight, while others did not halt until they were safely east of Jordan or even at Damascus itself.

The Franks, however, now fell victims to the same difficulties of communication and co-ordination that had contributed to Saladin's blunder. According to a story quoted in *L'Estoire de la Guerre Sainte,* the sight of a runaway horse pursued by a group of soldiers gave the impression that the leading Frankish troops had been routed, at which the rest turned back.[38] The theory that there was a misunderstanding is supported by Ibn Shaddād, who said that Saladin himself halted at the foot of Tell al-'Ayyāḍīya with five companions and rallied what he could of his centre.[39] From the Tell the Franks could see that the Muslim left was unbroken and they must also have been able to see Taqī al-Dīn to the north of them. Since any further advance would expose their flanks they began to draw back: but as soon as they started to retreat Saladin sent squadrons that he had rallied round the corner of the Tell to attack them. Some Franks were routed and Ibn Shaddād reported that when their main body saw them in flight pursued by the Muslims, they thought that the rest of the attacking force had been lost. The whole line now retired in confusion, pressed by the Muslim left and by Taqī al-Dīn, Qaimāz and Ḥusām al-Dīn who had now come back into action. The pursuit was only broken off when Frankish reserve squadrons came out to protect their camp. The Frankish losses were put at 7000 and the corpses were thrown into the river to pollute the water. Ibn Shaddād wrote: "I saw them after they had been carried to the bank to be thrown in and I estimated them at less than 7000."[40] Gérard de Ridefort, the Master of the Templars, who had been captured at Ḥaṭṭīn and released in return for having negotiated the surrender of Templar castles, was captured again and killed. Amongst the Muslim dead were the emir Mujalla ibn Marwān and al-Ẓahīr, the brother of Ḍiyā' al-Dīn 'Īsā.

A self-inflicted wound marred the Muslims' success. When the Muslim troops appeared to be on the verge of defeat, their servants took advantage of the confusion to ransack the tents and escape with what they could seize. According to 'Imād al-Dīn, Saladin was eager to press an attack before the Franks could recover from their losses, "but when they looked for the army, it had gone".[41] The fugitives, the looters and those pursuing the looters had all scattered and Saladin could do no more than issue orders for a general recall. The attack had to be postponed; the Franks made good their losses through reinforcements and many of the Muslim deserters never came back. Such goods as had been recovered were piled in Saladin's pavilion and "the heap was so huge that those seated on one side could not see those on the other side of it". Possessions were returned to whoever could swear to their ownership, but Ibn Shaddād wrote: "this episode had a more serious effect [on the Muslims] than the rout".[42]

'Imād al-Dīn now drafted an official letter in which he wrote that, though they had been weakened by earlier losses, the Franks were swarming like ants and had widened and deepened their trenches so that it had proved impossible to attack them; during the battle; "the troops of the east" had shown fear, only those of Sinjār standing firm, and "the eye of Ṭumān was refreshed in Paradise by the daring of his son"; the Franks were now dejected but "as long as the sea continues to supply them and the land does not repulse them, they will be a perpetual plague".[43] Al-Fāḍil wrote a private note to express his pleasure that 'Imād al-Dīn had escaped from the confusion of battle, "of which he said that he took his reins to fly from it not to it...and this was right... Congratulations on safety are better than felicitations on martyrdom."[44] In another letter he took on the role of military critic: the battle was a misfortune which God was asked to remedy; it was obvious to all clear-sighted men that the mistake lay in the fact that the Muslim army was too near to a numerically superior enemy; if so close a watch had to be kept in order to protect Acre and to maintain the morale of the garrison, then it should be done with cavalry in light order and not with heavy baggage; if Saladin was safe, however, then everyone was safe; as for 'Imād al-Dīn himself, instead of complaining about the loss of his possessions, he should be grateful for God's favour in his escape. 'Imād al-Dīn had asked him to help to track down the goods that had been stolen from his tent and al-Fāḍil replied that he had given instructions to the market officials, but that it was difficult to imagine that the plunderers would get as far as Egypt, especially since a watch was being kept for them.[45]

Saladin appears to have agreed in part with al-Fāḍil's criticism that he was too near the enemy and, as corruption had made the battlefield unhealthy, on 12 October he sent back the heavy baggage to his camp site on the hills some 6½ miles (10 km) south-east of Tell al-'Ayyāḍīya. After this he held a council, attended by both Ibn Shaddād and 'Imād al-Dīn.[46] He was said to have talked of the small numbers of the enemy – "only a few remain out of this multitude" – and pointed out that in the new year the Franks would be reinforced, whereas the Muslims could look for no more help except from al-'Ādil, who was on his way. Because of this, he urged an immediate attack. To counter his arguments it was remarked that the army's morale was low; they had been "under arms and on horse-back" for fifty days; the horses were saddle-sore and Saladin himself had a "disordered constitution", because of the strain that he had undergone; time was needed to regroup the fugitives, for al-'Ādil's arrival and "to collect infantry to stand in the face of their infantry";[47] Turkmans could be got by promises of land and gifts and "undoubtedly the Muslims will help";[48] there was time for Muslim reinforcements to arrive and overwhelm the Franks before the sailing season opened and the best plan, it was urged, was for the army to withdraw, leaving a masking force that could be relieved in rotation. This was what al-Fāḍil had recommended in his letter, but 'Imād al-Dīn apparently did not agree with it and claimed to have pointed out that the sea gate of Acre was still open, whereas a Muslim withdrawal would allow the Franks to renew their blockade. This was obvious enough, but was not allowed to outweigh the more important point that it would be dangerous to press the army beyond the limits of its endurance. As a result, the Acre garrison was ordered to shut the gate and Saladin drew off his baggage on the night of 15/16 October. In spite of his ill health, he then rode out each morning on a tour of inspection, showing on his return "marks of the hardship that he had endured".[49] The Franks were unloading their siege engines and entrenching their camp "from sea to sea".[50] Their wall, in which gates had been left through which they could charge, was strengthened with the spoil from the trenches and defended with mantlets, as well as being manned by guards. To 'Imād al-Dīn this showed the folly of the theory that if the Franks were left an opening, they would retreat.

He urged Saladin to send out the army to attack, and quoted him as replying: "they will not do anything unless I am riding with them and watching how they act."[51]

To add to Saladin's difficulties, rumours were now multiplying about the approach of Frederick Barbarossa with an army put at the lowest at 200,000 men. Frederick was said to be intending to march through the lands of Qilij-Arslān and of the Armenians and a letter came from the Armenian Catholicos of Qal'at al-Rūm, on the Euphrates, expressing fear for his lands. 'Imād al-Dīn added, however, "there was no doubt that he was inclined to favour his own filthy race", and spies were sent out to get definite information. "We said: 'the danger is clear, but the news is confused. The Muslims will rise up for us.' "[52]

On 23 October Ibn Shaddād was sent to put this optimism to the test by summoning reinforcements from Sinjār, Jazīrat ibn 'Umar, Irbil and Mosul, as well as from Baghdad.[53] His mission ran into an immediate difficulty. When he reached Aleppo, he met Saladin's official envoy to the Caliph, Ḍiyā' al-Dīn al-Shahrazūrī, returning from Baghdad, where he had been trying to bargain for troops in exchange for Shahrazūr. Ḍiyā' al-Dīn claimed that the necessary arrangements had been made and that it would only confuse the issue if another envoy approached the Caliph. Al-Ẓāhir did not want to interfere, saying that he could not turn back a messenger from his father, and Ḍiyā' al-Dīn arrived at Saladin's camp apparently in a state of jealous suspicion. A council meeting was held at which it was, belatedly, pointed out that Shahrazūr could not be given up as both 'Izz al-Dīn of Mosul and Zain al-Dīn Yūsuf of Irbil had offered money and troops for it and if they found that it had been given to the Caliph, "they would not send a single rider [to help us]".[54] Bektimur of Khilāṭ had been gathering men and showing open hostility to Saladin, and the implication was that a wrong move could produce an anti-Ayyubid coalition east of the Euphrates to break Saladin's power there while he himself was tied to the Coast. Saladin made the pious, but not wholly credible, point that he was willing to give the Caliph "all these lands",[55] and so could not refuse him Shahrazūr and Ḍiyā' al-Dīn was sent back to Baghdad to continue negotiations.

Ibn Shaddād himself said that the Caliph had made him "fair promises",[56] but 'Imād al-Dīn reported that his mission had not prospered and that the Caliph was delaying his reply, presumably until he had settled the question of Shahrazūr with Ḍiyā' al-Dīn. In the event, Shahrazūr was not handed over and Saladin seems to have relied on flattery and fear. 'Imād al-Dīn wrote an official letter in which he pointed out that "we are not faced by a single enemy who might be destroyed, but, rather, all [the Franks] beyond the seas are our enemies"; there was no Frankish city, town, island or district that had not sent out ships; they had proclaimed in their assemblies that their brothers in Jerusalem had been destroyed by Islam; those who left their homes to fight would have their sins forgiven them and those who were unable to make the journey could send arms and money; some were travelling by sea, and as for those who were coming on foot, news kept flooding in that their lands had been left empty behind them; with their arrival, the evil would be magnified: "polytheism will seek to exalt itself, but it will not be exalted as the religion of God has al-Nāṣir [the victor] as Caliph".[57]

In spite of this rhetoric, it must have been clear that at least for the time being Saladin could only count on his own resources. On 1 November al-'Ādil had moved from Birkat al-Jubb to Bilbais with a strong force, including a number of Negroes,[58] and they arrived at Acre towards the end of the month. Saladin himself had been collecting Syrian infantry and he tried to keep up some military pressure, but the weather closed in, with rain and cold ending all chance of serious fighting.

At this point, Saladin, who had already lost a nephew, 'Izz al-Dīn Mūsik, suffered another blow through the death at al-Kharrūba of one of his most valuable companions, Ḍiyā' al-Dīn 'Īsā. Al-Fāḍil wrote to express his sorrow and added that the situation into which the Muslims and their Sultan had been forced had disagreed with their patience just as the place had disagreed with their constitutions and there was fear for "the fruits of men's hearts".[59] This was a clear hint that dissatisfaction might breed sedition and it must have been obvious that if the siege was going to develop into a war of attrition, it would be vital for Saladin to keep up the morale of his men by arranging for their regular replacement. As a result, "the foreign troops",[60] presumably those of Mosul, Sinjār and Diyār Bakr, were given leave and Saladin stayed with a predominantly Ayyubid force amongst whose commanders were al-'Ādil, al-Afḍal and Taqī al-Dīn. In spite of the fact that it was not the sailing season, fifty galleys of the Egyptian fleet had put to sea under the command of Lu'lu' and they arrived at Acre on 26 December. They carried a number of emirs and their followers, who stayed to reinforce the garrison, and the sailors themselves were used to man the mangonels and to shoot Greek fire. They also disturbed the Franks by making a surprise attack on "the market of the wine shops and the brothels" in the Frankish camp. 'Imād al-Dīn added that the Muslims had heard that 300 Frankish prostitutes had arrived by sea and he noted that "the Franks do not consider it wrong for an unmarried woman to give herself to an unmarried man".[61]

20

THE FALL OF ACRE

The Muslim year 585 had started with Saladin enjoying unchallenged military supremacy in Palestine. He had admittedly lost the initiative to the extent that he had to wait for the Frankish counter-thrust, but he could still pick from a choice of targets – Tripoli, Tyre or Antioch – for his next attack. At the year's end he was faced with the prospect of having to fight, not for further conquest, nor even to maintain his position, but for survival. If the German crusaders reached northern Syria in full strength while he was tied to Acre and if the Franks there continued to be reinforced, the whole of Syria and then Egypt itself would be in danger.

He now sent out more requests for help, this time to Ṭughtekīn in Yemen, who had not answered his earlier summons, and to Qyzyl-Arslān, Lord of Hamadān.[1] Here the position was complicated by the fact that Qyzyl-Arslān's nephew, the young Seljuq Sultan Ṭughril, had escaped from his uncle's control. The Caliph had taken Qyzyl-Arslān's part and in May 1188 his vizier had been defeated by Ṭughril in battle, after which Ṭughril, who was now on the borders of Irbil, had sent messengers to Saladin asking for support. Saladin excused himself on the grounds that he was preoccupied with the Franks, but he wrote to a number of his officers and allies, including Zain al-Dīn Yūsuf of Irbil, telling them to give Ṭughril what help they could. He also sent an envoy to act as mediator between uncle and nephew, but the quarrel showed that he could expect little help from Qyzyl-Arslān. Another difficulty occurred when Zangī of Sinjār was too quick in sending out his troops under the command of his son, Quṭb al-Dīn. Saladin did not want them to arrive before the campaigning season opened and ordered them back. This offended Zangī and Saladin had to write that he had "wished to spare [Quṭb al-Dīn] fatigue, so that his army might be rested when it was summoned. For there would be more pressing need for it in the spring."[2]

Before the end of March 1190 the Germans were ferried across the Dardanelles and at Acre, the Franks restarted active campaigning in the month of Ṣafar (10 March – 7 April) with a surprise attack on the left wing of the masking force, while Saladin himself was off hunting. The Muslims claimed early success, but they ran out of arrows, and suffered casualties in a Frankish charge which drove them back to the river. This showed that it was time for Saladin to reassemble his armies, and the first to come were the Syrians, with the young Shīrkūh of Homs, Sābiq al-Dīn 'Uthmān of Shaizar, the son of Ibn Al-Muqqadam, and a number of Bedouin and Turkmans. After their arrival, on 25 April Saladin moved down from the hills to his old position at Tell Kaisān. Taqī al-Dīn was again on the right and al-'Ādil commanded the left wing, while al-Afḍal and al-Ẓāfir flanked the centre on the left and the right respectively. With the opening of the sailing season, the Frankish ships had returned and as the Egyptian fleet had no thought of challenging them, Acre was again cut off. 'Imād al-Dīn wrote that a wooden pigeon cote had been set up by one of Saladin's men, "and we had said: 'what is this enthusiasm for something that will be of no use?' " The pigeons were now pressed into service to carry coded messages to the town, "until there were few left because of the many messages". Divers were also used to swim into the harbour and 'Imād al-Dīn noted that, although some were killed, others were always prompted by poverty to volunteer, never believing that it could happen to them.[3]

Before fighting started again in earnest, Saladin had a belated success with the surrender on 22 April of the castle of Beaufort, on terms that covered the safety of the garrison and the release of Reginald, who was still being held in Damascus. Less encouraging was the arrival on the next day of an envoy from the Caliph. By way of reply to Saladin's pleas for the rescue of Islam, the Caliph had sent two loads of naphtha, five naphtha artificers and a note authorising Saladin to borrow 20,000 dinars from merchants and charge the loan to Baghdad. Al-Fāḍil had once spent 200 dinars in 15 days on his return from pilgrimage[4] and 'Imād al-Dīn spent 300 dinars on a 23-day journey from Damascus to Egypt in conditions where the prices of food and fodder must have been roughly equivalent to those at Saladin's camp.[5] 'Imād al-Dīn wrote merely that Saladin, while expressing his gratitude, did not take the money,[6] but, by any standards, it was a derisory sum, and according to another report he angrily recalled the million dinars that al-'Āḍid had given him during the siege of Damietta.[7] He claimed that he was now spending more than 20,000 dinars in a single day[5] and it is difficult to avoid the conclusion that relations were now so strained that the Caliph's gift was intended as a diplomatic insult.

For their main offensive effort the Franks had been concentrating on siege engines, and had built three moveable siege towers with imported wood, "as only rare forms of timber will serve for these huge structures".[8] The towers were covered in hides dipped in vinegar to protect them from Greek fire and they could be seen from the Muslim camp "looming over the walls of Acre".[9] According to the author of the Latin *Continuation*, the garrison were so alarmed that they had begun to negotiate surrender terms[10] and 'Imād al-Dīn confirmed that swimmers brought news to Saladin that the town was in danger.[11] As more reinforcements reached him, he began a series of diversionary attacks. 'Imād al-Dīn Maḥmūd, the Lord of Dārā, arrived on 27 April and joined the fighting which had started that day. On 28 April Saladin moved up from Tell Kaisān to Tell al-'Ayyāḍīya and ordered up the army market so that no one need leave to buy provisions. On 2 May the baggage train was brought up and the servants drew swords and shields from the armoury to join in the attacks. These were not proving effective, however, and on 3 May swimmers again brought news that the town was hard pressed. Saladin sent out urgent calls for help and he was reinforced the next day by al-Ẓāhir from Aleppo, followed by Keukburī. The Franks had divided their forces and some held the trenches while the others pressed the town and worked to fill in the fosse. The situation was now saved for the garrison by the son of a Damascus copper-smith. This man had earlier asked permission to enter Acre where his suggestions for burning the towers had annoyed the naphtha artificers, "as this was not his craft", while others had laughed at him, saying: "this man is wasting his money on what does not concern him". Eventually on 5 May he had been allowed the use of a mangonel for his own version of Greek fire which not only destroyed the towers but burnt other Frankish machines in the same blaze.[12] Letters were sent from Saladin's camp giving news of this success, describing the fosse as "a pool of fire with the tower as a fountain", and adding "God destroyed the violet with the pomegranate of fire".[13]

The immediate danger to Acre had gone, but further north the Germans were advancing through Asia Minor. Official rhetoric varied from the hopeful – they were the moths whom the flame of war would destroy[14]...and the rain flood which would be halted when it reached the firmly based mountain[15] – to the querulous: "where are the Muslims? God forbid that they should be abandoning Islam".[16] One letter throws some light on Saladin's general plans. It starts conventionally by noting the arrival of a message from the Caliph which had been read to Saladin's campanions to strengthen their resolution, "and it was as though they heard the voice of one summoning them to the Faith". Saladin then complained of the Frankish command of the sea: the sea was supplying them with ships more numerous than its waves and when one Frank was killed on the land, a thousand more would come by sea to replace him; "this long period and the heavy expenses have affected the ability, though not the obedience, of our companions and their circumstances, but not their courage". There were fears of an attack on Egypt and Saladin went on to say that work on the strengthening of the fortifications of Alexandria and Damietta was going on night and day and it was hoped that news of this would prevent an enemy landing. In an ominous reference to the Germans, he told the Caliph that Hama and Homs had been ordered to hurry on their harvesting and to store away their grain.[17]

Similar precautions were being taken elsewhere. One of Ibn al-Athīr's brothers was acting as agent for an emir in a Mosuli village. He wrote to ask his master whether he should sell any grain when it had been harvested and was told to store it all. The emir later explained: "when we heard of the arrival of the German King, we were sure that there was no place left for us in Syria".[18]

At Acre, according to the Latin *Continuation*, the Frankish camp was now between the hammer of Saladin's forces and the anvil of the town, as troops from two parts of the world, Asia and Africa, had combined to attack the third.[19] In fact, Zangī of Sinjār had arrived at the end of May and he was followed in June by Sanjar-Shāh of Jazīrat Ibn 'Umar and Zain al-Dīn Yūsuf of Irbil, together with 'Alā' al-Dīn, the son of 'Izz al-Dīn of Mosul. The Germans, however, effectively prevented Saladin from using his numbers to take the offensive. In another letter to Baghdad he claimed to have been ready to reinforce Qilij-Arslān, who had sent a stream of letters in March, April and May asking for help and promising support. This had been followed by a period of silence and then suddenly word had come that the Germans were in the middle of the lands of Islam, making for Syria. Peace had been made between them and Qilij-Arslān, who was helping to give them a safe passage – "yet the Holy War is obligatory for all Muslims" – and Saladin was alone in supporting the burden.[20] This was unfair to Qilij-Arslān and had Saladin seriously intended to support him, he should have sent troops earlier. Now, however, he had no choice but to split his forces and those whose lands lay on the invasion route were sent north, while he himself stayed with the easterners and the Egyptians. The first to leave was Taqī al-Dīn's son, Nāṣir al-Dīn, Lord of Manbij, who was followed by the son of Ibn al-Muqaddam, together with Bahrām-Shāh, Lord of Baalbek, Sābiq al-Dīn 'Uthmān of Shaizar and al-Ẓāhir with the Yārūqīya troops of Aleppo. Finally Taqī al-Dīn himself, with the troops of Hama, left on 14 July.

By this time, the edge of the danger had been blunted by Barbarossa's death. A letter came from Qal'at al-Rūm which gave a résumé of the situation: Barbarossa had left his lands in the charge of his eldest son and after moving through Hungary he had forced the Byzantine Emperor to give him passage; after a thirty-three-day running battle with the Turkmans he had defeated Qilij-Arslān's son Malik-Shāh outside Iconium and entered the city by force; he had stayed there for five days and had then taken twenty hostages from amongst Qilij-Arslān's emirs; later, however, he had fallen ill as the result of bathing in a river, and he had then died after a brief illness.[21] 'Imād al-Dīn mentioned this report, but quoted another that he had heard from a Christian eye-witness: the Germans having come through the mountains into the Cilician plain, were trying to cross the Cydnus by a single bridge; Barbarossa himself had been guided to a ford, but in attempting to cross, he had been swept away and drowned; after his body was recovered, the flesh was boiled off his bones, which were put in a sack so that they could be buried at Jerusalem.[22] His younger son, the Duke of Swabia, now took over command of the army, but al-Fāḍil wrote: "if the king of the Amān is broken, as is said, then after him the unbelievers will be building on a shattered foundation".[23]

At Acre, meanwhile, Saladin had arranged for supplies to be brought up by another squadron of the Egyptian fleet, estimated by the author of the Latin *Continuation* at twenty-five ships.[24] On 14 June the Muslims saw "many sails appearing at noon", and Saladin made a diversionary attack in which "both sides sold their lives for rest in the next world".[25] The *Continuation* claimed that two large Muslim ships were destroyed for the loss of one Frankish galley that had run on a rock,[26] and 'Imād al-Dīn put the losses at one on each side.[27] 'Imād al-Dīn had apparently been sending complaints to al-

Fāḍil who now wrote to say that, although a letter had arrived from him, it had contained nothing new. There had been good news recently, "so why have the noble letters been delayed?" The fleet had brought both provisions and joy to Acre, and al-Fāḍil was sure that 'Imād al-Dīn's next letters would show that his mind had been cleared of anxiety.[28]

Acre was now in no immediate danger and Saladin was content to wait on events. In the Frankish camp, however, according to western report, the common soldiers were restless.[29] "Desirous of a change, [they] began to tax the chiefs with sloth", and "on St James's day [25 July] a mournful and unpropitious one, the ill-fated crowd...burst forth". The attack was directed against "Tecadin, the Sultan's grandson,[30]...a man of active spirit and bold in arms, but of exceeding wickedness and implacable cruelty". The attackers were said to have had no commander; each man was his own leader and they could scarcely recognise their own banners. In fact, Taqī al-Dīn had left the camp more than a week earlier, and the attack was not as ill conceived as was suggested. 'Imād al-Dīn thought that the Franks were trying first to forestall the Germans and secondly to take advantage of the weakness on the Muslim right wing, where most of the northerners had been stationed.[31] Saladin, however, had taken the precaution of transferring al-'Ādil to take Taqī al-Dīn's place and he followed the tactics that Taqī al-Dīn had used in the battle of 3 October 1189, by drawing off to trap the attackers. He was supported by his immediate neighbours on the right wing, Ṣārim al-Dīn Qaimāz and 'Izz al-Dīn Jūrdīk, and when the Franks broke formation to plunder his camp, he turned back against them and charged. Saladin sent reinforcements from the centre, including his own guards, a squadron of Mosuli troops under the command of 'Alā' al-Dīn and Egyptians under Sonqor al-Ḥalabī. The Franks had gone too far to allow for a safe retreat; it was said that only Ralf de Hauterive, Archdeacon of Colchester, came out from the camp to help them and 'Imād al-Dīn reported the Frankish dead as stretching from the sand-dunes to the shore in nine lines, each with more than 1000 corpses.[32] Al-Fāḍil wrote to congratulate al-'Ādil, telling him that the day, the fame and the reward in heaven were all his.[33] Another letter gave news to an official at Damascus that God had destroyed the unbelieving devils; they had come out to attack the right wing and "the servant" had drawn up his line, but had then held back until he had excited their greed and lured them on; when at last the Muslims had charged, more than 12,000 Franks had been cut off, not one of whom had escaped; the Muslims had advanced up to their trenches and continued to pull the noose tight, without losing a single man. God was now asked to give them an easy victory over those who remained.[34]

The aftermath of the St James's day battle repeated the pattern of the previous October in that the Muslims failed to follow up their advantage. Saladin was said to have intended to attack, but he was occupied with news from the north, where the German army was crumbling. Perhaps Frankish peace feelers, noted by 'Imād al-Dīn at this point,[35] led him to underestimate the difficulties, but, at any rate, whatever opportunity there may have been was soon lost. Reinforcements were brought in by Henry of Champagne on 28 July and on 1 August Saladin withdrew to al-Kharrūba. One of the reasons for this was the corruption of the battlefield, but another was news from spies and deserters that the Franks, encouraged by Henry's arrival, were now planning a surprise attack on his camp. By the time that he moved back, they were reported to be even stronger than before.

In the north, however, the Germans were no longer formidable. The Duke of Swabia had been ill and 'Imād al-Dīn reported that most of his men were "carrying sticks and riding on donkeys".[36] The Catholicos of Qal'at al-Rūm wrote to say that he had watched them going over a bridge:

> a huge number crossed but I found only a few with shields or lances. I asked them about that and they said: "we stayed in an unhealthy plain for some days, running short of provisions and of firewood. We had to burn most of our equipment and we lost many men and had to slaughter horses for food."[37]

They had been split into three divisions in order to ease problems of supply, but their weakness made them an easy prey. Some went by Baghrās, apparently thinking that it was still in the hands of the Templars, and 'Alam al-Dīn Sulaimān, who now held Darbsak and Baghrās, wrote to say that he and a number of Aleppans had captured enough to lead to a glut on the slave market. 'Alam al-Dīn passed on news of their shortage of equipment and this encouraged the Syrians to capture another 500 before they managed to reach Antioch.[38]

According to the Latin *Continuation* the Frankish leaders had hoped to persuade the Duke of Swabia to stay at Antioch so as to prevent Saladin from concentrating his forces, but the Duke insisted on moving south.[39] He was said to have wanted to go by Hama and Homs, but was warned against this and, instead, he took the coast road by Latakia and Jabala, towards the end of August (map 3). Taqī al-Dīn's garrisons made no serious attempt to halt his march and on 8 September Saladin heard that he had been met by Conrad and taken to Tripoli. How many of his men were still left alive was not clearly known. Ibn Shaddād said that he had seen in an expert estimate a figure of 5000 horse and foot,[40] while 'Imād al-Dīn put the survivors at approximately 15,000.[41] What was certain was that they no longer threatened Syria and when the Duke of Swabia sailed from Tripoli to Tyre at the end of September al-Fāḍil echoed the bathos by writing: "as for the king of the Amān, God has given protection [*ammana*] from his evil doing... In spite of his arrival at Tyre by sea, he is still besieged, as sailing is a siege."[42]

For all their apparent failure, however, the Germans had forced Saladin on to the defensive for the whole summer. It was not until October that he was rejoined by al-Ẓāhir, Sābiq al-Dīn 'Uthmān, Bahrām-Shāh of Baalbek and the son of Ibn al-Muqaddam, while Taqī al-Dīn did not come back until November. In their absence, he had never seriously threatened the Frankish camp and as far as the siege was concerned, time was not on his side. Richard Coeur de Lion and Philip of France had left Vézelay on 4 July and, in the shorter term, Acre was plagued by a constant problem of supplies. In spite of the provision ships that had arrived in June, by August word had come of serious shortages. Saladin called up more supplies from Egypt, but as they were slow in arriving he gave orders to the governor of Beirut, who sent a ship disguised as a Frankish merchantman, with a clean-shaven crew and, according to Ibn Shaddād, pigs on its deck,[43] that slipped through the blockade. Within a fortnight, however, word came again that the city had no provisions left, and although this may have been an exaggeration, Ibn Shaddād reported that the situation was serious enough to force Saladin to conceal the news.[44] His three Egyptian supply ships had been held up for a fortnight by a contrary wind and al-Fāḍil wrote to say that when he was sure that they must have reached Acre, they had been found still at Damietta.[45] The winter storms had arrived early on the Coast, where the white tents of Saladin's camp were compared to bubbles rising above a flood, but eventually on 16 September the ships fought their way into the harbour with their escort of galleys. Al-Fāḍil noted that amongst their cargoes were approximately 4000 *ardabbs* of wheat and 300 loads of flour, as well as other foodstuffs, weapons, arrows and various sorts of luxury goods, all of which had been supplied by Saladin, while the Alexandrian merchants had more than doubled that amount. As a result, "the city is flourishing and the unbelievers are in difficulties". Al-Fāḍil went on to add: "letters from the Franks have been found and translated. These show that they have been abased. Their numbers, like their supplies, have diminished and sudden relief [for the Muslims] may not be long in coming."[46]

The Franks certainly had no reason to be content with their progress. After the arrival of Henry of Champagne they had tried a continuous mangonel barrage until the mangonels were destroyed in a sally and on the night of 2/3 September two more mangonels were burnt, on one of which Henry was said to have spent 1500 dinars. On 24 September they made an attack with fire-ships on the Tower of Flies, which Saladin described as the lock of the harbour.[47] He had garrisoned it, he said, with crossbowmen, archers, naphtha artificers and mangonel crews and the Franks had tried to burn the mantlets that were used to protect it. At the critical time, however, "the wind which was with them turned against them", and their fire-ships, filled with "fats, kindling, oil and wood", were blown back and destroyed uselessly.[48] The Pisans had prepared a special ship in the form of a floating castle for assaulting the walls, but on 6 October Muslim galleys made a surprise sortie from the harbour and burnt it. The story of failure was the same on the landward side. The Duke of Swabia arrived on 7 October, but 'Imād al-Dīn wrote: "his arrival made no impression... The Franks said: 'would that he had not come to us'."[49] An immediate probing attack that he made towards Tell al-'Ayyāḍīya was unsuccessful and on 14 October the formidable battering rams prepared by Henry of Champagne and the Archbishop of Besançon were destroyed by fire. On 17 October word came by pigeon that Franks from Antioch had tried a surprise raid, but the Muslims had been forewarned by spies and al-Ẓāhir's men had driven the raiders off with heavy losses.

In spite of this dismal record, al-Fāḍil's optimism about chances for a quick settlement was shortlived. Saladin had given orders that Jaffa, Arsūf and Caesarea should be abandoned and demolished and that Sidon, Jubail and even Tiberias should be stripped of their walls. Al-Fāḍil commented on this in a letter written later in the autumn: "the destruction of towns at this difficult time must undoubtedly strengthen the spirit of the enemy and weaken that of the Muslims...

We are saving the enemy the expense of destroying places that he would otherwise have to besiege". By way of encouragement al-Fāḍil noted that he had a dream in which a messenger had told him to write the good news of the German army, which had now been reduced to less than 5000 men, but for the rest, the situation was gloomy; Genoese ships had been allowed to enter the Muslim harbour of al-Mahdīya and were now carrying stores to the Franks; "the lands are not as they were. Communications are cut, jobs halted, markets sluggish and trade ruined"; Egypt had been drained of its gold coinage and were it not for the fact that its dirhams had no value elsewhere, they too would have vanished.[50]

The key to the situation was command of the sea and on 14 October 'Abd al-Raḥmān ibn Munqidh was sent as an envoy from Saladin to Ya'qūb ibn Yūsuf ibn 'Abd al-Mu'min, the Lord of the Maghrib, whose lands Ayyubid troops had been ravaging almost throughout Saladin's career. The Maghribis had the reputation of being the best Muslim sailors[51] and al-Fāḍil emphasised to 'Abd al-Raḥmān that if a strong fleet could cut the sea routes to Acre, the Frankish army would either starve or be destroyed; if there were ships ready, they should be sent as soon as possible, but if this could not be done, there were many other ways in which Ya'qūb could help. Al-Fāḍil's letter stresses the stalemate at Acre; the Franks, numbered at 100,000, did not dare leave their camp, but the Muslims could not force their way in because of the fortifications; to tilt the balance the western Muslims were asked to send more aid than was coming from the western Franks. The letter made no reference to the grievances that Ya'qūb might legitimately be nursing, but al-Fāḍil instructed 'Abd al-Raḥmān that, if he was asked about the Ayyubid commanders in North Africa, Yūzpah and Sharaf al-Dīn Qarā-Qūsh, he was to point out that "they are not amongst the leading emirs, *mamlūks* or *ṭawāshīs*" – "God forbid that we should order an evil-doer to act wickedly in the lands."[52] 'Abd al-Raḥmān had a meeting with Ya'qūb on 18 January 1191 and returned unsurprisingly empty-handed a year later.

In October deserters brought news that the Franks were looking for another battle. Saladin's war council advised a withdrawal to tempt them away from their fortifications and on 20 October he moved back some 10½ miles (17 km) from Acre to the hills of Shafar'am. He himself had been unwell and another sufferer was Zain al-Dīn Yūsuf of Irbil, who had been affected by what Ibn Shaddād described as two fevers coming at different times.[53] Saladin had refused him permission to go home, but he had been allowed to retire to the hills of Nazareth. He had rejected the services of Saladin's doctor, knowing, 'Imād al-Dīn added, "that his brother Keukburī coveted his position",[54] one of the few hints that Saladin's circle was not considered to be above the use of poison. Instead, he preferred to be treated by one of his own companions and he died on 19 October. Keukburī was said by 'Imād al-Dīn to have sat in a tent "as though to receive congratulations".[55] He took charge of all his brother's property and arrested those of his emirs who held castles, lest they break their allegiance. He then bargained with Saladin for Irbil, which was given him in exchange for Ḥarrān, al-Ruhā and Sumaisāṭ. According to Ibn al-Athīr, the people of Irbil itself offered the town to Mujāhid al-Dīn Qaimāz, but he refused it, either through fear of Saladin or because he thought that his master 'Izz al-Dīn might not allow him to keep it.[56] Keukburī stayed with Saladin until Taqī al-Dīn arrived from Hama on 3 November, and then left for the east. He later enjoyed an excellent reputation for piety and generosity, as well as for success in the Holy War, in which it was said that he had never lost a battle. This was true enough and due, in part, to his own merits, but also to the fact that after leaving Saladin at this critical point, whether by accident or design he never came back.

Zain al-Dīn Yūsuf's death coincided with trouble amongst the eastern contingents. Sanjar-Shāh of Jazīrat Ibn 'Umar, who was now in his fifth month at Acre, was refused leave to return home on the grounds that the Franks were putting out peace feelers.[57] This does not tally with the report that they were looking for a battle, and he pressed his point unsuccessfully in Saladin's pavilion on the feast of 'Īd al-Fiṭr (1 November). He then returned to his own camp, ordered his tents to be struck and marched off defiantly towards Tiberias. When Saladin was told of this, he wrote to remind him that he had joined the Ayyubid side because he was afraid of his uncle, 'Izz al-Dīn of Mosul. He also pointed out that he had "stretched out his hand against the wealth, blood and honour" of his subjects,[58] the implications being that he could expect no support from them, and if he deserted now, Saladin would no longer protect him. The messenger carrying this letter caught up with him at Tiberias, but he still refused to go back and continued up the Damascus road through the defile of Fīk. As it happened, this was the route by which Taqī al-Dīn was marching from Hama and he was quoted as saying that Sanjar-Shāh had spoken to him at first "as though I was one of his *mamlūks*. When I saw this behaviour, I told him that [it would be better for him] to go back sensibly, but if he did not, I would take him back by force... He started to weep and I wondered at his earlier stupidity and then at his abasement."[59] He successfuly cowed Sanjar-Shāh into returning and Sanjar-Shāh then camped beside him "in fear for his life". Saladin took no action, but was later quoted as saying: "I never heard ill of anyone without finding it less than had been reported, except in the case of Sanjar-Shāh."[60]

Although Sanjar-Shāh's defection was more spectacular, the pressure exerted by Zangī was probably more serious. Zangī had arrived at Acre at the end of May and claimed to be unprepared for the winter. Ibn Shaddād, who was acting as go-between, found both him and Saladin determined to have their own way. Zangī finally wrote a personal note containing both threats and promises and Saladin sent it back with a line of poetry added: "he who loses one like me, what, I wonder, can he gain?"[61] In addition to the implied threat Saladin was also reported to have negotiated with him over Jazīrat Ibn 'Umar, and for the moment he too was persuaded to stay. Al-Fāḍil, who commented on the restlessness of the easterners, was almost certainly right in coupling it with Saladin's need for money. There were too few prospects for expansion or plunder to encourage unwilling allies and al-Fāḍil added: "tongues are generous with advice but hands are miserly with help".[62]

Nothing more was reported by Ibn Shaddād of Frankish peace feelers, but on 11 November earlier warnings were confirmed by the sight of the Frankish army coming out in battle order and advancing to the wells that the Muslims had dug by Tell al-'Ayyāḍīya. Saladin's masking force drew back to Tell Kaisān and by way of precaution he sent off his baggage that night to Qaimūn and Nazareth. This was reported by Frankish scouts, who were quoted by Ambroise as bringing news that Saladin himself had left and that it would be "great folly" to follow him.[63] In fact, the Franks made no move towards the hills, but on 12 November they turned southwards in the direction of Haifa. Saladin drew up the Muslims across their line of advance, with the right wing extended to the hills by al-Kharrūba, and the left resting on the river Na'mān. The right wing had been strengthened since the St James's day battle by the return of the northerners and it now comprised Saladin's sons, al-Afḍal al-Ẓāhir with the troops of Aleppo, al-Ẓāfir, the Mosulis with 'Alā' al-Dīn, al-'Ādil, Ḥusām al-Dīn of Nablus, Ṣārim al-Dīn Qaimāz and 'Izz al-Dīn Jūrdīk, Ḥusām, al-Dīn Bishāra of Bāniās and Badr al-Dīn Dildirim.

On the left were the troops of Sinjār, Sanjar-Shāh with his contingent from Jazīrat Ibn 'Umar, Taqī al-Dīn, al-Mashṭūb with the Mihrānī and Hakkārī Kurds, and the Hakkārī emir Khushtarīn. Saladin's guard was in the centre, but he himself was too ill to take part in the fighting and stayed by the hills. Another absentee through illness was Zangī who had retired with the baggage, as had 'Imād al-Dīn.

The Muslims followed their normal tactics by sending out skirmishers to hold up the advance without committing themselves to closing their formation in order to block it. The Franks were said to have taken four days' supplies with them[64] and their march brought them down the Na'mān river until they were roughly halfway to Haifa, where they were said to have been looking for stores. If they had already used up half their provisions, any further advance would clearly have been dangerous and they now circled round the head of the river and camped by Tell al-Kurdāni on its western side. The Muslims drew off for the night and Saladin now ordered his right wing to close up to the river and his left wing to take up a new position between the river and the sea. His orders were that the Franks should be surrounded but the Muslims were not to press them too closely "until the day is advanced",[65] by which time he presumably hoped that their formation would have been broken. The Franks woke on the morning of 13 November to see "all the Turks in the world"[66] around them, but they moved off back towards Acre in tight formation around their banner, with infantry screening the cavalry.

This was the fiercest field action since Ḥaṭṭīn. The Frankish rearguard were moving backwards facing the enemy and keeping up a continuous fire with crossbow bolts and arrows, while Saladin sent squadron after squadron into battle until he had no reserves left. The Muslims were too impatient to obey orders and keep their distance; they were described as almost inter-mixed with the Frankish rear ranks and Ibn Shaddād noted many Muslim casualties, including the Asadi emir Saif al-Dīn Yāzkūj, who was wounded.[67] The Franks were said to have buried their dead where they fell and to have carried off their wounded. By noon they had covered little more than 2 miles (3 km) and had reached the bridge of Da'ūq. According to Saladin's plan this should presumably have been held by the right wing and Ambroise confirms that it was guarded.[68] Ibn Shaddād, however, merely reported that the Franks crossed and then cut down the bridge to block pursuit, after which they camped on the east bank.[69] Neither he nor 'Imād al-Dīn suggested that there was any longer either a chance or a plan to destroy them, and it may perhaps be assumed that the bulk of the right wing had already joined the battle on the west bank.

Saladin tried to arrange for a night attack by the Acre garrison on the Frankish camp, but got no reply to his message, and on the morning of 14 November the Franks moved off again. The Muslims followed, but without pressing an attack, and they were finally driven off by a charge from the camp. Imād al-Dīn was left to comment that had Saladin not been ill not one of them would have escaped and Saladin himself was seen by Ibn Shaddād weeping tears of vexation.[70] He certainly had reason to be distressed that the Franks could leave the shelter of their camp but, apart from this, they had done him no harm. The Muslims thought that they were trying to relieve pressure on their supplies and Ambroise confirmed that they had hoped to find stores at Haifa, which they then heard had been removed. Ibn Shaddād added that they wanted to take advantage of Saladin's illness[71] and presumably they knew of the unrest in the Muslim army. In the event, however, all that the fighting showed was that as long as caution and discipline were maintained, neither side could hope for a decisive victory and the stalemate continued.

Saladin now repeated the tactics that he had followed after the Muslim losses at the Litani and planned an ambush for 23 November. He succeeded in capturing a number of Franks, including Guy de Senlis, the Butler of France, and although Ibn Shaddād had spoken of intense heat on 13 November he now reported that Saladin gave the prisoners furs because of the cold.[72] Winter, in fact, had closed in and as the campaigning season was now ending, the easterners, 'Alā' al-Dīn of Mosul, Zangī and Sanjar-Shāh were at last allowed to leave, on the understanding that they were to return in the spring. From Acre to Mosul, however, is a straight-line distance of over 500 miles (805 km) and not surprisingly it was more than six months before the Mosulis and troops from Sinjār came back, while Sanjar-Shāh never returned at all. Saladin himself wintered in his camp on the hills, and although the Franks did not try to challenge him there, they kept up pressure on Acre itself. On 31 December seven supply ships arrived from Egypt, one of which was wrecked on a rock near the harbour. The Franks attacked to divert the garrison from unloading the others and while the fighting was going on, the rest were sunk by a sudden squall. Less than a week later a section of the city wall collapsed, destroying part of the outworks, and the

Franks rushed to the attack "like sombre night"[73] and were only beaten off with difficulty. All the builders and craftsmen of the town were collected to work under cover of a barrage of stones and arrows until the breach was repaired.

The garrison had now been besieged for some fourteen months. There was growing discontent, and Saladin decided to take advantage of the fact that the Frankish ships had been either beached or sent back to Tyre to send in replacements for those who wanted to leave. In theory this was a sensible move but 'Imād al-Dīn was critical of the way in which it was carried out. According to his figures there had been some 20,000 men in Acre, including sailors, servants and merchants, together with 60 "emirs and leaders". The emirs had employed – and presumably paid – the common people as a civilian work force to help with such tasks as shifting the mangonels; when they left, the common people left with them and only 20 emirs could be found to take their place. Qarā-Qūsh had stayed in Acre and the leader of the incoming garrison was the Kurd, al-Mashṭūb. Payment was offered to volunteers, but 'Imād al-Dīn added that the majority of the clerks who dealt with this were Christian Copts and the Muslims in charge of the treasury considered it virtuous to save what money they could. As a result, they annoyed would-be volunteers by insisting on "impossible conditions", to ensure that they actually did serve. Saladin urged generosity, but "the officials of the *dīwān* displayed their customary stupidity".[74] Al-'Ādil stayed on the coast at Haifa to supervise the operation, but it had not been completed by the time that the Frankish ships resumed their blockade in the spring of 1191.

The Muslims got some satisfaction from difficulties in the Frankish camp where plague coupled with famine claimed at its height up to 200 victims a day. For the most part, however, they were concerned with their own troubles. Al-Fāḍil arrived in the month of Dhū 'l-Ḥijja (30 December 1190 – 28 January 1191) and before he left Egypt he had written to say that acts of disobedience (to God) and injustices were obvious everywhere.[75] The war was causing shortages. In the case of weapons, demand had outstripped supply and he commented on the despatch of spears, that were now "not to be found in the lands".[76] 'Imād al-Dīn had complained of a lack of doctors in the camp and al-Fāḍil replied that there were fewer in Egypt and none who could be trusted. He repeated that "evildoers have multiplied and come into the open... They detect the scent of sedition, – may God cut off the noses with which they smell it."[77]

The grievances and difficulties were passed on by Saladin to the Caliph. In one letter the Caliph was told that the enemy had sunk their claws into Acre, and "Islam asks aid from you as a drowning man cries for help.": "the servant and those of God's riders who are with him have been eaten up by the gnawing war...their hopes are stretched out to their Commander who is their Imām".[78] At the end of February 1191 Saladin sent another repetitive and emotional plea for help. He referred to an interruption in his correspondence which had been caused by weariness and disgust at the news of this enemy "whose affair has grown so great"; one point of danger was now Seljuq Rūm, where Qilij-Arslān and his sons were quarrelling – "If these lands fall into the hands of the unbelievers, then there will be no more Islam"; Saladin had already sent messages and envoys, but the Caliph had a better right to command; Qilij-Arslān had told him that a number of the enemy had reached Italy,[79] from where they could find an easy passage to Acre early in the spring when the sailing season opened. In what may have been a deliberate attempt to alarm the Caliph he added that "the tyrant known as 'The Aid of Christendom', the Pope", was on the move, a story which he refused to believe himself when Quṭb al-Dīn ibn Qilij-Arslān produced it for him;[80] as for Acre, the Franks could not be attacked in their camp and in spite of their losses they would move out every day, sometimes with their whole force and sometimes with part of it; they had come from so many lands that in the case of prisoners and deserters, relays of interpreters were needed, one translating for another; "the slackness of the Muslims in aiding their comrades in the cause of truth is matched by the eagerness with which these people aid their comrades in falsehood". He himself, he wrote, had to keep his armies so long that he angered them and they angered him; when troops came from distant parts, they would begin their service by asking for leave and this had evil consequences, as the enemy heard of it and waited, expecting them to disperse; the men of Mosul and Sinjār had stayed throughout the summer and endured nobly, but the troops of Diyār Bakr had excused themselves on the grounds that they had to protect their own lands; more men were needed, Turkmans in huge numbers and Bedouin "to fill the eye of the damned enemy"; for the Franks were corn that could only be harvested by men numerous as locusts. Lest the Caliph think that he was asking for money that he should have provided himself, he added that his private property comprised only three estates, one in Egypt and two in Syria, all of whose revenues were being spent in the war: "the call goes out only to one who will answer and symptoms are described to none but the doctor"; it was the Caliph to whom every complaint was taken and it was beneath his banners that the Holy War was being fought.[81]

On 2 March, soon after this letter had been written, Taqī al-Dīn left camp. He had pressed his claims to the towns that Keukburī had exchanged for Irbil – Sumaisāṭ, al-Ruhā and Ḥarrān – and Saladin granted them to him on the understanding that he was to visit them and come back as soon as he had allocated their *iqṭā's*. The logic of Saladin's own career had tied him to the Coast to cope with the problems that his victories had created, but although this might distort the pattern of Islamic power politics, it could not halt the expansionist urge. Taqī al-Dīn, who already held Mayyāfāriqīn, was looking for a kingdom of his own. Saladin must have realised this, but he could not afford to leave a power vacuum in the east, and he merely stressed to Taqī al-Dīn that he must observe the agreement that had been made with the Ortoqid Lords of Āmid and Mārdīn.

A further source of weakness was the quarrel between 'Izz al-Dīn of Mosul and Sanjar-Shāh. According to Ibn al-Athīr, after Sanjar-Shāh's attempted desertion in November, Saladin had suggested to 'Izz al-Dīn that he should attack Jazīrat Ibn 'Umar, but he had been afraid of being tricked and had asked for written authorisation. After an interchange of messengers an agreement was made and 'Izz al-Dīn besieged the town for four months. He failed to take it, but terms were finally agreed by which some of its lands were given to Mosul.[82]

Saladin's information on the movements of the Crusaders from Italy was about to prove accurate. While he himself received some reinforcements with the return of Bahram-Shāh of Baalbek, 'Alam al-Dīn Sulaimān with troops from Aleppo, and Badr al-Dīn Maudūd from Damascus, his most formidable enemies, Philip and Richard, left Messina in March to cross to Sicily. At Acre, there was some minor skirmishing and on 5 April a number of Frankish prisoners were brought in from Beirut: Saladin's young sons asked to be allowed to kill one of them, but he refused, lest they should acquire a taste for blood, and he was quoted as adding: "at the moment they do not distinguish between Muslims and unbelievers".[83] Amongst the prisoners Ibn Shaddād saw a toothless and feeble old man who said through an interpreter that he had made a journey of "a number of months" in order to visit the Sepulchre, at which Saladin released him and sent him back to the Franks.[84] Some weeks later he showed the same attractive generosity when a three-month-old baby was stolen from the Frankish camp. The Franks advised the mother to approach Saladin himself – "he is a merciful man" – and she was brought to him by the Muslim guards. The child had already been sold in the market, but Saladin paid its owner and sent to have it fetched. Ibn Shaddād wrote:

> he gave it to the mother and she took it, with tears streaming down her face, and hugged it to her breast. The people were watching her and weeping and I was standing amongst them. She suckled it for some time and then Saladin ordered a horse to be fetched for her and she went back to their army.[85]

On 20 April, Philip of France arrived at Acre. He had brought six large transports with him and 'Imād al-Dīn reported that the Franks were disappointed by the smallness of his force, but that he had reassured them that there were more reinforcements to come.[86] Saladin's own army was by no means at full strength. He had lost Taqī al-Dīn; none of his easterners had returned and although he was trying to recruit Turkmans through Badr al-Dīn Dildirim, none had yet arrived. Al-'Ādil had been at Acre since November 1189 and although there is no record that his men had gone home, they can be assumed either to have been weakened or to have left, as a fresh force had now been called up from Egypt.

Saladin was still waiting in his camp by Shafar'am when serious fighting started again on 30 May and he had to cover over 14 miles (23 km) each day throughout the next week in order to relieve the hard-pressed garrison. The Franks had started a mangonel bombardment and were trying to fill up the fosse by throwing in dead beasts and even human corpses. The garrison split into working parties, one cutting up the corpses for easy removal and another taking them to be thrown into the sea. A third division covered the first and a fourth worked the mangonels and guarded the walls. The constant pressure was tiring them out and on 5 June Saladin moved up his camp to Tell al-'Ayyāḍīya.

In the meanwhile Richard Coeur de Lion had been getting nearer: the Muslims heard garbled versions of his seizure of Cyprus[87] and Saladin made vague arrangements to help the Emperor of Byzantium to attack it.[88] Muslim ships from Beirut and al-Zīb had been trying to intercept stragglers from the English fleet and they claimed to have captured six ships, but Richard himself arrived safely at Acre on Saturday 8 June with twenty-five galleys. According to Ibn Shaddād he was "inferior to Philip in kingdom and rank but wealthier and more famous in war and for courage",[89] while

Ibn al-Athīr described him as "the [first] man of his time for courage and guile".[90] Deserters told the Muslims that the main Frankish effort had been delayed until his arrival, and this "brought fear to their hearts",[91] but Saladin himself, 'Imād al-Dīn added, remained calm.[92]

Fierce fighting now followed. On 11 June a large Muslim supply ship from Beirut carrying some 700 fighting men was intercepted and sunk by Richard's galleys. There were major attacks on the city on 14 and 18 June, and on 23 and 24 June the Franks probed first along the line of the northern shore and then along the river. Ibn Shaddād reported that just before Richard arrived the Franks had asked Saladin to send an envoy for a parley, to which he had replied that they should send one of their own, as he was not concerned to start negotiations. Then on 18 June a messenger came from Richard to al-'Ādil, who passed him on to Saladin. Richard was asking for a meeting, but Saladin made an excuse that kings could not fight one another after having met. After this Richard fell ill and the Muslims heard, wrongly, that Philip had been wounded.[93]

Another piece of news that reached the Muslims was that Conrad had left the Crusaders' camp to return to Tyre on 25 June. 'Imād al-Dīn explained that the wife of Humphrey of Toron – Isabella – was the daughter of "the king who held Jerusalem when he died", that is, Amalric; kingship, in Frankish custom, passed to the son or, if there were no sons, to the eldest daughter; if she died without issue, the next daughter took the throne. "The former king", that is Guy de Lusignan, had taken the kingdom because of his wife (Sibylla, Amalric's eldest daughter), but lost it when she died (in the winter of 1190/1); Isabella was now the rightful queen and Conrad had argued that as Humphrey was not of royal blood, he could not have her to wife.[94] Ibn Shaddād wrote: "her first marriage was invalidated by a requirement of their religion, but their opinions about this were confused".[95] Conrad then married Isabella, although it was said that she was already pregnant and 'Imād al-Dīn noted later that pregnancy was not a bar to marriage in the religion of the Franks.[96] Both Guy and Humphrey were said to have complained to Richard on his arrival, as a result of which Conrad now fled to Tyre, fearing that he might be arrested.

Muslim reinforcements arrived in the last week of June. Although Zangī had stayed at home himself, he had sent troops from Sinjār who were now stationed on Saladin's left wing. Two divisions of Egyptians also arrived and 'Alā' al-Dīn brought up the contingent of

Mosul. Because of the threat from Taqī al-Dīn the easterners had not been joined by any troops from Diyār Bakr and Saladin was quoted as exclaiming: "this is the work of Satan".[97] He wrote to Mosul to tell 'Izz al-Dīn of the Frankish pressure: "they have mined the walls and the city is in danger... Nothing remains now except that God should overtake it with his grace."[98] In another letter he wrote: "if help does not come now, when will it come? Whoever comes, but not when he is needed, has not come at all."[99]

Richard's envoy now returned to the Muslim camp and was met by al-'Ādil and al-Afḍal, who took him to Saladin. He asked for a safe-conduct so that Richard could meet Saladin in the plain of Acre alone without their armies. Saladin replied: "he does not understand my language and I do not understand his",[100] and he suggested that the interpreter, whom they would have to use, could act as an envoy in the negotiations that must precede any meeting. This idea was not taken up, and it was then agreed that Richard should meet al-'Ādil. Nothing was heard for some days and it was rumoured that the other Frankish leaders had told Richard that this was too dangerous, but he then sent a messenger to deny the rumour and to say that he had been ill. He asked leave to send Saladin a present of falcons and hunting dogs, and asked for chickens on which to feed them, saying that they were not yet in good condition after their journey – a request which led al-'Ādil to suspect that he was concerned for his own invalid diet. His messenger asked for proposals, but was told that any initiative must come from the Franks. Discussions were then suspended until 1 July when an envoy came again, bringing as a gift a released Maghribi prisoner. Ibn Shaddād remarked that the purpose of these Frankish embassies was to test Muslim morale and that it was for the same reason that the Muslims received them.[101] There is no word in the Arabic sources of envoys sent in return by Saladin, but according to the author of the Latin *Continuation* he made frequent presents to the kings and promised them either money, or part of the Holy Land or all that lay to the west of the Jordan, but did so simply to gain time.[102]

To support their diplomacy the Franks launched another major assault on 2 July, forcing Saladin to relieve the pressure by attacking their camp. According to Ibn Shaddād, he took no food that day but urged his men on with tears in his eyes, while al-'Ādil joined in the fighting himself.[103] On 3 July a message came from the garrison to say that if nothing was done they would have to ask for quarter. Ibn Shaddād described this as "the gravest news that had reached the

Muslims". Acre contained "all the arms of the Coast, Jerusalem, Damascus, Aleppo and Egypt",[104] as well as those from other Islamic countries, and the prospects of disaster gave rise to fears for Saladin's health. Another abortive attack was made on the Frankish camp and al-Mashṭūb came out under a flag of truce to discuss terms with Philip. He pointed out that quarter had always been granted to the Franks when they had asked for it, but Ibn Shaddād and 'Imād al-Dīn heard that Philip angered him by referring to the Muslims as his "*mamlūks* and slaves",[105] and he went back, saying that Acre would now be defended to the last man. Morale, however, was deteriorating and on the night of 3/4 July a number of emirs slipped out of the harbour in a small boat. This was a serious blow to Saladin, as if he could no longer rely on his emirs, his whole position was at risk. He pardoned one of the deserters on condition that he returned to Acre that night and he cancelled the *iqṭā's* of the others, who included the son of 'Izz al-Dīn Chāūlī and the second-in-command of the Asadi emirs.[106] He wrote to tell Keukburī of the news, but added that the garrison was still fighting and making sorties against the Franks from the outworks and from the saps.[107]

He hoped to make a surprise attack at dawn on 4 July, but Ibn Shaddād wrote: "the army did not help him in that, and said: 'we are putting the whole of Islam at risk' ".[108] There was fighting later in the day, but meanwhile three messengers from Richard came out to ask for fruit and snow. They were presumably again testing Muslim morale and Saladin countered by allowing them to visit the army market, where the extent of the Muslim resources could be seen in more than 7000 shops. A single cookshop was described as having 28 cooking-pots, each capable of holding 9 sheep's heads, and by way of luxury there were over 1000 baths, where customers were prepared to pay a dirham or more to enterprising Maghribis who had dug holes in the ground, lined them with clay and filled them with heated water.[109] The Muslims spent the night of 4/5 July under arms, as it had been arranged that the garrison should try to cut their way out. The plan failed, apparently because the Franks had been alerted, and on 6 July there were more negotiations. The Muslims offered to surrender the town and its contents in exchange for the freedom of the garrison. When this was refused they increased the offer by promising to release one Frankish prisoner for every member of the garrison, and finally they offered the Cross as well. The Franks, however, were insisting on the return of "all their lands and the release of all their prisoners",[110] terms that were considered unacceptable. On 7 July a message came from the garrison saying that they were prepared to fight to the last man. Reinforcements arrived on 9 July with Sābiq al-Dīn ʻUthmān and on 10 July Badr al-Dīn Dildirim brought up a large force of Turkmans. Meanwhile in Acre an attempt had been made to build a masking wall behind the main Frankish breach, but there were other gaps and the town had become weaker.

If Acre was taken by storm, the garrison could expect no mercy. Their messages show that they were wavering. Saladin had been told on 3 July that they would have to surrender and on 7 July that they would fight to the death, since when they had presumably heard of the failure of his own negotiations. On 12 July the Franks attacked again and a swimmer brought news of the final collapse; Al-Mashṭūb had negotiated terms; the city and its contents, including the ships in the harbour, were to be surrendered; the Muslims were to pay 200,000 dinars and hand over the 1500 "unknown" prisoners and 100 nominated by the Franks,[111] in addition to the Cross. Conrad, who had returned to the Frankish camp, had acted as go-between in the negotiations and was to be given 10,000 dinars for himself, with another 4000 for his "companions". In return the garrison were to be allowed to leave with their families and personal property.[112] When this message came, Saladin called his war council. "His ideas were disturbed, his thoughts distracted and his state confused."[13] There is indication that al-Mashṭūb had been authorised to make offers that in effect pledged Saladin's own credit on such a scale and Ibn Shaddād said that Saladin intended to send out a swimmer that night to say that he did not approve the terms. At noon, however, the Franks "gave one shout"[114] and their banners were seen on the city walls. There was distress and weeping amongst the Muslim army. ʻImād al-Dīn wrote: "we consoled Saladin... 'Though the city has fallen, Islam is not lost' ",[115] and Ibn Shaddād wrote that he had tried to divert his mind to thoughts of the defence of the Coast and of Jerusalem.

21

STALEMATE

On the night after the fall of Acre the Muslim baggage train was sent back to Shafar'am while Saladin stayed in the forlorn hope that the Franks could be lured into a rash attack. From a strategic point of view, the fall of Acre was in itself no more than an unpleasant setback. The Franks already held ports on the Coast and Acre added no new factor to the military equation. The loss of arms and supplies and the waste of the money spent on Qarā-Qūsh's fortifications must certainly have been serious, but did not prevent Saladin from keeping his army in the field. Throughout the siege he had resigned the initiative to the Franks and at least he now had the chance to move again. To set against this, however, was the blow to his prestige. In the course of his career he had suffered a number of military checks, but his one actual defeat, at the battle of Ramla, had been a matter of chance and carelessness. At Acre, however, he had committed all the resources that he could muster on one single object and failed. The effect of this was bound to be serious in an army for which success was the main cohesive force. The Kurds, for example, were said to have complained about the fate of their fellow tribesmen in the garrison and to have suffered the heaviest casualties in the final assault on the Frankish camp.[1] If any one section of the army felt itself aggrieved, the result could prove disastrous.

Saladin blamed Taqī al-Dīn, who far from hurrying back from the east as he had promised, had been drawn into a war with Bektimur of Khilāṭ.[2] The basis of Saladin's tactics, however, had always been to let himself be attacked in as strong a position as possible and then to use the mobility of his men to break or trap the enemy. Even had he been reinforced, it seems unlikely that he could even have stormed the Frankish fortifications, and he obviously stood a better chance when the Franks were on the move again – provided that he himself was determined to fight the war to its end and that he could maintain the morale of his men. He wrote to tell Keukburī that the Franks were planning either to give battle or begin on a march, "and in both of these purposes, if God wills, is their destruction...for we shall oppose them wherever they go".[3]

For the moment the Franks made no move and at dawn on 14 July Saladin, still "sorrowful and concerned about future plans",[4] moved back to Shafar'am. The author of the Latin *Continuation* reported that the Franks were not sure whether or not he had agreed to ratify the surrender terms and on the day that he moved they sent out three envoys, together with a messenger from the captured Qarā-Qūsh.[5] According to 'Imād al-Dīn, a council meeting was now held at which it was agreed to accept the terms, after which the timing had to be settled.[6] The *Continuation* quoted forty days as the period originally allowed for the payment of the ransom and the release of the prisoners,[7] but 'Imād al-Dīn now wrote that the Franks wanted half the money, all the prisoners and the Cross produced within a month, calculated apparently at thirty days from the date of the surrender, after which the payment of the rest of the money could be delayed for another month.[8] Saladin sent an envoy to discuss this and Ibn Shaddād said later that it was agreed to make the settlement in three, monthly instalments.[9] The Frankish envoys were now allowed to go on to Damascus to inspect their prisoners and they returned with four whom they had selected on 24 July. On 2 August two more envoys from Richard and a Kurd from Acre came out and the envoys prostrated themselves before the Cross. In their discussion on the exchange of prisoners they told Saladin that a number, including Qarā-Qūsh, had been taken by Philip to Tyre. According to 'Imād al-Dīn, Philip had left "because of some matter that had gone wrong for him",[10] and he was said to be planning to go home, leaving al-Dūk (the Duke of Burgundy) to take his place. Saladin sent an envoy to Tyre with a gift in the hope of finding out what his real intentions were.

Saladin now occupied himself with collecting the prisoners and the money and on 11 August the Franks reminded him that the first month was ending. What was due, according to Ibn Shaddād, was the Cross, 1600 prisoners and 100,000 dinars,[11] all of which had been collected except for a number of the prisoners to be chosen by the Franks, who had not yet finished making their selection. There was a difficulty over the question of how to make the transfer, a point that had not been fixed in the original agreement. In return for handing over the first instalment, Saladin wanted all the garrison released and he offered the Franks hostages for the remaining 100,000 dinars. As an alternative, he suggested that if they preferred to keep the garrison, they should send him hostages of their own. Ibn al-Athīr had apparently heard that the Franks were willing to release some prisoners, but he added that it was thought that these would only be "servants, poor men, Kurds and people of no importance".[12] Both Ibn Shaddād and 'Imād al-Dīn said that they had refused to release anyone at all, insisting that what was due should be handed over.[13] According to the Latin *Continuation* Saladin was warned that if this was not done, the prisoners would be killed.[14]

The Franks could argue fairly that Saladin was inventing difficulties, while Ibn Shaddād later quoted "Richard's co-religionaries" as saying that he never had any intention of keeping his word.[15] The immediate result was that Saladin refused to hand over what was due and on 20 August Richard had some 3000 Muslim prisoners massacred on the plain between Tell al-'Ayyāḍīya and Tell Kaisān. When the Muslims inspected their dead, they found that only well-known leaders and those who were considered useful for slave labour had been left alive. Ibn Shaddād evidently thought that Richard was within his rights to consider the agreement broken, but he pointed out that in that case the prisoners should have been kept as slaves and not killed.[16] The Muslim advance guard had watched what was happening and Richard may have hoped to force Saladin to attack at a disadvantage, but in fact only skirmishing followed. Another explanation quoted by the Muslims was that Richard did not want to leave too many prisoners behind when he moved from Acre,[17] but this would only make sense if he really believed that Saladin was preparing to cheat him. Otherwise, he could have got rid of the garrison and taken the money, the Cross and the exchanged Franks by accepting Saladin's hostages. In crude terms of profit and loss, 200,000 dinars were probably worth more to Saladin than the lives of 3000 men of little rank or importance, and the Muslims' anger at the massacre might have been thought calculated to stiffen their determination. In fact, however, it seems to have had the opposite effect and it cannot seriously be suggested that Saladin intended to sacrifice his men. The most plausible explanation is that both sides were genuinely suspicious of each other. Saladin now retaliated in kind by killing Franks who fell into his hands in the fighting that followed, but on neither side was resentment strong enough to interfere with later negotiations.

On Friday and Saturday, 23 and 24 August, the Franks were seen to be making preparations for a march. Saladin had heard that they were planning to move down the coast towards Ascalon and he held a council meeting. The coastline, where the Franks would have the sea on one flank and thickets and sand dunes on the other would not suit the normal Muslim battle tactics, but two emirs were sent out to reconnoitre. They returned with news of some suitably open sites and it was decided to shadow the Frankish army and attack where possible.

On the morning of Sunday 25 August[18] the Franks were seen to have lit fires, this being "their custom when they intend to travel".[19] Word was passed to Saladin and he ordered the Muslim baggage to be sent off. Stores had been collected in the expectation of another stationary summer and a quantity of these had to be abandoned through lack of transport animals, but what could be removed was taken to Tell Qaimūn. The Franks now marched off in three divisions, each carrying its own baggage. Part of the Muslim army had gone ahead to Tell Qaimūn; Saladin himself was apparently moving parallel to the Franks' line of march, and al-Afḍal was in command of a division that was harassing them as they moved. There was some fierce fighting and al-Afḍal sent word that the Frankish rearguard was straggling; with a thousand men to reinforce him he could destroy them. Saladin sent off what reserves he could, but 'Imād al-Dīn wrote: "the Sultan was told: 'we did not come out with the intention of fighting a battle. The people [presumably the bulk of the army] have gone ahead to the camp and there is a better place for a battle by Caesarea.' "[20] Meanwhile Richard had ridden back to the rescue and when Saladin, with Ibn Shaddād in attendance, went "to the edge of the sand",[21] he was met by the news that the stragglers – the Duke of Burgundy's French – had rejoined the army and crossed the Kishon river by Haifa. To march behind them any further along the sea shore would only tire the horses and waste arrows.

The heights of Carmel which border the plain of Acre mark the edge of a spur of hill country that stretches over some 35 miles (56 km) south-east/north-westwards, cutting off the plain of Acre and valley of Jezreel from the plain of Sharon in the south (map 2). The high ground that forms the tip of the spur is roughly triangular. The Franks at Haifa had to march round the apex of the triangle and down its south-west side, while Saladin, from Tell Qaimūn, could move along its base through the pass that follows the line of the river Tut and come out ahead of them on the coast. On Monday 26 August he sent on his baggage train through the first section of this pass, but rather than allow it to come out too soon he appears then to have ordered it to turn south-eastwards across the easy slopes that separate the Tut Valley from the Iron Valley. Al-'Ādil went on ahead to the Iron Valley, while 'Alam al-Dīn Sulaimān and Ḥusām al-Dīn Bishāra were left at Tell Qaimūn to protect the rear against any surprise move by the Franks along the north-east flanks of Carmel. As a further precaution, 'Izz al-Dīn Jūrdīk was sent to watch their camp, while Saladin himself followed the baggage train and then rode off on a long reconnaissance.

The Franks were not in any hurry and Saladin, who had sent his baggage south to Majdal Yābā some 13 miles (21 km) east of Jaffa, had to call it back again, as the army was running short of supplies. A Frankish prisoner, who was questioned in Ibn Shaddād's presence, said that they had been waiting for their fleet with "men and provisions"; the cost of their food had gone up by a third since the first day of their march and they had lost 400 horses in the fighting.[22] Saladin was later told that Richard had been tempted out from Acre by a report that the Muslim army was now small and scattered and that the Bedouin who had given him this news had been executed. He himself wrote to Keukburī: "we have gone on to forestall them on their march", and he asked "how is it that the noble man [Keukburī himself] does not take vengeance for Islam?"[23]

The Franks made a short march on Wednesday, remained in camp on Thursday and on Friday 30 August they moved down the coast towards Caesarea, which had earlier been demolished by the Muslims. This stretch of their route had been recommended to Saladin as a suitable battlefield and he now committed his squadrons to an attack. Ibn Shaddād reported that the Franks were still moving in three divisions, the vanguards being commanded by Geoffrey de Lusignan, the centre by Richard and the rear by "the sons of the Lady of Tiberias", while the fleet was sailing alongside them.[24] In each division the cavalry was flanked by two columns of infantry, one between it and the Muslims and the other marching along the shore. These latter were carrying the baggage and the tents because of their lack of transport animals and this led Ibn Shaddād to exclaim at how the Frankish soldiers were willing to endure crushing toil without regular pay.[25] He also commented on the damage done by their crossbow fire and the ineffectiveness of the Muslims' arrows against their infantry. He saw Franks marching unconcernedly with more than ten arrows sticking out of their equipment and 'Imād al-Dīn described them on their march south of Caesarea as looking like hedgehogs, bristling with arrows.[26] Saladin was unable to block their march and they camped on Friday night at the Crocodile River (Nahr al-Zarqā'), $3^1/_2$ miles (6 km) north of Caesarea and some 20 miles (32 km) from the Carmel promontory.

On Saturday Saladin kept watch from the limestone ridge that overlooks Caesarea, but the Franks stayed in camp. Then on Sunday they made a short march of 5 miles (8 km) past the ruins of the town to the Dead River (Nahr al-Mafjir) and Monday saw a repetition of Friday's bitter fighting as they forced their way through heavy Muslim attacks to the Reed River (Nahr al-Qaṣab). The Muslims camped up-stream and here they buried one of Saladin's famous *mamlūks*, Ayāz al-Ṭawīl, a man said by Ambroise to have carried a lance twice as heavy as those of the Franks and to have been so strong that no one dared attack him.[27] He was killed, according to 'Imād al-Dīn, when his horse fell, being unable to get up because of the weight of his armour.[28] Saladin claimed that the Franks lost 1000 horses in this battle.[29]

On Tuesday 3 September Saladin moved to the forest of Arsūf. The Franks stayed in camp by the Reed River on Tuesday and Wednesday and then on Thursday 5 September, after having been reinforced by the sea, they moved a further 9 miles (14 km) down the coast and halted by the Nahr al-Fālik (river Rochetaille). Richard now decided to test the Muslims' morale again and 'Alam al-Dīn Sulaimān, who was in command of the masking force, was asked to fetch al-'Ādil for discussions. Saladin gladly agreed and told al-'Ādil to draw out the discussions for as long as possible in order to give Turkman reinforcements time to arrive. The plan failed. Richard came out with Humphrey of Toron – a handsome young man but clean shaven, as Ibn Shaddād described him[30] – to act as interpreter and repeated his demand for the whole of the Coast. Al-'Ādil, ignoring his instructions, replied "roughly" and the meeting was broken off. This seems to have taken Saladin aback. As soon as he heard what had happened, he sent off his heavy baggage. The light baggage followed "until it came up near the heavy baggage" and then Saladin changed his mind and called "them" – either the light or the heavy baggage train or both – back again. They arrived in camp after dark "and the people were very disorganised that night". Perhaps fortunately for the Muslims, the Franks did not move on the next day and Saladin had time to restore order and to send the baggage off once again.

On Saturday 7 September Saladin was told that the Franks were making for Arsūf, 5 miles (8 km) to the south of the Nahr al-Fālik. He decided on a general action, drew up his squadrons and sent out his skirmishers. The Franks were marching by the sea shore in open ground that led to orchards outside Arsūf. Inland was a ridge – "the crest of the hills", as Ibn Shaddād described it[31] – and beyond this the forest of Arsūf. The Frankish formation, with the Templars in the vanguard and the Hospitallers in the rear, was described by Ambroise in his famous account of the battle,[32] but no significant details are given in the Muslim sources. Saladin apparently drew up the Muslims in line parallel to the Frankish columns, with his own guard acting as a reserve. The battle was started by the skirmishers, presumably the 2000 "Turks" armed with bows, described by Ambroise,[33] and when the Frankish vanguard was getting near the orchards, Saladin committed the main body of his army. He himself rode along his line, urging on his men. Ibn Shaddād wrote: "I met him several times and he was only accompanied by two servants with two led horses. I also met his brother [al-'Ādil] who was in the same case and arrows were passing both of them." The Franks were hard-pressed and Ambroise reported urgent pleas made by the Hospitallers to be allowed to charge, because of the number of horses that they were losing. Saladin, however, was not acting with his usual caution. The temptation to rashness was obvious but the only occasion on which he had defeated a Frankish army on the march had been at Ḥaṭṭīn, where both the ground and his own superior numbers had been in his favour. Here he could not surround the Franks because of the sea and by pressing them closely while they were still unbroken he was exposing himself to a counter-attack.

By the time that the head of the Frankish column had reached the orchards, Ibn Shaddād thought that their cavalry had realised that only a charge could save them. According to Ambroise, Richard had planned a simultaneous attack from each division, but after a final plea from the Hospitallers, two knights, unable to restrain themselves, broke ranks and were followed by the rest. Ambroise claimed that had it not been for this premature thrust, the Muslims would have been destroyed, but his account is not confirmed by Ibn Shaddād. From his position in the Muslim centre Ibn Shaddād could see the Frankish cavalry mustering in the middle of their infantry and taking their lances. His picture is one of a concerted and well-ordered attack. The infantry closed up to leave gaps in the line. The cavalry shouted "like one man", and then charged the three Muslim divisions, centre, left and right simultaneously. The centre broke. Ibn Shaddād rode off to look for shelter in the left wing, but was met by the sight of its rout. He turned to the right wing, whose condition was even more serious. He then went back to Saladin's own guard, where he found Saladin himself with only seventeen men. All the rest had been thrown into the fight, but his banners were still flying and his drums were being beaten to rally the fugitives. Al-Afḍal, al-'Ādil, Ṣārim al-Dīn Qaimāz and the Mosulis under 'Alā' al-Dīn were said to have stood firm and after their first charge the Franks paused, fearing an ambush. They then charged twice more, driving the Muslims back to the ridge . Saladin himself went to a tell by the edge of the forest, where he again tried to muster his men. The Franks were afraid of being ambushed amongst the trees and so pursued no further.

According to Ambroise, after their rout the Muslims returned to the attack and 'Imād al-Dīn told his readers that had the Franks not been able to take shelter in Arsūf, they would have been destroyed.[34] Saladin, however, was under no illusion about his failure. He could only be got to take a very little light food and he refused to accept Ibn Shaddād's consolations.

There are no accurate figures for Muslim casualties, but Ibn Shaddād reported that a number of leading men were amongst the dead and that many horses were wounded. More important, however, were the implications of the battle for the future of the war. It had been proved at Acre that the Muslims could not defeat the Franks when they were entrenched. Now it was shown to be dangerous to attack them when they were on the move, and it was becoming hard to see what Saladin could do to free himself from the problems of a prolonged war in which there was little chance that he could ever force a decision. At that, however, if it was difficult for him to win, the Franks could still lose. They had scored an undoubted success, but the Muslim rout was, in fact, little more than an undignified and expensive version of their usual tactics. Saladin had not allowed his men enough room to avoid the weight of the Frankish charge and instead of opening out or retiring in good order, they had been forced to turn and flee. The Franks, however, had not been able to trap them and Saladin had rallied them successfully. He could expect reinforcements, and the Franks for their part had suffered losses and would certainly find it difficult to replace their dead horses. Moreover a long war needed a united effort. How much the Muslims knew about Frankish feuds is not clear. ʻImād al-Dīn and Ibn Shaddād were only concerned with the quarrel between Richard and Conrad, and there is an unfortunate dearth of letters covering this period, but Saladin must certainly have hoped that he could out-stay Richard. The morale of the Muslims was low but if Richard decided to turn inland, without enough baggage animals or a safe supply route, and move into the Judaean hills where his water and supplies would be at risk, the tables could immediately be turned.[35]

Whatever his losses and disappointments, Saladin took care not to show weakness. On the day after the battle he made a demonstration against the Frankish camp and when the Franks moved from Arsūf 8 miles (13 km) south to the ʻAujā' river on Monday 9 September, he challenged them with his skirmishers. Ambroise reported that "Caisac" (ʻAlam al-Dīn Qaiṣar) and 30 emirs, each with 500 Turks "of hardy race",[36] had asked Saladin to be allowed to attack[37] and according to Ibn Shaddād Saladin was hoping for another Frankish charge so that "God might give the victory to whom He wills".[38] The Franks, however, were not to be tempted, and in particular they were not prepared to turn inland where they might be surrounded. Ibn Shaddād appears to show that they were still following the line of the shore where he says that some crossed the ʻAujā' and others stayed on the "east side",[39] which may suggest that they were fording it by its last north/south loop where it reached the sea.

At this point Richard was some 3 miles (5 km) from Jaffa itself and Saladin now prepared to draw off. He sent his baggage camels to Ramla on the night of 9/10 September and followed himself on the next day. He tried to put the best construction possible on his long-running battle. He told Zangī of Sinjār that the Franks had taken seventeen days over a two-day journey,[40] and he explained to the Caliph that their route by the sea shore had been all "narrows, thickets, sands and places not wide enough for manoeuvring" – "Every time that we found open ground we pressed them"; al-Afḍal had cut off their rearguard on the first day; they had lost 1000 horses in the fighting by Caesarea and a great Count, known as Sīr Jāk (Jacques d'Avesnes) had been killed at Arsūf to the distress of the King of England.[41]

Saladin had earlier been warned that the Franks were making for Ascalon. He now held a war council at which, according to ʻImād al-Dīn, ʻAlam al-Dīn Sulaimān pointed out that at Jaffa Richard was equidistant from Jerusalem and Ascalon; each would need a garrison of 20,000 men; and the Muslims could not hold both; if the Franks captured Ascalon intact, they would strengthen it and use it as a base for further attacks, and its position on the coast road to Egypt would make it doubly dangerous. In view of this, he advised Saladin to demolish it.[42] His argument presupposed that the Muslims were intending to use fixed garrisons to defend the Coast rather than rely on a field army, and clearly Saladin himself was no longer hoping to defeat Richard on the march. He realised, according to Ibn Shaddād, that the Muslims would be unable to hold Ascalon "because of their recent experience at Acre and what had happened to the garrison there",[43] and he knew that he would have to husband their strength for the defence of Jerusalem. As a result, he decided to go to Ascalon himself to see to the dismantling of its fortifications, while al-'Ādil with ten emirs stayed to watch Jaffa.

Once the decision had been made, it was important to forestall any Frankish counter-move and after a night march Saladin reached Ascalon on Wednesday 11 September. He was in a gloomy mood and told Ibn Shaddād that he would prefer to lose all his children rather than have to remove a single stone from the walls.[44] 'Imād al-Dīn wrote of Ascalon: "I never saw a fairer or a stronger place",[45] and there was great distress amongst the townspeople when they were forced to leave. Transport to Egypt and Syria could only be hired at hugely inflated rates and what could not be moved had to be sold at sacrifice prices. The state granaries were thrown open, as it was impossible to take away grain and, on a humbler level, twelve chickens could be bought for a dirham. Ibn Shaddād wrote: "monstrous things took place and there was frightening discord".[46]

It was reported in the *Itinerary of Richard I* that Geoffrey de Lusignan was sent by sea to investigate what was happening and that Richard then tried unsuccessfully to get his allies to move south.[47] Ibn al-Athīr heard that Conrad had sent him a message of reproach, saying: "had I been with you, Ascalon would have been in our hands today with only one tower destroyed".[48] In fact, however, Saladin had moved so fast that Richard would have had little time both to reconnoitre and to move before serious damage had been done. On 13 September al-'Ādil sent word that the Franks had not heard what was happening and on the same day fires were started in Ascalon. On 14 September Saladin rode out to inspect the work, but "his constitution became disordered"[49] and for two days he could neither ride nor eat. The baggage train was then moved up to the town so that "the servants and porters" could help and by the time that Saladin himself rode north again on 23 September most of the wall had been destroyed. The masons with a cavalry guard were left behind to finish the demolition under the command of al-Afḍal.

The route from Jaffa to Jerusalem ran across the plain by Ramla and then into the Judaean hills near Latrun. While Saladin had been at Ascalon, Richard had started to fortify Jaffa for use as a base. Saladin's military reactions had always been conventional and by this move Richard could count on tying him down to sentry duty on the Jerusalem road for the rest of the autumn. It comes as no surprise, then, to find that on his return from Ascālon Saladin went to Ramla, where he ordered work to begin on the demolition of the castle. He allowed his men the contents of the state granaries of Ramla and Lydda and in Lydda he ordered the destruction of the Church of St George. There were problems in Jerusalem itself whose governor had written to complain of shortages of men and supplies. These letters were said to have been stolen by eastern Christians, who were discovered trying to smuggle them to the Franks, and Saladin now left on a flying visit of inspection. He rejoined his army on 30 September to find that one of Qilij-Arslān's sons, Qaiṣar-Shāh of Malaṭīya, had arrived to ask for help against his father and brothers and that Richard had almost been captured on the day before. Ambroise said that Richard had dismounted when out riding on the plain and had then fallen asleep,[50] but Ibn Shaddād and 'Imād al-Dīn reported that he had come to the rescue of Frankish foragers who had been ambushed by the Muslim advance guard.[51] He was in difficulties when one of his companions, William de Pratelles, showing a timely command of Arabic, had cried out that he himself was the *malik* (king). As a result William was captured and Richard escaped.

Rashness on Richard's part might, perhaps, suddenly tilt the balance, but, otherwise there was little to encourage Saladin. Al-Fāḍil, who had gone back to Egypt, noted how the standards of civil were falling. He wrote in his diary that there was unparalleled vice, fornication, sodomy, perjury and wrong-doing amongst all classes from the emirs downwards; so-called Muslims were eating in day-time during the fast of Ramaḍān and drinking wine at night with Christians in a way that earlier had been unheard of.[52] The background to the military situation was equally depressing. Saladin wrote to tell the Caliph that as there had been no respite from war for four years, the army's morale was low; because of the number of casualties horses were now hard to get; equipment was non-existent and armourers were working over-time in Egypt and Syria. He added: "the servant is undertaking this duty alone, helped only by the Lords of Mosul and Sinjār".[53]

Because of the difficulties, it is not surprising that peace talks became more important. While Saladin was at Ascalon, al-'Ādil had written to tell him that Humphrey of Toron had again come to discuss terms. The Franks were still demanding the whole of the Coast, but Saladin was now despondent enough to consider that there might be some point in negotiating. No immediate progress was made as on 8 October al-'Ādil sent on the "pleasant news" that Philip was dead[54] and that Richard had returned to Acre. Five days later, however, Frankish ships arrived at Jaffa carrying, it was said, both Richard himself and a large force with which the Franks were planning to march on either Ascalon or Jerusalem. On 17 October Richard met al-'Ādil's clerk, al-Ṣanī'a, and gave him a note, which was then passed from al-'Ādil to Saladin. In it Richard pointed out that the country was being destroyed and that both sides had suffered losses. He claimed Jerusalem as a Christian holy place and asked for all the land west of Jordan and for the Cross. Saladin replied that Jerusalem was holy to the Muslims – "it is greater in our eyes than it is in yours"[55] – and that its surrender could not even be discussed; the Muslims were getting "crops and advantages" from their territories, while the Franks could not "build up any stone" in the lands that they held; the Cross could only be returned in exchange for something of greater value to the Muslims.

Both Saladin and Richard knew that the point about "crops and advantages" was debatable. Saladin had just lost the grain-stores of three towns. One of his emirs had escaped from Acre by climbing through a latrine window and had brought the unpleasant news that the peasants of the hill country were providing Richard with "vast supplies".[56] Richard, however, was not in a strong enough position to press too hard and he now produced his most imaginative proposal, that al-'Ādil should marry his sister Joanna, the widow of William of Sicily.[57] He would give her whatever he himself held on the Coast and Saladin was to do the same for al-'Ādil. Al-'Ādil and Joanna would then live in Jerusalem, where there was to be no Frankish garrison, but only "priests and monks". The Templars and the Hospitallers were to be given villages but no castles. The Cross would be returned to the Franks; prisoners on both sides were to be released and the new kingdom would form part of Saladin's dominions. Al-'Ādil held a meeting of his advisers, including 'Imād al-Dīn and Ibn Shaddād. It was agreed to bring the proposal to Saladin, with Ibn Shaddād acting as spokesman. He was to say that, if Saladin agreed, then al-'Ādil was content, but if Saladin refused, Ibn Shaddād was to stress the importance of the affair by saying: "this is the final point reached in the peace negotiations and it is he [Saladin] who had decided to bring them to nothing". When they met, Ibn Shaddād repeated the question three times and each time Saladin agreed to accept the plan. In fact, according to Ibn Shaddād, he believed that it was a trick and that Richard would not keep his word, but 'Imād al-Dīn wrote: "we thought that the affair was now finished".[58] On 22 October an envoy representing both Saladin and al-'Ādil was sent to the Franks. He was met by the news that Joanna had now refused to play her part, according to 'Imād al-Dīn because of protests from the other Frankish leaders, and that Richard was trying to save his idea by suggesting that al-'Ādil should become a Christian. The exchange of prisoners and the return of the Cross were called off, but Ibn Shaddād wrote: "the door of discussion was left open".[59]

After the interruption of negotiations Saladin was warned by deserters that the Franks were planning to march on Ramla. He himself had earlier retired to Latrun, as the Franks had been too close for comfort and his men had been unable to graze their horses freely, but he now moved back to battle order. The Franks had advanced on Yāzūr, where his *mamlūks* "being accustomed to fighting against them and relying on their horses and equipment"[60] attacked their camp. As in the Litani battle, however, inexperienced volunteers pressed too closely and were killed in a Frankish charge. Then on 1 November Saladin told Ibn Shaddād to bring al-'Ādil, 'Alam al-Dīn Sulaimān, Sābiq al-Dīn 'Uthmān and the son of Ibn al-Muqaddam. When they arrived, everyone else was cleared from the tent and, according to Ibn Shaddād, Saladin took out a letter and began to weep "until we broke into tears as well, without knowing why".[61] This fresh disaster was the death of Taqī al-Dīn, news of which was followed next day by an angry letter from the Caliph complaining of his attack on Bektimur of Khilāṭ.

It was clear that Saladin was not going to find encouragement, let alone support, from Baghdad, but the Franks themselves were giving him an opening. Early in October he had sent an envoy to Tyre, where Conrad had been sounding out the chances of bartering an open break with Richard for Sidon and Beirut. Reginald of Sidon arrived at Saladin's camp on 5 November to negotiate on Conrad's behalf and three days later Richard and al-'Ādil had another meeting, at which they talked for most of the day, parting on friendly terms. Richard again asked for a meeting with Saladin, but again Saladin said that a settlement would have to be made first. On 9 November Saladin entertained Reginald, who told him that a number of Frankish leaders were supporting Conrad. Saladin stressed that any bargain would depend on Conrad's showing "open enmity to the sea Franks",[62] and on the same evening Humphrey of Toron came as an envoy from Richard. Richard's message, as quoted by Ibn Shaddād, ran:

> I wish for your friendship and affection. You have said that you have given these lands of the Coast to your brother and I wish you to act as an arbitrator between him and me. We must have a foothold in Jerusalem, but my aim is to see that you divide the lands so that the Muslims may not blame your brother and the Franks may not blame me.

On 11 November Saladin held a council meeting at which he explained the possible alliance with Conrad, based on the exchange of Sidon[63] in return for support, and also the terms suggested by Richard by which the Muslims would be given all the mountain villages and the Franks certain nominated coastal villages, or else all could be shared. In either case the Franks were to keep priests and churches in Jerusalem. The emirs were of the opinion that, since Frankish sincerity was doubtful, if peace was to be made it should be made with Richard. Ambroise quoted al-'Ādil as urging this "because there was no better man than Richard in Christendom",[64] but from the Muslim point of view he also had the attraction of being further away. There was an exchange of messages in which the marriage of Joanna was mooted again. Richard said that, in view of the disapproval of the Franks, he would have to ask leave from the Pope and if this was not granted, he would offer his niece. Saladin replied that if the Pope agreed to Joanna's marriage an agreement could be made, but Richard's niece had not been discussed before and could not be considered now. Ibn Shaddād wrote that what Saladin really wanted was to destroy any basis for peace and he quoted him as saying that he was afraid of Frankish treachery if peace were made: "if I die, these [Muslim] armies will hardly stay united and the Franks will grow strong. The best thing to do is to continue the fight until we drive them from the Coast or die."[65]

Richard had told Saladin that it would take three months before an answer could be expected from the Pope and in the meanwhile Saladin made no move to force a battle. On 17 November he retired to Latrun, leaving the Franks to advance to Ramla. According to 'Imād al-Dīn, it was thought certain that they now intended to march on Jerusalem and fighting patrols were sent out every day.[66] Then the weather broke and on 12 December Saladin moved up to Jerusalem, leaving his advance guard on the edge of the plain at Bait Nūbā, 3½ miles (6 km) east-north-east of Latrun. From Jerusalem he wrote to say that his army was tired, that the city needed men and supplies and that "if no help comes next spring, the affair will be hard".[67] This last phrase appears to prove that he did not expect a serious attack at this stage and in fact mud, rain and snow were making movement difficult. Ambroise wrote of "great rains and great storms",[68] and he complained of tents being battered down by hail and of the loss of horses and supplies. Meanwhile, Saladin kept up pressure on the Frankish lines. 'Imād al-Dīn wrote that while the Franks were at Latrun the Muslims "cut the road of their merchants".[69] Sābiq al-Dīn 'Uthmān attacked on 29 December and on 3 January Saif al-Dīn Yāzkūj and 'Alam al-Dīn Qaiṣar raided around Ramla. Saladin himself was strengthening the fortifications of Jerusalem and on 22 December it was reinforced by the arrival of Egyptian troops under Abū 'l-Haijā' the Gross.

For the Franks the temptation to ignore the difficulties and risk a march into the mountains must have been very great. 'Imād al-Dīn had commented on the old women who used to call out to them during the fighting that the Sepulchre was under the domination of the enemy.[70] Pope Gregory in his letter summoning Christendom to war had quoted the Psalmist: "O God, the heathen have come into Thine inheritance; Thy holy temple have they defiled; they have laid Jerusalem on heaps."[71] Jerusalem was the emotional focus and the tangible goal of the Crusade. Further, it could fairly be argued that so much of Saladin's own prestige was tied to it that he might be forced to fight even at a disadvantage rather than abandon it. According to the western sources, it was the Templars, the Hospitallers and the other survivors of the Latin Kingdom who argued against an advance.[72] Richard has been criticised for listening to their advice, but apart from the difficulties of supplies and transport, he knew well enough how far the odds were in the favour of the side that stood on the defensive. Ibn al-Athīr quoted the story that he asked for a plan of the city and on being told that it was surrounded by deep valleys "except for a short space on the north side", he said that it would not be taken "while Saladin lives and the Muslims are united".[73] As a result, the Franks drew back from Latrun to Ramla. According to 'Imād al-Dīn they "scattered to the coast" on 16 January, and on 20 January Richard himself marched on Ascalon.

Saladin had no intention of taking the offensive and he allowed his own troops to disperse, with orders, Ambroise had heard, to reassemble in May.[74] This is expanded in the *Itinerary*, which notes that his men "had conceived bitter anger" against him because he had failed in his promise to redeem the prisoners of Acre and "they left his army for a time with groans and lamentations".[75] Saladin had certainly subjected them to prolonged strain and, willingly or unwillingly, he now changed his tactics. Since the start of the siege of Acre he had stayed in close contact with the Frankish army and, although this had brought him some successes in the battles of the plain of Acre, in the long run it had proved a failure. He now waited for more than six months behind the walls of Jerusalem, daring Richard to attack him. Instead of being concentrated as a striking force, his army was extended north and south of Jerusalem along the Jordan valley and southwards to the Egyptian border. In Egypt itself he ordered precautions to be taken. In the month of Ṣafar 588 (17 February – 16 March 1192), according to Maqrīzī, women and children were evacuated from Tanis and Damietta and at Damietta orders were given for trees to be cut down – lest they should be used for enemy siege machines – and for the fosse to be dug out.[76]

Although his strategy was primarily defensive, he was still concerned to score small tactical points by allowing his men to attack Frankish communications. On 28 January, 'Izz al-Dīn Jūrdīk raided Yubnā, some 13 miles (21 km) south of Jaffa, and on 18 February he took troops from Jerusalem and attacked the outskirts of Ascalon. On 1 March Fāris al-Dīn Maimūn moved by Tell Gezer and raided Yubnā and then Jaffa. On the Frankish side, Richard, who had decided to rebuild Ascalon, surprised and defeated Saif al-Dīn Yāzkūj and 'Alam al-Dīn Qaiṣar, who were camped nearby. Saladin himself, meanwhile, was living in "the house of the priests by the Sepulchre"[77] and supervising work on the fortifications of Jerusalem. Two thousand Frankish prisoners were used as slave labour and 'Izz al-Dīn of Mosul sent fifty masons to help. Efforts were concentrated on the vulnerable northern approach where it was planned to construct "a new deep fosse"[78] and new towers were built from the Damascus gate on the north to the Jaffa gate on the west.

Al-ʿĀdil and Saladin's sons took their share of the work and Saladin himself carried stones on his saddle-bow, helped by a mixed crowd of camp followers and dignitaries of Jerusalem.

In February 1192 Richard went back to Acre. From there he sent a messenger to ask for another meeting with al-ʿĀdil and Saladin thought it worth sending al-ʿĀdil "to join our troops in the Jordan valley, Kaukab and those parts".[79] Al-ʿĀdil was to tell Richard that negotiations had already dragged on without result and unless there was some reason to think that things would now be different, there could be no point in meeting. Al-ʿĀdil's own instructions, however, were to settle things if he could, but if not, to prolong the talks until the troops returned later in the spring. He was given an *aide-mémoire* of the settlement terms, and for the first time there is a reference to the fact that Richard was to be allowed Beirut, if he pressed for it, provided that it remained unfortified; the Cross was to be given up and the Franks could have a priest and pilgrimage rights in Jerusalem, on condition that they did not carry arms. There was no longer any talk of Joanna's marriage. Al-ʿĀdil left Jerusalem on 20 March and sent back a message from Baisān to say that he had met Humphrey of Toron. Richard wanted an equal partition of lands; if the Franks were holding more of the Coast than the Muslims, it must be evened up, and vice-versa; the Franks must have Jerusalem, while the Muslims could have the Rock. Al-ʿĀdil was told that he could accept these proposals in principle, but he then sent Saladin a message to say that he had decided not to meet Richard himself until the details had been worked out. He also said that there had been further discussions about Jerusalem in which Richard had agreed that the Muslims should have the Rock and the Citadel, while the rest of the city and its villages were to be shared; no "well-known" Frankish leader was to stay there.[80] Al-ʿĀdil himself returned to Jerusalem on 1 April to give an account of what had happened.

At this point the negotiations were again interrupted by quarrels. On the death of Taqī al-Dīn his twenty-year-old son Nāṣir al-Dīn, fearing lest Saladin should deprive him of his father's *iqṭāʿs* east of the Euphrates, had been showing signs of disaffection and there was a suspicion that he might desert and ally himself with Bektimur. This could not only ruin Saladin's position east of the Euphrates but, if it led to another coalition of his Muslim enemies, could even threaten Syria. Al-Afḍal had left Jerusalem in February and on 16 April Saladin wrote to tell him to cross the Euphrates and take over Nāṣir al-Dīn's lands. Nāṣir al-Dīn now wrote to al-ʿĀdil asking him to intercede. Saladin was perhaps too tired or preoccupied to handle the matter well, a mood which may have been responsible for the order that he gave during this period for the execution of al-Suhrawardī at Aleppo. According to Ibn Shaddād, he was particularly distressed by Nāṣir al-Dīn "because none of his family had ever feared him or sought an oath from him".[81] First he accepted al-'Ādil's intercession but on 14 May, in a fit of anger, he tore up the document setting out the terms of agreement. He then changed his mind again and recalled al-Afḍal, who was so annoyed that he stayed in Damascus until the danger from the Franks was grave enough to force his father to summon him. Al-'Ādil himself was sent across the Euphrates in mid-May to settle affairs, thus further weakening Saladin's position, and Ibn Shaddād suggested that it was news of the start of this quarrel that had led Richard to interrupt his search for peace.

The situation was complicated by Richard's own feud with Conrad. Ibn Shaddād reported that another messenger had come from Conrad to continue the negotiations of the previous autumn.[82] Saladin again insisted that Conrad should fight his fellow-Franks. He could then keep whatever he took from them himself, and similarly the Muslims would keep what they took by themselves. Places captured jointly were to go to Conrad, but Saladin was to have their prisoners and money and all Muslim prisoners in Conrad's lands were to be released. If Richard were to entrust him with any territory, this was to be treated on the terms agreed upon between Saladin and Richard, "except for Ascalon and what lay beyond it" (to the south), which was not to be included in a peace treaty.

In April the situation changed again. The dispute over the title of King of Jerusalem had eventually been resolved and all the Franks, including Richard, had agreed that it should go to Conrad. This was not reported by 'Imād al-Dīn or Ibn Shaddād, but Ibn Shaddād quoted Conrad's envoy, who had now returned to Saladin, as saying: "the affair has been settled between Conrad and the Franks; if he succeeds in making peace with Saladin now, the French will leave by sea, but if there is any delay, then peace talks with him must be abandoned".[83] Ibn Shaddād gave no further details of the terms, but on 24 April Saladin sent al-'Adl to Tyre in order to draw up a peace agreement. On 1 May al-'Adl sent back word that three days earlier Conrad had been killed by the Assassins. One report was that the murderers had claimed to be working for Richard,[84] while according to a story quoted by Ibn al-Athīr, it was Saladin who had offered to pay Sinān for the murder of both Richard and Conrad.[85] This is a problem without a solution, but the postponement of a settlement was perhaps more nearly in the interests of the Assassins themselves than of any other group.

Desultory attempts at diplomacy continued after Conrad's death. According to 'Imād al-Dīn, Richard was still pressing for an equal division of lands, while Saladin suggested that if the Franks abandoned Ascalon and Jaffa, they could keep what else they held.[86] The Byzantine Emperor Isaac tried to use the friendship that he had been claiming with Saladin to establish his own position in Jerusalem. His envoy arrived on 15 May with a request for the Cross. He was also asking for the Sepulchre and the other churches of Jerusalem to be put in the hands of his priests and for a joint attack on Cyprus, all of which was refused. As for Cyprus, al-Fāḍil noted that Guy de Lusignan, to whom Richard had given Cyprus, had been negotiating with Saladin.[87] He was said to have broken with Richard and al-Fāḍil added that this disunity was an obvious source of advantage to the Muslims: "there is no doubt that the master will receive Guy... He had become a friend"; the promise that Saladin would help Isaac take Cyprus had been made when Cyprus was held by an enemy and could not apply now. Isaac, al-Fāḍil went on, either as a friend or as a foe would neither help nor harm Saladin and the same was true of the Lord of the Maghrib who had by now rejected Saladin's appeal for help.

Saladin must have known far more about Richard's feuds and difficulties than the Arabic sources record and the *Itinerary* makes Richard say, with no more than a touch of exaggeration: "does not Saladin know all that goes on in our camp?"[88] In fact, Saladin may well have been negotiating on the strength of reports that Richard would have to leave the Coast in the early summer, but in spite of calls from England, he took the decision to stay, and then set about strengthening his position by attacking Dārūm on 23 May. The Muslims were relatively weak; al-'Ādil had left Jerusalem for the Euphrates on 22 May; al-Afḍal was still absent and the troops from Mosul and Sinjār had not yet arrived. Dārūm had been left in the charge of 'Alam al-Dīn Qaiṣar, who preferred to remain outside it. He may have been hoping that the Franks would make their customary slow work of the siege, but Richard had with him a troop of renegade Aleppan miners who apparently drove their saps under the walls on the first day of the attack. The garrison asked to be allowed to consult Saladin before surrendering, but this was refused.

Qaiṣar made no move to help and the place was taken by force. 'Imād al-Dīn claimed that only a small number of Muslims were captured, but admitted that this was a great loss to Islam and with Ascalon and Dārūm in Frankish hands,the coast road to Egypt was again blocked to all but strong forces.[89]

There was some further manoeuvring in the south and then on 6 June a messenger brought news to Saladin that the Franks "with horse, foot and a vast crowd"[90] had camped at Tell al-Ṣāfiya, some 19 miles (31 km) east-north-east of Ascalon at the foot of the Wādī al-Sanṭ. The Muslims had already begun to muster and by 31 May Saladin had been joined by Turkmans under the command of Badr al-Dīn Dildirim and by the son of Ibn al-Muqaddam with "a fine force".[91] By 9 June the Franks, moving northwards along the line of the Shephelah hills, had camped beyond Latrun and intercepted some raiding Bedouin returning from Jaffa, six of whom escaped to bring news to Saladin. "Spies and information agents"[92] told him that the Franks were halting to bring up supplies and equipment and that they then intended to march against Jerusalem. On 10 June a Frankish envoy arrived with a servant belonging to al-Mashṭūb to discuss the ransom of Qarā-Qūsh. Ibn Shaddād added cryptically "and they were talking of peace".[93] Meanwhile, Saladin had brought in supplies to Jerusalem and allotted his emirs their battle stations on the walls. According to Ambroise, the Franks were waiting for Henry of Champagne who had been sent to Acre to fetch reinforcements,[94] and while they delayed there was constant skirmishing around their camp and attacks on their supply lines. It was at this time that in one sortie Richard was reported to have reached Qalunīya, within 5 miles (8 km) of Jerusalem.[95]

While the Franks were waiting, Richard had been following the progress of a large caravan and its military escort coming from Egypt. It had mustered at Bilbais and according to Ibn Shaddād Richard had been kept informed of its march by "corrupted Bedouin",[96] identified by Ambroise as a native-born spy named Bernard with two companions.[97] On 22 June word reached Saladin that Richard had left camp on the previous afternoon, with a force put by 'Imād al-Dīn at 700 (heavy) cavalry, 1000 Turcopoles and 1000 foot.[98] No one knew where he was going, but Saladin was alarmed for the safety of his Egyptians and sent off a detachment to warn them of danger. The Egyptians can be assumed to have taken the coast road to al-'Arīsh and then to have turned towards Beersheba to follow the caravan route by Hebron and the spine of the

Judaean hills to Jerusalem. Richard moved back to Tell al-Ṣāfiya and then by Qaratayyā to the Wādī al-Ḥasī, to the west of this line. The Egyptian commander, al-'Ādil's half-brother Falak al-Dīn, had taken the precaution of reconnoitring the Wādī al-Ḥasī, but his men had left before Richard's arrival, and reported it clear. Falak al-Dīn then camped by Tell al-Khuwailifa,[99] south-east of the head of the Wādī, at the start of the Judaean range. Aslam, the leader of Saladin's detachment, advised him to march through the night, but according to 'Imād al-Dīn, he had told the caravan that the danger had now passed and that they need not move until morning.[100] A second suggestion made by Aslam was that he should camp on "the mountain",[101] perhaps Ra's al-Nukb to the east of Tell al-Khuwailifa, and when he refused, Aslam went there himself with his men.

Richard's timing had been faultless. In another twenty-four hours the caravan would almost certainly have escaped and had he come too early, he might have been discovered in the Wādī al-Ḥasī. He now made a final reconnaissance. Ibn Shaddād heard that he had ridden out himself in Bedouin dress,[102] but although Ambroise reported an encounter between his Bedouin and the caravan guards, he made it clear that Richard was not with them.[103] The caravan was preparing for a dawn start on 24 June and according to one of Ibn al-Athīr's friends who was travelling with it they had just finished loading the camels when Richard's attack took them by surprise.[104] They scattered, with the Frankish cavalry in pursuit and the infantry was left to collect the booty. Aslam, who had not been noticed on his hill, claimed to have attacked and recovered part of the spoils, but his force was too small to turn the tables on Richard, who was left master of the field. Ibn Shaddād put the Muslim prisoners at 500. He added that some 3000 camels had been taken in addition to horses, the muleteers, camel-drivers and grooms being pressed into Frankish service.[105] Of the survivors, some made their escape back to Egypt and others were guided by Bedouin round the south end of the Dead Sea. Ibn al-Athīr's friend said that he himself fled without knowing where he was going and went on until he saw a large building on a hill. He asked what it was and was told "Kerak".

A postscript to the story was added by the geographer and traveller al-Harawī, some of whose research notes were lost with the caravan.[106] The Franks could be expected to look through captured correspondence for military secrets but, remarkably, they took the trouble to study al-Harawī's notes and identify the author. Richard, who throughout his stay on the Coast was conspicuous for the contacts that he had made with individual Muslims, sent him a personal message to say that his property would be returned to him if he came to visit the Frankish army, an invitation which regrettably he failed to accept.

Late on the day of the attack a groom arrived at Jerusalem to give the news to Saladin. Ibn Shaddād was present and reported that Saladin could scarcely be consoled and that "no news ever came that grieved his heart more".[107] By his success Richard had not only supplied himself with money but now had enough baggage animals to allow his army free movement. Saladin had particular reason to be anxious about Egypt. At the start of the Crusade he had been warned that the Frankish effort would be divided between Syria and Egypt[108] and Richard had several times been heard threatening to march south.[109] The Egyptian army had been weakened by the removal of the detachments that had come with Abū 'l-Haijā' in December, as well as those routed at Tell al-Khuwailifa. 'Uthmān, who had been left in charge, had never had to face a serious emergency and if Richard moved Saladin would almost certainly have to leave Jerusalem and follow him. In that case, if he went by Eilat, the Franks could double back, but on the coast road, with Ascalon and Dārūm in Frankish hands and the Franks in command of the sea, he could find the Ḥaṭṭīn position reversed and his own army cut off without supplies.

Jerusalem, however, was still too strong a magnet for the Franks. Richard moved back to Bait Nūbā on 29 June and Saladin gave orders that cisterns were to be destroyed, "so that there remained around Jerusalem no drinking-water at all".[110] On 2 July al-Afḍal arrived with al-Ẓāfir and was posted to the west of the city and in the evening Saladin held a council. Al-Mashṭūb and all the Asadi emirs were present, as well as Abū 'l-Haijā', who was described as attending with great difficulty and having to sit on a chair. Ibn Shaddād was asked to address them and he suggested that they should meet by the Rock and bind themselves to fight to the death. Saladin remained silent for a long time and the emirs stayed motionless, "as though birds were perched on their heads". He then told them that all the Muslims were depending on them and that it was for this that they had "eaten from the public treasury". Al-Mashṭūb replied that they would support him to the death.

Saladin was said to have been encouraged by this meeting, but after the evening prayer he asked Ibn Shaddād to stay behind and told him that Abū 'l-Haijā' had sent him a note. A number of *mamlūks* were objecting to the preparations for a siege and saying that they were afraid lest the disaster of Acre should be repeated. They advised battle, in which victory would give them the Coast and defeat would allow them to escape. If Saladin was determined to hold the city, they insisted that either he or a member of his family must stay in it, as otherwise Kurds would not take orders from Turks and vice-versa. Saladin, on hearing this, had wanted to stay himself, but in view of the danger to Islam, it was decided that his place should be taken by Farrukh-Shāh's son, Bahrām-Shāh of Baalbek. Ibn Shaddād stayed with Saladin until dawn and suggested that the issue must now be left to God. On 3 July Saladin performed the Friday prayer in the Aqṣā Mosque and Ibn Shaddād wrote: "I saw him prostrating himself and repeating words with the tears pouring down on to his prayer mat."[111]

The dramatic crisis never came. On the evening of 3 July 'Izz al-Dīn Jūrdīk, who was in command of the Muslim advance guard, sent word that the Franks had moved out from their camp on that day and then marched back again. On 4 July, spies reported that the French wanted to advance but that Richard was concerned by the shortage of water, and on the morning of 5 July the whole Frankish army turned in retreat towards Ramla. The Muslims heard that a council had been appointed to decide whether or not to attack Jerusalem and when they had made up their minds to withdraw "it was not possible to disobey them".[112]

Their success at Tell al-Khuwailifa, their newly-acquired baggage animals and the absence of some of Saladin's troops might reasonably have encouraged the Franks, but had they attacked they would have been challenging Saladin on his own ground. Muslim demoralisation could have given them a quick victory, but the hills of Jerusalem were a very different setting from the plain of Acre where the Franks' unchallenged command of the sea had disheartened their opponents. Had the Muslims seen the Franks held up by Jerusalem's new fortifications, short of supplies and water and exposed to attacks by reinforcements from al-'Ādil, al-Afḍal and the easterners, it cannot be doubted that they would have taken heart again. From a military point of view an attack on Egypt would have been a far graver threat to Saladin, and, according to Ambroise, Egypt, Beirut and Damascus were the three targets that were now suggested.[113] The Crusading force, however, was too deeply disunited and too urgently in need of a quick solution to follow the dictates of grand strategy. Its discipline and unity depended on the prospect of an attack on

Jerusalem and when this finally vanished, it was obvious that, at the very least, the initiative had at last returned to Saladin.

Richard did his best to cover his position by a diplomatic rearguard action. An envoy came from Henry of Champagne, whom the Franks had agreed to leave as King of the Coast, to say that Richard had given him all that he himself held there and to ask Saladin for those parts of it which were in the hands of the Muslims, "so that I may be one of your children".[114] This disingenuousness angered Saladin, but he later told the envoy that they could discuss the position of Tyre and Acre on the terms agreed with Conrad. Richard himself then sent word to say that peace should be made, "not because of any weakness on my part but in our [common] interest", the Muslims should not be deceived by his withdrawal – "the ram draws back to butt". On 9 July another message from Richard urged the need to spare both Franks and Muslims the destruction entailed by war. Richard added that Henry of Champagne was to be at Saladin's service and he and his troops would help Saladin in the east, if he summoned them; as for the Sepulchre, "a number of monks and solitaries have asked you for churches and you have not been ungenerous. I [now] ask you for a church."

Saladin held a council, whose unanimous opinion was that the peace terms should be accepted because of the weariness and low morale of the Muslims and their load of debt. It was agreed that Richard should be given the Sepulchre. He was to be allowed to keep the lands that he held by the Coast, while the Muslims kept "the mountain castles". The districts in between were to be shared, while Ascalon "and what lies beyond" (to the south) were to be left desolate and held by neither side. With the settlement apparently complete, at this point negotiations again faltered and on 12 July another envoy returned from Richard. There was some bargaining about the position of the Franks in Jerusalem, where Richard was now asking for a force of twenty men in the citadel, but the envoy added on his own initiative that the Franks had really given up all claims there except for the right of pilgrimage. The stumbling-block was Ascalon, on which, as the envoy pointed out, Richard had spent large sums of money. Saladin eventually agreed to offer Lydda by way of compensation, but on 19 July his envoy returned alone and reported that Richard was refusing to "destroy one stone" of the walls of Ascalon. At this, Saladin broke off negotiations.

The Muslims were now almost at full strength. 'Alā' al-Dīn of

Mosul, Quṭb al-Dīn Sūqman of Āmid and troops from Sinjār under the command of Mujāhid al-Dīn Yurun-Qush had reached Damascus. Al-Ẓāhir had arrived at Jerusalem on 17 July and al-'Ādil came on 23 July. He found that Saladin had left on the previous day, having heard a report that Richard himself had gone to Acre and that the Franks were planning to attack Beirut. To counter this al-Afḍal was sent to Marj 'Uyūn, where the eastern troops who had gathered at Damascus were ordered to join him. Saladin himself moved by al-Jīb down the mountain to Bait Nūbā. On 25 July he camped between Lydda and Ramla and next day he reconnoitred Jaffa. At a council meeting it was decided to press an attack and on 27 July the army was drawn up outside Jaffa, with al-Ẓāhir in command of the right wing and al-'Ādil on the left.[115]

The mangonel crews and the sappers began the attack and according to Ibn Shaddād the Muslims were sure that they could take the town within a day, but the fierceness of the resistance "weakened their hearts". More mangonels were set up on the next day and the Muslims were inclined to wait for their barrage to take effect. Saladin, however, was determined to waste no time and launched an assault. A number of Muslim leaders were wounded, but the garrison now sent out envoys to discuss the surrender terms. They asked for a three-day delay until 31 July and promised that, if no reinforcements had arrived by then, they would surrender. Saladin refused and when the envoys returned with the same request he refused again, but by this time the sight of these diplomatic manoeuvrings had blunted the edge of the Muslim attack. On 29 July part of the curtain wall collapsed, but the Franks fired piles of brushwood behind the breach so that no one could pass. Ibn Shaddād wrote: "what fighters they were – in spite of all this they did not close any gate but continued to fight outside their gates until nightfall."

Saladin was disconcerted by the resistance and according to Ibn Shaddād he spent the night in a state of anxiety. On 30 July the attack was concentrated on the breached curtain wall, and eventually, after a concentrated assault by the whole army, the wall fell. Ibn Shaddād wrote that at first no one dared to approach for fear of fire, and then when the smoke and dust cleared, they saw that the Franks had "replaced the [stone] wall by one of lance points". This stout defence, he added, "filled the Muslims with great awe". At this stage envoys again came to discuss surrender terms. Saladin agreed to exchange knights, Turcopoles and foot-soldiers for their Muslim equivalents held by the Franks, while non-combatants were to pay the Jerusalem ransom. The envoys then asked Saladin to halt the attack, but he said that he could not hold back his men. The Franks should retire to the citadel, leaving the Muslims to "busy themselves" with the town. This was done and the Muslims began to ransack Jaffa, where amongst their spoils they found a quantity of plunder taken from the Egyptian caravan.

Late that same afternoon Saladin got word from Ṣārim al-Dīn Qaimāz, who was watching the Franks at Acre, that Richard had given up his march on Beirut and was returning to the rescue. According to Ibn Shaddād, Saladin was anxious to take over the citadel as a matter of urgency, but the Muslims were too tired to obey orders and were busy looting. Rather than try to enforce discipline, Saladin retired to his baggage train and early on the morning of 31 July a Frankish trumpet sounded to show that ships had been sighted. There was a curious lack of urgency about Saladin's reaction. He told Ibn Shaddād that the army would prevent any landing, but many of the Muslims were still out of control in Jaffa and he himself made no move to the shore. Ibn Shaddād was sent to the citadel, with 'Izz al-Dīn Jūrdīk, 'Alam al-Dīn Qaiṣar and Durbās al-Mihranī "to strengthen the advance guard",[116] and he was ordered not only to bring out the Franks, but to make an inventory of all the money and weapons found there, which was to be passed to al-Ẓāhir. He left immediately and found that al-Ẓāhir, on a tell by the sea, had slept through the trumpet calls. "He got up with the sleep in his eyes...and we entered the town, came to the citadel and ordered the Franks to come out."

The garrison apparently thought that there were too few ships for a rescue and as those that were in sight showed no signs of attempting to land, they agreed to leave. At this point Jūrdīk told Ibn Shaddād to wait until the Muslims were cleared from the town. He was evidently afraid that discipline had broken down to such an extent that the Franks might be seized for private ransom and he began "to beat the people and drive them out", a move that supplied the background to Ibn al-Athīr's story that Saladin's *mamlūks* had plundered other Muslims as they left Jaffa.[117] Ibn Shaddād reproached Jūrdīk for time-wasting – "the Muslims were not gathered together in any one place, so how was it possible to drive them out?" – but to no effect. A total of forty-seven Franks came out of the citadel but by this time some thirty-five ships had arrived and the remainder of the garrison began to show signs of defiance. Ibn Shaddād came down from the citadel hill to warn Jūrdīk, but the

Franks now launched a sudden charge, killing a number of Muslims. The attack, however, was premature. The relief force had not landed and as they could only see Muslim flags waving and hear the Muslims shouting, they thought that the citadel had fallen as well as the town. As a result, when Saladin ordered his drums to beat for a general assault, the bishop and the castellan came to present their excuses and to ask for the surrender terms to be renewed. By this time about fifty Frankish ships were cruising off shore and a man, identified by Ambroise as a priest, "chanting his Mass",[118] jumped down on to the beach from the citadel and swam out to them. He was brought to Richard, whose red galley now turned for the harbour. There was no effective resistance and the disorganised Muslims were cleared from the town. The army drew off to Yāzūr and a large quantity of booty which could not be moved in time had to be abandoned.

On the morning of 1 August Richard moved outside Jaffa to the place from which Saladin had directed the siege. He sent invitations to his Muslim friends "and there were talks and much jesting beween them".[119] According to Ibn Shaddād, he combined a taunt, asking why Saladin, the greatest king of Islam, had drawn off at his arrival, when he was wearing only his "sea-boots", with a compliment on the speed with which he had stormed the walls of Jaffa and he ended by saying that there must be peace, "for my lands beyond the sea are ruined".[120] The bargaining now started again. Saladin conceded that the Franks could keep the Coast from Caesarea to Tyre. Richard asked for Jaffa and Ascalon as well, and Saladin then agreed to let him keep Jaffa, but insisted that Ascalon must be given up. On 2 August an envoy came to say that Richard thanked Saladin for Jaffa, but was asking again for Ascalon. The envoy added that if peace was made within six days Richard would leave, but otherwise he would have to winter on the Coast. The reply was that the Muslims could not give up their claim to Ascalon and that Richard would certainly have to winter on the Coast, as the Muslims would take what the Franks were holding when he was gone, or even before; Saladin could afford to wait indefinitely; he was able to relieve his troops so that those on duty in winter were not on duty in summer; he himself was an old man in the middle of his own lands, surrounded by his family, and he had already renounced the pleasures of the world; Richard, on the other hand, was in the prime of life and far from his home.

In fact, neither side could afford to wait indefinitely and unless the problem could be solved by battle, both were going to be forced to compromise. For the Franks, if the Latin Kingdom was not to be re-established in its old borders, what was needed was a base for future expansion and this was provided by Antioch and Tripoli in the north and by Tyre, Acre and Jaffa to the south. Ascalon, with its strategic position on the coast road, was more important to Saladin than to an attenuated Frankish state that could no longer hope to control traffic between Egypt and Syria. Richard, however, was not going to let it go without a struggle and Saladin had to find some means of forcing the issue without demoralising his army any further.

From Yāzūr the Muslims had withdrawn to Ramla on 2 August. Saladin now heard that a Frankish force was marching from Acre to reinforce Jaffa and he decided to send his baggage back to the hills and march north to challenge it. If an opportunity came, it could be attacked; if not the Muslims could draw off in safety and he was quoted as saying: "this is better than waiting for the enemy's armies to join and then going to the mountains like a beaten force. Now we shall go like pursuers."[121] He left on the morning of 3 August, but he had got no further than the 'Aujā' river when he heard that the Frankish column had entered Caesarea. He decided that it could no longer be attacked, presumably because he might be trapped between it and Richard, and he also heard that Richard himself was camping outside Jaffa with few tents and a small force. This was too tempting a prize to ignore and at dawn on 4 August, he made a surprise attack. Ibn Shaddād was with the baggage train at the time and had to rely on eye-witness reports. He said that Richard had only 10 tents, not more than 17 horses and less than 1000 foot. The Muslims charged, but when the Franks held firm, they withdrew and surrounded the camp. Saladin then ordered them to charge again, but only al-Ẓāhir was willing to obey. The debacle of Jaffa and, in particular, the conduct of Saladin's *mamlūks*, had brought discontent to a head. Al-Janāḥ, the brother of al-Mashṭūb, was quoted as telling him to get "his servants who beat the people at Jaffa" to attack. Ibn Shaddād added: "I heard that Richard took his lance that day and rode from the end of the right wing to the end of the left and no one came out against him." Saladin saw that to remain passively confronting this tiny force was "pure loss" and he moved off in a fury to Yāzūr. Ibn Shaddād wrote that it had been thought that this blatant display of disobedience might lead him to crucify some of his men but, in fact, he recovered from his anger and that night he invited the emirs to share fruit that had been sent him from Damascus.[122] It was clear, however, after this fiasco, that peace would have to be made before indiscipline became endemic.

The actual advantage that Richard had gained was brief. Saladin retreated to Latrun on 5 August and on 7 August his envoy returned from the Frankish camp. He had not been allowed to enter Jaffa, but Richard had spoken to him outside the town and told him that as nothing had come of his overtures, he had now made up his mind to stay and there was no room for further negotiations. On the same day 'Alā' al-Dīn brought up the Mosulis, who had been withdrawn from Marj 'Uyūn, and on 20 August reinforcements arrived from Egypt. Richard had fallen ill and Saladin heard that all the French had retired. They had run short of money and were now intending to sail for home. Richard in his illness sent messengers to ask for fruit and snow and from them Saladin learnt that there were from 200 to 300 knights in Jaffa. The Franks were not repairing the town wall but only that of the citadel. The opportunity was obvious and on 27 August Saladin moved to Ramla with the intention of attacking Jaffa if he could or, if not, Ascalon. His advance guard had been sent to make a probing attack and reported that only 300 riders had come out of Jaffa, some mounted on mules.

At this point a Frankish envoy came with al-Ḥājib Abū Bakr, for whom Richard had asked in his illness. Richard was in no position to fight, but for all his seemingly overwhelming advantage, Saladin could not rely on his men. According to 'Imād al-Dīn, his emirs pointed out that the lands were ruined, the peasants miserable and the army tired. There was a lack of food and fodder and corn prices were soaring. If the Franks despaired of peace, they would fight to a finish, whereas a truce would allow "the inhabitants to return to the lands", and grain could then be collected for the renewal of the war.[123] Abū Bakr reported that Richard was now prepared to sacrifice Ascalon, although he was asking Saladin to give him something by way of compensation – a request that was dropped on 28 August. According to 'Imād al-Dīn, Saladin himself would still have preferred to fight, but he could not act without support.

Badr al-Dīn Dildirim, who was on friendly terms with Richard, was sent "to take his hand on the matter". He was to say: "the Sultan has assembled the armies and I cannot talk to him about this truce unless I am sure that you will not draw back".[124] Dildirim returned next day to say that Richard had agreed to a settlement. Saladin had a register of the land of the Coast brought before him. The Franks were to have the country from Jaffa to Tyre, but he removed from the list Ramla, Lydda, Yubnā and Majdal Yābā, which formed part of the territories of Jaffa, and Nazareth and Sepphoris, which belonged to Acre. The emended list was sent to the Franks on 30 August and the envoy was told that an agreement would have to be reached on the next day. Later that same afternoon more Frankish envoys returned. Saladin's own messenger said that Richard had objected to receiving no compensation, but when his envoys saw Saladin on 31 August they phrased this more tactfully and quoted him as saying: "if you give me more it is through your goodness and generosity". Saladin sent the envoys with Dildirim to al-'Ādil and on 1 September the final terms were drawn up. Richard was, in fact, given compensation, as the Franks were allowed to share the revenues of Ramla and Lydda. Ascalon was to be demolished, and both sides were to confirm that this had actually been done. The truce, to run for three years and eight months, was to cover land and sea and apply to the territories of the Assassins as well as to those of Tripoli and Antioch. Saladin's envoy presented the document to Richard, but he was too ill to read it and said: "I have made peace: here is my hand."[125] Henry of Champagne and the other Franks took the oath on 2 September and envoys were then sent to Saladin's camp. They required a number of Muslim leaders to swear to the truce terms including al-'Ādil, al-Afḍal, al-Ẓāhir, al-Mashṭūb and Dildirim. Envoys were to travel to Antioch to administer the oath to Bohemond and to those Muslim lords who lived near Frankish lands. Saladin then held a reception; "they took his noble hand",[126] and peace was proclaimed.

Neither side had won. For all their losses and sacrifices the Franks had not recovered Jerusalem. Saladin, having had the Coast apparently at his mercy after Ḥaṭṭīn, had seen his resources drained, his lands endangered and his army's morale sapped. On land, both sides had fought each other to a standstill, but Saladin had not been able to challenge the Franks' command of the sea. There was nothing that he could do to stop them sending reinforcements to the bases that they still held in order to prepare for another attack. He could hope to have discouraged them by the damage that he had inflicted on them, but it was not clear when he himself would be strong enough politically or economically to fight on such a scale again. He may well have felt that his own strength had been overtaxed and he told Ibn Shaddād:

> I do not know what will happen to me and the enemy will grow strong. He has those lands left him so that he can come out to recover the rest. You will see all these [Muslim leaders] sitting at the top of their towers and saying: "I shall not come down", and the Muslims will be destroyed.

On 5 September he moved back to Latrun. "The two armies mingled",[127] and a number of Muslims went to Jaffa to trade, while many Franks came to Jerusalem to visit the Sepulchre. Richard, who, according to the *Itinerary*, was trying to pay off old scores against the French,[128] asked Saladin to admit only those who had his permission, but Saladin tried to ensure that as many as possible made their pilgrimage so that they would be content to return home "and the Muslims might be protected against their evil".[129] 'Alam al-Dīn Qaiṣar was sent, together with a Frankish detachment, to demolish Ascalon. There was a brief delay as the garrison at first refused to leave, claiming that they had not received their pay, but when this was settled, Richard left Jaffa and on 10 September Saladin allowed his troops to disperse.

The rest of Saladin's life was no more than a brief postscript to the war. On the day that peace was made Ibn Shaddād had suggested to him that he should now make the pilgrimage to Mecca.[130] He had agreed to this and had lists drawn up of other would-be pilgrims and of the stores etc that would be needed. What Ibn Shaddād had forgotten, however, was the Caliph's fear that Saladin had designs on Baghdad. Saladin had to be reminded by al-Fāḍil that he would have to tell the Caliph of his intention "lest he think that you are doing something of which you are guiltless", – and al-Fāḍil added: "it might be said that the Sultan had come to take revenge, shed blood or disturb the pilgrimage". Al-Fāḍil also pointed out that there were still Franks on the Coast and they had not forgotten Jerusalem. Further, "the investigation of injustices is the most important of the ways in which God's favour can be sought", and in the districts of Damascus there was sedition and violence, as the peasants were suffering from oppression by the *iqṭā'* holders; the treasury was empty; "one of the most important tasks is to establish sources of revenue... There was much discussion of this earlier, but things occurred to divert the master's attention."[131]

Al-Fāḍil reported in another letter that an uneasy start had been made to the truce by the capture at sea of a ship carrying an envoy from Isaac of Byzantium. The circumstances were not explained and this was presumably an act of piracy and not of war, but al-Fāḍil wrote that the plundered goods had been sold openly in the markets of Acre. He was also concerned about Jerusalem. Letters written after Saladin's death complain of disrepair and neglect in the city, but al-Fāḍil dates the start of the decay to Saladin's lifetime. That this supreme prize of the Holy War had been allowed to suffer from lack of funds shows in the clearest light the strains on the finances and administration of Saladin's state. It alarmed al-Fāḍil. He was afraid that indignation amongst the Franks might lead to another Crusade and he wrote that news of what had happened was even more dangerous than what Frankish pilgrims could see with their own eyes, as often "scandalous reports have roused those who were heedless".[132]

As a result of these pressures Saladin changed his mind about the pilgrimage and instead he went to Jerusalem on 13 September. Then, after consulting with al-'Ādil he sent an envoy to Baghdad to discuss how best to improve relations. On 6 October al-Ẓāhir took his leave. Ibn Shaddād wrote that Saladin recommended him to fear God, this being "the root of all good", to be chary of shedding blood "for blood does not sleep", and to conciliate his subjects and his emirs – "I have only reached my present position by conciliation." "He then kissed al-Ẓāhir's face, rubbed his hand on his head and left."[133] On 15 October he went for a brief visit to Beirut, where Bohemond surprised the Muslims by visiting him without a safe-conduct, and on 4 November he returned to Damascus, for the first time since April 1189. He now thought of going to Egypt, which he had not seen for ten years, but changed his mind again and spent the winter at Damascus or on hunting trips in the country round it. On 16 February 1193 he greeted Ibn Shaddād, who had just arrived from Jerusalem, with tears in his eyes. It had been a wet winter with water "like rivers on the roads",[134] and Saladin was not in good health. His movements were lethargic and "it was as though his body was full".

On 20 February he rode out to meet the pilgrims returning from Mecca and at midnight he fell ill.[135] On the fourth day of his illness he was bled. On the sixth day Ibn Shaddād was present as he drank some tepid water, but the disease was getting worse and his mind was wandering. On the ninth day he stopped taking liquids and broke out in feverish shivering. From then on he was only occasionally conscious. Fear spread through Damascus and the traders removed their goods from the markets. Al-Fāḍil and Ibn Shaddād used to go every evening to see him or to get news of his condition and Ibn Shaddād wrote: "the people read the state of his health from our faces". On the tenth day he was given a clyster and took some barley water. Sweat broke out on his legs and this was taken as a good sign. On the eleventh day, 3 March, the sweat had penetrated the bed coverings and the matting and stained the floor. That evening his condition grew worse and Ibn Shaddād and al-Fāḍil were not allowed to see him. Al-Afḍal offered to accommodate them for the night, but al-Fāḍil was afraid that if they did not leave the citadel as usual, there would be a disturbance in the city. The *imām* Abū Ja'far and al-Fāḍil were with him on the morning of 4 March. The *imām* was reciting from the Quran. "It is said that when he reached the words: 'There is no god but God and in Him do I put my trust', Saladin smiled; his face cleared and he surrendered his soul to God."

22

CONCLUSION

To his admirers, Saladin on his death-bed at Damascus can be seen as the hero of Islam, the destroyer of the Latin Kingdom and the restorer of the shrines in Jerusalem. Eulogy, however, must accommodate itself to the fact that such a view was not accepted by numbers of his Muslim contemporaries. He can be pictured by his detractors as manipulating Islam to win power for himself and his family and only then launching on an adventure which still left a Frankish state poised to strike, if Europe were willing to support it, at an overburdened and impoverished Muslim empire. The praise and blame implicit in such assessments may be irrelevant to a historical study, but the assessments themselves serve to underline the problem of Saladin's relationship to his background. In turn, this must be related to his own qualities, in so far as they can be seen to determine how far he controlled events, rather than merely reacted to them.

As a war leader, Saladin has to his credit two decisive victories in field actions against Muslim troops, at the Horns of Hama and at Tell al-Sulṭān, as well as his defeats of the Franks at Marj 'Uyūn and at Ḥaṭṭīn. In terms of the length of the action and its bearing on his career, an equally important success was his crushing of the Negroes in the street fighting in Cairo, while his reverses included the battle of Ramla, the loss of Acre, the battle of Arsūf and the debacle of Jaffa. His defeat at the battle of Ramla was caused primarily by his carelessness, but elsewhere his tactics and strategy were marked by caution against the Franks and daring against the Muslims.

It must be emphasised that at this period poor battlefield communications limited the tactical effectiveness of any commander when once battle had been joined, this being the reason for Saladin's nearly disastrous mistake in the battle of October 1189 at Acre and his failure to co-ordinate his ambush at Tibnīn earlier in the same year. In view of this, judgement should be based on the manipulation of time, distance and numbers. Of these, Saladin at his best handled time and numbers with remarkable economy, notably at the Horns of Hama and earlier in his first march on Damascus. Ḥaṭṭīn was the climax of a campaign conspicuous for the concentration of force at the critical moment, but Saladin's earlier delay at Kerak and his indecision in the orders sent to al-Afḍal show a possible weakness of planning. It may be noted that in an almost identical position Napoleon criticised the son of the Pasha of Damascus, who re-enacted al-Afḍal's part and scattered his forces, for laying himself open to Murat's counter-blow.[1] At the siege of Acre Saladin was faced with an immensely complicated problem in his attempt to muster an army from the Nile, the Euphrates and the Tigris, and then to arrange for regular reliefs, while maintaining his offensive capacity. As has been shown, he had a number of failures, but these must be set against his overall success in keeping his men in the field.

He had an impressive record of success in siege warfare, but against this has to be set the time that he wasted at Aleppo and Mosul and his crucial failure at Tyre. It must also be remarked that he did not press home his attack at Baisān in 1182 or at 'Ain Jālūt in 1183. In part this can be explained in terms of razzia strategy, or it may be argued that the Baisān and 'Ain Jālūt campaigns were primarily political camouflage for the grand design against Mosul. A wider criticism can be directed against his apparent willingness to surrender the initiative to the Franks after Guy's march on Acre, and, in fact, his tactics throughout the Third Crusade can be seen as careful but unimaginative. Here again, however, the factors involved and, in particular, numbers, supplies and morale must not be forgotten, and although at times the Muslims were ineffective, Saladin's tenacity and organising ability allowed him to recover from what might have been a losing position.

A point in his favour was the excellence of his intelligence service. He was surprised by Baldwin at Marj 'Uyūn and he failed to save the Egyptian caravan from Richard, but, in general, he was able to base his plans on more or less accurate information. If this can be attributed to efficient organisation, the converse is true of his most conspicuous failure, which was at sea. The siege of Acre showed conclusively that he could not challenge Frankish naval supremacy and it appears that, in spite of his concern to improve his fleet, his administrators were unable to carry out his orders effectively.

The administrative machine itself consisted of an inherited bureaucracy, within whose framework operated a system of patronage with Saladin at its head. It was patronage, rather than formal administration, that appears to have occupied his own time and so many requests were forwarded to him that he was quoted as saying: "before me, subjects were afraid of kings and fled from them...but now they come on missions to me until they weary me".[2] Patronage was diffused through the social structure. Al-Fāḍil wrote that Saladin would have the (heavenly) reward for the difficulties that he had faced in collecting money, while his sons had to labour at giving it away.[3] Saladin's treasurer paid out money to Imād al-Dīn's protégés without asking for his master's authorisation[4] and as a gesture of respect for the emir Najm al-Dīn ibn Maṣāl payments recommended by him were continued after his death.[5]

The co-existence of bureaucracy and a patronage system is a common and often harmless phenomenon. Weaknesses are produced by the overlapping of particular interests and by the concentration of patronage in a way that interferes with efficiency. It is not surprising, then, to find at this period that money promised by patrons was withheld by administrators or that administrators ran foul of the system by ignoring the favoured position of its protégés. These difficulties were increased by the fragmentation of Saladin's empire. Tūrān-Shāh in Syria gave 'Imād al-Dīn a grant from the revenues of 'Aidhāb – "they told me: 'at least it is nearer than Aden' "[6] – after which he had to send the document in the diplomatic bag to al-Fāḍil, who was charged with taking it himself to 'Aidhāb on his way to Mecca.

A definition of administrative power given in a letter to Baghdad lists amongst its principal functions appointments and dismissals.[7] As has been shown, Saladin was quick to move his own family. His brother Būri was given the *iqṭā's* of the Fayyūm in the year 576 A.H. (1180/1 A.D.) and these were then transferred in the same year to Taqī al-Dīn.[8] Tūrān-Shāh was sent to Egypt almost immediately after Ibn al-Muqaddam's surrender of Baalbek and al-Ẓāhir was recalled in the winter of 1183 after less than six months in Aleppo. The motive for such moves seems generally to have been short-term advantage and Saladin did not make a habit of preventing the continued occupation of power bases within his lands. One example of this is the fact that Nāṣir al-Dīn Muḥammad ibn Shīrkūh was left in charge of Homs until his death and, more significantly, in spite of the embarrassment caused by Ṭughtekīn in Yemen, nothing positive was done to dislodge him.

Further down the scale, non-Ayyubid allies, such as Dildirim of

Tell Bāshir and Mankūrus of Bū Qubais, were confirmed in the possession of their lands, presumably with a view to stability and good administration as well as out of reluctance to antagonise supporters. It should also be noted that a number of enforced appointments were made. A letter dated to 1179 reported that the emir 'Izz al-Dīn Mūsik had resigned from his position as governor of the eastern province of Egypt but had been reinstated against his will,[9] while the castle of Kaukab after its fall was forced on Ṣārim al-Dīn Qaimāz. Saladin's commanders were not always successful as civilian administrators – Abū'l-Haijā' had to be replaced in Niṣībīn in 1183 and there were complaints about al-Mashṭūb in Nablus in 1192[10] – and his conscription of the reluctant may, in part, reflect an absence of competent governors, just as the employment of Christian and Jewish clerks underlines a similar problem at a lower level. Money, however, is at least an equally obvious factor. Saladin's letter to Farrukh-Shāh about the fortifications and garrison of Damietta emphasised the point that the *iqṭā'* holder had to bear the expenses of the defence of his holding,[11] as did his orders to Taqī al-Dīn and al-Mashṭūb in 1178-9 to "increase the number of their men and to employ the cream of the warriors".[12] This must have kept emirs from volunteering to take over places needing large garrisons and expensive repairs and 'Alam al-Dīn Sulaimān, whom 'Imād al-Dīn criticised for selling grain from Baghrās to the Franks, should probably be seen as recouping losses rather than as making an illicit profit.

Saladin's own financial difficulties can be seen reflected in his own letters and in the complaints of al-Fāḍil and 'Imād al-Dīn. At the upper end of the scale, the link between power and borrowed money is shown in the huge sums owed by Tūrān-Shāh at his death. There was an ambivalent attitude towards extravagance. Generosity was one of the Bedouin virtues enshrined in the *Ḥamāsa*, which, as has been noted, supplied Saladin and his contemporaries with many of their conventions. Al-Fāḍil wrote that "debt is the disease of the generous",[13] and he quoted an anecdote about Hārūn al-Rashīd who was told by his treasurer that an expedition which he was planning would be expensive, to which he replied: "no money is wasted that leaves a legacy of praise".[14] On the other hand, there are al-Fāḍil's complaints about the overburdened economy of Egypt and in a letter to Saladin's treasurer in Damascus he pointed out that to mortgage more than the land could produce emptied the treasury and took wealth from the Muslims.[15]

Saladin himself subordinated money to men and, as al-Fāḍil

reported, he used the wealth of Egypt for the conquest of Syria, that of Syria for the conquest of Jazīra and that of the Jazīra for the conquest of the Coast.[16] In such a process, however, as al-Fāḍil also noted, "hopes of expansion can never come to an end".[17] The difficulties that arose when expansion was halted can be seen in reports of violent disturbances amongst the peasants around Damascus at the end of the Third Crusade,[18] poverty in Jerusalem both in Saladin's lifetime and after his death and complaints after his death that "salaries in Egypt remain in name only and have no meaning".[19] To set against this it can be argued that the economy, which had to be flexible enough to cope with periods of famine and natural disasters, could accept short-term distortions. William of Tyre noted that liberality was one of Saladin's most dangerous weapons,[20] and, whatever strains and disappointments were involved, he unquestionably succeeded in his own main aim, the collecting of raw material for war in the form of men, money and supplies.

Liberality as a weapon in the power struggle was allied to diplomacy, both on a personal level and in dealings between states. Although Saladin prided himself on his ability to handle men, his record is not without blemish. The main – and insoluble – enigma remains his relationship with Nūr al-Dīn, where perhaps the fairest comment is that, whatever Nūr al-Dīn's feelings, no open breach was made. His early quarrel with the Qāḍī Kamāl al-Dīn was generously made up: it was unremarkable that a rival, such as Quṭb al-Dīn Ināl, should refuse to join his service or that al-Za'farānī should leave it, but the fact that he could not win over his old comrade, Jūrdīk, is surprising. Later in his career the arrest of Keukburī and the defection of Sanjar-Shāh were setbacks, but, on the other hand, considering the difficulties involved, his family relationships were generally successful. Admittedly, he was on the verge of a break with Taqī al-Dīn at the time of his recall from Egypt in 1186 and it was Taqī al-Dīn's quest for independence that later seduced him from the Holy War. Tūrān-Shāh was a source of embarrassment over the problem of Baalbek and Ṭughtekīn was both an embarrassment and a disappointment in Yemen. There were rumours of discontent on the part of Tūrān-Shāh and of Nāṣir al-Dīn Muḥammad ibn Shīrkūh, but in spite of this the Ayyubids as a family unit worked well together and it was not until after Taqī al-Dīn's death that there was a serious threat to their coherence.

On a wider front, Saladin's diplomatic manoeuvres are open to misinterpretation. It should be noted that the volume of diplomatic correspondence was very large indeed and the incompletely recorded exchanges must be seen as part of a continuous process, one of the main aims of which was the gathering of information. Illustrations of this can be seen in 'Īsā's embassy to the camp of al-Pahlawān outside Khilāṭ and in exchanges of messages with the Crusaders. Further, the proposals made in Saladin's letters are not to be taken literally, but rather as fixing the limits of his bargaining position. He is found at various times negotiating with the Byzantines, Raymond of Tripoli, Conrad de Montferrat and, apparently, Guy de Lusignan against the Franks. The joint move on Mosul that he suggested to 'Imād al-Dīn Zangī matches what he wrote to the Emperor Isaac and to Conrad and it can be inferred that the offer of an offensive alliance was merely an opening gambit. He later dropped all mention of this when he settled terms with Conrad and his dismissal of both Isaac and Raymond as men whose friendship or enmity did not affect him can be taken as true to the extent that he was probably prepared to settle for neutrality. In view of this technique suggestions that he planned a far-reaching diplomatic campaign to isolate the Franks of the Coast by means of treaties with the Italian cities and with the Byzantines should not be pressed too far.

A similar interpretation should be applied to what appears to be the cynical opportunism of some of his letters. His references to Amalric's death, for instance, merely give the appropriate formulae for external and internal use and cannot be taken as showing any personal feelings. By the same token, congratulations sent him after the capture of Jerusalem must not be interpreted as showing that his success had won over his rivals. The Holy War propaganda and the continuous self-justification of his letters to Baghdad are examples of coloured rhetoric in which everything is shown in extremes and internal contradictions are glossed over or ignored. This too can be seen as a matter of convention. His claims were inflated and their justification dubious, but he should at least be acquitted of the charge of cynicism.

It is, of course, true to say that Saladin blurred the distinctions of the Holy War by adding Muslims, such as the Almohades, to the list of possible enemies and, instead of being confined to the recovery of the Coast, the concept was thus almost infinitely extendable. In part, this may be accepted as the idealist's view of the obligation to fight until the word of God is established, but it can also be linked to the fact that in the politics of expansion war appears as an integral part of a cyclic process, conditioning the expectations of society and the reactions of the holders of power. Seen in an internal Islamic context, the process involved was one of continuous realignment, either of the cells of a cellular society or of the classes and individuals who controlled the transmission of power. The fact that this power was based in the first instance on military force had the advantage of providing society with a ready-made defence against external threats, but the lack of balance, and in consequence the maladministration that it encouraged, can be seen in the loose organisation of Saladin's empire, where 'Aidhāb, formally part of his dominions since he first took power in Egypt, could be pictured by Ibn Jubair in 1183 as semi-independent[21] and where, for all Saladin's successes east of the Euphrates, in his illness al-Fāḍil could stress that he should be moved from Ḥarrān to "his own lands".[22] This can, perhaps, be seen as an illustration of centrifugal force, balanced by the centripetal attraction of the centres of power, and it may be noted that to the old Byzantine–Arab world of parallel institutions, where schools, colleges, hospitals and careful bureaucratic supervision were duplicated on both sides, it was the hordes of "Franks", Turks and Kurds attracted to these centres who were the barbarians.[23] The accommodation to or assimilation of these war-bands by other groups could virtually monopolise the energies of a whole society, but although glimpses of this pattern can be seen almost throughout Saladin's career, his Holy War propaganda must be seen as an attempt, conscious or unconscious, to canalise energy and direct it outwards. The attempt failed and, together with the other problems whose roots lie in this period, notably the economic impact of Saladin's wars and the social consequences of the importance that they added to the military élite, the results of this failure must be studied further before a final judgement can be made of the effect of the Crusades on Islam.

In this, it is Saladin's actions rather than his personality that are of relevance, but the broader investigations required, which are outside the scope of a biography, must still take account of what lies beyond the balance sheet of success and failure, the quality of mind and, by extension, the measure of originality of the man himself. 'Imād al-Dīn paints a consistent picture of a hero whose life was based on contempt for the "spider's web" of the world[24] – "the old woman loved by young men"[25] – and on a devotion to the Holy War, "whose abandonment is a sin for which no excuse can be brought to God".[26] Satire's view of the Holy War can be seen in al-Wahrānī's recommendation to Taqī al-Dīn: "the servant's advice is that you should resign from this service, settle in the orchards of Damascus, turn from repentance and collect together the sinners of Damascus, the prostitutes of Mosul, the panders of Aleppo and the singing girls of Iraq, delighting the five senses...and relying on the forgiveness of the Forgiving and Merciful God". To ignore the existence of this type of humour is to distort the picture of Saladin's age, but it may fairly be argued that the conventional view of Saladin is of importance, in spite of the details and attitudes that it obscures or ignores, specifically because it reflects a conventional mind.

Napoleon's secretary, Bourrienne, wrote:

> almost every day during the siege [of Acre] Bonaparte and myself used to walk together at a little distance from the sea-shore... He said to me: "Bourrienne, I see that this wretched place has cost me a number of men and wasted much time... If I succeed, as I expect, I shall find in the town the pacha's treasure and arms for 300,000 men. I will stir up and arm the people of Syria, who are disgusted at the ferocity of Djezzar... I shall then march upon Damascus and Aleppo. On [my] advancing into the country the discontented will flock around my standard and swell my army. I will announce to the people the abolition of servitude and of the tyrannical government of the pachas. I shall arrive at Constantinople with large masses of soldiery. I shall overturn the Turkish empire and found in the east a new and grand empire... Perhaps I shall return to Paris by Adrianople or Vienna, after having annihilated the house of Austria."[27]

In similar circumstances, Ibn Shaddād was in Saladin's company on a winter's day by the coast of Acre during the Frankish siege. Ibn Shaddād had only recently seen the sea and he was so awed by the waves that he wrote:

> were I to be offered the whole world to put out to sea for one mile, I would not do it... While I was thinking of this, Saladin turned to me and said: "Shall I tell you something?" "Certainly." "It is in my mind that when Almighty God facilitates the conquest of the rest of the Coast, I shall divide up the lands, give my instructions and take my leave. Then I shall cross this sea to the islands of the Franks and pursue them until no one remains on the face of the earth who does not acknowledge God or until I die."[28]

Al-Fāḍil knew perfectly well that, even if Saladin were able to take the Coast, he could never attack Europe and he wrote: "not one of the

Franks beyond the seas fears that if Syria is conquered his own lands will be taken".[29] Saladin, in Ibn Shaddād's account, is merely painting a conventionally romantic picture of the future where inconvenient difficulties disappear in visions of death or glory. By contrast, Napoleon's plan, similarly grandiose and equally unsuccessful, was based on the logic of the possible. It might not have worked, even had Acre fallen, but unlike Saladin's day-dream it showed the practical imagination of genius.

Saladin, who objected to a poetic reference to silvery leaves, "because leaves are green",[30] clearly adopted "the plain man's" approach and his conventional quality reflects one aspect of Islam, in its capacity not as a religion but as an assimilative social force. Here the unconventional, such as the mystical philosophy of al-Suhrawardī, is dangerous and the common denominator is to be found not in reason but in emotion. Saladin himself, as has been seen, was an emotional man, who is shown weeping over the death of Taqī al-Dīn and over the return of the baby to its Frankish mother at the siege of Acre. Perhaps significantly, he admired the line:

> "a year passes; another year follows it:
> a month returns, and then another month"[31]

The simple expression of this conventional idea skirts banality but is aimed at the common ground of emotion that can be identified without thought. It is the generosity of feeling derived from this common ground – co-existing with hypocrisy and brutality – that gave the Crusades their mythopoeic quality, where the Muslims admired the Franks who were fighting not for money or through fear or because of compulsion by a ruler, but "purely out of zeal for the object of their worship",[32] while, on the other hand, "had they [the Muslims] not been unbelievers", the Franks would have said that there were no better men born.[33] This, in turn, is the basis of the western legend that elevated Saladin from being a "patron of prostitutes" to the company of Hector, Aeneas and Caesar amongst the virtuous pagans of Dante's *Inferno*.

It is surely this that serves to explain much of what can be known about Saladin himself. He cannot be thought of as an innovator, but as a man who was content to act on ideas supplied him. He was a good, but not a great, strategist and tactician, an open-handed but not far-sighted administrator and a man with his share of faults, mixed motives and weaknesses. His reputation, however, in history and legend, is based on his identification with conventional emotion.

He appears to have held instinctively to the middle ground. The conventional mind was matched by virtues that were no less attractive for being themselves conventional. He was not concerned to question the relevance of his ideals or even apparently, to check how far he was guilty of distorting them. They were part of the heritage of Islam, to be accepted emotionally, not intellectually, and with such an attitude he could be presumed to ignore contradictions. The attractiveness of such a position must depend largely on the fundamental sincerity, however intellectually muddled this may be, of its holder. This is a test that Saladin must be allowed to have passed. Not surprisingly, he failed to win over his Muslim enemies, but he impressed the Franks and, as for his friends, Ibn Shaddād wrote of his death: "I have heard people say that they would like to ransom those dear to them with their own lives, but this has only been said figuratively in my hearing, except on the day of his death. For I know that had our sacrifice been accepted, I and others would have given our lives for him."[34]

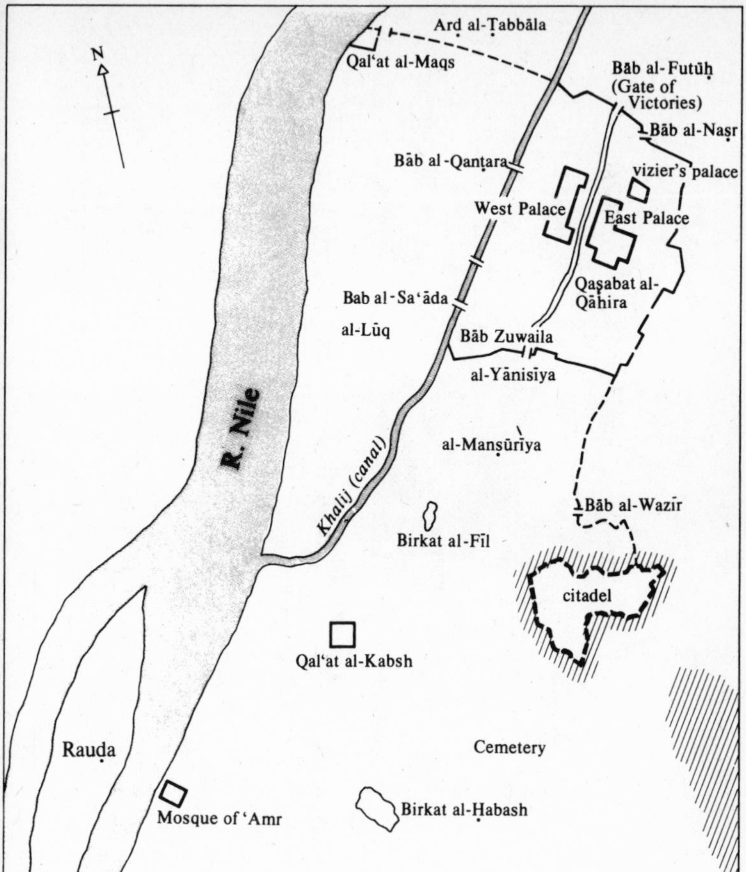

Plan of Cairo

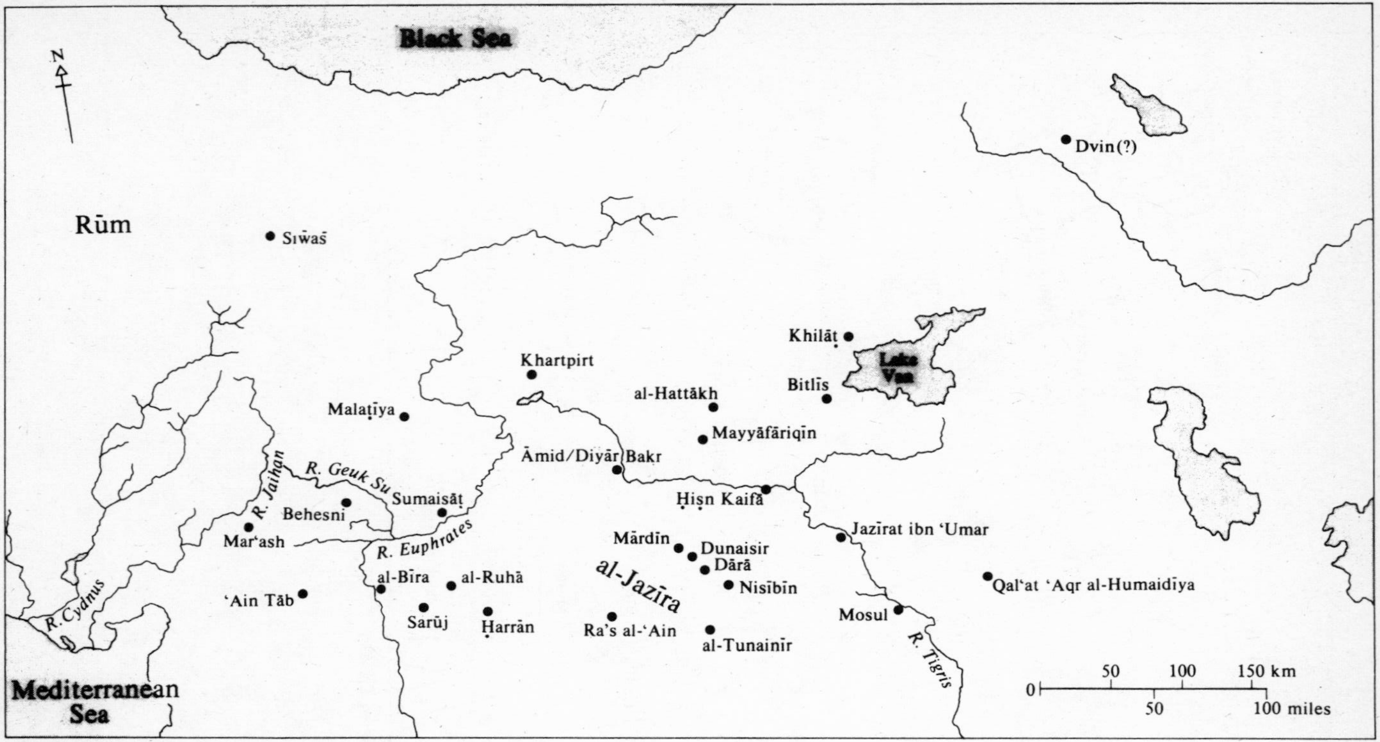

Map 1. Turkey East

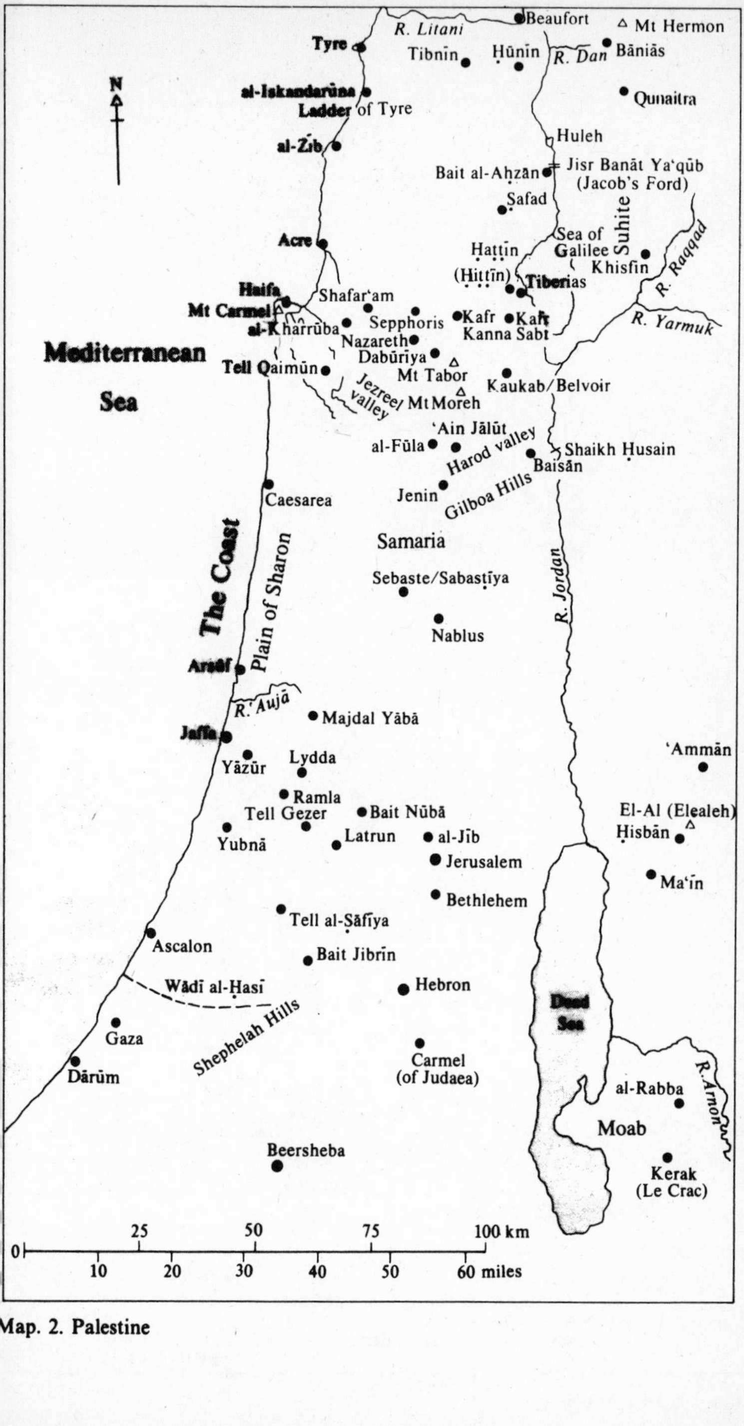

Map. 2. Palestine

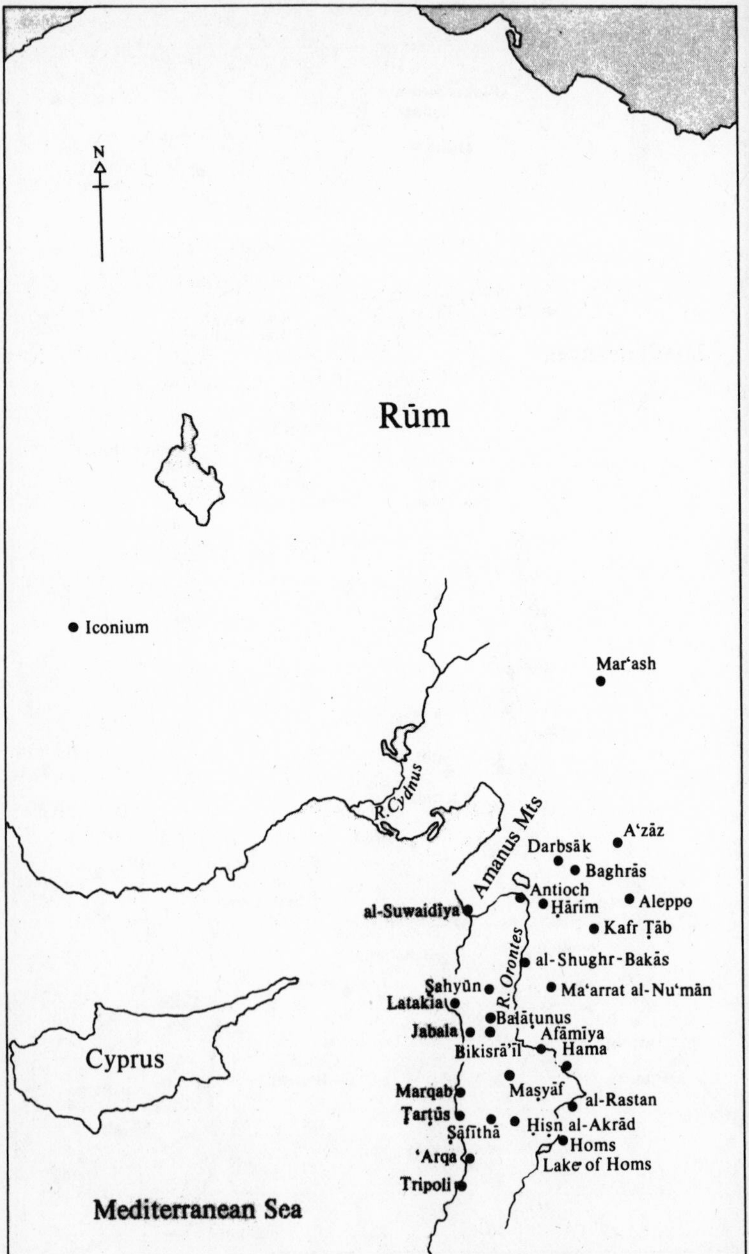

Map. 3. Turkey West

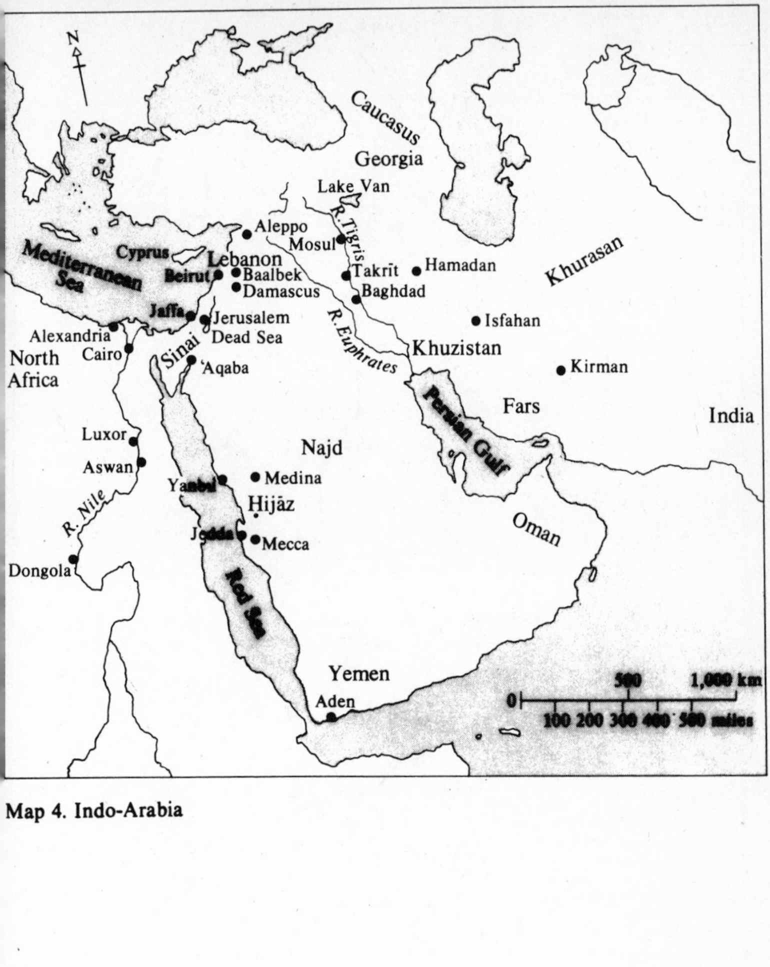

Map 4. Indo-Arabia

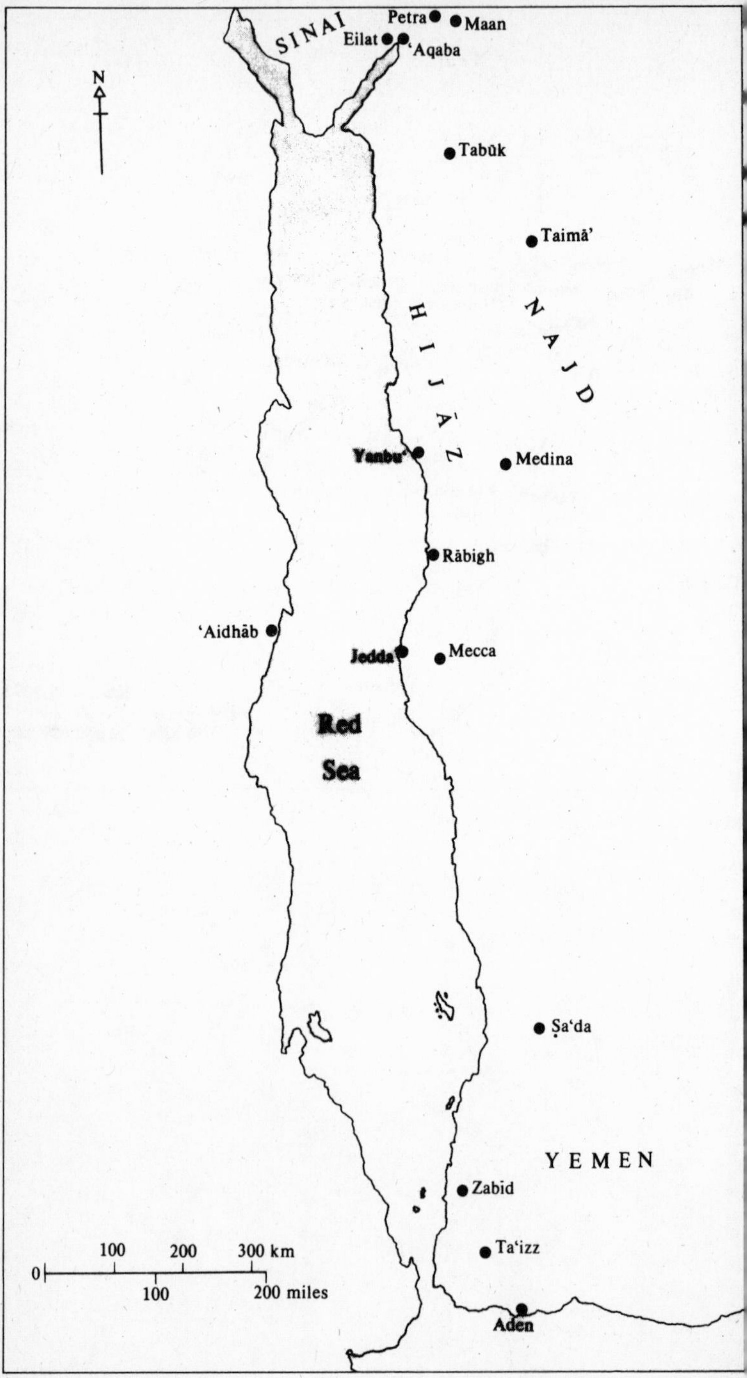

Map 5. Southern Arabia

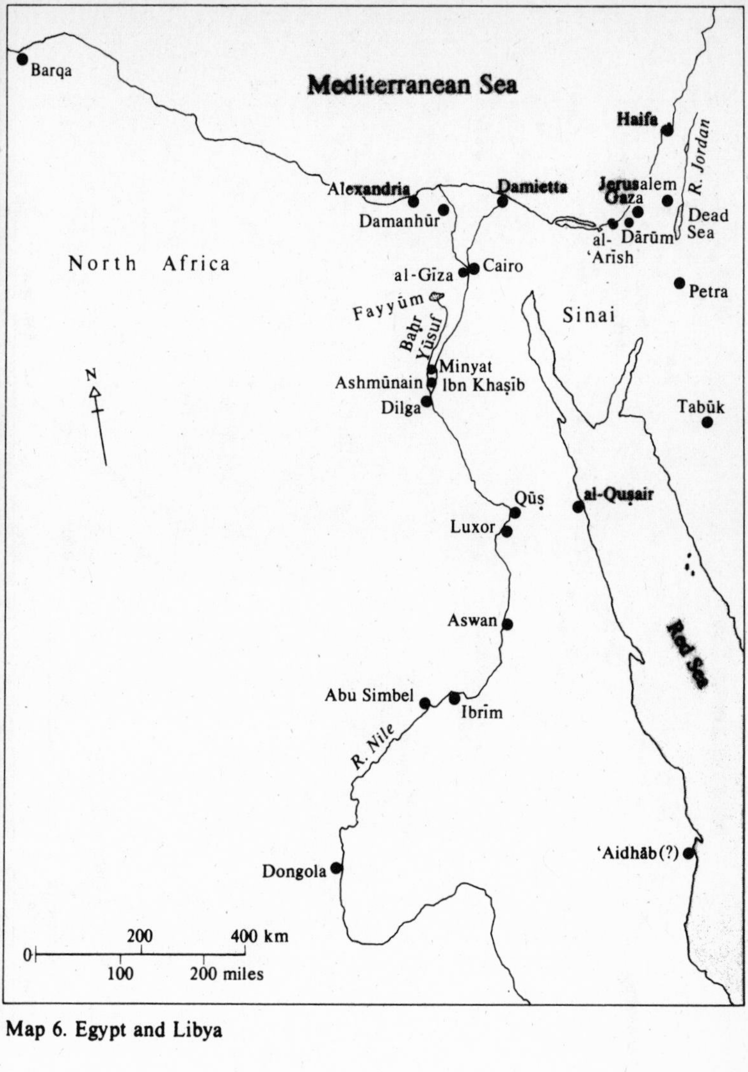

Map 6. Egypt and Libya

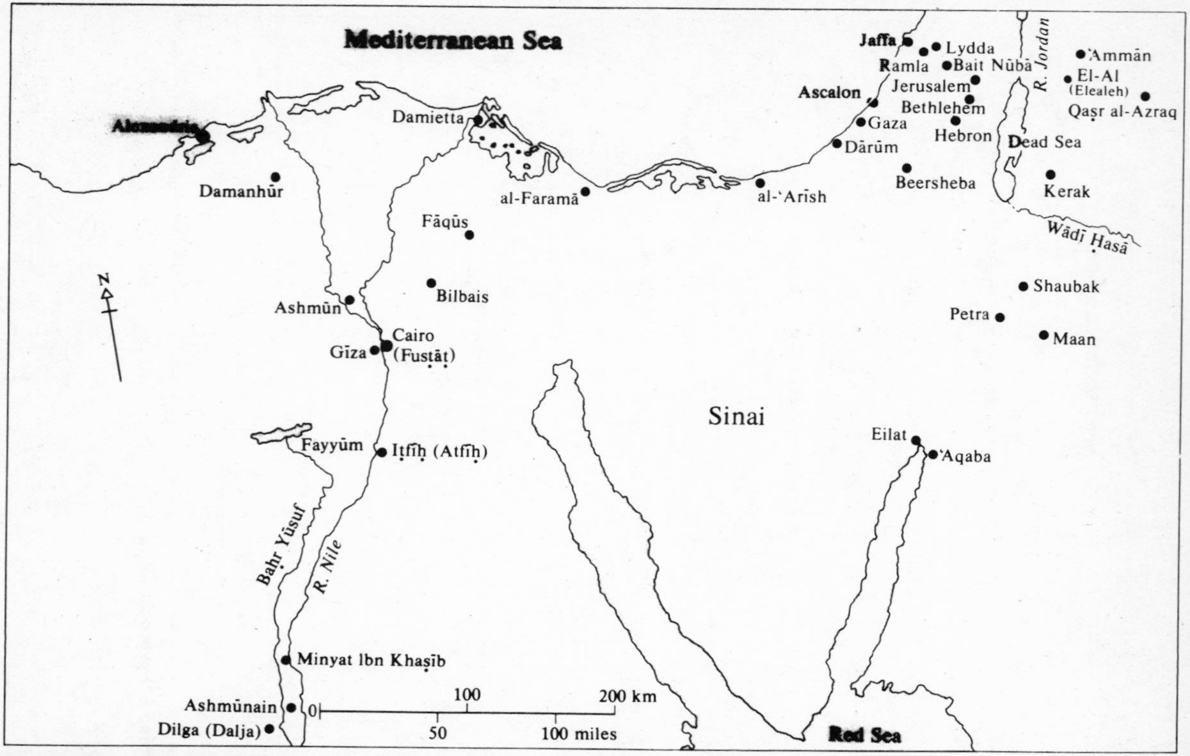

Map 7 Nile Delta and Sinai

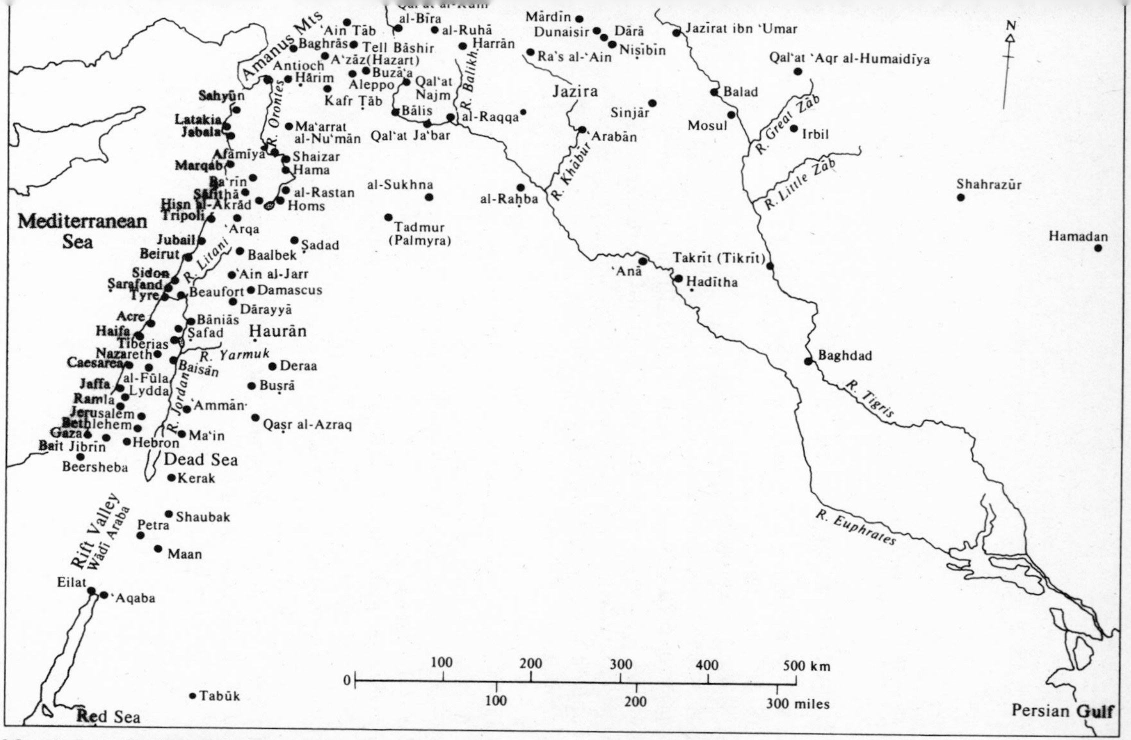

Map 8. Iraq, Syria and Lebanon

NOTES

Abbreviations, etc, used in the Notes

A.S. = Abū Shāma, ed. Aḥmad and Ziyāda, vol. 1.1.2.
A.S. 1 = Abū Shāma, Cairo, vol. 1.
A.S. Ra. 2 = Abū Shāma, Cairo, vol. 2.
B.A. = *Shifā 'l-qulūb*; see Anon.
Barq = *al-Barq al-Shāmī*; see under 'Imād al-Dīn.
Bundārī = *Sanā al-Barq*; see under 'Imād al-Dīn; references are to Şeşen's edition.
Daulat al-Akrād; see Muḥammad b. Ibrāhīm.
Ehrenkreutz = *Saladin.*
Fatḥ = *Kitāb al-fatḥ al-qussī;* see under 'Imād al-Dīn.
Gibb = *The Life of Saladin.*
I.A. = Ibn al-Athīr, *al-Kāmil.*
I.F. = Ibn al-Furāt.
I.S. = Ibn Shaddād.
Kharīda; see under 'Imād al-Dīn.
Khiṭaṭ; see under al-Maqrīzī.
Nur. = *Dīwān rasā'il*; see under 'Imād al-Dīn.
Q. = al-Qalqashandī.
Sanā = *Sanā al-Barq*; see under 'Imād al-Dīn; references are to F. El-Nabarawy's edition.
W.T. = William of Tyre.
For Berlin, Cairo (= *al-durr al-naẓīma*), Cambridge, Leiden, Mosul, Munich, Paris, TC. (= Top Kapu), 7307, 25756, 25757; see al-Fāḍil.

Early adventures

1 Cf., in particular, Gibb, 'The Arabic Sources for the Life of Saladin'; Elisséeff, *Nūr ad-Dīn*, 1.1 sq.; Sauvaget and Cahen, *Introduction to the History of the Muslim East.* One narrative not noted by these authorities is the disappointing history by Ibn Abī' l-Haijā', whose author is claimed to have been contemporary with Saladin (cf. *Fihris al-Makhṭūṭāt al-Miṣrīya* (Cairo n.d.), pt. 2, *al-Tārīkh*, sec. 3, p. 56).

2 *Sanā al-Barq al-Shāmī*, pt 1, ed. Şeşen. For the unpublished portion of this work reference is made to "A Critical Edition of the Abridgement by al-Bundārī of the *Kitāb al-Barq al-Shāmī* by 'Imād al-Dīn", by El-Nabarawy.

3 Gibb's attack on the reliability of Ibn al-Athīr and on his part as "devil's advocate" against Saladin ("The Arabic Sources for the Life of Saladin" 71) is of importance but is based on too favourable a view of the impartiality of 'Imād al-Dīn.

4 Cf. A.H. Helbig, *Al-Qāḍī al-Fāḍil, der Wezīr Saladin's* (Berlin 1909). There is no reason to doubt the general authenticity of the correspondence. Letters quoted by the narrative historians generally agree with the manuscript versions; they are self-consistent and there are few valid motives for forgery. On the other hand, in the case of official letters, attribution of the drafts to al-Fāḍil need not be correct. In the present work, as a matter of convention, quotations from official letters are attributed to Saladin.

5 Al-Fāḍil *'Al-durr al-naẓīma.*

6 MS. Nūri Osmāniye (Istanbul) no. 3745. Autobiographical details show that the author left Mosul for the service of al-Afḍal. The manuscript also includes a letter attributed by the copyist to 'Umāra al-Yamanī.

7 MS. Ayasofya (Istanbul) no. 4299.

8 *In Search of Cultural History* 39.

9 Cf. Minorsky, "The Prehistory of Saladin".

10 A.S. 535-6.

11 Cf. Michael the Syrian XVIII. 10.325.

12 A.S. 539.

13 Cf. Ibn Abī' l-Haijā' 201.

14 Cambridge 12. Folio references are to the *incipit* of the letters.

15 25757.39.

16 7465.5. For the conventional background to this, cf. Abū Tammām, *Ḥamāsa*, 2.362.

17 Munich 113.

18 Wahrānī 228.

19 I.S. 34.

20 Bundārī 349.
21 Wahrānī 228.
22 *Travels* 288 sq.
23 *Itinerary of Richard I* 71; cf. the Latin *Continuation* of William of Tyre 59: "parentum non ingenuorum proles, nec tamen obscuri sanguinis humilitate plebescens".
24 Usāma ibn Munqidh 154.
25 Munich 122.
26 Cf. Lapidus, *Muslim Cities in the Later Middle Ages*, 90; Ritter, "Irrational Solidarity Groups".
27 W.T. 925. The Bedouin are listed after the "Turks", apparently in order of importance; cf. Napoleon, *Guerre d'Orient*, 2. 41.
28 Cf. I.A. 12.25.
29 Usāma ibn Munqidh 84.
30 25757.15, cit. Q. 13.81 (also TC. 65, Leiden 207).
31 For the dominant position of the Banū 'l-Dāya, see p. 72.
32 Cf. p. 20.
33 For the background to this decline, cf. Ehrenkreutz 13 sq.
34 Wahrānī 4.
35 Cf. p. 20.
36 Wahrānī 4.
37 *Continuation* 61.
38 W.T. 893: "nam summo eorum principi pro minimo est uter de contendentibus aut succumbat aut obtineat, dummodo non desit qui sua et regni negotia procuret".
39 I.S. 40.
40 I.A. 11.298.
41 A.S. 418.
42 *Ibid.*
43 I.A. 11.299.
44 25757.15.
45 *History of the Atabegs* 126.
46 Cit. A.S. 421; cf. also *Khiṭaṭ* 1.338.
47 I.A. 11.299.
48 For details of the fighting, see A.S. 419 sq.; *Khiṭaṭ* 1.338.
49 Cf. A.S. 402; Q. 10.310.
50 A.S. 420.
51 Cf. note 42.
52 I.A. 11.300; for a note on the fortifications of Bilbais, see *Khiṭaṭ* 1.174.
53 A.S. 423.
54 Cf. Bundārī 61; A.S. 423.
55 Cf. I.A. 11.300; W.T. 892: "pusillus statura, pinguis multum et corpulentior".
56 Sibṭ 295; B.A. 10.

57 543 A.H.

58 A.S. 408.

59 For Shīrkūh's two sons, cf. *Kharīda* 1.193.

60 Gibb (4 sq.) follows Ibn Abī Ṭayy's account (A.S. 1.100) and states that Saladin was appointed deputy military governor/commandant of Damascus in 1156. It should be noted that Ibn Abī Ṭayy's account is inaccurate, as Abū Shāma points out: first, it makes Saladin succeed Tūrān-Shāh in this office after Tūrān-Shāh's death and, secondly, although it is entered by Abū Shāma under the heading of the year 550 A.H. (= 1156), it neither states nor implies that this was the year of the appointment. Ibn Abī Ṭayy goes on to report that Saladin resigned his office after some days and Gibb together with Ehrenkreutz (32) states that he was reappointed later. It can be seen from later evidence (cf. Sibṭ 327; *Daulat al-Akrād* 1) that Saladin's tenure of this office was the subject of gossip and it must be stressed that the evidence connected with it is untrustworthy.

61 *Travels* 298 (*ṣāḥib al-shurṭa).*

62 A.S. 1.100; B.A. 15.

63 *Itinerary of Richard I* 72; Latin *Continuation* 60.

64 Wahrānī 28.

65 Bundārī 222.

66 W.T. 902.

67 *Ibid.* 903.

68 I.S. 37.

69 W.T. 905.

70 A.S. 424.

71 Cf. A.S. 399 sq.

72 I.A. 11.324; it is not clear in this context whether Ibn al-Athīr intends this figure to cover all Shīrkūh's cavalry or only Nūr al-Dīn's additions, but later (11.326) he applies it to the whole force.

73 25757.15.

74 W.T. 925; according to this passage, by the time of the battle of Bābain, Shīrkūh had collected 10,000–11,000 Bedouin.

75 A.S. 424.

76 W.T. 908.

77 Bundārī 62.

78 W.T. 904.

79 *Ibid.* 905.

80 A.S. 400.

81 *Ibid.* 425.

82 Cf. Cairo 34.

83 A.S. 426.

84 *Ibid.* 425.

85 W.T. 918.

86 *Ibid.* 921.
87 Cit. A.S. 426.
88 7307.103.
89 Cit. A.S. 426.
90 W.T. 925.
91 Sibṭ 269.
92 I.A. 11.325 sq.
93 Bundārī 63.
94 Cit. A.S. 426.
95 Leiden, *al-kitāb al-thālith fī'l-iftikhār.*
96 Cit. A.S. 426; William of Tyre (925) put Shīrkūh's numbers at 12,000 "Turks" and 10,000–11,000 Bedouin. He gave Amalric 374 knights and a number of Turcopoles, whom "many accounts" criticised as being of no use during the battle. In addition, there were the "worthless and effeminate" Egyptians.
97 Bundārī 63.
98 'Umar b. 'Abd al-'Azīz, *Sūq al-Fāḍil,* 3.
99 I.A. 11.326.
100 W.T. 928.
101 *History* 3.1.89.
102 W.T. 928.
103 *Ibid.* 929.
104 *Ibid.* 934.
105 *Ibid.* 938.
106 *Khiṭaṭ* 1.174; Maqrīzī adds that Saladin had 1000 horse.
107 W.T. 933.
108 *Ibid.* 932.
109 A.S. 427.
110 W.T. 933.
111 *Ibid.* 934.
112 Bundārī 64.
113 I.S. 38.
114 Bundārī 64.
115 *Khiṭaṭ* 1.339.
116 W.T. 936.
117 *Ibid.* 937.
118 *Ibid.* 938; *Khiṭaṭ* 1.175: "he came out to Amalric, King of the Franks, and sat with him".
119 W.T. 938.
120 *Khiṭaṭ* 1.175; according to A.S. 428, Ibn Maṣāl was arrested.
121 A.S. 428.
122 Cf. p. 5.
123 *Muqaddima, passim.*
124 Cit. A.S. 383.
125 Bundārī 66.

126 A.S. 394.
127 I.S. 39.
128 Bundārī 70.
129 W.T. 945.
130 *Ibid.* 948.
131 A.S. 430.
132 I.A. 11.335. "Coast" is used as a translation of the Arabic *al-sāḥil*, referring to the Frankish-held section of the Levant littoral.
133 I.S. 39; Quṭb al-Dīn had succeeded his brother Saif al-Dīn (cf. p. 21) on the latter's death in 544 A.H..
134 A.S. 389.
135 Bundārī 74.
136 For the confusion in the form of this name, cf. A.S. 415: "Shāwar had three sons, Ṭayy, al-Kāmil and Sulaimān"; Ṭayy has been restored for Abī Ṭayy in A.S. 431 and 434; in 455 there is a reference to "the two sons of Shāwar, al-Kāmil and his brother, that is, al-Ṭārī".
137 A.S. 431.
138 I.F. 4.1.23.
139 A.S. 431.
140 I.A. 11.336.
141 W.T. 951.
142 Cf. A.S. 432; *Khiṭaṭ* 1.339.
143 *Khiṭaṭ loc. cit.*
144 Cf. A.S. Ra. 2.33.
145 Cf. I.F. 4.1.33.
146 *Khiṭaṭ* 1.339.
147 Bundārī 74; A.S. 433.
148 W.T. 953; A.S. 433.
149 W.T. 953.
150 *Khiṭaṭ* 1.214.
151 Cit. A.S. 432.
152 A.S. 391.
153 Bundārī 74.
154 W.T. 954: "homo inverecundus, clamosus, detractor, seditiosus".
155 I.A. 11.338; Ehrenkreutz (51) suggests that Shīrkūh hesitated: "perhaps he thought an expedition too risky". This should not be accepted. 'Imād al-Dīn notes Shīrkūh's eagerness to return (cf. Bundārī 71, 75) and Nūr al-Dīn's remark quoted by Abū Shāma (394) ("if you delay in going to Egypt, then expediency will require that I go myself") is to be taken as rhetorical emphasis, underlining the importance of the move.
156 Bundārī 75.
157 W.T. 950; cf. Bundārī 76.
158 I.F. 4.1.26-7.

159 W.T. 955; for the story that when Shīrkūh was reported to have reached Ṣudr, Shāwar sent out Shams al-Khilāfa to ask Amalric to return some money, cf. A.S. 434. Amalric is quoted as saying: "I know that you are an intelligent man and that Shāwar is a king. You would not have asked me to give you this large sum except because of something that has happened."

160 A.S. 434.

161 W.T. 956.

162 I.A. 11.339 (reading Rabī'a 2 for Jumādā 2).

163 Cf. A.S. 435.

164 Bundārī 78.

165 A.S. 398.

166 Cf. A.S. 398-9, 436; I.A. 11.430; Sibṭ 277.

167 Bundārī 78.

168 A.S. 435.

169 Cf. I.A. 11.339; A.S. 396.

170 Ehrenkreutz 57.

171 Cf. *Khiṭaṭ* 2.92 and 378 for the career of Masrūr, one of the Palace servants, who rose to the position of commander of Saladin's *ḥalqa* (division).

172 Cf. al-Makhzūmī 44.

173 Cf. p. 6.

174 W.T. 957.

175 There is a discrepancy in the dating of their death; this is given in Bundārī 85 and A.S. 455 as "Monday 4 Jumādā 2" (= 5 March). Ehrenkreutz (58) follows a later version that reads Jumādā 1 for 2 (= 3 February). This is supported by the story that Shīrkūh was presented with al-Kāmil's head (cf. I.F. 4.1.33), but a stronger argument in its favour is that 5 March was a Wednesday and 3 February a Monday.

176 I.A. 11.340 cf. Lapidus, *Muslim Cities in the Later Middle Ages*, with reference to fourteenth-century Cairo: "in most of these events... there was no pattern of popular support or opposition to the régime. The mobs had no will of their own" (165); "as long as the opportunity to plunder was controlled by the Mamluks, the masses could be manipulated in a way which forestalled their being organised against the régime" (184).

177 *Khiṭaṭ* 1.339.

178 *Travels* 54.

179 A.S. 437.

180 *Ibid.*

181 Cf. I.F. 4.1.54.

182 I.S. 40.

183 A.S. 438.

184 Leiden, *al-kitāb al-thānī fī'l-rithā'*.

185 I.A. 11.343 mentions both the army command and the Fatimid vizierate as objects of ambition for the "Nūrid emirs in Egypt", but does not imply that they were separable.

186 I.A. 11.343; Ehrenkreutz (67), while noting that "the expeditionary army constituted the most effective military contingent in Egypt", suggests that "there are certain indications... that in spite of Saladin's dynamic personality, al-'Āḍid hoped to bring him under the influence of the palace establishment". He also (64) notes a Fatimid plan, which he quotes on authority of the *Itti'āẓ al-ḥunafā'*, that the Palace should take into its own service the cavalry commanded by Bahā' al-Dīn Qarā-Qūsh and appoint "a local Fatimid military man" as vizier.

187 Wahrānī 5.

188 Bundārī 81.

189 A.S. 407.

2 Vizier of Egypt

1 W.T. 913.

2 *Ibid.* 925.

3 Bundārī 214.

4 *History* 3.1.87.

5 Cf. p. 25.

6 I.S. 40.

7 A.S. 440.

8 *Itinerary of Richard I* 73; cf. *Continuation* 61.

9 Cit. Q. 10.91.

10 Cit. A.S. 410.

11 25757.15.

12 A.S. 455.

13 *Ibid.*

14 I.A. 11.344; A.S. 408. According to one story (Ibn al-Athīr, *History of the Atabegs,* 143) Nūr al-Dīn at first refused to send Saladin's family on the grounds that this would cause dissension. He changed his mind on hearing that the Franks were mustering to attack Egypt. This account is followed by Ehrenkreutz (72, 76).

15 Cit. A.S. 440.

16 A.S. 441.

17 Cf. I.F. 4.1.66.

18 A.S. 407.

19 Bundārī 84.

20 For a description of the Palace, cf. *Khiṭaṭ* 1.384.

21 Cf. Bundārī 82; A.S. 450; *Khiṭaṭ* 2.2.
22 Cf. Bundārī 83. For Fatimid army numbers, 40,000 horse and 30,000 black foot-soldiers, cf. *Khiṭaṭ* 1.94.
23 For this phrase, cf. Abū Tammām, *Ḥamāsa*, 1.41.
24 Abū Ṣāliḥ 92.
25 *Khiṭaṭ* 2.3. Maqrīzī notes that the crowd numbered 50,000, but elsewhere (*Khiṭaṭ* 2.20) he says that the square could accommodate (only) 10,000 horse and foot.
26 Cf. I.F. 4.1.69 sq.
27 Cf. Bundārī 84; I.F. 4.1.71.
28 A.S. 452.
29 Abū Ṣāliḥ (92) wrote: "a body of Armenian Christians overcame the blacks, and drove them away and killed many of them". This may suggest that the Caliph's archers now helped the Syrians.
30 Cf. Bundārī 84.
31 Nicetas 208.
32 Cinnamus 278.
33 Nicetas 209.
34 *Ibid.* 208.
35 W.T. 961; for the Muslim figure of forty horses per *ṭarīda*, cf. Ibn Mammātī 339.
36 25757.15; Maqrīzī, *Khiṭaṭ*, 1.214, set the figure at more than 1200 ships.
37 Bundārī 88.
38 Cf. Q.2.385.
39 I.S. 41.
40 Cf. Röhricht, *Regesta*, 122.
41 Cinnamus 279.
42 W.T. 964 sq.
43 *Khiṭaṭ* 1.215.
44 I.A. 11.352.
45 W.T. 964.
46 Bundārī 87.
47 Nicetas 214.
48 W.T. 969.
49 Nicetas 216.
50 *Ibid.* 212.
51 W.T. 966.
52 Nicetas 210, 214.
53 *Ibid.* 213.
54 W.T. 969.
55 Nicetas 217.
56 W.T. 969.
57 Nicetas 219.
58 25757.15.

59 *Khiṭaṭ* 1.215.
60 A.S. 460.
61 I.A. 11.352.
62 Cit. A.S. 465.
63 Bundārī 89.
64 I.A. 11.352.
65 *Khiṭaṭ* 1.46.
66 I.F. 4.1.69.
67 For a report that al-ʿĀdil went to Egypt with Shīrkūh and Saladin, cf. Ibn Khallikān, "Abū Bakr Muḥammad al-Malik al-ʿĀdil", *Kitāb wafayāt al-aʿyān.*
68 Cf. Bundārī 92.
69 Bundārī 91.
70 Michael the Syrian XVIII. 10.338.
71 Bundārī 92.
72 W.T. 971 sq.
73 I.A. 11.355.
74 Cf. A.S. 482.
75 Cf. Bundārī 94.
76 Bundārī 96.
77 Cf. I.A. 11.365.
78 I.A. 11.365.
79 For futher details of Tūrān-Shāh's *iqṭāʿ*s, cf. A.S. 488, Ehrenkreutz 82.
80 W.T. 973.
81 Cit. A.S. 489.
82 W.T. 975.
83 *Ibid.* 978.
84 Cf. al-Ṭarsūsī, MS. (Bodley) Huntington 264, f. 205.
85 For a note on the term *ṭulb*, cf. Lyons and Riley-Smith, *Ayyubids,* 1.217; 200 men is a not unreasonable figure for this period. Abū Shāma (*Ra.* 2.9) reports Taqī al-Dīn as taking 200 out of 800 horse for a night attack and Saladin took 20 men from each of his *ṭulbs* as bait for an ambush (cf. I.S. 101) in a context where one-tenth of the total force would be appropriate.
86 A.S. 489.
87 W.T. 977.
88 *Khiṭaṭ* 1.185; cf. A.S. 486.
89 Q. 7.27.
90 It is clear that this date (Bundārī 108) is wrong and that "Rabīʿa 2" should be read for "Rabīʿa 1".
91 The author of the *Tārīkh Mayyāfāriqīn* (135) saw this caravan, which left Damascus, reportedly with 70,000 camels, on 31 December; it comprised the children of Tūrān-Shāh, "and of his brothers", together with their wives and retainers. This suggests

that Saladin returned to Cairo at the end of February and that Jumādā 1, given by A.S. 486 and *Khiṭaṭ* 1.185, is a better reading than Jumādā 2, found in Bundārī 109.

92 Cf. Ehrenkreutz 84.

93 Wahrānī 95-6.

94 *Khiṭaṭ* 1.359.

95 Cit. A.S. 498.

96 Bundārī 114.

97 For a full account, cf. Ehrenkreutz, "Saladin's coup d'état in Egypt", *Medieval and Middle Eastern Studies in Honor of Aziz Suryal Atiya*.

98 A.S. 493.

99 I.F. 4.1.157.

100 *Ibid.* 4.1.130.

101 A.S. 499; for variants, cf. also Sibṭ 290.

102 A.S. 494.

103 I.A. 11.370.

104 *Khiṭaṭ* 1.358.

105 A.S. 440.

106 There is a discrepancy in this dating. Abū Shāma (504) quotes from 'Imād al-Dīn's *Dīwān* to show that the *khuṭba* was introduced on 14 May 1171 in Alexandria and on 4 June in Fusṭāṭ and Cairo. This is linked by Gibb (8) to the report that Nūr al-Dīn's messenger brought news of the *khuṭba* to Baghdad on 25 September. The introduction of the *khuṭba* in Alexandria, a Sunnī stronghold, would have been typical of Saladin's cautious approach, but there is no support for the detail or the date in Bundārī.

107 I.A. 11.369.

108 Cit. A.S. 499.

109 Details can be multiplied, cf. Ehrenkreutz 85 sq. Ehrenkreutz underlines an important point where he refers (85) to the Fatimid Caliphate as a "prestigious institution". The lack of demonstrably effective power in the Palace may lead to an underestimation of the importance that contemporary observers could reasonably attribute to it.

110 *Khiṭaṭ* 1.86; for a decree promulgated on 4 September moving the tax year so as to make it coincide with the solar year, cf. Q. 13.54.

3 Lord of Egypt

1 25757.114.

2 Bundārī 112.

3 *Ibid.*

4 Bundārī 117.

5 I.A. 11.371 sq.

6 W.T. 993.

7 Bundārī 118. Ehrenkreutz (105) refers to "a major defeat at the hands of hostile Bedouin warriors", but this is not confirmed by 'Imād al-Dīn. Maqrīzī (*Sulūk* 44) reports that Saladin lost 5000 beasts.

8 Cit. A.S. 506.

9 *Khiṭaṭ* 1.427; cf. Q. 3.351.

10 Bundārī 149; for the report that Saladin never found the Fatimid treasures, cf. *Khiṭaṭ* 1.435.

11 For details of these taxes, cf. *Khiṭaṭ* 1.104.

12 Cit. A.S. 522-3.

13 Munich 93.

14 Q. 3.470.

15 Maqrīzī, *Sulūk*, 45.

16 *Khiṭaṭ* 1.108.

17 *Travels* 42.

18 *Khiṭaṭ* 1.108.

19 *Travels* 62 sq.

20 For a parallel, cf. Robinson and Smith, *Biblical Researches in Palestine*, 1.43: "the people in general do not ascribe their oppression so much to the Pasha (Muhammad Ali) as to his subordinate agents. They suppose that if the murmurs of the peasantry could reach his ear, the immediate and pressing evils would be remedied."

21 Cf. Ibn Mammātī 78; Q. 3.285.

22 Cf. Gibb 10.

23 For a monetary study, cf. Ehrenkreutz, "The crisis of *dīnār* in the Egypt of Saladin". In his book (103 sq.) he stresses the difficulties caused by Saladin's shortage of gold. Neither the letters nor other literary sources add substantially to the available evidence.

24 *L'Économie Royale des Lagides* 492.

25 Al-Nābulsī 18.

26 *Khiṭaṭ* 1.97.

27 *Ibid.* 1.85.

28 Ibn Mammātī 336 sq.

29 For notes on Ayyubid *iqṭā's*, cf. Poliak, "The Ayyubid feudalism"; Rabie, *The Financial System of Egypt*, 26 sq. Saladin is credited with following the example of Nūr al-Dīn by introducing a hereditary system (cf. *Khiṭaṭ* 2.216). As is shown in the case of the Byzantine *pronoia,* this latter can be seen as a natural development rather than as an innovation (cf. Ostrogorsky, *Pour l'histoire de la feodalité byzantine*, 83). In

general, Bloch's remark on the history of feudalism applies at least as appositely to the east as to the west: "to write the history of feudal inheritance would involve compiling statistics, period by period, of the fiefs which were inherited and those which were not – a task which in view of the meagerness of the source material can never be performed" (*Feudal Society* 196).

30 Al-Makhzūmī 100.
31 Ibn Mammātī 201 sq.; cf. Q. 3.450.
32 Al-Makhzūmī 51.
33 Ibn Mammātī 319.
34 Al-Makhzūmī 77.
35 Al-Nābulsī 24.
36 Al-Makhzūmī 113.
37 Cf. Rabie, *The Financial System of Egypt*.
38 TC. 145.
39 25757.12.
40 TC. 126.
41 Al-Makhzūmī 103.
42 *Khiṭaṭ* 2.367.
43 'Umar b. 'Abd al-'Azīz b. al-'Adīm, MS. 4.
44 Ibn Mammātī 66.
45 Q. 1.41.

4 The shadow of Syria

1 *Barq* 3.106B.
2 Cit. A.S. 501.
3 A.S. 507.
4 *Sulūk* 45-8.
5 Abū Ṣāliḥ 5.
6 *Sulūk* 46.
7 25757.15; the letters unfortunately add little of importance to the well-known documents dealing with trade – cf. Amari, *I diplomi arabi*; Röhricht, *Regesta*; Heyd, *Histoire du commerce du Levant*.
8 Cit. A.S. *Ra.* 2.71.
9 7465.65.
10 Cit. Q. 6.506.
11 Cit. A.S. 531.
12 Q. 6.511.
13 Cf. I.A. 11.387.
14 By contrast, Abū Ṣāliḥ (265) describes Dongola as a great city with "many churches and large houses and wide streets. The

king's house is lofty, with several domes built of red brick, and resembles the buildings in al-'Irāq."

15 I.A. 11.386.

16 Cf. p.23: see Bundārī 75.

17 A.S. 524.

18 Bundārī 123. As 'Imād al-Dīn notes, this is adapted from a line by Abū Tammām (*Dīwān* 1.71).

19 Bundārī 130.

20 Cf. W.T. 994.

21 Bundārī 125.

22 Cit. Bundārī 299.

23 W.T. 1046; cf. Wavell, writing of the First World War, *The Palestine Campaigns*, 13: "the Bedouin of Sinai, again, were concerned merely to extract profit to themselves by service as guides or as spies to the nearest or best paymaster, or by entirely impartial looting, whenever opportunity offered".

24 Bundārī 126.

25 I.A. 11.393.

26 *Ibid.* 11.391.

27 For a reference to remission of taxes to attract Turkmans, cf. Q. 13.36.

28 Nicetas 227.

29 Bundārī 134.

30 I.A. 11.391.

31 A.S. 544.

32 Cf. Bundārī 138.

33 I.A. 11.393.

34 W.T. 995.

35 Cit. A.S. 558.

36 Cit. A.S. 559.

37 Cit. Bundārī 298.

38 A.S. 552; Bundārī 349.

39 25757.15.

40 Cit. A.S. 552.

41 A.S. 553.

42 I.A. 11.396.

43 Q. 5.37.

44 *Travels* 133–4.

45 I.A. 11.397.

46 Berlin 51.

47 Cambridge 17.

48 A.S. 561; cf. also a Fāḍilī letter to Nūr al-Dīn, cit. A.S. 562.

49 I.A. (11.399) mentions both the anonymous Christian and Zain al-Dīn 'Alī; 'Imād al-Dīn refers to a *jundī* in the *Kharīda* (3.103) and to Zain al-Dīn in the *Barq* (cf. Bundārī 148, cit. A.S. 560); Ibn Abī Ṭayy names Ibn Maṣāl (cit. A.S. 561).

50 Cit. A.S. *Ra.* 2.5.
51 Cf. p. 276.
52 Wahrānī 191.
53 I.A. 11.402.
54 *Ibid.* 11.372.
55 I.S. 47.
56 A.S. 442.
57 25757.8; cf. p. 62.
58 Cambridge 17; the letter was obviously sent before news of Nūr al-Dīn's death had reached Egypt.
59 I.A. 11.403.
60 W.T. 1000.

5 Independence

1 Cf. Maqrīzī, *Sulūk*, 48.
2 Cf. Bundārī 161.
3 Cf. I.A. 11.406-7.
4 Bundārī 154; for the term *khādim* ("servant") applied to eunuchs, cf. al-Makhzūmī 106.
5 W.T. 1000.
6 Cf. Bundārī 156; A.S. 589.
7 Cit. A.S. 594.
8 Cf. Bundārī 155.
9 25757.8, quoted in part in A.S. 587.
10 25757.6; TC. 59; cf. Bundārī 156; A.S. 587. The editor's substitution of 14 for 4 Dhū'l-Qa'da in the text of Bundārī, based on later sources, is almost certainly wrong, as the 14th was a Sunday.
11 Bundārī 156.
12 7465.215; cf. A.S. 594.
13 25757.146; cf. A.S. 596.
14 Cit. Q. 7.115.
15 25757.146.
16 25757.15.
17 Bundārī 170.
18 *Ibid.* 170.
19 *Sulūk* 56.
20 Bundārī 172.
21 Saladin added details which, he said, had been confirmed by captured knights. The Sicilians had come with a cavalry force of 1500 men, 1000 of whom were armed with lances, while the remaining 500 were lightly-armed Turcopoles. They had 200

galleys, each carrying 150 fighting men, giving a total of 30,000 men. There were 36 *ṭarīdas* carrying horses and 6 ships loaded with weapons, siege equipment, large timbers, etc. There were 40 provision ships, which also carried the mangonel crews, as well as servants and artisans, and these brought up the total number to 50,000. Of the 1000 lancers, 700 drew monthly pay at rates ranging, for the most part, from 15 to 20 dinars for a 5-month period, while some "famous men" among them drew up to 100 dinars a month. The rank-and-file Turcopoles were paid from 5 to 10 dinars a month.

22 Cf. Maqrīzī, *Sulūk,* 57; I.A. 11.414.

23 I.S. 48.

24 According to a letter (Leiden, *al-kitāb al-thālith fī'l-iftikhār*) the battle took place "south of Esna on the east bank of the Nile". The letter confirms that "Bedouin, slaves and Negroes" took part in the revolt.

25 Munich 14.

26 Bundārī 161 sq.

27 *Ibid.* 165.

28 Cf. I.S. 49.

29 A.S. 596.

30 I.A. 11.415.

31 Cf. I.A. 11.406.

32 Gibb (12): "loyalty can only be the consequence of loyalty", reading *wafā' for wafāt,* but cf. 7465.170 (see p. 235) for the clearly expressed, conventional sentiment.

33 Bundārī 168-9.

34 I.A. 11.415.

6 From Egypt to Syria

1 Bundārī 176.

2 A.S. 602.

3 Cf. 7465.3.

4 Cf. I.A. 11.416.

5 25757.145.

6 7465.222

7 B.A. 11.

8 Leiden, *al-kitāb al-rābi' fī'l-rithā'*.

9 I.A. 11.416.

10 7465.222.

11 According to the author of *Tārīkh Mayyāfāriqīn* (109), Ibn al-Muqaddam came out to meet Saladin at Dārayya. He adds, less convincingly, that Raiḥān also visited him.

12 Bundārī 177.
13 W.T. 1012-13.
14 I.S. 50.
15 Cit. A.S. *Ra*.2. 177.
16 Cf. *Fatḥ* 456.
17 7465.222.
18 7465.220.
19 *Ibid.*
20 7465.222.
21 *Ibid.*
22 7465.220.
23 *Ibid.*
24 Bundārī 178.
25 7465.122.
26 7465.222.
27 A.S. 607.
28 Bundārī 179.
29 Cit. A.S. 612.
30 25757.141.
31 Munich 135; 7465.122.
32 TC. 62.
33 25757.141.
34 Cit. A.S. 607.
35 Cit. A.S. 608.
36 *Travels* 250.
37 25757.147.
38 25757.146.
39 Cit. A.S. 609.
40 I.A. 11.418.
41 Bundārī 181.
42 25757.143.
43 Cf. 25757.143.
44 Cf. Bundārī 182; A.S. 611.
45 W.T. 1016.
46 *Ibid.* 1017.
47 25757.71.
48 Cit. A.S. 614.
49 Bundārī 182; the letter 25757.128 gives this as eighteen days – apparently a copyist's error.
50 25757.128.
51 Cit. A.S. 612.
52 Cit. A.S. 612.
53 Bundārī 183.
54 25757.128.
55 25757.112.

56 I.A. 11.420; A.S. 637.
57 TC. 110.
58 Bundārī 187.
59 Cf. p. 85, note 29.
60 Cit. A.S. 631.
61 Cf. p. 33.
62 Cf. I.S. 156.
63 Mosul 49.
64 Cf. p. 88, note 42.
65 Or, reading *muṣālaḥa* for *maṣāliḥ*, "to be reconciled with".
66 25757.144.
67 The text has Quṭb al-Dīn, which appears to be a copyist's error.
68 Mosul 49.
69 Bundārī 188.
70 I.A. 11.421.
71 Mosul 49.
72 Cf. A.S. 639; W.T. 1018.
73 For a parallel from a not dissimilar period, cf. Tarn, *Hellenistic Military and Naval Developments*, 24: "for a time, until settled kingdoms again formed, a type of warfare prevailed in which the object was not to destroy the enemy – nobody wanted to destroy useful mercenaries – but to compel him to surrender and then enlist him yourself".
74 Cf. I.A. 12.32.
75 Mosul 49.
76 TC. 110.
77 Bundārī 190 – the phrase is in rhymed prose and may be purely rhetorical.
78 Mosul 49.
79 Cf. A.S. 639.
80 Cit. A.S. 639.
81 Mosul 49.
82 Cf. p. 101.

7 War and diplomacy

1 Mosul 49.
2 Cf. Wavell, *The Palestine Campaigns*, 62: "over the soft sands of the Sinai Desert... twenty-five miles – covered mostly at the walk – [was] an exhausting day for cavalry". A slower pace meant that more supplies had to be carried.
3 25757.15.

4 Cf. Q. 10.135. In another reference, Q. 1.194, the Caliph is found quoting from the Quran (49.17): "they claim that you owe them a debt of gratitude in that they have embraced Islam. Say: 'you have conferred no favour on me'."

5 Mosul 49.

6 Sibṭ's reference to operations against the Assassins (329), dated to 570 A.H. (August 1174–July 1175), noted by Gibb (17) and Ehrenkreutz (141), is not taken up by 'Imād al-Dīn or mentioned in the letters.

7 Bundārī 194.

8 W.T. 1018–19.

9 Bundārī 193.

10 25757.144.

11 Bundārī 195.

12 Cf. A.S. 648.

13 I.A. 11.427.

14 Bundārī 200.

15 Cit. A.S. 648.

16 Mosul 69.

17 I.S. 51.

18 TC. 63.

19 25757.136.

20 Cit. A.S. 663.

21 TC. 63.

22 I.S. 51, reading *tadmīran* for *tadbīran*.

23 Bundārī 201.

24 I.A. 11.429.

25 *Ibid* 11.428.

26 A.S. 653. Gibb (18) is right in noting that Ibn Abī Ṭayy's reference to Tūrān-Shāh's part in the battle is mistaken. This is not a textual error, as the context shows that Tūran Shāh is the intended subject, but presumably a mistake on the part of Ibn Abī Ṭayy.

27 Bundārī 201.

28 Cit. A.S. 652.

29 I.A. 11.428.

30 25756.86.

31 Bundārī 204.

32 Cit. A.S. 655.

33 I.A. 11.429.

34 Cit. A.S. 655.

35 Bundārī 208.

36 *Ibid.*

37 W.T. pt I, 305.

38 Bundārī 209.

39 I.A. 11.430.
40 Cit. A.S. 661.
41 Bundārī 211.
42 Cit. A.S. 659.
43 Bundārī 209.
44 *Ibid.* 212.
45 *Ibid.* 214.
46 Cit. A.S. 657; for details of the flight of Quṭb al-Dīn Qaimāz, cf. I.A. 11.424.
47 A.S. 662.
48 Bundārī 216.
49 Cf. A.S. 662.
50 "So-and-so" and "such-and-such" have been substituted for proper names in the manuscript.
51 Munich 40.
52 There is some confusion here in the manuscript and this sentence might conceivably belong to another letter. Nevertheless, it accurately reproduces Saladin's concern for propaganda.
53 Ibn al-'Adīm 29.
54 I.A. 11.431.
55 A.S. 669; cf. I.S. 52.
56 Bundārī 217.
57 I.A. 11.431.
58 Bundārī 218.
59 I.A. 11.436.
60 Cit. A.S. 669.
61 W.T. 1020. The dating of this raid to 1175 (cf. Grousset, *Histoire des Croisades*, 2.627) cannot be accepted, as Saladin himself was then in or near Damascus.
62 W.T. 1021.
63 I.A. 11.437.
64 Cf. I.A. 11.437; Bundārī 219.
65 W.T. 1022.
66 *Ibid.* 1023.
67 *Ibid.*
68 I.A. 11.437.
69 *Kharīda* 2.232.
70 Bundārī 225.
71 *Ibid.* 231.
72 I.A. 11.436.

8 Egyptian interlude

1 Munich 19; for what can be construed as an analysis of the power

of the common people in their role as producers of wealth, cf. al-Makhzūmī 28.

2 25757.8.

3 25757.108.

4 Bundārī 239.

5 Munich 2.

6 Cit. A.S. 689.

7 Bundārī 241.

8 Paris 10.

9 Cairo 41–2.

10 *Fatḥ* 81.

11 *Khiṭaṭ* 2.194 (cf. also 515).

12 W.T. 960.

13 For further details, cf. Gibb 44; Ehrenkreutz, "Saladin in the naval history of the Mediterranean Sea", 100 sq.

14 Maqrīzī (*Khiṭaṭ* 1.233) notes that there was a Fatimid rising at Qifṭ in 572 A.H. (July 1176–June 1177), as a result of which 3000 of the inhabitants were killed by al-'Ādil. This is partly confirmed by a letter (Leiden, *al-kitāb al-thālith fi'l-iftikhār*) which refers to a rising in upper Egypt led by "a *khārijī* claiming the Imamate". He attacked Qūṣ, but was defeated and killed by its governor, Ṣārim al-Dīn Yurun-Qush.

15 Munich 29.

16 *Khiṭaṭ* 2.93.

17 Bundārī 244.

18 Munich 33.

19 *Ibid.* 28.

20 *Ibid.* 53.

21 W.T. 1030 sq.

22 Bundārī 233.

23 *Ibid.* 237.

24 *Ibid.* 234.

25 *Ibid.* 235.

26 Wahrānī 81.

27 *Ibid.* 106.

28 *Ibid.* 104–5.

29 *Ibid.* 61 sq.

30 *Ibid.* 68.

31 *Ibid.* 67.

32 *Ibid.* 55.

33 *Ibid.* 207.

34 *Dīwān* 210.

35 *Ibid.* 182.

36 *Ibid.* 130.

37 *Ibid.* 236.

38 *Ibid.*
39 *Dīwān* 94.
40 Wahrānī 76.

9 Defeat and difficulties

1 W.T. 1037.
2 25757.152.
3 Munich 35.
4 *Barq* 3.7B; Bundārī 252; A.S. 697.
5 W.T. 1043.
6 *Khiṭaṭ* 1.86. Such figures must be used with caution. Q. 4.16 notes the custom of concealing army numbers. Maqrīzī (*Khiṭaṭ* 1.95), after giving a figure of "12,000 and no more" for Saladin's Egyptian army, remarks that an individual soldier might have up to 100 servants, of whom at least some can be assumed to have been militarily effective.
7 W.T. 1040.
8 *Ibid.* 1043.
9 Bundārī 255. Sibṭ (342), followed by the *Daulat al-Akrād* (3), says that Saladin was on his way to Tell al-Ṣāfiya.
10 Even this can be reckoned at some six hours' march from Ascalon.
11 I.A. 11.442; Bundārī 255.
12 W.T. 1041.
13 I.S. 53.
14 W.T. 1045.
15 I.A. 11.442.
16 Bundārī 256; for Taqī al-Dīn's customary place on the right wing, cf. *Khiṭaṭ* 1.217.
17 The influence of 'Imād al-Dīn's literary background on his style must always be weighed when his accuracy is assessed. For the phrase that he attributes to Taqī al-Dīn (*'ud, yā Aḥmad, fa-inna 'l-'aud aḥmad;* Bundārī 256), cf. Ḥarīrī 398. ("Go back, Aḥmad, for to return is more praiseworthy.")
18 W.T. 1043.
19 *Ibid.* 1045.
20 Cit. A.S. 701.
21 W.T. 1046.
22 Bundārī 260.
23 *Ibid.*
24 Q. 8.291.
25 *Barq* 3.19A.

26 25757.150. The report quoted from Maqrīzī (*Sulūk* 65) by Ehrenkreutz (159) that Kurdish troops were blamed for the defeat is not confirmed by contemporary sources, but is of interest in showing how in later tradition Saladin was dissociated from his Kurdish background (cf. Q. 4.343 for a story of his massacre of a group of Kurds).

27 Bundārī 266; *Barq* 25A.

28 Cf. Munich 3.

29 Bundārī 266.

30 W.T. 1036.

31 Bundārī 266.

32 25757.153; cf. A.S. 706.

33 Bundārī 269.

34 Ibn al-ʿAdīm 36.

35 W.T. 1047.

36 Cf. I.S. 177.

37 Cf. Ibn al-ʿAdīm 37.

38 Bundārī 268.

39 I.S. 53.

40 25757.70. Gibb ("The Arabic Sources for the Life of Saladin" 61) attacks Ibn al-Athīr for "carelessness...or deliberate falsehood" because of his remark that the Frankish attack on Hama (see p. 126) was caused by Saladin's defeat. It can be suggested, however, that Ibn al-Athīr was not following the *Barq*, as Gibb supposes, but a report mentioned by Saladin (Munich 7) that the Franks were now on their way back to Hama. The folios of the Munich manuscript are unfortunately disordered here, but it seems that Saladin used the rumour of this second threat to claim credit for the speed of his reaction.

41 Bundārī 270.

42 *Ibid.* 280.

43 *Ibid.* 282.

44 *Barq* 3.46B.

45 *Ibid.* 3.42A.

46 *Ibid.* 38B.

47 Bundārī 274.

48 Munich 7.

49 *Ibid.* 29.

50 Bundārī 320.

51 *Barq* 62B.

52 Bundārī 298.

53 *Ibid.* 301.

54 *Ibid.* 299.

55 Cit. A.S. Ra. 2.2

56 Bundārī 307.

57 *Ibid.* 309.
58 Cf. I.A. 11.378.
59 7307.65.
60 Munich 101.
61 Bundārī 309.
62 *Barq* 105A.
63 Bundārī 310.
64 *Barq* 103B.
65 Mosul 76.
66 *Barq* 103B.
67 W.T. 1050.
68 Bundārī 314; the distance is over 50 miles (80 km).

10 Consolidation and expansion

1 *Barq* 48B
2 Q. 7.90.
3 For her name, cf. *Khiṭaṭ* 2.462.
4 Bundārī 317.
5 *Barq* 118B.
6 Bundārī 321; *Barq* 121B.
7 Wahrānī 187.
8 Bundārī 323.
9 *Barq* 122A.
10 Cit. Bundārī 323.
11 *Barq* 137B.
12 Cf. *Barq* 137B; Bundārī 332; A.S. Ra 2.9.
13 W.T. 1053.
14 *Barq* 125B.
15 Bundārī 324.
16 W.T. 1054.
17 Mosul 75.
18 W.T. 1055.
19 For 'Imād al-Dīn's account of the battle, cf. *Barq* 128A sq.; Bundārī 326.
20 TC. 86.
21 W.T. 1050. For the account of the fall of the castle, see *Barq* 138B; Bundārī 333; TC. 86.
22 W.T. 1059.
23 *Barq* 145B.
24 A.S. Ra. 2.11.
25 Wahrānī 187.
26 *Sulūk* 69.
27 Cf. Wahrānī 182 sq., for details given in this paragraph.

28 TC. 86.
29 25757.36.
30 Bundārī 341.
31 W.T. 1063.
32 Bundārī 345.
33 W.T. 1062.
34 Bundārī 342.
35 I.A. 11.459.
36 *Ibid.* 11.460.
37 Mosul 78.
38 W.T. 1064.
39 Bundārī 345.
40 *Ibid.* 347.
41 I.A. 11.465.
42 Cf. *Khiṭaṭ* 1.60.
43 Munich 32.
44 I.A. 11.463.
45 Bundārī 357.
46 Cf. A.S. Ra. 2.17.
47 Q. 10.135.
48 Cit. A.S. Ra. 2.17.
49 I.S. 54.
50 Bundārī 347.
51 *Ibid.* 348.
52 Ibn Abī Ṭayy, cit. A.S. Ra. 2.18.
53 Cf. I.A. 11.469.
54 B.A. 11.
55 Bundārī 349.
56 Maqrīzī, *Sulūk* 71.
57 Wahrānī 182.
58 TC. 55.
59 Cf. Bundārī 353.

11 Opportunities

1 A.S. Ra. 2.19.
2 *Khiṭaṭ* 2.124.
3 Cf. *Sulūk* 73.
4 *Ibid.* 71.
5 *Ibid.* 74.
6 Cf. al-Makhzūmī 111 for a reference to Bedouin attempts to cheat the *dīwān*. On parades – used to check the number and type of troops provided by the tribes – after the cavalry had been

inspected, the foot-soldiers would borrow their mounts, in order to qualify for higher rates of pay.

7 25757.93.

8 *Sulūk* 72.

9 Cit. *Khiṭaṭ* 1.185.

10 *Sanā* 209.

11 *Ibid.* 210.

12 *Ibid.* 211 sq.

13 Berlin 56.

14 Mosul 73.

15 Cf. Berlin 47.

16 Cit. A.S. Ra. 2.21.

17 A.S. Ra. 2.21.

18 Cit. A.S. Ra. 2.22.

19 I.A. 11.473.

20 Ibn al-ʿAdīm 46.

21 Cit. *Sanā* 207.

22 Cit. *Sanā* 208; cf. A.S. Ra. 2.23; Ibn Wāṣil 110.

23 Paris 66; cf. A.S. Ra. 2.24.

24 Paris, A.S. *loc. cit.*

25 A.S. Ra. 2.23.

26 See *Sanā* 211.

27 See *Sulūk* 77.

28 Cf. *Khiṭaṭ* 1.407.

29 I.S. 55.

30 Cf. Ibn al-ʿAdīm 48–9.

31 Ibn al-ʿAdīm *loc. cit.*

32 I.A. 11.474.

33 Cf. Ibn al-ʿAdīm 52.

34 W.T. 1087.

35 *Sanā* 218, cit. A.S. Ra. 2.27.

36 W.T. 1063; for the conventional terms of such agreements, covering lives, property and merchandise, cf. Q. 14.58 and 67.

37 Cit. A.S. Ra. 2.26.

38 *Sanā* 211; A.S. Ra. 2.27; such statements are to be used with caution as they need represent no more than vague generalisations.

39 Cf. an anonymous poem in the *Ḥamāsa* of Abū Tammām (2.71); for its attribution to ʿAbd Allāh al-Qushairi, cf. al-Karmi, *Qaul ʿalā Qaul*, 2. 327.

40 Paris 42; cit., in part, Munich 111; 25756.101; A.S. Ra. 2.28.

41 W.T. 1087.

42 *Sanā* 219; cf. A.S. Ra. 2.28.

43 W.T. 1091.

44 *Ibid.* 1087.

45 The alternative form, al-Qurain, is found in Wahrānī 162.
46 25757.9.
47 W.T. 1089.
48 25757.9.
49 W.T. 1091.
50 25757.9.
51 *Sanā* 221.
52 For details of this action, cf. W.T. 1092 sq.; Paris 42.
53 *Sanā* 222.
54 *Ibid.* 224.
55 Cf. W.T. 1097.
56 *Ibid.* 1096.
57 Paris 51.
58 W.T. 1098.
59 Cf. W.T. 1100; the Franks had sent out a fleet of thirty-three galleys, but the Egyptians had left before it arrived.
60 I.S. 56.
61 *Sanā* 227; *Barq* 5.6A; A.S. Ra. 2.29.
62 I.A. 11.482.
63 Paris 63; 25757.56.
64 Paris 42; Munich 111.
65 Paris 56; 25757.22.

12 The capture of Aleppo

1 Paris 28
2 *Sanā* 227; *Barq* 5.7B.
3 25757.62.
4 I.S. 58
5 I.A. 11.482.
6 *Sanā* 227; cf. A.S. Ra. 2.30.
7 Cf. Ibn al-ʻAdīm 56.
8 Paris 12; 25757.27; cf. A.S. Ra. 2.31.
9 Cit. A.S. Ra. 2.30.
10 Bundārī 330.
11 *Sanā* 239.
12 I.A. 11.491.
13 *Sanā* 243.
14 I.A. 11.484.
15 25757.5; Berlin 41.
16 Nur. 52.
17 *Sanā* 230.
18 *Ibid.*
19 *Travels* 239.

20 I.A. 11.484.
21 For details, cf. Ibn al-'Adīm 59.
22 Cf. W.T. 1101 sq.
23 W.T. 1106
24 *Sanā* 230.
25 I.A. 11.485.
26 *Sanā* 230.
27 I.S. 57.
28 *Ibid.*
29 Paris 56.
30 I.A. 11.485.
31 *Ibid.*
32 Cf. *Sanā* 231; A.S. Ra. 2.32.
33 I.A. 11.486.
34 For this and details of the negotiations, cf. *Sanā* 231 sq.
35 I.A. 11.487.
36 Cf. *Sanā* 235; A.S. Ra. 2.33.
37 I.A. 11.487.
38 I.S. 57.
39 Cf. Paris 10.
40 Cf. 25757.36.
41 Cf. I.S. 57; Gibb (35, note 1) mistakes the position of Sa'd al-Dīn and assumes that he was granted the *iqṭā'* of Sinjār and that Ibn Shaddād's account is wrong. It is confirmed, however, by Munich 137.
42 I.A. 11.488.
43 Cf. *Barq* 14A; 23A.
44 Paris 10.
45 *Ibid.* 110; Mosul 66.
46 I.A. 11.488.
47 Paris 17; TC. 48.
48 25757.96.
49 25757.36.
50 Cf. 25757.29.
51 Paris 113; Leiden 13.
52 *Sanā* 242; A.S. Ra. 2.35.
53 I.A. 11.490.
54 *Travels* 59.
55 *Khiṭaṭ* 2.86.
56 Paris 113; Leiden 13.
57 *Travels* 60.
58 *Khiṭaṭ* 2.86.
59 Paris 114.
60 Cf. *Sanā* 243; Paris 114; 25757.131.
61 *Travels* 59.

62 *Barq* 43B; cf. Q. 4.155.
63 25757.29; A.S. Ra. 2.36.
64 Berlin 54; A.S. Ra. 2.36.
65 A.S. Ra. 2.36.
66 25757.29.
67 Cf. I.S. 58; I.A. 11.488 sq.; *Sanā* 238.
68 *Barq* 55A.
69 *Sanā* 247; the *Daulat al-Akrād* 7-8 doubtless exaggerates the numbers of the Egyptian reinforcements, putting them at 5000.
70 Berlin 57.
71 *Barq* 56A.
72 *Ibid.* 57B.
73 7465.197.
74 Berlin 57.
75 Cf. *Sanā* 248.
76 W.T. 1113.
77 Cf. *Kharīda* 1.197.
78 *Sanā* 245.
79 *Ibid.* 248.
80 25756.10; cf. A.S. Ra. 2.40.
81 Berlin 51.
82 I.A. 11.493. Gibb (36 note 2) is unnecessarily sceptical of Ibn al-Athīr's explanation. In view of the small size of the professional armies of the period, successful defence of towns required civilian co-operation, which normally had to be bought (cf. p. 200).
83 *Sanā* 249.
84 The date quoted by Ehrenkreutz (181), 6 May, cannot be reconciled with that of a letter (Paris 19; Munich 113) sent from Sarūj on Saturday 7 May (12 Muḥarram).
85 Cit. A.S. Ra. 2.39.
86 *Barq* 64B.
87 Munich 137.
88 *Ibid.* 126; A.S. Ra. 2.41.
89 Munich 123; Paris 3.
90 Munich 113; Paris 19; *Barq* 34A; A.S. Ra. 2.49.
91 Munich 117.
92 Cf. Munich 129; Berlin 6.
93 Berlin 10.
94 *Barq* 79A.
95 Cf. Ibn al-'Adīm 63 sq.
96 *Barq* 80A.
97 Berlin 69.
98 *Barq* 80B
99 W.T. 1113 sq.
100 Berlin 64.

101 *Sanā* 257; cf. the *Dīwān* of Abū Tammām 1.93.
102 Ibn al-'Adīm 66.
103 I.A. 11.497.
104 Ibn al-'Adīm 67.
105 TC. 19.
106 Ibn al-'Adīm 71.
107 *Sanā* 260; *Barq* 96B; for the dating, cf. I.S. 60; A.S. Ra. 2.44; Gibb 38; Ehrenkreutz 181.
108 Cf. Ibn al-'Adīm 69.
109 A.S. Ra. 2.44.
110 Berlin 75.
111 *Ibid.* 56.
112 Munich 140.
113 Berlin 58.
114 *Ibid.* 75.
115 A.S. Ra. 2.43.
116 Munich 140.
117 Cit. A.S. Ra. 2.43.
118 I.A. 11.497.
119 Ibn al-'Adīm 68.
120 Ibn Wāṣil 143.

13 Empire-building and the Holy War

1 Cf. p. 86.
2 A.S. Ra. 2.46.
3 *Sanā* 259; *Barq* 89B.
4 Cit. A.S. Ra. 2.46.
5 A.S. *loc. cit.*
6 *Barq* 89B.
7 Munich 131; Paris 36; Berlin 83; A.S. Ra. 2.48.
8 Berlin 72.
9 *Ibid.* 78.
10 Cit. A.S. Ra. 2.49.
11 Munich 140.
12 25757.30; Berlin 38; A.S. Ra. 2.47.
13 Berlin 44.
14 *Barq* 100 sq.
15 TC. 97.
16 Cf. W.T. 1115.
17 Paris 77.
18 *Ibid.* 70.
19 *Sanā* 265; *Barq* 112A.

20 W.T. 1118.
21 *Ibid.* 1122.
22 *Sanā* 266; *Barq* 112B.
23 W.T. 1119.
24 Cf. I.S. 62.
25 W.T. 1120.
26 *Ibid.* 1123.
27 Judges 7.12.
28 W.T. 1123.
29 *Sanā* 266.
30 *Barq* 114A.
31 W.T. 1124.
32 Paris 72.
33 *Sanā* 267; *Barq* 117A.
34 Cit. A.S. Ra. 2.52; cf. Ibn al-'Adīm 75.
35 *Sanā* 268; *Barq* 118A.
36 W.T. 1124.
37 *Sanā* 268; *Barq* 118B; W.T. (1129) gives this as eight mangonels – six in the township and two outside it. That this was an adequate figure for a siege-train can be seen from the figure of nine mangonels quoted for the second siege of Kerak (cf. p. 217).
38 25757.33 'Imād al-Dīn (*Sanā* 267) represents Taqī al-Dīn as having accompanied Saladin to Kerak, but must have telescoped his account.
39 W.T. 1126; the story that Saladin did not bombard the tower in which the young couple were housed is ignored in the Arabic sources.
40 *Barq* 126B.
41 Ibn al-'Adīm 74.
42 *Sanā* 268; *Barq* 118B.
43 *Barq* 126B.
44 *Sanā* 270; *Barq* 126B.
45 Cf. *Sanā* 321.
46 A.S. Ra. 2.53.
47 7465.2.
48 7465.3.
49 7465.10. The well-known Fāḍilī quotation (*Khiṭaṭ* 1.100) gives a figure of 4,653,029 dinars for Egyptian revenue covering the country "from Alexandria to 'Aidhāb", excluding the *thughūr*, the *arbāb al-amwāl al-dīwānīya*, and "a number of regions". The present quotation is self-consistent, in that the daily expenditure of 17,000 dinars gives an annual total of 6,205,000. The disparity between it and the figure given in the *Khiṭaṭ* calls into question the importance of the exceptions listed there, but it may also represent accounting differences, i.e. whether certain expenses

are set off against income, which is then not listed, and also perhaps variants in the treatment of the *jaishī* dinar. It underlines the fact that totals given by contemporary authors cannot be accepted at face value until it is clear how they have been reached and precisely what they cover.

50 *Sanā* 273; *Barq* 130B.

51 I.A. 11.499.

52 *Barq* 134A.

53 7465.24.

54 Ibn al-'Adīm 77.

55 I.S. 64.

56 *Sanā* 271; *Barq* 128B.

57 7465.20; Mosul 80.

58 *Sanā* 273; *Barq* 130B.

59 *Sanā* 272; *Barq* 129B.

60 *Sanā* 273 sq.; *Barq* 130B sq.

61 Cf. the refusal of Saladin's gifts by Bektimur at Sinjār in 1182 (p. 183).

62 *Sanā* 288.

63 I.A. 11.504.

64 7465.20; Mosul 80.

65 *Sulūk* 87.

66 Cit. *Sanā* 277.

67 *Sanā* 278.

68 *Sulūk* 84.

69 I.S. 66.

70 Ibn Wāṣil 157.

71 *Sanā* 278.

72 A.S. Ra. 2.55–6.

73 *Sanā* 279.

74 *Travels* 298 sq.

75 *Sanā* 280.

76 Ernoul 105.

77 *Sanā* 280.

78 *Travels* 299.

79 *Sanā* 280.

80 7307.27.

81 I.S. 67.

82 *Sanā* 281 – "Saladin sent [*ajrā*] his cavalry to Nablus – the army took spoils – on his/its way back he/it halted at Sebaste – we joined forces at al-Fawwār."

83 Cf. letter quoted by Raoul de Diceto, *Ymagines historiarum*, 2.27 – "Salahedinus... Neapolim venit."

84 *Sulūk* 84.

85 *Travels* 300 sq.

86 *Sanā* 279.
87 I.A. 11.509.
88 *Sanā* 281.
89 Nur. 52.
90 I.A. 11.509.
91 *Sanā* 282.

14 The end of empire

1 Sulūk 85.
2 *Travels* 309.
3 Cambridge 23; the attribution of the letter to al-Fāḍil is perhaps supported by its tone and, in particular, by the reference to disapproval of Taqī al-Dīn's actions; on the other hand, there is no other evidence that al-Fāḍil went to Hama on this occasion.
4 Munich 22.
5 7465.38; Mosul 84.
6 Cf. I.S. 67.
7 Cf. I.S. 67.
8 Cf. p. 215.
9 *Sanā* 293.
10 7465.45.
11 7465.46.
12 7465.50
13 *Sanā* 294 sq.
14 7465.46 (2).
15 I.A. 11.511.
16 *Sanā* 295.
17 I.S. 68.
18 7465.174.
19 I.S. 68.
20 He failed in his attempts on the first two towns, but established himself at Khartpirt. Saladin was urged to take back Āmid, as his advisers were suspicious of the "behaviour and secret thoughts" (*Sanā* 303) of those who were in charge of Nūr al-Dīn's heir, Suqmān. Ibn al-Farrāsh was sent to investigate. On his advice, Suqmān was presented to Saladin by the vizier al-Qawwām and then confirmed in possession of Ḥiṣn Kaifā and Āmid.
21 *Sanā* 297.
22 *Ibid.* 297 sq.
23 I.A. 11.512.
24 Ibn al-'Adīm 81.
25 *Sanā* 309.
26 Gibb (42 note 1) prefers the earlier date for the incident. He

rejects the suggestion, followed by Barhebraeus (*Syriac Chronography* 319) that two approaches were made.

27 *Sanā* 299: the text of Ibn Wāṣil (167) gives "west".
28 *Sanā* 299.
29 *Ibid.* 300.
30 Munich 19.
31 *Sanā* 300. The proposal was not without recent precedent; for a plan to divert the Oxus, in 568 A.H., cf. I.A. 11.378.
32 I.A. 11.513.
33 Cf. *Sanā* 302.
34 *Sanā* 301.
35 Cit. *Sanā* 302.
36 I.A. 11.515.
37 *Sanā* 304.
38 *Mu'jam al-buldān*, 5.237.
39 *Sanā* 305.
40 *Ibid.* 306.
41 7465.50.
42 7465.156.
43 7465.158.
44 7465.154.
45 Munich 72.
46 *Sanā* 303.
47 *Ibid.* 307.
48 *Ibid.* 308.
49 I.S. 69.
50 Cf. 7465.162.
51 *Ibid.*
52 *Sanā* 308.
53 I.S. 70.
54 *Sanā* 308.
55 Munich 70.
56 *Sanā* 308.
57 Munich 11.
58 *Ibid.* 59.
59 7465.170.
60 7465.172.
61 7465.167.
62 Munich 88.
63 *Ibid.* 45.
64 *Sanā* 311.
65 7465.161.
66 *Sanā* 317.
67 7465.166.
68 7465.163.

69 25757.117.
70 7465.164.
71 *Sanā* 313.
72 Al-Fāḍil, cit. A.S. Ra. 2.67.
73 Cf. I.A. 11.518.
74 I.A. *loc. cit.*; for a report that he was poisoned by his wife, Saladin's sister, cf. Ibn Abī'l-Haijā' 182.
75 I.S. 70.
76 Cf. Munich 65. For the last sentence, cf. al-Mutanabbi, *Dīwān*, ed. Dieterici (Berlin 1961), 579.
77 Munich 83.
78 Cit. A.S. Ra. 2.64.
79 I.S. 70.
80 Ibn al-'Adīm 83.
81 Cit. A.S. Ra. 2.65.

15 Preparations

1 *Sanā* 323.
2 I.A. 11.518.
3 Quran 4.10.
4 *Sanā* 324.
5 *Ibid.* 325.
6 *Ibid.*
7 Munich 26.
8 Cf. Munich 72.
9 Cf. Munich 63.
10 Munich 57.
11 Details in this and in the following paragraph are derived from *Sanā* 325–6.
12 I.A. 11.525.
13 I.S. 72.
14 *Sanā* 327.
15 *Ibid.*
16 *Ibid.*; an example of this obstinacy was his refusal to surrender the *iqṭā'* of Hama when he moved to Egypt (cf. *Sanā* 322).
17 Cit. A.S. Ra. 2.70.
18 Quran 11.80.
19 I.A. 11.524.
20 *Sanā* 328.
21 *Ibid.* 335.
22 Cf. Wahrānī's definition of *fiqh* as the science of "spitting in the face of one's opponent" (101).
23 Michael the Syrian XVIII.10.398.
24 *Sanā* 330.
25 *Ibid.* 331.

26 *Ibid.* 350; A.S. Ra. 2.80.
27 *Sanā* 337 sq.; I.A. 11.526.
28 *Continuation* 64 sq.; for an account of these events, cf. Riley-Smith, *The Knights of St. John in Jerusalem and Cyprus,* 81.
29 *Continuation* 66.
30 *Sanā* 338.
31 *Ibid.*
32 *Sanā* 339.
33 *Ibid.;* I.A. 11.527.
34 *Continuation* 58.
35 Munich 83.
36 The reference is to Umm Jamīl bint Ḥarb, who dropped thorns in front of the Prophet.
37 Munich 71.
38 Cit. A.S. Ra. 2.75.
39 Cf. Munich 84.
40 *Fatḥ* 104.
41 *Sanā* 342.
42 *Sanā loc. cit.*; cf. I.A. 11.531.
43 Anon., *Libellus* 5.
44 *Ibid.* 6.
45 *Itinerary of Richard* I 70.
46 *Libellus* 5.
47 Cf. *Sanā* 342; I.A. 11.531.
48 Nur. 3.
49 *Continuation* 67.
50 Munich 84.
51 I.S. 75.
52 7465.209.
53 7465.54; for this episode, cf. Brand, "The Byzantines and Saladin", 168–9.
54 I.A. 11.527.
55 *Continuation* 67.
56 Cf. Munich 82.
57 I.S. 75.
58 *Fatḥ* 15.
59 Paris 90.
60 *Sanā* 342; I.A. 11.531.
61 Cit. *Continuation* 80.
62 Cf. *Continuation* 72.
63 Munich 84; but cf. a letter quoted by A.S. Ra. 2.82, which suggests, without specifying the time, that most of the emirs were in favour of a battle.
64 Nur. 5.
65 I.A. 11.532.
66 *Ibid.* 11.533; cf. *Sanā* 344 – "lives are not guaranteed... I must do battle."

16 Ḥaṭṭīn

1 *Sanā* 343.
2 I.S. 76; this term (*saṭḥ*) is used more appropriately later in this passage to describe the plateau of the Horns of Ḥaṭṭīn. A possible emendation here would give *safḥ* ("foot" of the mountain).
3 *Fatḥ* 105.
4 Nur. 5.
5 *Ibid.*
6 Cf. *Sanā* 344.
7 Paris 90; TC. 29.
8 Cf. *Estoire d' Eracles* 52.
9 I.A. 11.533.
10 Cf. *Libellus* 68.
11 *Fatḥ* 22.
12 Cit. *Continuation* 81.
13 It must be stressed that Gibb is indulging in conjecture where he writes (53) that Ibn al-Athīr "hits off Raymond's attitude correctly, at least in the first part of the argument".
14 Cf. *Libellus* 69: "per turmas suas processerunt"; for the implications of this phrase, cf. *Continuation* 103: "procedit acies ad delicias intuencium prudenter digesta, nam nec simul nec sparsim, sed per turmas incedit".
15 Cf. A.S. Ra. 2.82.
16 Paris 90; TC. 29.
17 A valuable description of the roads in question, together with a survey of the sources, is found in Prawer, "La bataille de Hattin".
18 Paris 90; TC. 29.
19 Paris, TC. *loc. cit.*
20 Cf. Ansbertus 4.
21 Prawer, "La bataille de Hattin", comments on the vulnerability of horses at this period; a reference to Frankish horse armour is found in I.S. 150.
22 *Sanā* 348.
23 *Ibid.* 345.
24 *Ibid.* 345 sq.; *Fatḥ* 22 sq.
25 *Libellus* 71.
26 *Fatḥ* 24.
27 Cf. Nur. 5; William of Tyre, writing of the battle of Antioch in the First Crusade, noted: "according to their usual method, they set fire to the stubble" (pt 1, p. 292).
28 Cf. Ansbertus 3.
29 *Libellus* 71.
30 Cf. I.A. 11.535; *Fatḥ* 24.
31 *Continuation* 70.

32 Nur. 5.
33 Paris 90; TC. 29.
34 Nur. 5.
35 I.A. 11.536.
36 *Sanā* 348.
37 For this account, cf. I.S. 78.
38 *Continuation* 71.
39 I.A. 11.537.
40 *Sanā* 350.
41 Nur. 5.
42 *Ibid.*
43 *Sanā* 349.
44 I.S. 77.
45 *Fatḥ* 27.
46 A.S. Ra. 2.82.
47 *Sanā* 349 sq.; cf. *Fatḥ* 28.
48 *Continuation* 71.
49 Paris 90; TC. 29.
50 Cf. A.S. Ra. 2.82; *Khiṭaṭ* 2.234 puts the Frankish force at 50,000.

17 The capture of Jerusalem

1 *Sanā* 353.
2 Cit. A.S. Ra. 2.86; for a note on al-Qāsim b. al-Mahnā (Zambaur, *Manuel de Généalogie* 114) cf. Q. 4.300.
3 *Sanā* 351.
4 I.A. 11.539.
5 *Sanā* 353.
6 I.A. 11.539.
7 *Ibid.* 12.25; the quotation need not necessarily be authentic but must represent what could reasonably be believed of Saladin.
8 Cit. Ansbertus 4 sq.
9 *Sanā* 355.
10 I.A. 11.541.
11 I.S. 80.
12 *Sanā* 356.
13 I.A. 11.543.
14 *Fatḥ* 37.
15 *Continuation* 74.
16 *Fatḥ* 39 sq.
17 *Sanā* 358.
18 I.S. 80.
19 *Fatḥ* 44.

20 Cf. *Continuation* 73, note 163.
21 *Continuation* 73.
22 I.A. 11.544.
23 *Sanā* 360.
24 *Ibid.*
25 *Sanā* 361.
26 I.A. 11.545.
27 TC. 98.
28 Ḥusām al-Dīn Ibrāhīm al-Mihrānī; cf. *Sanā* 361.
29 Cf. *Sanā* 362.
30 W.T. pt 1, p. 383.
31 I.A. 11.546 sq.; I.S. 81; *Sanā* 364.
32 *Sanā* 363.
33 *Continuation* 75; this was echoed by Saladin, who wrote that the refugees thought that the church (of the Holy Sepulchre) would intercede with God for them (Cairo 15; Q. 6.496).
34 *Libellus* 87.
35 W.T. pt 1, p. 360.
36 I.A. 11.548.
37 *Libellus* 88.
38 *Ibid.* 89; cf. *Kharīda* 1.158 for a line by the poet al-Adīb al-Qaisarānī addressed to Nūr al-Dīn: "nothing can cleanse Jerusalem except flowing blood".
39 Cf. Cairo 15; Q. 6.496 (Paris 79; TC. 103; 25757.119).
40 For the figure of 3000, cf. A.S. Ra. 2.92; for 5000, cf. *Sanā* 365; according to Ibn Jubair (*Travels* 306) a similar proposal had been made by Muslims before the capture of Tyre by the Crusaders but had not been carried out.
41 *Fatḥ* 55.
42 *Continuation* 75.
43 *Libellus* 90.
44 *Fatḥ* 60.
45 *Sanā* 368.
46 *Fatḥ* 55 sq.
47 I.A. 11.550.
48 *Fatḥ* 60.
49 *Sanā* 374.
50 TC. 137.
51 7307.89.
52 Cairo 15.
53 *Sanā* 368.
54 *Fatḥ* 63; *Sanā* 369; amongst the preachers was Zain al-Dīn 'Alī (cf. p. 68).
55 Cairo 15.
56 *Fatḥ* 61 sq.; *Sanā* 369, 371.

57 *Fatḥ* 69; cf. W. T. pt 1, p. 334 for a proposal made by the Muslims at the time of the First Crusade "to overthrow from its very foundation the Church of the Resurrection of the Lord and utterly destroy the Sepulchre of the Lord contained therein. This action would, they hoped, keep away in the future the great concourse of pilgrims who flocked thither."
58 *Fatḥ* 60–1.
59 *Ibid.* 55.
60 *Ibid.* 56.
61 I.S. 82.
62 *Sanā* 374–5.

18 Success and failure

1 Cf. 7465.180.
2 Cf. *Continuation* 78.
3 *Sanā* 376.
4 I.S. (83) dates his arrival to 21 November, but 'Imād al-Dīn appears to suggest that he came after Saladin had moved to the Tell (*Sanā* 376).
5 *Fatḥ* 79.
6 7465.182.
7 7465.180.
8 *Sanā* 379.
9 *Fatḥ* 96 sq.
10 *Ibid.* 97.
11 Cit. A.S. Ra. 2.122.
12 *Fatḥ* 99.
13 7465.181.
14 *Fatḥ* 99.
15 7465.183.
16 Cit. *Continuation* 88.
17 *Fatḥ* 80.
18 *Ibid.* 81.
19 *Sanā* 380.
20 Cf. *Sanā* 383.
21 I.A. 11.556.
22 *Fatḥ* 88.
23 Cf. *Itinerary of Richard I* 81.
24 *Fatḥ* 89.
25 According to I.S. (82) the Franks who left Jerusalem went to Tyre, but the Latin *Continuation* (75) reports that they were allowed a choice of Alexandria, from where they could sail to Europe, or Antioch.

26 I.A. 11.555.
27 De Bourrienne, *Memoirs of Napoleon Bonaparte*, 158.
28 Cf. *Sanā* 381.
29 Cf. *Sanā* 383; for a note on Saladin's monetary crisis at this time, cf. Rabie, *The Financial System of Egypt*, 173.
30 Nur. 44.
31 Cf. I.A. 11.559.
32 *Sanā* 392.
33 Cf. *Fatḥ* 101; A.S. Ra. 2.123; Ibn Abī'l-Haijā' 187.
34 I.A. 11.559.
35 Cf. Berlin 64.
36 *Fatḥ* 117.
37 *Ibid.*; this phrase is found almost *verbatim* in the *Continuation*: "quasi clavis erat tocius regionis" (113).
38 Cf. *Fatḥ* 110.
39 *Fatḥ* 128.
40 *Ibid.* 130.
41 Cf. *Fatḥ* 132.
42 7307.24.
43 Cit. A.S. Ra. 2.128.
44 *Fatḥ* 141.
45 I.A. 12.10.
46 *Ibid.* 12.11.
47 *Fatḥ* 146.
48 I.S. 92.
49 I.A. 12.15.
50 *Fatḥ* 151.
51 A.S. Ra. 2.131.
52 I.A. 12.17.
53 *Fatḥ* 153.
54 Cit. A.S. Ra. 2.131.
55 Cit. A.S. Ra. 2.132.
56 I.S. 93.
57 TC. 37.
58 *Fatḥ* 157.
59 7307.28.
60 I.S. 94; *Fatḥ* 158.
61 *Fatḥ* 157; a *ghirāra* was the "moderate amount of wheat that a man could carry under his arm" (*Itinerary of Richard I* 143).
62 I.S. 94.
63 *Ibid.* 95.,
64 Cit. A.S. Ra. 2.134.
65 I.A. 12.20.
66 *Fatḥ* 161.
67 I.A. 12.22.

68 *Fatḥ* 166.
69 Cit. A.S. Ra. 2.136.
70 I.S. 96.
71 *Fatḥ* 166.
72 Cit. A.S. Ra. 2.136; Q. 7.23.
73 7465.62.
74 7465.71; Mosul 43.
75 7465.65.
76 7465.76.
77 7465.65.
78 7465.69.

19 Crusaders at Acre

1 Cit. A.S. Ra. 2.137.
2 I.S. 98.
3 I.A. 12.27.
4 *Ibid.*
5 TC. 34.
6 *Continuation* 110.
7 I.S. 98.
8 7465.52.
9 I.A. 12.29.
10 *Fatḥ* 182.
11 *Ibid.*
12 I.S. 100.
13 *Ibid.* 101.
14 *Fatḥ* 180.
15 I.S. 103.
16 *Continuation* 113.
17 *Ibid.*
18 Cf. *Fatḥ* 186; I.S. 104.
19 *Fatḥ* 188.
20 I.S. 103.
21 I.S. (104) explained the detour on the grounds that this road was the only one which could accommodate the army.
22 *Continuation* 114.
23 Cit. A.S. Ra. 2.143.
24 I.S. 105.
25 7465.80; Mosul 46.
26 7465.90; Mosul 3.
27 'Imād al-Dīn, cit. A.S. Ra. 2.143.
28 *Ibid.* cit. A.S. Ra. 2.144.

29 *Fatḥ* 191; 'Imād al-Dīn is glossing over a genuine difficulty (cf. also p. 169). The earlier an action begins, particularly in hot weather, the more likely it is that a second watering will be needed; cf. *Field Service Pocket Book*, pt 2, India: "animals do not drink well in the early morning... Opportunities to feed, water, and rest men and horses should be found even during the progress of battle" (15).
30 I.S. 106.
31 *Ibid.* 107.
32 7465.90; Mosul 3.
33 Nur. 19.
34 7465.96.
35 Cf. *Fatḥ* 200.
36 I.S. 111; *Fatḥ* 198.
37 *Fatḥ* 198.
38 Ambroise, *L'Estoire*, 1.2997 sq.
39 I.S. 111.
40 *Ibid.* 112.
41 *Fatḥ* 207.
42 I.S. 113.
43 Cf. *Fatḥ* 201 sq.
44 7465.100.
45 7465.85.
46 Cf. I.S. 114; *Fatḥ* 209.
47 A.S. Ra. 2.146.
48 *Fatḥ* 210.
49 *Ibid.* 211.
50 *Ibid.* 212.
51 *Ibid.*
52 *Fatḥ* 216.
53 *Ibid.* 216 sq.
54 *Ibid.* 219.
55 *Ibid.*
56 I.S. 115.
57 Cf. *Fatḥ* 221.
58 Cf. 7465.87.
59 7465.94.
60 *Fatḥ* 214.
61 *Ibid.* 230.

20 The fall of Acre

1 *Fatḥ* 234.
2 *Ibid.* 233.

3 *Ibid.* 239.
4 Cf. 25757.36.
5 Bundārī 236; these figures coincide well enough, providing a daily total of some 13 dinars. They do not refer to purely personal expenditure, but to the general expenses of a body of servants. The same average would translate Saladin's 20,000 dinars into a force of just over 1500, which would then have to be multiplied by the number of their own followers. This would represent only one division of the Muslim army (Saladin's *ḥalqa*), as other commanders would be responsible for the pay of their own troops.
6 *Fatḥ* 243.
7 Cf. B.A., year 586 A.H.
8 I.A. 12.45.
9 I.S. 120.
10 *Continuation* 120.
11 *Fatḥ* 243.
12 Cf. *Fatḥ* 247; A.S. Ra. 2.154.
13 Cf. 7307.58; 25756.68.
14 Cit. A.S. Ra. 2.151.
15 Cit. A.S. Ra. 2.157.
16 Cit. A.S. *loc. cit.*
17 Munich 4; Paris 87; cit. A.S. Ra. 2.157.
18 I.A. 12.50.
19 *Continuation* 123.
20 *Fatḥ* 267.
21 *Ibid.* 263.
22 *Ibid.* 262.
23 7465.101; this is not to be taken as a scribal error for Almān, as al-Fāḍil plays on the root *amina* (cf. p. 316).
24 *Continuation* 125.
25 A.S. Ra. 2.154.
26 *Continuation* 125.
27 *Fatḥ* 257.
28 7465.101; 25756.80.
29 *Itinerary* 120.
30 Correctly given here in the Latin *Continuation* as nephew (126).
31 *Fatḥ* 272.
32 *Ibid.* 274.
33 7465.113.
34 TC. 135.
35 *Fatḥ* 279.
36 *Ibid.* 265.
37 Cit. A.S. Ra. 2.157; I.S. 127.
38 Cit. *Fatḥ* 266.

39 *Continuation* 128.
40 I.S. 137.
41 *Fatḥ* 287.
42 7465.106.
43 I.S. 135.
44 *Ibid.* 138.
45 Cit. A.S. Ra. 2.166.
46 Munich 81.
47 *Fatḥ* 290.
48 *Ibid.* 292.
49 *Ibid.* 287.
50 Cit. A.S. Ra. 2.176.
51 Cf. Munich 29.
52 A.S. Ra. 2.171; cf. also Q.6.526.; Gaudefroy-Demombynes, "Une Lettre de Saladin au calife Almohade", 289 sq.
53 I.S. 144.
54 *Fatḥ* 298.
55 *Ibid.*
56 I.A. 12.56.
57 Cf. I.S. 145; I.A. 12.60 sq.
58 I.S. 145.
59 I.A. 12.61.
60 *Ibid.* 12.62.
61 I.S. 146.
62 Cit. A.S. Ra. 2.167.
63 *L'Estoire* 1.4001.
64 I.S. 147.
65 *Ibid.* 148.
66 Ambroise *L'Estoire*, 1.4023.
67 I.S. 149.
68 *L'Estoire* 4070.
69 I.S. 149.
70 *Ibid.* 150.
71 *Ibid.* 147.
72 *Ibid.* 151.
73 *Ibid.* 153.
74 *Fatḥ* 212 sq.
75 Cit. A.S. Ra. 2.166.
76 7465.92; Mosul 4.
77 Munich 104.
78 Nur. 23.
79 The Arabic gives "Antioch"; for this confusion, cf. p. 342, note 54.
80 Cf. I.S. 220.
81 7465.107; cf. A.S. Ra. 2.185.
82 I.A. 12.61.

83 I.S. 156.
84 *Ibid.*
85 I.S. 158.
86 Cit. A.S. Ra. 2.183.
87 Cf. *Fatḥ* 329.
88 Cf. A.S. Ra. 2.178.
89 I.S. 157.
90 I.A. 12.65.
91 I.S. 161.
92 *Fatḥ* 337.
93 I.S. 164.
94 *Fatḥ* 342.
95 I.S. 199.
96 Cit. A.S. Ra. 2.196.
97 Cit. A.S. Ra. 2.186.
98 Cit. *Fatḥ* 346.
99 Cit. *Fatḥ* 349.
100 *Fatḥ* 348.
101 I.S. 166.
102 *Continuation* 140.
103 I.S. 166.
104 *Ibid.* 168.
105 *Ibid; Fatḥ* 352.
106 'Izz al-Dīn Arsal; cf. *Continuation* 140, "Essenditi", wrongly identified by the editor as 'Izz al-Dīn Jūrdīk.
107 *Fatḥ* 353.
108 I.S. 168.
109 Maqrīzī, *Sulūk* 94.
110 A.S. Ra. 2.187.
111 I.S. 170; Ambroise (*L'Estoire* 1.5204) gives this as 2000 nobles and 500 men of inferior rank, and the *Continuation* (141) as 200 knights, 1000 men of lesser rank and the 500 Franks held in Acre itself.
112 This is contradicted by Ambroise (*L'Estoire* 1.5207), who says that the terms did not cover property.
113 I.S. 171.
114 *Ibid.*
115 *Fatḥ* 358.

21 Stalemate

1 Ibn Abī'l-Haijā' 201.
2 *Fatḥ* 358.
3 Cf. *Fatḥ* 368.

4 *Ibid.*
5 *Continuation* 142.
6 *Fatḥ* 359.
7 *Continuation* 141.
8 *Fatḥ* 359.
9 I.S. 173.
10 Cit. A.S. Ra. 2.189.
11 I.S. 173.
12 I.A. 12.68.
13 I.S. 173; *Fatḥ* 371.
14 *Continuation* 142.
15 I.S. 174.
16 *Ibid.*
17 I.S. 175 – this was the reason given for Napoleon's massacre of his prisoners at Jaffa. Grousset's remark (*Histoire des Croisades* 2.61), "cet acte de barbarisme inouie...produisit dans tout l'Islam un effet désastreux", is ill-founded. There appears to have been no significant reaction.
18 There are a number of familiar problems and inconsistencies in the accounts of this march, to which nothing new can be added here. In part these may be due to the fact that the Franks do not always appear to have moved as a single unit. The *Itinerary of Richard I* (230) notes that the army advanced to "a town called Merla" (al-Mallāha) "where the king had spent one of the previous nights". This suggests that where circumstances allowed, the advance guard was detached. Difficulties of dating derive from the fact that, although Arabic and western sources agree on the days of the week, the Arab writers take Sunday 25 August to be 1 Sha'bān, whereas it should be 2 Sha'bān (for this difficulty cf. Stevenson, *The Crusaders in the East*, 356.361). Ibn Shaddād's account is, in general, the clearest and should be preferred.
19 I.S. 175.
20 *Fatḥ* 376.
21 I.S. 175.
22 *Ibid.* 178.
23 Cit. *Fatḥ* 378.
24 I.S. 179.
25 *Ibid.* 180.
26 *Fatḥ* 380.
27 *L'Estoire* 1.6025; the *Itinerary of Richard I* (231) dates his death to the previous day's march.
28 *Fatḥ* 381.
29 Cit. *Fatḥ* 386; cf. A.S. Ra. 2.191, where this is referred to as the battle of "Monday 9 Sha'bān when the enemy left Caesarea".

30 I.S. 182.

31 *Ibid.* 184; Ibn Shaddād's account of the battle is given on pp. 183–5.

32 *L'Estoire* 6137 sq.

33 *Ibid.* 6212.

34 Cit. A.S. Ra. 2.191.

35 Grousset (*Histoire des Croisades* 2.78) underestimates the difficulties by writing of Richard: "au lendemain de la victoire d'Arsuf, il aurait pu sans doute marcher droit sur la Ville Sainte, alors sans défense, et l'emporter de haute lutte".

36 *L'Estoire* 6898.

37 *Ibid.* 6871.

38 I.S. 185.

39 *Ibid.*; it is, of course, impossible to determine with exactitude the course of the river at this period.

40 Cit. A.S. Ra. 2.193.

41 *Fatḥ* 385.

42 *Ibid.* 389.

43 I.S. 186.

44 *Ibid.*

45 *Fatḥ* 390.

46 I.S. 187.

47 *Itinerary of Richard I* 247.

48 I.A. 12.71.

49 I.S. 188.

50 *L'Estoire* 1.7097.

51 I.S. 190; *Fatḥ* 391.

52 Cit. *Khiṭaṭ* 2.24.

53 *Fatḥ* 392.

54 I.S. 191; the text states that Philip died of illness at Antioch – perhaps another instance of confusion between Antioch and Italy or Antaliya (cf. p. 324, note 79).

55 I.S. 194.

56 *Ibid.* 195.

57 *Ibid.* for inter-marriages in the eleventh century between Christian princesses and Muslim rulers, cf. Lévi-Provençal, *Histoire de l'Espagne Musulmane*, 2.241–2.

58 *Fatḥ* 394.

59 I.S. 196.

60 *Ibid.* 197.

61 *Ibid.*

62 I.S. 202.

63 The omission of Beirut from the text of I.S. (203) may represent a scribal error.

64 *L'Estoire* 1.8700.

65 I.S. 202-3.
66 *Fatḥ* 398.
67 *Ibid.* 413.
68 *L'Estoire* 1.7631.
69 Cit. A.S. Ra. 2.194.
70 *Fatḥ* 231.
71 Cf. *Continuation* 82.
72 Cf. Ambroise, *L'Estoire*, 1.7691; *Continuation* 146.
73 I.A. 12.75.
74 *L'Estoire* 1.7933.
75 *Itinerary of Richard I* 261.
76 *Khiṭaṭ* 1.180; cf. Maqrīzī, *Sulūk*, 111.
77 *Fatḥ* 399.
78 *Ibid.* 401.
79 I.S. 205.
80 *Ibid.* 206.
81 *Ibid.* 207.
82 *Ibid.* 206.
83 *Ibid.* 207.
84 Cf. Ambroise, *L'Estoire*, 1.8885.
85 I.A. 12.78.
86 *Fatḥ* 422.
87 Cit. A.S. Ra. 2.178; cf. *d* version of the *Continuation* of William of Tyre; "apres ce que le rei Guy ot paie les .lx.m. besants au rei d'Engleterre, il ala en Chypre, et mena partie des chevaliers qui estoient deserites dou reiaume. Ensi come il fu saissi de l'isle, il manda ses messages a Salahadin requerant lui de conseill" (MS. Lyon. bibl. mun. 828, f. 330*a*). For this reference we are indebted to the kindness of Dr Ruth Morgan.
88 *Itinerary of Richard I* 301.
89 *Fatḥ* 423.
90 I.S. 211.
91 *Ibid.*
92 I.S. 212.
93 *Ibid.*
94 L'Estoire 1.9817.
95 *Fatḥ* 424.
96 I.S. 213.
97 *L'Estoire* 1.10269.
98 *Fatḥ* 425.
99 Wavell (*The Palestine Campaigns* 131–2) described Tell al-Khuwailifa as "a dominating height some ten miles north of Beersheba...which not only gave observation over all the surrounding country but commanded the best supplies of water in the neighbourhood".

100 *Fatḥ* 425.
101 I.S. 215.
102 *Ibid.* 214.
103 *L'Estoire* 1.10340 sq.
104 I.A. 12.82.
105 I.S. 214.
106 *Kitāb al-ishārāt* 3.
107 I.S. 215.
108 Cf. A.S. Ra. 2.137.
109 Cf. I.S. 218.
110 I.S. 215.
111 *Ibid.* 216.
112 A.S. Ra. 2.199.
113 *L'Estoire* 1.10208.
114 Details of these negotiations are quoted from I.S. 218 sq.
115 For Ibn Shaddād's account of the fighting at Jaffa, see I.S. 222 sq.
116 The text of I.S. (223) gives *yad*; the correct reading, *yazak*, is found in Ibn Abī'l-Haijā' (204).
117 I.S. 12.84
118 *L'Estoire* 1.11111.
119 I.S. 227.
120 *Ibid.* 228.
121 *Ibid.* 229.
122 *Ibid.* 30.
123 *Fatḥ* 435.
124 I.S. 232.
125 *Ibid.* 234.
126 *Ibid.* 235.
127 *Ibid.* 236.
128 *Itinerary of Richard I* 331.
129 I.S. 236.
130 *Ibid.* 237.
131 Cit .A.S. Ra. 2.205.
132 Mosul 68.
133 I.S. 238.
134 *Ibid.* 242.
135 Details of Saladin's last illness are quoted from I.S. 243 sq.

22 Conclusion

1 *Guerre d'Orient* 82.
2 Cit. A.S. Ra. 2.138.
3 7307.21.

4 Bundārī 287.
5 *Ibid.* 306.
6 *Ibid.* 352.
7 Munich 113.
8 Abū Ṣāliḥ 204.
9 Wahrānī 182.
10 Cf. I.S. 239.
11 See p. 88.
12 Bundārī 322.
13 Cit. Bundārī 298.
14 Cit. Bundārī 279.
15 TC. 75.
16 Cit. A.S. Ra. 2.177.
17 TC. 147.
18 See p. 361.
19 7465.137.
20 See p. 83.
21 *Travels* 71.
22 See p. 236.
23 Cf. similiarities in detail and tone between the account of negotiations between Taqī al-Dīn's Turks and the inhabitants of Libyan Tripoli (A.S. Ra. 2.38) and Nicetas' description (397) of the capture of Thessalonica by the Latins.
24 7307.98.
25 7465.238.
26 7465.222.
27 Bourienne, *Memoirs of Napoleon Bonaparte*, 85.
28 I.S. 22.
29 Cit. A.S. Ra. 2.148.
30 Cit. A.S. Ra. 2.210.
31 The author is Kamāl al-Dīn al-Shahrazūrī (cf. *Sanā* 398) and the line is based on one by al-Misjāḥ b. Sibā' cit. Abū Tammām, *Ḥamāsa*, 1.417.
32 7465.81.
33 Ambroise, *L'Estoire*, 5069.
34 I.S. 246.

BIBLIOGRAPHY

BEO = *Bulletin d'Études Orientales*
BFA = *Bulletin of the Faculty of Arts, Cairo University*
JAOS = *Journal of the American Oriental Society*
JESHO = *Journal of the Economic and Social History of the Orient*
JRAS = *Journal of the Royal Asiatic Society*
MMIA = *Majallat al-majma' al-'ilmī al-'arabī*
MMII = *Majallat al majma 'al-'ilmī al-'irāqī*

WORKS REFERRED TO IN THE NOTES: (A) EASTERN
(B) OTHERS

(A) Eastern

Abū Ṣāliḥ al-Armanī: *The churches and monasteries of Egypt and some neighbouring countries,* ed. and trans. B.T.A. Evetts, Oxford 1895.

Abū Shāma, 'Abd al-Raḥmān b. Ismā'īl: *Kitāb al-rauḍatain fī akhbār al-daulatain,* vol. 1.1–2, ed. M.H.M. Aḥmad and M.M. Ziyāda, Cairo 1956, 1962; vols. 1 and 2, Cairo 1870.

Abū Tammām, Ḥabīb b. Aus: *Dīwān,* ed. M. 'Azzām, 3 vols., Cairo 1951–7.
Dīwān al-Ḥamāsa, reprint of the 1331 A.H. edition, 1969.

Aḥmad b. Yūsuf b. 'Alī al-Azraq: *Tārīkh Mayyāfāriqīn wa-Āmid,* MS. Brit. Mus. Or. 5803; page-references are to "A critical edition of the Artuqid section in *Tārīkh Mayyāfāriqīn wa-Āmid*", A. Savran, unpublished thesis, St Andrews University.

Anon.: *Shifā' 'l-qulūb fī manāqib banī Ayyūb*, MS. Brit. Mus. Add. 7311 (attributed to Aḥmad b. Ibrāhīm al-Ḥanbalī by M. Kurd Ali, "al-Shāmiyyūn wa'l-tārīkh", *MMIA*, XVII (1942), 101).

Barhebraeus, Abū'l-Faraj: *Syriac Chronography*, trans. E.A.W. Budge, London 1932.

al-Fāḍil, 'Abd al-Raḥīm b. 'Alī al-Baisānī: *al-durr al-naẓīma min tarassul 'Abd al-Raḥīm,* ed. A. Badawi, Cairo n.d.
MSS.: Berlin We 1264
Brit. Mus. Add. 7307
7465
25756
25757

Cambridge Qq. 232
Leiden cod. or. 287
Mosul 93.3
Munich 402
Paris MS. ar. 6024
Top Kapu 2497
(Cf. also Vatican v.946).

al-Harawī, Abū'l-Ḥasan 'Alī b. Abī Bakr: *Kitāb al-ishārat ilā ma'rifat al-ziyārāt*, ed J. Sourdel-Thomime, Damascus 1953.

al-Ḥarīrī, al-Qāsim b. 'Alī: *Maqāmāt al-Ḥarīrī*, Beirut 1965.

Ibn Abī'l-Haijā': *Tārīkh Ibn Abī'l-Haijā'*, MS. Ahmadiya (Tunis) no. 4915.

Ibn al-'Adīm, 'Umar b. Aḥmad: *Zubdat al-ḥalab min tārīkh Ḥalab*, ed. S. al-Dahhān, Damascus 1968.

Ibn al-Athīr, 'Alī b. Muḥammad: *al-Kāmil fī'l-tārīkh*, Beirut 1965 (photomechanic reprint of the edition by C. J. Tornberg, Leiden 1867–76), 12 vols. and index.

al-Tārīkh al-bāhir fī' l-daulat al-Atābakīya, (*History of the Atabegs*), ed. A.A. Tolaymat, Cairo n.d.

Ibn al-Furāt, Muḥammad b. 'Abd al-Raḥīm: *Tārīkh al-duwal wa'l-mulūk*, vol. 4, ed. H.M. al-Shammā', Basra 1967.

Ibn Jubair, Muḥammad b. Aḥmad: *Tadhkira li akhbār 'an ittifāqāt al-asfār, (The Travels of Ibn Jubayr)*, ed. W. Wright, Gibb Memorial Series, Leiden 1907.

Ibn Khaldūn, 'Abd al-Raḥmān b. Muḥammad: *al-Muqaddima*, Cairo 1867.

Ibn Khallikān, Aḥmad b. Muḥammad: *Kitāb wafayāt al-a'yān*, Cairo 1882.

Ibn Mammātī, al-As'ad b. al-Khaṭīr: *Kitāb qawānīn al-dawāwīn*, ed. A.S. Atiya, Cairo 1943.

Ibn Shaddād, Bahā' al-Dīn Yūsuf b. Rāfi': *al-Nawādir al-sulṭānīya, sīrat Ṣalāḥ al-Dīn*, ed. J. al-Shayyāl, Cairo 1962.

Ibn 'Unain, Muḥammad b. Naṣr Allāh: *Dīwān*, ed. Khalīl Mardam, Damascus 1946.

Ibn Wāṣil, Muḥammad b. Sālim: *Mufarrij al-kurūb fī akhbār banī Ayyūb*, vol. 2, ed. J. al-Shayyāl, Cairo 1957.

'Imād al-Dīn, Muḥammad b. Muḥammad, al-Kātib al-Iṣfahānī: *al-Barq al-Shāmī*, sec. 3, MS. (Bodley) Bruce 11; sec. 5, MS. (Bodley) Marsh 425.

Sanā al-barq al-Shāmī, abridged by al-Bundārī, Fatḥ b. 'Alī, pt 1, ed. R. Şeşen, Beirut 1971; see also "A Critical Edition of the Abridgement by al-Bundārī of the *Kitāb al-Barq al-Shāmī* by 'Imād al-Dīn", by F. El-Nabarawy, unpublished thesis, Cambridge University Library [published Cairo, 1979, after this work was prepared].

Kitāb al-faiḥ (Landberg: *fatḥ*) *al-qussī fī' l-fatḥ al-Qudsī*, ed. Landberg, Leiden 1888.

Kharīdat al-qaṣr wa-jarīdat al-'aṣr, vols. 1-3, ed. S. Faisal, Damascus 1955–64.

(*Dīwān rasā'il al-Kātib al-Iṣfahānī*, MS. Nūri Osmāniye (Istanbul) no. 3745, wrongly attributed to 'Imād al-Dīn.

al-Karmī, Ḥasan Sa'īd: *Qaul 'alā Qaul*, Beirut 1968.
al-Makhzūmī, 'Alī b. 'Uthmān: *Kitāb al-minhāj fī'ilm kharāj Miṣr*, MS. Brit. Mus. Add. 23483.
al-Maqrīzī, Aḥmad b. 'Alī: *(Khiṭaṭ) Kitāb al-mawā'iẓ wa'l-i'tibār*, reprint Baghdad 1970 of the Cairo 1953–4 edition, 2 vols.
Kitāb al-sulūk, ed. M.M. Ziyāda, vol. 1.1 (2nd edition) Cairo 1956.
Itti'āẓ al-ḥunafā', MS. (Istanbul) Ahmed III, no. 3013.
Michael the Syrian: *Chronique de Michel le Syrien*, ed. and trans. J.-B. Chabot, 4 vols., Paris 1899–1910.
Muḥammad b. Ibrāhīm b. Muḥammad al-Anṣārī: *Tārīkh daulat al-Akrād wa'l-Atrāk*, MS. Maktaba Hekimoglu Pasha, no. 695.
al-Nābulsī, 'Uthmān b. Ibrāhīm: *Tārīkh al-Fayyūm*, ed. B. Moritz, Cairo 1899.
al-Qalqashandī, Aḥmad b. 'Alī: *Ṣubḥ al-a'shā fī ṣinā'at al-inshā'*, 14 vols., Cairo 1332–46 A.H..
Sawīrus b. al-Muqaffa': *History of the Patriarchs of the Egyptian Church*, trans. Y. 'Abd al-Masīḥ and O.H.E. Burmester, vol. 3, Cairo 1968–70.
Sibṭ ibn al-Jauzī: *Mir'āt al-zamān*, Hyderabad 1951.
Tārīkh Mayyāfāriqīn see Aḥmad b. Yūsuf.
al-Ṭarsūsī, Murḍā b. 'Alī: *Tabṣirat arbāb al-albāb*, MS. (Bodley) Huntington 264.
'Umar b. 'Abd al-'Azīz b. al-'Adīm: *Sūq al-Fāḍil, fī manāqib al-qāḍī al-Fāḍil*, MS. Arif Hikmat (Medina) no. 410 (*tārīkh*).
Usāma ibn Munqidh: *Kitāb al-i'tibār (An Arab–Syrian Gentleman and Warrior)*, trans. P.K. Hitti, Columbia University Press, 1929.
Yāqūt, b. 'Abd Allāh al-Ḥamawī: *Mu'jam al-buldān*, 5 vols., Beirut 1955.
al-Wahrānī, Zakī al-Dīn Muḥammad b. Muḥammad: *Maqāmāt al-Wahrānī wa-rasā'iluhu*, MS. Ayasofya (Istanbul) no. 4299, ed. Sha'lan, Cairo 1968.

(B) Others

Amari, M.: *I diplomi arabi del R. Archivio Fiorentino*, Florence 1863.
Ambroise: *L'Estoire de la Guerre Sainte*, ed. G. Paris, Paris 1897.
Anon.: *Chronicon Terrae Sanctae seu libellus de expugnatione*, ed. H. Prutz, Danzig 1876.
Ansbertus: *Gesta Frederici Imperatoris in Expeditione Sacra*, Monumenta Germaniae Historica: Scriptores, 1892.
Bloch, M.: *Feudal Society*, trans. L. A. Manyon, London 1961.
Bourrienne, F. de: *Memoirs of Napoleon Bonaparte* (trans.), London 1905.
Brand, C.M. : "The Byzantines and Saladin, 1185–1192: Opponents of the Third Crusade", *Speculum*, XXXVII (1962), 167–181.
Cinnamus, John: *Epitome Historiarum*, Corpus Scriptorum Historiae Byzantinae, Bonn 1836

Continuation of William of Tyre: *Die Lateinische Fortsetzung Wilhelms von Tyrus*, ed. M. Salloch, Leipzig 1934.

Ehrenkreutz, A.S.: "The crisis of *dīnār* in the Egypt of Saladin", *JAOS*, LXXVI (1956), 178–84.

"The place of Saladin in the naval history of the Mediterranean Sea in the middle ages", *JAOS*, LXXV (1955), 100–16.

"Saladin's coup d'état in Egypt", *Medieval and Middle Eastern Studies in Honor of Aziz Suryal Atiya*, ed. S.M. Hanna, Leiden 1972.

Saladin, State University of New York Press, 1972.

Elisséef, N.: *Nūr ad-Dīn, un grand prince musulman de Syrie au temps des croisades (511–569 H./1118–1174)*, 3 vols., Damascus 1967.

Ernoul: *Chronique d'Ernoul et de Bernard le Tresorier*, ed. L. de Mas-Latrie, Paris 1971.

Estoire d'Eracles, Recueil des Historiens des Croisades: Historiens occidentaux 1.2.

Field Service Pocket Book, pt 2, Government of India Central Publication Branch, Calcutta 1928.

Gaudefroy-Demombynes, M.: "Une lettre de Saladin au calife Almohade", *Mélanges René Basset*, Paris 1925.

Gibb, H.A.R.: "The Arabic Sources for the Life of Saladin", *Speculum*, XXV (1950).

The Life of Saladin, Clarendon Press, Oxford 1973.

Gombrich, E.H.: *In Search of Cultural History*, The Philip Maurice Deneke Lecture, Clarendon Press, Oxford 1969.

Grousset, R.: *Histoire des Croisades et du Royaume Franc de Jérusalem*, 3 vols., Paris 1934–6.

Heyd. W.: *Histoire du commerce du Levant au moyen âge*, Leipzig 1923.

Itinerarium Peregrinorum et Gesta Regis Ricardi, ed. W. Stubbs, Rolls Series, London 1864; trans. *Itinerary of Richard I*, Bohn, London 1848.

Lapidus I.M.: *Muslim Cities in the Later Middle Ages*, Harvard University Press, Cambridge, Mass., 1967.

Lévi-Provençal, E.: *Histoire de l'Espagne Musulmane*, 2 vols., Paris and Leiden 1950.

Lyons, U. and M.C., and Riley-Smith, J.: *Ayyubids, Mamlukes and Crusaders*, Heffer, Cambridge 1971.

Minorsky, V.: *Studies in Caucasian History*, London 1953.

Napoleon: *Guerre d'Orient: Campagnes d'Egypte et de Syrie*, Paris 1847.

Nicetas Choniates: *Historia*, Corpus Scriptorum Historia Byzantinae, Bonn 1835.

Ostrogorsky, G.: *Pour l'histoire de la féodalité byzantine*, trans. H. Grégoire, Brussels 1954.

Poliak, A.N.: "The Ayyūbid feudalism", *JRAS* (1939), 428–32.

Prawer, J.: "La bataille de Hattin", *Israel Exploration Journal*, XIV (1964), 160–79.

Préaux, C.: *L'Économie Royale des Lagides*, Brussels 1939.
Rabie, H.: *The Financial System of Eygpt, A.H. 564–1741/A.D. 1169–1341*, Oxford University Press, 1972.
Raoul de Diceto: *Ymagines historiarium*, ed. W. Stubbs, Rolls Series, London, 1876.
Riley-Smith, J.: *The Knights of St. John in Jerusalem and Cyprus 1050–1310*, London 1967.
Ritter H.: "Irrational Solidarity Groups", *Oriens*, I (1948).
Robinson, E., and Smith, E.: *Biblical Researches in Palestine, Mount Sinai and Arabia Petraea*, 3 vols., London 1841.
Röhricht, R.: *Regesta Regni Hierosolymitani*, Oeniponti, 1893.
Sauvaget, J.: *Introduction to the History of the Muslim East*, 2nd edition revised by C. Cahen, University of California Press, 1965.
Stevenson, W.B.: *The Crusaders in the East*, Cambridge 1907.
Tarn, W.W.: *Hellenistic Military and Naval Developments*, Clees-Knowles Lectures in Military History, Cambridge 1930.
Wavell, A.P.: *The Palestine Campaigns*, 3rd edition, London 1938.
William of Tyre: *Historia Rerum in Partibus Transmarinis Gestarum*, Recueil des Historiens des Croisades: Historiens occidentaux, vol. 1. Pt 1. trans. Babcock and Krey, Columbia University Press, 1943.
Zambaur, E. de: *Manuel de Généalogie et de Chronologie pour l'Histoire de l'Islam*, Bad Pyrmont 1955.

GENERAL BIBLIOGRAPHY

Abel, F.M.: *Géographie de la Palestine*, 2 vols., Paris 1933–8.
Abū Makhrama, 'Abd Allāh al-Ṭayyib: *Tārīkh thaghr 'Adan*, ed. O. Löfgren, 2 vols., Leiden 1936.
Ahmad, M.H.M.: "Some notes on Arabic historiography during the Zengid and Ayyubid Periods", in B. Lewis and H.M. Holt (eds.), *Historians of the Middle East*, London 1962.
al-'Arīnī, E.E.: *Miṣr fī 'aṣr al-Ayyūbiyīn*, Cairo 1960.
Ashtor, E.: *Histoire des Prix et des Salaires dans l'Orient Médiéval*, Paris 1969.
Atiya, A.S. *The Crusade, Historiography and Bibliography*, Bloomington, Indiana University Press 1962.
Crusade, commerce and culture, Bloomington–London 1962.
Ayalon, D.: "L'Esclavage du Mamelouk", *The Israel Oriental Society*, Oriental Notes and Studies, Jerusalem 1951.
Baldwin, M.W.: *Raymond III of Tripoli and the Fall of Jerusalem (1140–1187)*, Princeton 1936.
Balog, P.: "History of the dirhem in Egypt from the Fāṭimid conquest until the collapse of the Mamlūk empire", *Revue numismatique*, 6e série, III (1961).

al-Barrāwī, R.: *Ḥālat Miṣr al-iqtiṣādīya fī ʻahd al-Fāṭimiyīn*, Cairo 1948.

El-Beheiry: *Les institutions de l'Egypte au temps des Ayyubides*, Cairo 1971.

Ben-Ami, A.: *Social Change in a Hostile Environment; The Crusaders' Kingdom of Jerusalem*, Princeton 1969.

Ben Shemesh, A.: *Taxation in Islam*, vol. 1 *Yaḥyā ben Adam's Kitāb al-Kharāj*, Leiden 1967; vol. 2 *Qudāma b. Ja'far's Kitāb al-Kharāj*, Leiden 1965; vol. 3 *Abū Yūsuf's Kitāb al-Kharāj*, Leiden 1969.

Benvenisti, M.: *The Crusaders in the Holy Land*, Jerusalem 1970.

Cahen, C.: *La Syrie du Nord à l'époque des Croisades, et la principauté franque d'Antioche*, Paris 1940.

"Un traité d'armurerie composé pour Saladin", *Bulletin d'Etudes Orientales de l'Institut Français de Damas*, XII (1947–8).

"Le régime des impôts dans le Fayyūm Ayyūbide", *Arabica*, III (1956).

"Un traité financier inédit d'époque Fatimide–Ayyubide", *JESHO*, V (1962).

"Douanes et commerce dans les ports méditerranéens de l'Egypte médiévale d'après le *Minhādj* d'al-Makhzūmī", *JESHO*, VII (1964).

"L'évolution de l'iqṭā' du IXe au XIIIe siècle", *Annales: Économies, sociétés, civilisations*, VIII (1953).

al-Dawādārī, Abū Bakr b. 'Abd Allāh: *al-Durr al-maṭlūb fī akhbār banī Ayyūb*, MS. Sarayi, Istanbul, no. 2923 VII.

Deschamps, P.: *Les châteaux des croisés en Terre Sainte, ii. La défense du royaume de Jérusalem*, Paris 1939.

al-Dhahabī, Muḥammad b. Aḥmad: *al-'Ibar fī khabar man ghabar*, ed. Ṣ. al-Munajjid and F. al-Sayyid, 5 vols., Kuwait 1960–6.

Dichter, B.: *The Maps of Acre: An Historical Cartography*, The Municipality of Acre 1973.

Du Cange, C. du Fresne: *Les familles d'Outremer*, ed. E.G. Rey, Paris 1869, reprinted Burt Franklin, New York 1971.

Dussaud, R.: *Topographie historique de la Syrie antique et médiévale*, Paris 1927.

Forand, P.G.: "Notes on 'ušr and maks", *Arabica*, XIII (1966).

Gaudefroy-Demombynes, M.: *Les institutions musulmanes*, 3rd edition, Paris 1946.

Gibb, H.A.R.: "The Armies of Saladin", *Studies on the Civilization of Islam*, Boston 1962.

Goitein, S.D.: *A Mediterranean Society: The Jewish Committee of the Arab World as Portrayed in the Documents of the Cairo Geniza*, Berkeley and Los Angeles 1967.

"The exchange rate of gold and silver money in Fatimid and Ayyubid times", *JESHO*, VIII (1965).

Hackett, J.W.: "Saladin's Campaign of 1188 in Northern Syria", unpublished thesis, Oxford 1937.

Haq, M.: "Al Qaḍi-al-Fadil and his diary", *Proceedings and Transactions of the tenth All-India Oriental Conference*, 1940.

Ḥasan, Z. M.: *Kunūz al-Fāṭimiyyīn*, Cairo 1937.

Herde, P.: "Die Kämpfe bei den Hörnern von Hittin und der Untergang des Kreuzritterheeres (3. und 4. Juli 1187)", *Römische Quartalschrift für christliche Altertumskunde und Kirchengeschichte*, LXI (1966).
Hodgson, M.G.G.: *The Order of the Assassins*, The Hague–Paris 1955.
Ḥusain, A.S.: *al-Abad al-Ṣūfī fī Miṣr*, Cairo 1971.
Ibn Abī Uṣaibi'a, Aḥmad b. al-Qāsim: *'Uyūn al-anbā' fī ṭabaqāt al-aṭibbā'*, Beirut 1965.
Ibn al-'Amīd, al-Makīn Jirjis: *Akhbār al-Ayyūbiyyīn*, ed. C. Cahen ("La chronique des Ayyoubides", *BEO*, XV (1955-7)).
Ibn Ba'ra, Manṣūr al-Dhahabī: *Kitāb kashf al-asrār al-'ilmiyya bi-dār al-ḍarb al-Miṣriyya*, ed. A. Fahmī, Cairo 1966.
Ibn Bassām, Muḥammad b. Aḥmad: *Kitāb anīs al-jalīs fī akhbār Tinnīs*, ed. J. al-Shayyāl, *MMII*, XIV (1967).
Ibn Shaddād, Muḥammad b. 'Alī: *al-A'lāq al-khaṭīra fī dhikr umarā' al-Shām wa'l-Jazīra*, ed. S. al-Dahhān, Damascus 1963.
Ibn Taghrī Birdī, Yūsuf: *al-Nūjum al-zāhira fī mulūk Miṣr wa'l-Qāhira*, 12 vols., Cairo 1929–56.
Jāmātī, H.: *al-Nāṣir Ṣalāḥ al-Dīn*, Cairo 1962.
Jarrār, F.A.: "Usṭūl Ṣalāḥ al-Dīn al-Ayyūbī", *Al-Abḥāth*, XIII (1960).
Johns, C.N.: *Palestine of the Crusades*, 3rd edition, Jerusalem 1946.
Johnston, R.C. (ed.): *The Crusade and Death of Richard I*, Anglo-Norman texts 17, Oxford 1961.
Kraemer, J.: *Der Sturz des Königreichs Jerusalem (583/1187) in der Darstellung des 'Imād al-Dīn al-Kātib al-Iṣfahānī*, Wiesbaden 1952.
al-Kutubī, Muḥammad b. Shākir: *Fawāt al-wafayāt*, Cairo 1866.
Labib, S.Y.: *Handelsgeschichte Ägyptens im Spätmittelalter*, Wiesbaden 1965.
Lambton, A.K.S.: "Reflections on the iqṭā' ", *Arabic and Islamic Studies in honor of Hamilton, A.R. Gibb*, Leiden 1965.
Lane-Poole, S.: *Saladin and the Fall of the Kingdom of Jerusalem*, London 1898.
Le Strange, G.: *Palestine under the Moslems*, reprint of the 1890 edition, Khayat, Beirut 1965.
Lewis, B.: *The Assassins: A Radical Sect in Islam*, New York 1968.
"Kamāl al-Dīn's biography of Rašīd al-Dīn Sinān", *Arabica*, XIII (1966).
"Government, society and economic life under the Abbasids and Fatimids", *Cambridge Medieval History*, 2nd edition, 1966, vol. 4, pt 1.
Majīd, A.M.: *Nuẓūm al-Fāṭimiyyīn wa-rusūmuhum*, Cairo 1953.
Mason, H.: *Two Statesmen of Mediavel Islam, Vizier Ibn Hubayra (499–560 A.H./1105–1165 A.D.) and Caliph an-Nāṣir li Dīn Allāh (553–622 A.H./1158–1225 A.D.)*, The Hague–Paris 1972.
Mayer, H.E.: *Bibliographie zur Geschichte der Kreuzzüge*, Hanover 1960; see also *Historische Zeitschrift. Sonderheft*, 3, for a supplement.
Möhring, H. *Saladin und der Dritte Kreuzzug*, Frankf. Hist. Abh., 21, 1979–[published after the completion of this work].

Moustafa bey Munir Adham, M.: "Le Caire au XVe Siècle d'après les données de Maqrizi", *Bulletin de la Société Royale de Géographie d'Égypte,* XIII (1924), 131–80.

al-Nābulsī, 'Uthmān b. Ibrāhīm: *Kitāb luma' al-qawānīn al-muḍiyya,* ed. C. Becker, and C. Cahen, *BEO,* XVI (1958–60).

Prawer, J.: *Histoire du Royaume Latin de Jérusalem,* Paris 1969.

Qal'ajī, Q.: *Ṣalāḥ al-Dīn al-Ayyūbī,* Beirut 1966.

Ravaisse, P. "Essai sur l'histoire et sur la topographie du Caire de 'après Makrizi", *Mémoires publiés par les membres de la Mission Archéologique Française au Caire,* pt 3, 409–80; pt 4, 33–114, Paris 1887.

Rey, E.G.: *Les colonies franques de Syrie au XIIe et XIIIe siècles,* Paris 1883.

Rikabi, J.: *La Poésie profane sous les Ayyubides et ses principaux représentants,* Paris 1949.

Riley-Smith J.: *The Feudal Nobility and the Latin Kingdom of Jerusalem 1174–1277,* London 1973.

Rodinson, M.: "Histoire économique et histoire des classes sociales dans le monde musulman", *Studies in the economic history of the Middle East from the rise of Islam to the present day,* London 1970.

Röhricht, R.: *Beiträge zur Geschichte der Kreuzzüge,* 2 vols., Berlin 1874–8.

"Amalrich I., Konig von Jerusalem", *Mitteilungen des Instituts für österreichische Geschichtsforschung,* XII (1891).

Rosenthal, F.: *A History of Muslim Historiography,* Leiden 1952.

Runciman, S.: *A History of the Crusades,* 3 vols., Cambridge 1951–4.

Sa'dawī, N.H.: *al-Tārīkh al-ḥarbī al-Miṣrī fī 'ahd Ṣalāḥ al-Dīn,* Cairo 1957.

al-Ṣafadī, Khalīl b. Aibak: *Al-Wāfī bi' l-wafayāt,* Bibliotheca Islamica, 9 vols, Leipzig *et al.* 1931–74.

Schlumberger, G.: *Campagnes du roi Amaury Ier de Jérusalem en Egypte au XIIe siècle,* Paris 1906.

Semenova, L. A. *Salakh-ad-Din i Mamliuki v Egipte,* Moscow 1966.

Setton, K.M. (ed.): *A History of the Crusades,* Philadelphia 1958.

Sivan, E.: "The Beginnings of the Faḍā'il al-Quds Literature", *Israel Oriental Studies,* I (1971).

Smail, R.C.: *Crusading Warfare 1097–1193,* Cambridge 1956.

Smith, G.R.: *The Ayyūbids and Early Rasūlids in the Yemen (567–694/* 1173–1295), Gibb Memorial Series, London 1974, vol. 1, being a critical edition of *Kitāb al-Simṭ al-Ghālī al-Thaman fī Akhbār al-Mulūk min al-Ghuzz bi'l-Yaman* by Badr al-Dīn Muḥammad b. Ḥātim al-Yāmī al-Hamdānī.

al-Subkī, 'Abd al-Wahhāb b. 'Alī: *Ṭabaqāt al-Shāfi'iyya al-Kubrā,* 6 vols., Cairo 1906–7.

al-Sulamī, 'Abd al-Raḥmān Muḥammad: *Ṭabaqāt al-Ṣūfiyya,* Leiden 1960.

Surūr, Jamāl al-Dīn: *al-Daulat al-Fāṭimiyya fi Miṣr,* Cairo 1970.

Tafel, G.L., and Thomas, G.M.: *Urkunden zur älteren Handels-und Staatsgeschichte der Republik Venedig mit besonderer Beziehung auf Byzanz und die Levante,* 3 vols., Vienna 1856–7.

Tāmir, 'A.: *Sinān wa-Ṣalāḥ al-Dīn*, Beirut 1952.
Theodoric: *Libellus de locis sanctis*, ed. T. Tobler, St Gallen 1865.
Tyan, E.: *Histoire de l'organisation judicaire en pays d'Islam*, 2nd edition, Leiden 1960.
Vasiliev, A.A.: *History of the Byzantine Empire*, University of Wisconsin Press, 1961.
Vatikiotis, P.J.: "The Rise of Extremist Sects and the Dissolution of the Fāṭimid Empire in Egypt", *Islamic Culture*, XXXI (1957).
Yūsuf, J.N.: "Dirāsa fī wathā'iq al-aṣrayn al-Fāṭimī wa'l-Ayyūbī", *BFA*, VIII (1954).
Ziyāda, M.M.: "Dīwān al-zakāt", *al-Thaqāfa*, CCXI (1943).

INDEX

(a) People

'Abbās b. Shādhī 77
'Abd al-Karīm b. Zain al-Dīn 'Alī 68
'Abd al-Laṭīf al-Baghdādī, Muwaffaq al-Dīn 56
'Abd al-Masīḥ, Fakhr al-Dīn 40, 72, 105
'Abd al-Nabī b. 'Alī 65
'Abd al-Raḥmān b. Munqidh, Shams al-Dīn 318
Abu Bakr (al-Ḥājib) al-'Ādilī 359
Abū Bakr b. Qarā-Arslān (brother of Nūr al-Dīn Muḥammad 148, 227
'Abū'l-Haijā' the Gross, (al-Samīn), Ḥusām al-Dīn 35, 77, 183, 345, 352, 368
Abū Ḥassān b. Ḥassān, (al-Ḍarīr) 110
Abū Ja'far, (al-Shaikh) 363
Abū Ṣāliḥ, al-Armanī 34, 59
Abū'l-Ṭāhir al-Iṣfahānī, 'Imād al-Dīn, Aḥmad 114
Abū Tammām, Ḥabīb b. Aus 3
al-'Adid, Abū Muḥammad 'Abd Allāh (Fatimid Caliph) 6, 24, 31, 44, 45 (d.), 310
al-'Ādil - al-Malik al-'Ādil, Saif al-Dīn Abū Bakr Aḥmad b. Ayyūb 39 (in Egypt), 77 (in upper Egypt), 113, 129 (left in Egypt), 131, 135, 143, 158, 164 (marriage of his daughters), 165 (left in Egypt), 170, 186, 187, 208 (leaves Egypt), 211 (given Aleppo), 214, 217 (at Kerak), 238 (at Ḥarrān), 240, 244, 267 (summoned after Ḥaṭṭīn), 271 (urges attack on Jerusalem), 275 (at Jerusalem), 280 (at Tyre), 283, 291, 295 (returns to Egypt), 307 (at Acre), 314, 320, 323 (at Haifa), 327, 328, 335, 336, 337 (at Arsūf), 342 (suggested marriage to Joanna), 347, 348, 355, 360 (swears to truce terms), 362
al-'Adl, Najīb al-Dīn Abū Muḥammad b. 'Abd Allāh 224, 252, 348
al-'Adl b. al-'Ajamī, Shihāb al-Dīn Abū Ṣāliḥ 72, 78, 79, 90, 126
'Aḍud al-Dīn, Abū'l-Faraj b. Ra'īs al-Ru'asā' 112, 129
al-Afḍal (al-Malik al-Afḍal, Nūr al-Dīn Abū'l-Ḥasan 'Alī b. Ṣalāḥ al-Dīn), 114, 135, 221, 240, 243, 246, 252, 263 (at Ḥaṭṭīn), 267, 277, 280 (at Tyre), 283, 302 (at Acre), 320, 328, 334, 338 (at Arsūf), 341, 347, 348, 352, 353, 360 (swears to truce terms), 363
Aḥmad b. Taqī al-Dīn 124
'Ain al-Daula, al-Yārūqī 29, 33
'Alā' al-Dīn b. 'Izz al-Dīn Mas'ūd b. Maudūd b. Zangī 312, 314, 320, 322, 327, 338 (at Arsūf), 354, 359
'Alā' al-Dīn Mas'ūd, Abū Bakr b. Muḥammad 203
'Alam al-Dīn Qaiṣar (Caisac) 339, 345, 346, 349, 356, 361
'Alam al-Dīn Sulaimān 160, 164, 202, 245, 291, 315, 325, 335, 336, 339, 343
Alexander the Great 283
'Alī *see* Shams al-Dīn 'Alī
'Alī b. Abī'l-Fawāris, Mubāriz al-Dīn 90
Almohades 76, 194, 222, 370
Amalric I (King of Jerusalem) 8 (siege of Bilbais), 11 (joins Shāwar), 14 (at Bābain), 17 (siege of Alexandria), 19 (leaves Egypt), 20 (returns), 22 (siege of Cairo), 24 (leaves Egypt), 36 (attacks Damietta), 73 (attacks Banias), 75 (d.), 370
Ambroise 320, 321, 322, 337, 339, 344, 345, 346, 350, 351, 353, 357
Ammianus Marcellinus 190
Andronicus, I, Comnenus (Emperor of

(b) Places